DEATH AND
THE ENLIGHTENMENT

DEATH AND
THE ENLIGHTENMENT

*Changing Attitudes to Death
among Christians and Unbelievers
in Eighteenth-century France*

JOHN McMANNERS

CLARENDON PRESS · OXFORD
OXFORD UNIVERSITY PRESS · NEW YORK
1981

Oxford University Press, Walton Street, Oxford OX2 6DP
London Glasgow New York Toronto
Delhi Bombay Calcutta Madras Karachi
Kuala Lumpur Singapore Hong Kong Tokyo
Nairobi Dar es Salaam Cape Town
Melbourne Aukland
and associate companies in
Beirut Berlin Ibadan Mexico City

Published in the United States by
Oxford University Press, New York

British Library Cataloguing in Publication Data
McManners, John
Death and the Enlightenment.
1. Death
I. Title
155.9'37'0944   BF789.D4
ISBN 0-19-826440-2

Set by Western Printing Services Ltd
and printed in Hong Kong

Acknowledgements

Inevitably, I must begin by admitting my debt to the multitude of French historians, brilliant and inventive, whose names figure so often in the references—more especially Michel Vovelle, Pierre Chaunu, Robert Favre, and Philippe Ariès. Though I would hope to have contributed something original, for the most part, I would describe my book as an attempt to make English readers aware of the methodological ingenuity of contemporary French historians, and to combine the findings of a great deal of their recent research and speculation into a comprehensive synthesis.

The English author of a book of this kind needs support to work in Paris. I am most grateful to the British Academy for research grants, and to Michel Fleury, President of the *IVe Section* of the École Pratique des Hautes Études, for the hospitality of the Hôtel Chalon-Luxembourg, so agreeably situated in the Marais. This note of acknowledgement is being written in Paris, where I am enjoying, in every sense of the word, the office of Directeur d'Études étranger under Professor Fleury's presidency: the research I am now doing is for a study of a different kind, and my renewed gratitude will be recorded in a later publication. I must also thank the Rockefeller Foundation for allowing me a month of agreeable retreat at Bellagio, where the first four chapters of *Death and the Enlightenment* were put into final form—a chronicle of disease and misery written in palatial surroundings while looking out reflectively over the waters of Lake Como. By good fortune, Professor Walsh McDermott visited Bellagio when I was there, and generously put his technical and medical knowledge at my service.

His aid was one of many examples which demonstrate that authors who venture on themes which straddle the boundaries of disciplines need long-suffering friends—who are willing to be trapped into conversations designed to tap their erudition and ideas. First among my victims I must thank Bruno Neveu, for so many hours of lively discourse in his flat and in restaurants in Paris, at my home and in Oxford Senior Common Rooms. But there have been many others. What I say about the history of medicine has been improved by the criticisms of Ludmilla Jordanova; on the history of spirituality, I have benefited from conversations with Père Rayez. Alban Krailsheimer, Ron Truman, and Robert Dingley will now be reflecting with satisfaction, I imagine, that death is no longer a compulsory subject of discussion at lunch in Christ Church. To two friends I must give especial thanks for disinterested help on a scale and to an extent that is manifestly unreasonable. Richard Fargher of St. Edmund Hall has read every word of this book, both before it went to press and in proof, and I am enormously indebted to him for broad-ranging criticism, scholarly guidance, and precise corrections. Mary Fargher has also cast her critical eye over the volume, to my great profit. They are long-standing allies who have performed this selfless task on almost everything I have published, and I am deeply grateful to them.

With astonishing forbearance, Marion Stowell and the staff of the History Faculty Office here at Oxford have laboured over the past four years transforming my drafts into typescript and, in the process of interpreting my handwriting, have acquired skills worthy of professional code-breakers and palaeographers. My thanks of a somewhat similar apologetic flavour must be expressed to all concerned at the Oxford University Press—to Robin Denniston who haunted me until I handed over an incomplete manuscript on which I had too-long ruminated, to Robert Shackleton (then Bodley's Librarian) who promptly devoted his next weekend to reading it; to Phoebe Allen who has performed an astonishing feat of copy-editing on my unsystematic references and inspirational prose; also to Audrey Bayley, the most patient and encouraging of editors. It was a gratifying experience to find oneself 'produced' in such a genial and professional fashion.

The gloomiest moment of an historian's life is when his publisher demands an Index. To my wife, who has relieved me of this and so many other burdens, I am deeply grateful.

In four chapters in *Death and the Enlightenment* I have reproduced paragraphs substantially identical with those I have published elsewhere. I am grateful to the Oxford University Press, *The Times Literary Supplement*, the S P C K, and the British Society for 18th Century Studies for permission to do so.

Contents

A Personal View   1

1   Death's Arbitrary Empire   5
2   Defences against Death: Eighteenth-century Medicine   24
3   The Shadow of Death and the Art of Living   59
4   Statistics, Hopes, and Fears   89
5   The Soul, Heaven, and Hell   120
6   The Afterlife: Doubts and Reconsiderations   148
7   Preparation for Death   191
8   Deathbeds   234
9   Funerals   270
10   Graveyards: Patriotism, Poetry, and Grim Realities   303
11   Death as an Instrument: The Public Execution   368
12   Suicide   409
13   Living, Loving, and Dying   438

References   467

Bibliography
   A. Eighteenth-century works   569
   B. Secondary works   588

Indexes   605

A Personal View

'One cannot look directly at the sun or at death,' said La Rochefoucauld.[1] The historian of death is not writing about an event which can be assessed from the reminiscences—and subsequent conduct—of those who have experienced it. We never have reports from the inside; we are always external observers. Maybe there is a way to instinctive, spiritual comprehension, open to those who love and who identify themselves with the dying: 'ubi amor ibi oculis'.[2] Maybe we can sense what lies after death by meditating upon the mystery of the purpose of life. Kierkegaard[3] said that 'immortality is no learned question', but something only to be understood by looking into one's own soul. By allying our destiny to the destiny of another, and by looking into the depths of our own nature, we can strive to understand death. But these are not the ways of the historian who, whatever affinities or introspection he uses to work towards his conclusions, must always start from solid evidence. Some testimony, however fraudulent, some artefact, however humble, must come down to him to form the starting-point of the working of the historical imagination. In truth, the historian is never really writing about death. He is writing about the attitudes of the living to death, to the dying, and to the dead—or rather, we should say, the attitudes of those who *have* lived, for there is the continual sad irony involved in the universal and ordinary fact that those who console or kill, mourn, commemorate, or vilify, must go the same way themselves and be remembered, then forgotten, in their turn.

The attitude of men to the death of their fellows is of unique significance for an understanding of our human condition. Man is distinguished from the animals by knowing that he must die, and by his invention of ceremonies of remembrance and commemoration. According to Vico, religion, marriage, and the burial of the dead are the institutions, the external principles on which all nations were founded and which continue to preserve them. (A

1

modern commentator has sardonically observed that, of these three institutions, only the burial of the dead seems likely to continue.[4]) If the foundation of the social order rests on Vico's respect for the dead, it may also be said that the awareness of the shadow of mortality is at the expanding centre of the human personality, the essential catalyst for the reactions creating and affirming individuality.[5] The knowledge that we must die gives us our perspective for living, our sense of finitude, our conviction of the value of every moment, our determination to live in such a fashion that we transcend our tragic limitation.

Such is the importance of the subject that it might seem, both to the historian of society and to the historian of ideas, that a study of attitudes to death, conducted on the grand scale, would lead to significant philosophical generalizations about the 'epochs of historical evolution'. By this means an attempt has been made to divide civilizations into the categories of 'death denying', 'death defying', 'death accepting', and 'death transcending'.[6] I confess that I do not have confidence in interpretations of the whole sweep of human destiny. These chapters on eighteenth-century France are simply an attempt to sympathize with, and so far as one can create the illusion, to live again the hopes and fears of four or five past generations. They are written with a certain scepticism concerning the possibility of learning the secrets of the heart from the more obvious external evidence. In facing death[7] we cling to rituals, observances, and folkways, not necessarily because we are committed to their significance, but simply to keep despair at bay, to occupy the empty and defeated mind. We set up monuments, however incongruous, because no other way is left to show our affection or pride. Liturgiologists, preachers, poets, artists, and undertakers go on their way professionally, refining and achieving within the closed world of their own expertise, obeying its current conventions and seeking the applause of their peers. Their patrons, the mourners, are not often exigent, for in the face of death we are at our least critical: having lost so much, what is there left to gain? The historian may read too much into the evidence, forgetting the numbness that takes over the mind at the parting of friends, and analysing as if they were spontaneous the automatic or contrived gestures behind which we take refuge and seek to rebuild our lives.

The joke contrasting us with the Victorians: we are frank about sex where they were reticent, and reticent about death where they were frank—may still be true of popular practice, but clearly no longer applies to authors and publishers. The taboo on the investigation of death was broken by Geoffrey Gorer's famous article, 'The Pornography of Death' in 1955, and since then there has been a flood of works on the subject; a recent count[8] of titles, mostly sociological, medical, psychological, and religious, shows the rush to publish in full swing about 1963, and reaching a peak in 1976. Among historians, Philippe Ariès has been pioneering death for fifteen years, and his articles have now been collected and expanded into a volume, *L'Homme devant la mort*.[9] His broad view, tying changes in attitudes to death over two thousand years of Europe to the story of the development of individuality and to changes in the structure and ethos of the family, seems to be confirmed by a closer study of eighteenth-century France. Others have followed Ariès, more especially the French historians of the *Annales* school, and they have naturally concentrated on their own country and on the seventeenth and eighteenth centuries, where the sources are appropriate to their methodology. It is then that parish registers begin to provide demographical information in detail (see Lebrun's volume on Anjou in 1971[10]); the last will and testament is more generally used and provides unusual materials for statistical findings (see Vovelle on the wills of Provence in 1973[11]); the expansion and elaboration of personal correspondence and the fashion for writing memoirs encourages psychological interpretations; the literature of the Enlightenment, concentrating on intellectual debates, provides a quarry of information for the history of ideas (see Favre's recent study of death in thought and literature[12]); discussions of both human nature and society become more sophisticated and provide us with better evidence in the century of *L'Esprit des lois* and *Les Liaisons dangereuses*.

It was through reading Lebrun in 1971 and Vovelle in 1973 that I decided to choose the title *Death and the Enlightenment* for the Birkbeck Lectures in Cambridge five years ago. But no doubt I also had subconscious motives for writing these essays. It does not need Freud[13] to tell us that we labour under the illogical hope that time and fate will make a stop for us. This was an eighteenth-century commonplace: 'All men think all men mortal but themselves,' say the *Night Thoughts*. There are two ways of trying to maintain the illusion. One is to follow the formula for happiness which Pascal satirized, refusing to consider those evils which we cannot cure. The other is to take the opposite tack, to face reality with bravado and to find reassurance in reducing it to routine. Some of the spirituality of the seventeenth and eighteenth centuries has this obsessive quality of haunted insistence. The manifold writings on death in our own day may, *mutatis mutandis*, reflect the same determination to take refuge from fear in clinical and learned analysis, or even, as an American commentator says, to be 'one up on death because of these cute exercises and intellectual niceties'.[14] In a matter of this kind, we cannot know our own motivation, for as we can but use the mind to search into the mind, we have no means to distinguish our instruments from the subject-matter they work on. But whatever my motives, as I write on death I am reminding myself continually of a hope that I have glimpsed, a hope implicit in the spiritual writers discussed in these essays, and set out most simply and clearly by a Calvinist divine of the seventeenth century: 'Christ is our eternal friend and it is the law of friendship that friends support one another.'[15] No doubt it is an impropriety in someone claiming to be a historian to end on such a personal note, but I do not see how I can conclude my researches into death without admitting that, in the last resort, it is a personal affair. 'Il n'y a pas de mort,' says one of Malraux's characters. 'Il y a seulement moi qui vais mourir.'[16]

1

Death's Arbitrary Empire

In eighteenth-century France, 'death was at the centre of life as the graveyard was at the centre of the village'.[1] Speaking in averages, and confounding in one the diversity of the whole country and the fortunes of all classes, we find that something like a quarter of all babies born in the early years of the century died before reaching their first birthday, and another quarter before reaching the age of eight. Of every 1,000 infants, only 200 would go on to the age of fifty, and only 100 to the age of seventy. A man who had beaten the odds and reached his half-century would, we may imagine, have seen both his parents die, have buried half his children and, like as not, his wife as well, together with numerous uncles, aunts, cousins, nephews, nieces, and friends. If he got to seventy, he would have no relations and friends of his own generation left to share his memories. If this is a description of the average, what can we say of the unfortunates whose sombre ill luck weights down the figures to this mean? The task of our first four chapters will be to try to picture the expectations and fears, so different from our own, of the folk of two centuries ago, and to assess their influence upon mental attitudes and social customs.

A new understanding of the eighteenth century comes to us when we review its history in terms of disease and mortality. In narrow fetid streets and airless tenements, in filthy windowless hovels, in middens and privies, in undrained pools and steaming marshes, in contaminated wells and streams—and, for that matter, in the gilded corridors of Versailles, where excrement accumulated—infections of every kind lurked. The files of the administrators, more especially those of the Royal Society of Medicine at the end of the *ancien régime*, are full of information sent in by medical experts about local epidemics and peculiar illnesses, but it is often difficult to deduce from their accounts what the specific

5

diseases were. They spoke essentially of symptoms. Fevers were 'bilious', 'putrid', 'autumnal', 'red', 'purple', 'intermittent', 'malignant', 'inflammatory'. The spitting of blood so often mentioned could have been the result of cancer of lungs or larynx, infection of the trachea, or pulmonary tuberculosis; their 'scurvy', deduced from bleeding gums and painful joints, could include arthritis and pyorrhoea. An autopsy frequently produced a report of 'worms' in lungs or stomach, without any other evidence to bring precision. Even so, the process of identification of the diseases of the past has proceeded, facilitated partly by the grim fact that the researcher need not concern himself overmuch with anything but the most deadly of illnesses. 'With their bodies assaulted on all sides, these people were carried off before the more subtle disorders had a chance to strike.'[2] The main killers were influenza and pulmonary infections, malaria, typhoid, typhus, dysentery, and smallpox, striking in waves across a debilitating pattern of routine afflictions—mange, skin disorders, gout, epilepsy. The grimmest scourge of all was smallpox, which seems to have become a more common and more virulent disease from the late seventeenth century.[3] A doctor of Montpellier in 1756 described it as being 'everywhere', as it were 'naturalized' and 'domesticated', especially at Paris, 'where it never relaxes its grip'.[4] According to d'Alembert's calculations, there were eight chances out of ten of catching 'la petite vérole', and of those who were attacked, the chances of dying were one in seven.[5] Not surprisingly, then, the army records on new recruits continually speak of marked faces—'visage picoté', or 'cicatrisé', 'greslé', 'gravé', 'marqué', 'grené'.[6] This was, indeed, a disease which destroyed the beauty of so many of those it did not slay. A novelist's character who wishes the worst for her enemy calls down this infection upon her, together with recovery, and 'un visage à faire trembler'.[7] Prévost's hero comes back to find Helena unrecognizable: he can only make love to her in the dark.[8] And it was a most terrible way of dying, in misery and disfigurement—a new form of death, said Montesquieu; nothing like those pastoral metaphors of flowers falling under the reaper's scythe.[9] It is now becoming possible to trace the geographical and chronological patterns of certain epidemics, even of diseases with a less clear definition than smallpox, and within these patterns to make a surer identification of the disease itself. For long, as a result of the documentation produced by government precautions, the day-to-day movement of the great plague of Marseille of 1720–1 along the roads of Provence has been known; with rather more difficulty, the progress of typhus coming into the port of Brest on warships throughout the century has been charted,[10] and, with more sophisticated techniques, that of the pneumonia which came over the border to Lorraine in 1782, reached Dijon early next year and the Pyrenees in November, then circled to Poitou by October 1784—a deadly scourge, which killed no less than 35 per cent of those that caught it.[11] Eventually a map of epidemics in eighteenth-century France will be produced, giving their places of origin, times of attack, staging points, and hiding-places, and the zones of susceptibility and immunity; pathogenic bacteria and viruses will have achieved their own sinister and independent history.

In 1766, Messance, publishing his researches on population, drew attention to the dangerous month of the year, which he said was March.[12] Contemporaries knew, of course, about the hazards of different seasons, but had not put their fears into statistical form. Since Messance, technical demography has completed the picture. There were two seasons when mortality was at its highest, winter and early spring on one hand, and autumn, especially the month of September, on the other. In some places, winter was the cruellest season, in others autumn.[13] From December to March, pneumonia and pulmonary afflictions abounded, and the sheer cold took its toll of those who were ill-clothed and lacked the means to keep warm. And these were numerous. Wood was in short supply in the cereal-growing plains and in the cities. Heating arrangements were rudimentary; even in Versailles, wine froze at the royal table in winter, and the heavily padded and decorated coats of courtiers were not just for display. Clothing passed from upper to lower classes and from older to younger generations, getting more and more threadbare on its journey. The poorer streets of cities were a motley pageant of rags, anonymous or with prestigious social origins. There were peasants who never changed their linen, and when they discarded it, it was too worn to be sent to the paper-mills. Even the more prosperous peasants (as we know from the 'contrats de vie à pot et à feu' drawn up when the old people handed

7

the farm over to the management of the younger) made do with two shirts and two coats a year, and a cloak every five.[14] There was not much in the wardrobe to keep them warm and dry in the snow or rain of winter. In August, September, and October, dysentery would strike, and before illnesses encouraged by the excessive heat had declined, there would come the onset of those which flourished in the ensuing dampness—'les maladies d'automne lors de la retraite du soleil'.[15] These were fevers—malaria (coming, as contemporaries noted, with the floods[16]), typhoid, and 'purple fever' which was often confused with the ubiquitous scarlatina or measles. Generally, it was adults, especially the aged, who succumbed in winter, and the younger children in the autumn—though there were exceptions: the cold in some places carried off more babies under the age of one than the intestinal infections of the hotter weather.[17] Superimposed upon this yearly cycle of menace was the arbitrary onslaught of great epidemics, sometimes driving the death rate up to double and treble the monthy average; there was the dysentery in Anjou in 1707 and 1779, highly infectious and lethal within two or three days, the influenza in the same province which caused devastation in 1740, the typhoid and enteric fever in Brittany from 1758 onwards which was largely responsible for reducing the population of that province by 4 per cent; there were more localized outbreaks, like the military fever in Pamiers in 1782 which killed 800 people.

Being born was a hazardous business for both mother and child. 'Don't get pregnant and don't catch smallpox' was Mme de Sévigné's advice to her married daughter—'Ne devenez pas enceinte, ni n'attrapez la petite vérole'[18]—although she had only simple ideas of how to avoid either. The proverbial pride in pregnancy of primitive societies was overwhelmed, in eighteenth-century France, by fear. Medical manuals considered a pregnant woman to be suffering from an illness, and even cited Scripture in ascribing the pains of childbirth to the transgression of Eve.[19] Many women, especially those of the poorer classes, came to their ordeal in wretched health, and the prevalence of rickets caused deformities which made delivery difficult. There were hardly any hygienic precautions, the technique for arresting haemorrhages was not yet developed, and the manipulation of forceps (supposed to be limited to qualified surgeons alone) was clumsy. Until the reign of Louis XVI, there was hardly any attempt to train midwives. In reporting to their bishops or to the secular authorities, parish priests described how the office of midwife came to be filled in their parish. 'Providence gives to each village enough knowledge among the women to be able to aid each other free of charge,' said an optimistic *recteur* in Brittany.[20] A *curé* in the diocese of Boulogne in 1725 said that his midwife inherited the job from her mother—'the women have a reasonable amount of confidence in her.' Another *curé* said that 'ours has worked here for thirty years: she took up the office of her own accord, the women of the parish accepted her, and it has not been thought fitting to oblige her to undergo further training.'[21] Horror stories about midwives abound—beating on the stomach to 'hasten delivery', cutting the umbilical cord too close or failing to tie it, forgetting the placenta, crippling babies by rough handling, and—even—showing off by turning the infant round so that the feet emerged first.[22] Louis XIV made a clean break with tradition when he called in a man, the surgeon Jacques Clément, to the *accouchement* of the Dauphine in 1686 (Dr Hecquet showed courage as well as prudery when he published his *De l'indécence aux hommes d'accoucher les femmes* in 1708). But were surgeons much more use than midwives? Clément bled his patient, wrapped her in the skin of a newly flayed sheep, and kept her in a dark room for nine days without so much as a single candle.[23] And how good was the gynaecologist whose advertisement in Paris has been preserved as a curiosity?—'Montodon, ci-devant pâtisseur, boulevard Bonne Nouvelle, est actuellement chirurgien et accoucheur.'[24] In fact, there was little that even the most expert practitioner could do if things went wrong. If the baby's head stuck, there would be a week of agony and the vileness of gangrene before inevitable death. The Caesarian section without anaesthetics left one chance in a thousand for the women. It was a sensation for the French medical world when the surgeon Sigoult performed a completely successful Caesarian in 1777, and a colleague at Quimper followed suit in 1778.[25] Many babies were stillborn, or died within a few days, or were maimed for life. A memoir to an intendant in 1773 describes young people coming out of a parish mass, marked by inexpert deliveries—atrophied, hunchbacked, deaf, blind, one-eyed, bandy-legged, bloodshot of eye, lame and twisted, hare-lipped, 'almost useless to society and fated for a premature end'.[26] Many women too were killed, or crippled, or mentally scarred; a *curé* blames the rise of contraceptive practices in his parish on the neurotic determination of so many women never to undergo the experience of childbirth again.[27]

'One-third of the human race perishes before reaching the age of twenty-eight months,' said Buffon; 'half the human race perishes before the age of eight years.'[28] He was not exaggerating. Between 20 and 30 per cent of babies born died in their first year: in a particularly wretched hamlet in the early part of the century, over 32 per cent died in their first year and over 22 per cent in their second.[29] There were, of course, healthy and unhealthy areas, depending on the peculiar combination of advantages and disadvantages in food supplies, geographical features, and climate. The national average in the eighteenth century for children surviving to the age of ten was, roughly, 55 per cent; at Crulai in Normandy it was 65 per cent; in poverty-stricken villages amidst the stagnant malarial pools of the Sologne or of the Mediterranean littoral, it was 40 per cent. In Sérignan, amidst the coastal marshes and with a silted port which ensured the continuing poverty of the village, of 1,091 children born between 1716 and 1783, only 427 survived to their tenth birthday.[30] The deadly season of the year for infants was early autumn, when heat, humidity and flies, and unhygienic ways of living brought the intestinal infections for which no remedy was known. These visitations were facilitated by the custom, prevalent among richer people and town dwellers, of sending infants away to be nursed by foster mothers. Towards the end of the century, of the 21,000 babies born each year in Paris, only 1,000 were fed by their mothers, another 1,000 by wet-nurses brought into the home, 2,000 to 3,000 were sent to places near the city, and the rest to more distant localities—concentric circles within which the proportion of deaths became higher as the distance from home increased.[31] In smaller towns, the fashion had less hold: in Meulan, for example, the *petit peuple* kept their babies, and only professional people and better-off artisans sent them away.[32] For families of the urban working class, like small shopkeepers or the silk workers of Lyon, it was an economic necessity to get the wife back to counter or loom quickly. For the leisured class, a satisfactory explanation is harder to find; a certain harshness of mind, an unwillingness to become too attached to a pathetic bundle whose chances of survival were so limited, the desire to resume sexual relationships as soon as possible, the belief that loss of milk diluted the quality of the blood of the mother, a reliance on the therapeutic qualities of country air to give the baby a good start or (very doubtfully) some subconscious reaction against an infant's 'oral sadism'[33]—whatever the reasons, a compelling social custom had arisen. In 1774, a reformer, appealing to have children 'brought up in the order of Nature', described the sensation when a mother declares her intention of breast-feeding her first child: protests from her parents, and all the ladies lamenting to see her risking her life for a new-fashioned theory.[34] Given the demand, around the cities a wet-nursing 'industry' had arisen. In some villages near Limoges, girls married earlier to qualify.[35] Such glimpses as we get of this peculiar interchange between town and country show an unfeeling and mercenary world—women who take on two or three babies in addition to their own, knowing that there will be competition for survival, who go on drawing their pay when they know their milk is drying up and their client's infant will have no chance, specialist 'sevreuses' who wean children knowing there is every chance of killing them.[36] These practitioners are preying on legitimate children, with parents to look after their interests and hoping against hope that they will be trundled back home in nine months' time. What then of the illegitimate ones, the multitude of foundlings, the *enfants trouvés*?

The fate of these unhappy infants throws a harsh, cold light on the cruel underside of the century of crystalline wit and rococo delicacy. Increasing numbers of children were being abandoned. An average of 2,000 a year came to the Enfants Trouvés of Paris in the 1720s, rising to a record total of 7,676 in 1772; thereafter, royal edicts forbade the bringing-in of foundlings from the provinces, and the Parisian total stabilized at about 5,800 a year.[37] In Bordeaux at the mid-century, there were about 300 admissions annually; in Metz, in the winter of 1776, no less than 900, so that an administrator extrapolating statistics for a century ahead, foresaw a time when all the children in France would be without parents.[38] These numbers swamped the organizational abilities of the *ancien régime*, at least in so far as *seigneurs hauts justiciers*, the Crown, and (in Flanders and Brittany) the parishes were willing to pay,[39] and the hopeless problem they presented deadened the charitable instincts of those who cared. A Genevan doctor reports a nun of the Parisian foundling hospital taking refuge in the reflection that these innocent souls would go straight to eternal bliss, since the revenues of her institution could not feed any more of them anyway.[40] There was a prejudice against making immoral conduct easier by spending money on those 'unhappy fruits of debauchery' (though it is true that some children were abandoned by married parents who were too poor to maintain them).[41] Many illegitimate children were doomed before ever they reached the shelter of an institution—physically impaired by the mother's attempts to conceal her pregnancy or to produce an abortion,[42] infected with veneral disease,[43] or hopelessly weakened by a journey from some distant place, crowded in baskets on the back of a donkey, or of a porter travelling on foot, or jolting in a wagon.[44] The infants who got through the crucial first week in which so many died had to survive the grim and crowded conditions in the hospital, and the rigours of the system of putting out to nurse (with private families paying more to pre-empt the healthiest and most reliable foster mothers).[45] Only one foundling in ten lived to reach the age of ten: nine had perished. Such survivors as there were would live gloomily learning a trade in some institution full of prostitutes, layabouts, and madmen,[46] or in some ruthlessly disciplined orphanage;[47] a very few might be found again by their parents[48] or left with some sympathetic country family—but the chances of a decent existence were infinitesimal. One who did get through the hazards and succeeded was the *philosophe* and mathematician d'Alembert, left as an infant on the steps of the church of Saint-Jean-la-Ronde. An expert on the calculus of probabilities, he must often have reflected on the odds that he had beaten.[49]

Driven to despair by poverty, some parents abandoned their children: there were suspicions that others did not strive officiously to keep them alive. The synodal statutes of various dioceses ordered the *curés* to warn their flocks against the dangerous practice of putting children to sleep in the beds of their parents, where so often they were suffocated.[50] Perhaps these accidents were the result of risks knowingly run, though what judgement can be made amidst

the promiscuity and confusion which grinding poverty engendered? A surgeon described the injuries suffered by babies in the
vineyard country around Reims: while their mothers toiled among
the vines they were sometimes attacked by animals—eyes pecked
by turkeys, hands eaten off by pigs.[51] And for the healthy grown-
up, the ordinary routines of life were precarious. Society was
ill-policed, unable to take effective measures to suppress highwaymen and discipline vagabonds. Rural life was violent. Wife-beating
was common.[52] Unpopular *curés* were kept awake by nocturnal
tapages which could degenerate into riots. There were affrays with
cudgels and clubs at fairs. In Languedoc, where the hunting rights
of the lords had been bought off, peasants went around with guns;
poachers returned the fire of gamekeepers; and pot-shots were
taken at *seigneurs* and other unpopular local worthies.[53] The youths
of villages were organized, quasi-officially, into bands, the 'garçons
de paroisse', who fought pitched battles with those from other
places at fairs, marriages, and the draw for the *milice*, or when
communities quarrelled over boundaries or grazing rights. In 1752,
in the Lyon area, the *jeunesse* of Échalas allied with three other
villages fought those of Hillery and their allies; there were many
injuries, but no one available to give evidence to the authorities.[54] In
towns, the police force was inadequate to maintain order at festivals
or to organize precautions against accidents. A panic at the fireworks in Paris for the marriage of the Dauphin in 1770 led to more
than 1,000 being trampled to death; two years later, the great fire at
the Hôtel-Dieu claimed many victims.[55] There were, indeed, few
precautions against fire—for long the only Parisian fire brigade was
the Capuchin friars, swarming into action in frocks and cowls, with
axes and ladders. Narrow streets, ramshackle buildings, and an
abundance of wooden construction made the old parts of cities
hopelessly vulnerable, tinder dry in summer, and underpinned
with extra fuel in winter when the cellars of the rich were crammed
with firewood and grain. That was how the historic centre of
Rennes was burnt out in December 1720, with few fatal casualties,
but causing enormous damage, and hardships which took their
indirect toll of lives.[56] Buildings, especially the parish churches for
whose maintenance a local rate had to be levied, were often left
unrepaired and dangerous; every year there were floods from

unbanked rivers, wreaking devastation and leaving legacies of fever.[57] In the streets and in the countryside, savage dogs, some with rabies, wandered; in remote areas wolf packs hunted—there was a government bounty for each one killed, the parish priest to issue a certificate on the production of the ears; in 1750, 126 were killed in the province of Anjou alone.[58] Our modern concept of 'accident' as some technical failure—burnt-out wire, slipping flange, broken lever—obtruding into well-organized habitual comfort, was almost unknown in the eighteenth century. Life was hazardous throughout, with a lurid penumbra of danger from violent men and savage animals on the margins. It seems almost idyllic, by contrast, to read of the ancient dame of Meulan whose quiet death at home is solemnly recorded: 'tombée dans sa cheminée après s'être endormie'.[59]

Up to the last two decades of the *ancien régime*, hardly anything was done to regulate dangerous trades or to prevent industrial accidents. The Italian, Bernardino Ramazzini's *De morbis artificium*, which began the serious study of these problems, published in Modena in 1700, was translated into English in 1705, but not until 1771 did it appear in a French version. Philippe Hecquet, however, used Ramazzini's work in his *La Médecine, la chirurgie et la pharmacie des pauvres* (1740), though his opening sentence, describing the poor as playing the role in the State which shadows play in a painting, demonstrated the fatalistic presuppositions which he brought to his subject.[60] Even so, though nothing was being done, contemporaries were becoming aware of the terrifying hardships which crippled industrial workers and abbreviated their lives. Diderot, whose *Encyclopédie* did so much to draw attention to the skill and precision displayed by ill-rewarded craftsmen, expressed surprise, in 1773, that there was a slight excess of births over deaths in France, given the conditions he had seen in some workshops—as bad as those of the mines in Saxony where a woman might outlive a dozen husbands.[61] Conditions in French mines were grim enough: twelve hours a day underground, in continual danger from explosions (because fires were burning to suck air along the galleries) and from flooding (if the horse-turned pumps failed).[62] The workers who polished mirrors, their feet continually in water and hands continually getting cut, were worn out by the interminable pushing to and fro of the heavy weight; printers received fractures and bruises from the levers of their presses; candle makers stifled in the heat around the furnaces; hemp crushers invariably got asthma; gilders became dizzy within a few months from the mercurial fumes which eventually poisoned them; workers who handled unwashed wool were recognizable by their pale and leaden countenances, upon which would be superimposed the permanent stains of the colours used in dyeing.[63] Alarming examples of the effect of bad conditions of working and living on mortality rates can be studied in the armed forces. In war, few sailors were killed by cannon-balls. The seventy-four-gun ship *Ajax* patrolled in the Atlantic and Indian Oceans from February 1780 to June 1784; during that period 228 of her crew of 430 died. Battle accounted for only thirty (and of these half perished from the explosion of one of the ship's own cannon); nine were drowned (6 after falling from a mast, 1 swept off the ship's latrine by a freak following wave); no less than 185 were killed by diseases: scurvy, dysentery, malaria— infections that ran riot among men cooped below decks for most of their time afloat, and living on food lacking in indispensable vita- mins (they paid good prices to the *caliers* living in the hold for fresh rat meat).[64] It could be said that war killed soldiers, but essentially indirectly. The mortality rate in a particular regiment from 1716 to 1749 was five times higher in war years than in those of peace, but the deaths occurred principally from December to April, when the troops were in winter quarters.[65] In the barracks built in the eight- eenth century (always at the expense of the local authorities, not of the Crown), the standard size for a room was 16 by 18 feet, to contain thirteen to fifteen men crammed into four or five beds.[66] These stifling conditions, rampant epidemics, the cold outside, and venereal disease killed many more in winter quarters than the shot and steel of the enemy in the summer campaigning season. It was a rule under the *ancien régime* that life in State institutions was abbreviated. When *dépôts de mendicité* were set up in 1767 to clear vagabonds off the roads, the inmates died off rapidly. They were by definition poor physical specimens, and contractors received only 6 sous a day for maintaining them. At Rennes, of 600 initially arrested, 137 died within a year, though it is true there were a lot of infections about at the time. At Saint-Denis, the death rate in the *dépôt* was consistently double that for the town, not excepting the high infant mortality from the latter total.[67] Contrary to the traditional egalitarian theme of the *danse macabre*, still relished in the popular literature of the eighteenth century, death was not without deference to rank and possessions, to the well-to-do with their log fires, warm clothing, protein diet, and spacious houses. To keep death at bay, the historian Muratori noted during the plague at Modena in 1714, space and time, the prerogatives of the rich, are needed—private rooms, changes of clothing, leisure to take precautions, freedom to move away from danger to the open country.[68] True, in this age of multitudinous servants, it was difficult to erect effective barriers of unofficial quarantine—in the last resort, infections got through: 'the guard at the gate of the Louvre' of Malherbe's famous poem was no security against them. No doubt there were special afflictions to descend upon the self-indulgent; moralists (with some injustice to the sufferers) liked to instance apoplexy, paralysis, and gout. Cynics would add the dangers from the medical profession; the peasant, who distrusted blood-letting and could not afford to pay the surgeon to do it, was at least free from his attentions. Even so, the life expectancy of the rich was much better than that of the poor, and the men of the eighteenth century knew it. In statistical terms, we might guess that the advantage was something like ten years above the average and seventeen years above that of the very poor.[69] Peasants, living crowded together in single-roomed cottages, were very vulnerable, and even more so were the poor of the towns, whose debilitating conditions of working were allied to crowded, insanitary accommodation. Disease spread quickly where there was only one bed for a family. A doctor in the countryside complained of the way in which people 'occupy the beds of those who are dead of the malady [typhoid] on the same day the corpse is taken out of it',[70] and it was well known that the communal bed was one of the reasons why the great plague of 1720 in Provence so often swept off a whole family, though the flea-borne method of transmission was not yet understood.[71] The churchwardens of the poverty-stricken parish of Saint-Sauveur in Lille complained that the death rate of their parishioners in the epidemic of 1772–3 had been much higher than in the wealthy parish of Saint-André. 'The higher numbers here', they said, 'can only be because the inhabitants are poor, more numerous and crowded into little houses, often occupied by many families, and situated in very narrow streets called alleyways . . ., they breathe the less pure air here, and because of the dirt which is virtually inseparable from poverty, they propagate all the diseases which catch a hold among them.'[72] In Lyon, the silk workers lived twelve to fifteen in a garret, forty to fifty families in a house in the tall buildings around sunless courts, stinking of the chickens, pigs, and rabbits that they reared, and of latrines. In 1783 Menuret de Chambaud published an essay on the 'medico-topography' of the city. 'The workers', he said, 'live a life very different from that of well-off people. They are usually thin and shrivelled, short of stature; the contamination of the air they breathe, the poor quality of the food they eat, the lack of exercise, the filth in which they exist, the cramped position in which they have to operate their machinery completely change their nature, and render them entirely different from the other inhabitants.' And he added that they died quickly, more especially of tuberculosis.[73]

When the Royal Council on 29 April 1776 set up its commission to investigate epidemic diseases in the provinces, one of the questions it posed was: 'Why do epidemics sometimes seem to spare a particular class of citizens?' Probably, the intention was not to look at the obvious overcrowding of the slums, but at the food and water supplies and at the dietary habits of the different classes. Seventy years earlier, during the misery at the end of the reign of Louis XIV, the economist Boisguilbert, in a burning tirade, had censured the maldistribution of food supplies which cut short so many lives. There are men, he said, who sweat blood in their toil, with no food other than bread and water, in the midst of a land of abundance, who 'perish when only half their course is run', and whose children are 'stifled in their cradles'.[74] At about that time, Vauban estimated that a weaver of Rouen who missed a single day's work would leave his family hungry. Estimates later in the century—at Arles in 1750, by the agricultural society of La Rochelle in 1763, by the owner of a carpet factory in Abbeville in 1764—show that the poorer peasants and urban workers, though far from being reduced to bread and water, lived all their lives on the margins of danger: any loss of working days had to be paid for by starvation later.[75]

17

There was a cycle of illness, debt, and hunger which made death almost certain on the next round of visitation, and it was not unusual for wretches who had struggled fiercely against starvation to give up on hearing that they had caught some disease, knowing that the future had little hope.[76]

Most people in France lived on cereals, because this was what they could afford. A modern attempt to work out a typical budget for a family of the poor majority in an ordinary year, suggests 50 per cent of expenditure on bread, 16 per cent on fats and wine, 13 per cent on clothing, and 5 per cent on heating.[77] So far as the proportion on bread is concerned, eighteenth-century estimates studied more recently confirm the generalization.[78] The ration in hospitals was one and half *livres* a day, and this was the amount an employer generally allowed to a servant in Paris. The Auvergnats who migrated from home to do back-breaking work as building labourers and navvies needed more and could afford it: according to Moheau they ate prodigious quantities, five to six *livres* a day.[79] Judged on the scale of calories, in a fair year, the workers of France were fed efficiently, so far as potential energy was concerned, but, as more than 90 per cent of these calories came from cereals (including maize porridge in the south and beer in the north), the dietary deficiencies are obvious. The food consumption of the inmates of the hospital of Caen (bread, and the unusual advantage of plenty of Norman cider), of the conscripts doing guard duty at the citadel of Saint-Malo in the mid-century (unimaginative bread, biscuits, and salt meat, with none of the coastal fish which ought to have diversified their diet), of the peasants of Périgord (chestnuts and maize in fearful stews kept simmering all day), of the peasants of Basse-Auvergne (bread, soup of nut oil, and water tinctured with wine)—all show the same deficiencies: a lack of meat, fish, dairy produce, and fresh vegetables.[80] That meant a deficiency of vitamins, animal fats, calcium, and trace elements, leaving the way open for rickets, scurvy, skin eruptions, loss of teeth, the breaking down of the natural power of resistance to cold, and the stunting of growth, both physical and mental. It was a matter for wonder that men from mountain areas (where the pastures offered milk and meat) were so tall—as in Auvergne, where they towered over the puny inhabitants of the cereal-growing plain.[81] The suggestion that the weaker force of gravity at high altitudes had allowed them to spurt upwards found some currency.[82] The ill effects of the inevitable deficiencies were increased by ignorance. Apart from Duhamel du Monceau's excellent advice about fruit and green vegetables as a prophylactic against scurvy (1759), and Dr Tissot's sage counsels against overeating (1761), there was little knowledge of what constituted a balanced diet.[83] Even the rich did not know what was good for them. They ate a large amount of meat—the records of butchers' cattle taken into Paris and into the small town of Saint-Jean-de-Losne show that there would have been a ration equivalent to what we get today had it been equally divided.[84] But an analysis of the meals eaten by a magistrate of Toulouse and of the pupils at a boarding-school for young nobles show, even so, a lack of calcium and some vitamins.[85] The food available to ordinary people was not always wisely used. The regulation stew-pot of the peasants boiled away the vitamins (an intendant, trying to convert them to the use of rice, recommended seventeen hours' simmering, a receipt for edible glue).[86] Fresh bread was unusual, since for economy, huge loaves which lasted for two or three months were baked in communal ovens.[87] The oft-recorded obstinacy of peasants in refusing to eat unusual food like potatoes, even when starving, is paralleled by the refusal of the Parisians to accept the government economy bread of wheat, rye, and barley, invented during the dearth of 1767.[88] And of course, the people were spendthrift; living on crusts and onions all week, they would go to drinking booths on Sunday night, or swig a tot of *eau-de-vie* on their way to work in the mornings.[89] But statistics of vitamin, calcium, and trace-element deficiencies can prove too much. Like the analysis of wages in eighteenth-century France, they go to show that half the population ought not to have been alive at all. Life, for these people, was 'an economy of makeshifts', patching up a living by all sorts of incongruous combinations of earnings; no doubt they supplemented their food supplies by tilling odd corners, keeping animals in hutches, gleaning in hedgerow and common, begging, poaching, and pilfering. That was why it was so dangerous to become institutionalized, whether shut up in a *dépôt de mendicité*, a hospital, a madhouse, or on shipboard. Survival became difficult when there was no scope for enterprise.

Whatever mysterious and useless medicines they prescribed, the doctors of eighteenth-century France knew the primary importance of sound nourishment to aid the sick to recovery. Meat soup was the standard prescription for all convalescents; in Languedoc when the lawcourts awarded damages to a victim of assault, the cost of those 'bouillons' generally figured on the list, and it was customary to observe, when one of the neighbours was seen at the butcher's, that there must be someone ill in the house.[90] 'Remedies and advice are useless unless there is a foundation of solid nourishment,' said a physician called in to investigate the outbreak of dysentery in Anjou in 1707, and he asked for 'bouillons' to be dispatched daily to all who had been afflicted. 'Bread, wine, and blankets' were the prescriptions of the doctors of Anjou who dealt with epidemics of dysentery in 1768 and typhus in 1774.[91] In times of dearth, the poor were driven to eat contaminated or unripened grain, and were poisoned in consequence; 'all the bad foodstuffs which shortages condemn us to use, abridging our life in the hope of supporting it,' said Voltaire—insisting that deaths from this cause should be counted under the heading of 'famine'.[92] Officials in Brittany in 1769 and 1771 reported diseases (one called them of an 'epileptic' kind) which were sweeping the provinces because the crop failures had driven the people to eat grain that had been damp when stored and had fermented and grown musty. The parish priests in 1775 ascribed a 'putrid fever' to a similar cause.[93] In the Sologne, there were outbreaks from time to time of ergotism caused by infected grain—the disease was called 'St. Anthony's fire' and 'dry gangrene': it led to the loss of fingers, noses, or whole limbs, and eventually to madness.[94] And the greatest killer of all was contaminated water. Springs and wells would become infected as they dried up or floods overflowed them from dubious catchment areas, or were permanently dangerous because of defective masonry in cisterns, or because animals had access to them. Typical complaints concern effluent from flax-crushing or animal manure getting into drinking supplies, or froth from the oxen's mouths still floating on the top of buckets brought in for domestic consumption. In some villages without a well, water was collected in shallow holes dug here and there and had to be filtered through linen.[95] And any Parisian who gave a thought to where his water supply came from

20

would confine himself to drinking wine always—if he could afford it.

Certain seasons of the year brought the shadow of food shortages. There were the dangerous months of *la souture* from April to July, when the previous year's grain was being used up, and before the new crop was harvested. There was a danger period too in winter, especially for townspeople, for freezing weather might ice up the canals along which the supply barges came, or stop the water-mills from grinding the flour. And, worst of all, the crop might fail, damaged by unseasonable cold or rain or hail; rumour would race ahead of truth, encouraging the hoarding which transformed fear into the first instalment of grim reality.

It is generally said that the era of great famines ended in 1709; thereafter came shortages, serious indeed, but not deadly, 'les disettes larvées'.[96] 'In the seventeenth century people died of hunger: in the eighteenth they suffered from it.'[97] This is true so far as dying as a direct result of starvation is concerned, though local historians can always find a catastrophic year to form an exception worthy to qualify as the last of the crises—perhaps 1730 at Saint-Maurice-du-Désert in Normandy, 1739–40 in the Cotentin, 1752 in the Toulouse area, while Richard Cobb paints a sombre picture of Rouen in Year III and Year IV of the Republic, with grain prices tripled and a cruelly hard winter.[98] A common-sense review of the probabilities of dying might suggest a logical sequence: famine, hunger weakening the resistance of the population, the resort to contaminated food causing illness, the onset of some killing disease, and the starving poor forced into vagabondage acting as carriers for the infection. In practice, in the eighteenth century this proposed pattern of death's operations is only occasionally borne out by comparisons of the graphs of corn prices, illness, and mortality. At Dijon in the 1740s, it seems clear that famine must have been the essential cause of the increase in the number of deaths, though an epidemic could strike at a particular place with an overwhelming impact only explainable by its own virulence.[99] Over the large area where the Parlement of Paris had jurisdiction, there was a dearth of a classical pattern between 1738 and 1741: a wet summer in 1738 and a poor crop, a normal harvest in 1739 but preceded by a rainy period which had encouraged hoarding, a long winter in 1739–40, with a freezing January damaging the sowing of the previous autumn, followed by a wet July and August wreaking further havoc on the harvest, and floods in December to disorganize transport. There were food riots in Paris in the autumn of 1740. Yet the mortality figures do not fit in with the rise in grain prices, and in 1741 it was in distant Brittany and not the Paris Basin that a significant increase in the death rate occurred.[100] At Meulan, near the capital, bread reached its high in 1740, but there were fewer deaths that year than in 1738, a year of epidemic (78 as against 101). Here, the periods of high grain prices had been 1709–10 and 1740: the years of epidemic 1706, 1716, 1738, 1743—showing no obvious connection.[101] At Strasbourg[102] in 1719–21, 1733–5, and 1742–4, grain reached a high price without there being any deficiency in the harvests—a result of the fevers and influenza outbreaks which discouraged the corn-dealers from supplying the city.

It has been argued, with eighteenth-century England as the example, that malnutrition does not weaken resistance to disease, except in the case of afflictions arising directly from deficiencies of diet, and tuberculosis and dysentery.[103] A historian who has never known what it is to be hungry for very long instinctively feels inclined to doubt this assertion. True, studies of the Third World today show how deprived peoples can sometimes maintain themselves in calorific and protein balance on a diet that would mean starvation to the inhabitants of advanced countries. While bodily size and appearance are affected by the food supply, the same does not necessarily apply to resistance to infection. But there is a distinction to be made. While the nutrition taken by individuals seems not to have much effect on their chance of becoming infected with most diseases, it is of the utmost importance in deciding what their ultimate fate will be. 'Malnutrition does not particularly favour or impede the acquisition of infection, but it goes a long way to determine the course of the resulting disease.'[104] The relationship between dearth and epidemic among the poorer classes of eighteenth-century France is not so much a short-term correspondence, but a general pattern of attrition by the alternations and the accumulated onslaughts of hunger and disease. The point may be taken, however, that pathogenic bacteria and viruses do not need to wait to find a human population weakened by famine before they strike;

some apparently hopeless human groups may have built up an immunity, while some apparently flourishing ones may be unprotected. One disease may fade out, leaving the weak as predestinate victims for another; thus the plague vanished from Languedoc after 1655, and malaria took over, its victims forming a new reservoir of infection to pass on to future generations.[105] We may picture death as vigilant but unhurried and patient. Sometimes hunger served its purposes, as in the terrible dearth in the spring of 1740 in Auvergne, where a *curé* reported that the women let their children die so that the adults could live, and the men, to avoid conceiving children, resorted to unnatural practices with animals.[106] Sometimes some overwhelming contagion, like the plague of Marseille, swept away all human defences. It could be, in these disasters, that the swift succumbing of the physically weak was a precondition for a widespread pattern of infection which trapped the rich, who might otherwise have escaped. 'La famine amène la peste,' said the bishop of Chartres moralizing, 'et la peste est pour tout le monde':[107] more often, the continuing cycle of disease, hunger, renewed disease, and despair brought life to an end. There is a story of Louis XV encountering a funeral procession and asking what the man had died from. 'Starvation, Sire.' It was an indictment of his government, and the answer would have been true, indirectly, of many other deaths from infections and accidents. 'C'est de misère que l'on meurt au dix-septième siècle' says Lebrun.[108] Though the situation was changing in the eighteenth century, this grim generalization was still broadly applicable. Particular diseases were the indispensable infantry in Death's dark armies, but his generals were Cold and Hunger.

Defences against Death:
Eighteenth-century Medicine

Amidst the melancholy grandeur of his declining years, Louis XIV was an illustrious survivor: he had outlived his own generation and his immediate heirs. In April 1711 his son Monseigneur, le Grand Dauphin, was stricken down by smallpox. France then looked towards the duc de Bourgogne, son of Monseigneur and grandson of Louis XIV, and to his charming duchess, for the inauguration of a new era of reform. On 5 February 1712, sinister red pustules showed that the duchess had measles. The doctors gave her tobacco, opium, and emetics and she died on the 12th. On the 16th, the deadly signs appeared on the duc, and within three days he was gone. At the beginning of March, measles struck down the duc de Bretagne, another grandson of the Sun King, and he died with nine doctors bleeding him. The heir was now a four-year-old boy, Louis duc d'Anjou, the second son of the duc de Bourgogne. The ladies of the court would not allow the doctors to come near to bleed him, and he survived. The long reign of Louis XIV had been made possible by good luck and by virtue of an iron constitution – he had hunted at the age of seventy-four, and in the following year stopped the frenzied horses of his carriage when they bolted. He had survived[1] gonorrhoea, typhus, measles, malaria, and renal colic, and all the while in his later years he had been vexed by gastric afflictions (a result of gluttony), constipation, vertigo, gravel, carbuncles, and gout (his physicians had stopped him drinking the wine of Champagne and put him on to that of Burgundy, leading to a national quarrel of the vintners). In a fearful onslaught on his decaying teeth in 1685, the surgeon-dentists had split his left upper jaw, so that when he drank the liquid spurted from his nose. He had been purged 2,000 times (occasionally and on the last day of every moon), had been subjected to hundreds of clysters (enemas), and

24

had bleedings galore, until he told the doctors he would have no more of them. One medicine had been extraordinarily effective—cinchona bark, which provided pints of quinine to allay the effects of his malaria. One operation had been brilliantly successful, the removal of an anal fistula in 1686, after practice incisions on less illustrious sufferers. On 15 August 1715, the great king finally yielded to an illness which had been dogging him, and took to his bed.[2] Gangrene developed in the left leg below the knee and was rising. On 24 August the King made his confession, and received the viaticum and extreme unction. On the following day he said goodbye to his family and the assembled courtiers, asking pardon for the bad example he had set. 'I am departing, but the State will always remain . . . I hope that you will remember me sometimes.' He told the Dauphin that he had loved war too much, and urged him to care for his people (that he was still planning extensions to the park and stables at Marly should not be taken as proof of insincerity: Louis XIV's humanitarian dying words were not meant to include recommendations for the reduction of royal splendour). Fagon, the *premier médecin du roi*, called in four other doctors, to no avail. On 28 August an empiric from Provence, called Brun, arrived, with a secret elixir against gangrene. After a dispute, the doctors allowed it to be tried. The King took ten drops in wine of Alicante and felt rather better. The court ladies clamoured for Brun's remedy to be tried again, and so it was. There was no hope. The courtiers faded away from the bedside, and on Sunday 1 September, at 8.15 in the morning, the King died. Through the bonfires of rejoicing in the streets of Paris, a carriage brought the Dean of the Faculty of Medicine of the University, one of his colleagues, and two surgeons, to Versailles, to join Fagon and the other royal physicians for the autopsy. Once it was over, the doctors enjoyed a substantial collation, the surgeons being excluded, since the long-standing feud between the two branches of the medical profession did not allow of friendly social relationships.[3] The story of Louis XIV's illnesses during life and of his death is instructive. The medicine of the age had only two effective remedies: mercury for venereal disease and quinine for fevers. Surgeons were capable of inflicting terrible maimings, but also of feats of astonishing dexterity. The feud between the surgeons and the official Faculties hampered the progress of knowledge. For most illnesses, the supposed cures were either harmful or useless. A wandering charlatan could turn up, even at the royal bedside, and his elixir be tried. This was all that could be done for the greatest monarch in Europe. Rousseau's verdict in *Émile*, fifty years later, may serve as a commentary on the events of that second half of August 1715 at Versailles. The physician's art, he said, is fraudulent, and merely increases the bitterness of death. 'Cet art mensonger . . . recule moins la mort qu'il ne la fait sentir d'avance.'[4]

There were twenty-four Medical Faculties in France, offering courses of three-year study following on the two years necessary for the *maîtrise ès arts*. The formal teaching, in Latin, and based on the aphorisms of Hippocrates and Galen and ancient textbooks superficially revised, was of less use than the practical experience which might or might not be gained, depending on the presence of some expert professor, or on the student's own curiosity and determination. At Montpellier, until a Collège Royal de Chirurgie was set up in 1757 (at the instance of Lapeyronie, a patriotic citizen who had become Chief Surgeon to Louis XV[5]), the work of the professors was hampered by the administrators of the hospital of Saint-Éloi, who refused access to their wards to all academic teachers; students queued for tickets to accompany the hospitals' *chirurgien major* on his rounds.[6] All together, there were only half a dozen Medical Faculties that had a solid reputation. In the west, it was proverbial that you sent for a doctor who had qualified at Montpellier, and not at Nantes or Angers[7] (which was something of a libel on Angers, where there were some prestigious teachers[8] even though the official standards in the examinations were contemptible). These were litigious days. The Faculty of Nantes went to law before the Parlement of Brittany to try to get graduates of Montpellier disbarred from local practice;[9] about the same time, the Faculty of Paris staged a three-month strike in protest against the setting-up of the Royal Society of Medicine.[10]

When they were not engaged in scoring off each other, the physicians were united to keep down the surgeons, who belonged to a separate profession for long tied up with the guild system. Only in 1692 had they been finally separated from the barbers by royal edict. But they were rising in the world.[11] In 1731 an Académie Royale de Chirurgie was founded – not a learned society, but a teaching and professional organization. Then in 1743 (for Paris) and 1756 (for the provinces) surgeons were formally made members of a liberal profession, provided they produced a thesis for the *maîtrise ès arts*. Ludicrously, some grey-haired and highly qualified practitioners had to learn their Latin again to qualify. There were opportunities for first-rate training – at the Collège de Chirurgie in Paris, as a lay pupil with the Frères de Saint-Jean de Dieu, at the courses for naval surgeons at Saint-Malo and Brest, or in the military hospitals. Even so, most surgeons who were installed in country villages had only rudimentary skills. Yet, including all those who had technical qualifications, however unsatisfactory, there was still not a great deal of professional medical advice available in most parts of France. A survey carried out by the Royal Society of Medicine on behalf of the government in 1786,[12] showed that, lumping together all doctors and surgeons, the intendancies of Amiens, Dijon, and Soissons had only 59 medical practitioners per 100,000 inhabitants, while the Rennes area had only 24, and these unevenly distributed—an independent investigation by the intendant showed that the west of the province was particularly ill-provided.[13] These surveys also showed most towns were generally three times better served than rural areas. At Nantes, there were nine doctors and forty surgeons, as well as an indeterminate number of naval medical officers, whereas villages would only have a single surgeon anywhere near at hand, and not necessarily competent at that. Such a one the *subdélégué* of Villers-Cotterets described as 'a public assassin, licensed to kill the sick with impunity'.[14]

Except when they were carried off to the hospital, often enough to die there, or in times of epidemic, when the government sent experts round, the peasants and urban workers saw little of the medical profession. The parish priest, with his contacts outside the village, was expected to be knowledgeable in matters of health. When he met his brother clergy socially, or at the bishop's *conférences ecclésiastiques*, or when he went up to the cathedral city to pay his clerical taxation, collect the consecrated oils, or see to other business, he would hear news of what the gazettes reported concerning new remedies. Sometimes he would receive instructions from the intendant about hygienic precautions, to be read from the pulpit, or, if a disease was rampant in the parish, would be put in charge of the distribution of free medicines – the peasant cheerfully put them in his soup and thought them 'sweeter than honey because they cost nothing'.[15] Some *curés* became specialists. We hear of one growing medicinal herbs, in the belief that 'healing the body and the soul are two ministries which the pastors ought to exercise simultaneously', of another applying the new-fangled pseudo-science of mesmerism to the healing art.[16] In 1775, the chronicler of the town of Le Mans recounts how four *curés* had a theological argument so heated that one collapsed and died—alas! he was the only man in town who could cure maladies of the eyes.[17] In October 1789, a parish priest of Poitou wrote to the government saying that he had been 'apostle, judge, surgeon and doctor' to his people for thirty-four years.[18] The sisters of charity (the Sœurs de Saint-Vincent-de-Paul), who went round the countryside, would do bandaging and, even, bleeding—'extracting the blood of commoners without worrying about qualifications to do so'.[19] A doctor of Saint-Brieuc in 1779, less jealous of professional monopolies than most of his colleagues, said that the sick at Plérins could quite properly be left to the sisters of charity there, and he was happy to help with advice in difficult cases.[20] Such tolerance towards the clergy and religious orders was rare,[21] and was never extended by the profession to unqualified amateurs unprotected by the uniform of the Church. The government and intendants kept getting complaints against fairground charlatans, peasant wiseacres who graduated from dosing cattle to treating human beings, the 'venomous horde' of empirical surgeons, grocers who acted as apothecaries, muscular characters who set up as dentists, public executioners who (with their sinister experience of breaking victims on the wheel) were adept at bone-setting.[22] In towns, the apothecaries' shops had medicines available for the credulous with money to spare. Traditional and reputable was *orviétan*, a mixture of dried vipers and twenty-five other substances, in treacle. Among the novelties were Agirony's 'anti-venereal balsam' (1769), the 'golden drops' of General la Mothe, a Transylvanian soldier whose wife carried on the preparation after his death in 1757, and Arnoult's 'poudre antiapoplectique' (1741), which was supported by a testimonial

28

from Cardinal de Polignac—prince of the Church, author, and international diplomat, one could hardly expect a better recommendation.[23] For the countryside, there were handbooks of do-it-yourself medicine, like the collection of 'simple household remedies' allegedly put together by Mme de Foucquet, mother of Louis XIV's minister,[24] and almanacs which noted the proper dates for bleeding and purging. But pamphlets of popular medical advice were comparatively few in the literature hawked by pedlars.[25] While the book trade proper abounded in medical treatises for the edification of hypochondriacs among the bourgeoisie, the peasants seem to have been dourly satisfied with personal advice from someone who counted locally, or with traditional remedies passed down in the village.

It would be interesting to know more about the diffusion in rural France of knowledge of these traditional herbal medicines; some of them, examined in the light of modern pharmacological knowledge, turn out to contain drugs, narcotics, antiseptics, soothing or purging elements—wild thyme, digitalis, ergot of rye (used by some eighteenth-century midwives to stop bleeding), gentian, root of bryony, leaves of borage, fennel, burdock, juniper, artemisia, greater celandine.[26] For the pious, religion offered saints who specialized in various maladies—Laurent and Lazare for burns because they had been tortured by fire, Eutrope and other decapitated saints for migraine, Aldegunde and Agathe for tumours. There were wells, springs, and pools, chapels and shrines for pilgrimages, with far-distant folk-memories echoing behind the prayers and floating in the incense which Christianized an antique paganism. In Normandy, the victim of fever ought to say, to allay the symptoms, 'I do not shake or tremble' because Christ had said these words to a Jew who accused him of showing fear on the way to Golgotha; for burns, say five Paters and five Aves, and add 'let fire lose its heat as Judas became pale when betraying Jesus'. For toothache, drive a nail into a tree, declaring 'enbornus, et dognus et diminuet'.[27] With what degree of conviction these ceremonies were performed, the folklorists cannot tell us. There were peasants who were bled by the calendar, and those who refused to be bled under any circumstances: like their property or their pig, their blood was theirs and remained theirs. No doubt, so far as religious observances or superstitions were concerned, there was a willingness to try any-thing. But characteristic all the while of village life was a universal, sceptical fatalism: whether it was God or the Devil involved, what would happen would happen, and in due time, early or late, death would claim its due.

Hospitals were for the poor. A survey in the early days of the Revolution shows that there were about 2,000 institutions worthy of the name in France.[28] Some were tiny, but for those (more than half the total) about which details are available, the average number of beds was ninety or so. The provinces of Guyenne, Languedoc, Dauphiné, and Alsace were better provided, according to their population, than provinces like Anjou (where there were only twenty institutions with a total of 717 beds);[29] the reason for the imbalance may be that Catholic piety had been more active in this respect in areas where there had been a confrontation with Protes-tantism. And everywhere, hospitals essentially served the towns. More than half of them were in places with over 2,000 inhabitants; 57.27 per cent of them were available to 18.8 per cent of the population. In 1662, Louis XIV had ordered the foundation of institutions to care for the sick in every town, and had sent round Jesuit preachers to exhort municipalities to fulfil their obligations. The standard pattern for any sizeable place had become an Hotêl-Dieu for the sick, and a sort of 'workhouse' in the Victorian sense of the term, under the name of 'l'Hôpital Général', for the old, infirm, foundlings, and prostitutes.[30] Control of these institutions was generally vested in a Bureau with a membership of municipal and judicial officers, clergy and elected notables, with the bishop or his deputy presiding, while the day-to-day administration and the care of the sick would be in the hands of an order of nuns. Sometimes, as at the Hôtel-Dieu of Paray-le-Monial,[31] the sisters did all the nursing single-handed, but it was more usual for them to have women auxiliaries and paid servants for the heavy work. At the Hôtel-Dieu of Paris, which had 2,500 to 3,000 patients, there were sixty-nine Augustinian nuns (with ten novices and twenty girl postulants) in charge of 162 male and 146 female orderlies, 38 laundry assistants, and 20 assorted servants.[32] We know the stan-dard daily roster of the nuns: one in charge of each group of two wards, fifteen on night duty, five on the apothecary's counter, two in charge of porters and visitors, three in charge of the big laundry and two of the small (the latter the worst job in the hospital, dealing with the foul linen of the sick), others in charge of supplies, the depository of patients' civilian clothes, and of the shirts which were their hospital garb.[33] As in every institution of eighteenth-century France, however worthy its object, feuds and confusions abounded. The administrators at Béziers were at war with the city fathers; at Orléans, at war among themselves (the three canons of the cathedral versus the six laymen); the 'recteurs' of Trets were accused of lending the funds to each other; the nuns of the Hôtel-Dieu of Provins of laying out English-style gardens with 'immodest statues' and buying a billiard table.[34] At the Hôtel-Dieu of Paris there was a running battle between the nuns and the medical practitioners; the latter accused the sisters of admitting the homeless and hungry even if they were not seriously ill, of overfeeding their charges, of refusing to dismiss useless servants, and of monopolizing the right to give good news to patients; the nuns replied that the doctors were perfunctory in their visits, introduced their licentious students into the wards, and tried to seduce the novices.[35] But it was sheer penury, not maladministration, which made the hospitals of France so destructive of human life. The age when testators left great estates to the poor was over. More people were pushed into the hospitals just when less money was being given to them. At Aix-en-Provence[36] the annual collection for the Hospital General was only half as much in the mid-century as it had been fifty years before, and charitable bequests in wills became fewer. This does not necessarily mean that the springs of generosity were drying up, but it does mean that the hospitals were losing their share. And their finances were ill-administered. Law's scheme under the Regency ran away with so many investments. The patchwork inheritance of odd pieces of property accumulated over the generations could not usually be organized into efficient agrarian units. Almost everywhere the administrators resorted to loans, and loans to pay off the loans, so that by the sixties at Aix and other places there was a threat of total bankruptcy and closure. The story of the institutional care of the sick in the eighteenth century is one of nuns pinching and scraping and treasurers inventing hand-to-mouth expedients. Every resource was intensively and pathetically exploited. The best

31

hospital in Paris, the Saint-Jean Baptiste de la Charité, fortunate in having substantial property, had on its accounts annual alms from the king, the *fermiers généraux* and the Comédie-Française (there was a *droit des pauvres* levied on all theatres in the kindgom),[37] the rent of chairs in the chapel, the contents of offertory boxes, collections from processions in the city, and two tragic items, 'Ventes d'habits des malades décédés' and 'Argent trouvé dans les poches des décédés'.[38] The clothes were worth ten times the cash: the chief possessions of the poor were the battered garments they stood up in. The Quinze-Vingts of Paris, a home for the blind, had as its essential sources of income its levy of half the property of anyone admitted, and the proceeds of the begging tours of the inmates, recognizable at the doors of the churches of the capital by the fleur-de-lis badge of yellow copper which they wore. La Charité at Lyon lived by selling annuities; in the seventies, the servicing of its debt cost 400,000 livres a year; those who accepted office as 'recteur' or 'trésorier' had to hand over huge sums free of interest and with a limited hope of recovering them—it was cheaper, though much less prestigious, to buy out of the office when the turn came round.[39] Some small places kept going because the nuns in charge accepted wounded soldiers (the Crown paying 14 sous a day[40]) rather than the local sick, others because the families of the nuns had given 'dowries' and added extra contributions to them to enable their daughters to carry on their charitable labours.[41]

The horrors of the old hospitals of France were the result of poverty, not of ignorance or heartlessness on the part of administrators or staff. With its solid income from two farms, fifty-seven houses, and a windmill, and almost as much again from investments, the hospital of Saint-Jean Baptiste de la Charité at Paris was well organized (it was here that the greatest inventive surgeon of the century practised, Jean Baseillac, son and grandson of surgeons of Tarbes, Frère Cosme by name in religion). There were six wards arranged according to the nature of the disease or the severity of the operation; each patient had his own bed, cup, spittoon, urine flask, and *chaise de commodité*, and received nourishing meals throughout the day, ending with beef tea at nine o'clock at night. But to get in required influence, as one of the *frères* proudly told a visiting *abbé* from Normandy who was expressing his astonished admiration.[42] At the Hôtel-Dieu of Paris, things were very different: the sick were six or seven to a bed in stifling cavernous halls, operations took place in the wards in the sight of the next batch of victims, and the gloomy corridors were filled with the stench of suffering. In some of the provincial institutions, all kinds of misery were crammed together incongruously. At Rodez, at one desperate period, there were only four nuns to oversee the staff who looked after 160 bedridden patients, 260 ailing poor, 122 geriatrics, and 50 dangerous lunatics.[43] The Salpêtrière at Paris was a byword for horror—prostitutes in sackcloth shut up in regimented droves, and lunatics, four to a cell on straw, crawling with vermin and bitten by rats.[44] Smaller hospitals rarely had facilities to cope with crises; in Malestroit, the administrator reported that they had to push extra people into the damp and freezing chapel.[45] Richeprey, touring the south at the end of the *ancien régime* gathering information for a scheme of tax reform, saw other things which needed reform also; the hospital at Marcillac, he said, was a room like a stable, with three palliasses, 'the very sight of which made me feel ill myself'.[46] No wonder the poor, more especially the peasants, were obdurate in their protests when carried off to one of these crowded and miserable institutions. But to those living on the margins of survival, illness meant unemployment, unemployment meant starvation, and families could not spare women or children from their work to look after one of their members. So poverty drove the sick into the hospitals, and there, poverty killed them.

The *ancien régime* is seen at its worst and at its best, so far as the treatment of the sick is concerned, in the arrangements of the army for its soldiers.[47] An officer described a hospital at Strasbourg in the winter of 1734/5 during the War of the Polish Succession: four to five hundred men were being looked after by two *infirmiers*; treatment and food were available only once a day; there were no sheets, and the smell was overpowering. These were the hospitals run by contractors for profit. The troops much preferred the *hôpitaux ambulants* with the regiments, where their captains ensured that they got their rations, and the surgeons were genuine military personnel. Best of all for the wounded soldier was a chit from his officer to go off to one of the watering-places, such as Bourbonne-les-Bains or Saint-Amand-les-Eaux; typically, this was done by preference when the medical inspector was coming round to weed out the unfit—absence for convalescent treatment was a guarantee against being struck off the payroll. When warships came back to port laden with sick, the numbers might be too great for the naval hospitals, and the civilian ones would be suddenly and dangerously filled, maybe with sailors with typhus or some other fearsomely infectious disease. Malouet's attempts, as Intendant de la Marine, to improve the facilities at Toulon are instructive concerning the shortcomings in the humanitarian programmes of this sentimental age. In 1781, he proposed to transfer the naval hospital from a few unsatisfactory rented houses to the extensive buildings of the old Jesuit *collège*. The nuns, the *Sœurs Grises*, however, fought him until the summer of 1787 before they accepted a new contract for the nursing. Their limitations can be seen in their refusal to look after sailors with venereal disease (nearly half the total); the government's in its refusal to pay a reasonable capitation fee for the sick treated—the sisters were asking double what Malouet was offering.[48] The institutionalized sick and poor of eighteenth-century France were subjected, if that is a fair word, to a great deal of compulsory piety, but even anticlerical reformers never really believed that the nuns could be replaced. As the days of the Revolution were to show, appeals for patriotic women to take over met with no response. What the nuns did in the hospitals was not well done: the wonder was that it was done at all.

What of the minority of Frenchmen who could afford and were willing to pay a doctor's bill; what treatment was offered, and what did it avail them? Though there were signs of a change of attitude, the wits throughout the country carried on the satrical tradition of Molière. The doctor is depicted as burying his mistakes, and duping the survivors into gratitude by impressive jargon—such as Desportes' Doctor Rhubarbini used on the stage in 1721. Like Chamfort's Doctor Delon, the best physicians could explain away everything: 'il est mort guéri'—he was cured, but unfortunately, he died. In his notebooks Voltaire put the activities of the medical profession alongside warfare and the counsels of the theologians as prime destroyers of the human race: if we had common sense, we would rely solely on 'Nature'.[49] Death should be represented as a genial figure, said the Prince de Ligne, a stately old lady welcoming us into an endless field of poppies; it was the sorrows of life—or perhaps a physician—who should be the allegorical figure wielding the sinister scythe of the reaper. [50] It was an old joke, but Messance, the statistical expert on living and dying, asked the question soberly: whether the doctors killed more than they cured. And it was another old joke to refer to licensed assassinations—as when in January 1787 Mme de Sabran wrote to the chevalier de Boufflers in far-off Senegal to tell how 'poor M. de Mailly' perished; his physicians bled him to cure his indigestion—'jamais assassinat n'a été mieux prouvé'. [51] Somewhat later, Florian devised his verse fable, *La Mort*. Death, 'queen of the world', assembles her court in Hell to choose a First Minister who will make her realm even more populous than it is now. Fever, Gout, and War appear, then Plague, looking very convincing. But a doctor pays his visit, and immediately becomes the favourite. However, they had forgotten the vices; in they troop, and Death finally chooses Intemperance. [52] It had been a close-run thing.

It is easy today (though, like all anachronistic commentary, unfair) to give instances to justify the suspicions of the satirists that eighteenth-century medicine was almost useless to the individual patient. By sheer trial and error the curative properties of mercury and cinchona bark (quinine) had been discovered. Apart from these two major remedies and some of the herbal concoctions traditionally in use, the pharmacopoeia of the age was a catalogue of marginally useful and occasionally harmful receipts, not without connections with sympathetic magic. Nicolas Lémery's *Pharmacopée universelle* (1738) and *Dictionnaire universel des drogues simples* (new edition, (1759)—compiled by a member of the Academy of Sciences—included such items as the powdered skull of a young man who has died a violent death, human excrement, viper broth, and ground-up jewels. For gout or 'hysterical vapours', two or three glasses of *eau de mille fleurs* first thing in the morning was recommended; this was cow's urine, which had to be fresh from source. It was also said to 'remove obstructions', which is not surprising. [53] Between the unenlightened empiricism which prescribed the doses (and which had discovered the medicines efficacious against venereal disease and malaria), and the professed ambition of the physicians to be scholars of universal scope, widely read

in humane literature, and interpreting and explaining every devi-
ation of the human mind and every failing of the body, there was an
enormous unbridged gap. Hence the unreality of so much of the
controversy within the Medical Faculties, its portentousness, and
sensation seeking. The question as to whether tea and coffee were
dangerous was discussed with sociological declamations. What was
the explanation for monstrous births, for the revolting phenomenon of cretinism in the Valais? Can love-sickness be cured by
herbal remedies? (This was the title of the thesis of Boissier de
Sauvages, the most distinguished professor of the Faculty of Montpellier in the century[54].) Erudite analyses of scatological subjects
were a favourite exercise, for example, Nicolas Chambon de Montaux's *Traité des maladies des filles*, published in two volumes in
1785.[55] The most successful medical treatise of the Enlightenment,
running into numerous editions, was the Swiss Dr Tissot's *L'Onanisme, ou dissertation physique sur les maladies produites par la
masturbation* (1760); to masturbation he ascribed impotence,
epilepsy, indigestion, coughs, spots, madness, and decline into
death, with a permanent haunting remorse that was a foretaste of
Hell.[56] The medical theorists of the early eighteenth century were
learned, and historically minded in a fashion peculiar to their own
encyclopaedic age. Like Bayle, they loved the curious anecdote for
its own sake and for its relevance to wide-ranging generalizations
about human life; compiling evidence about health and disease
from all centuries of the past and from their own time, they treated
it all as of equal importance. The last great exponent of this sort of
medical erudition was Jean Astruc, who was appointed physician to
the Regent in 1726. Six hundred authors were quoted in his treatise
on venereal disease (1736) and he followed up with a supplement of
new information from Chinese history.[57] Even more ancient lore
was found in his *Traité des maladies des filles* (2 v. 1762), and his
learned volume on the art of midwifery four years later began with
the observation that he had never himself been present at the
delivery of a baby. Did God tell Adam how to cut Eve's umbilical cord
or did he make the discovery himself?[58] These sort of questions
were Astruc's speciality, and he is remembered today for his scholarly ingenuity in detecting the different strands of narrative in the
Pentateuch. After him, medicine had no more great encyclopaedic

analysts. If Antoine Portal of the Faculty of Montpellier began his seven-volume history of anatomy and surgery with a chapter on 'The anatomists and surgeons who lived between the Flood and the Fall of Troy',[59] this was a harmless piece of swank, not an attempt to make the sons of Noah or the companions of Hector relevant to surgical operations in the Hôtel-Dieu of Paris.

'If the atmosphere is dry and the barometer is very high, bleeding is useful and, even, necessary.'[60] So said the ordonnance of the Royal Council of 29 April 1776, setting up a modern system of comprehensive inquiries into epidemics. The tragic effect of the unbridged gap between the actual treatment given to the sick and the claims of the medical profession to provide comprehensive explanations of sickness and health in general, is exemplified in the continuance, throughout the eighteenth century, of the harmful old practice of bleeding, allied to the use of weakening emetics and purges. A doctor in Alsace, in 1786, coping with an outbreak of a 'bilious, putrid, venomous, purple fever' made all sorts of intelligent observations: the epidemic prevailed among the poor, the cause was contaminated food, hygienic precautions were necessary, quinine helped, psychological measures like forbidding the tolling of church bells would contribute toward allaying the panic. Nevertheless, he spent most of his time prescribing emetics and enemas and bleeding his patients from neck, arms, and feet; thereby undoing most of the good he had achieved in other ways.[61] The nuns of the Visitation of Auxerre recorded in their register the death of Sister Louise-Edmée-Marie Davigneau, in 1787, with an undertone of bitterness: 'They gave her as many as fifty bleedings in a year, and the other torments which medicine prescribes were in proportion. It is easy to understand that after this our dear sister was for long unable to undertake even the lightest of tasks.'[62] This is Molière without the irony, a secret protest of common sense against the tyranny of the experts. The long-standing reliance on the efficacy of bleeding, purging, and emetics was derived, in origin, from the Galenic belief that the digestion turned food and drink into the four humours—blood, phlegm, yellow bile, and black bile, these being supposed to be allied with the four temperaments, sanguine, phlegmatic, choleric, and melancholic. Galen had died fifteen hundred years ago, but his doctrine had carried on through the Middle Ages, refined and distorted by its passage through Byzantine and Arabic sources. By the beginning of the eighteenth century, almost everything that was supposed to support the Galenic hypothesis had been experimentally overthrown. Autopsies did nothing to confirm the view that ill health arose from the imbalance of the humours, and in the sixteenth century Vesalius had shown that Galenic anatomy was derived from the study of animals, rather than of man. Observations with the thermometer did not correspond to Galen's doctrines of heat and cold, and Harvey's work on the circulation of the blood made it clear that the heart must be regarded as a pump, not as a sort of fireplace. The best seventeenth-century physicians therefore turned away from Galen as the founder and patron of their art, and gave their allegiance to Hippocrates— taking him to be the exemplar of precise and accurate observation. Even so, 'the fall of the Galenic scheme of medicine was not identical with the fall of the Galenic practice of medicine',[63] and dependence on bleedings, purgings, and emetics continued. This professional inertia was possible, in part because of the complexity of the inheritance of the past: Hippocratic, Galenic, and Aristotelian doctrines; Christian, Arabic, and Jewish lore; and fragments of empirical discovery—all confounded into a vast system of technicalities hallowed by the centuries. It was possible also because there was no one comprehensive theory moving in to the attack, and Galenism became incorporated in each new hypothesis that tended to displace it. At the end of the seventeenth century, the explanation of diseases by hydrostatics (obstructions, eddies, excessive viscosities in the arteries, lymph channels, and the like) and by chemical action (the impact of sulphurous or other dangerous particles from the air on particles in the bloodstream) was combined uneasily in the new medicine.[64] Later, when 'vitalism' took over at Montpellier (Théophile Bordeu's *Recherches anatomiques sur la position des glandes et sur leur action* of 1752 was the key work, ascribing to each gland the power to choose those parts of the blood appropriate for its secretion[65]), the ancient medical heritage was still not rejected. 'Much of Aristotle and Galen', observes Temkin, 'can be perceived in the vitalism growing in the eighteenth century and dominating the early nineteenth.'[66] So long as the physician was dominated by the idea of keeping equilibrium in the patient's mind and in his body, bleeding and its allied devices of evacuation could be defended—on the grounds of temperamental adjustment, preserving the balance between fluids and liquids or blood and bile, or as regulating the pulse (whether the pulse was too fast or too slow made no difference to the treatment).[67] True, the quest for equilibrium also tended to encourage the idea of letting Nature take its course—keeping the patient's mind distracted and his body well nourished and exercised until his natural balance was restored. On these grounds, voices against bleeding began to be raised in the medical profession; Philippe Hecquet's splendidly entitled *Le Brigandage de la médecine* (1732), the anonymous *Les Abus de la saignée* (1755).[68] But they were concerned with the 'abuse' of the remedy; they did not say it was useless. Even enthusiasts for the *vis medicatrix naturae* could continue to accept bleeding as necessary under certain circumstances. In the enlightened *Encyclopédie méthodique*, published in over 100 volumes from 1787 and through the revolutionary era, medicine is treated as a science, linked with all the other sciences, and there are sophisticated descriptions of the respiration, of the circulation of the blood, and of the workings of the neuro-muscular system; yet the 'humours' remain, influenced by the weather and the passions, so too do the discussions of when to bleed and when to purge.[69]

Under the old humoral pathology, the physician was treating the whole man, not seeking the proximate cause of a specific illness.[70] The symptoms he detected pointed towards a disequilibrium in the humours reflected elsewhere, and once its peculiar nature was ascertained, the choice between bleeding, purging, emetics, and sudation could be made, with some minor supportive remedies and—to be fair—some advice about mental and temperamental adjustments. What was lacking—and this deficiency was the barrier to progress—was the concept of a specific disease, with its unique cause. The Medical Faculties were searching ingeniously for a comprehensive explanation for all ill health. At the end of the *ancien régime* the major subject of investigation, backed by the government, was the relationship between the weather and epidemics. 'The medical profession', Meyer writes of this meteorological research, was 'in desperation . . . seeking a "corpus of doctrine" which would act like the wave of a magic wand solving all problems.'[71] Searching for a total explanation and failing to find one, the doctors were left with nothing better than the old humours, and the practice of bleeding. They were aware of the importance of accumulating data, but what selective principle should direct their observations and reduce them to patterns of meaning? Sydenham's attempt to classify diseases as the botanists had classified plants, on the basis of similarities of structure and function, was taken up by Boissier de Sauvages at Montpellier.[72] His *Nosologia* (1763) turned out to be a catalogue of symptoms enlivened by touches of historical circumstance and inferential psychology. 'Syphilitic epilepsy as in Bonet's [book] *Sepulchretum*', 'simulated epilepsy' (as manifested by the Jansenist convulsionaries), hysterias of various brands, 'verminous', 'chloratic', 'menorrhagic', 'febrile', 'visceral', and 'libidinous' (the latter a revival from the old Galenism)[73] were classifications by appearance and anecdote. In fact, the *Nosologia* was a faithful handbook for the diagnostic techniques of the physicians of the Enlightenment: learned, encyclopaedic, unselective, and recording such symptoms as would serve to interpret the imbalance of the whole man. Presentiments of a 'germ' theory of disease in the seventeenth century, some brilliant observations in the eighteenth about individual diseases (diphtheria, rickets, and rabies),[74] and even the sensation caused by a new empirical breakthrough against smallpox, did not suffice to ensure the concentration on specificity which was to be the way ahead for medicine (that is, until our own day, when the sulpha drugs and antibiotics have encouraged a return to a generalized pathology).[75] The change of attitude came at the end of the eighteenth century (by clinical observations and autopsies Pierre Bretonneau defined typhoid separately from the undifferentiated mass of fevers),[76] and the discovery of specific, pathogenic microorganisms came more than half a century later.

The doctors could do little to save a patient who had been struck down by one of the major killing diseases; except for malaria and syphilis, they had no effective remedy. The deathbed scene with its last farewells was a religious and social phenomenon, but it was made possible and, as it were, fitting, by the state of medical knowledge: the physicians knew no cure, but they were expert readers of symptoms, and recognized when death was inevitable.

That is not to say that their ministrations were useless. They knew the value of sound diet and cleanliness, and the importance of conveying assurance; when the worst came to the worst they could administer opium to relieve pain. On the relationship between mental tensions and physical disorders they were perceptive and sympathetic—witness their studies of the 'vapours' among young ladies and the 'nostalgia' which caused the breakdown of so many new recruits to the army.[77] The demand that Nature takes it course, accepted by Rousseau and Voltaire, was adopted by some enlightened practitioners, like Voltaire's own doctor, Tronchin. ('Nature' is ambiguous, however. In 1767, Le Clerc, a former medical officer in the French and Russian armies, published a two-volume appeal for a medicine strictly according to Nature, in which he said some good things—ignore the 'why' and concentrate on 'second causes', forget old traditions, accept inoculation against smallpox, distrust the remedies in chemists' shops. Yet he believed in the efficacy of bleeding, and rejected quinine: 'I do not think that Providence has put the fever in our climate, and the remedy in America.'[78]) And, though it saved few lives, there was one branch of eighteenth-century medical practice which was brilliant and inventive. The surgeons had the advantage of not needing to know the 'why'; they could consider the body as a Cartesian machine, study its interlocking parts by anatomical dissection, and practise on dead bodies before they came to live ones. For long, anatomical studies had been held in honour. They revealed the wonders of the Creator's handiwork, and appealed to macabre curiosity. In the reign of Louis XIV fashionable society went to see dissections, and since methods of preserving organic tissue had been invented, the 'cabinet anatomique' came into vogue along with more bearable collections of natural history.[79] It was customary to open the bodies of kings and the great after they died, a routine check against foul play which nevertheless exalted the anatomist's art.[80] Though stories of the nocturnal raids of medical students on cemeteries abound,[81] and there were occasional explosions of popular prejudice (riots at Lyon in 1767 and Caen in 1782[82]), there was no religious prejudice against anatomical experiment, and the law encouraged magistrates and hospital administrators to make corpses available in the cooler months from October to April.[83] As yet, only a few enthusiasts donated their own bodies for research, but the gesture was approved as a patriotic singularity.[84] Against the background of educated approval, there was a remarkable development of surgical instruments and techniques during the eighteenth century. The growing sophistication of the operation for the 'stone' is the best example. Nicolas Le Cat (1700–68) of the Hôtel-Dieu of Rouen invented the 'grand appareil' (the probe in the urethra met by the 'conductor' behind and guiding the 'dilator' to the bladder, followed by the pincers to grip the stone). Surgeons at Bordeaux refined on the method,[85] but Frère Cosme at Paris changed to the new lateral lithotomy, after many trials on corpses at the hospital of La Charité. He also invented improved instruments, the 'lithotome caché' and the 'sonde à dard', using the devices of retractable blades and arms to work inside the bladder.[86] Here is a case of progress by concentration on specific details, with no attention to ultimate causes. Like the porters of Paris, the surgeons knew all the streets but not what went on in the houses. It was the old joke of the physicians, but it unwittingly revealed the reason for the surgeon's superiority. These excruciating manipulations were performed without anaesthetics; the surgeon Antoine-Michel Leroux in 1792 refused to subject himself to the operation, on which he had published a learned work of reference, and took an overdose of opium.[87] Everything had to be done at lightning speed, because of the agony of the patient, and because there was as yet no means of arresting the flow of blood but the pressure of an assistant's fingers. Without antiseptics and hygienic precautions, fatal infectious complications often set in. Major operations were undertaken when there was no alternative. In these cases, the new techniques and fearsome dexterity of the surgeons saved a few lives.[88] It was, maybe, in less spectacular manipulations that the surgical skill of the eighteenth century made its greatest contribution to human welfare—in improvements in dentistry,[89] in operations on the eyes,[90] in dealing with fractures and crippling accidents; not so much prolonging life, as making longer life worth while.

Prevention is better than cure. The aphorism was never surer than in the eighteenth century, and the medical profession saved more lives by the advice it gave in the offices of the administrative bureaucrats than at the bedside of patients. From the early seventeenth century, doctors had warned of the dangers of polluted air and water,[91] and successive kings had issued ordinances to improve hygienic conditions, especially in Paris. By the early eighteenth century, jokes about chamber-pots emptied from upstairs windows were anachronistic, unless the prompt arrival of the police was also described, and anecdotes of the twenties tell of heavy fines on the contractors emptying latrines when they disposed of their spoil in the gutters or left their carts in the streets after daybreak. They were supposed to cart the sewage to the dump at Montfaucon, 'le seul dépôt de la vidange des fosses d'aisances de toute la ville', and in 1726 regulations were made to ensure that collectors drawing off manure only did so in winter, and after a three-year maturing period. The city built a new, stone-lined sewer on the right bank in 1737, attempted to clean the streets by various methods, including watering-carts, and in the eighties encouraged the companies armed with newly invented suction-pumps which took over the emptying of the cesspits of the capital.[92] Even so, Mercier was able to describe the cycle of horrors from latrine to gutter, gutter to Seine, Seine to the receptacles of the water-carriers—and three-quarters of Paris still depended on them. In the provincial towns, the same story can be told—enlightened officials struggling against the thrifty complacency of the inhabitants; unless an epidemic struck, and then suddenly the doctors were listened to, offal and manure dumps vanished from the streets, and bonfires burned everywhere, to destroy the rubbish and 'clear the air'.

When fear of death drove, ruthless administrative efficiency and frenzied co-operation from below suddenly appeared in the sprawling, unhygienic confusion of eighteenth-century France. On 25 May 1720, *Le Grand Saint-Antoine* berthed at Marseille with a cargo of bales of cotton from the Levant, bound for the fair at Beaucaire.[93] Eight people had died on board during the voyage. The captain had landed at Toulon to inform the owners, and they had used influence to get permission for the unloading of the cargo. The passengers were allowed out of quarantine on 14 June. On 9 July the doctors reported to the municipality that there was plague in the city. It rained on 21 and 22 July, and humidity activates fleas, and these fleas were carrying the deadly disease. On 23 July fourteen people died and the rich began to flee. A week later, the Parlement of Aix put the city under interdict, but in the interval 10,000 citizens had escaped to endanger the rest of the province. By the middle of August, 400 people were dying every day, and the 'corbeaux' (generally galley-slaves) who collected the bodies had a life expectancy of two days. The plague spread along the main roads—wherever human beings and their flea-infested clothing or possessions moved, so that the big towns of Aix and Arles were the first to be hit. The whole of Provence lived in terror, and turned to the government for the enforcement of the traditional drastic precautionary measures. The doctors[94] recognized plague infallibly from the characteristic hard dry tumours behind the ears, the knees, and in the armpits, and by the coughing of blood. They knew that the disease was encouraged by rain, but faded away in winter cold; they knew it passed—somehow and mysteriously—from person to person, and that the poor tended to be victims rather than the rich. But they had no remedies except bleeding (which was positively harmful) and the administration of certain medicines (which were, in fact, toxic). They knew that cleanliness was a sound precautionary measure, and they recommended abstinence from sexual intercourse to preserve energy (this might have helped if it kept immoral characters out of dubious localities). One thing, however, was clear to the doctors and the authorities—the only way to stop the spread of plague was to isolate completely the areas where it was detected.[95] There was already a well-established system of quarantine for the passengers and crews of ships. If this barrier was breached, there were customary precautions all around the port; municipalities would set up *conseils de santé*—to take emergency measures, setting up a local quarantine station, keeping out all travellers except those armed with a *billet de santé* (signed by a notary and *curé* and presented on the end of a long stick), hoisting a black flag on a church tower if the disease broke through, and organizing the burial of the dead in quicklime and the burning of their clothes and furniture. When the Parlement of Aix pronounced its interdict on Marseille, soldiers drew a line of blockade around the city. No one could escape. Commissioners were in charge of each *quartier*, distributing such food as could be obtained, seeing that the carts took away the corpses, and supervising the burning of infected possessions. Belsunce, the bishop, a difficult and intolerant character, showed himself a hero; his palace became a hospital, and he went round encouraging his clergy in their ministrations. Meanwhile, most towns of Provence had isolated themselves by a *mur de la peste*—to stop anyone getting in. The Vice-Legate of the Comtat built a drystone wall six feet high with a ditch of an equal depth all the sixty miles from Bonfas to Sisteron, which did no more than delay the arrival of the plague at Avignon.[96] In the tense period of waiting for the first casualty which showed the defence had been breached, the towns of Provence had never been so clean—rubbish removed, streets swept and garnished.[97] The only way to pass a plague wall was to go into quarantine and have your clothes baked in an oven or steeped in vinegar. The soldiers fired on sight, and executed those who broke the regulations. At Brioude, a woman who had passed the line was shot; at Gévaudan a man who had concealed some woollen cloth in an infected area was executed by the alternative military method, clubbing to death—'la tête casseé jusqu'à ce que mort s'ensuive'. The same savage punishment was ordered by the military commander in Gévaudan for a *corbeau* who had deserted from Mende—the inhabitants of the house where he had lodged were sent into quarantine and the furniture in the room where he had slept was burned.[98] Once the danger seemed to be over in any place, an official investigation was made, for there were lessons to be learned for the future from the analysis of the details of the movements of the pestilence. At Corréjac, Doctor Rochevailler arrived on 6 May 1721 and assembled the inhabitants to question them about the outbreak of last November. It turned out that the scourge began when one of the inhabitants accepted a gift of a shirt and a pair of stockings from a relative at the fair of Saint-Clément; the man, his wife, and three children, and the heirs who collected their possessions all died, for the shirt and stockings were loot from Marseille stolen by a convict who had been pressed into service as a *corbeau*. In other villages it was established that the disaster began with the arrival of a soldier, an itinerant harvester, a team of muleteers, or a load of woollen cloth.[99] The emergency regulations which various towns had published were preserved in their archives for future reference. The chevalier d'Antrechaus, who had presided over the municipality of Toulon in 1720–2, published in 1756 (on rumours of plague in

Algiers) an account of the methods he had used for quarantine and food distribution,[100] and in 1771, the Controller General, the abbé Terray, circulated to all towns in the kingdom copies of the Marseille regulations. For the rest of the century, the memory of the great plague of 1720 ensured that the coastal quarantine system was ruthlessly effective, sometimes even endangering the lives of ship-wrecked sailors who needed warmth and treatment which could not easily be given in isolation. In Roussillon, there was a sort of coastguard watch against dubious landings, manned by the *corvée*.[101] In 1771, the *subdélégué* of Elne called out the peasants to man the look-outs on news of an infected Dutch ship in the Mediterranean; on 25 October the watchers went home, but were immediately recalled on rumours of plague in the far-distant Baltic. The craftier inhabitants armed themselves with certificates of medical incapacity from their *curés*, and the villagers put their most idle and irresponsible youngsters on these coastal excursions; it was left, as usual, to the administrators and their medical advisers to keep precautions going, until some sudden mysterious epidemic struck to alarm the countryside and produce demands for the traditional old governmental regulations.

Clubbing with musket butts the skulls of violators of plague cordons might, with a certain cynicism, be described as one of the effective devices in the early history of preventive medicine. This particular brutal instance, and the principle involved—that of losing a few lives to save many—was cited in 1724 by a writer defending the new idea from the East of inoculation against smallpox,[102] the first great empirical breakthrough in the art of prevention rather than cure. The fable of heroic *philosophes* leading the battle against reactionary churchmen and magistrates is now exploded. Voltaire supported inoculation, so too, and earlier, did the Jesuit *Mémoires de Trévoux*; the abbé Prévost and La Mettrie were opposed to it, though it suited Voltaire's book to pretend that his only opponents were churchmen clamouring for submission to the decrees of Providence. D'Alembert's statistical essay concluded in favour of progress, but he had reservations. Bishop de Barral of Castres had none, and took Doctor Icard around with him on his pastoral visitations.[103] The ban of the Parlement of Paris in 1763 on inoculation in towns, until the Faculties of Theology and Medicine had pronounced, was not unreasonable in so far as it was motivated by the fear that an epidemic for the many might be the price of conferring immunity on the few. Even so, the story of the victory of the new technique was sensational, evoking hundreds of publications and an abundance of lively anecdotes. When Choiseul sent Dr Galti to La Flèche to inoculate all the cadets of the École Militaire in 1769, the battle was officially won, the victory being celebrated by the Abbé Roman in *L'Inoculation, poème en quatre chants*, and in the fashionable hair-style for ladies, *coiffure à l'inoculation*, with a sun rising over a laden olive tree, fruit, and flowers, with an entwining medicinal serpent.[104] How many lives were saved in the course of the eighteenth century? It is difficult to say. In Franche-Comté the new idea was quickly taken up, in Anjou it was largely ignored. The total of deaths directly from smallpox may not have been much reduced, but it was a weakening malady, and those who were saved from it had a better chance of resisting other diseases. If it is true that the cycle of smallpox had been becoming increasingly virulent, inoculation (and the vaccination that followed) seems to have arrested the process.[105] Probably, the demographical expansion of France up to 1800 owed little directly to this innovation, whose statistical significance lay in the future. But the psychological effect was enormous. There was a new and unexpected glimpse of hope about the possibility of medical progress, and there was a corresponding increase in the prestige of the members of the medical profession. Molière himself would have had to praise them. The worst that could be said of them was that the Muslims and the Chinese had been first to make the discovery.

The new hope of medical progress, which the success of inoculation created, is reflected in the multiplication of medical books after 1760.[106] Among educated people there was an increased concern with problems of health, a growing reluctance to accept illness fatalistically, and an intensified shrinking in face of pain. There is a cheerful illustration of the changing attitude in the story of the rise of watering-places, and a bizarre one in the panic about being buried alive. The therapeutic properties of mineral springs had been recognized in the seventeenth century, but the golden age of the watering-place came in the second half of the eighteenth, under the influence of the Rousseauistic cult of Nature, creating a predisposition to take 'natural' medicines, and a certain free and easy tendency in social relationships. Théophile Bordeu began his great reputation by a treatise on the mineral springs of Béarn[107] and Jean-Philippe de Limbourg made a fortune by advocating those of Spa in the principality of Liège. The prince de Ligne describes how at Spa he met the Emperor Joseph II, English archbishops and their wives, French bishops and their nieces, dubious young beauties of Paris affecting gaiety, bearded Jews, dancing masters dressed as Russian majors, stolid Dutchmen watching the exchange rates in the gazettes, retired generals nursing pretended wounds, princes incognito who would have been more anonymous under their real names, Americans, duchesses leaning on big walking-sticks.[108] Those who could not afford these excursions and their promenades, riding, and billiards, could at least enjoy the health-giving mineral water, with its iron which gave the bodily fibres elasticity, and its 'volatile vitriol' stimulating the nerves. In 1775, the Royal Council made regulations obliging the proprietors of springs to put on each bottle they sold a certificate of authenticity and date; by 1787, twenty-two different varieties of water were on sale in Paris.[109] As for the very different manifestation of hypochondriacal zeal—the panic about being buried alive—what had been vague unease became acute alarm after the *Dissertation sur l'incertitude des signes de la mort* of 1740.[110] Some grisly stories circulated: the abbé Prévost the novelist cried out under the anatomist's knife—too late; luckier, a worthy of Châteaudun sat up in his coffin in the chancel when the band of the regiment of dragoons struck up; less fortunate was the wretch in Anjou who hammered on his coffin during the church service, but the only member of the congregation who heard him 'did not think that he had an obligation to speak rather than the others, and was worried by the idea of disturbing the ceremony'; in Paris, a girl dug up by body-snatching medical students revived and was taken home; there were also reports of exhumations which provided evidence of desperate struggles underground to escape from the tomb.[111] Doctors wrote treatises about the signs which prove death, and invented resuscitation treatments to be tried on all corpses.[112] Wills prescribed delays before interment, and tests of various kinds—in 1770, one proposed that the servants of the household should watch by the body in relays for forty-eight hours, with a reward of 300 *livres* for any who noticed signs of consciousness.[113]

This sort of enhanced susceptibility may be one of the reasons why the attitude of the public towards the medical profession began to change in the 1760s, and certainly, the prestige of inoculation had much to do with it. Though satirical observations of the old kind lingered on, the doctors now had a magical receipt to preserve the lives of men and the beauty of women. Dr Galti put down a wager of 12,000 *livres* against all comers that the method was infallible (it was not, and the duchesse de Boufflers caught smallpox because she had been inoculated too lightly; but Galti, being the first to know, rushed off and collected his own prize money).[114] The recognition of the enhanced status of the medical profession began at Court.[115] Though ten times as many *avocats* bought their way into the nobility, when it came to letters of nobility granted for merit alone, the physicians predominated—thirty-five of them between 1724 and 1786, as against sixteen *avocats*. Significantly, twelve of these ennobled medical practitioners had served at Court, and sixteen in the armies; participation in the honourable profession of arms and in the care of the royal person were responsibilities which did not fall to lawyers. At Versailles and at Paris, the most successful doctors cut splendid figures. The *premier médecin du roi* drew a salary double that of a *maréchal de camp* and five times that of a magistrate of the Parlement. Théophile Bordeu, consultant to the duchesse de Chartres and the prince de Conti, rode in a four-horse carriage and dined every Friday with the court banker Laborde.[116] Henri Grandjean, chief oculist to Louis XVI, was an ornament of society who proved himself a man of aristocratic sensibility when he refused the Order of Saint-Michel when it was first offered because a senior colleague was being passed over.[117] Vicq d'Azyr, consultant to all the great, secretary of the Royal Society of Medicine, and adviser to the government on epidemics human and animal, was the first representative of a new phenomenon on the eve of the Revolution: the medical statesman. A playwright in 1733 had abandoned the old satirical stereotype of physicians as pedants, and portrayed them as courtiers, 'braided, powdered, and curled', giving themselves the airs of officers of the royal guard—'vous les croiriez d'aimables mousquetaires'.[118] In

49

1774, the duc de Lévis described a further stage in the climb to social success: the doctor had become the indispensable confidant of the ladies. 'I can only compare the feelings of the ladies for their doctors to those that their grandmothers had at the end of the reign of Louis XIV for their spiritual directors.'[119] There was, of course, a gulf between Parisian consultant and local practitioners. Yet, at the end of the *ancien régime*, doctors and surgeons were being well spoken of in the provinces and a minority were rising to affluence and a position of local distinction comparable to that of the great in the capital. In Nantes in 1788, of nine doctors six paid 100 *livres* capitation tax, which put them near the top of the social hierarchy; the forty surgeons were inferior, but two of them were richer even than the richest doctors.[120] Indeed, the most rapidly rising occupational group of the century was the surgeons, gaining a recognition as a liberal profession and appropriating increased rewards, and establishing the view that past distinctions between them and the doctors had been solely due to 'vanity and sloth'.[121] Professorships in University Faculties now fell to experts with surgical experience, especially after service on a warship, or a vessel of the Company of the Indies, or a slaver—for these tragic voyages from Africa could hardly have made a profit without intelligent medical advice on the selection of merchandise and on hygienic precautions.

The approval of public opinion helped to swell the pride of the medical profession. La Mettrie, himself both a *philosophe* and a physician, had no doubt which vocation was the more important. 'Doctors are the only philosophers who are useful to the Republic . . . . the others are idlers and drones.'[122] The obituary orations of Vicq d'Azyr on distinguished colleagues in the last dozen years before the Revolution give an impression of men conscious of belonging to a highly intellectual international confraternity, extending from Uppsala to Halle, from Leyden to Bâle; they are widely read in physics, chemistry, botany, and meteorology; they are sensitive souls in the Rousseauistic vein, and they usually die from overwork or through the hazards of their 'ministry'; they are dedicated 'citizens', true 'patriots'.[123] Pamphleteers at the beginning of the Revolution take up this theme of 'ministry'. One suggests dividing the revenues of the Church between the *curés* and the doctors, another suggests that it is a pity to confine the genius of the physician to 'the sad, dry analysis of millions of infirmities'; they should direct private hobbies and reading, public fêtes and theatre programmes, and arrange marriages.[124] The *cahiers* of 1789 ask for more doctors in the countryside, and those of some of the nobles ask for the right to practise medicine without infringement of noble status.[125] During the Revolution, the old idea of 'charlatanism' and the new one of 'the medical aristocracy' caused the abandonment, for some years, of regulations about qualifications.[126] But the ideal of social leadership devolving upon the profession survived. 'In certain respects', said Cabanis, 'the profession of medicine is a kind of priesthood, in others, a magisterial office.'[127]

The Académie Royale de Chirurgie had been founded in 1731, a centre where ideas were exchanged, and a repository for the corporate privileges of the surgeons; the documents conferring these privileges were published by the Academy in 1744, with a proud preface claiming equality with the physicians and a vast superiority over the Ancients, who had not known how to deal with a simple stoppage of the urine, and did their trepanning with hammers.[128] In 1777, the King gave the pharmacists a central institution, the Collège de Pharmacie, where lectures were to be given on chemistry and natural history as well as on the art of preparing medicaments. Though as yet there were few discoveries to help the patient, the alliance between the chemists and pharmacists marked the way of future progress. The alliance had begun when the Faculty of Montpellier defeated the Faculty of Paris over the use of antimony (as against the Galenic principle of purely herbal remedies), and developed when the brothers Geoffroy of the Academy of Sciences gave chemistry courses for apothecaries, followed by the apothecary François Rouelle's lectures, from which the chemists, even Lavoisier, profited.[129] In 1776–7, the King also set up the Société Royale de Médecine, initially a group of eight experts under the *premier médecin du roi*.[130] The immediate task of the new foundation was to consider measures against a cattle plague in Gascony, but there was also a far-reaching scheme of medical research—to obtain from local correspondents information about the incidence of disease and death as related to social class, geographical features, and, above all, weather conditions, as well as maintaining some check on the health statistics of hospitals, prisons, army camps, and naval vessels. The Society not only initiated these inquiries: it also produced a plan for the reform of medical education, a system of teaching identical for physicians and surgeons, based on practical work in the dissection laboratory and in hospital wards, leading to a diploma of uniform standard for the whole country.[131] Calling in the medical consultants to deal with a cattle plague was an illustration of Vicq d'Azyr's aphorism that 'medicine is one', and the next step was the creation of a central institution for veterinary teaching, which would foster research activities, linking human with animal problems.[132] Up to now, the school at Alfort had taught reading, writing, and simple rustic medicine, including the farrier's art of shoeing horses. In 1782 two new chairs were created, one anatomical, for Vicq d'Azyr himself, and another on rural economy for the chemist Fourcroy. In the second half of the eighteenth century, the medical profession was being endowed with corporate institutions for research and the dissemination of information. At the same time medical journals began—*Le Journal de médecine, de chirurgie et de pharmacie*, followed by the *Gazette de Santé*.[133] Medicine had been held back from progress by the custom of 'solo practice'; physicians followed the traditions of their guild, seeing only a limited number of cases, with little chance of exchanging information with colleagues, while the hospitals were religious and humane institutions, not geared to continuous scientific inquiry. Apart from the rare possibility of another empirical discovery, day-to-day practice would not have led to a decisive breakthrough. Corporate institutions, specialization, machinery for the co-ordination and dissemination of information were necessary for progress. As Comte said, the prospects for astronomy would have been unpromising if all research in that science had been left to sea captains.[134]

In assessing the contribution of medicine to the civilization, comfort, or numerical expansion of mankind, we ought to give more weight than we normally do to the bureaucrats and administrators, and their ideal of public service. The professional organization of medicine prepared the way for its eventual triumph as a scientific discipline. More than this, in the second half of the eighteenth century, the activities of reforming administrators established the main principles of public hygiene and social medicine as we know them. [135] In a few uncompromising quotations from writers of the Enlightenment the theory of the modern Welfare State can be found—the rights of the poor to the abundance of the rich (Turgot), to food, clothing, and a way of life not damaging to health (Montesquieu), and to 'prompt, free, certain and complete' assistance (La Rochefoucauld-Liancourt). [136] These are generous statements by men whose riches had not blinded them to justice, but one doubts if reformers at the end of the *ancien régime* were consciously moved by such extreme convictions. There was a long tradition of government intervention, whether on Christian, populationist, mercantilist, or Enlightenment principles: the King's ministers had a duty to keep down the price of bread and ensure its supply, and to stop the spread of infectious diseases. There were no more visitations of the plague after 1720, but whenever any other serious epidemic was reported, the intendants called in medical experts to investigate, and sent round the *boîtes d'Helvétius*, boxes of medicines, originally prepared by the Swiss physician of that name. [137] Once convinced that inoculation was safe, the government promoted it. After a resounding controversy (which we must study later) had established the danger of burials in inhabited areas, orders were given for the removal of the graveyards. This was an age of municipal improvements—evident not only in splendid façades, pavements, and street lighting, but also in hygienic reforms—and the aldermen imitated the government in calling on the local Medical Faculty for advice. [138] These interventions became more fashionable still in the second half of the century with the rise of *sensibilité*, which caught the imagination and moulded the language of polite society. Behind the *clichés*, there was genuine delicacy of feeling, and behind the pretensions and insincerities, there was a new sense of duty towards fellow citizens, and a deepening of affections within the intimate family circle. Now, for the first time, there was serious concern for the artisans who worked in dangerous and unhealthy conditions. Rousseau complained that they suffered to provide luxuries for the rich; an inspector of manufactures wrote to the Royal Society of Medicine arguing that our sophisticated culture depends upon their obscure toil (engravers, for example, transmit faithful representations of the works of great artists), and he appealed for 'natural' conditions of work, with free currents of air circulating.[139] Moheau used the populationist's argument and asked for a State inquiry into 'the trades that are destructive to the human race', and Necker began the collection of information about them. 'The field of inquiry is vast,' Moheau had said, 'the subject practically untouched, and the object is noble.'[140] In Rousseau's *Émile*, the charter of *sensibilité* so far as children are concerned, the arguments of enlightened doctors for mothers breast-feeding their babies were enumerated with moving conviction. The appeal to family affection and duty was more effective than the new statistics of differential mortality and the old fears about the transmission of dangerous passions. Marie-Antoinette was convinced: 'Je veux vivre en mère, nourrir mon enfant et me consacrer à son éducation.'[141] Consciences were stirred about the wretched *enfants trouvés*, but what could be done? The King forbade their carriage from the provinces to Paris, and the doctors experimented to find a hygienic way of feeding them with animals' milk. Though there were no significant improvements in midwifery, the government tried to ensure that the best knowledge was available, and in the seventies, experts were sent round to give demonstrations. The famous Mme Du Coudray, with her anatomical doll, is said to have trained about 5,000 midwives on her tours between 1760 and 1783. Bankrupt, the government of Louis XVI could offer little to the population by way of medical services except in the crises of epidemics, but it at least could disseminate medical information. On the bridges and on posts by the riverside the municipalities displayed its latest circulars: how to rescue the drowning and give them artificial respiration.

Up to the reign of Louis XVI, a detached observer might have taken Chamfort's observation seriously: hospitals existed, not to look after the sick, but to hide them from sight so they would not embarrass the pleasures of the healthy. From 1774, however, reforms began. Six new hospitals were built at Paris, as many as in the preceding century, and four new military establishments were set up at Lille, Metz, Strasbourg, and Toulon.[142] In 1784, the abbé de l'Épée published an account of the school where he taught the deaf and dumb by sign language. Two years later, Valentin Haüy described the success of his method of teaching blind children; they learned to read by the use of embossed characters, and excelled at singing and instrumental music—all the while, they were treated as ordinary children, not as invalids. [143] The scope of social medicine was being extended to new categories of disability, and its aims were becoming more ambitious: to make the handicapped into first-class citizens. During Necker's ministry, the hospitals (a special concern of his philanthropic wife) were directly under the Controller General. He appointed a layman, Jean Colombier, a former doctor with the army, as inspector (replacing the clerical Grand Aumônier with his archaic visitation rights), and devised a plan for centralizing hospital funds under the control of the Sovereign, 'le caissier général de ses pauvres sujets'. [144] (The scheme was received with justified distrust: the Sovereign had too often been interested in confiscating funds irrespective of the merits of the case.) After the fall of Necker, control of the hospitals passed to the Minister of the King's Household, the Baron de Breteuil, an opponent of *lettres de cachet*, a supporter of tolerance towards Protestants, and an advocate of hygienic reforms. After the great fire at the Hôtel-Dieu in 1772, there had been plans, now abandoned, to move this vast institution out of the capital. In 1785, Breteuil appointed a committee, which included the scientists Lavoisier and Laplace, the naturalist Daubenton, the astronomer Bailly, and Jacques Tenon the surgeon, to re-examine the question. [145] A hospital with as many patients as the population of many a town of France, they reported, was an absurdity, a vast centre of infection, and they asked for four smaller hospitals to be built on the fringes of Paris, each with its own pure water supply and sewage system. Though the fall of Breteuil in July 1788 and the Revolution prevented further progress, some imaginative memoranda were published which reveal the ingenuity of the new social medicine. Their generally accepted idea, that of a hospital divided into *pavillons* for different kinds of illness, and to separate operations and treatment from the wards, was taken from English models, and from the French naval hospital at Rochefort, built in 1780 after the study of designs across the Channel. Jean-Baptiste Le Roy, of the Academy of Sciences, said each *pavillon* should be 'a kind of island in the air', containing about a hundred patients, men on one side, women on the other, with ventilation coming up from the floor in the central aisle. Condorcet, as befitted a mathematician, said the way to plan the size of a ward was to ask how many patients a single night nurse could cope with, and he himself wanted a multiplicity of small parish hospitals, forty in all for Paris.[146] Tenon the surgeon insisted that every patient was a 'citizen' with all his rights intact, and, being statistically minded, worked out exactly the amount of oxygen these rights included—in the present Hôtel-Dieu, he said, the sick get only one-sixth of their entitlement. Similarly with space for sleep and movement—according to a colleague, Tenon never went to a funeral without measuring the grave to see if its dimensions were adequate. He wanted all hospitals under State administration, with the physicians in control of the patients and (remembering the feud between nuns and surgeons at the Hôtel-Dieu) lay nurses trained from among the orphans brought up at public expense. These humanitarian ideas flourished in the autumn days of the *ancien régime* as the State slid into bankruptcy. The *cahiers* of 1789 believed that society should care for the poor and infirm, but had no coherent view of how this was to be done or who should pay for it.[147] War and conscription was to create a new emergency medicine in France on a vast scale, and give grim new experience to hospital surgeons. But by Year V, the ideal of social security had been abandoned.

'Whether physicians are many or few, whether they are skilled or ignorant', said Sénac de Meilhan, 'the figures in the tables of mortality do not vary.'[148] This pessimism—from the son of a great doctor—about the achievements of the medical profession in the eighteenth century, was justified, in so far as the progress of medical science in the narrow sense is concerned. But improvements in treatments and technique did something to improve the quality of living, reducing the number of crippled births, scarred faces, broken teeth, blind eyes, mis-set fractures. And what did save lives was the work of administrators and doctors to restrain the spread of epidemics and to improve hygienic conditions. Even so, much of what was done and projected—like the proposals for hospital reform—was to be effective only in the future. Lavoisier, with the scientist's impatience, complained of this slow progress in a world where civilization was so brilliant. 'All the arts', he said, 'are moving rapidly to their state of perfection; that of living in society, of preserving in their full force and health a great number of individuals gathered together, to make big cities more salubrious and the communication of contagious maladies less easy, is still in its infancy.'[149] The medicine of the eighteenth century, concentrating on the two extremes of encyclopaedic accumulation of detail and the search for the single grandiose explanation,[150] had not yet found the way towards a scientific study of diseases. Yet the breakthrough had been brought nearer. The Montpellier school had contributed by insisting that medicine was autonomous, not subject to chemistry or to other sciences.[151] By the time of the *Encyclopédie méthodique*, medical men regarded their subject, not only as autonomous, but also in some way as the discipline within which all the other sciences could find their focus; they looked forward to a synthesis of earth science with environmental medicine.[152] Contributors pressed cartography into the service of medicine, especially for plotting the incidence of tropical diseases; the therapeutic qualities of electrical treatments were noted; developments in the chemistry of gases were used in the studies of diseases borne by the atmosphere; the effects of climate, heat, light, magnetism, gravitation, and the heavenly bodies were subjects for reflection. Hallé, who had been a member of the Faculty of Paris under the *ancien régime* and became Professor of Medical Physics and Hygiene after the reorganization of medical education in 1795, planned a systematic study of the physical environment as an aid to public hygiene—a subject in which the English and Americans admitted that the French led the world. Conscious of belonging to an international community of learning, the medical profession was looking outwards, ready to accept the results of research elsewhere. Mauduyt, writing on the medical relevance of electricity in 1792, was citing English, Scottish, and German sources, as well as French ones. All the while, the expectations of the public and the professional pride of the doctors created a psychological pressure for new achievements, and the government's encouragement of corporate organization, and the setting-up of machinery for collecting and disseminating information created possibilities of research for the future. The Revolution swept away the old hospitals and universities, and in the chaos of war, a new medical organization had to be created. The process was painful, but the old clichés and technicalities of medicine were discredited, and the doctors, retaining their professional status and role of leadership, were encouraged by the experiences of war towards a ruthless practicality. The medical philosophy of Cabanis, *phénoménisme*,[153] was fitted to the new age, refusing to seek for causes or the essence of things, and simply observing and analysing. Thus, it has been said, a new medicine was born 'out of a political and technological revolution'.[154] But this technological revolution had been prepared under the *ancien régime*. The idea of clinical research and instruction on the hospital wards, already tried at Leyden and Edinburgh, was seen with J.-J. Sachs at Strasbourg in the fifties, and the hospital attached to the Paris College of Surgery in the seventies, in some military establishments, and in the eighties in La Charité under Desbois de Rochefort and, above all, in the Hôtel-Dieu with Pierre-Joseph Desault.[155] The clinician's case-book was to become a decisive instrument of research once it was systematically co-ordinated with the practice of morbid anatomy. Vicq d'Azyr spoke of interrogating 'the organs of the dead to find the causes of diseases', but he spoke in vague terms and included the solution of problems of morals and sentiment.[156] Bichat in 1801 put the alliance of clinical study and the autopsy into a sharper, harsher light. The notebook, he said, will reveal only 'a succession of incoherent phenomena', 'but open a few corpses—*ouvrez quelques cadavres*' and all the confusions will vanish. Foucault[157] sees here a new attitude to death: man, having constituted himself an object of scientific investigation, is seizing on the tragedy of death as just another opportunity for unsentimental observation. But how new is this attitude? Throughout this century of precise anatomical dissection, the mystery of death had never deterred the surgeons. Diderot[158] has a story of Frère Cosme turning up at La Charité to collect a corpse, and being thunderstruck on hearing that the man had recovered. 'Mon cadavre!', he lamented, and was only pacified when they found him another one.

3

The Shadow of Death and
the Art of Living

If the bell indeed tolls for every man, death was very near to life throughout the eighteenth century. But its shadow was even darker than a statistical appraisal would assume. Accidents, affrays, public executions, and the customary fashion of dying in public combined to make the last agony and the livid corpse a familiar sight. Hospitals did not afford the opportunity for slipping out of life quietly in our modern fashion, under the care of medical technologists. In their hovels and slums, the poor died as they lived, huddled together, and even the houses of the rich were not organized for privacy. Reminders of the crudeness of death were evident in the crudeness of living[1]—blood on the pavements from the butchers' shops, slivers of corpses thrown out into the street from the lecture rooms of the anatomists, dead animals in the gutters. As if to compensate for the confusion and promiscuity, social arrangements were formal: mourning was a rigorous observance marked, for those who could afford it, by black clothing with bands of white linen at the sleeves and a long black cloak overall. For a parent, the official period of grief was six months, four and a half for grandparents, and two for a brother or sister. The Court led the way in imposing mourning for members of the families of princes of the blood and for foreign royalty; a series of deaths among the great of Europe could bring the merchants of silk and taffeta of Lyon to the verge of ruin. Normally, the King's example fixed the duration of the observances of the Court, though close family and private individuals might choose for themselves a longer period. The King mourned six weeks for the duchesse de Berry in 1719, her father the duc d'Orléans and his household at the Palais Royal for three months, and Mme de Saint-Simon, whose eccentricity it was to be over-scrupulous in these matters, for six.[2] Citizens of Paris who could afford mourning clothing aped the great of Versailles, gaining some quiet satisfaction at being dressed in a fashion which concealed distinctions of rank; an English visitor to Paris in 1776 found that he could not decently go round sight-seeing until an urgent visit to the tailor had fitted him out in black to show respect to the prince de Conti, lately deceased.[3] Eight years earlier, the abbé Coyer, always in the van of innovation, had urged the abandonment of mourning apparel; in affliction, he thought, we should dress cheerfully, for the only true sorrow is that which we feel secretly in our hearts.[4] His proposal received no support, though in the next reign, the commercial problems of the textile manufacturers of Lyon persuaded the government to reduce the time of mourning for foreign princes.

'Man has no need to strive to think of death. It presents itself so often to him that he can regard it as incorporated, as it were, in his being!' Having thus disclaimed any need to do so, Caraccioli carried on with his substantial volume, *Le Tableau de la mort*.[5] There was a massive religious literature on preparation for death, and books meant to be consoling, and even those that actually were, constituted grim reminders all the same. 'O Dieu mon père!', Tallement des Réaux had exclaimed at the sight of a solid work in quarto by a Protestant divine enumerating the 'Consolations against the terrors of death', 'ce gros livre me fait plus de peur que la mort mesme.'[6] Preachers were eloquent on 'the importance of salvation, the brevity of our days, the duration of eternity', and with deaths so frequent, there was often enough some fearful recent example to alarm the hearers. Mme de Parabère, the hard-drinking mistress of the Regent, was converted (though not from drink) by a sermon on 'eternity' just after her valet had dropped dead while pouring the coffee.[7] 'Think of death, it is nearer than you suppose', said the bishop of Dol, censuring a parishioner who had maligned his parish priest—the man was dead within the week, his wife as well.[8] When Bridaine, the great missioner, was preaching near Lyon in 1735, two men who ridiculed him met with fatal accidents; one fell off a wall while performing an imitation, another collapsed in a drinking bout—crowds flocked to see the corpse: 'cet exemple fit un effet prodigieux'.[9] One could wish that the pulpit orators had played less upon the emotion of fear, yet with the incidence of death so heavy and so arbitrary, it would not have been easy to do otherwise. Like the novelists, who brought their plots to a *dénouement* and their villains to punishment with easy verisimilitude,[10] in harping on death they were simply talking in terms of everyday reality. Significantly, the clergy by common consent had the social role of exhorting their flocks to practical action in preparation for death: they were expected to warn against delay in making a last will and testament, and to insist that this document was scrupulously fair to the rights of natural heirs and the reasonable expectations of loyal servants. There is scarcely a religious treatise on preparation for the end which does not warn of the injustices, disputes, and lawsuits which are laid to the account of those who neglect their testamentary duty.[11] Throughout the year, the liturgy of the Church commemorated the departed, and families would remember their dead at grace after meals, on the occasion of a First Communion, a marriage, or the first mass of a priest. Once a year, on All Souls' Day, the faithful were called to pray for all the departed without exception; there would be processions of parishes, monasteries, and chapters to their cemeteries for the solemn asper-sion of the tombs.[12] On that day the grim *Libera* was said or sung after mass, and the *Te Deum* and the *Gloria* were omitted from all offices.[13] The observances of the Church were supposed to replace the whole twilight world of popular superstition which had evolved around the idea of death and the memory of the departed. But liturgical observances were no substitute, in the countryside, for the old portents of mortality. In Brittany, it was an ill omen to see a magpie alight on a roof or to be startled by a cock crowing near by, and more dangerous still was the sight of a candle going out at a wedding, or hearing the church clock strike in exact coincidence with the ringing of the handbell by the server at the elevation of the mass.[14] And what of the frequent sighting of ghosts in bedrooms and churchyards? Secular writers joined with churchmen to explain them away: they are frauds, false alarms, the product of a bad digestion; they come from the heat generated in graves throwing up a hazy outline of the corpse below.[15] Instead of imagining the return of the dead, one did better to pray for them. The magistrates of certain towns provided all citizens with extra opportunities for doing so by sending round at night the *Clocheteur des trépassés*.

In distinctive dress (black dalmatic with a white cross front and back, or a tabard with skull and cross-bones), lantern in one hand, bell in the other, he would walk the streets crying, 'Priez Dieu pour les trépassés', prefaced maybe by 'Réveillez-vous, gens qui dormez', or rounded off by 'Pensez à la mort'. The dogs barked and there was many a sleepy oath at his 'vain and tragic sermon',[16] and if some prayed for the dead, others made a different use of the opportunity—the wits parodied the *clocheteur*'s cry, 'Prenez vos femmes, embrassez-les.'[17]

What effect did constant familiarity with death have on the minds of the men of the eighteenth century? The oversimplified question, 'Did they fear death more than we do?' is impossible to answer. The comparison would have to be sustained through differing social and geographical milieux which were not, and are not, homogeneous. More than that, earlier centuries, unlike our own, were subject to demographic crises, general or local, of varying intensity. There came a point, in times of famine and epidemic, when a 'panic threshold'[18] was crossed, somewhere just short of the doubling of the death rate among those over ten years of age who had got through the dangerous early years and had seemed to have a reasonable chance of survival. And what measurements can we devise to classify fear? How do we compare a gnawing, barely recognized unease, with a series of forced reactions to specific alarming examples, or the sudden sickening realization that interrupts euphoria, with the long haul of twilight apprehension? Most of us are too preoccupied with living to brood on death; when we do so, it is with fear, though with resignation too, for this is our necessary lot (in the words of one of the abbé Prévost's charming heroines, 'death is just one of the thousand necessities to which we are subjected'—'C'est notre sort').[19] We are afraid, we are resigned, and we concentrate on living. These are the eternal human attitudes, always present in our minds and interchanging in their domination—on rare occasions totally transformed by love or courage, on most occasions overlaid and disciplined by social conventions and traditional formulas.

That familiarity breeds contempt can hardly be postulated of death, so far as our own final dissolution is concerned, but it may breed callousness to the deaths of others. 'No one wept for the dead,' said the fourteenth-century chronicler of the plague in Sienna, 'because everyone expected to die himself.'[20] Restif observes, sardonically, that in Paris it was only porters, cobblers, and laundresses whose children shed tears for them; Mercier says that when a funeral procession went by no one paid attention: 'qui veut être pleuré après sa mort ne doit pas mourir à Paris'.[21] As in 'la Ville' so in 'la Cour': Versailles[22] was coldly indifferent to the departure of its luminaries and to public disasters. The dancers stepped over the blood on the floor where the chevalier de Fénelon had killed himself; the corpse of a duke, hidden under an old blanket, was ferried out by a couple of lackeys; the ball for the marriage of the Dauphin went on with undiminished splendour on the evening of the day when a thousand Parisians had been trampled down in the great firework panic. In this private universe of gilded unconcern, Louis XV learned his sadistic evasiveness, forbidding all mention of death—save when he spoke of it himself to the aged. 'Where do you wish to be buried?' 'Sire, at the feet of Your Majesty.' Even those who mourned sincerely, it was commonly said among ordinary people, soon forgot. There were popular jokes about the quiet satisfaction of heirs, and widows who were not inconsolable. Chateaubriand was to go so far as to say that a man returning from the grave would not be welcome, even among those who had most sincerely mourned him—so easily do we form new friendships and adopt new habits.[23] Another commonplace was to say that the deaths of others do not drive us to think of our own. This was not just a complaint by the theologians. The death penalty, said a lawyer in 1790, is useless as a deterrent for, though 'every instant we acquire new proofs of our mortality', we refuse to complete the syllogism.[24] Even if we weep sincerely for others, said Maine de Biran, the impression on our minds is fleeting: 'nous ne songeons presque jamais à la mort.'[25] Men are subject to death, misery, and ignorance, Pascal had said, and as they know no cure, they refuse to think of them.[26] This was Mme du Deffand's formula, to avert her gaze from death as much as possible, just as Restif did not wish to see clocks on mantelpieces—'vous voyez votre vie s'écouler.'[27] When death had to be spoken of, there were anodyne synonyms available, and even those who refused to accept the possibility of an afterlife talked of a 'journey', 'voyage', 'sleep', of the 'harbour', the 'door', and the 'refuge', with their ambiguous implications of a progress and a goal. Or, more rarely, the explicit could become a burlesque device, limiting the confrontation with reality to a humorous context. There is the 'hole', the 'trou' Piron speaks of in one of his mock epitaphs for himself:

Enfin je me vois au trou
Que n'évite fou ni sage.[28]

Dom Lobineau the Maurist historian complains of the same dark passage, the burrow of the mole down which he had to go to an eternal reward—though he would rather have stayed with his books: 'Ce diable de trou de taupe par où il faut aller au paradis.'[29] Yet were people really unconcerned, did their evasions and euphemisms avail them, was their apparent callousness anything more than a shield against unbearable pain, a conformity to a convention? The losses that are more frequent and the losses that are expected are not thereby easier to bear. Versailles appears in a different light when we see Louis XV standing on the freezing balcony as Mme de Pompadour's coffin passed through the court- yard below—only one of his mistresses, but the last of his friends. When the folk of the eighteenth century can be glimpsed with their defences broken down, it is the same grief that we know. There is the same bitterness of parting, the same struggle to break through cliché and the ordinariness of life and of dying to express undying affection. 'I am like the lost dove which laments its fate unceasingly until it dies of sorrow,' says a letter from a soldier, dying in a military hospital in Bavaria, to his wife at Lyon. 'I would have to have a heart as hard as marble to forget the object that my heart adores. My dear heart, I will never forget you, even when it pleases the Lord that I be carried off into a clime unknown to human kind. I swear that I will never fail to think of you. I pray my sister to look after my father always and not forget him nor abandon him, nor my mother Dominique, and to look after little Philbert, to have him taught to read and write and pray to God.'[30] Behind the elaborate conventions of formal mourning which the century imposed, there was the same hopelessness and loneliness before the empty chair and the silent house, and the same polite struggle to offer the accustomed social responses, the same attempts to forget that become merely a crueller form of remembering—'l'on vous croit consolé, mais souvent l'on n'est que distrait.' For days after the death of his seven-year-old daughter, Moreau could see her everywhere: 'Je ne sais comment j'ai pu survivre'—'I do not know how I kept on living.'[31]

We have asked about the impact of the continual presence of death on the minds of the men of the eighteenth century: only an impressionistic answer can be given. But a more precise question can be formulated if we consider social structure. Compared to us, these folk faced heavy odds: they had none of our complacent expectation of a standard life span. What effect did their limited expectation and continual sense of uncertainty have on the way in which their lives were organized and on their attitudes to human relationships? Did they accept life's responsibilities earlier and hasten on their decisions, or did they drift through lack of confidence, or did they take more care than we do to associate the next generation with their projects? Did they clutch more frantically at pleasure, or did it seem less desirable because more ephemeral? Were they more cynical—or more tender—in human relationships? Of course, there never has been and never is time enough for ambition, love, pleasure, or reflection, and it is not easy to think of death without hope of postponement. 'O temps suspends ton vol' comes in the works of an eighteenth-century poet as well as in those of Lamartine.[32] Similarly, among those who could not foresee the possibility of a more secure expectation of living, there was a fatalistic acceptance of their lot and a determination to do the best they could with it which are curious to us only because of our anachronistic privilege of making a comparison with a more predictable existence. This is not a comparison in terms of an average life span, but in terms of expectation. Their permissible hope, so far as duration is concerned, was much the same as ours, except that theirs was barely permissible and ours is a confident assumption. We are examining the effect upon conduct and social relationships of a severely limited expectation of reaching this theoretically possible boundary. The prize in the lottery was the same for them as for us, but the number of blanks in the draw was vastly greater.

Poets divided the life of man into infancy, adolescence, manhood, and old age to correspond to the four seasons of the year:[33] the medical practitioners of the eighteenth century wanted greater exactitude, and preferred to use a succession of seven-year periods. This was the system of 'révolutions septennaires' adopted by Cabanis in his famous *Rapports du physique et du moral de l'homme* (1802),[34] but the idea was well established before him. According to La Curne de Sainte-Palaye's *Mémoires sur l'ancienne chevalerie* (1759), this was how the training of the medieval knight had been organized: educated by the women up to the age of seven; from seven a page; from fourteen a squire; and then a true knight at twenty-one.[35] Daignan, a doctor of the Medical Faculty of Montpellier, who published a *Tableau des variétés de la vie de l'homme* in 1788, divided life into fifteen periods, each of six or seven years, in seven cases allowing a year of overlap. The first period he passes over quickly. It is 'l'âge des hasards'; the chances of survival are limited—'l'enfant le mieux constitué peut périr à chaque instant.'[36] We have seen the statistics of this grim uncertainty; Buffon's 'One-third of the human race perishes before reaching the age of twenty-eight months; half the human race perishes before the age of eight years.'[37] There were variations in the death rate in different areas, but everywhere in France the slaughter of the innocents went on, and the death of young children was part of the routine of family existence. To understand the mentality of the eighteenth century, the first step is to try to recapture the instinctive harshness, resignation, and fatalistic determination of people who saw their children born to die rather than to live.[38] An infant was baptized on the day of birth—or, at the latest, on one of the two following days[39]—this ensured salvation, if death intervened before the age of reason: 'il a été baptisé,' says the duc de Luynes of such a case, 'il est heureux.'[40] If the godparents lived at a distance, they would be called together before the birth to prevent delay.[41] Episcopal and royal ordinances threatened penalties on parents who neglected their duty in this respect, though usually there were recent examples of mortality enough to encourage the faithful to make haste in securing their child in its eternal destiny. A provincial notary, whose son was baptized at the time of a local epidemic, was inspired to make a curious entry in his journal in praise of the fear of death. 'This child is born in a time of calamities by the sudden deaths which afflict this area and, indeed, all the province.

May God manifest his anger thus to him all through his life, so that he may conduct himself with fear and merit his mercy.'[42] When, in high society, we hear of 'baptisms' some weeks after the birth (for example, Christophe de Beaumont, the future archbishop, was born on 26 July 1703 and baptized on 10 August, by permission of the bishop of Sarlat, and the duc de Croy was baptized six weeks after his birth in 1718), this refers to a formal, complete ceremony in church—there had always been a private baptism (*ondoiement*) before this.[43] Parents had a subconscious awareness of emotional danger in becoming too fond of infants—best keep them at a distance in the care of wet-nurses until the balance of probability tilted in favour of their survival.[44] The accepted attitude to the death of a child was stoical resignation: 'God has afflicted us, . . . we must submit to his will: let us pray that he will see fit to conserve to us the only one that is left,'[45] and the name of the deceased child would often be given to the next, the family replacement.[46]

The years from seven to fourteen Daignan describes as 'l'Adolescence', 'the age of hopes', characterized by curiosity, idleness, and impatience. From the beginning of this period of life, we are dealing with a moral being, capable of knowing the difference between good and evil. This is in accordance with the regulations of churchmen and lawyers. At seven, a child was expected to make his confession; he would be catechized and confirmed and, if he fell gravely ill, he would receive extreme unction.[47] He could also be put on trial in a law court, and at the age of fourteen, the magistrates would sentence a juvenile criminal to the same punishment as an adult. According to the statutes of most dioceses, between the ages of ten and twelve a young person would receive the First Communion—in the diocese of Arras the age was ten, in that of Auxerre eleven, in that of Autun twelve.[48]

At the age of seven, boys began to take their place in the adult world of work. It was then that the sons of great nobles, as in the days of chivalry, left the household of women to come under the direction of a tutor, while the sons of the lesser nobility and the bourgeoisie were sent off from home to a *collège* or *pension*.[49] At this age the son of a peasant would be sent out to do the less physically demanding tasks of the fields—minding a cow or a couple of sheep, gathering sticks. At Marseille, where there were

more interesting opportunities, boys would evade whatever school-
ing was provided and go off with the fishing fleet or even on
voyages, condemning themselves to a lifetime of ignorance which
was the reason—said the local bishop—why so many of them
finally became renegades to the Turks in the Levant.[50] Once they
reached fourteen, boys were apprenticed to a trade or assumed the
full burden of agricultural labour as a *valet de ferme*; at about that
age girls left home for domestic service in the town, though this was
rather too early by the standards of the Enfants trouvés of Paris
(this institution paid 40 *livres* a year to country foster-parents
looking after orphans, reducing to 35 *livres* for boys at the age of
twelve and ending at fourteen, but continuing for girls to sixteen—
'it can be presumed that boys reaching the age of fourteen and girls
at sixteen will be in a position to be useful to those who are looking
after them').[51] In any case, a young person of either sex was
regarded as an adult at sixteen. Until the Commission des Réguliers
in the seventies, this was the age at which monastic vows could be
taken.[52]

A census of Flanders taken in 1764 divides each of the categories
(nobles, male commoners, female commoners, male servants, and
female servants) into two—up to sixteen and older. The clear point
of decision was the issue of military service. According to royal
ordinance, this was the age at which an enlistment was valid
(though military opinion later in the century thought this too
early, and the Revolution was to take its conscripts at eighteen).[53]
By this stage of life young people had entered the next of Daignan's
categories, 'puberty'—though the good medical expert had to concede that the neatness of this scheme is compromised by the variation
of the age of achieving full sexual growth, depending on climate,
diet, and social *milieu*. For a boy of prosperous background in the
South of France, puberty might be reached as early as thirteen years
of age (eleven for a girl); for a boy in poor circumstances in the
North, it might be as late as nineteen (seventeen for a girl). Not
surprisingly Daignan regards this as the most difficult period of
life—marked by 'desire, vanity, and the thirst for independence'.[54]
Significantly society was well organized to keep youthful high
spirits in tutelage—in the severe discipline and long working hours
of the *collège*, the army, and apprenticeship. In rural France the

young people beginning adult work, though still subject to paternal authority, gained a sort of disciplined independence by moving into the comparatively sophisticated organization of village youth with its hierarchy and sense of belonging. In many places, especially the South, there were formal associations of youth under various names (*guet, vogue, bravade, corps de jeunesse*) which took a leading part in communal festivities and had a recognized independent role in the community. Since marriage among the peasants was so late, a tight and active organization for youth was a social necessity.

Daignan's next two categories are Youth (*la Jeunesse*) from twenty-two to twenty-eight, a time of love, enthusiasm, and emotional sensitivity, and Virility (*la Virilité*) from twenty-nine to thirty-four, the age of ambition and of the full play of the passions. Our medical doctor is interested in sexual potentiality, but his observations are superficial. He does not discuss the age of marriage. In fact, this varied greatly according to social class. Free from economic constraints and with lineages to perpetuate, great aristocrats married early. Most of the dukes with peerage status (*ducs et pairs*) married before the age of twenty-five.[55] A financier with his way in the world to make would delay founding a family. Only 13.6 per cent of those who became *fermiers généraux* in the century had married before the age of twenty-five—the average age was thirty-three years six months. Handling money professionally made men cautious: thirty-one was the age for the *bourgeoisie* of Geneva. Merchants of Bordeaux married at about thirty, though they generally chose as their wives girls in their early twenties.[56] From sheer economic necessity, the peasants married late—the men, on the average, at twenty-seven to twenty-eight, the women at twenty-five to twenty-six. This postponement of marriage was the keystone of the old demographic structure, the essential contraceptive device keeping population and resources in equilibrium. As life was shorter and more precarious than today, one might have expected that men and women would live at a faster tempo, making maximum use of the time available. But in peasant France, prudence and economic necessity overwhelmed the sense of the brevity of existence, imposing a long delay before sexual fulfilment was legitimate—almost the same length of time as a marriage could

be expected to last before death intervened. As between the anecdotal evidence about free love in hayrick and hedgerow and the
statistical evidence of few illegitimate births in the countryside,
there is room for speculation about what really happened during
this long waiting period of doctor Daignan's enthusiastic and
passionate *Jeunesse*.[57]

As far as sexual activity in later life is concerned, Daignan is
oversimplifying in concentrating on physical potentiality, as if he
was dealing with a human activity of a given proportion which
inevitably declined, and was not susceptible of transformation, of
growing in depth and refinement. Le Maître de Claville, in his
famous moralizing treatise earlier in the century, had taken the age
of thirty as the point where the passions come under intelligent
direction: up to the age of twenty-five, men look for a beautiful
woman, over the next five years, for an attractive one, and thereafter for an intelligent one—after thirty, 'une femme raisonnante'
pleases them best.[58] This analysis, of course, was a long way from
describing how matrimony was organized in practice, since it refers
to the feelings without taking into account questions of money and
an establishment—the all-important dowry among the aristocracy
and *bourgeoisie*, the workshop inherited by the artisan's widow,
the flock of sheep left to the widow of the *laboureur*, the few
hundred *livres* that the peasant girl had amassed by eight or nine
years' work in the town. The customs and, indeed, the laws of the
social order were directed, where marriage was concerned, to
protecting the interests of families and their property. According to
the decrees of the Council of Trent, which laid down the official
view of the Church, mutual consent makes a marriage valid,
irrespective of the consent of the parents. But these decrees did not
run in France (they did at Avignon, which was a sort of Gretna
Green in this respect). By the law of the French State, a man under
thirty was disinherited if he married without parental permission,
as was a woman under twenty-five, and since to the lawyers inequality of fortunes established a presumption of *rapt de séduction*,
one of the partners might be in danger of the death penalty.[59] A free
choice based on affection alone was rare—among odd, rich individuals indifferent to social position, the younger sons of richer
peasants, and artisans and lower middle-class couples where the

wives shared in the work of shop, counting-house, or loom. For prudential reasons—whether the ingrained instinct of peasant society to keep population within subsistence limits, or private choices made for material or family motives—the age of marriage was not regulated by Daignan's 'passion', the pressures of sexual impulse at differing ages.

The economic reasons which delayed the age of marriage would not normally operate to prevent a second union when one of the partners died, certainly not in the case of the man who, indeed, might have children to be looked after and household problems needing a woman's care. There was a prejudice against early re-marriage—revealed in satirical observations in literature, in local customs of licensed buffoonery, and, in some provinces, by legal disqualifications from inheritance. Yet there was usually very little delay in forming a new union; widowers especially were quick to find new partners. In one place in Anjou, out of 181 widowers in the eighteenth century, 65 remarried within a year. In villages in Touraine, the average delay before a man remarried was thirteen months; in one place, half the men had found a new partner within six months. In Lyon most widowers had remarried within a year and 30 per cent of them within two months; in the Norman village of Crulai, 70 per cent within two years. In Meulan, it was quite common for a man to find consolation within two months; sometimes even within three weeks, barely enough time to have the banns read.[60] It was more difficult, of course, for a woman to find a new husband, especially if advanced in years, or with young children to burden the family budget. Hence the sad plea (in 1737) to the ecclesiastical court of the diocese of Cambrai from a woman of thirty-eight with five children seeking permission to marry within the prohibited degrees. 'She is already advanced in age without hope of having any chance other than the aforesaid . . . relative; she does not wish to let the opportunity pass.'[61] In any case, there were ecclesiastical canons and royal ordinances to impose an initial delay on even the most eligible widows, the so-called 'délais de viduité' which ensured the legal status of children born after the death of their father. On the other hand, a widow whose husband had left her some property was a good catch, and in certain towns which were growing rapidly (like Versailles in the early years of the century), the shortage of women enhanced their matrimonial chances. And even in Meulan, where there were no particularly favourable circumstances, practically all women who lost their partners before the age of thirty remarried, half of them within two years. In one village in Auvergne, the average delay for widows was only nine months and a few days. In the Bas-Quercy among the peasants, the average delay for women before remarrying was three and half years, as against the masculine average of fifteen months.[62] A pathological variant of this haste (as it seems to us) to remarry is seen after the great plague of Marseille in 1720, when there was a wild rush of survivors to remarry (some with their plague swellings scarce healed) so that contemporaries reflected on the aphrodisiac effect of the contagion, as if it impelled them to replace the missing population—a madness to conclude in the space of twenty-four hours the most important affair of a lifetime, and to consummate the marriage almost on the very ground where it was celebrated.[63] But this carnival of sexuality at Marseille, baroque and hysterical, can be prosaically interpreted. The marriage rate tripled just when property was made available by sudden deaths and the labour shortage caused high wages.[64] Even so, there was astonishing haste.

'How quickly we pass by on earth', cried Rousseau—the first quarter of our lives we know not how to live; in the last quarter we are beyond enjoying it; in the interval we spend three-quarters of our time in sleep, toil and unhappiness. Yet, in spite of his lament, Jean-Jacques suggested a sophisticated—almost a paradoxical— reaction. We should not strain to extract the utmost from the time available: we should learn how to waste it, to live at our own rhythm, to find contentment in travelling rather than arriving.[65] How right he was—if only time had been available! To love at leisure, to saunter a little and dream of passion, to have opportunities to redeem our mistakes and make up our quarrels, to find affection growing slowly and surely over long years together; this is loving, but few generations on only part of the globe have ever known it. The duration of marriage was abbreviated by the Malthusian pressure of economic necessity dictating the customs of society at one end, and by death at the other. When two people fell in love—or when a marriage was arranged between them—the combination into one destiny of their joint hazards loaded the dice of unhappiness more heavily still against them. A marriage rarely lasted for more than twenty years before one of the couple died (at Crulai, 51.5 per cent of unions lasted less than fifteen years, and 37 per cent less than ten; at Azereix, by the age of forty-five half the men had been widowed); in a particularly unhealthy village in Basse-Auvergne, no less than 43 per cent of the first marriages were broken within ten years by the death of one of the partners.[66] And in their time together, a husband and wife would have seen as many children die as live. Whether with the child arriving every year among the silk workers of Lyon, or arriving every two years among the peasants (later because breast-feeding, or sexual taboos connected with it, delayed conception), death ensured that there were few children together round the same hearth. The numerous patriarchal family of the *ancien régime* is more evident in sentimental literature than in the statistics of demography. Big family groups were assorted survivors. Few children knew their grandparents, and to live long meant, most often, loneliness among a generation of strangers.

Since the shadow of death made the partnership of husband and wife so fragile, the custom of the age devolved family responsibilities on a wider circle of relatives.[67] Uncles and aunts in particular had a responsibility for nephews and nieces; they would join in discussions about suitable marriages and have a say in the dispositions of the contract; they might be called in by an ecclesiastical court, together with other relatives, to act as a family council to settle a dispute between parents and children; they would provide a refuge for a niece or nephew in disgrace; if both parents died, they would offer a place at their own fireside to the very young and help to promote the careers of older ones. It also seems to have been understood that they had a right to intervene to protect their own side of the family if a second marriage caused tensions; thus in Restif de la Bretonne we find an aunt rescuing a niece from a tyrannous stepmother, and a second wife released from the persecutions of malicious stepdaughters. And, just as the arbitrary incidence of death extended family obligations over a wider circle, it also strengthened the moral obligations of neighbourhood. There was a strong prejudice in rural France against a girl marrying outside her village; but conversely, there was a village provision, in even the crudest and poorest areas, to do something to help orphans.

Among sensitive souls in comfortable surroundings, the omnipresence of death and the uncertainty of life could weave nuances of sombre and, maybe, deeper feeling into the affections than bound together husband and wife, parents and children, lover and mistress. But in the harsh environment of peasant France, death came savagely, in alliance with poverty, imposing a timetable of existence which brutalized those who passively accepted its arbitrary dominion. We have an example in the village of Sennely,[68] where the death rate was higher than in most rural areas; it was in the Sologne, a land of trees, dark pools, mists, and sandy, infertile soil. The inhabitants were pale and puny, their eyes lustreless, their temper suspicious and secretive. Marriages generally took place after the death of a parent, which gave the opportunity of a roof to shelter under and land to cultivate. The average duration of a marriage before death intervened was ten to twelve years. Not many children survived to adulthood, and few parents lived to see their grandchildren; a family would consist of four or five persons. In any case, children did not stay long by the parental hearth, for poverty drove them out to work for richer people at the age of seven. The years of family companionship were brief. There were numerous orphans; the village assembly would put them under the charge of a *tuteur*, who himself was likely to die before his charge reached the age of fourteen, the precocious threshold of independence. Widowers and widows remarried quickly—sometimes within a few weeks: the average delay was eleven months, and half the marriages celebrated were second or third unions for at least one of the parties. According to the parish priest of Sennely early in the century, marriages were mercenary affairs; the number of sheep a woman possesses is all the man needs to know, apprentices marry the widows of their masters, a modest fee will find a husband for a pregnant girl. So too with family relationships, they were harsh and unfeeling. Yet, says the *curé*, the folk were not ungenerous and would share their miserable crust with starving beggars. The statistics of life and death provide a clue towards understanding the paradox: the timetable of existence reduced human relationships to the elemental tactics and sympathies of a programme of survival.

Daignan's formula for the years from twenty-nine to thirty-four is 'the age of ambition', which suggests that the young men of the upper classes, in whom he was principally interested, would be preoccupied with rising in the world. This would be true, though with the proviso that they had already moved into an assured place in society during the period of *Jeunesse*. By our standards, the major responsibilities of life were assumed at an early age. No doubt the difference has something to do with instinctive calculations of chances and time available affecting the pace at which life is lived—but it was also the result of a social system in which offices were sold and priority in promotion given to high birth. The profession of arms was the mainstay of the poor provincial nobility—a profession which they would have wished reserved to them—and a man did not need to be very old to risk his life as an officer in the army. At the age of fourteen or fifteen, a boy would arrive at his regiment from the École Militaire, maybe with the brevet of second lieutenant (in 1778 the Minister of War made fifteen the minimum age); maybe, if his studies had been unsatisfactory, to serve for a time before commissioning. To get into the select École de Mézières (founded 1749) which trained the engineers, a boy had to be fifteen (as well, of course, as of noble birth or the son of a serving officer in good standing). Sixteen was the normal age for a second lieutenant to go on active service—thus the future bishop of Saint-Pol-de-Léon fought in a campaign at that age, and at seventeen entered the seminary of Saint-Sulpice (as the standard joke had it, he preferred to have his head shorn rather than broken).[69] There are stories of mere boys from aristocratic families who tried out their military vocation even earlier: the prince de Montbarey was wounded in battle at the age of twelve with his tutor by his side[70]—but this example, and others like it, concerned a young man who was serving under a very close relative. Officially, the minimum age for promotion to a captaincy was eighteen, and five years' service in that rank was needed before the full colonelcy could be obtained; a reforming ordinance of 1776 prescribed a further six years as lieutenant-colonel, thus lifting the minimum age for the command of a regiment to thirty. But the rules were rarely observed. Since the rank of full colonel was obtained by purchase for a vast sum and its duties were nominal, it was monopolized by great aristocrats of the Court, often in their twenties. This was a different story from the the normal *curriculum vitae* of the generality of serving officers—a provincial noble would expect to become a captain at thirty-three; and the limited number of officers promoted from the ranks would have served as sergeants up to their mid-thirties.

The official minimum age to become a magistrate in one of the Parlements or other Sovereign courts was twenty-five. In the Parlement of Bordeaux, 76 out of the 162 *conseillers* who sat between 1775 and 1790 had received royal dispensations as being under age, and a greater proportion still, fully three-quarters of the total, in the Parlement of Toulouse.[71] The average age of entry to the Parlement of Paris during the reign of Louis XV was twenty-two years and seven months, and when the Revolution began, most of the magistrates were under the age of thirty-five.[72] Given appropriate lineage and the standard payment, the examination of a candidate was a formality: reading a few words of a Latin discourse normally sufficed. It did not require much learning or many years' experience to condemn a man to death—and incidentally twenty-one years of age was the minimum for the public executioner.[73] The intendants, who ruled in the provinces in the king's name, had practically all passed through the magistracy in their early twenties; thereafter, they had bought offices of *maîtres des requêtes* (legal and administrative officials of the Royal Council) at an average age of twenty-five, and had been appointed to their intendancies at an average age of thirty-five.[74] Thus, they had passed a decade doing exacting work on one of the branches of the Council and on its investigative commissions, constituting a thorough training for a future provincial administrator. The abusive privileges of the *ancien régime* did not extend to tolerating youthful inefficiency in the essential business of the Crown. Even in the Parlements, new magistrates were supposed to be under a sort of apprenticeship in their early years. A financier who did not have influential connections might have spent about twenty years in the offices of the *Ferme Générale* in Paris and on *tournées* of inspection in the provinces before he was permitted to buy in as a *fermier* himself (the average age was forty-one).[75] The legend of absurdly young bishops, 'évêques à la bavette', has been exploded, so far as the eighteenth century is concerned. If the special unsatisfactory case of the 'election' of Rohan by the Chapter of Strasbourg is omitted from the calculation, the average age at which the bishops of 1789 had been nominated originally is seen to be thirty-seven; of the total of 130, no less than 86 had been between thirty-four and forty-five when appointed. Unlike the magistrates of the Parlement of Paris, the bishops, on the eve of the Revolution, were not a youthful corporation—only 23 were under forty-five, 88 were between forty-five and seventy, and 17 were over seventy.[76] Revolutionary pamphleteers complained, with reason, of the exclusively aristocratic birth of the prelates of the Gallican Church, but practically all of them had pursued a serious course of academic study and had passed a decade or more as a *grand vicaire* in a diocese—the same length of time that an intendant had served in the business of the Royal Council. Like the younger sons of poor provincial nobles who sought the brevet of lieutenant which was their passport to death, these sons of great families were at once enjoying an exclusive privilege and following a serious vocation. A few scandalous examples apart, they were well qualified to serve the king and, indeed, the Gallican Church.

The years from thirty-six to forty-two—the period of life when, for the most part, aristocratic *grands vicaires* received the welcome news of an episcopal see awaiting them—figured in Daignan's scheme as 'middle age' (l'Âge moyen), characterized by 'consistency', potentiality for leadership, and desire for fame. Next, from forty-three to forty-nine, came a period of fulfilment ('l'Âge mûr'), a time of 'possession', when pride is satiated, the fire of the passions moderated, and wisdom has been attained. Apart from the shadow of the awareness that time is running out, the forties seem to Daignan to be an enjoyable decade in life, at least for those whose careers had been successful—status achieved, the mind cultivated, experience gained, while sexual desire and physical strength have not yet seriously faded. Buffon, following a popular common-place,[77] had said that a man's 'vitality' (meaning all-round capacity for living) was at its height at forty-two. Daignan was inclined to put this peak rather later, at forty-nine.[78] But after that date, there could be no argument: it was downhill all the way.

'A cinquante ans nos beaux jours sont passez', Le Maître de Claville had said.[79] There was general agreement on this sad aphorism: the best of life was over at fifty. Indeed, those who put the peak of 'vitality' in the forties did not deny that physical decline was setting in. We grow in stature, Buffon had said, to the age of eighteen, and thereafter thicken out and strengthen to the age of thirty; from thirty-five onwards (rather later for women), the cartilages harden, the skin wrinkles.[80] Cabanis also takes thirty-five as the age when the hardening of the substance of the body begins to cause difficulties for the working of the heart, arteries, and nerves.[81] His contemporary Senancour agreed that this precise age marked 'the end of youth', though he put the 'progression rétrograde de nos facultés' as beginning seven years later.[82] Whatever 'youth' was, everyone agreed that it was lost by thirty-five. D'Argenson, defining it as the time 'when a man thinks himself immortal' and 'imagines projects of long duration', thought this the extreme of optimism: more probably, the decisive change came at thirty.[83] An apothecary of Caen, who invented a remedy for fever, adjusted his dosage to fit such suppositions: the standard dose of his medicine was to be decreased from the age of forty, until by seventy the amount was identical with that for small children.[84] The view that the peak of 'vitality' was reached in the forties only meant that mental development and social experience were, so far, compensating for the onset of physical decline.

By the age of fifty, this decline was such that a labouring man would be worn out. There is nothing for such a one to look forward to, says Mercier, but a place in the hospital where he can die in peace.[85] This was the time of life, according to Mirabeau, when ordinary folk who could afford it ought to be buying their annuity. In Marseille, artisans invested their savings against an annual *rente* from one of the city's two major hospitals at the average age of fifty-five; this was later than Mirabeau had supposed, but by definition, these were healthier people than most—they had been fit enough to earn a surplus, and they expected to live long enough to enjoy their income: the hospital administrators complained of their untoward longevity.[86] In poverty-stricken rural areas, the peasants broke down earlier. A medical observer in the *bocage* country of Normandy in 1776 describes the inhabitants as looking old at forty and, indeed, regarding themselves lucky to get so far; in their view, a man of twenty had only a dozen years ahead of him.[87] At fifty, even for someone not worn out by manual labour, the shadow of future ineffectiveness lay heavily on the imagination. Toulesjours, one of Restif's characters, at the age of fifty-two says that he has passed through all the stages of life when a man is a man—'je touche à celui où il cesse de l'être'; he is glad to be able to describe himself as of 'a ripe age' rather than 'old', but he is at the point of crossing the boundary.[88] Fifty marked the beginning of loneliness. Then, said Le Maître de Claville, hardly any of those are left whose company gave us pleasure when we were twenty.[89] Few, if any, near relatives would be still alive: Restif himself, partly because of his career of shady adventures, and partly because of the incidence of death, was alone in the world in his early forties. 'Depuis cinq ans, mon âme était morte,' he says, at the age of forty-six. 'For long, I had lived alone. I spoke to no one; I no longer knew the tenderness of affection; such feelings were denied to me, for my friends were dead. I was alone, an isolated stalk of wheat in the midst of the sheaves that the sickle of time had harvested.' He worked by day and wandered the streets at night, and then, unexpectedly and disastrously, he fell in love again.[90]

Up to about the middle fifties, moralists could still find compensations for growing old. A novelist tells of women of the upper class who retain their looks and vivacity along with their great experience of life.[91] Daignan talks of the slowing-down of mind and body being accompanied by gifts of tranquillity, prudence, and foresight; Diderot roguishly congratulates himself on finding modest, timid girls attractive now, instead of brash, red-lipped charmers with low necklines;[92] more seriously, Buffon was glad to know that his reputation was secure, his work almost completed, and his peace of mind immune from the slings and arrows of envious critics.[93]

But at fifty-six, the age which Diderot calls 'terrifying', there was little cheerful left to say. 'C'est ici que commence l'amertume de la vie', is Daignan's gloomy comment—'the bitterness of life', an existence marked by regrets, worry, bad temper, and unreasonable lust to dominate other people.[94] Decline is swift; sixty-four, he says, marks 'the end of pleasure'. He may have meant pleasure in general, but certainly implied sexual pleasure in particular. Given the standard medical view of the eighteenth century, that sexual activity weakened the body (with onanism totally destroying it), it was impossible to be optimistic about the love life of the aged; indeed, they would only shorten their days by trying—'for an old man, each sacrifice to Venus is a spadeful of earth on his head'.[95] Senancour agreed with Daignan that sixty-four was the sinister age, the year in which life ends, the first year of death, the onset of creeping annihilation.[96]

The doctor of Montpellier puts his formal category of old age (*Vieillesse*) in the years sixty-four to seventy; his next two divisions are 'Décrépitude' and 'Caducité'. His 'décrépitude' comes a little earlier than most authorities would have put it. For centuries, the melancholy game of classifying old age into chronological compartments staving off to the last moment the admission of uselessness, had gone on. Hippocrates' green springtime of decline to seventy, old age to seventy-five, and feebleness thereafter had been reflected, earlier in the eighteenth century, in Astruc's 'incipient' and 'confirmed' old age, with 'decrepitude' at seventy-five.[97] Generally, seventy seems to have been the accepted age for being 'old'. A dictionary of 1768, whose author himself was prepared to apply this term to women of fifty and men of sixty, said that,'selon le langage du monde', sixty-five does not come within the definition of 'vieillesse' but seventy definitely does so, and he expresses surprise that language assumes such a rapid transition.[98] Once the cape of seventy had been rounded, a man or a woman was the survivor of a forgotten generation. Old men customarily tell their grandchildren, said Daignan, that they alone remain of the old branch of the family.[99] The younger people often showed small respect to these mysterious ancients—to them, they are like intruders from another planet, said Mercier. A writer on old age talked of the danger of becoming a stranger in one's own home by dint of staying there too long.[100] A poet put it

> Malheur à qui les Dieux accordent de long jours,
> À la race nouvelle il se trouve étranger.[101]

Medical men had unflattering observations to make about human nature when they spoke of these lonely old people; they talk of moral decline as well as physical. Daignan lists suspicion, avarice, boasting, love of flattery, self-centredness, and indifference to others; the reason is, he says, 'à mesure que tout nous abandonne, nous nous concentrons plus en nous-mêmes'.[102] This was the standard medical view: the old care only about themselves and their miserable, joyless survival, because of the introversion of their nature. Bichat describes the ancient figure by the fireside, 'concentré en lui-même', 'a stranger to all that surrounds him . . . happy to feel that he still exists, when all other feelings have virtually abandoned him.'[103] Of such a case Cabanis says, 'son égoïsme est l'ouvrage immédiat de la nature'—his selfishness arises from the tendency of life to turn inwards upon itself.[104] More imaginatively, Diderot talks of this inner psychological withdrawal as a sort of instinct for self-annihilation; the child is a fluid mass seeking development, and the old man is another shapeless mass, but drying up and shrinking, 'which withdraws into itself and tends to reduce itself to nothingness'.[105] One effect of this contraction of spirit is a turning to the world of memory. To 'self-love' as one characteristic of the sexagenarian, Sénac de Meilhan adds another, 'the admiration of the past'.[106] Within, the recollection of pleasures lost for ever was likely to cause bitterness, 'the general discontent of the old with present pleasures' of the abbé Joannet.[107] Without, facing the world, the aged edit their memories to support their boasting, claiming to have been what they would have wished to be, says Daignan, to compensate for finding themselves nothing at all.[108] A stock figure for the writer of *caractères* was the old braggart telling of his heroism in battles and sieges; another was the ancient bore praising former times to prove the degeneracy of the present—in my days peas had more flavour, women were more beautiful, and men more courageous. Why can't they recognize that no one admires them, or loves them, except for their money?[109] The old, says a poet unkindly in 1782, are 'objects of ridicule and, often, of fear'.[110] Surrounded by incomprehension and aversion, where can they turn for consolation? Looking back at time past causes vexation: looking forward inspires apprehension—the antithesis is from Dom Pernety's Rousseauistic treatise on the maladies of the soul.[111] Children know nothing of death, grown men are not really convinced that they must die, but the old have neither ignorance nor illusion to help them: so Diderot sums up the evolution of our minds in face of the shadow of death—'le vieillard se berce en tremblant d'une espérance qui se renouvelle de jour en jour.'[112] What sort of a life is this that limits its horizon to the gift of a single extra day? Such gloom was the stock-in-trade of the cruder religious apologists and humanistic moralizers. 'Quelle affreuse chose que la vieillesse!'[113] A time of shame for those who have no claim to respect but their numerous years (a sentiment from Seneca);[114] a time of despair in face of the realization that the following of ordinary decency ('l'honnêteté morale') falls far short of pious duty;[115] a time of hopelessness when it is no longer possible to win merit by doing active things in the service of God and man;[116] a time of distraction by the pains of illness (even a sensitive spiritual writer like Duguet is specific about stiff backs and incontinent bladders);[117] a time when the hand of death is visibly upon us, so we resemble 'un sépulcre mouvant', a walking grave.[118] The medical profession did not regard the aged as more particularly afraid of death—rather, said Cabanis, they sink into apathy, without terror or regret, speaking of their own approaching demise as of that of a stranger.[119] This was also the view of the religious apologists. Sheer panic, perhaps, at the very end, but in the declining years before that a hopeless inability to find mental or spiritual inspiration: a warning to all of us to repent while we are still capable of doing so.

What consolations were there for old age? A religious man could take refuge in acceptance of the decrees of Providence, in continuing to offer to God what services he could still perform, and in cultivating an ever-increasing detachment from the world. The humanistic version of the Christian attitude was expressed by Delisle de Sales; whatever 'sophists' say, the old still have the pleasure of helping other people, 'a sublime pleasure indeed'.[120] But for those who wanted pleasures more tangible than those of altruism, there was nothing better to fall back on than the argument that each age of life has its own peculiar satisfactions. This was the formula of Mme du Châtelet's *Discours sur le bonheur* (written 1746–8, published 1779).[121] She had to admit, however, that those of old age were difficult to obtain. Divertissement, study, and gratification of the palate depended on continuing mental lucidity and physical capability; *la considération*, the enjoyment of respect for one's assured status in society or one's achievements, was available only to members of the upper class or to the achieving minority. There was a similar difficulty about proclaiming the satisfactions to be derived from memory. What of those who look back, like Rousseau, and see only that they are 'dying without having lived', whose recollections put them in Lesbros de la Versane's category of the 'gens qui meurent très vieux sans avoir existé'?[122] As for the pleasure of finding oneself alive for another day when one's contemporaries are dead, La Fontaine had demolished it: 'qu'on me rende impotent, cul-de-jatte, goutteux . . . pourvu que je vive'—to cling miserably to a worthless existence is one of the less noble of human instincts.[123] Unrestrained by Christian scruples, Mme du Châtelet had drawn the logical conclusion: 'Happily,' she concluded, 'we have it in our own hands to hasten the end of life if it is too long delayed.' There was, however, a less drastic alternative. Religious writers sometimes recommended the setting-aside of the last years as a period of preparation for dying—perhaps devoted to some humble task, like teaching poor children, perhaps solely to mental discipline.[124] Saint-Simon lists some great names of the court of Louis XIV who had set 'an interval between life and death'.[125] Such retirement was common practice among widows who could afford to buy an *appartement* in a convent, where they could end their days in peace and relative comfort—saving enough, perhaps, to pay their husband's debts or to provide a little extra for their children to inherit.[126] It could be said that the nunnery where some aristocratic lady had been educated as a girl was the very place for her to die—Choderlos de Laclos among novelists seized on the dramatic possibilities of a life thus turning through a full circle. The idea was appropriated by non-believers. Toussaint claimed to be looking forward to this interval between life and death when he published his *Éclaircissement sur 'Les Mœurs'* (1762),[127] and Roucher, the deistical and anticlerical poet, spoke of his intention to seek such 'an interval of peace and repose between death and the active life'.[128] The age of sixty-four, Daignan's 'end of pleasure' and Senancour's beginning of creeping death, might be the occasion to will one's ordinary existence to an end, and to start living in fellowship with the dead, consoled by their writings and their memory',[129] a time for coming to terms, if not with God, at least with oneself.

But in the course of the eighteenth century, the attitude to old age was changing. When his wife died, and with his daughter safely married, one of the abbé Prévost's heroes retires, at the age of fifty, to a monastery, as a lay guest of the Community, withdrawn from society and mourning his lost companion. Yet after three years he comes out of seclusion to accompany the son of a great nobleman on an educational tour, and once back in the world, falls in love again. The story is a parable of the psychological change which was fulfilled in the second half of the century. Before they knew for sure that the pattern of mortality was improving, some of the affluent minority were abandoning fatalism about growing old and dying. Against logic, they were wanting to live longer, and they were discovering the logic to insist on enjoying life and being useful at a greater age.

This may have been a subconscious reaction to the fact that the increasing life span (see below, Chapter 4) of the older generation was delaying promotion for others. In the eighties, episcopal candidates[130] surveyed their prospects with gloom. 'I see no movement in the Clergy,' said Talleyrand; it was not his morals which were holding him back, but simply the lack of suitable vacancies.[131] Parish priests were also living longer and blocking the horizon of lesser ecclesiastical ambitions. In the diocese of Boulogne up to 1757, half the clergy were aged between forty and fifty-five; in 1790, only 41 per cent were in this age group, while no less than 47 per cent were older.[132] The Assembly of Clergy of 1775, complaining of the decline of vocations to the parochial ministry, speculated on possible reasons, psychological and financial. Probably the cause lay, not in the fading of the propulsive force of vocation, but in the weakening of the magnetic field of attraction, as fewer benefices became vacant.[133]

Since the prizes would come later, ambition must needs be patient. And it was easier to wait since existence was becoming more comfortable. To live long became more desirable. The great were no longer expected to pass their days in public parade and tiring display, to freeze in vast apartments, to flog down treacherous roads on horseback or jolt in creaking carriages, to hunt, roister, declaim, and duel. A less demanding and more intimate life-style was becoming possible and fashionable. There were well-sprung carriages; travel became easier—the times of the stage-coach runs from Paris to Angers, to Rennes, and to Caen were halved between 1765 and 1780.[134] Private life withdrew from marble halls and antechambers to smaller warmer rooms, with furniture made for relaxation rather than show. Meals became more sophisticated. Though cookery books began in the seventeenth century, and Louis XIV dined in overwhelming splendour, it was a coarse abundance that reigned at his table: the *maître d'hôtel* who ran himself through with his sword in 1671 was atoning, not for the quality of the dishes, but for the shortage of roasts on two tables and the late arrival of the fish.[135] The Regent in his intimate suppers and Louis XV were more delicately served. According to the Jesuit editors of *Les Dons de Comus, ou les délices de la table* of 1739, a culinary revolution was taking place, and evidence of its progress was provided by the success of *La Cuisinière bourgeoise* seven years later, which went through thirty-two editions by 1789.[136] Conduct, like the cuisine, was evolving towards refinement. Boisterous exercises and buffoonery continued to give place to the life of the *salon*, conversation, poetry readings, attendance at theatres and musical concerts, and dabbling in matters scientific—visits to anatomical dissections, gathering specimens for geological and botanical natural history collections, getting electric shocks from the abbé Nollet or being hypnotized by mesmerists. The arts of war, statecraft, and diplomacy were becoming more highly organized, and self-consciously professional. Manœuvre, administrative skill, the well-turned argument, the ingenious appeal to well-informed opinion came to count for more; intelligence and experience were more important than they had been for the successful conduct of affairs.

Through devotion to her family and confidence in God, Rousseau's Julie was determined to go on living to her last breath. For less elevated reasons, older ladies began to reject the notion of putting an interval between life and death by withdrawal from the world. At a certain age, Helvétius had said, women forsake rouge, abandon pleasure, and take to piety. Diderot replied that this had become rare. 'They stay in society, they are indulgent to the amusements of the young, they play cards and converse (and talk well because they have experience to draw on); they go to the country, on promenades, to the theatre—and they rarely indulge in malicious gossip. Their principal concern is for their health, and they are fastidious about all the little comforts of life.'[137] As for men, Buffon advised those of an intellectual bent never to regard their work as done. At eighty and even eighty-six (the old astrological idea of eighty-four being a dangerous 'climacteric' is implicitly rejected), a man has an expectation of another three years ahead of him—much can be done in this time. The philosopher will plan on this basis then dismiss the idea of death from his mind, taking each day as it comes.[138] In 1810 the Swiss Meister was consoling himself with Buffon's device of statistical therapy: there is no age at which we cannot hope for a couple of years more.[139] 'Old age diminishes the force of the body, but augments the insight of the mind,' the *Encyclopédie* had said.[140] The century afforded examples—Fontenelle, Chaulieu, Voltaire, Buffon, Fleury—men who contributed to science, poetry, wit, and statescraft in defiance of the years. (Fontenelle, the greatest prodigy for longevity, was not the ideal example, for his trick of survival seemed to be to abjure laughter, tears, and friendship.)[141] The professional cynic Chamfort was willing to concede that he had learned most, in his lifetime, from 'Sleeping with women of forty and listening to old men of eighty'.[142] The career of the outrageous maréchal de Richelieu was evidence that sleeping with a man of eighty might also have been instructive in its way. In 1802, a doctor writing on the influence of the Revolution on the population, declared that the patriarch of sixty going to the fair was no longer looking at the girls to find a daughter-in-law, but a wife for himself;[143] sexual potency, like intellectual achievement, might carry on longer than the gloomier writers had assumed.

From the sixteenth century there had been a tradition of splendid old men in literature[144]—hermits or pagan pontiffs in pastoral idylls who gave sage advice or sanctified the union of virtuous lovers; from the *Astrée* early in the seventeenth century there were 'Druids', and the imaginary voyages added further variants of the ancient who served as the touchstone of arcadian or utopian morality. Any connection between these respected apparitions and the real old men by the fireside, suspected or ignored by the younger generation, was purely coincidental. But from the middle of the eighteenth century, the patriarchal myth found embodiment in a real personage, *le bon curé*, the virtuous parish priest, who acted as spiritual guide, doctor, agricultural adviser, dispenser of charity, reconciler of conflicts, and protector of star-crossed lovers within the rural community in which his lot was cast. Reformers used the stereotype as a device to criticize the excessive wealth of prelates and monks; so too did the *philosophes*, glad to make practical utility the criterion for assessing the value of the clergy. Some *curés* lived up to their image. A young man too shy to propose marriage was helped by his parish priest, and when on his honeymoon the coach lost a wheel, he found a refuge with his bride in a hospitable presbytery while repairs were made.[145] This was what always happened in novels: a bearded sage in a red hat trimmed with ermine was constantly available on the barren shores of Sardinia to give shipwrecked heroes bed and board and talk about religion.[146] The tradition of the pastoral patriarch or pontiff had been agreeably ambiguous: in the land of fable, he might serve as a symbol of all worthy priesthood, Christian included (this was the case in Fénelon, and Chateaubriand was to have Père Aubry, an ordained Christian pastor in the American wilderness), or he could be a deistical substitute, an illustration that revelation was not indispensable. Anticlericals kept the latter idea going by utopian imaginings which made a priesthood a social function developing upon old age. Restif's 'Australians' entered the ranks of the clergy at the age of seventy, the oldest male inhabitant always being 'the Sovereign Pontiff'. During the Revolution, the idea was carried a stage further, and the father of the family was assumed to be, *ex officio*, the minister of a sort of social religion. 'It was a favourite idea of the revolutionaries', writes Mathiez, 'that the father of the family was, by virtue of his position, a natural priest or pontiff.'[147] Theophilanthropy, the most sophisticated of the invented cults, was supposed to be ruled by a council of 'pères de familles', or at least of the oldest ones, provided they were recognized to be wise and of irreproachable conduct. The place given by the Revolution to old men in its theatrically organized processions and invented religions was, even at the time, vaguely ridiculous. But revolutionary anticlericalism was appealing to instinctive new currents of thought. Family affections were deepening, the aged were being accorded more respect, and, for their part, were beginning to insist on living their lives right through, seeking enjoyment and trying to be useful to the end of their days. They still were hardly aware that mortality was being rolled back, but so far as the choice was theirs, they were choosing to get more out of their span and to put more into it; they were refusing to accept 'social death' before their actual physical demise.

4

Statistics, Hopes, and Fears

I

The population of France was rising throughout the eighteenth century. Within the present geographical limits of the country, there were, maybe, 21,000,000 people in 1700. (This is a recent estimate by M. Dupâquier: earlier guesses had preferred nineteen, or even seventeen millions.) More certainly, the figure for 1740 is 24,600,000. Since the forties were a decade of hardship, by 1750 the population may have been rather less. Thereafter, there was a steady increase: 25,000,000 in 1759; 27,500,000 in 1780; 28,100,000 in 1790; 30,000,000 in 1810.[1] On the basis of these figures, the increase must have been fully as great in the first forty years of the century as in the similar period after 1750, so that what was once the standard view, that the expansion was a phenomenon of the second half of the century, would be an illusion reflecting the impressive recovery after the forties—and also, it must be admitted, reflecting the weight of local studies, which so often put the population rise late rather than early. The increase was far from uniform over the country; there were zones of stagnation and, even, of regression, in sharp contrast to zones of dynamic expansion, and from area to area, the chronological pattern of the movement varied.

Brittany and Anjou were provinces where the 'old demography' continued to the Revolution. After a recovery in the fifties, from 1770 deaths were more numerous than births, a result of raging attacks of dysentery and enteric fever.[2] In this broad pattern there were geographical variations; the disastrous mortality figures in Brittany in 1772, for example, were the result of epidemics largely confined to four out of the nine Breton dioceses.[3] Normandy was a province of feeble growth, just 5 per cent over the century, though there were areas where expansion was greater, reaching half the national average rate, because of new land being brought into

89

cultivation.[4] The population of Languedoc had been falling from 1680 to 1740, witness the phenomenon of the 'dead villages' from which the inhabitants had departed, fleeing from malaria and the iniquitious system of inflexible global taxation, which laid the burdens of the dead on the survivors. About the mid-century, expansion began, though not everywhere: the unhealthy Rhône delta and the Camargue remained inimical to human existence until the nineteenth century.[5] Provence had been expanding in the seventeenth century up to 1689, the decline after that date being hastened by the great plague of Marseille of 1720–1. The revival in the second half of the century did not do much more than compensate for the losses of 1689 to 1730. Marseille itself regained its original size by the Revolution, but Aix, which had lost 8,000 of its 24,000 inhabitants during the plague, had still not recovered.[6] What plague did for Aix, industrial decline did for Reims; the drapery trade went downhill, and the 32,000 population of 1675 had become 25,000 towards the end of the *ancien régime*.[7] Both Angers and Le Mans had been more populous in the middle of the seventeenth century than they were in 1789; the former city was growing, but slowly, the latter was contracting.[8] Though declining towns were few, there were others which were expanding without necessarily adding to the population at large. It was a commonplace in the late eighteenth century to refer to the cities as death-traps, killing off a population which was constantly being replenished by immigration from the countryside. Paris rose from 450,000 in 1684 to 500,000 in 1700, to 600,000 in 1789. recruiting massively at first from the provinces, but less so later on.[9] After the great fire of December 1720, Rennes became a vast builders' yard for twenty years, drawing in thousands of workers.[10] Against the background of the decline of Brittany, Nantes doubled its population, again by immigration. In the 1780s, only 21.6 per cent of the men and 38.5 per cent of the women who married there had been born in the city.[11] The expansion of Toulouse by 5,000 souls between 1750 and 1790 was also the result of an influx from outside.[12] There were some 'new' towns. Charleville, a centre of armament manufacture and a garrison strong point, was a creation of the seventeenth century which began its own demographical rise in the second half of the eighteenth.[13] The classical example of an artificial creation is Versailles where, on an undrained unhealthy spot, Louis XIV created a town of craftsmen and labourers for the construction of his palace. Growth went on long after the royal *château* was completed; from 10,000 in 1730 the population rose to 40,000 in 1789. Marriages were frequent and numerous children were born, but the death rate was extraordinarily high, and recruitment was by immigration. In 1792, 52.7 per cent of the inhabitants had been born elsewhere.[14]

By contrast to these examples of decline or growth by trans-ference, there were areas of massive population increase: a doubling of numbers in Alsace and Lorraine, and in the *généralité* of Valenciennes; a 70 per cent rise in that of the Île de France; 50 per cent in those of Pau and Auch and in the Toulouse region; a modest 22 per cent in the intendancy of Tours. In each area, the story of expansion had its detours and complexities. Lorraine rose from half a million in 1710 to 1,200,000 in 1780. But in the forties, floods, dearth, typhus, and cattle plague devastated the province, so that in 1747 deaths exceeded births; the Seven Years' War was another crisis for the frontier lands, and during the grain shortages of 1770–1 and 1784–5 emigrants departed to settle on the newly reconquered Hungarian lands of the Emperor.[15] Alsace rose from 348,000 in 1709 to 642,000 in 1786, an upsurge which lost impetus in years of war or bad harvests. The increase took place in certain zones—forest country and the towns,[16] perhaps because there was land to spare in the wooded terrain and industrial jobs available in the cities. The demographical map of the Toulouse region shows dapplings of light and shade; in the broad sweep, the *généralité* of Montauban was booming; everywhere else there were villages in decline scattered among those that were flourishing. Generally, however, progress ceased after 1770, and the years from 1789 to 1792, as harsh as any in the reign of Louis XIV, were regressive.[17] In the Paris basin, rises and falls here and there, and from year to year, cancelled each other out until 1750, when an upsurge came, increasing the population by 32 per cent by 1791.[18] The same chronological pattern is found in Auvergne; here, the *généralité* of Riom showed a fall from 650,000 inhabitants in 1690 to 500,000 in 1730, then a rise after 1760 to 700,000 in 1789—and this in spite of the continual emigration of labourers from the province.[19] For the most part, the towns of France were taking the lead in the expansion, a fact noted with satisfaction by the abbé Expilly in his famous geographical dictionary. From 1700 to 1789, Lyon increased by between 30 and 50 per cent, Nancy by 50 per cent, Strasbourg by 60 per cent.[20] Some towns doubled: Tarbes had 2,370 citizens early on and 6,058 at the Revolution; Dôle went from 5,000 to 9,000; in 1715 Bordeaux had 55,000 and in 1790, 110,000; the corresponding figures for Auch are 4,000 and 10,000. The little town of Meulan went from 1,200 in 1700 to 2,105 in 1790.[21] Each town and hamlet had its chronological peculiarities. At Meulan, the increase took place solely after 1740. At Sérignan on the malarial Mediterranean coast, there was no improvement until after 1760 (was the introduction of viticulture the reason?). At Villedieu-les-Poêles in Normandy, a centre of the manufacture of pots and pans, the rise was confined to the first half of the century.[22] In one village in Touraine, births exceeded deaths only between 1730 and 1739 and 1760 to 1789; in another in Normandy baptisms exceeded burials consistently all the while from 1714 to 1780.[23] From the multitude of variations it is clear that all sorts of factors must be involved in the population rise—details of local circumstance, of weather and crops, the ups and downs of manufacturing and trading, the longer term effect of earlier demographical crises creating the 'classes creuses' with fewer families to procreate, local pressures concerning the age of marriage and sexual conduct, changes in psychological predispositions affecting fecundity, opportunities for social or geographical mobility, and, more mysteriously, the changes in the virulent force of particular epidemics. Maybe, in one of these or in some combination of them lies some broad and comprehensive explanation for the population rise of the eighteenth century, but if so, this total answer has so far eluded us.

The principal immediate 'cause' of the population growth was that death was being defeated. The average duration of life in the decade 1740–9 was 25.9 years; between 1790 and 1799, it was 32.1. The number of deaths per thousand in Strasbourg from 1730 to 1740 was 41.4; in 1789 it down to 35.5. The figures for Marseille are 44 in 1659 and 32.5 in 1754. In Lyon, in spite of the increase of the population, the number of deaths in 1783 was no higher than in 1730, and half as many as in 1693.[24] These figures are confirmed by what we know of demographical progress elsewhere, especially in the Île de France, Languedoc, and Auvergne. To assess the psycho-logical impact of the improvement it would be important to know which ages of the population were being spared, but in the present state of our knowledge it is impossible to generalize with con-fidence. The remarkable figures of the decline of infant mortality in the Vexin français (262 per 1,000 in the mid-seventeenth century: 138 in the 1770s)[25] are not matched in many other places; things got worse in Strasbourg, for example, and there was a widespread deterioration elsewhere in the last decade of the *ancien régime*. But there can be no doubt (with the inevitable exceptions, like the Toulouse area) that, in the expanding areas of France generally, adults were living longer. On the national figures so far available, a girl of five years of age in the 1740s would have had, by the law of averages, rather more than forty-one years ahead of her; fifty years later, she would have had forty-seven years.[26] The death rate for adults in Strasbourg was 34 per 1,000 in the thirties and 25 per 1,000 in the eighties.[27] Consolidated figures for some convents in the dioceses of Langres, Auxerre, and Dijon show that 48.3 per cent of the inmates reached the age of sixty in the period 1650–1719; later, between 1720 and 1790, no less than 62.6 per cent were getting there.[28] Evidence of a similar kind concerning the longer duration of marriages and increased life expectancy has been pro-duced for Auvergne and Languedoc. One might hazard a guess that adults were living longer over most areas of the population ex-pansion, but that the reduction of infantile mortality was a rarer phenomenon, though with a more decisive effect on the expansion in the places where it occurred.

Between 1700 and 1800, fully ten years were added to the average life span of Frenchmen. It would be of the utmost interest if we could demonstrate that the improvement marked the beginning of our 'modern' attitude to death (the idea that we live out our standard ration of years, barring accidents—'boys don't die unless they get run over'). The burden of death on the mind, however, would not correspond too closely to its incidence. The fatalistic acceptance of the deaths of infants is one thing, the calculation of chances among adults is another; two different sets of statistics of mortality are needed, and two different kinds of apprehension are involved. The chances of famine, epidemic, or war causing mass fatalities on the one hand, and the routine chances in ordinary living on the other, are two different and separable pressures on the mind. To assess the fear of death we need to know the reasonable expectation of length of life which a man might entertain year by year (a figure varying more especially according to social class); we also need to know the reasonable expectation which he might have that 'accidental' intrusions of the type of plague or famine would not suddenly lengthen the odds against him (a figure varying with geographical area, but with social class determining the possibility of evasive measures). In each case, two different sets of figures or estimations are involved: the real statistical odds as the historian subsequently knows them, and the imagined ones as contemporaries saw them—for a man may at once be calculating logically on what he regards as sound information, yet simultaneously and subconsciously be aware of the real chances of the case. These are the sort of questions the historian asks, without always being able to suggest an answer, and it was in the eighteenth century that these sorts of questions suddenly became meaningful. The educated strata of society came to think in a new fashion which has been, ever since, one of the distinguishing marks of Western civilization. This change in mental attitudes is one of the most revolutionary and neglected aspects of the thought of the Enlightenment: the beginning of the statistical study of human living and dying.

II

From the latter years of the seventeenth century, political theorists and governments embarked on the collection of statistics and their interpretation in a more comprehensive and scientific fashion. Thus arose 'Political Arithmetic'. Under this heading a French encyclopaedia of 1778 described the rise of a new and 'separate science' over the past ninety years, beginning appropriately in England, the land of Newton, but now widely studied in France, Germany, Holland, and Switzerland.[29] Governments had always been aware that statistics were needed for the efficient levying of taxes and the conscripting of soldiers; this was one of the points on which Bodin gave advice in his *République* (1576). But the Englishmen Graunt and

Petty, the founders of the more professional Political Arithmetic, spoke of the importance of knowing, not only about taxable wealth and conscriptable bodies, but also about the numbers of doctors, lawyers, and clergy needed, and about the numbers of excessively rich and excessively poor subjects; all this a necessity for 'good, certain and easie Government'. John Graunt went further and said we should all be interested in the results of his 'laborious bustling and groping'. We are afraid of death, and seek to understand the hazards of the world in an attempt to alleviate our anxiety. Remembering this, governments should give us a weekly record of deaths when there is a plague scare—honest, to carry conviction, though with a marginal possibility of falsification in times of sweeping epidemic, to preserve us from despair. In the early eighteenth century, English theologians joined in the praise of the newly fashionable statistical study, for it revealed the workings of God's economy in the Universe: how births and deaths are complementary, and how the balance of male and female is nicely contrived to encourage the institution of marriage.[30] But it was France rather than England which became the land of official statistics, and the inhabitants did not praise their rulers for their zeal to illustrate the workings of Providence. Whenever an inquiry about population was made, it was assumed that a tax was in the offing. The record would be adjusted accordingly. The magistrates of Strasbourg in 1774 sent an immediate and precise reply to a circular of the Controller General asking for the total number of citizens; they omitted clergy and nobles and their households, the inhabitants of the forts and the citadel, and everyone else exempt from normal taxation. They did not trust the tax officials in Paris to do subtraction sums.[31] In 1783 the intendant of the Pays de Foix reported that he was being offered the figure of 800 inhabitants for the parish of Bonnac, whereas ten years before, the *curé*, going from house to house, had made it 1,578; it was all a question of whether the information was needed for taxation purposes or for channelling government help to the starving.[32]

In the reign of Louis XVI, Colbert established the practice of nation-wide statistical questionnaires addressed to the intendants; in 1664, he wished to know, not only about nobles, clergy and commoners, but also about crops and criminality—with especial insistence on the number of counterfeiters of the currency.[33] He also began the practice of publishing monthly details of births, marriages, and deaths in Paris.[34] In 1686, Vauban published anonymously his famous fifteen-page booklet on the methodology of census-taking.[35] Its influence is seen in various local reviews—the house-to-house survey of Valenciennes in 1693, the village-to-village survey of Provence in the same year (concerning crop failures), and the analysis of the diocese of Albi by families in 1695 (concerning assessments to the new capitation tax).[36] In 1697, the great *enquête* for the instruction of the duc de Bourgogne, the heir to the throne, took place; the questionnaire said the 'old registers' were to be consulted, 'to see if the population in former days was more numerous than it is now', and reasons for the rise or fall were to be suggested.[37] As the example of Provence in 1693 shows, the government was not only concerned with exacting money; it was also attempting to fulfil another of its major tasks—redistributing food supplies in time of famine. In 1709, a circular of the Controller General asked the intendants for population figures (they were to use the hated tax rolls and add the non-paying ecclesiastics and children) to enable the government to feed the starving.[38] There was, too, another type of crisis census. During the great plague of Marseille which devastated Provence in 1720–1, the intendant insisted that each community send to him, every ten days, a statement of population, giving the number of those who had died and the number of those who had recovered, together with recapitulative totals brought up to date, and a running estimate of the expenditure which would be needed to bring life back to normal.[39] In 1713, 1730, and 1762, major inquiries were addressed by successive Controllers General to the intendants (chiefly for taxation purposes, though economic development was also being studied), and in 1771, the abbé Terray ordered the completion of an annual return giving the statistics of baptisms, marriages, and burials in each *généralité*.[40] This comprehensive scheme was possible only because the parish priests had been gradually brought under orders to keep accurate records. In 1714, they had been instructed to ensure that the deaths of even the youngest infants were duly included; from 1736, they had to make a second copy of each entry; from 1746, they were to keep baptisms, marriages, and burials in separate registers. (Alas! *curés* were not always conscientious, and there was an established procedure for taking depositions from parishioners to reconstitute missing entries when the death of an incumbent or an episcopal visitation revealed negligence.[41]) Among other things, Terray's annual census was meant to establish whether the population was rising or falling; the Estates of Languedoc in 1744 had been asked to produce comparative figures for 1684, 1700, and the present day, and there had been various other inquiries directed towards laying the bogy of a nation in decline. Turgot, maintaining the principle of these statistical returns, in 1775 said they could 'give rise to useful observations concerning the influence of climate on the population and on the duration of human life'.[42] From preoccupations with taxation, conscription, food supply, and plague control, government was moving towards the support of medical research. Not that the old harsh necessities were forgotten. In the last decade of the *ancien régime*, the chevalier des Pommelles made three journeys round France at government expense to calculate the number of potential conscripts for the *milice* in different provinces, and in 1789 he published the tables he had drawn up. Brittany, La Rochelle, Tours, and Orléans, he said, were *généralités* where the population was declining, while in others such as Valenciennes it was increasing rapidly. Thus Brittany, where deaths exceeded births in the ratio of 12 to 11, was an unfavourable area for recruitment, but a good one for raising loans by selling annuities—subscribers died off quickly here.[43] For large-scale planning of any kind, including hygienic reform and, even, moral improvement, said Condorcet, statistics were necessary, and only the power of the State would suffice for their collection. 'Social mathematics can only establish the facts with the help of *la puissance publique*.'[44]

Human statistics are full of human interest. Educated people were becoming more numerate. The household notebooks (*livres de raison*) of the seventeenth century had contained more entries about family history, the weather, and culinary receipts than accounts; now they tended to precise budgeting.[45] The growing sophistication of mathematics, the expansion and diversification of commerce, and the extension of education made their impact on personal attitudes, helping to create 'les débuts de la fascination des chiffres exacts'.[46] More inclined to use precise calculation in the business of living, and seeking statistical ammunition to use in the dispute of Ancients versus Moderns and pessimists versus optimists in the Population controversy, in discussions of France's power relative to Great Britain, to bolster proposals for reform or merely to damn government exactions, the reading public was interested to know the secrets that were accumulating in the files of the Controller General and intendants. In 1709, a commercial attempt was made to satisfy this curiosity, the bookseller Saugrain of Paris publishing a *Dénombrement du Royaume* in two volumes, full of information from official sources, though much out of date and, often, inaccurately interpreted. A new edition in 1720 added more reliable statistics from a census in the *généralité* of Rouen in 1713 and from the taxation records (of the *taille*, the land tax) for 1717–18. According to the editor's own story, he later sent round 20,000 printed questionnaires to local correspondents, but, as few were returned and of these few were intelligently filled in, he reprinted his *Nouveau dénombrement* in 1735 without revision.[47] A leap forward in technique came with the abbé Expilly's *Dictionnaire géographique, historique et politique des Gaules et de la France*, published in six volumes between 1762 and 1770.[48] Expilly had detected the major error in Saugrain, the assumption that 'feu' in the tax records meant a family (this was not so in most of the south and west), and he had got the system of local correspondents working by persuading parish priests in five intendancies to fill in his *fiches*. He had also devised a rule-of-thumb method for establishing a figure for the total population without alarming the inhabitants by inquiries about taxable details: multiply the number of annual births, taken as an average over a dozen years, by a fixed coefficient (differing as between town and country). His findings were a decisive blow in the great Population controversy. France, he said, had never been so thickly populated—a result of peace, improved communications, developments in agriculture, and the extension of the area of cultivation. The good abbé became famous, though at his own expense: for long afterwards he was trying to get financial, as well as honorific, recognition from the government.[49]

The first major technical contribution to modern demography came in 1766: *Recherches sur la population des généralités d'Auvergne, de Lyon, de Rouen et de quelques provinces et villes du Royaume, avec des réflexions sur la valeur de blé tant en France qu'en Angleterre depuis 1674 jusqu'en 1764.* The author, Messance, had been secretary to an intendant of Auvergne, and had moved with him to Lyon, then Rouen, and in each area had gathered statistics, which he published to refute the anti-patriotic myth that France was in decline.[50] He used Expilly's multiplication of births method, but made allowances for the mobility of the population, and for the approximations in the statements of age at death which were found in the registers of the *curés*. His information was sifted through more sophisticated meshes—he compared France with England, and one province of France with another; he examined the proportion of ecclesiastics to total population in various places, and established the average number of people per house in crowded Paris; he worked back from dates of baptism to find which months had seen most sexual activity (July, May, June, and August), and he noted the months when deaths were most frequent (March) and fewest (August).[51] Like Expilly, Messance argued that the population was increasing, and in his *Nouvelles recherches*, published in 1788, he produced a formula to describe the process which, so far as it goes, is as good as any we can find today: there was a small in-built surplus, enough to make up the losses of war and major crises of epidemic or famine; if these losses by unusual disaster became less frequent, the population would rise.[52] Clearly the offices of the intendants (where Messance had worked) were the places where statistics were available, and some intendants were themselves becoming specialists in their interpretation. At Vienne, Boula de Nanteuil had dossiers on the population of twenty-three out of the thirty-two *généralités* covering the years 1770–4, which he was analysing for the use of the military authorities.[53] The baron de Montyon, who ruled successively at Riom, Aix, and La Rochelle, collected statistics about criminals from the records of the Parlement of Paris,[54] and was almost certainly the author of the next major work on the population question, *Recherches et considérations sur la population de la France*, published under the name of 'Moheau' in 1778.[55] Like Expilly and Messance, 'Moheau' was a patriotic exponent of the theme of an expanding nation: at the current rate, he argued, the country's population would double in two-and-a-half centuries—indeed, would go on expanding until either the atmosphere was polluted or food supplies ran out. This grim *dénouement*, however, lay in the distant future; for the moment it was important to encourage a dense population, since prosperity comes from the division of labour fostering the growth of specialist skill. So he exhorted his readers to marry to increase the numbers and ensure the happiness of ensuing generations.

The statistics provided by these writers on Political Arithmetic had a personal and highly individual interest as well as a public one—perhaps they served to alleviate Graunt's 'anxiety', or, maybe, to intensify it, for who can say that any information about death is really consoling? Messance gives figures derived from five parishes of the Lyon area between 1740 and 1760. Half those born die within twenty years, two-thirds within forty, three-quarters within fifty; only one in eight gets to seventy, and one in twenty-two to eighty. These findings, he shows, correspond almost exactly to those from eight parishes and two towns in the Rouen area, the only significant difference being one concerning the chances of reaching extreme old age; around Lyon, one in 165 gets to ninety: around Rouen only one in 413.[56] 'Moheau' gives a table of expectations. At seven, it is reasonable to hope for another forty years, at twenty for another thirty-one or thirty-two; at forty, for another twenty-one; at sixty, for another twelve.[57] Both writers offer advice on where to live to live longer. Stagnant pools and marshes are dangerous, high ground and dry soil propitious, both by reason of their clean air and by their purer drinking water. 'Moheau' compares La Napoule, on a marshy plain, where the average life span is eight years, with Apt, in a valley surrounded by snow-covered mountains, where it is thirty-two, and with the parish of Ambrun, in the mountainous diocese of Condom, where, of the 130 inhabitants, 21 are over seventy and 10 over eighty. And he recommends especial care at certain seasons; for children, in the early autumn, for the aged, at the end of winter and early spring.[58]

The study of the individual's chances of living or dying was not, however, the invention of the writers on Political Arithmetic. Before Expilly, Messance, or 'Moheau' had published, it had been brought to a fine art by statisticians offering the financiers of governments a basis for the calculation of insurance risks. The lawyers were also interested, since if a man vanished, the courts had to prescribe the rights of his heirs, striking a mean between a reasonable certainty that he would not reappear, and the common-sense presumption that no news is bad news. Towards the end of the century, with the aid of the mathematicians, the elapse of time for presumption of death was taken to be enough to have brought the missing man up to between the ages of seventy-two and seventy-five.[59] But it was in selling annuities especially that governments needed the advice of statisticians. This was a standard device for raising revenue, and it was not easy for people with savings wanting to make provision for their old age to find a satisfactory alternative. Hence the popularity of the *rentes viagères*, sometimes constituted on two persons together (theorists argued that this promoted family amity),[60] but more often on a single individual. A variant, used by the French government since 1689, was the *tontine*, an investment in which the subscribers were divided into 'classes' according to age (each class generally covering five years), then subdivided into 'societies' of 150 to 200 *rentiers*; within each society, the annuities of those who died were transferred to the survivors. Another kind of *tontine* was the *tontine composée*, in which only half the annuity passed on, the other half being extinguished to the profit of the government. Investors in a *rente viagère* or a *tontine* naturally gave careful thought to their chances of living long and, if they had a conscience, to the rights of their dependants. It was a matter of common jest that the best way to be healthy was to join a *tontine*—it was a declaration of optimism in the first place, and it provided an ever increasing incentive to survive.[61] Mme de Polastron, who ignored the expectations of her children and put her heritage into a high-yield annuity to be extinguished when she was eighty, was censured by public opinion; she lived on in penury until the age of eighty-eight—'elle fut punie par où elle avait péché'.[62] On the other hand, the government had to be careful. As the administrators of the two big hospitals of Marseille discovered, those who borrow money by selling annuities are up against the determined longevity of their customers: their investors died at the surprisingly late average age of seventy for men and seventy-three for women.[63] Necker's notoriously wasteful borrowings were annuities at 8 and 10 per cent, without division into classes according to age, and assuming an average paying-out time of twenty years—a naïve method of raising money which was exploited by the inhabitants of Geneva. Thirty girls from the healthiest families in town, all successfully vaccinated, and kept on a healthy diet with the best medical attention, were the nominal beneficiaries of the 'Genevan system', living on and on, at immense profit to their backers. When, in July 1788 Pernette Elisabeth Martin of Geneva died, two millions of *rentes* went down with her—she had been worth more than Marie-Antoinette.[64]

In France, the key work on life expectancy had been published in 1746, Deparcieux's *Essai sur les probabilités de la durée de la vie humaine*. A controversy about its methodology in the pages of the *Journal de Trévoux* and the *Journal de Verdun*, in which the author was backed by the Académie royale des sciences,[65] brought the book to notice, and its lucidity encouraged the general reader. Deparcieux summarized the works of earlier writers: Halley's statistics from Breslau in Silesia, Moivre's treatise on annuities, and a recent analysis of the incidence of death in Sweden, but his chief sources were in France. The deaths he considered were those of the subscribers to the various tontines, of monks and nuns as entered in monastic registers, of the parishioners of Saint-Sulpice as recorded by the *curé* over thirty years, and of members of the Academy of Sciences. He was aware of the danger of taking a particular group as typical—those who think they are healthy invest in tontines, and monks and nuns have their physical fitness tested during their noviciate (so they last better than other people for a couple of decades, then decline because of their austerities).[66] He also realized the difference between *la vie moyenne* (the sum total of the ages divided by the number of people) and *la vie médiane* (the number of years marking the time when half of them would be dead)—a point on which even Buffon was to be confused.[67] Deparcieux had some clear findings. Women live longer than men (the popular belief that the age of forty-five to fifty is dangerous to them is a delusion). Big cities kill off their populations. The average life expectancy at birth is twenty-one years in Paris; in Laon it is thirty-seven years; in the Cévennes, forty-one years. The children of richer parents have a better chance of survival in their early years (the suggestion is that their wet-nurses are better paid and more closely supervised). As for the question which we all wish to ask, an approximate answer is given from the records of the tontines from 1689 to 1742—it being understood that the subscribers are a healthier group than average. At the age of forty, it would be reasonable to hope for another twenty-seven and a half years (today, there would be a life expectancy of thirty-seven); at fifty, life expectancy was twenty years (today, nearly twenty-eight).[68] In a way Deparcieux was conveying reassurance. It was commonly said that the life of a man, on the average, was twenty years;[69] having shown that there were parts of France where this figure was greatly exceeded, he was now doing the calculation for adults, excluding from the sum the terrible infant mortality. Buffon carried optimistic calculation further. Our first fifteen years, he argues, do not count—our ideas do not form part of the same succession as later, we only begin to live 'morally' when we become consistent and forward-looking. Thus, while by statistics I have lived a quarter of my life by the age of twelve, morally, it is only at twenty-five that this point is reached; life is only half gone at thirty-eight and even at fifty-six a quarter is still left.[70]

In the second half of the eighteenth century, anyone who wished to speculate on the hazards and hopes of life had to start from Deparcieux, and Buffon's prodigious success ensured that this sort of speculation was fashionable. When an epidemic which killed adults only struck in a poor parish of Lille in 1772, a know-all alderman refused to believe the figures in the *curé*'s register: all the writers on population, including the famous Buffon, he said, have told us that one-third of the deaths recorded must be those of children under twelve.[71] Daignan, a medical expert from Montpellier, brooded over Buffon's figures, and travelled in his own country and in the Low Countries and Germany from 1762, studying the statistics of life expectancy before publishing his essay on the stages of human life in 1786. But what advice could he give to help us to live longer? Just what Deparcieux, Buffon, Messance, and 'Moheau' had said: live on mountain tops and avoid marshes.[72] But mortality tables and the statistics in the files of the intendants might be used by the State to help us in the gloomy circumstances when we would be unable to help ourselves. Claude-Hubert

Piarron de Chamousset, a wealthy Parisian philanthropist, in 1754 published his *Plan d'une maison d'association*, a precocious design for national health insurance. Hospitals, he said, are for the poor, and the rich are looked after at home: the middling sort of people should become members of a contributory hospital scheme. On the eve of the Revolution, the famous scientist Lavoisier proposed a similar insurance contribution against sickness and old age,[73] and a reforming pamphleteer worked out the actuarial details of a plan for husbands to buy State pensions for their wives. At the National Assembly in 1790, a more radical welfare proposal was made: a free old-age pension for everyone.[74]

III

Educated Frenchmen at the end of the *ancien régime*, knowing their Buffon, Expilly, Messance, and 'Moheau,' whether directly or through the fashionable encyclopaedic, sentimental, or reforming journalism, were aware how death operated. They knew the expectancy of life at different ages, and gloomily reflected upon their own chances. If they were in the way to inherit property they reflected on those of other people. They were haunted by the devastating figures for infant mortality; they speculated on the reasons for differential expectations as between the sexes. Reformers complained of the adverse chances of the poor, and of the unhealthy occupations which abbreviated men's lives; everyone knew the importance of good food, living space, and cleanliness in the battle for survival. There were stock jokes about the untoward longevity of those who purchased annuities. Anticlericals maintained that the selfish introversion of the cloister shortened the life span of monks and nuns—or, alternatively, excessive self-indulgence; churchmen replied that the religious lived longer because of their joyful self-dedication.[75] Differing life expectations as between town and country, and between the various provinces of France, were discussed, and it was known that certain types of terrain favoured survival. Everyone knew where to find the best information about when to buy an annuity, joint or single, and what the terms ought to be. They knew something about statistical methodology, how to juggle with incomplete or dubious information to get reasonable conclusions about the chances of living or dying.

But in this generation obsessed with the statistics of life and death and, maybe, more intensely devoted to the sheer secular pleasure of living than others before it, we do not find an awareness of what is obvious to us now—that this was the age when the 'new demography' was rising, the beginning of the lifting of the shadow of death from the human mind. Given the complexity and startling contrasts of the demographic map of France, as revealed by modern research, it is understandable that a coherent view of a general progression was hidden from contemporaries. They assumed the continuance of the pattern of history as their fathers and grandfathers remembered it: the terrible later years of Louis XIV, the recovery; the grim forties, recovery again, and the dearths of the seventies; it is left to modern historians to distinguish major crises from *crises larvées*, and to know that the great holocausts of the seventeenth century were not to recur. The growth of the cities was, often enough, regarded as a superficial and unhealthy phenomenon. The increase of population in the smaller villages rather than the larger (something we do not yet entirely understand—was it because larger numbers provided a bigger target for epidemics?)[76] was calculated to hide away expansion from superficial observation. It is a truism to say that we see what we have been looking for, and what we look for, very often, is something logically necessary to our present picture of the world, something for which we have a ready-made explanation. In this matter of changing beliefs about the way in which the population was moving, presuppositions were all-important. In 1802, an enthusiast for the Revolution, a medical doctor proud of the potency of his art, looked back on the last decade and described France as a land of rapidly rising population.[77] He discounted the devastation of the wars, and took his stand upon the wrecking of monasticism, the legislation prescribing the equal division of inheritances among children, the sale of Church property, the progress of medicine, and, even, the closing of the institutions which had cared for foundlings, and the libertinage of the numerous soldiers, as the reasons for the sensational new departure. Statistically his knowledge was limited, but political and professional enthusiasm convinced him that the conditions were right and mankind must be flourishing. Under the *ancien régime*, there was no such compelling argument to encourage expectation of an increase in population or an increase in the human life span. This is not surprising, since we still do not know for certain the reason why it happened, and of the two most likely explanations,[78] one is based on postulates which the eighteenth century would not have understood, and the other needs careful definition going behind superficial appearances. There is agreement that the great 'crises' of mortality of the seventeenth century—crises in which disease and starvation interlocked, but played quasi-independent roles whose lethal effects still need more precise assessment—had given way in the eighteenth century to crises of a less deadly kind. Granting, as appears to be the case, that what is to be explained is a defeat for death rather than some significant increase in fecundity, the reasons for the improvements may well be found in some change in the nature of some of the principal killing diseases, or some improvement in the food supply. The first proposed explanation—the hypothesis of some mutation in the strain, or some other accident in the life cycle of certain of the pathogenic bacteria and viruses, so that epidemics became less frequent and less virulent—is only the beginning of an uncircumstantial guess, but, unlike the men of the eighteenth century, we can at least understand how this might have been so. The other proposed explanation is the hypothesis of an improvement in the food supply, whether as an initial factor encouraging the population rise, or as evoked by that rise[79] but being a pre-condition of its continuation. In either case it has been forcefully argued, especially by M. Morineau, that there was no increase in the production of grain; that maize and potatoes merely made up deficiencies in the grain harvest; that there was no 'agricultural revolution' in France; and that contemporaries never supposed there was.[80] This view understates the importance of maize in changing the two-year rotation of crops in the Midi to a three-year cycle, and of the introduction of the potato into arid soils in mountainous areas.[81] There were also other diversifications of cultivation, maybe not significant in adding to the bulk of available cereal protein, but providing nutritional elements which had been lacking before. The decline in cereal yields is partly a result of the change to cattle rearing in some areas, and it has been observed, in the dairy-farming country of Normandy, that infant mortality was lower there, since there was milk available for the children, a more varied diet for all, and the mothers of babies were not exhausted by the desperate toil of the harvest season.[82] And in the eighteenth century, the food supply became more strategically available because of improvements to barns and storage facilities and to communications, more especially by river and canal.[83] In famine times, life and death depended on finding a solution to 'le problème des arrivages',[84] whether bringing in grain from other provinces, or from overseas. It may be, too, that industrial expansion, more particularly in cloth manufacture, paid for increased imports of food from abroad. But these developments were spread over the century and were not obvious. Amid the dearths of the seventies, Frenchmen's view of the agricultural progress of their country was that held by M. Morineau. They had no reason to expect an increase in population. As it happened, there was a contrary belief of long standing that the population was falling, and that the government ought to be taking serious measures to rescue the nation from decline.

It seems astonishing today that some of the most serious political and economic thinkers of the Enlightenment should have shown such zeal in warning their countrymen against a non-existent menace. When Messance published his optimistic and patriotic collection of statistics in 1766, Grimm said that his bold assertion of a population expansion ran contrary to the records of the parlements for the past fifteen years, all writings on politics, and public opinion generally.[85] To be fair to the theorists of decline, they were often talking of the long-term movement of history, in which figures from three or four *généralités* about what had happened in the last two or three generations had little relevance. In the *Lettres persanes* in 1721, Montesquieu asked why the Europe of Roman antiquity had been ten times more populous than the continent of his own day, witness the colossal ruins to be seen in the wastes of Sicily and Spain, and the history of the waves of northern barbarians sweeping southwards for centuries driven by the pressure of their own numbers.[86] The sophisticated modernity of Montesquieu as a historian and social analyst riveted upon the minds of his readers the dubious old commonplace of decline which they were already predisposed to believe because of their education in the moral and rhetorical ambience of the ancient Latin authors. If, in the quarrel of Ancients and Moderns, the Moderns had won, thanks to science, technology, and Christianity, classical antiquity was at least still allowed to retain its numerical superiority. There was also another line of reflection, derived from the spectacle of more recent historical events, which helped to maintain the theory of population decline in its unauthenticated sway over men's minds. The glittering achievements and disastrous legacies of Louis XIV compelled critical and patriotic assessment, which could not be done too openly. The persecution of Protestants and Jansenists and the waging of dynastic wars had to be described in formulas which would allow the policies of the Sun King to have been right in his time but wrong for posterity to continue. In his reign, the vast taxation system, so destructive of agricultural progress, had been elaborated; this was how the despots of Spain had driven their vast empire down the path to decadence. A shorthand way of drawing the parallel and describing Louis XIV's ruinous legacy was to refer to the decline of the population. According to Quesnay,[87] physician to Louis XV and the chief of the Physiocratic school of reformers (who wished to rejuvenate agriculture, making it the primary source of national wealth and the essential object of governmental solicitude), there had been 24,000,000 inhabitants in France in 1650; in 1701 there had been 19,000,000; and in 1750 only 16,000,000. (From these figures the inference could be drawn, that the earlier part of the Sun King's reign had lost 5,000,000 people, and the miseries of his declining years had lost the best part of 3,000,000 more.) Thus, the most influential and, indeed, the only coherently thought-out theory of economic reform of the century had as its postulate, its spur to action, its critique of past mistakes, the depopulation argument. As the hypothesis of decline was solidly reaffirmed by reputable authors, reformers—clerical and anti-clerical—found it a useful foundation to build on. Among churchmen, the abbé Jaubert's *Des Causes de la dépopulation et les moyens d'y remédier* (1767) blamed libertinage and warfare, destructive of human life in themselves, and calling down divine vengeance; he also blamed the persecution of the Huguenots and regretted monastic celibacy.[88] On the other side, Christian marriage was blamed by the more outrageous writers. The maréchal de Saxe would have all unions temporary, limited to five years, and not renewable except by special dispensation, if there were no children.[89] *A fortiori*, there was a hue and cry against clerical celibacy. Monasteries, said Montesquieu, are 'gulfs that swallow up future generations'. Diderot did the calculation to show how splendidly the future could be reinforced by the progeny of 40,000 lusty *curés*; Ange Goudar did another sum to show that over a 3,000-year term monasticism would wither off the entire French race. Voltaire liked to give statistical demonstrations of the evil of clerical intolerance: counting the Crusades, the Spaniards in the Indies, and persecution generally, Christianity had so far been responsible for 9,468,800 deaths.[90] Neutral writers made practical suggestions: let the State pay children's allowances for all additions to the family beyond the third[91] or, even, said a daring publicist of 1787, distribute plots of land to the people.[92]

In their defence against the *philosophes*, churchmen had not forgotten the providential argument, as it had been used by English theologians in the early days of 'Political Arithmetic'. The *Journal de Trévoux* denied the allegations of decline and, equally, the possibility of expansion—at least on the world-wide scale. The Creator wished to keep the population of the globe constant. Boys and girls were in fairly equal numbers, but with rather more boys because they had to face more dangers during life. The figures for life expectancy were so arranged that the world's population was kept constant at 720,000,000.[93] Another respectable writer, vaguely convinced by Messance, conceded an excess of births over deaths, but held this was just a temporary divine expedient to provide against any recurrence of the plague and to enable the foundation of colonies. Another theorist on the religious side called in the principles of mechanics to prove that the number of human beings could never vary, since the weight of each planet had to remain constant: 'one grain more or less would cause a derangement in the general system of all the heavenly bodies and their orbits.' Even so, he recommended the keeping of records of births and deaths: one could never be too cautious.[94] Faignet de Villeneuve was unusual in that he denied, not the proposition of decline, but the reasons advanced for deploring it: numbers were unimportant. As against the mercantilist ideal of power and the newer idea of the advantages of the division of labour, he simply said that our aim should be to perfect men. True, he would also wish to augment numbers according to our needs—perhaps he deserves a place in the history of contraceptive practices.[95]

It took time for Voltaire,[96] the sardonic and scintillating defender of simple common sense, to see through the Physiocratic thesis of population decline. In 1732 he was explaining the vast numbers of the northern barbarians of the past by their practice of polygamy (a point to vex populationist Christians). In 1759 he was blaming smallpox from Arabia and the other pox from America for the drastic reduction of the number of inhabitants in Russia—the fault of Muhammad and Columbus. He was appalled by the revelations of statistical studies about the huge mortality among infants; of every twenty-six marriages, he said, only four leave children who become fathers in their turn. Then, in 1763, Voltaire was seen to have changed his mind; France, he said, was more populous now than in the fourteenth century. It was the first time that a major writer had challenged the thesis of decline, though the perpetual secretary of the Academy of Auxerre had done so in 1758, and aroused a preliminary controversy.[97] Voltaire was entering the lists before Messance, and the reason for his conversion is significant. J.-B.-F. de la Michaudière, intendant of Auvergne, the patron of Messance, had passed on to Ferney the statistics concerning the *généralité*; not for the first time Voltaire was in advance of public opinion because he had inside information. Even so, in 1771 he was describing France as having 20,000,000 inhabitants, that is, he was doing no more than backing the stationary hypothesis, giving the figure which Vauban had put forward for the later years of Louis XIV. To the extent that the Physiocrats maintained that there had been a fall to 15,000,000 or 16,000,000, Voltaire was defying them, but their 'intellectual terrorism' probably accounts for his unwillingness to push further the case for expansion. A modern historian[98] has put together the statistics of baptisms and burials which had been collected in France in the second half of the century—those in the files of the Controller General Terray, those held by the intendants Boula de Nanteuil and Montyon (that is

'Moheau'), and some published in the *Gazette d'agriculture* between 1776 and 1780. From these, comparative totals have been
compiled for the years 1770 and 1780 (with a few gaps filled by
other years) for each of thirty-five *généralités*. In every case,
baptisms exceed burials except in Lille in 1770, and in Bourges,
Orléans, Rennes, and Tours in 1780. Some figures on life expectancy collected in the last decade of the *ancien régime* were, in 1806,
tabulated and published by Du Villard—revealing that Frenchmen
had been, at that time, enjoying a longer life span that had been
postulated by Buffon, from earlier evidence, in 1777.[99] But cor-
related evidence of these kinds had not been available to contemporaries. Everyone knew how the sweep of death's scythe was arbitrary, sparing certain areas, reaping brutally in others, active
viciously in certain years and decades, and not in others. It was hard
to believe that there was now a basic pattern of change, and that for
the better.

IV

'The days of our age are threescore years and ten; and though men
be so strong that they come to fourscore years, yet is their strength
then but labour and sorrow, so soon passeth it away and we are
gone.' The Psalmist, it was generally agreed, had defined man's
allotted span. This is what people of the eighteenth century looked
forward to, though with a totally different estimate of the chances
of getting there compared with our own unthinking assurance. And
then, as now, the achievement of a hundred years was a matter of
news, of celebration, more especially in the second half of the
century. As usual, the almanacs reported such prodigies: thus the
Almanach de Liège in 1760 recorded the death of an aristocratic
lady in the south of France at the age of one hundred and three—at
ninety, her teeth had been renewed.[100] But specialists were taking
over this branch of journalism; in the following year, one Lottin,
publishing an *Almanach de la Vieillesse, ou notice de tous ceux qui
ont vécu cent ans et plus*, asked all centenarians to send their names
'written very legibly', for insertion in the next issue.[101] Meanwhile,
Voltaire was writing to those he heard of: between 1759 and 1762
three old ladies received his congratulations; one had three deaf-

111

and-dumb children surviving—they conversed cheerfully by sign language and knew all the latest news.[102] In Lyon, an abbé established that no less than forty-seven inhabitants had passed the hundred mark in the last twenty years, a result, he thought, of the benign climate of the city.[103] In 1777 and 1779 Buffon added to his great work information about other heroes of longevity, with an especial interest in their propensity for marriage: it was no mean feat to take a wife at the age of one hundred and eleven.[104] In the eighties, we hear of a peasant twenty-two years beyond his century, who lived in a cave,[105] and of an artisan of the Faubourg Saint-Antoine almost as old. Everyone in Paris could direct you to him, Mercier said, whereas when Rousseau had lived in the capital, no one knew his address.[106] In 1788, the nobles of Dauphiné, defending the Parlement of Grenoble against the Crown, sent their petition to Versailles in the charge of the hundred-year-old marquis de Viennois; the Revolution was to see other centenarians as envoys to the sovereign power, proclaiming the patriotic sentiments of their locality before the assembled legislators of the nation.

Was it only extreme good fortune and an enduring constitution which got a man into the select company of those who managed to exceed the psalmist's span by twenty or so years? Perhaps there was some medicine or dietary regimen which could help—the eighteenth century had inherited some traditional lore of this kind, and some enthusiasts professed to find it still helpful. Arnauld de Villeneuve, a French physician of the Middle Ages, had invented a formula in which saffron, aloes, and viper juice were the principal ingredients—but as he had also recommended cheerfulness and moderation in eating and drinking, he may not have done much harm. He had also discouraged sexual intercourse and any exercise violent enough to raise a sweat, so that he had never been a favourite with the younger generation.[107] His receipts, pharmaceutical and psychological, were recommended to his countrymen by M. de Longeville de Harcouet in the last years of Louis XIV, together with additional proposals for a vegetarian diet. From the sixteenth century came the advice of Cornaro, a Venetian who had reformed from a career of self-indulgence at the age of forty and had gone on to pass the hundred mark—he too forbade sex and strenuous activity, and limited meals to 12 oz of food and 14 oz of wine. The *Journal de Trévoux*, at the beginning of the century, was sceptical about the validity of the Cornaro method, since even monks are allowed 30 oz, and each Israelite in the wilderness was officially allowed by God to gather 50 oz of manna.[108] In 1761, Lottin, the compiler of statistics about centenarians, produced the standard formula: moderation in bed and at board, but he also recommended packing up the furniture and moving house to the more salubrious areas of Europe—the two best places were a breezy little village in Hanover and an island off Norway where people felt so bored with their interminable lives that they tended to migrate elsewhere as a respectable form of suicide.[109] Chomel in 1772 was willing to predict who would live long—those with healthy ancestors, sound physique, and the ability to sleep long and profoundly—there was only one curable element here, and he did not know how to deal with insomnia.[110] Delisle de Sales and Erlach, in tune with Rousseauism, enviously noted that savages often lived to a century and a half, but they did not propose to adjourn to the woods to qualify. A patriot of eighty-two years of age in 1789 shared with the public the secret of his *huile odiférante*; he ascribed to it his continuing fitness, and proposed to retire for a while from active business to reorganize himself for a new spell of work—like Nature preparing for Spring.[111] Jean-Claude Chappuis sent a *Plan social* to Necker in this same year of national regeneration; his reforms, he said, would have as one effect the lengthening of the life span to between 90 and 120 years, though he warned the Minister that this extra population would cause food shortages unless rationing was introduced along with his utopia.[112] During the Revolution similar prognostications were heard—that a free government, equality, and the disciplining of youth in the army would prolong the average life span—more especially in Lanthenas's *De l'influence de la liberté sur la santé* (1792);[113] but disillusionment set in as war and Terror added new hazards to the struggle for survival. The revolutionary formula for longevity had proved as useless as the ancient counsel of moderation.

The medical profession, as might be expected, had no time for the amateur tradition of do-it-yourself longevity. By the eighteenth century, the Aristotelian and Galenic accounts of the working of the ageing process—that the 'interior fire' dies down and the 'radical humidity' dries up—were no longer fashionable.[114] In their place, the medical experts had adopted two more circumstantial explanations, mutually complementary, and in neither case leaving much room for discoveries which might delay the final end. Our organs are worn out, it was said, by friction, 'le frottement insensible des corps hétérogènes';[115] food and drink wear their way down, artificial light wears out the eyes and noise the ear-drums.[116] A rather different version of this theory of exhaustion by use was Delisle de Sales's description of the vital fluids within us becoming degraded. There were experiments with blood transfusions in the eighteenth century, but the blood was only part of the problem; the more important *suc* in our nervous system is evaporating, and as even the most powerful microscope cannot detect it, what chance have we of coping with its loss? The only hope of surviving would be to cease from activity and live in a perpetual coma, husbanding our fluids and doing nothing.[117] The second line of explanation of aging concerned the hardening process. Our growth, Lecat said, turns inwards from the age of twenty-five: we solidify. The only way to escape this ultimately fatal development would be to continue to grow outwards, becoming a giant.[118] The hardening forces the heart, lungs, and nervous system to work more strenuously against increasing pressures, a burden which ultimately proves too much for them. The conduits in the nerves, which operate hydraulically, transmitting pressures to and from the brain, causing feeling and movement, are especially adversely affected. Microscopically invisible though they are, Lecat describes how they become encrusted, as it were with stalactites. Thus, said Marat, while artificial machines break down because their material wears out, the animal machine is unique in that it perishes by acquiring increased solidity. It is growth, life itself, that destroys life.[119] 'La vie est un minotaure,' said Buffon, 'elle dévore l'organisme,' but he could hold out no hope of delaying the timetable of decline. There were, of course, certain healthy ways of life which would give a chance of a few extra years—like breathing the pure air of the mountains, or moderating one's appetites. But 'since the time of David' all men have the same 'term', the standard expectation of life.[120]

Granted that the term of human existence was fixed by the laws of God and of physiology, there was an abundance of arguments, going back to Cicero, Seneca, and Marcus Aurelius, for the fatalistic acceptance of the inevitable. Life is repetitive, the same old passions bringing about the same results. Its interests are exhaustible: a man who has lived a hundred years has seen everything. [121] We accept the fact that we are living once and for all, since no one (the idea was St. Augustine's) would be willing to return to infancy to start all over again. [122] Our views of what constitutes a long or a short life are arbitrary—an insect whose span is but a single day has achieved what self-fulfilment is possible to it; the nigh on a thousand years of Methuselah are nothing in comparison with eternity. [123] And what use would it be to live longer if, in the end, you must die anyway? This was Bossuet's tremendous theme: live a hundred years, live as long as the great oaks under which your ancestors are buried and which will shade your descendants, the day will come when the breath of death destroys you like a house of cards. [124] Sadly, thanking an author for sending him a table of the probabilities of the duration of life, Voltaire conceded the point. 'Everybody dies at the same age; for it makes no difference, when you reach that point, whether you have lived for twenty hours, or for 20,000 centuries.' [125] Given extra years, said the Christian Dumas, our knowledge would increase, but so too would the area of our conscious ignorance; our achievements would be more numerous, but our moral status would be unimproved—all we are entitled to ask is time enough to prepare for the life to come. Besides, he said, using the more fashionable social arguments of the century, our deaths are necessary to society, lest the old become a burden on the young, the gap widen excessively between the older and younger generations, and the poor acquire intelligence above their station. [126]

In practical terms, the hope to live longer was a yearning to join the few—favoured by fortune or Providence or aided by their own self-denial in following courses of moderation—who reached the far barrier which the ageing process imposed, somewhat above the Psalmist's four score years. The idea of lifting this barrier altogether, and greatly extending the allotted span, is something different, an imaginative fantasy which, no doubt, flitted often through the minds of mortal men, though rarely with any serious interest; it is the myth of the Hyperborean clime beyond the icy gales, the fountain of youth, the alchemist's potion. The eighteenth century did not take kindly to these old magical reveries: one writer applauded the Mongols who, when they invaded China, burned all the books concerning the manufacture of the elixir of life.[127] But since the rise of modern science, the seventeenth century had seized on the idea that Nature might be manipulated and controlled— leading to speculations on the possibility of breaking the barrier on the human life span; Descartes and Bacon touch on the idea in their vision of a scientific future.[128] Logically, though perhaps not psychologically, the biblical view of death as the punishment of sin was no bar to these imaginings, for even if death is postponed, it still comes to us all eventually with the same sombre implications. The various scriptural texts which seemed to prescribe a maximum age—the Psalmist's eighty and the reference in Genesis 6 to a hundred and twenty—were taken, not as evidence for limits, but as statements of fact applicable to their own time only. Aquinas was cited for the view that God would not impose an arbitrary rule on the workings of the natural order.[129] The sceptical conditioning imposed by the Latin authors—inculcating a view of life as an artistic unity, as it were a play, complete once every human experience had been savoured, and of history as a cyclical process whose workings can be fully understood in the course of a normal lifetime—still remained influential with moralists and theologians, but by the early eighteenth century, the classical mortgage on the European future was being lifted. In the quarrel between Ancients and Moderns, both sides agreed that history is a continual series of innovations. What was in dispute was whether they were inferior or superior to what had gone before. The progress of invention, science, and commerce rapidly became accepted as indisputable. As a result, a long-enduring myth about the changing pattern of the human life span collapsed, a myth in whose cause fanatical enthusiasts for the literal interpretation of the Scriptures had been incongruously allied with those who praised the superiority of classical antiquity to degenerate modern times. The Bible tells of the patriarchs before the Flood, with Methuselah, dying at 996, as the longest lived. Then, after the Deluge, came Abraham, with 'only' 275 years; and after him, with a long but successively deteriorating span, Isaac, Jacob, and Joseph (who was down to 110), though Job was compensated for his tribulations with 217. The old explanation—that the 'year' of the sacred writers was a unit of shorter measurement—was abandoned in the light of modern science, since the operations of the planetary system, and hence, the rotations of the seasons, would have to be accepted as fixed from the start. That God should have allowed the patriarchs a privileged life span was not unreasonable; as M. de Longeville Harcouet early in the century said, Adam had lost his right to eat of the tree of life, but he and his immediate descendants needed a generous allocation of years, so that they could discover the arts and sciences and populate the globe.[130] This would not entirely explain why our lives are so much shorter now; one view was that Nature generally was running down, and man grows feebler in the process, the plants on which he feeds having lost their primeval qualities of intensive nourishment. This hypothesis suited the Ancients as against the Moderns—a reason to account for the superior greatness of the heroes of antiquity. And even when the Ancients had lost the battle, the myth of a declining life span still lingered on. Buffon, whether ironically or not is hard to say, gravely discussed the hypothesis of botanical exhaustion, though he preferred the theory that gravity had been less powerful in the early days, and men's bodies, moving around with less resistance to overcome, were less subject to the hardening process which abbreviates life. As late as the 1770s echoes of the old story about the world running down were heard. A journalist thought that we live shorter lives than the Ancients, shorter indeed than the men of the seventeenth century (witness the case of a London worthy who died in 1635 at the age of 152, having done penance in a white sheet at the age of 100 for seducing a girl).[131] On the other side, a rival publicist cited the Maréchal de Villers commanding the French troops in Italy at the age of eighty: the Romans had been astonished when Pompey mounted his horse in battle at the age of fifty-eight.[132] Yet these were the last flickers of the old controversy. With Montesquieu and Voltaire a new concept of history arose; the past was no longer a linear movement from Greece through Rome to Western Europe—there was a vast world panorama with all sorts of excellences, and the future might be still more rich and complex. And the implica-

117

tions of the vast time-scale of the future began to be the subject of speculation. The abbé de Saint-Pierre had been the first to think in this way, though he had been concerned with moral rather than scientific achievement.[133] Once the future appeared open and virtually endless, all sorts of glittering possibilities could be imagined. Any intelligent man would be curious to glimpse them. The idea of resuscitation, as against unbroken long-continued survival, became a fashionable whimsy in the eighteenth century, and in 1766 the anatomist John Hunter was experimenting with freezing carp then trying to revive them as a prelude to storing away human beings in ice. What would America look like in a hundred years' time?—a good question, for here was the land of potentialities and opportunity. If people could be embalmed like flies in wine then revived in the sunshine, Benjamin Franklin would have wished to be immersed in a cask of madeira with a few chosen friends to await the full flowering of the greatness of his nation. Or maybe, men could do more than dream of reviving to see their ambitions realized, they might one day be able to live on and on and share in the achievement. Condorcet's vision of perpetual progress included the hope of an indefinite prolongation of human existence by medical skills and selective breeding. Such a comfortable consummation, progress to end progress, was to be anathema to Malthus, who foresaw the advent of the last selfish, static generation of humanity, which would cease to reproduce itself and monopolize the sweets of existence, while so many greater and more virtuous ones had vanished into dust. But Condorcet was untouched by the ethical problems arising from monopoly and immobility—and untroubled too by the evidence all around him that men are incorrigible and self-destructive. His dream of life unlimited in a world at peace, the *Esquisse d'un tableau historique des progrès de l'esprit humain*, was written in hiding in the last six months of his life, just before he took poison in a revolutionary gaol to escape the grim formalities of execution by the guillotine. Ten years after the death of Condorcet, Cabanis,[134] the philosopher of Medicine, who had hardly been optimistic about the possibility of medical innovations revolutionizing society, dreamt of a transformation of the race by disciplined social engineering on a long time-scale. 'In virtue of his organization,' he wrote, 'man is endowed with a perfectibility to which it is impossible to assign a limit.' True, there must be such a limit imposed by Nature, but we are very far from reaching it. Physical education and eugenic manipulation (he cites the way in which the breed of animals has been perfected) will create new faculties and new senses; as the generations go by, men will be transformed, 'they will no longer be the same men, no longer the same race'. These were dreams, and élitist ones at that, lacking the imaginative substantiality of modern science fiction. Diderot was ironical at his own expense about his interest in such speculations. 'Accord to man', he pictured himself saying earnestly, 'I don't say immortality, but simply double his present life span, and you will see what will happen.' To which d'Alembert replies, 'And what do you want to happen? But what has this to do with me? Let what will happen, happen, I'm off to bed, goodnight.'[135] D'Alembert, as portrayed by Diderot, represented the standard verdict of eighteenth-century intelligence. Longer life was a distant utopian dream. Let us do what we can with the meagre allocation fixed for us by Nature and defined by the Psalmist. What good is speculation? Some things are pre-ordained. 'Goodnight!'

The Soul, Heaven, and Hell

Theologians spoke of man as body and soul: the body which decomposes into dust, the soul which lives on to face the judgement of God and be sent to its eternal destiny. What happens when we die and soul and body are sundered? And, to start at the beginning, what is the soul and how can we be sure that it has this property of immortality?

In attempting to define and describe the soul, the Christian apologists centred their argument on the word 'moi'. I have a feeling of individuality, of being a single, coherent, unique being—myself. The soul is 'le moi', 'ce qui constitue le *Moi* de l'Homme'.[1] Sensations from the outside world are appropriated by 'le moi' and woven into its own existence;[2] it does things of its own volition and is conscious of undergoing things which happen to it.[3] It compares ideas, and affirms, doubts, or suspends judgement; it balances contradictory sides of an argument against each other without any consciousness of being divided against itself.[4] Because I have a soul—perhaps one should say, because I *am* a soul—I know myself as a single, unique individual. Here is the basic intuition on which personality is founded: 'ce sentiment individuel de notre existence', says the comte de Valmont in the abbé Gérard's improving novel, 'qui fait évidemment de chacun de nous une seule personne . . . ce sentiment du *moi*, si unique, si simple.'[5]

To define the soul as the principle of individuality made it difficult to think of mind and soul as two separate things; Christian apologists, indeed, spoke of mind as being within the soul. Para de Phanjas in 1774 speaks of 'l'esprit' (that is, a man's understanding, closely allied with 'reason') as being one of the soul's faculties. He contrasts it with 'le cœur moral' which is not so much a faculty of the soul as the soul itself 'envisagé relativement aux différents sentiments qu'elle éprouve'.[6] His use of the words 'esprit' and 'cœur' in combination to sum up the whole personality was an established literary *cliché*; the abbé Prévost, for example, refers to his hero Cleveland as having received from nature 'un esprit et un cœur extraordinaires'. According to the marquis de Charost in his *Réflexions sur l'esprit et le cœur* (1736), mind and heart added together form the soul: united, they are 'un tout qu'on appelle l'âme'.[7] A qualification might, perhaps, be made to his statement: heart and mind are within the soul, but the soul is greater than the mere sum of them. The total personality is judged by moral criteria, and this fact keeps the mind in its true and subordinate place and ensures that the feelings of the heart are not taken for the whole duty of man. The abbé Rose speaks of the beauty of the soul as consisting in 'the proportion of its sentiments to all that is bound to it in the order of its duties';[8] it is not every reaction that counts, but reactions to duties. Only when we act with the whole personality do we reach the highest elevation of which we are capable. Watelet accepts this idea of the theologians as a device of analysis in art criticism; he wants the painter to throw his 'soul' (*âme*) into the figures he paints to give them 'la vie morale'. If you cannot do this, he says in his advice to artists, limit yourself to still life, perspectives, flowers, and landscapes, which do not require the communication of your soul—'ils exigent au moins des émanations de votre esprit'.[9]

All souls come from the hand of God. Speculation was allowable about the timing of this great creative act. There might have been a vast bank of souls set up at the beginning of the world, awaiting the production of bodies by the processes of sexual intercourse and generation. These pre-existent souls might even have lived through some earlier life span; the disciples had asked Jesus 'who did sin the man or his parents that he was born blind' (John 9:7), and Origen had explained our miserable confinement in the body as a punishment for the sins of an earlier existence.[10] But these were no more than permissible speculations. The established theological view, which had prevailed since the Middle Ages, was that God creates each soul individually at the time he places it in the body— thus, the theologians had never succumbed completely to the view of God as the supreme machine maker who gave the universe an initial push then abandoned it: his creation, like his providence, was continuous.

Accepting this hypothesis of special individual creation, the question arose—it was of particular interest to moral theologians and medical men—at what precise moment was the soul implanted? On the Preformationist theory (that is, that the totality of human bodies which would ever exist was enshrined in regressive miniatures within the body of Adam—or of Eve) it was possible to think of soul and body as having had a long connection before the moment of birth. But the progress of science and the inherent improbability of the idea made Preformationism a declining cause, and the involvement of the soul in the wasteful processes of sexual generation was unsatisfactory anyway, so the theologians came to limit their questions to the developing foetus in the womb. Apart from the reference to St. John the Baptist leaping for joy in the womb of Elizabeth, the Scriptures gave no guidance about the moment of the soul's implantation, so the answer had to be given from first principles. The ideal time was taken to be when the foetus had reached its recognizable bodily shape.[11] Some problems—insoluble ones—remained. Was it just that the soul of a stillborn child should be excluded from Heaven, seeing that baptism could not be administered? (In these circumstances, there were sometimes 'miraculous' signs of life by popular demand to constrain the clergy or the *sage-femme* to administer the sacrament.)[12] And what if a monster was born—could it be assumed that an immortal soul was involved? A good deal of unedifying medical and pastoral ingenuity was expended on the problem, without getting further than the common-sense idea of conditional baptism in doubtful cases.[13] More seriously scientific was the question, How did the affinities between the personalities of children and their parents come about? Père Tournemine, at the beginning of the century, gave the only answer which was possible without slipping into the heresy of Traducianism. God must be supposed to create a soul to suit the body which awaited it: 'Les qualités naturelles de chaque âme sont proportionnées aux dispositions naturelles du corps qu'elle doit animer.'[14] And how is Original Sin transmitted? Is it a corruption passed down from body to body, or is it some flaw in the linkages between soul and body, such as a loss of the control of the senses; does the brain of the mother transmit to the brain of the child some deep-rooted perversity? Or must God be assumed to be more directly responsible by creating souls that are deficient, either because he makes them like Adam's, lacking in the original grace which the first man squandered, or because in adjusting the soul to suit the body the imperfections of the parents are inevitably perpetuated? If none of these methods of transmission was accepted, what was left but the sinister hypothesis of imputation?[15] The writers of the Enlightenment were sapping the weakest buttress of Christian doctrine when they attacked the concept of Original Sin. The arguments for its transmission were improbable or dubiously ethical, and for its imputation, unethical altogether. As Voltaire pointed out, cab horses are whipped, but it is not rational or moral to suppose that this is because one of them had once eaten forbidden oats. There was, however, a parallel proposition of the theologians which was easier to understand. Adam's disobedience had subjected all his posterity to death. It was possible to deny the doctrine of man's perversity and to regard human nature as perfectible, but no one could deny the necessity of dying. If Nature was benevolent, it was hard to see why this must be so: there was a curse on man after all.

Since the soul was defined as 'le moi', the principle of individuality, the theologians were under no necessity to point to any place in the body where it resided. Medical investigations and philosophical speculations about 'le siège de l'âme', said the abbé Joannet, could at most determine the particular organ which first received the soul's action, the 'point d'appui' upon which it operated.[16] The soul eluded the anatomist because it was nonmaterial. This being so, death was a phenomenon which affected the body alone. The soul, having nothing perishable about it, was naturally immortal. Père Hayer was careful to distinguish here: Christians do not regard the soul as an emanation from God as enduring as its divine source—this is what Tertullian called making it 'more than immortal'; what they say is, God creates and sustains the soul, each moment of its existence being 'a new favour from the Infinite Being'.[17] Gros de Besplas manœuvred the opposite way to cover the remote possibility of some future physiological investigation discovering a material element in the soul; whatever its substance may be, he said, God can make the soul immortal; indeed, it may exist within our body like one of the *germes* which the microscope reveals in seeds, ready to spring up to life eternal out of the corruption of the body when it dies.[18] For a different, technical reason, a Swiss writer took the same line—the *moi*, our individuality, can only be said to subsist if our memories are preserved, thus our resurrection body must exist somewhere in miniature within our present one, ready to take over the memory-laden fibres of the brain when we die.[19]

Generally, however, the religious apologists insisted that the soul was non-material. This led to complex debates as to how spiritual and material entities could inter-react, but it promoted the argument for man's immortality. Material particles, the argument ran, are infinitely divisible, and material objects are thought of as consisting of specific parts; our bodies we recognize as containing such parts; we consciously move some of them and we are conscious of others moving themselves. But the soul we cannot think of as other than indivisible; we have no concept of its parts, and we feel our acts of will and desire as straightforward motions emanating from a single centre. I can be doing different things simultaneously—writing, thinking, distracted by events around me, feeling cold, and so on, but everything is being done by or happening to one person with a continuous, unified memory.[20] With his usual *naïveté*, the apologist Caraccioli makes the argument ridiculous by citing dreams as evidence of the soul's independence of the body in thinking or imagining; Bergier, with his usual sophistication, reduced the indivisibility proof to a 'sentiment intérieur' of individuality which carries with it a conviction of immortality.[21]

There were, of course, many scriptural references to prove the immortality of the soul, or at least to affirm the certainty of judgement and a life after death. The *philosophes* sought to discourage the devout by chronological surveys of the evidence to show that the Jews had picked up the idea late in their history from Chaldean sources; Bergier has eight columns of citations to prove the contrary.[22] But this was peripheral harassment. Even if belief in an afterlife arose late in the literature of Israel, it was firmly rooted in the teaching of Christ and his apostles. More than this, the scriptural teachings pointed on to an appeal to the principles of morality and justice which we assume must underlie the workings of the universe. God has implanted in us a hope and a yearning, he cannot wish to mislead us; he has inspired us with a desire for happiness, surely he must offer us a way to achieve it; he has made us reasonable beings, so we expect to see justice prevail—look around and see how everywhere virtue is persecuted; this alone is sufficient proof of the necessary existence of a land beyond the grave where injustices will be rectified. Or, to appeal crudely to this-worldly considerations: the belief in a future life and its rewards and punishments is the only foundation of morality.[23] To affirm death as the end is to undermine civilization: 'Le partisan de l'anéantissement est l'ennemi de la société.'[24]

Whatever else happened in the life after death, one item of the scenario was clear: there would be a vast organization of reward and punishment to redress the injustices of this earthly life. Theologians and Christian publicists had this organization, with all its various possibilities, worked out to the last embarrassing detail. It was done by taking Scripture literally, then proceeding in sharp logical steps to reconcile all the circumstantial indications found there—and, in the process, ignoring the general spirit of the New Testament.

The tiny minority of saints could hope to go directly to Heaven. As St. Stephen fell beneath the hail of stones he saw the heavens open and Christ at the right hand of the Father. The act of dying, said St. Paul, simply, is 'to depart and be with Christ'.[25] This splendid translation of the élite few directly to God's presence might, perhaps, stop just short of complete felicity of body and soul for, according to the abbé Bergier, a meed of joy was reserved to be bestowed at the moment of the general resurrection.[26] The words of Jesus to the Penitent Thief, 'Today shalt thou be with me in Paradise', were held by some to be an additional proof of the instantaneous elevation to Heaven of the chosen few, but there was a problem here, for Christ did not ascend himself until forty-four days after he made the promise; perhaps 'today' was merely an emphatic way of saying 'soon', and the repentant and redeemed criminal spent the intervening time in the limbo where the just of the Old Testament awaited the news of their deliverance.[27]

But the saints are few. For ordinary Christians the heavens are not opened without trials, formalities, and tribulations. For practically all men, immediately after death there is an individual, lonely judgement; this is irreversible, the Great Assize at the end of time 'necessarily' confirming the verdict already given.[28] The foundation of this first judgement is the sudden, definitive revelation of what our lives have been like: 'In God, as in a great mirror, we see, in the twinkling of an eye, the whole history of our lives, and at the same time we are conscious of every tiny detail.'[29] Broken by this self-knowledge and confronted with Christ, we judge ourselves as surely as we are judged. There was a comfortable theory, reflected sometimes in the formulas of wills, that three days were allowed after death during which the prayers of relatives and friends might avail to help the waiting soul before the irrevocable sentence was pronounced;[30] but the best authorities were sterner—according to them, the judgement was immediate, and where the tree fell, there it would lie. 'Entre la mort et le jugement particulier, nul milieu; l'arbre restera éternellement du côté où il sera tombé.'[31]

Judged and forever deprived of hope, the incorrigibly wicked were dispatched straight to Hell. This did not mean, however, that they would escape the Last Judgement. Père Bridaine, the famous hell-fire preacher, described how they would be taken out of their fiery dungeons, put back into bodies suitably dirty and revolting, and appear at the Great Assize to be publicly condemned and sent back to burn for ever.[32] Those Christians who were to be saved were sent, after the individual judgement, to Purgatory, there to be cleansed by tribulation. This was the standard belief, though there was, perhaps, a more attractive alternative for a select minority—those who were not in the highest category fit for direct promotion to heaven, but who had worked single-mindedly for their salvation and had died piously. These, said the Jansenist Duguet, would be rewarded with a long and restful sleep until history came to its conclusion: they would not suffer, they would but await their ultimate felicity.[33] The bishop of Alais, in a pastoral letter on the death of Louis XV, described the King's soul as waiting underground in perpetual silence until the Last Trump sounds and the Ancient of Days arrives to pronounce upon his happiness or doom;[34] this was a convenient supposition, respectful to monarchy and also enabling the good bishop to avoid deciding whether Louis XV was in Purgatory or in Hell, a difficult problem. At least, he had not made the error of the preacher at the funeral of Francis I in the sixteenth century who (so the story ran) had proclaimed the King's direct promotion to Heaven, thus arousing the Sorbonne to angry protest at this affront to the doctrine of Purgatory.[35] The theme of repose after death for those who were worthy (or, as a dubiously invented exception, for those of worldly eminence who were not) was a throw-back to the ancient Christian belief which had preceded the elaboration of the doctrine of Purgatory. When the Church conquered the world and the world infiltrated the Church, Purgatory could rise from the status of hypothesis to a formal doctrine: it was a special institution to cater for nominal Christians. It also proved profitable to the clergy. Its proofs had been hammered out in controversy with the Protestants.[36] Christ's victory has removed the guilt of our sins, but the penalty remains, and expiation must be assumed to be graduated according to the gravity of our offences. Some sins cannot be forgiven in the next world, we are told (Matt. 12:32), therefore the others can be. The Jews believed in prayers for the dead (Tobit 4:18; 2 Macc. 12:45), so did St. Paul (2 Tim. 1:18), and the Church has always done so. Thus, the offering of prayer by the living for souls in Purgatory was an essential part of the Catholic religion. Devotional writers systematized the intercessory duties of the Christian year: pray for a relative on the anniversary of his death, and for all you have loved on one day each month; on All Souls' Day, however, you are not to think of individuals but to petition God on behalf of all men;[37] remember too, that prayer for baptized infants is not required or proper—at their obsequies we say the mass of the day or, perhaps, of the Blessed Virgin or of the Holy Angels, and not the sombre requiem for the departed.[38] And the old system of indulgences to alleviate the sufferings of souls in Purgatory, or on their way there, still operated, in spite of Jansenist attacks on the frivolous concept of a God whose punishments could be bought off so cheaply,[39] and anticlerical grumbling at the profits accruing to the clergy ('Le purgatoire', said the atheistic *curé* Meslier, 'est le brasier qui fait bouillir la marmite du pasteur'). Indulgences were attached to particular churches, feasts, services, and processions (with or without candles); at death, the uttering of the name of Jesus brought a plenary indulgence, and there was another special one for the silent turning of the mind to Jesus and his mother, provided the supplicant had been accustomed in life to

127

use the greeting 'Jesus Christ be praised' in Latin or in the vulgar tongue.[40]

And what were these sufferings, terrible, yet finite and a prelude to glory, which could be abbreviated by prayers and indulgences? Did they consist of ordeal by fire, and if so was the fire identical in kind with the fire of Hell?[41] Or was there, as a lay apologist suggested, a blinding radiance, not to burn, but to show up all the depths of our guilty consciences, and a long period of alienation during which God repulsed the yearning soul from union with himself until all its offences had been purged?[42] These were matters for speculation, but whatever the severities of Purgatory, there was no need to fear, for the Christian who was sent there knew that he was saved by being guaranteed the gift of infallible perseverance,[43] while the saints and all the faithful would be sustaining him by their prayers.

When a soul in Purgatory had served out its sentence, presumably it slept to the end of the world. Dom Calmet, the biblical commentator whose naïve diligence provided Voltaire with so much of his ammunition, and the acknowledged expert on vampires and werewolves, was prepared to describe from Holy Writ the exact chronology of the Final Catastrophe, from the arrival of the Beast from the abyss to the three-and-a-half years' reign of Antichrist preceding the Second Coming and the Last Judgement.[44] The sophisticated abbé Bergier would have none of this. There is warrant in the Fathers for believing that the Gospel writers conflated in one description the signs preceding the end of the world and those announcing the fall of Jerusalem; in any case, 'le monde finit pour tous ceux qui meurent'—*our* world ends when we die, and that is all we need to know.[45] Bergier clearly thought of the end without apocalyptic embroideries; the professional poet and panegyrist Thomas, equally suspicious of lurid details, described how sun and stars would cool into dead ashes in an undramatic silence—though God's judgement would intervene all the same.[46] However the end came, cataclysmically or gradually, the consummation would be the Great Assize, when Christ would pronounce judgement, and his angels would separate the righteous from the damned.[47] Everyone would appear at the Last Judgement in the body, for there would be a general resurrection. The wicked would be seen in stinking corpses, the just in glittering radiance. This universal embodiment of so many generations caused problems, since the same material particles would have taken their places in various bodies throughout the course of history; how to decide, for example, when allocating them, between cannibals and their victims? Bergier, as usual, produces a judicious explanation. When we speak of the 'body' in this connection we do not mean the total mass of material particles, we mean the *stamina originalia* of Leibniz and Clarke, the interior secret of memory and selfhood.[48] The whole subject of the general resurrection lent itself to such unedifying conundrums. Would the bodies be clothed? (probably not, though this could hardly matter to the just in their radiance); would acquired deformities be reproduced? (no—the nail marks in the Lord's resurrection body were a concession to the disciples, to assist identification); at what age of their life then would people appear? (in their prime, or at the age of Christ's resurrection, maybe); and what of very small children?[49] Where could space be found to assemble such a vast multitude? One particularly naïve commentator expected all the planets to be pressed into use, with God moving round aloft on clouds in space.[50]

But the concept of the Last Judgement raised a much more serious problem, more serious because it was of a moral nature. Since the individual judgement immediately after death was definitive, irreversible, why was this tremendous and sombre charade necessary? How could the Great Assize be reconciled with the principle of economy in the universe and with the generosity and dignity of God? One explanation was derived from the necessarily provisional nature of the punishment imposed after the initial condemnation. Only after the general resurrection would the bodies of the wicked become available for torment along with their souls, and if there were to be gradations of pain in Hell, there were some crimes (for example the propagation of heresy) which could not be assessed until all their consequences had worked themselves out in the whole sweep of human history.[51] Another explanation was: justice must be seen to be done. Hypocrisy must be confounded: the whole world would learn about those amorous intrigues, those dubious readings, those libidinous thoughts and mental treacheries.[52] Guardian angels, confessors, and friends would all testify, giving 'an exact account of all their warnings'.[53] In the face of evidence, publicly rehearsed for everyone, the damned would be obliged to recognize the justice of their sentence. 'We justify ourselves normally by comparison',[54] and all possible comparisons would have been made. 'People sometimes ask why, at the end of time, there will be a universal judgement,' says Père Collet: the answer is obvious when you look around in a society where, to preserve the hunting pleasures of seigneurs, a peasant can be sent to the galleys for killing a rabbit. In the face of such horrors, God feels obliged to demonstrate before all the nations that the mighty have been brought low.[55] And the cruelties and injustices of the world had been turned against the Son of God himself during his earthly sojourn; the Great Assize would serve as a vast ceremony of reparation for insults which had constituted a crime of cosmic proportions.

This, we must remember, was an age when rewards and punishments were dealt out with a maximum of colourful or macabre ceremony, an age which was incapable of conceiving of majesty without due outward splendour, and of hierarchy without manifest patterns of deference. And finally, for the most insensitive of the Christian apologists, there was the argument that the elect needed an opportunity to exult in their superiority and in their new-found glory, and that the punishment of the wicked would not be complete until the tremendous spectacle of the joys they had lost reduced them to hopeless and envious despair.[56] The trouble was, of course, that every device for increasing the misery of the damned was equally effective in cheapening the bliss of the righteous.

What then of the joys of Heaven which some had won and some had lost for ever? The biblical language about pearly gates, streets of gold, and foundations of jasper and sapphire was generally agreed to be metaphorical, an aid to the 'weakness' of our imagination.[57] Bergier was prepared to go so far as to guess at the geographical location of heaven—probably in the endless spaces beyond the furthest stars—but with his usual reticence he abjured picturesque details: the final end of the righteous consisted of union with God and with all those who loved him, a union in which our own individuality and all individual affections will be preserved.[58] By contrast, the lay apologist Caraccioli was lyrical in his precision and saw Heaven as situated on planets scattered throughout the universe, with the redeemed, resplendent in their spiritual bodies, sweeping at will between them with the stars as their landmarks.[59] Other speculations about Heaven concerned the nature of its social organization. It could be assumed that distinctions of worldly rank had vanished; true, Bossuet had given the kings of France (provided they qualified for salvation) thrones to sit on, but this, maybe, was just loyal rhetoric. Contemporaneously, the Jesuit Père Rapin was declaring that there would be 'hardly any' distinction among the elect, who would be uniformly clothed in light, as the angels are—'hardly any' made allowance for the saints to enjoy some pre-eminence.[60] Bridaine the mission preacher, on the other hand, expected to find a hierarchy of degrees of sanctity, but without any feelings of envy.[61] Bergier's insistence on the preservation of individual affections was important: in God's other kingdom earthly loves and friendships will be renewed. This was generally assumed, though not always stated; indeed, in 1700 Nicole spoke of man as created 'to live in an eternal solitude with God alone', and came to the verge of describing human relationships as expendable raw material with which we can work out our salvation.[62] Yet his argument is not so austere as it may seem, for if all are united to God, through him they must be united to each other. Nicole was mainly concerned to eliminate the sentimentality with which we surround our earth-bound affections, and to show them continuing only as seen through the pure illumination of the divine centre— and, in any case, he spoke with Jansenist austerity. By contrast, his contemporary Bossuet urged his hearers not to grieve for the dead as if they were separated for ever, 'rather let us strive to render ourselves worthy to rejoin them'. The great proof text for this consoling doctrine was of course, St. Paul's picture (I Thess. 4: 17–18) of the redeemed 'caught up together in the clouds'—'comfort one another with these words'.[63] Even so, except when it was a question of pastoral care for individual grief, it was more usual to concentrate on the concept of the Church in general than on the continuance of the narrower alliances which we form on earth, with their inevitable exclusive undertones—that is, until Rousseau intervened to bring his peculiar intensity of personal feeling into imaginings about the future life.

United to God and to those they had loved (assuming that all had made a Christian end), what would the redeemed actually *do* in Heaven? It was difficult to give a convincing answer—a place of unearthly bliss is presumably beyond description. All the senses will be satisfied, Père Rapin had said, 'selon leur intégrité', and he went on to describe how universal chastity would reign. One did not need to be a Muslim to wonder how much enjoyment was left in the 'integrity' of the senses. Caraccioli absurdly cites the feeling of release and comfort which we experience after sleep or a hot bath as an indication of the delights of living in a spiritual body.[64] The theologians thought of Heaven as static; thus they were deprived of the idea of the progressive achievement of new degrees of acquired perfection building up through eternity which had attracted Leibniz and which informed the speculations of M. Bonnet of Geneva.[65] In fact, the religious writers of eighteenth-century France, who were so eloquent about the horrors of Hell, had little specific comment to make about the joys of Heaven. Dom Calmet, with much to say about the scenario of judgement and of the infernal regions, could find only three lines of commentary for the heading 'Vie éternelle'. Was Catholicism then essentially a religion of fear? We should beware of the inference. There is a great deal in the spiritual writers about drawing near to Christ and seeking union with God, and this concerned Heaven without mentioning it. Punishment ought to be precisely definable, while the scope of supernatural gifts would eternally expand as the soul became more aware of the mysterious depths of the personality of the Giver. Perfect bliss is a subject which does not lend itself to literary eloquence. 'On ne s'intéresse guère à des êtres parfaitement heureux,' said Chateaubriand.[66]

The converse was also the case. There was a great deal of interest, of a macabre or homiletic kind, in the fate of beings who are totally unhappy. According to Dom Calmet,[67] the rabbis had had seven hells, which the Christians had economically reduced to four—Purgatory, Limbo (for unbaptized children), the Bosom of Abraham (where the Patriarchs had awaited the coming of Christ to release them—a place which, maybe, was identical with Limbo), and Hell proper for the vast multitude of the damned. Not much was said about Limbo and Abraham's Bosom. There were no terrifying volcanic landscapes to attract the haunted imagination in these islands of repose, and they were reserved for special categories of souls which, by definition, were not available to listen to the exhortations of preachers and theologians. The arrival of Christ in the shades to beatify the just of the Old Testament was, however, a moving theme which attracted the attention of the abbé de La Baume in his prose epic, *La Christiade* (1753). Christ asks for Adam; Abraham reports that he is alone and silent, brooding over the enormity of his transgression. 'Adam, où êtes-vous?' It is the the same divine voice that was heard in Eden, but this time there is no condemnation. Four thousand years of penitence are over.[68]

Theologians proper had no interest in these literary inventions. For them and for their readers, only one hell was practically relevant, the Hell of the damned. To a degree which is almost incomprehensible today, hell fire was a prominent ingredient in Christian apologetics, spiritual writings, and sermons. Its lurid terrors had their parallel in the savage penal code of the law courts; these horrors, in this world and the next, were assumed to be necessary to compel men to be moral. In the eighteenth century, death was an everyday occurrence; its shadow at once bred familiarity in the hearers of sermons and encouraged those who preached them to terroristic emphasis. In evangelistic missions, which took place in some parishes at roughly decennial intervals, the central theme was, usually, death and the last things. The thunderous Bridaine, the greatest of the missioners, whose voice could be heard streets away from the church and whose surplice sleeves dripped with sweat as he preached, made death his speciality and 'Eternity' his watchword. In 1736 he laid down a programme for a 'retreat' for women lasting four days; day one was on death, day two on judgement, day three on Hell, leaving only a quarter of the time for salvation and other cheerful things.[69] One of the mission canticles of Père Badou (who died in 1727) was an apostrophe to the damned asking them to give an account of their torments—

> Racontez-nous, impudiques,
> Les douleurs que vous sentez,
> Pour vos amours frénétiques,
> Et vos sales voluptés.

133

With a chorus

> Dites-nous, dites-nous
> Quels tourments endurez-vous?[70]

It was especially appropriate in missions to invoke the sanctions of
the afterlife for sins of pride and luxury which human laws did not
punish and—as the canticle suggests—for sins done in secret, more
especially those of a sexual kind. When denouncing lascivious
winks, signs and kisses, and the 'dernières libertés' before marriage,
Bridaine[71] does not fail to remind his hearers of the Hell awaiting
them: it was an axiom among moralists that only supernatural
terrors would avail to cool the hot blood of youth. But in
fashionable churches as in parish missions, innumerable sermons
invoked death. It was the great argument against the preacher's
most insidious foe, delay. We think ourselves secure for today, for
this week, maybe for this year, 'and so we build for ourselves a sort
of eternity.'[72] 'La conversion commence par la frayeur,' said a
handbook of the pulpit published in 1712.[73] No doubt this invocation of fear was an appeal to a sub-Christian motivation. But it
gave to the clergy the opportunity, in a harsh hierarchical society,
indifferent to poverty and organized for the benefit of a tiny
minority, to proclaim the Christian ideal of equality at the one
point where it became indisputably effective. The power of even the
most despotic kings was humiliated: 'what proportion can there be
between a reign of a few days and the immensity of eternity?'[74] All
human pride became futile. 'Quel droit avez-vous à tirer vanité des
dons de Dieu?', asked Père Élisée in the mid-century; 'Y a-t-il
encore des cendres de qualité?'[75] Bossuet had asked. The religion of
fear was also the religion of frankness. When the justice of man was
silent it was possible to speak in the name of the justice of God.

When Père Badou's lechers told the singers of canticles what
torments they suffered, they might also be expected to provide
clues about their topographical location. The centre of the earth was
no longer the stock answer. The expert on infernal geography in the
early part of the century, the Englishman Swinden (translated into
French in 1728), calculated that the accumulation of successive
generations had already outrun the sub-terrestrial storage space,
and that insufficient air could penetrate to the core of the globe to

keep the furnaces hot enough for reasonable efficiency. The sun seemed more appropriate, both in size and temperature, to provide an adequate Hell for the foreseeable future.[76] Wherever it was, what was it like? 'An ocean of fire in the midst of eternal night'[77] was the standard formula. Worms and serpents also figured in Dom Calmet's picture, but the sounder commentators were sceptical about them. Was the fire a real fire, as St. Augustine had maintained, or an allegorized one, as Origen had thought? Probably it was real: 'il n'y a aucune raison de penser que ce n'est pas un feu matériel', said Bergier.[78] Were there devils in charge? Writers of Christian epics, who knew their Milton without sharing in his inspiration, found the possibility too interesting to miss. La Baume mentions Belial, Moloch, and Belzebub, with Satan their over-lord—huge, deformed, with lopsided wings because Michael had clipped them. Another epic writer, Boesnier, identifies the false Gods of the New World with the Miltonic demons.[79] But judicious theologians were not enthusiastic about the hierarchy of the in-fernal court and the structure of power in the realm of eternal torment. A Devil there must be, but they did not wish to elevate his status by giving him subordinates and constitutional authority.[80]

It was not difficult to picture a suitably lurid Hell, but there were technical difficulties in making it work efficiently. Obviously, the damned would bitterly reflect upon their loss of eternal happiness: this was the meaning which Bergier found for 'the worm that dieth not'—it was mental torture, the gnawing of regret.[81] But, given that it was material fire, the working of the fiery torment was less easy to understand. If the wicked had no bodies, how could the flames inflict pain? If they had bodies, would they not rapidly consume and vanish? According to one school of unedifying speculation, God provided a body for the damned to suffer in and kept it renewed; or, maybe, the flames had the peculiar quality of burning without destroying. According to another school of ex-planation, no body was required, since 'a sensation of burning' could be divinely created without it, just as an amputated limb can cause pain by the illusion of its presence. Cartesian principles were invoked to give the argument a scientific flavour; the adventures of the body were just 'the occasional cause' of the feelings of the soul, and God can add to these occasional causes as he sees fit, directly as it were, without being obliged to resort to corporeal afflictions.[82] The theologians hardly seemed to notice how their explanations affected their concept of God: for them, God had not only abandoned the souls who had rejected him, but he was also actively engaged throughout eternity in keeping the system of torment working, in crushing the wicked 'without ever annihilating them', in ensuring that sinners were continually 'reborn for suffering'.[83]

God's sinister activities were not limited to technological details: he also had a grim psychological role to play. The great Judgement would necessarily, in many a case, separate king from subject, master from servant, confessor from penitent, pastor from flock, friend from friend, husband from wife, parent from child. Could those who were saved be happy in the knowledge that those they had loved were lost? Bridaine's thunderous sermons exult in this separation, in the 'implacable hatred' which replaces the old worldly affections: 'O l'étrange séparation! et qui des hommes pourrait le comprendre?'[84] Père Griffet describes how even the greatest saints will not be allowed to help their friends—God will expunge from their minds all feelings of regret: 'Dieu ne permettra pas qu'ils aient pour les réprouvés le moindre sentiment de compassion!'[85] As for the damned, some of them will now try to repent. This was not a theme the theologians relished (possibly, they considered that no repentance amidst the horrors of Hell could possibly be sincere[86]), but it figured luridly in popular preaching. Bridaine turns the screw of spiritual terrorism to its final degree, describing how Christ will refuse to listen, how 'anathemas and maledictions' will issue from his mouth, and how the Blessed Virgin herself will appear 'like a bear deprived of her whelps breathing blood and eternal death'.[87] In Bridaine we find too—what is rare in the eighteenth century—a description of how the saints enjoy heightened pleasure in Heaven from watching the sufferings down below. Occasionally, it is possible to find also the grim old picture of the God who adds to the torments of the damned by showing himself more splendidly to them than to the elect—this theme is found in Massillon.[88] A lay apologist for Christianity, publishing in 1768, used this concept in its more nauseating form. 'The God they have lost' will show himself in Hell in all his splendour to excite the miserable castaways to 'the sharpest movements of a violent and jealous love'; their hearts will race up to him 'like an arrow from a powerful bow', but will be repulsed and thrown back into impotent rage and blasphemy.[89]

The stolid battalions of the theologians and the irresponsible cavalry of hell-fire preachers and menacing apologists who skirmished on their flanks were, they believed, defining and elaborating on the picture of God's workings as found in the Scriptures. The abbé Bergier cited Matthew 25:46 as establishing eternal punishment as 'a dogma no Christian can change'—those who failed to succour the sick, the hungry, and the stranger 'shall go into everlasting punishment, but the righteous into life eternal'.[90] Less sophisticated commentators cited the lake of fire and brimstone in Revelation 20:10. Dom Sinsart, a specialist on eschatological themes, drew attention to the assumptions concerning the future life which underlay Christ's teaching, more significant, perhaps, than direct statements—the fate of Sodom and Gomorrah was to be preferred to the doom hanging over Capernaum, and it had been better for Judas if he had not been born; something worse than mere annihilation awaits the wicked. The tacking-together of texts about Hell inevitably led to inferences about the nature of God, and Dom Sinsart did not shrink from the furthest logical extreme. In the Old Testament, God is described as visiting his people with pestilence and punishing David by killing his child. We shudder at such ruthless justice, for the Creator has implanted in us the emotion of sympathy, which is aroused at the sight of suffering. But this is but 'une vertu de tempérament'; it is not present in God, in whom inviolable equity rules.[91] We have been warned. Those who scorn the obvious means to happiness deserve to be unhappy 'for ever: this plan is in conformity with reason and with the majesty of God'.[92] Père Claude Judde, a Jesuit writer on the spiritual life, contrives to make this grim theme of a divine justice operating independently of the human virtue of sympathy even more repellent, by personalizing God's reactions to the sinner; you refused to accept any suffering in his service, and so he does not love you enough to watch over you with particular care; when temptation comes, you will lack grace and fall away into condemnation. Do not take comfort from the parable of the Prodigal Son—if he had come back three times or more, would he have received the same reception? 'Grand sujet d'en douter.' You spurn God and he will spurn you. 'In a word, Gods treats us as we treat him.'[93] But what of the Second Person of the Trinity, our advocate, the intercessor for sinners? Even his intervention in the judgement could be used to obscure God's love—'measuring his vengeance on the grand scale of his gifts', said a *curé* in an Advent sermon; adulterers will face the Son of the Virgin, debauchees the ascetic who fasted in the wilderness, men of angry words the lonely victim who stayed silent before Pilate.[94] Judde and *curé* Chevassu drag God down to our level; a contemporary lay apologist went to the opposite extreme and defended the divine justice by talking of its olympian, indifferent superiority—is the potter unjust if he throws away the clay?[95] In another writer, the concept of justice, all too appropriately described by the Old Testament term of 'vengeance', was carried to the point where God seemed to be under a constraint which operated against his own nature. Gros de Besplas,[96] giving a grim warning to the 'esprits forts', threatens them with 'these burning abysses, into which his inflexible vengeance will oblige him to let you fall'—*le forcera*; there is a sense in which, confronted by the obligations of justice, God is not free.

The theologians thought they were conserving God's majesty by emphasizing the inflexibility of his justice. If sin is considered merely as an occurrence in finite time, it will not seem worthy of eternal punishment, but if it is considered *sub specie aeternitatis*, as contempt and defiance of God, it gains a cosmic significance. A slave who stabs his king, says the bishop of Boulogne, must not expect to escape with a painless execution. Hell has no torment sufficient to avenge the blood of a God, says Père Griffet;[97] we do not know, says Bergier with more nicely measured language, what punishment is appropriate for an affront to infinite justice and mercy.[98] Judde refines the argument still more by introducing the concept of holiness. God's severity to the sinner is proportionate to his abhorrence of sin; to perfect holiness, every act of disobedience is an affront of infinite proportions.[99] Perhaps the theologians were also preserving God's majesty by emphasizing his final and total immunity from suffering; as it were, by imposing the utmost and irretrievable suffering on the damned he was showing himself totally free from all shadow of the consequences of man's disobedience. In a literary epic the crude assumptions behind a theological position may be incautiously revealed; in his *Christiade*, the abbé de la Baume depicts the Father as silent, emotionless, and inexorable, watching the torments of his Son nailed to the cross.[100] If he was impassive then, he would not be likely to be moved by the fate of the wicked in Hell. When we have a study of 'le Christ des lumières',[101] we may find that the theme of the impassivity of God is closely bound up with the grim old theology of judgement. If it is possible to believe in Hell today, it could only be a belief in some realm of silence and futility, where personalities disintegrate because they have turned away from the source of life. But the theologians of the eighteenth century thought they had found in Scripture the fiery Hell of torment, and they were reluctant to accept anything less than unclouded splendour and omnipotence for God. That was why Dom Sinsart insisted: 'the Devil does not command as master: he simply obeys the orders of God', he is 'the executor of divine justice'.[102] In short, God was responsible for the system of eternal torment.

To what extent were French churchmen touched by civilized scepticism about eternal punishment—whether influenced by common sense, the revival of interest in the universalist theories of Origen dating from Huet's *Origeniana* in 1668, by English speculations about limits to the duration and intensity of the pains of the damned, or by the writers of the Enlightenment? The way being narrow and the gate strait, few were assumed to gain entry to eternal life. The abbé Nonotte, confuter of Voltaire, saw no difficulty here, the principle being the same, however many go down to destruction—they all have free will, they make their own decisions, and their actions settle the final statistics. The abbé Troya d'Assigny, in a three-volume treatise[103] on 'the small number of the Elect', took the same view; the blood of Christ is available to justify all who believe in him and live Christian lives. The idea that few are saved simply arises from the observed facts of the way people live; it is, as it were, a sociological, not a theological inference. But not everyone was so ruthlessly logical; perhaps a careful examination of special cases could reduce the vast numbers of the legion of the lost. All baptized children who died before the age of reason—a very large number in those days—were safe. According to Aquinas, unbaptized children were lost, though they did not suffer pain; in spite of this ruling, Bergier thought they might still be saved, as the Holy Innocents had been.[104] The Patriarchs of the Old Testament had been granted a special dispensation, Christ going to preach to them after his crucifixion—perhaps the same privilege had been extended to the virtuous pagans? There were sequences in the Gallican liturgies which spoke of Christ, between his death and his resurrection, breaking the gates of Hell and constraining the underworld to release the generations which had been engulfed.[105] True, most theologians lacked enthusiasm for the salvation of those who had never been believers, but they betrayed their unease by trying to find reasons beyond mere ignorance to account for their damnation. Perhaps the apparently self-sacrificing conduct of the sages of antiquity had been inspired solely by secret, overweening pride?— this was the argument which Voltaire found so contemptible. As for those who have lived after Christ, they have not made enough effort to discover the truth. Perhaps in the case of the Jews, notoriously impervious to the Gospel, their unwillingness to learn may be the result of the inherited curse which has perverted the whole race since the crucifixion (such was the terrifying anti-Semitic argument of Bourdaloue).[106] For others, the fault must lie in their worldliness and idleness. In his *Traité de la joie de l'âme chrétienne* (1779), P. Lombez appeals to the light that lightens every man coming into the world: infidels who sincerely follow this illumination would not rest until they found the Christian secret—geographical distance, apparently, would not hamper them. More realistically he concedes that children may be unable to accept the Gospel because their fathers have conditioned their minds against it, or have driven away the missionaries; but, he says, they are none the less damned—'have children the right to demand back the provinces that their fathers have lost by waging an unjust war?'[107] This was harsh logic of an Old Testament kind, and not all theologians were satisfied with it.[108] From Saint François de Sale's discussion of the fate of Epictetus, there was some authority to hope for a special dispensation for all men everywhere who worshipped the Supreme Being and observed the Natural Law. This civilized argument was anathema to the Jansenists.[109] The great Arnauld censured it in an essay, 'On the necessity of faith in Jesus Christ' (written in 1641 and published in 1701)—a title which was to be taken in its narrowest possible meaning. Reluctantly, Louis Racine, true to his Jansenist origins, defended the hypothesis of the small number of the elect (in a poem of 1724) with no better explanation than the arbitrary will of God: 'I adore a hidden God. I tremble and keep silent.'

By contrast, the doctrine of the salvation of virtuous pagans was proclaimed by Jesuit writers (P. Sirmond in the seventeenth century and P. P. Ségaud and La Marche in the 1750s and 1760s), and by theologians in the Jesuit camp, like Fénelon. Though the *philosophes* could always goad the orthodox into foolishly intolerant outbursts by welcoming pagans into heaven (the Sorbonne so reacted against Marmontel's *Bélisaire* in 1767, giving anticlericalism one of its most important psychological victories), there was no gainsaying the abbé Bergier's point: 'l'Église ne l'a point décidé'— there was no authoritative doctrinal ruling, and no necessity to damn the sages of antiquity. At least five reputable theologians (the abbé Baudraud was the most significant) defended their case in the 1770s; they were not sure how God's salvation would operate, whether by miraculous revelations or manœuvres of judicial accountancy, but they were sure that all who were damned would have only themselves to blame. Para du Phanjas, greatly daring, not only suggested that virtuous pagans were saved, but also all baptized heretics who were alienated from the Church by invincible ignorance; taking these two categories as saved and adding all young children, and also counting in (a dubious device to swell the statistics) the multitude of the angels, he concluded that the redeemed would finish up as a majority.

Another device to make Hell respectable was to suggest gradations of punishment. No one, it might be argued, was ever entirely wicked; what reward then did the damned receive for their—admittedly few—good actions? One answer was that they were given their reward in this life (here also was a convenient solace for the just who resented seeing the wicked flourishing like a green bay tree).[110] But a much more generally accepted idea was that of gradations of torment in Hell itself. According to the famous *Pensez-y bien*, the fire had a selective quality, it was 'un feu sage et raisonnable'; it would burn sensualists and voluptuaries more severely, and make a concentrated attack on the tongues of blasphemers. Père Judde has punishments meted out in proportion to the gravity and frequency of sins and to the status of the sinner—Judas, priests, and monks will be singled out for extra severities. A man's crimes, with suitable adjustments for his opportunities and the grace made available to him, said Dom Sinsart, would define his precise and unique fate: probably no two places in Hell would be alike. [111] In logic, the same might be expected to apply to heaven— there are 'many mansions' in the Father's house; the promise of 'a hundredfold' reward to the disciples suggests 'une récompense spéciale et particulière'. [112] Lawyers, in their utilitarian way, insisted on punishment being proportionate to the crime, and some of the theologians, forgetting the parable of the labourers in the vineyard and the Christian idea of God's uncovenanted and uncalculating generosity, found a way of rationalizing the penal structure of eternity. 'On ne recueille dans l'éternité que ce que l'on a semé dans le temps,' said Dom Morel early in the century. [113] Apart from making nonsense of the doctrine of salvation, this made the Heaven–Hell structure illogical, for there would have been no great gulf between them, and a good deal of 'bunching' of examination candidates around the borderline could have been expected. And as for Hell, if it had graduated zones of torment, was it possible for its denizens to move between them? Nothing they could do of their own volition could avail them, and nothing could ever contrive their escape—granting these two principles, a case might just possibly be made out for the efficacy of the prayers of the living on their behalf. The general view of the theologians (claiming the authority of Aquinas) was that prayer was efficacious only for souls in Purgatory, but towards the end of the century the more generous view of St. Augustine revived. A professor in the seminary at Lyon (M. Emery, later to become the great reforming head of Saint-Sulpice at Paris) wrote, though he did not publish, an essay, 'De la mitigation de la peine des damnés', arguing that, while the damned suffer eternally, the intercessions of the just may avail to render their torments less harrowing. [114] The same theme was expounded powerfully by Mgr de Pressy, bishop of Boulogne, in a pastoral letter of 1776, the third in a series reconciling faith and reason. In confidence, he told his clergy, Hell is not quite as bad as preachers make out—this secret could be revealed to believers who suffered from excessive fears and to opponents of religion who blasphemed against God's system of justice. The damned have 'pleasure' of a kind—indeed, this is why their sufferings are eternal, since they can never stop desiring the things which hurt them. Very probably, the 'fire' and the 'worm' are just metaphors; for some of the damned, there may be no actual pain involved at all, but simply the obsessive realization of eternal futility. The torments of Hell do not prevent some sort of independent living—the devils can muster the leisure and concentration to tempt us, and Dives could think of his five brethren. God punishes us less than we deserve, and in ways which even the objects of his wrath are obliged to recognize as just; grim as their fate is, the denizens of Hell would probably prefer to go on there rather than be granted the annihilation which English liberal theologians assume is so merciful. The specific statement— it were better for Judas if he had 'never been born'—presumably implies the existence of others in Hell who are marginally better off than the non-existent. In all logic, there must be hierarchies of punishment; there are 'many mansions' in Heaven and—no doubt—various departments in Hell (a convenient supposition for dealing with virtuous pagans without having to open the gates of Paradise to them). Nor does 'eternal' punishment necessarily imply a single unchanging level of doom—a war can have its truces, a perpetual flame can burn low (just as in Heaven the four Beasts who worship the Ancient of Days 'day and night' must be assumed to have rest periods). Therefore, following St. Augustine and the Greek Church, we may reasonably expect the prayers of the living to be efficacious, not only for souls in Purgatory, but also for those in Hell itself: the damned may be promoted to less rigorous departments, or may be allowed periods of intermission.[115]

Once the efficacy of prayer for the damned is recognized, the whole structure of eternal torment begins to totter. The inference is: God never abandons anyone, and earthly affections go on, collaborating with him in seeking to redeem the lost; perhaps, even, there is a human solidarity in judgement, something almost forgotten by the exponents of individual striving for salvation, who confined it to the destiny of souls in Purgatory. True, M. Emery and the bishop of Boulogne were not typical. The theologians continued to rehearse the old *clichés* about eternal punishment, sometimes maybe reinforcing them in defiance of the attacks of *philosophes* and *libertins*. But times were changing, and the volcanic scenario of the underworld was becoming gravely suspect. Fables about devils and their incursions into the affairs of mortals and visions of Hell by medieval saints were rejected, on the principle of the abbé Lenglet-Dufresnoy's treatise on apparitions (1752): miraculous events specifically described in Scripture can be accepted, but all others are suspect.[116] Preachers were becoming less inclined to dwell literally on the macabre traditional horrors. The abbé Poulle defined eternal punishment as simply being left alone in sin.[117] (A *curé*, who was inclined to agree, ruefully reflected that some of his flock would never come near the confessional if they thought Hell was nothing worse than the deprivation of the vision of God.)[118] Writing during the Revolution, Père Grou, a severe Jesuit who was clumsily literal in some of his pictures of the afterlife (he depicts graduated rewards, with those in the lowest 'mansions' of Heaven bitterly regretting 'the lack of diligence' which has consigned them to such 'a small degree of glory'), nevertheless agreed with Poulle in abandoning the imagery of devils and conflagration. 'Heaven is the abode of love, as Hell is the place where there is no love; this is the most exact notion we can form of these two states.'[119] Those set-piece sermons of specialist evangelists or monks preaching at parochial missions or the 'stations' of Lent and Advent are not typical of the run-of-the-mill preaching of country *curés*. According to one bishop, it was impossible for him to preach menacing sermons, as his office tied him indissolubly to his people, and his salvation was dependent on theirs.[120] Even without these elevated sentiments, parish priests, in daily and often friendly relations with their people, may have acted as he did in practice. Certainly they did not approve of sombre Capuchins intruding into their parishes breathing doctrines of vengeance,[121] and the desire to frighten the ladies on Advent Sunday would be offset by the fear of ridicule from the better educated parishioners.[122] Towards the end of the century, said one observer, it became impossible to pile up declamations about judgement, for the fashion had turned against them.[123] Indeed, as early as 1738 a canon of Reims was complaining that the incontrovertible doctrine of the eternity of punishment was being neglected in the pulpit—'a subject neglected today by many preachers, who seek rather to sparkle, to please'.[124] It was a question of ridicule, but, more importantly, a question of the meaning of the idea of a God of love. 'Conversion begins with fear'—a history of the progress of Christian thought in the eighteenth century could be written around the theme of the abandonment of this harsh un-Christian maxim.

No doubt most people imagined themselves as likely to qualify, after death, for something less than the extreme penalty. Hell was for the others, so whatever pressure there was for humanitarian reform in the eschatological sphere was concentrated on Purgatory. Here, the abbé Gaudron incautiously conceded (contradicting the preachers' eloquence about the small number of the elect), would congregate all the 'fidèles lâches et négligens'.[125] The whole comfortable idea was anathema to Protestants, of course. The French Calvinists,[126] like the Catholics, regarded the wicked as bound for Hell immediately they died, and the saints as entering directly into heaven. In prayers for individuals and in letters of consolation to the bereaved, they tended to enlarge the category of the blessed: he has entered the heavenly Jerusalem, 'il est arrivé à sa patrie par un plus court chemin'. But according to the considered theological view, the majority of the faithful would sleep in their graves until on Judgement Day the Spirit of God would breathe life into their bones, and the voice of Christ would order Death to release its grip and the bonds of corruption to fall away. Jansenists could not reject the doctrine of Purgatory, but they followed the Protestant controversialists in their criticisms of it: God was not to be 'bought off' easily. Under the pressure of such criticism, and in the interests of morality, the clergy of France were anxious to get rid of the superstitions and facile hopes which were associated with the idea of a treasury of merits. Collet, the good monk who lists all opportunities for indulgences with uncritical fervour, was also making careful qualifications: confession, true contrition, and the performance of penance are all necessary; the duration of time in Purgatory may be adjusted, but God still regulates as he wills the intensity of pains—indeed, we do well to desire a longer time of expiation if this is needed to increase our supply of Grace.[127] If the rules were being tightened up, however, the décor of Purgatory was becoming less lurid. While the theologians were, mostly, keeping Hell as hot as ever, by common consent the temperature of Purgatory was declining. In Provence,[128] artists working for churches and confraternities had dropped out devils long ago, and were now allowing the fire to burn low. Grimaces of pain were being replaced by the dawning signs of the euphoria of deliverance; in 1787 began the new fashion of grey neoclassical pilasters and urns as a setting for skulls and angels—the macabre faded into conventional symbols. Religious art, said a canon in 1788, rejoicing at the destruction of one of the old frescoes of judgement, should express 'pity or devotion to the Mother of God', and never sheer horror. Diderot, who did not mind if Christianity made itself ridiculous in the cause of art and strong emotion, regretted the decline of lurid imagery, and objected to a picture, *The Passing of Souls from Purgatory to Heaven*, in the Salon of 1761 because it had no gulf of fire, no crowds of men and women ravaged by every passion and intensity of feeling. The sort of picture he wanted, he said, would spring from the brain of an artist who shuddered at his own imaginings, who would wander sleepless and barefooted at night through the deserted house, casting his sketches on to paper by the pale glow of his night lamp.[129]

On reading Diderot's observations, one wonders if, maybe, Hell was not so much an article of religious faith imposed on the credulous by the theologians (as the *philosophes* were inclined to say) but rather a popular institution with majority support—a majority composed of divergent elements, of course: sadists and masochists,[130] the self-righteous and the self-humiliating, men of the establishment who feared popular envy, and the disinherited poor who had nothing to look forward to in his life, monastic celibates who subconsciously felt thay had given up too much, facile publicists who relished their opportunities for sombre eloquence, preachers making a name for themselves, apologists brought to bay who defiantly asserted their marginal doctrines, would-be reformers who saw no possible hope of the advent of social justice, lovers of curiosities and speculations on the margins of the known universe, those who enjoyed the thrill of strong and vicarious emotions, artists and publicists who liked to have humdrum reality embroidered in vivid colours. Like the Ottoman and Habsburg powers in the nineteenth century, Hell was an empire with nothing to recommend it except that there were so many people interested in its survival.

6

The Afterlife: Doubts and Reconsiderations

I

The French theologians of the eighteenth century had inherited and
were engaged in refining a Platonic doctrine of the soul, as against
an Aristotelian one. They did not think of the soul as the 'form' of
the body, they did not take seriously the part played by the vicissitudes of the body in the formation of the personality, and they had
no insight into the process by which individuality grows and defines
itself; individuality, to them, was an initial gift which undergoes
modifications. They thought of the soul as a substance, albeit
spiritual and ethereal. There was, implanted in the body, an immaterial, substantial self, which could well have existed long before
and which certainly carried on for ever after the body had dis-
appeared. Christian thinkers today could not possibly accept this
idea of a ready-made self inhabiting a body; whether working from
philosophical or psychological insights or from interpretations of
the Bible, they would regard man as a psychosomatic unity, however mysterious. To some modern theologians, the uncompromising statement of this unity would involve the acceptance of the total
reality of death—the abandonment of the serene philosophic expectation of the survival of the immortal soul, and its replacement
by the strictly biblical, Jewish, and primitive Christian hope of the
resurrection of the dead. In any case, the soul would certainly not
be regarded as starting off as a self in miniature, ready to grow and
to be tested by moral choices. It would, rather, be a potentiality for
selfhood, which could be achieved—as a distinguished recent writer
has put it—by bringing the dimensions of past, present, and future
into an ever-tightening unity, by the acceptance of the past and by
commitment for the future.[1]

The eighteenth century was on the verge of scientific investigations of both body and mind which were to yield a rich new
harvest, but the ghostlike Platonic soul of the Christian apologists

148

could not be enriched or diversified by new discoveries, nor could it play any part in new hypotheses. It did, however, in its time have advantages corresponding to its disadvantages, for while it could not be incorporated or enriched by new systems of thought, it also could not be contradicted by them. It was in the powerful defensive position, from the point of view of abstract logic, of being irrelevant.

The soul, as described by the theologians, non-material, purely spiritual, individually created by God for implantation in the foetus at a certain stage of its development in the womb, was a spare, smooth concept which did not lend itself to hostile grapplings by scientists or sceptics. Things would have been different if St. Augustine's dictum, 'Deus creavit omnia simul', had been developed into a doctrine of pre-existence; in this way, the soul would have become entangled with all the difficulties of the Preformationists[2]—the choice between Adam and Eve as the vehicle encapsulating all future generations, the problem of the status of the multitudinous 'animalcules' of the Adamic hypothesis which were wasted in the process of conception, the problem of the 'monsters' which God must be supposed to have planned from the very beginning of creation. In the case of the Siamese twins of Vitry (1706) and the monstrous sheep of 1733, the scientists of the Preformationist school were prepared to vaunt God's ingenuity at the expense of his wisdom; the theologians had, at least, rescued the soul from this perverse sort of praise. The theory of spontaneous generation, which in the course of the century came to dominate biological thinking, did for the body very much what the theologians had already done for the soul—gave it a clearer and a cleaner start. True, atheists liked epigenesis because no divine intervention in the natural process was postulated, but the problem of the birth of monsters illustrates how it was not always to the advantage of religious apologists to insist on God's direct involvement. Buffon's theory of spontaneous generation by an interior moulding force was at once self-consciously independent of the ideas of the theologians and parallel to them. The immaterial and immortal substance in man is admitted to exist, but is thenceforward dismissed from the discussion; all we can know about it must come from the study of the mind—'il nous est impossible d'apercevoir notre âme que par la pensée'.[3] On the other hand, the idea of an original *moule* dating from Creation, which makes each organ shape and use molecules to reproduce itself under the direction of an over-all *moule* for the whole body, a process working 'sympathetically' like gravitation and chemical affinity, is—almost—a soul-making machinery built into the fabric of the universe. The mind of Adam is not a Lockean *tabula rasa*; there is, rather, in the first man, an inner sense, a *moule* enabling him to think creatively, to become aware of himself and his unique identity, and experience all the tensions of moral decisions. 'An imperfect Lockean and a grudging Cartesian, Buffon had arrived, by the route of his own theories, at an affirmation of the dual nature of man, a product both of eternal *moule* and of contingent environmental pressures, that was roughly comparable with the soul–body dualism of the theologians.'[4]

Since the soul was non-material, the investigations of the anatomist could not disprove its existence or describe its destiny. Yet, indirectly, there was always some danger to the theologians along the frontiers of medical speculation. It was a Galenic principle, almost universally accepted, that the emotions had their effects on the state of the body; even Descartes with his dualism had not denied the proposition. What if the mysterious channels of this influence could be used to create a counter-effect by the discovery of drugs to affect the body and through it to influence the mind? This quest of Jerome Gaub,[5] of Heidelberg, set out in his *De regimine mentis* (1747), was taken up pugnaciously by Antoine Le Camus in 1753; he proposed cures for 'defects of the understanding and of the will' by medical treatments for the body; these would replace the 'advice, precepts, education, and lessons' which had so often proved ineffective in the past.[6] It was a proposal to minimize the importance of the work of the clergy, both intellectual and pastoral, and to elevate the status of the medical profession. To the iatromechanists of the school of Descartes as modified by Boerhaave, the body operated by reason of its mechanical properties; the various secretions of glands, for example, were produced because of the differing sizes of tubes and pores, the differing elasticity of fibres, viscosity of fluids, and alteration of hydraulic pressures. This autonomous model of the body's working posed no threat to the soul, but, as the abbé Pernetti in an essay of 1746 on the relation of character to facial appearance urged, it reduced to unimportance those who theorized about the soul's properties—let their 'presumption' yield place to the anatomists who at least study something tangible, that is, the soul's operations on the body.[7] In the early eighteenth century the mechanical view lost favour among the medical experts, being replaced by Stahl's 'animism'—the theory of an indwelling 'soul' directing the body purposefully, sending secretions to their appropriate places: saliva to the mouth, the gastric juices to the stomach. There were insoluble problems as to the relationship of this 'soul' which directed the routine bodily functions to the rational, spiritual soul of the theologians. These problems faded as fashionable medical speculation took a new turn about the middle of the century, with Bordeu's publication on the glands (1752), a work which turned the Montpellier Faculty to 'vitalism'.[8] The 'être spirituel' within the brain did not have to descend from rational and moral reflections to run the digestive processes—the routine bodily functions were inspired and controlled by the 'sensibility' of the nervous fibres. The monarchical constitution of animism gave place to the federal constitution of vitalism, with heart and stomach and brain being quasi-independent centres of life. Haller was to replace the concept of 'sensibility' or 'sensitivity' with that of 'irritability', so that purposive as well as routine activities of the body became explicable, at least in part, as reactions to external stimuli. La Mettrie was to go the whole way and assume that the accumulation of knowledge about the complexities of the body pointed to a circular explanation of its workings which excluded any reference to non-material entities. Even so, once the existence of the soul was granted (as it usually was), its immateriality preserved it from the challenges of experimental science. As the abbé Joannet pointed out, the most the anatomists could do was to discover the *point d'appui* in the body where the soul makes its contact.[9] The theologians therefore considered the speculations of medical men with complacency.

As distinct from the ideas of classical antiquity, the eighteenth-century anatomists favoured the brain as the general area where the *siège de l'âme* might be found; Descartes had chosen the pineal gland, others the *corps calleux*, others the peripheral membranes where the nerve endings come into this 'grand laboratoire du fluide animal'. The skill of surgeons, however, tended to disprove their own hypotheses; every operation on the brain which left the patient behaving rationally excluded the part removed or damaged as a possible location for the activities of the soul. Perhaps the soul was not dependent on any part of the body, but could choose its own point of intervention to collect and manipulate sensations.[10] One of the most attractive physiological models of the century fitted neatly with this view. The mass of the body, so the theory ran, bones, tissue, organs, could be regarded as an autonomous organization which went on its own way digesting, circulating, and breathing; it was related to the essential man only as the soil is related to the plant growing in it, or as the trellis-work is related to the vine which it supports. The essential man is found in the nervous system, which lies within the body like a tenuous insect with multitudinous arms and branches, and is animated by the soul from some minuscule 'filament nerveux', no bigger than an atom, hidden away in the labyrinth.[11] The naïve, deistic marquis de Culant wrote an epic poem and an 'opinion' of a 'Chinese mandarin' using this medical theory as an explanation of the soul—a 'substance sensible' which contains all the facilities for seeing, hearing, and feeling, which runs along the nerves during life, and draws together at death, immortal and indestructible, by virtue of its inherent centrifugal force.[12]

But all this concerned only the *modus operandi* of the soul, not its essence. Generally, there was no clash between medicine and theology. The anatomists conceded to the theologians the autonomy of their discipline. Most medical men, said the composer of an *éloge* on Boissier de Sauvages, a famous member of the Faculty of Montpellier, recognize 'a principle of vital movements, superior to ordinary mechanism', and do not inquire any further.[13] The great physician Lecat having conceded, in parenthesis, that God contributes to man some pure substance of which he only knows the nature, rushes on to describe in detail his own equally mysterious 'esprit universel', which we breathe in from the air, which goes in the blood to the brain, and is here separated to form 'animal fluid' and the 'fluid of sentiment' for the nervous system.[14] Marat, the future revolutionary, describes the body as 'a machine of the hydraulic type' (again, it is a question of fluids from the brain flowing in the canals of the nerves), but does not venture to guess how the hydraulic movements can become sensations of taste, smell, sound, and colour. 'O ténèbres impénétrables, c'est ici vraiment que la sagesse est confondue.' We must not strive to lift the veil, he concludes—we should be content to adore these mysteries.[15]

Marat abandoned the attempt to understand and worshipped at the point when pressures on the fluids in the nerves were transformed into sensations; he had no formula to bridge the gap between mind and matter. Nor had anyone else. Fontenelle had spoken for both the sceptics and the scientists when he admitted: 'Whatever system you adopt when you try to follow sensations right through to the point when they reach the soul, you find yourself lost in the immense chaos between soul and body.'[16] The theologians therefore were not downcast when they failed to show how soul and body interacted. Descartes had invoked 'occasional causes': the cannon ball does not demolish the wall, but God takes the occasion of its impact to do so. Leibniz relied on God's power of foreknowledge of all vicissitudes of the body to imagine him creating a pre-established harmony. Père de Tournemine, in his *Conjectures sur l'union de l'âme et le corps* (1703), rejected these explanations and spoke, with some show of being more realistic, of the divinely ordained interdependence of soul and body. The soul was not a ghost in a machine; it was genuinely affected by the body's health or sickness—if the humours were out of balance, the soul fell into melancholy; if all physical functions responded smoothly to the will, the soul was filled with pleasure. Yet there was no gainsaying the criticism of the abbé de Belmont; Tournemine gave a better description than the others of what happened, but no better explanation—the union of body and soul remained 'inexplicable'.[17] This became the accepted opinion of the theologians and, indeed, of the deists of the century. However etherealized or subtle we imagine matter to be, we cannot understand how it can act upon the spirit;[18] we will never know how the 'vibration of a fibre' can produce an idea;[19] we must accept, uncomprehendingly, a 'mutual dependence' which is the work of 'the Supreme Arbiter of Nature';[20] God has given us the great book of Nature to read, but he has taken away the preface and the chapter headings which would have provided the explanation.[21]

Though religious apologists were undismayed by their inability to explain the interaction of soul and body, they were disturbed by the implications (or what they thought were the implications, or what *philosophes* suggested were the implications) of the sensationalist epistemology of Locke, which was 'proposition One of the Enlightenment'.[22] Locke had never denied the immateriality or immortality of the soul, but he had incautiously suggested that God might have endowed matter with the power of thinking, and this was taken as a clue towards the interpretation of his general philosophical position—his denial of innate ideas and his empirical theory of knowledge. 'If all our knowledge is but sensations, says the Jansenist Chaumeix, 'it follows that man would have no knowledge if he had no senses, no body. Hence the body, that is to say, matter, is the physical and necessary cause of thought.'[23] Locke reduces all our ideas to the flow of sensations, complains Père Hayer, this makes matter fundamental to the life of the soul.[24] What then happens to the soul's autonomy, and to its overriding obligations to morality? A vicious churchman, the 'abbé T. . .', in d'Argens's pornographic novel, *Thérèse philosophe* (1760), uses a cynical deduction from Locke's doctrine to corrupt young women: 'the soul controls nothing, . . . it acts only as a consequence of the sensations and faculties of the body.'[25] In fact, the danger from Locke was exaggerated. It was well established, from the middle of the century, that these simplified versions of his philosophy were psychologically untenable. As Hume saw, a mind which begins as a *tabula rasa* will never be able to do anything with the ebb and flow of sensations, and Rousseau made the crucial distinction concerning mental operations: to perceive objects is to have sensations, to perceive relationships is to judge.[26]

Even so, the theologians remained watchful. As some of them saw, Locke's followers, to avoid the disintegration of personality which would follow if the soul was regarded as a mere bundle of perceptions, would have to postulate some principle of identity and organization, like the 'simple substance' of Condillac, 'differently modified by the impressions made on the parts of the body'. The key to the nature of this principle would be found in the memory, and Buffon, Voltaire, and d'Holbach were suspiciously anxious to elevate the memory's importance. This was enough for a school of religious apologists (Rousseau agreed with them) to found their epistemology on a *sentiment de l'existence* by which every man is conscious of his continuous selfhood irrespective of the build-up of chains of recollection. The most sophisticated of these writers was the abbé Lelarge de Lignac. 'Le sentiment de l'existence', he wrote, 'est en nous antérieur à toute connoissance, et à tout raisonnement.' That is why Condillac's allegory about bringing a statue to life by endowing it with one sense organ after another is misleading—the feeling of our identity precedes every other sensation, both chronologically and logically.[27] It is the greatest of innate ideas, giving the soul its independence of the Lockean doctrine of sense perception. Without Lelarge de Lignac's subtlety, other theologians followed similar courses, defending Descartes and innate ideas, or enumerating the faculties of the soul so as to have sensations created within it, with material objects providing only the initial stimuli. Their emphasis on defining the soul as 'le moi', the unique principle of individuality, was a standing repudiation of any view which limited its functions to those of a recording tablet, a mere accumulator and classifier of sensations. The abbé Joannet, who took his stand with Socrates, Plato, and Descartes for innate ideas, as against Locke and Condillac, describes in detail the *sens externes* (sight, hearing, etc.) and the *sens internes* (memory, imagination, a sense of beauty and of moral perfection) which are the endowments of the soul, and carries the analysis into an imaginative new field, by insisting on the relations of the soul with the Spirit World, 'more habitual and more essential than relations with the world of matter'. 'Le moi', he says, is provided with other senses than those which put it in touch with the world of material bodies—it has intellectual senses and yearnings, which are necessary to direct its progress in 'le monde des Esprits'.[28] In this way he covered the questions of moral responsibility in this life and immortality in the next—indeed, we are already partly living in the world which is to come.

II

Joannet's zeal to elaborate the faculties of the soul was not unconnected with his other philosophical speciality—his two volumes,

Les Bêtes mieux connues (1770), were an intelligent and sympathetic answer to the famous old question, 'Do animals have souls?'. The theologians, who had cheerfully sailed round the cape of the inexplicable interaction of soul and body, and had weathered the storm of Locke's sensationalist philosophy, at this point on their voyage found all the hazards they had evaded looming up before them again in a series of menacing rocks and shoals. Descartes had said: animals are machines. This ruthless statement had proved acceptable to Jansenists, vivisectionists, fervent Cartesians who did not question the master's *obiter dicta*, Christian apologists who liked to have difficult problems simplified, and citizens who disliked their neighbours' dogs; it was also to prove useful to the atheistical materialists for, as Voltaire remarked, man's supremacy to brute creation might be merely a question of degree, the great clock at Strasbourg being more complex than a roasting spit. All the anecdotes about the intelligence of animals, from Montaigne onwards, went against Descartes's view; Bayle disapproved of the Cartesian hypothesis; so too did Jesuit writers of the end of the seventeenth century, who revived Aristotle's idea of the 'sensitive soul', intermediate between matter and spirit, to provide the animals with a compensatory prize. In 1737, the Cartesian abbé Macy admitted that the theory of animal automatism had lost all credit.[29] By the second half of the eighteenth century, the currents of humanitarian and sentimental feeling evident in changing attitudes to relationships within the family were extended to animals also. In so far as the crude Cartesian view survived, it did so equivocally in the revision of Keranflech, who based his argument on the ambiguity of the word 'soul' and who, one suspects, was using the word 'machine' ambiguously himself.[30]

If Descartes was mistaken, what could be said about the life principle in animals? In a flippant essay of 1739, the Jesuit Bougeant proposed to allow them immortal souls—they were, perhaps, fallen angels. His book was much read, and he was exiled to La Flèche. Other writers, free from the constraint of ecclesiastical discipline and fascinated by the exotic atmosphere of the East, interested themselves in the transmigration of souls which, in its Indian form, included animals in the cycle of transformations on the way to reconciliation with the divine essence.[31] As Montesquieu observed, the doctrine conveniently gets rid of the embarrassing idea of a God who has to be ready to manufacture a suitable soul at the behest of every human pair which chooses to have sexual relations, while Voltaire thought that this 'antique system' was at least 'equitable'. Turgot agreed: transmigration would provide a logical cadre within which suitable rewards and punishments could be awarded and imposed. As a Physiocrat, he liked the idea of a single change in the market mechanism transforming the whole economic order, and here was a single, sweeping contrivance to revolutionize the world to come. His friend, Dupont de Nemours, said he would not object provided he was guaranteed the role of a well-bred dog in his next incarnation.[32] In fact, the *philosophes*' interest in metempsychosis was light-hearted (though Diderot and d'Holbach denounced it as ridiculous altogether). As they well knew, this 'equitable' system could not possibly have a serious moral content, since we must assume that the memory of past existences is erased, and if it is, what personal identity remains to be the subject of rewards and punishments? These exotic speculations were just another of those excursions into comparative religion undertaken chiefly because manifold opportunities turned up in this field for twisting the tails of the clergy (if this metaphor is permissible in the context).

Churchmen could hardly connive at the acceptance of the doctrines of the Brahmins, but some of them were willing to join with other thinkers in conceding to animals something like a soul, provided it was not immortal. The ancient Greeks had discerned in man a rational soul and a sensitive one, the latter described by the abbé Barthélemy as 'une nature lumineuse et subtile, image fidèle de notre corps, sur lequel elle s'est moulée, et dont elle conserve à jamais la ressemblance et les dimensions'.[33] Dom Calmet, rigidly orthodox but always athirst after strange wonders, was tempted to annex this sensitive soul to man along with the rational one—how else but through such an astral body could the angels in Genesis have had intercourse with the daughters of men? and what other explanation can we give of the ghosts and flickering lights which nocturnally haunt our graveyards?[34] The theologians, however, afraid of mechanistic vitalism, would only allow one soul in man, and that purely spiritual. Even so they were sympathetic to attempts to revive Aristotle's sensitive soul to explain acts of will and intelligence in animals. Boullier in 1728 spoke of 'un principe actif qui a des sensations et qui n'a que cela' which operated in brute creation; this was something halfway between Cartesian mechanism and the *âme sensitive*, and was taken over by the *Encyclopédie*.[35] The abbé Joannet in *Les Bêtes mieux connues* got rid of the Cartesian drag on the active principle which he made into 'un principe sensitif et intelligent' to provide animals with 'une âme purement sensitive'. God's creative agent for this purpose is 'an electric fluid', the same force that makes the planets move, seeds grow, and the *fluide nerveux* circulate in the channels of the nerves of the human body.[36] Thus, there is an affinity between men and animals, for although men do not share in the *âme sensitive* of brute creation, their highest bodily operations are inspired by its electric fluid. Para du Phanjas in 1774 was more cautious, and made sharper distinctions. He describes a special substance which God uses to animate brute creation, neither matter nor spirit but intermediate between them, 'une substance immatérielle, douée de sensibilité, privée d'intelligence, incapable de moralité'.[37] The theologians were adopting a civilized attitude to animals, but were treading dangerous ground. Without scriptural or scientific warrant they had invented a new substance to suit their doctrinal presuppositions. There was a non-material soul in man beyond the scope of empirical verification, and there was now a sensitive soul or immaterial substance, capable of feeling but not of morality, in animals—equally incapable of verification. The existence of one unproven entity was being bolstered up by imagining another. Instead of an explanation, they were inventing new entities under the cover of the divine omnipotence.

Perhaps the theologians were also damaging some of their arguments for the immortality of the human soul. This principle of feeling and intelligence in animals, this substance endowed with 'sensibilité' was, presumably, immaterial and indivisible, and in arguing about the human soul, these qualities had been said to prove indestructibility.[38] And what of this 'sensibilité' without morality? The bishop of Boulogne, misanthropically, was concerned with the apparent 'vices' of brute creation—'cats are perfidious and ungrateful. Monkeys are maleficent, dogs are envious'; like mankind, the animal kingdom must have fallen from the state of innocence in which God created it.[39] More seriously, what of the apparent 'virtues' of animals? They have no ability to progress (the spiders' webs on the roof beams of Noah's Ark were the same as those on our barns today),[40] but they can demonstrate loyalty and affection and, undoubtedly, they suffer. They therefore deserve some reward. The beasts feel just the same as we do, said Condillac—they differ from us only because, lacking language to form a protective screen between themselves and things, they cannot shake off dependence on the exterior world. Thus, they are condemned to unrewarded suffering; we must assume, he says with sardonic orthodoxy, that God wills it so. D'Alembert joined Condillac in censuring this arbitrary and unfair exercise of omnipotence, and Bonnet asked why God refused to the animal creation the opportunity to climb up on to the moral plane.[41] In Maupertuis, Buffon, and Diderot the century saw the beginning of the idea of an evolutionary link between man and the animals; the question, 'why are the beasts not allowed to climb?' was bound up with the hypothesis that men had already done so.

Sophisticated debates about the soul are not likely to undermine conventional religion except in so far as they create, illogically, an atmosphere of doubt among those (the majority of the educated minority) who are vaguely aware of the controversies without following the details. The mere discussion of the affinities between men and animals, irrespective of the merits of the case and the nature of the conclusions, was the significant thing; it suggested that man was not unique and that the body could not be shrugged off as irrelevant to the inner personality. Caraccioli, the most simplistic of the apologists (and therefore the most easily alarmed), complained revealingly, in 1761: 'it seems that it is no longer permissible to speak of the soul except to attack it and to confound it with the instinct of the animals.'[42] The magical complexity of the mechanism of the great Strasbourg clock, by being continually compared with the roasting spit, began to look ordinary. Man's lofty spiritual destiny was being forgotten as he was drawn back, by comparisons, into the routine patterns of natural processes and instinctive reactions.

III

The opponents of religion, without necessarily being sincere or having genuine opinions of their own, had various ways of using the affinities between men and animals for sceptical purposes. If animals are machines, men are just more complex variations: 'si c'est là une machine, vous en êtes une autre,' said Diderot.[43] God was unfair in ignoring the sufferings of brute creation; or he was equal-handed in injustice, and men, like the animals they resembled, were but transient creatures; or, since a God who was unjust or indifferent was not worth bothering about, there was no God at all. On all these hypotheses, the soul of man was not immortal. These deductions were part of the pessimistic tradition which rejected the belief in a life after death, a tradition derived from classical antiquity and certain marginal writers of the Renaissance, passed on through the seventeenth-century *libertins*. The central question was that of evidence: there was nothing to prove the existence of a life after death, there was only the inspiration of our wishful thinking—'le désir de toujours être', as Saint-Évremond sadly defined it. Christian apologists who adopted the over-subtle device of annexing the sceptical argument, leaving the earnest inquirer with nothing to cling to but the guarantees of the Church, helped unwittingly to reinforce the *libertin* position.[44] In the early eighteenth century, this sceptical tradition carried on underground, occasionally revealing itself in café conversations recorded by police spies, in crafty asides in the writings of medical men, in manuscripts clandestinely circulated, and at the deathbed of some notorious *esprit fort* who took leave of his friends with ostentatious finality. The standard old arguments as they were revised and adapted by the sceptics of the Regency were powerfully and crudely summed up in the late 1720s or early 1730s in a manuscript compilation, *L'Âme matérielle*: there is no tangible evidence for the existence of the soul and no explanation of how it can affect or be affected by the body; the myth of its immortality arises merely from our wishful thinking; men are closely related to the animals, and the malfunctioning of the body in illness, intoxication, and old age manifestly affects the mind and personality; what we call the soul is, in effect, a sort of fire circulating in the blood, and is destined to extinction when the body dies.[45] About the same time as this clandestine manuscript was becoming known, the *esprits forts* began to talk about the philosophical Testament of Jean Meslier, another surreptitiously circulated manuscript. The character and circumstances of its author gave it an added piquancy. Meslier, for forty years *curé* of Etrépigny in Champagne, exercising there a blameless ministry (excessively young housekeepers apart) had often read the Church's suffrages at the burial of his parishioners, but when he died himself in 1729 he revealed what he had really thought on these occasions, for he left behind him this atheistical testament. For this life, he proclaimed the doctrine of absolute equality, enforced by the weapon of the general strike against the oppressors; for the next, it did not exist. He was going to join the dead, he said, who were no longer concerned with anything, who no longer cared: 'soon, I shall be nothing'. It was the doctrine which was to be proclaimed, notoriously, during the Revolution by another ecclesiastic, when Fouché, the ex-Oratorian, *représentant en mission* at Nevers, ordered the placarding of the gates of cemeteries with the motto, 'Death is an eternal sleep'.

An atheist, so far as the soul was concerned, would have to be a materialist, though there were nuances. In the *Nouvelles Libertés de penser* (1743), Mirabaud got on without a soul altogether. His rule was, not to multiply entities unnecessarily. Man differs from the animals only in so far as his brain is better adapted for reasoning by its greater complexity; he is 'un être qui pense, rien de plus'.[46] This is also what Helvétius said—we can feel and think, there is no need to say more. In d'Holbach too there was virtually no place for any kind of 'soul', which he defines in his notorious *Système de la Nature* (1770) as 'le corps envisagé relativement à quelques-unes de ses fonctions plus cachées que les autres'—it is but the mysterious side of the body's workings.[47] Even so, this lapidary statement cannot head us off from further speculation. In his universe consisting only of matter and movement, uncreated and never-ending, d'Holbach sees a principle of self-conservation operating, which in objects and in beings like ourselves creates a sort of field regulating the movements of matter; this is 'inertia' or 'gravitation sur soi'. This *gravitation sur soi* deserves more examination: it does not fit too easily into the closed system of deterministic patterns which is 'Nature' and all reality.

La Mettrie, by contrast, talked more seriously about the soul and, indeed, wrote a 'natural history' of it. He even used the Greek idea of the 'âme sensitive', which he said was found in both animals and man, and of the 'âme raisonnable', a higher level to which a very few men manage to elevate themselves. To him, the soul is 'the active principle in the body', deriving its animation from the Ether, delicate moving matter in the atmosphere, and having its location, in a general way, in the brain. But his soul, of purely material origins, dies with the body.[48]

This was La Mettrie's theory when he wrote his history of the soul; by the time he produced *L'Homme machine* (1748), his views had changed—he had come to consider the human organism as self-moving, independent of any immaterial force. He was influenced by Spinoza and Leibniz (these thinkers would not, of course, have approved of his conclusions), but his chief inspiration had come from his medical studies. He knew how muscular action took place, not only from nervous impulse, but also from some principle of 'irritability', and this he takes as the foundation of a biology totally divorced from metaphysics. Tremblay in 1744 described how polyps reproduce themselves from severed pieces: La Mettrie saw here the key to the understanding of the whole history of life in the universe. Nature is inherently creative. In his *Système d'Épicure* he put this insight into a cosmic context. There are seeds of all life, animal and vegetable, in the atmosphere, and by a process of natural selection over a vast time-scale new possibilities are tested; what is fit to generate and survive goes on until, at the end of the process, man emerges. 'Nature, having made, without seeing, eyes which see, now makes, without thinking, a machine that thinks.'[49]

Poor La Mettrie, the mountainously fat and atheistical doctor, who perished in exile in distant Prussia of a surfeit of eagles' lard *pâté*,[50] and made matter the ultimate reality because he carried round so much of it himself—he was harshly treated by his contemporaries, who looked on him as the oracle of the crassest materialism. In fact, he was a more confused and a more sympathetic character than his reputation and the uncompromising title of his

L'Homme machine suggests. Behind his impudent proclamation of unfettered self-indulgence he was a practical supporter of bourgeois industry and morality ('he who lives as a citizen should, can write as a philosopher');[51] he urged people to enjoy themselves and suffered himself from fits of deep depression; he honestly said that he thought human nature was evil and thus abandoned the main tenet of his own side in the feud with churchmen; he reduced everything to matter and was much concerned with art and literature and problems concerning the working of the imagination and the origin of genius. And he rejected Descartes's harsh verdict on the animals; indeed, he published an essay in 1750, *Les Animaux plus que machines*, which contrasts oddly, in title and content, with his notorious book on mankind. He was using 'machine' as a shocking word, but he knew its ambiguities, and in a biological context he thought of something much more sophisticated and elevated than clockwork: 'a machine that winds up its own springs', 'un Assemblage de ressorts, qui tous montent les uns par les autres, sans qu'on puisse dire par quel point du cercle humain la Nature a commencé.'

The knock-down, bludgeon argument of the materialists against the churchmen was the effect of illness or accident, such as damage to the brain, in destroying a man's rationality. 'Un rien,' says La Mettrie, 'une petite fibre . . . eut fait deux sots d'Erasme et de Fontenelle.'[52] A man's moral nature can be sapped by indulgence in opium, or by long imprisonment; his character is affected by physical debility or advancing years. How can the soul be spiritual if it is thus at the mercy of the body? The point could be carried further. Everyone is conscious of being a unique individual (this is one of the theologians' 'proofs'), but how can purely spiritual souls differ from one another? Do not these differences necessarily hinge upon the bodies? And if the body is responsible for differences in souls, might it not have been ultimately responsible for the development of the whole mental complex which the theologians are so keen to spiritualize? Bayle had speculated on the dog with the 'organs' (he included the brain) of Aristotle or Cicero—such a creature would have become fully as knowledgeable as these two great men. D'Argens and La Mettrie took up this theme, and Helvétius carried the idea of biological transformism still further by suggesting that the tool-making and manipulative faculty of the

163

human hand is the ultimate source of our difference from the animals and of all our culture—give horses hands instead of hoofs and they will soon surpass us.[53]

The apparently crude materialism of some eighteenth-century thinkers needs to be evaluated against the background of the medical science of the day. In most respects, medicine was barely out of the twilight of the Middle Ages. By contrast, anatomy, surgery, and microscopy had reached astonishing heights of detailed knowledge and skilled manipulation. True, the secret of life had not been revealed; the anatomists, said Fontenelle, are like the porters of Paris, knowing all the streets but not understanding what goes on in the houses.[54] Even so, then as now, the discovery of the ultimate secret hardly seemed a reasonable possibility; one could only hope to find some convergence in the evidence, some coherent way of looking at the relationship between mind and matter. And this convergence, this coherence seemed to be near. The labyrinthine subtleties of the body's working were a continual subject for admiration, and the point had been reached when sheer interlocking complexity might take the place of an explanation. The century was conscious too of standing on the brink of a new and detailed understanding of the workings of the mind; in novels, memoirs, works on morals and aesthetics, and in letter-writing, the intricacies of motivation and inspiration were being analysed as never before. The mind itself had become sufficiently complex to be, almost, a substitute for the soul. Some of the commonplace materialistic sentiments of the time sound insensitive. Fréret's (really d'Holbach's) *Lettres à Eugénie*, one of the most intelligent of all the works against Christianity, speaks of the body as a machine producing sentiment, thought, and reflection, all of which taken together 'Fréret' is willing to call 'soul'.[55] But this is not the heavy-handed materialism of nineteenth-century German scientific publicists (Moleschott's 'no thought without phosphorus', and Vogt's 'thought comes from the brain like urine from the kidneys'). It is, rather, the materialism of men who had a vivid, naïve, and newly-aroused sense of wonder, both at the intricacies of the mind and of the body; these intricacies they saw in a mysterious interlocking system, which, in a circular way, explains life and is a worthy setting for art, poetry, and, indeed, morality.

Eighteenth-century materialism developed its own cosmology, one which made God unnecessary, even as first mover. As compensation for his loss of immortal life, man was offered a place (honourable because he alone, of the known creation, was self-conscious and conscious of the process) in a grandiose and universal harmony. One of the key words of the century was 'Nature', and Spinoza's formula, *Deus sive Natura*, was at the heart of contemporary cosmological disputes. In the clandestine literature circulating in the 1720s, the idea that movement is a property of matter is found. Newton, as interpreted by Voltaire (that is, with God made indifferent to mankind and his intervention in natural phenomena limited to the initial push), became a help to the cause of materialistic vitalism. According to the Cartesians, matter was inert; according to Newton, it had the property of attraction. Why should it not also have the property of movement, and is not movement a significant stage on the way to thought?[56] Christian apologists had been fond of the idea of the 'Great Chain of Being' and its accompanying principle of 'plenitude' which causes God to fill the universe with an infinitely graduated hierarchy of created being. At the lowest level of argument, the idea had been used to defend the existence of angels and devils (and, for that matter, of mermaids) as indispensable links in the universal progression; at the highest, it had contributed towards a solution of the problem of evil, since it explained why God withholds valuable endowments from some of his creatures.[57] But the chain broke if at any point there was a qualitative jump. La Mettrie seized on this problem of discontinuity and asked just where in the series the theologians proposed to phase out the soul; for himself, accepting the principle of plenitude, he declares 'tout est donc plein d'âmes dans l'univers', every living being must have a soul, right down to the oyster clinging to the rocks, a vantage point, he adds sardonically, for observing the eternal verities.[58] But a similar difficulty occurs still further down the scale: if all Nature is comprehended, how can you draw a line between animate and inanimate? There are three possible ways in which a universe can be built up, said Maupertuis in 1745: by chance, by God's direct operation, or by 'the elements themselves uniting to fulfil the Creator's wishes'. He preferred the last method, as requiring one miracle rather than many, and he added the possibility of 'accidents' which might prove fruitful in causing new species to arise.[59] Thus, into the discussion came the concept of a blind, yet intelligent Nature, bringing forth new beings continually in multiple essays. Maillet's *Telliamed*, published three years after Maupertuis's *Essai*, envisaged an evolutionary process of fantastic length, suns succeeding suns in relays: given such a time-scale, a thousand million false starts are unimportant, and a blind, enduring purpose can create anything.

Diderot[60] took up the speculations of materialism at the point where La Mettrie had stopped, and asked if the distinction between dead and living matter had any validity. He had begun as a deist, thinking that the movement of particles can explain the physical order, but not the advent of life. But in his *Lettre sur les aveugles* (1749), Sanderson, after nearly a lifetime of blindness, turns to the concept of an indifferent, dynamic Nature, throwing up cruelly deficient worlds and destroying them continually in the wastes of space. Eventually, Diderot came to regard feeling as a property of matter itself; animals, including men, constitute, as it were, Nature's laboratory where *sensibilité* is developed from an inert to an active stage. Perhaps he had not gone so far down the path of atheistical materialism as many believed. The experimental nature of life would account for the tragedy of Sanderson's blindness, but hardly for the prevalence among men of the intense individuality which Diderot so much cherished (if everyone could express himself fully, he said, there would be as many languages as there are people[61]); the tendency of molecules to co-ordinate and resist disorder and chaos was, maybe, a more purposive force than he cared to imagine. In the final form of the theory there are three forms of life—in the animal, in each organ, and in the individual molecules. Only in the molecules is life indestructible; feeling here goes on for ever—'la mort s'arrête là'.[62] In a curious and moving letter to Sophie Volland, Diderot draws out the implications for our human dreams of reunion beyond the grave. Maybe the lovers who ask to be buried side by side are not so foolish as we tend to think. Mutual attraction surviving in the individual molecules of their dust may operate to draw them together into unity, a strange sort of immortality in which some residual memory of passion remains imprinted for ever on the ultimate particles of the material universe.[63]

IV

Men thirst for immortality. Diderot did not deny it. As one of his invented characters observes, the 'wise man' regrets that there is no evidence about the essence of the soul and, being afraid of annihilation, prays to be allowed to go on after this life 'in contemplation of the author of Nature'.[64] But when this life wanes, what is there to look forward to? No one would feel pleasure in anticipating the faint residual attraction left in molecules after his own individuality had been destroyed, and pride at being a briefly self-conscious nexus in a vast blind process would not give more than momentary satisfaction. But Diderot offered more. To him, our true immortality consists in the survival of the memory of our deeds in the minds of future generations. The idea was universally familiar, from the pages of the Old Testament, from the practice of the Church in making saints, and above all from the Latin classics, which were the basis of the education given in the *collèges* of France—as models of literary style, of elevated sentiments and patriotic duty. The ideal of the 'citizen', taken over from the Roman Republic, was Christianized by the Jesuits and secularized by the *philosophes*. Diderot was the great apologist for virtue. He condemned La Mettrie's hedonism as wicked, as showing a frivolous contempt for the immense tree of moral duty, whose topmost branches were in Heaven and whose roots extended down to Hell. The references to Heaven and Hell were, or course, rhetorical: there was no supernatural sanction for morality. Man lives in the family and society, and his duty lies to these two units within which his destiny is fulfilled. 'The height of perfection is to prefer the public interest to all other.'[65] A man's reward is to be remembered affectionately by his family round the fireside, and to be commemorated by his fellow citizens.

Thus, religious rewards and punishments in a future life are replaced by the verdict of future generations, a verdict which goes on century after century, accumulating, in the case of great men, at compound interest. With a confidence in the continuance of civilization which we no longer share, Diderot asks us to imagine 'wars upon wars . . . interminable troubles . . . for a hundred million years'—yet Voltaire's works will be read and his name will remain;

'you will have changed nothing but its pronunciation'. Whether crowning the truly great or shaming the tyrants or vindicating the anonymous poor and oppressed, the verdict of posterity is the true, the only immortality. 'O holy and sacred Posterity, support of the unhappy and the oppressed; thou who art just, thou who art incorruptible, avenging the good, unmasking the hypocrite, dethroning the tyrant—O just and consoling concept, do not ever abandon me! Posterity is to the philosopher what the next world is to the religious believer.'[66]

Though few welcomed his dismissal of a life beyond the grave, practically all Diderot's contemporaries agreed with his emphasis on the verdict of posterity. The ideal of glory, which had been essentially heroic, by the mid-century was changing into an ideal of utilitarian and philanthropic conduct,[67] though still retaining patriotic overtones. We must live in the light of our duty to future generations: 'Those who survive will be happy or unhappy because of us. Why not spare them pain?'[68] Looking forward to their happiness, we will be happy ourselves. They will remember us with thankfulness, just as we must look back and celebrate the examples of virtue and citizenship which previous generations have bequeathed to us. Here was an inspiration which d'Holbach made into the foundation of his new atheistic morality. There is no God, the soul is material and dies along with the body, but once they realize there is no directing providence and no world to come, men will bend all their endeavours to the improvement of this one. As we strew flowers on the tombs of Homer, Tasso, and Milton and the most virtuous of the Roman Emperors, we will resolve 'to merit, in our sphere, the praises of mankind'; not, maybe, of our immediate contemporaries, for even Corneille, Locke, and Newton died regretted only by their friends, but of future generations, better able to assess our talents and our virtues.[69] This call to self-sacrifice could evolve its own religious fanaticism: 'la postérité a ses dévots, comme la béatitude éternelle a les siens'.[70] An apologist for Mirabeau, making the best of his confused deathbed scene, spoke of the 'two majestic images' which 'filled his vast imagination: posterity and the National Assembly'. Another of these *dévots* of posthumous fame (which was one of the psychological forces of the Revolution) was to be Saint-Just, who went to the scaffold defiantly, confident in the achievement of secular immortality: 'Je défie qu'on on m'arrache cette vie indépendante que je me suis donnée dans les siècles et dans les cieux.'[71]

There were difficulties about this enthusiasm for posthumous glory. The Christian argument—a man stands or falls to God alone—was too austere for the age. At the end of the seventeenth century Mme Deshoulières had softened the ruthlessness of Pascal into a more humane form. Let nothing odious or cowardly sully your memory, but do not go beyond this negative ideal to strive for future glory. Such a quest is dangerous. For one thing, temptation lurks, since 'great crimes immortalize as surely as great virtues'; for another, by focusing your attention on the future you may miss the opportunity for true happiness and usefulness in the present.

> L'avenir remplit notre idée
> Pour obtenir qu'un jour notre nom y parvienne,
> Nous perdons le présent, ce temps si précieux,
> Le seul bien qui nous appartienne.[72]

This moderation, this deliberate restraint of ambition, does not seem to have held much attraction for the eighteenth century; the ideal of posthumous fame was beginning to take on a moral content of its own as it became entangled with dreams of unlimited progress by enlightenment. The arguments against it took a different form. One was severely practical, the other severely and democratically moral. Falconet put the practical argument to Diderot: even great historians have been proved mistaken, so how can you be sure of reaching posterity without being misrepresented; the process of transmission is a 'lottery'. Others had doubts about a fame which depends so much on paper and ink; worms eat books as well as men, and who knows what volumes the twenty-second century will wish to republish? And eventually, even though the time may be very far distant, everything comes to an end. The optimistic eighteenth century sometimes faced this possibility squarely. On the shorter term, Mercier pictures Paris destroyed by war, plague, or revolution; medical writers and Montesquieu foresaw a degeneration of the race; Buffon thought the cooling of the earth sets a term to human life, some 93,291 years; Maupertuis in 1742 pictured the earth pulled away from the sun as a satellite of a comet; Senancour envisaged a dying planet of marshes and barren rocks when the rivers had finished their work of eroding the soil and carrying it down to fill the sea; Cousin de Grainville at the end of the century depicted the sombre fate of the *Dernier homme*.[73] However long glory might endure, it could not last for ever.

The moral difficulty concerned the uselessness of the ideal of glory as a spur towards noble conduct to the majority of mankind. The Assembly General of the Clergy in 1775 made this point against the *philosophes*; all men have duties, but few can hope to be recorded in the annals of history—there must be some other hope, some other incentive.[74] 'Let us now praise famous men' is an aristocratic invocation which needs to be offset by reflections on 'those that have no memorial, and are perished as though they had never been'. Diderot, who was devoted to the ideal of élitist leadership and occasionally proclaimed something like the doctrine of the small number of the elect so far as fame was concerned, was also genuinely democratic in temperament and in love with ordinary people and their everyday skills that kept mankind clothed, fed, and housed. His attention was drawn by Hubert Robert's paintings of classical ruins (Robert returned from Rome in 1765 and exhibited in the Salon of 1767), not only because of their brooding sense of human transience, but also because they taught the reversal of values, the humiliation of 'les puissants de la terre' and the exaltation of the humble, anonymous men and women who keep the human race going. A barn within the shell of an imperial palace, a cottage leaning against a broken column, a few figures moving slowly through the overgrown ruins—a ragged woman with her baby, a horseman muffled against the wind—life goes on, and these humble folk are more worthy than the luxurious proconsuls and sanguinary tyrants who ruled the world.[75]

Thus, the Enlightenment came to have two very different ideas of survival in posthumous memory. For men of real greatness there would be enduring glory throughout the ages. True, the mechanism for the transmission of their memory presented problems. Thomas, the professional panegyrist of the age, looked sadly on the splendours of Pigalle's mausoleum for the maréchal de Saxe, for, in the end, even marble will crumble. Yet, he claims, writers can immortalize: we do not know where the urn containing the ashes of Agricola reposes, but his virtues live on in the pages of Tacitus.[76] What then of the biased or incompetent historians, and the worms that eat the books? The answer seemed to be: progress must be a reality, so the noblest ideas must ultimately prevail. 'Errors will pass,' said d'Holbach; 'truth will remain.'[77] And, as Truth went on its predestined way, the men who fought for it would be remembered with it. This explains the otherwise dubiously logical *cliché* of the times: virtue does not ask for pompous *éloges*, nor monuments of brass or marble: 'le Temple de Mémoire est dans le cœur des hommes.'[78] It was safer to be remembered, incidentally, within the perpetual triumph of truth within the human heart, than to be celebrated individually and separately. On the other hand, the mass of mankind will have to be content with the vague satisfaction of feeling they are contributing to a continuous process, and with the more specific happiness arising from the thought that their children will inherit the world which they are striving to build and maintain. Every man ought to be able to think of himself as aristocrats now do, finding his fulfilment in the continuation of his line, though without selfish pride, and only in the context of the common good. Though Helvétius aloofly ridiculed *postéromanie*, the fashion arose—and passed on to the festivals of the French Revolution—of celebrating the virtuous fathers of families whose achievements lived on in their well-brought-up children, the citizens of the future. In *Les Jours*, a reply to Young's *Nights*, the abbé Rémi declared that death has no rights against 'pères de familles', for they hand on, not only their name and possessions, but also their very souls, and so 'journey on through the centuries under the auspices of Nature.'[79] There was a corollary: a man ought to accept death so as to leave room for his descendants to have their turn on earth. According to Dupont de Nemours, there was not enough matter in the universe to suffice for the continual multiplication of a race which was immortal, and the moral is drawn in his fable *Oromasis*. When the demon Arimane tries to ruin the work of the Creator God by introducing death into the world, he merely succeeds in elevating man to his supreme glory. Without death, says Oromasis the Creator, 'it would not have been in my power to grant him Love . . . He could not have been a son, a husband or a father . . . He would have sunk to a status below the vegetables.'[80]

This view of the role of posterity in the motivation of the virtuous man—whether remembered by the nation for centuries or by his family for a few generations—was, to an extent, shared by Christians. Bronze, marble, stucco, and proud inscriptions in churches were a perpetual reminder of great services and great lineage. But there was a difference: God does not judge as man judges; what seems to us a momentous achievement may be a crime or a folly in his eyes.[81] Those 'gilded tombs of frail and sinful mortals' are, essentially, reminders of human transience.[82] And God is democratic. There are no two separate hierarchies of memory in his kingdom. For the vast majority of men and women, the gratitude of posterity can only be anonymous. 'Au bout de l'année, quelque souvenir encore,' says Père Judde, 'et puis, pour la plupart, un éternel oubli.'[83] By contrast, with all its harshness, the Christian picture of the hereafter was of an eternity in which no single individual, for good or for evil, was ever forgotten.

V

Hope was not the monopoly of Christians; there were few indeed in the eighteenth century who rejected the possibility of a future life. There was general alarm at the systems of materialists and atheists; thanks to the fact that the word 'âme', as we have seen, had its ambiguities, it was possible to suspect the presence of their machinations in comparatively innocent scientific speculations. The main current of the thought of the Enlightenment was deistic,[84] not atheistical or even agnostic; there were doubts about revelation, about the Christian plan of salvation, but few about the goodness of God or the existence of a life to come—which, indeed, became a less demanding and uncomplicated hope when the sombre Christian theme of judgement was abandoned or modified. To the Voltairian poet Roucher, the afterlife was to bring man to the crown of his achievement: only then would he fulfil his true possibilities:

> Si l'homme veut régner, if faut que l'homme expire,
> Au delà de la tombe est placé son empire,
> C'est la mort qui l'enfante à l'Immortalité

—this is an ode read to the Loge des Neuf Sœurs at an obituary celebration for Court de Gébelin in 1785.[85] If, at the gates of Heaven, some celestial official asks us what we believe, Parny, the satirical poet, advises us to say 'The immortal soul: a God who rewards and punishes: nothing more'. This severely limited reply will win full marks. 'In that case', says the angel, 'enter and choose a place to suit yourself.'[86] Perhaps, even, it does not matter what we believe at all; a philosopher who had wandered into the Elysian Fields by accident and managed to return (according to the fable of the deistic marquis de Culant,) reported the sole qualifications for entry as being—be useful, serve God and country, and do not be jealous of others.[87]

This sort of hope of a life beyond the grave touched Voltaire, though in this, as in most other matters, he was more sceptical than his followers. Since any stick would do to beat a dogma with, he did not fail to use arguments calculated to embarrass the clergy; the doctrine of the immortality of the soul is not found in the Old Testament, and the early Fathers thought the soul was a material object. On the other hand, since the Jews were barbarous and ignorant, an idea missing from their scriptures may simply be just another example of a civilized speculation which was beyond their comprehension. And in any case, downright scepticism is not for public proclamation, since the idea of a future life is necessary to keep the people in order and to restrain rulers from excesses: 'The common interest of all men demands that we believe the soul to be immortal.' Generally speaking, Voltaire's God is too aloof to concern himself with the puny affairs of mankind; we are rats on a ship bound for an unknown destination, mice lost in the castle constructed by the divine architect for his own mysterious purposes. And yet, who can tell what may happen as these great designs unfold; a man brooding alone could not help wondering if 'God would conserve for himself the purest part of our being'; death, maybe, is the point at which the caterpillar is metamorphosed into the butterfly.[88]

In contrast to this feeble intermittent hope, Rousseau had achieved a lyrical and highly personal certainty. To him (speaking in the person of the Savoyard *vicaire* in *Émile*), God's goodness is our certain guarantee; in creating us, God has assumed obligations towards us, to authenticate the hopes and longings implanted in our hearts. The mere sight of 'the triumph of the wicked and the oppression of the just', a 'shocking dissonance in the universal harmony', is proof enough that death cannot be the end of the story. And the intensity and sincerity of earthly loves prefigures eternity. Julie dies happy because she is hastening to a realm where there will be no more conflict between love and duty, and where she will be able to give herself again to Saint-Preux for ever. Poor Rousseau! He was striving to perpetuate in the life to come the intense and stable relationships which he himself had never enjoyed; his Heaven, like the city of his *Contrat Social*,[89] is built for us, and not for him—except of course, in the world beyond the grave, Jean-Jacques will find peace because all hearts will be open and transparent and his sincerity will be recognized. Indeed, he will escape altogether from the tyranny of having to live in the eyes of others. Within himself, he was conscious of his 'soul', the 'active and knowing substance' immune from the dissolution of the body, but imprisoned and weighed down by it, living only half the potential life for which it was destined. Released from the bonds of the flesh, the soul would spring up, vigorous and jubilant; he looked forward to the moment when, set free by death, 'I shall be *myself* without contradiction, without division, and will have no need of anyone but myself to be happy'.[90] Strange as Rousseau's enthusiasm may seem to us, it was an authentic emotion, an unselfconscious inspiration of the new Deism, a naïve and generous creed which had not yet come to its years of disillusionment. In this same euphoric mood, Mme Necker, with some insensitivity, criticized poor, blind Mme du Deffand's passive gloom and feebleness of sentiment. 'La mort même, cette grande circonstance, n'a été pour elle qu'une pensée triste, mais superficielle.' Rich, beautiful, and influential, it did not seem unfair to the wife of the great banker that she should also excel lesser mortals in rising to the height of welcoming death itself as a new achievement and experience; to her, death was to be an inspiration of our highest thoughts, an opportunity for us to savour the happiness engendered by virtue, to demonstrate the existence of God and the consolation to be found in him.[91]

Haunted by a persecution complex, Rousseau instinctively looked to an afterlife where the malicious would be put to silence, and the innocent, freed from their unjust censure, would achieve self-fulfilment and peace. In the overturn of the Revolution, among successive generations of revolutionaries who were disowned and destroyed by the movement they themselves had created, the justification of death as the providential machinery by which God redresses the injustices of life was transformed from a deistic platitude to a fervent conviction of the Rousseauistic kind. Fouché was to proclaim the finality of death at Nevers, but Robespierre contradicted him at the Festival of the Supreme Being and in the debates of the Convention: death is 'the beginning of immortality', the 'safe and precious asylum that Providence has reserved for *vertu*'.[92] Phillipeaux wrote to his wife from prison urging her to teach their son to believe in the Être Suprême and in the immortality of the soul, 'this consoling dogma is the only refuge for virtue, oppressed and put to shame'.[93] In the invented religions of the Revolution, the immortality of the soul was to be the essential doctrine for, as the manual of the cult of Theophilanthropy argued, without this belief men would cheerfully do evil, since 'their crimes would be buried forever with them in the tomb'.[94] If the afterlife was to be the sanction of moral conduct, the just would clearly be rewarded, as surely as the wicked were punished; at their last hour some, who, maybe, had thought little about Providence in their lifetime, rediscovered it through the hope of a reunion beyond the grave with those they loved.[95] 'C'est dans le sein de l'Éternel que nous nous reverrons'; our separation will be but temporary: in God we meet again. These farewell letters are moving documents, though more touching still is the last message of a young aristocrat (the son of General Custine) to his wife, which faces frankly the possibility that hope may be an illusion of wishful thinking. 'Adieu! Je n'érige pas en axiome les espérances de mon imagination et de mon cœur; mais crois que je ne te quitte pas sans désirer de te revoir un jour.'[96] And there were those, like Hérault de Séchelles and Danton, who courageously faced the guillotine asking nothing from the future but the exonerating verdict of history. The scaffold of the Revolution, retaining the secular ceremonies of the public execution of the *ancien régime* but excluding the religious ones, provided a forum for the public examination of the beliefs of the sentimental deism of the century.

VI

With a rare lyrical enthusiasm, intellectual sophistication, and moral earnestness, Rousseau was expressing the religious beliefs of so many, probably most, of the educated men of the age of the Enlightenment who had become doubtful about the Christian revelation. They were convinced of the existence of a creator God who had given man an immortal soul and who would dispense rewards and punishments in a future life, redressing thus the inequalities of this one and providing an incentive for moral conduct. The rewards were no problem: they were to be expected from a benevolent Supreme Being; the difficulty was, what of the punishments?

The conventional answer offered by the theologians was: the incorrigibly wicked would burn in Hell eternally. But during the seventeenth century,[97] thinkers on the fringes of orthodoxy—liberal Anglicans, Protestant theologians moving along the margins of Arian speculation or universal toleration, Platonists, students of the early Fathers who had rediscovered Origen's universalism, enthusiastic chiliasts—had devised or adapted all possible arguments against this grim conclusion. It was not the punishment itself which was in question, so much as its eternal duration; maybe the wicked would be annihilated, or simply be left, unredeemed, to the processes of natural death; maybe they would flit from existence to existence, being progressively refined, until the restoration of all things; the fires of Hell might be stoked for only a limited period, or there would be pauses in the routine of torment to allow opportunities for repentance. But the arguments against the endless duration of punishment—in the end, all reducible to one, its incompatibility with the love of God—had not been widely discussed; they had remained in manuscripts clandestinely circulated, or in books anonymously or posthumously published. One reason for caution was that doubts about Hell had for long been regarded as a peculiarly Socinian opinion, not unconnected with doubts about the divinity of Christ; indeed, there was some vague consonance between an infinite expiation and an infinite doom for those who rejected, or were excluded from its saving efficacy. To an age which took Scripture literally, but was just beginning to see the difficulty in continuing to do so, the standard proof texts for Hell seemed either irrefutable or too firmly welded into the sacred structure to be detached for sceptical criticism. To outflank the biblical evidence, Tillotson was reduced to the astonishing supposition that God would break his word rather than execute his salutary but cruel threats, being bound by his promises only when he offered rewards. In the light of the problem to be solved, Locke's *The Reasonableness of Christianity* (1695) was a masterpiece of exegesis, marshalling an unusual run of biblical citations to show how the penalty laid down for Adam's sin was simple death, not torment, how those who had lived before Christ would be saved if they had believed the messianic promises, and those who had never heard the promises would be judged according to the light of nature.[98] But the essential reason for concealing daring speculations about universal redemption or a temporary Hell was a concern for public morality which, it was confidently believed, would collapse once the common people ceased to fear for their eternal destiny. As late as 1720, Thomas Burnet was anxious to limit the happy secret of universal redemption to the learned few, a wish not entirely congruous with the four Latin, one French, and two English editions (within eleven years) of his *De statu mortuorum et resurgentium liber*.[99] In the seventeenth century, it seems, only sects which believed the end of the world to be imminent were forward in proclaiming their disbelief in eternal torment—no doubt because they saw less point in struggling to maintain the structure of order for the brief period in which it would still be necessary.[100]

The thinkers of the Enlightenment did not invent new arguments against Hell: they used the old ones freely and openly, and assessed them in a wider context. Louis XIV's persecution of the Huguenots had done more than discredit intolerance; it had also clinched the proof that religious differences among Christians were here to stay. The question of Hell had always been complicated by the consideration of who would be in it. With the Christian church permanently fragmented, even the most fanatical Catholic apologist could see the difficulty of adding the bulk of the population of civilized England and Holland and his own blameless Calvinist neighbours to the vast legions of virtuous pagans which had already marched down to perdition. This seems to have been the consideration which drove Pierre Cuppé, a *vicaire* of the diocese of Saintes, and an intellectual disciple of Locke, to write his famous *Le Paradis ouvert à tous les hommes*, a reply to the abbé de Cordemoy's gloomy *L'Éternité des peines de l'enfer* (1697).[101] Cordemoy published his diatribe to promote conversions among the Protestants of Saintes and, no doubt, only succeeded in exasperating them. Cuppé replied to him in statistical terms. Given the orthodox doctrine of Hell, how many people must have gone there? Of every thirty people who have lived on earth, there will have been something like 19 pagans, 6 Muslims, 2 Christians of heretical persuasions, and 2 nominal Catholics who had no true love for God—leaving 1 good Catholic, at the most, to qualify for a place in Heaven. Flatfooted literalists were soon using this sort of computation to settle the details of infernal geography: Hell must be in the sun as there would be no room for all its multitudes in the centre of the earth.[102] But Cuppé was making the calculation as a blow at the false concept of the divine majesty which was supposed to justify the enormity of the punishment inflicted on sinners: could waste on such a scale be part of the divine plan of Creation, and could God's splendour remain untarnished if his love was so decisively defeated? Cuppé's treatise was not published in French until 1768, though it became known earlier in an English version. In the meantime, however, the force of his argument was being increased by the widening of the horizons of the Enlightenment. To the despair of Christian apologists, Bayle had discovered the 'virtuous atheist'; now, more exotic figures appeared, the noble savage, the Chinese sage, and the deistic philosophers of imaginary utopias. The numerical superiority of the damned was becoming qualitative also. Christianity was coming to be regarded as one variant expression of the religious instinct in men, and its Hell was becoming a local phenomenon.

'Il est ridicule', said Voltaire, 'de penser que Dieu s'occupe pendant une infinité de siècles à rôtir un pauvre diable.'[103] This is a summary of the general opinion of the writers of the Enlightenment. Hell was absurd, and was unworthy of God's goodness.

Hell was absurd, partly because it did not work: it was useless. The preachers did not think so, for they dangled men over the pit to frighten them into moral conduct. To some extent, albeit condescendingly, Voltaire agreed with them. Men have to invent some psychologically satisfying explanation when they see the wicked escaping from the vengeance of the law, and a legendary place of torment may help to keep the servants in order. In theory, it looked as though Hell was useful as a deterrent. But what happens in practice? It was a matter of everyday observation how joyous sinners ignored the fiery ordeal ultimately awaiting them. 'Temptation is too near', said Diderot, 'and Hell is too far away.'[104] No doubt they would repent at the end, but the worldly tenor of their lives would be unaffected. The eighteenth century was rational and utilitarian: if punishment was to be inflicted, precise questions were to be asked about its actual deterrent force. In 1764, Beccaria was to lay down his famous criteria: legal penalties were to be prompt, public, the least possible in the circumstances, proportionate to the crime, and fixed by law. By these tests, Hell was inefficient and unreasonable. The punishment was long delayed rather than prompt, the maximum rather than the minimum, concealed behind the opaque barrier of the future rather than public, fixed by a law subject to the arbitrary vagaries of a doctrine of forgiveness, and proportionate to the crime only by a lofty and inhumane concentration on the idea of God's offended majesty. Thirty years before Beccaria, Marie Huber had used the argument of utility (put into more spiritual terms) to demonstrate why Hell must be a failure. In the end, such lurid threats insensitize the conscience; a man cannot believe that he has incurred such disproportionate penalties, or that they can be enforced against him in any possible rational organization of the universe.[105] D'Holbach, writing after Beccaria, applies utilitarian logic to the God he did not believe in as well as to the affairs of men. Hell is ridiculous, so it does not serve as a deterrent; by definition, those who are supposed to be in it are not allowed to repent, so it cannot serve a reformatory purpose. Perhaps then it is a punishment to serve a symbolic and declaratory purpose? But, unlike the Roman emperors and other tyrants, God enjoys a supremacy beyond all question, so it is pointless for him to use terror to vindicate a greatness which none can challenge. God knows the dispositions of our hearts, and he knows what our future conduct will be; the whole business of earthly trials leading to divine rewards or punishments is an empty game, as immoral as it is pointless.[106]

Hell was absurd, then, because its vast and creaking machinery

179

was ineffective. But maybe it was also absurd in another sense?—too ridiculous to be credible at all. Satan and his attendant devils were the most improbable element in the traditional picture of the infernal regions. Since Bayle and Bekker, the men of the Enlightenment had been reluctant to believe in them, or, at least, to accept any of the so-called evidence for their existence from their interventions in human affairs. The great wave of witch-hunting hysteria which had swept over western Europe in the late sixteenth and early seventeenth century, costing, according to Voltaire, 100,000 lives, was a reminder of the dangers of credulity. Louis XIV's edict of 1682, by what it left unsaid rather than by what it explicitly states, removed witchcraft and sorcery from the catalogue of criminal offences. Practitioners of the black arts would from henceforward be tried for sacrilege or fraud. The grim (and given the premisses) logical legal procedures devised over the generations by demonologists and lawyers to detect commerce with the Devil were repudiated.[107] True, in the eighteenth century mortal man still continued to try to contact and use the powers of darkness—or believed that others were doing so. Decadent socialites dabbled in black magic; the duc de Richelieu[108] and the duc de Chartres[109] were supposed to have seen the Devil, evoking him in blasphemous parodies of the mass involving goats and toads and (in Richelieu's case) an Armenian with his throat cut; scoundrels swindled great aristocrats with demonic pacts written on goatskin, and in 1752 two fashionable ladies had their clothes stolen at a Luciferian liturgy specially devised to encourage them to take them off.[110] Searchers for hidden treasures had their *grimoires* of prayers to Lucifer, Beelzebub, and Astoroth, and they hired renegade priests to say masses to conjure up the denizens of the underworld[111]—who would, presumably, rejoice at the opportunity to get their claws into a soul and also at being instrumental in putting corrupting riches back into circulation. Hysterical girls claimed to be possessed by demons, impotent husbands blamed their enemies for bringing in the powers of evil against them by use of *l'aiguillette nouée*,[112] rustic sorcerers claimed to cure men or cattle, not always by white magic. Churchmen or, at least, abbés on the fringe of ecclesiastical affairs and interested both in curious lore and the profits of publication, wrote treatises to defend the existence of devils and their commerce with human beings.[113] There was also a rather halting apologetical point to be made—as crudely expressed by the Parlement of Rouen in 1672: 'en doutant les mystères d'en bas, on ébranle dans beaucoup d'âmes la croyance aux mystères d'en haut.'[114] That was why Dom Calmet's *Traité sur les apparitions des esprits et sur les vampires*[115] was such a masterpiece of naïve and subtle temporization; most demonological stories are untrue, he tells us, but a few are well authenticated, each age has, its own supernatural marvels, witches who confess they have been to the *sabbat* are suffering from illusions, but illusions are the way the Devil operates. It was a demonstration of scholarship and pseudo-scepticism with enough credulity to avoid any threat to the 'mystères d'en haut'.

In fact, rural superstitions, fashionable black magic, lunatic treasure-hunting schemes, fraudulent occultism, and learned compilations of supernatural anecdotes did the cause of Satan no good. His empire had fallen. The hysterical days of witch scares and the *possédées* of Loudun were gone for ever and remembered only for discredit. Those who dabbled in the occult did not believe they were in touch with the hierarchy of Hell; they were merely experimenting in the shadow world on the fringes of reality, where there were more things in heaven and earth than philosophers dreamed of. Mesmerism was to provide a more respectable outlet for such unhealthy curiosity. Sensible men doubted if Satan had ever existed. Voltaire showed how the Jews in exile had picked him up from the Chaldean myths, and the story of the fallen angels from the Brahmins; they had applied these fables, and the Christian Fathers after them, to prop up the evil doctrine of Original Sin.[116] Diderot dismissed devils on aesthetic grounds: they were much inferior to the classical furies with serpents in their hair, they were 'gothic, and in thoroughly bad taste'.[117] Watelet, the art critic and painter, even thought Michelangelo's *Last Judgement* ridiculous—being a mix-up of history and fable, profane and sacred, diversified with grotesques and obscenities.[118] Intelligent churchmen agreed with the *philosophes* in at least one respect: they were not prepared to see the devils running loose in the world behind every popular superstition. They were more inclined to allow a loophole for supernatural happenings, but if there were such things as diabolical interferences in human affairs they did not wish to have notice taken of them. Malebranche[119] had said that there are a few real witches, and that in any case they should be treated as if they were mad; certainly they should not be punished, for this merely provokes new outbreaks of folly. This was the attitude of eighteenth-century theologians to diabolical manifestations. Bishops would use *lettres de cachet* to lock up girls who claimed to be possessed and the priests who dared to exorcise them. When charges of sacrilege were made in affairs of black magic, the ecclesiastical courts would impose lighter penalties than secular ones.[120] The Devil reigned in Hell, in accordance with certain scriptural passages, but he had nothing to do with this world. After the coming of Christ, said Hecquet, the Jansenist, the demons are no longer allowed to intervene among men. 'There are two powers, and two alone, which can bring about the significant events of the world, God and nature. For to admit the intervention of the Devil is to make his power rival that of the Creator.'[121] Satan as an epic figure, distinct from the traditional medieval grotesque, had come into European literature with Calderon, Vondel, and Milton at a time when men were dreaming of transcending human limitations in their quest for knowledge and power. But on grounds of religion and good taste, Boileau had banned him from France. Here, Voltaire's rule prevailed: the supernatural could only be depicted with 'vraisemblance' and 'goût'. Not surprisingly, French attempts to emulate and catholicize Milton were pedestrian,[122] and the myth of Orpheus was used to illustrate the creativity of the poet and the triumph of art over death rather than themes concerning Hell and human destiny.[123] Except among the pious, Hell, its inhabitants and furniture, became a comic subject. It was the most stable of empires, said the wits—after all 'heaven and earth will pass away'; it had excellent communications—the roads leading to it were 'broad' and the gates 'wide'; and it was full of agreeable company, ranging from popes to good-looking women.[124] Satan was treated with frivolity. The century began with *Le Diable boiteux* and near its end came *Le Diable amoureux*.

In an age when every educated man had been brought up on the literature of classical antiquity, and when the curiosities revealed by geographical Discoveries were a staple of polite conversation, one of the commonest procedures of argument, whether about civilizations or religion, was by comparisons. This was an obvious way of attacking—or of defending—Hell. All peoples in every age and everywhere have believed in judgement and a place of torment, the argument of justification ran. But the many parallels,[125] with their wildly imaginative details, were not entirely reassuring. The Formosan bamboo bridge over a pit of filth, the Mississippi Indians' barren hunting-grounds, the icy mountains of the natives of Florida, Tartarus, the underworld of Pluto, the seven gates of doom of the Muslims, the Christian eternal fire—a great deal of allowance, it seemed, should be made for human inventiveness. Perhaps the ideas of other religions were better than the standard Catholic doctrine. The ancient Romans and the followers of the Prophet allowed escape from torment after long expiation—they were more merciful; the Brahmin idea of the transmigration of souls seemed more logical and did not demand strange extra-terrestrial paraphernalia of vengeance. The universality of the belief in Hell was not necessarily evidence of its real existence. It might just be an illustration of the tendency of priestcraft all the world over to invent supernatural terrors, or it might be an indication of some predisposition or weakness in the human psychological make-up. The idea of Hell, said Toussaint, came from 'des cerveaux noirs et mélancoliques',[126] while Delisle de Sales spoke of the fanatic's twisted enjoyment in making himself 'an object of odious vengeance'.[127] A future of fiery torment haunts man's imagination, says Buffon, because of the persistence of an atavistic memory; primitive man, trembling amidst the volcanic chaos of the forming earth, had permanently imprinted on his mind the obscure conviction that his race would one day perish in some universal conflagration.[128]

'Il est ridicule de penser que Dieu s'occupe pendant une infinité de siècles à rôtir un pauvre diable.' Every word of Voltaire's sardonic observation was precisely chosen. The victim is unlucky, rather than iniquitous, the punishment, albeit with a farcical, culinary flavour, is eternal, eternity being defined as infinite duration, and God is portrayed as giving personal and permanent attention to its sordid details. Apart from the skilful touches of verbal malice, Voltaire was, however, just reflecting what the theologians were saying: Hell is eternal, and is willed by the omnipotent God. The essential argument of the Enlightenment was, quite simply, that this doctrine is incompatible with any civilized idea of God's nature, and with the Christian idea in particular. Christians pray: 'Our Father'. What father could act in this terrible fashion? Voltaire pictures St. Louis in the shades as saying: do not believe that the punishment of the wicked exceeds their crimes—this is how tyrants on earth take vengeance, 'but here it is a Father, who punishes his children'.[129] You say that God owes nothing to sinners, Toussaint observes, taking up one of the arguments of the theologians; true, but he owes something to himself, to show himself a true Father, indulgent to his children.[130] God must have created the Devil, says 'Fréret', he must have foreseen the Fall, and he foreknows all my transgressions, yet he lets things run and exacts the vengeance as he has foreknown it; there is no parental affection here, just the conspiratorial frenzy of a Caligula.[131] 'What son could love such a Father?', asks d'Holbach.[132] Step by step, Diderot pursues the illogicalities of damnation.[133] There is no proportion between eternal punishment and any possible career of sin, however outrageous, in this finite existence; there is no possible profit in prolonging the punishment of the wicked once the world is ended and the righteous have triumphed. If the penalties for a misspent life are infinite, we ought to strangle our children at birth before they have a chance to incur this fearful hazard. Diderot did not believe in the Christian God, but he was willing to argue within the hypothesis to confute the clergy or to gratify an anxious friend. To such a one, lying feverishly in the darkness of his bedroom, curtains drawn, meditating on the 'great gulf' and the cries of the damned, he provided his own private definition of the only sin for which there is no forgiveness: to distrust the mercy of God.[134]

The theologians proved Hell from Scripture. Diderot's comprehensive demolition of Hell swept away all their proof texts without bothering about the validity of any of them (except that he does venture into technicalities on the question of how we get the word 'eternal' in our translations).[135] It is essentially a question, he says, ironically, of where Christians decide to place the emphasis of their belief. There is one single argument for eternal punishment, he says, in the notorious *Encyclopédie* article on 'Damnation'—that is, it is 'clearly revealed in Scripture', against it are the central doctrines of the Church—God's glory, his goodness, and the efficacy of the sacrifice of his Son, all of which are devalued by the notion of everlasting torment. He was putting in ironical form the principle soberly laid down by Marie Huber: the Bible must not be interpreted so as to go against the verities which are the essence of all religion.[136] Rousseau says the same. An argument from biblical texts which finishes up with an unworthy idea of God is like a demonstration in geometry leading to an absurd conclusion—there must be an error in the original information. We cannot maintain the infallibility of the Scriptures at the expense of having to describe God as unjust or cruel.[137]

Nor can we maintain the infallibility of the Church by this expensive method. Churchmen claimed to speak with authority: to the *philosophes*, this simply meant that the Church was to blame for the deplorable betrayal of the character of God in the interests of institutional power. When Toussaint 'retracted' his *Essai sur les mœurs* in 1762, he astutely made his concessions to fix the blame in the right quarter. He had been mistaken, he humbly admitted, in casting doubts on eternal punishment. True, reason did not establish it, but the Church did: 'Je m'en rapporte à ce sujet à l'Église Universelle, qui fait un dogme précis et absolu de l'éternité des peines de l'enfer.'[138]

The case against the Church could be more sharply defined still. What of the virtuous pagans and noble savages who had never heard of the gospel and the heretics who misunderstood it? Were they not being excluded simply to make the Catholic clergy and their ministrations indispensable? It was an old difficulty, but one that had not become any easier to explain as the years went by. As we have seen, some churchmen were offering concessions on this point. But the general opinion of theologians was still inflexible. Rousseau, through his Savoyard *vicaire*, with intense seriousness was eloquent on behalf of those who are damned because of their lack of information. A God has died two thousand years ago in an unknown little town at the far end of the world. If this is an event which I am obliged to know about, why has it taken place so far from me? Is it a crime to be ignorant of what has happened at the Antipodes? Is my father lost because of the laziness of your missionaries? If it be true that there is only one religion within which a man can be saved, the work of the world will come to a standstill as all men feverishly go on pilgrimage to seek it.[139] Mme Roland, reflecting on the argument of Jean-Jacques, her spiritual mentor, carried his attack to a final degree of harshness: must I have heard, she asks, not only of Christ but also of one particular Church among those preaching him, of 'a Roman pontiff preaching a severe morality which he himself does not always practise?'[140]

Catholics, Protestants, and almost all deists agreed on one proposition about the afterlife: there must be rewards and punishments to redress the inequalities of this world and to provide a sanction to compel men to take the obligations of morality seriously. Ridiculous details apart, the quarrel with Hell was with its eternity, rather than with the concept itself. A few theologians were manœuvring towards concessions: perhaps there will be fewer in Hell than we imagined; perhaps something would be done for the virtuous pagans and heretics; maybe there are gradations of pain in the underworld and possibly, the prayers of the just might avail to promote some members of the confraternity of the damned into less rigorous compartments. But if God's goodness was to be vindicated, a more radical rethinking was called for, though it did not need to go outside the Christian tradition (Marmontel was not saying anything improbable when he claimed that the liberal argument of his hero Belisarius was derived from his own reading of the Fathers on the subject of the love of God). If God is love, there are two alternatives. Morelly, in his *Code de la Nature* (1755), was responsible for their utterly precise formulation, in decisive words which clearly influenced Rousseau and Marmontel. If supreme power and infinite wisdom are indeed united in a single person, he said, such a divine being could not punish—'elle perfectionne ou elle anéantit. Choisissez.'[141] The choice of annihilation was made, at the end of the seventeenth century, by Pierre Poiret, a liberal Protestant who published a vast and masterly treatise on 'the economy of universal Providence'.[142] In this world or the next, God would save those virtuous pagans and all who honestly sought him; but he would not override man's free-will; those who rejected his grace would finally be left to themselves—like owls, they would be allowed a corner of darkness in which to hide from the burden of

God's luminous glory, and there, in the shadows, their personalities would disintegrate. This is the 'strange work' of God referred
to in the Bible when a nation or person must be destroyed. Poiret
had many followers, though not among the Catholic theologians.
Maybe, however, those who talked of eternal punishment emphasizing, not the mechanism of torture but its irreversible and
hopeless quality, were on the verge of Poiret's theory without
realizing it. The seventeenth-century jest about the souls in eternal
fire becoming used to their environment like fishes in the sea was
not entirely frivolous as a criticism of orthodox pictures of Hell. If
that did not happen, the personality would assuredly be changed in
some other way, and in a totally hopeless and meaningless eternity
it is hard to imagine any alternative to disintegration. Maybe
preachers who ranted about millions of years of torment were
really talking about something like Diderot's 'life' surviving only in
isolated molecules, in this case endowed with some faint residual
aura of evil, rejected and meaningless.

The alternative to the idea of annihilation was universalism—all
men ultimately will be saved. This was a solution to the problem of
human destiny which scholars had to consider seriously because of
the authority of Origen—whose reputation was steadily growing in
the second half of the seventeenth century; though such an optimistic doctrine was, perhaps, more suited for promotion in the
friendly and sentimental atmosphere of small conventicles than in
the established churches preoccupied with the maintenance of public order. As the eighteenth century came to have civilized doubts
about the deterrent effects of the lurid punishments of the criminal
code, universalism aroused more interest as a religious speculation,
and its cause was powerfully promoted by the publication, in 1731,
of Marie Huber's remarkable analysis of the theological arguments. She took Purgatory much more seriously than the Catholics
did: its punishments cannot be bought off, it really is effective, and
effective for all. It operates, not to give us forgiveness, for that is
granted already, but to allow us time to see ourselves as we really
are and to allow our evil habits to die away; when the long process is
completed, we will achieve freedom and peace. The very devils may
hope to share in this cleansing discipline and be saved. In the end,
all will participate in beatitude to the degree of which they are

capable, all will pay homage to the divine justice, and God's saving purpose will be triumphant, without shadow of failure. What then of all those specific and circumstantial texts in the Bible? Marie Huber discounted them all against the dominant proposition of the love of God.[143] Seven years later, d'Argens, who could turn his hand to every sort of journalism, from aesthetics to pornography, and who was the intelligent echo of enlightened opinion, showed how a reassessment of scriptural evidence and the presuppositions of Christian doctrine demanded a revision of the official view of Hell. God is love, and if he is omnipotent he ought to be able to set aside all abstract rules of justice. The Bible often portrays him as persuaded not to punish his people, to turn aside his wrath, to change his mind. The 'despair' of the damned which the theologians talk of as part of their punishment is proof that they now know better and are not incorrigible; the standard belief in Purgatory is evidence that suffering can have a saving and purifying action—why then is an arbitrary line drawn between those who can be saved by suffering and those who can't?[144] (D'Argens, of course, was caricaturing the theologians' view of Purgatory—the souls there had been in a right disposition towards God at the time of their judgement; it was not their punishment that was converting them.) This idea of abolishing the boundaries of Heaven, Hell, and Purgatory was adopted later, in 1782, in one of the sensational publications of the century, *Le Ciel ouvert à tout l'univers*, whose title is an uncompromising proclamation of the doctrine of universalism. The author, Dom Luis, was a Rousseauistic monk who contrived to abolish Hell without mixing up the company in Heaven too incongruously—there was no need for the average church-goer to imagine himself hobnobbing with Caligula and Nero. The theologians were speculating about 'many mansions' in Heaven and gradations of pain in Hell. Dom Louis accepted their logic about a hierarchical stratification in the afterlife, but rejected the concept of a 'great gulf' fixed between the saved and the damned. To him, the end of all things became a symphony without bass undertones, an Alice-in-Wonderland eternity in which all had won and all would have prizes. Men would no more strive to be moral to avoid Hell fire, rather they would compete like athletes in virtue to obtain places nearer to God in an all-embracing Heaven. 'I saw the various stages of happiness which the Eternal has made ready for all men, not excepting a single one of them'. Even Ravaillac, the assassin of Henry IV, would be saved. All men can die in absolute confidence in God's great love.

> Qui s'endort dans le sein d'un père
> Ne doit point craindre le réveil.[145]

Dom Louis is here quoting his master, Rousseau—Julie's dying words of confidence in God. But the master himself would not have subscribed single-mindedly to such facile optimism. To Rousseau, universalism was just one possible solution—in his writings, the full implications of the religious thought of the Enlightenment are drawn out. So often the other thinkers are ambiguous on religious matters—their deference may be ironical, their orthodoxy merely precautionary, their scepticism a device to twist the tails of the clergy rather than a genuinely held opinion. But Rousseau, with all his neuroses and fears, always stated his genuine convictions, with a transparent honesty which was the fruit, not of simplicity or single-mindedness, but of the self-torturings of an over-subtle intellect continually demolishing its own subterfuge and poses. From liberal Genevan pastors and latitudinarian English churchmen, from English deists and Protestant mystics he synthesized the broad principles which were to revolutionize religious thought in the coming century—the necessity of qualifying all doctrine by the paramount assertion that God is love; the rule of interpreting all Scripture in the light of God's nature, and not as a quarry of information, even about spiritual things; the acceptance of the limitation of our knowledge of God to what is morally necessary, light enough to live by. Inspired by these principles he rethinks the whole question of rewards and punishments after this life. The goodness of God excludes eternal torment as part of this design. What punishment there may be, men inflict on themselves. Survival as a continuous entity includes the continuation of memory, and with memory there is always remorse. Thus, there is a Hell now in the heart of the wicked, and their self-punishment can intensify after death, when they face the full reality of the crimes they have committed. But their Hell, so defined, is not eternal.

Whether the wicked are finally annihilated or whether they are ultimately saved, Rousseau does not know, and he regards the question as a useless speculation. Sufficient for us to strive to do our duty and to know we go to the merciful God.[146]

7

Preparation for Death

I

'Quel doit être le plus grand soin d'un Chrétien?
C'est de bien préparer à la mort.'
'Bien mourir, c'est la plus grande et la plus impor-
tante action de l'homme.'[1]

Salvation depends on the dispositions of the soul in its last hour;
thus, the most important act of a lifetime is the act of dying, and a
Christian's chief duty is to prepare himself for death. This was the
standard teaching of the theologians.

True, it is always possible to be converted at the last, even after
long years of neglect and without any preparation at all. 'A single
act of love towards God can efface the sins of a lifetime.'[2] Until the
last breath has left the body, it is not too late. This also was
Christian doctrine, and preachers and moralists were obliged to
proclaim it. But they looked with displeasure on the multitude of
lukewarm believers who took courage from the thought that there
was always hope and postponed their amendment accordingly—
some, like Louis XV, until their last illness was upon them. 'Il fait
bon mourir là,' said someone of a luxurious worldling who had
reformed and died on a bed of straw as a monk in La Trappe; 'Et
vivre ailleurs,' said a cynical listener.[3] Since the proclamation of
free redemption and continuing hope was so dangerous, the theologians were universally sceptical about the practical possibility of a
genuine deathbed conversion; such an event, they thought, would
be a 'miracle'.[4] What sincerity could there be, they asked, in such a
sudden repentance, more especially as it would almost certainly
have been imagined beforehand as a last-minute expedient. We are
creatures of habit, and we grow more and more fixed in our ways,
very probably ways we learned in our youth; indeed, says Père
Gobinet, 'le salut dépend ordinairement du temps de la jeunesse'.

191

As we grow older, any sharp change of course becomes more and more unlikely. Besides, victories against great odds are usually the result of long preparation. David had essayed his courage against a lion and a bear before he challenged Goliath—how would he have fared if he had come untried to the ordeal?[5] Not surprisingly then, those who have lived good lives are those who make a good end: it is a fact of common observation. 'A holy death is the usual outcome of a holy life.' 'Ordinarily, a man does not die in grace and charity unless he has lived well.'[6] Dying is not an act which we can perform in isolation from the rest of our lives; it is an integral part of life and, humanly speaking, it is destined to fit into the general pattern. As Drexelius had said, dying is the final term in a syllogism, and a syllogism is valid only if its antecedent terms are in order.[7] We are gambling recklessly if we imagine we can live as one sort of a person and die a different one.

Postponing reconciliation means staking your soul on the chance that time will be available: but death does not always give warning. If, luckily, there is time, what distraction and confusion there will be—the sighs of servants, the tears of friends, the lamentations of your wife, the imprecations of creditors, and the murmurs of discontented heirs, says the writer of a laborious work of 400 pages on the dangers of delaying conversion.[8] And how dependent on the goodwill of other people the unprepared sinner will be! 'It happens all too often', says Père Griffet—no doubt casting a specialist eye over cases he has known—'that something is lacking in the conditions necessary for reconciliation,' enough to close the gates of heaven for all eternity.[9] And even if friends and the clergy do their duty, what a weight of responsibility rests on the wretched man whose life is ebbing away. Imagine yourself in his situation. A general confession is required. Maybe if you have been negligent, it is only then you will realize that your whole life has been a process of self-deception: what you had thought was love was just sensuality allied to the play of the natural affections, what you had thought of as abstention from wrongdoing was simply idle complacency, while others drifted into positive sin because of your silence and indifference.[10] The confessor's task is to disentangle these confusions and instill true penitence. But what happens if he is incompetent? What if he happens to be the very one whom you have deceived continually over all these years? Will you know how to be frank with him, and will he know how to insist and clarify?[11] The Church prescribes prayers for the use of the dying: what meaning will they have for you; indeed, how can you hope to pronounce even the formal words unless they are already familiar? Will pain, or the clouding of the mind, prevent you from reciting them with due fervour?[12] (Remember, says Père Berthier, hollow repetitions are not just futile, they are also dangerous: new sins, in fact, to swell the total of the old ones.[13]) Acts of faith, love, and submission to Providence are also prescribed: what meaning will they have amid the tensions of the end? You can answer this question by applying an empirical test. Look at the worldly folk who have made such acts of devotion during a serious illness and have since recovered. Their lives are unchanged. They live on for a few more years as evidence of the futility of a deathbed repentance.[14] And the last hours of life are particularly hazardous; they are unlike any others, because of their unique temptations, for it is then that the Devil puts forth his final, desperate effort: 'il dresse alors toutes ces machines'.[15] His ultimate weapon is—paradoxically—despair: despair coming too late to goad to penitence and reformation, but descending like a dark cloud to hide God from your eyes.[16] If you have no practice of the divine presence to fall back on, how will you know how to reach out to him then? If you are bereft of good works, what answer will you return to the Devil when he gloats over your deficiencies? The ceremonies designed to comfort the dying can work in precisely the opposite way on a mind which has lost its grounding in hope; each unction will serve as a reminder of the complicity of different parts of the body in sin, the figure on the crucifix will appear as a reproach, its wounds like mouths uttering decrees of condemnation.[17] The priest's consoling words will evoke memories of the very different sentiments you heard from him in pulpit and confessional about the doom of sinners.[18] Thus, having made you presumptious in life, the Devil will succeed in making you despairing in death, and you will be lost.[19] True, the divine forgiveness will always be near at hand, there for the taking, but how, amidst the confusions and fears of the end and the final assaults of the tempter, can you hope to lay hold on it without the assistance of some special, additional grace; and having neglected God for so long, how can you expect to be singled out for such exceptional gifts? There will be no spiritual investment to draw on when temptation reaches its crescendo and human powers are at their lowest ebb. 'Les hommes ne sont jamais moins en état de penser à la mort que lorsqu'ils en sont plus proches.'[20] So act now, be prepared, buy oil for your lamps while the shops are still open.

A scoundrel who ignored all this good advice could—however improbably—be saved at his last breath. Alas! the converse also was true: a good man at his last breath could throw away the merits of a lifetime. The theologians were grimly and reluctantly logical: they supposed a man's disposition in his dying moments decided his eternal destiny—the possibility of the salvation of the wicked and the fall of the just followed automatically from this premiss. In a Pastoral Letter on the death of Louis XV the bishop of Alais drew the attention of his diocese to 'two truths', one 'consoling', the other 'terrifying'. After a career of crime, the Penitent Thief had been saved: equally, 'after a life entirely given to good works and saintliness a man can, through a single mortal sin, become anathema'.[21] This could happen, the famous handbook on death, *Pensez-y bien*, had said, to even 'the greatest saint'.[22] Here was standard doctrine. 'I am always at the gate of Eternity; the moment I shall enter it is known only to God. If I have at that moment the love of God in my heart, I shall be saved for ever; if I have it not, I shall be lost without hope.' So wrote Père Grou, an aged French Jesuit in exile in England during the French Revolution. His insistence on the importance of the last moment almost makes the chance of salvation into a gambler's throw: 'how can you be sure that death will not come while you are admitting the first inroad of a sinful thought?'[23] In a volume of advice for the laity published in 1764, Collet, a monk and an expert on casuistry, tells an alarming parable. Two men are on their way to confession, and both turn aside, one to visit a pious lady, the other to go drinking with dissolute friends. Both die suddenly. The first has time to cry, 'Mon Dieu, ayez pitié de moi,' the second, in a drunken stupor, goes down to damnation, to the 'second death' from which tears and penitence can bring no deliverance. Ironically, the debauchees who had lured him to destruction are subsequently converted: they go into a strict religious order and are saved: 'How mysterious are the judgements of God!'[24]

No doubt there are deep-rooted psychological and, perhaps, sociological reasons why the grim idea of the decisive importance of the dispositions of the last hour had won acceptance. The significance of the individual and of his intense personal responsibility was emphasized; the comfortable idea of a corporate salvation was abandoned; the status of the clergy was enhanced by the demonstration of the importance of their ministrations.[25] Maybe there was also an element of intellectual accident involved: the pieces of the jigsaw fell into place this way as the attempt was made to guarantee God's omnipotence, his goodness, and man's free-will simultaneously. Perhaps there was, too, a sort of logic involved, connected with the beginnings of doubt about the over-lurid apocalyptic panorama of the Last Judgement. The first stage of this doubt had been the rise of the idea that the decisive judgement takes place, individually, immediately after death, with the Great Assize 'necessarily' confirming the verdict. Some writers speak of 'eternity' as beginning—at least for the wicked—immediately this individual judgement is pronounced. Early in the eighteenth century, a Jesuit explained the way in which the soul is fixed for ever in its dying state. 'Eternity undergoes neither change nor vicissitude. There is no going back to make amends, . . . all that remains is an eternal regret . . ., and repentance then is useless.'[26] Another writer speaks of the will remaining locked in the perversity which led to the one last mortal sin, another of that sin as becoming 'en quelque sorte . . . éternel'.[27] They seem to see no contradiction in postulating the beginning of a timeless state for the wicked, but allowing a continuance of duration for those who have qualified for Purgatory, nor do they notice how time will have to start rolling again to allow the wicked to attend in person at the Last Judgement. In all the discussion of eternal punishment there was a standing ambiguity as between a timeless state and infinite duration. The terror of the punishment was associated with the second concept, the impossibility of repentance with the first.

The theologians proclaimed the decisive importance of the last moment: but there was always some qualification, some safeguard. Most took care not to be obsessive and literal about the very last minute, but described the events of the deathbed as a unity, a series of acts of penitence, reparation, reconciliation, and adoration which were all of a piece. For all his ominous warnings, Père Grou seems to have accepted this view, at least so far as pious souls are concerned. Granted, precautions had to be taken to avoid breaking the pattern of the observances of Grace; for example, after he has been shriven, a man must not see his former mistress again, or have any other contact which might encourage him to look with complacency on his past sins. The sin which would be ruinous at the end must be a mortal sin, and this would require the full complicity of the will (was Grou playing fair with his 'admitting the first inroad of a sinful thought'?—this could easily be misunderstood). It was not so easy to fall away at the end as timorous souls might suppose, or as some hectoring writers might imply. Père Griffet described the damned as those who die 'dans la haine et dans la disgrâce de Dieu', that is, in actual hostility to God on their part or in the disgrace God imposes on them because of their wicked lives.[28] They had not drifted accidentally into impious death and damnation. Père Crasset, another Jesuit, writing in the late seventeenth century, made three qualifications to the alarming doctrine of the decisive deathbed. Firstly, those who have prepared themselves are never caught out: God would not allow it—'because of his goodness and justice God would never take by surprise someone who had almost always (*presque toujours*) been on his guard'. Secondly, a well-prepared Christian needs only a brief moment anyway, just enough time to reiterate and ratify his allegiance. Thirdly, as we know from a revelation to St. Gertrude, good works and other precautions we have taken in life will be allowed to supplement whatever may be lacking at our end.[29] These three points cover every possibility; they establish a clear connection between the life of faith and good works on the one hand and the reactions of the last hour on the other, a connection going beyond ordinary common-sense probabilities and allowing for accidents, mental illness, and so on. Père Judde later spoke of a 'secret and invisible judgement' of God during the course of our lifetime to decide whether the opportunity of a pious death should be allowed to us. (He does not specify whether God provides time, a strengthening of the will, or other special graces—presumably, as much of each as is required.) Thus, he said, 'the judgement after death depends on the state of the soul at death, but the state of the man at death depends on the judgement passed during his life.'[30] For Judde, there was a sort of Cartesian relationship between the life as lived and the events of the deathbed; God, working in the realm of occasional causes, brings them into equivalence. 'No good action is ever lost', said the Jansenist Duguet: 'God will always give a recompense.'[31] Preachers of homilies on alms-giving could be more specific; a charity sermon of 1783, on behalf of a hospital for old soldiers and retired ecclesiastics, spoke of the mollifying of the divine justice and the 'protection' and 'consolation' to the soul at the moment of death which the gratitude and prayers of the inmates of 'this patriotic edifice' would bring.[32] St. Augustine had laid down as an axiom, 'non potest male mori qui bene vixerit'.[33] In some way, whether by earning an intervention on God's part or by the psychological and spiritual conditioning which a well-spent life afforded, a man could ensure that he would not fall a victim to chance or the Devil at the end.

II

There were a great many books devoted to preparation for dying. The sort of titles available may be seen from the inventory of a bookseller of Rennes in 1725: *Consolations contre les frayeurs de la mort, Préparation à la mort, L'Importance du salut, Prières pour bien mourir, Saint désir de la mort, Douce et sainte mort du père Cracet, Le Chemin du ciel.*[34] This literature was essentially a creation of the seventeenth century. Its ideas were often derived from the accumulated store of Christian theology and speculation. Some writings are essentially compilations of scriptural texts or take the form of commentaries on parts of the Bible; borrowings from St. Augustine or Erasmus, at first or second hand, abound; the rejection of the world, sometimes to complete to be truly Christian, often has echoes of the *Imitation* (no less that 35 editions of translations of Thomas à Kempis appeared between 1735 and 1789). But the presentation and treatment were essentially the work of the seventeenth century. The classics of the art of dying of earlier centuries were not republished. The *Ars moriendi* of the Middle Ages and the writings of Gerson were no longer circulated, and little was heard of sixteenth-century humanists like Clichtove. The *De preparatione ad mortem* of Erasmus, which had been one of the best sellers of its time, was no longer popular, though there was a Latin edition in 1685 and French one in 1711.[35] In this respect, as in so many others, the seventeenth century was the creative epoch of spirituality in the French Church. Its patterns of devotion, formalized and established in the writings of the end of the century and the beginning of the next, were generally accepted by the churchmen of the Age of the Enlightenment. On official lists of titles of religious books authorized for printing in the provinces for the years 1778 to 1789, works dating from about a hundred years earlier constitute two-thirds of the reprints.[36] As many new books on preparation for death were published in the last quarter of the seventeenth century as in the following fifty years, and five times as many as in the fifty years after that, while the best sellers of the reign of Louis XIV went on triumphantly—forty editions of Père Crasset's *La Douce et la sainte mort* before 1800, and at least a dozen of *L'Ange conducteur*.[37] Until a detailed analysis of the devotional literature of the French eighteenth century is made, it will be difficult to say with confidence what new elements were being added to this seventeenth-century treasury of piety; one thing, however, is clear, everything was becoming more highly organized and systematized. The emphasis of the titles changes; the word 'new' is almost entirely missing, while the word 'method', sometimes supported by the adjectives 'easy', 'short', or 'abridged', is more frequent. 'A short and easy method of preparing for Christian death' and 'An easy method to be happy in this life and win assurance of eternal bliss' may seem indicative of an excessive confidence in methodology, though it is too ruthless a judgement to say that the age regarded religion as 'a closed field of study, like a language or a disease where, for the achieving of a certain objective, an array of techniques was at the disposal of the faithful'.[38] In no branch of devotion were these techniques more systematized than in preparation for dying. But if they were 'easy', they were not so in any psychological sense; they were sombre and harrowing.

We die but once—this is the basic proposition from which the manuals start—therefore we must ensure that we make no mistakes, we must 'rehearse', we must 'serve an apprenticeship to death'. It is important not to leave our preparation until late in life; indeed, children should be taught to reflect on the precarious nature of existence and the importance of 'making a good end'. Caraccioli's tearful *Les Derniers adieux de la maréchale de *** à ses enfants* (1769) was recommended by the censor as suitable for the education of children. Manuals of piety for convent schools were not squeamish.[39] For all ages, preparation for death was to take the form of a regular routine and be part of a life of prayer. Mark each hour of the day with an *Ave Maria* and a reflection on how many hours may still remain; on going to rest, remind yourself how sleep is the image of death and ask, 'What shall it profit a man if he gain the whole world and lose his own soul?' As you climb between the sheets reflect, this very linen may one day form my shroud.[40] Spend a day or more each year in retreat to ponder the fateful moment which comes to us all. Once a month—or, perhaps, annually,—receive the sacrament with the same rituals of preparation as are prescribed for a dying man before he receives the viaticum.[41] Choose appropriate subjects for meditation. The greatest subject of all is the Passion of Christ: here is the 'model for all those who wish to die the death of the just'.[42] There are all the stories of how the saints gave up their lives and, indeed, any other stories concerning mortality—Belshazzar's Feast, Saladin's banner, the Emperor Charles V and his itinerant coffin; read one of these accounts each morning, note the warning, 'pensez-y bien', and assimilate the lesson.[43] More prosaically, bear in mind the example of your friends and acquaintances; visit them in sickness and at the end, go to their funerals. Keep a little book, and on the first day of each year inscribe in it the names of those who have died in the past twelve months—their age, occupation, state of health, time and place of their last illness, how long they had for preparation, what they did and said towards the end, with what sentiments they received the last sacraments. Once a month, refer to this book, and compare yourself to those entered in its pages.[44] Or a man might meditate on the horrors of Hell—'Descendons en esprit dans l'Enfer'[45]—or of the grave. Caraccioli urges the daily descent, in the imagination, into the tomb, there to contemplate the workings of corruption, beginning at the eyes, moving to the ears, the lips.[46] Accept this fate. 'Ô cendre, ô vers, je vous reçois . . . comme les instruments de la justice de mon Dieu,' says a prayer dating from 1711 and used in the second half of the century by the Pénitents Blancs du Saint-Sacrement of the diocese of Dié.[47] The actual moment of death and all its lugubrious procedures could be imagined, whether of someone else 'dying before our very eyes',[48] or of oneself, with a deliberate rehearsal of the duties of the dying, culminating in the making of a 'fervent communion' and, perhaps, receiving 'spiritual extreme unction'—imagining each of the anointings with appropriate prayers. Then one could think of the moment immediately after death and the instantaneous judgement; we must not choose to reflect too often on the consoling aspects of our faith, says one writer, sometimes as least we do well to adore Jesus Christ in his quality as Judge, and not to wait until the very end to make this fearful recognition.[49] Another and more seriously reflective method of preparation originated from the *Testament spirituel* (1669) of Lalemant: the making of an inventory of beliefs and hopes to be re-read frequently for adjustment and reconfirmation, so that it was there, ready in the foreground of the mind for the last confirmation of all.[50] Most of the writers of these pious handbooks were members of religious orders, and this becomes obvious when they use death as a test to be applied to all actions, sometimes with a severity which would make life impossible except within the walls of a monastery. Check each action, omission, or desire, says Père Griffet, by the criterion: would I wish to be found so acting, omitting, or desiring with my expiring breath? The ideal, according to Père Judde, is to progress from acting always on the assumption that I may die at any time, to acting as if death is near, and finally to living all my life as if dead already, dead to the world, in 'perfect detachment'.[51]

These are the recommendations of systematizers and specialists (the spirituality of dying, like every other human activity, has its professional exponents). Taken in isolation, they do not give a representative picture of the piety of the age. Though in gloomy enthusiasm for their theme the experts sometimes forgot the duty of consolation, one of their avowed aims was to free the mind from obsessive worries, and not to cultivate unease into more complex and demanding forms. Meditation was meant to give positive employment to the imagination in place of the immobility and paralysis induced by fear: 'il est d'un grand secours à tous d'avoir à la main de certaines règles déterminées et les sujets de con-férence.'[52] Most treatises warned against excessive fear. 'The only thing you have to fear', said Arnauld, the great seventeenth-century Jansenist, to a bewildered soul, 'is to fear too much, and not to trust sufficiently in God's mercy.'[53] The idea is re-echoed in most reputable treatises; everyone describes hope as a necessary virtue. And it was an accepted maxim that brooding on death for thera-peutic spiritual purposes was an affair for the heyday of life, not for its decline. As the years go by, confidence in God's mercy should take over. 'Fear is good during life,' said a seventeenth-century Jesuit, 'but it is dangerous at death.'[54] Quesnel, the contemporary Jansenist leader, said the same: towards the evening of his days, a man should turn to meditation upon the final vision of God, before which theology, St. Paul, and the Gospels themselves become irrevelant, lamps burning in the darkness and due for extinction at the coming of the day.[55] In a work published posthumously in 1779 the austere Capuchin Père Lombez urged confessors to inspire the dying with confidence—this consoling ministry was not limited to pious souls; on the contrary, it was especially meant for those 'who have strong reasons for fearing the judgements of God'—'Fear greatly during life, and hope greatly when dying.'[56] We must remember that the specialist writers on death are not necessarily typical of theologians in general; the leading theologians of the earlier and later part of the century certainly disapproved of ex-cessive emphasis on the terrors of dying. In 1715, Languet de Gergy, bishop of Soissons, complained of the way in which the faithful had been terrorized in recent years by the idea of God's judgement.[57] In 1762, another bishop condemned the religious literature which undermined the confidence of pious souls, leaving them 'withered, desolated and imprisoned.' Twenty years later, the abbé Bergier deplored the compulsive reading of books on death by 'souls already oppressed by fear', like panic-stricken children who are unable to close their ears to tales of horror. Such books, he said, were not suited to earnest Christian readers: they had been written as counterblasts to Protestant heresies concerning predestination, or to counteract the enervating effect of laxist moral teachings within the Catholic fold, and their authors were townsmen, alarmed at the corruptions of urban life, which they mistakenly assumed were an indication of the depravity of the whole of society.[58]

In the best writings on death, hope and consolation outweigh the burden of judgement and fear. In them we find the two traditions of evangelism in tension: the tradition of the pulpit and the tradition of the confessional, with the latter predominating. On the one hand there is a public proclamation, primarily directed to hardened sinners (to preachers, all sinners are hardened) to alarm them and warn them while there is still time for amendment. On the other hand, there is advice of the kind the director of souls gives to earnest penitents in the confessional or in spiritual letters, countering or sublimating the fears which the thunders of the sermons excited, insisting on and interpreting the other side of the preacher's message, the love of God and his acceptance of sinners. By nature of their different status and duties, preachers and confessors had differing attitudes to death. Every priest, of course, was both a preacher and confessor as circumstances demanded, and he was always a penitent. A sophisticated writer on death would show an awareness of himself as acting in these three very different roles. A real-life example of their fulfilment can be found in the career of the abbé Augustin Boursoul of Rennes, famous for his sermons on judgement—he was a proclaimer of 'terrible truths' (though, as it happened, 'the happiness of the elect' was his subject when he collapsed and died in the pulpit on Easter Monday, 1774). Writing to an aristocratic lady, one of his penitents, on the death of her pious father, he speaks of the certainty of salvation without reservation: 'You have every reason to believe that God has received him in his great mercy,' you and your family will be reunited, and you can hasten their happiness by your intercessions.[59] In his private prayers, Boursoul speaks of his own approaching end with confidence, but with a subtle difference, for he avoids asking for happiness. He desires death for the same reason he desires Heaven, because only by this way can he come to love God perfectly; he fears Hell only because it is impossible to love God there—'O God, I love you, and I fear Hell only because the sweet liberty to love you is there lost for ever.'[60] The preacher's public emphasis on judgement and punishment became the confessor's private emphasis on forgiveness and happiness, with a special concentration of the affections and twist of the imagination when applying the forgiveness to himself as a penitent, to keep pride and complacency at bay.

Though the specialists on death did not always make this clear, their devotional exercises were to be understood in the light of the full Christian message. The deists of the century, for the most part, believed in rewards and punishments in the afterlife; the originality of the Christian picture of the judgement was that the decision was in the hands of Christ. This means, said Languet de Gergy in his *Traité de la confiance en la miséricorde de Dieu*, that we are judged by one who was a man like us, who was tempted as we are, who did not call us servants but friends, who taught us to speak of God as our Father and whose very glory depends on the effectiveness of the redemption which he wrought on our behalf. Even Judas, had he not despaired, could have been forgiven.[61]

But, as the Jansenists well knew, Languet's theology was deficient. He says little of the Cross, and here was the focus of the Christian message about dying, even in the rationalistic eighteenth century. The believer was to accept illness, pain, and death in the shadow of, and in the illumination of the passion and death of Jesus. Here was the supreme point of moral example and tragic emotion which was not lost on the deist—a continuing inspiration for artists, said the abbé du Bos;[62] a death which, by contrast with the death of Socrates, was that of a God, not a man, said Rousseau.[63] But to the Christian, Calvary was much more. The Cross was both the scene of the great triumph over sin, death, and the Devil from which the Christian hope is derived, and the tragic spectacle of torture which arouses sinful man to penitence and gives him confidence in God's forgiveness. 'Ah Lord! if you had wished to damn me,' says Père Crasset, 'you would not have mounted the Cross: I put my soul, my salvation and my eternity into your pierced hands.'[64] The *Christus Victor* theme, crudely interpreted as a divine deception luring the Devil into combat and defeat,[65] was not easily conciliated with the exemplarist theory of the Atonement; the century's admiration for the majesty and wonder of creation made it difficult to give convincing content to the concept of triumph through suffering. Duguet, who insists on the reality of the agonies of Jesus (or how, in our tribulations, can we convince ourselves that

God cares?), also speaks of the dying Christ as 'the Lord of life and death', choosing his own way to die, and of his body, 'from the myrrh of the Magi to the myrrh of Nicodemus', as being spiritual, not animal like ours.[66] (Contemporary artists faced a similar dilemma in portraying the Crucifixion: was it triumph or tragedy? was Christ 'the fairest of the children of men' or the haggard figure of medieval iconography? was he in-dwelt in death by the divine serenity, or was his the grim corpse of Ruben's *Descent from the Cross*, like an executed criminal taken from the wheel in the place de Grève.[67] Writers on preparation for death, depending on whether they were emphasizing the divine triumph or the human suffering, invited their readers to identify themselves either with the spectators on Calvary, learning from or being judged by the divine example, or with Jesus himself in defeat and loneliness. The sight of the Blessed Virgin and St. John would remind them of Christ's message of filial piety and the duties of friendship; of the mourning women, of the importance of corporate prayer for the dying; of the Pharisees, of the offensiveness of hypocrisy; of the Penitent Thief, of the hope of salvation.[68] Or, with the Master, they could follow the path which they themselves must one day tread—learning to yield up their lives as a willing sacrifice, to forgive their enemies, to face the temptation of doubt ('This is your hour and the power of darkness') or of despair ('Why hast thou forsaken me?').[69]

In these sorts of meditation there was a narrow borderline between edifying reflections and an excessive ingenuity which trivialized the great Christian story. Chertablon's *La Manière de se bien préparer à la mort* (1700) is an illustration of a style of piety barely comprehensible to us now. The devils grinning out of the illustrations and the sub-plot of the scheming second wife and the three children are embarrassing, and the pictures of the Passion of Jesus, shown to the dying man in handsome frames upheld by cherubim under the supervision of the Guardian Angel, are often only artificially made relevant; Simon Peter wants his hands and head washed (a full general confession is required), the disciples sing on the way to the Mount of Olives (rejoice now the end is near), 'Whom seek ye?' (we must offer our lives), Pilate's wife intervenes (wives can be a dangerous distraction—this in spite of the fact that she gave her husband good advice!), Pilate finds no fault (it is dangerous to rely on our good works), 'We know that his witness is true' (is our last will and testament in order?).[70] Duguet, the master of allegorical interpretations of the Passion, scorns such pedestrian ingenuities and avoids detailed moralizing. His most attractive work begins with Christ in the tomb: I must go there to visit him, says Duguet, in silence; the angels have not come yet, the disciples are scattered and far away—I come alone. If the wounds were showing and the face tormented by the agony of death, I would not dare to approach, but the body is covered with a shroud and I can lose myself in the darkness. My life is hid with Christ in God. In the sepulchre, I learn to begin the life of renunciation.[71]

Here we come to the heart of the matter. The anecdotal and sentimental recapitulation of the events of the Passion was but a device of meditation, a means to an end, and the end is the Pauline 'dying daily', being 'crucified with Christ'. Thus, a man is brought into union with Christ in his suffering, death, and resurrection, he is transformed, and receives the imprint of the life of Jesus. 'How happy is the soul in the crucified life', said a grimly austere hermit of Bordeaux, an exile from the Court in the early years of the Regency; 'in the midst of this life of continual dying to self, it receives the imprint of the life and suffering of Jesus Christ, working within it a marvellous and perfect transformation, which is its entire felicity.'[72] By seeking to suffer with Christ we perfect our love for God. 'To love a God crucified for our salvation', said the abbé Boursoul at Rennes, 'is to love for our own sake; to love a God who crucifies us, is to love God for himself.'[73] So the best preparation for death was to accept the cross willingly, perhaps to seek it. To some, even in the Age of Voltaire, this meant the mortification of the flesh by deliberate self-torture. Flagellation, learnedly defended in the early eighteenth century as a recognized discipline of the Church by J.-B. Thiers, a rigorist *curé*,[74] was still practised in the secret, largely clerical society called the 'Aa'. At Lyon, Cahors, and Toulouse we hear of whipping sessions on Fridays. At Toulouse, in the crypt of Saint-Sernin, with mattresses fixed against the windows to muffle the noise and to the accompaniment of the reading of the Passion narrative and the recitation of the *Miserere*, the *De Profundis*, and litanies of Our Lady, the *confrères* met to administer floggings to each other, and their chronicler records that there was never need to complain of their lack of mutual zeal.[75] But these fierce austerities were only for the few, and were kept secret to gain merit and to avoid ridicule. More commonly, spiritual directors talked of sacrificial living, not of the literal re-enactment of the flagellation of the Passion. The cross was to be taken up in the daily affairs of life. This was the Sulpician tradition as laid down by the great Louis Tronson at the end of the seventeenth century. The body must be cared for as an instrument of service (it is the temple of the Holy Ghost, and what would you do if you had a chapel which was falling into ruin?). Even so, in work, leisure, marriage, or any other activity, a man should seek 'une bonne croix', some burden to be borne willingly, for Christ's sake.[76] This was the central theme of Jesuit spirituality also, reaching its highest point of refinement in Père de Caussade: to accept all, good or ill, as coming from God's hand, to say continually, in sunshine or in rain, 'Fiat', 'Thy will be done'. Dying daily in the service of and in union with a crucified Master, the Christian could appeal to the sacrifice of Christ when he too came to his end: the confessor would give him the crucifix to cling to as his last agony began. When we meditate upon the tomb of Christ, said Duguet in 1731, we are not so much meditating upon his death, as upon our own baptism, for it was then we were buried with him in his sepulchre and began the lifelong process of dying to sin and rising again to righteousness, a process triumphantly completed on the day the breath leaves our mortal body. Nothing then remains but for the stone to be rolled away and the eternal day to dawn.[77]

III

To the impious, said a theologian writing in the 1770s, death appears as the worst of all evils; 'ordinary souls' face it with a sense of submission to the will of God, but 'fervent souls' desire it 'as the end of their exile and the happy arrival in harbour after a long burdensome voyage'.[78] This defines the two essential attitudes required of a Christian at his end: at the least, submission; ideally, joyful acceptance.

Joyful acceptance needed careful definition. Some writers took the dangerous—almost dualistic—view of the Christian as a stranger and pilgrim on earth, who looks forward all the while to being released from his temptations and yearns for the heavenly Jerusalem; indeed, he may be inspired with a 'holy curiosity' about the time and circumstance of the day of his deliverance, and if he prays for recovery from illness, he will not do so with an ardour which suggests that it is a matter of great importance.[79] Some writers waxed unconvincingly lyrical: 'O death . . . I take you for my sister, my wife and my friend!' Others expressed an unedifying disgust with earthly existence. Old age is a 'sewer', said a late seventeenth-century tract, and we should be glad to escape from its degradations. Life is tedious, said Caraccioli; no one complains at the theatre when the curtain falls on a boring play. Lafitau even upbraids parents who wish for a few more years to bring up their children piously. God can educate them better than you, he comments, and the desire to postpone death is merely 'a pretext to cover one's own imperfections'.[80] There were, however, more sophisticated and less heartless ways of looking at the duty of the acceptance of dying. When St. Paul wished to depart and be with Christ, it was not the departure which he yearned for so much as the closer union with his Master. 'It is not death which we desire,' said Bossuet, 'but to live with Jesus Christ.'[81] The desire to be with Christ should in no way detract from the fulfilment of worldy duties—to station and office, relatives and friends, dependants and the poor, and death is not to be regarded as an escape, but as the final act which completes a life lived in God's service. We should be continually setting a Christian example, and our deathbed is the last opportunity to do so—and in circumstances which will imprint the lesson on the minds of all who love us.[82] Dying is our greatest opportunity to do penance, and our lives are the most splendid offerings we can make to God; by surrendering them willingly, we can do homage to the divine majesty and recognize the divine justice. And, above all, here is our supreme opportunity to unite ourselves to Christ. 'Submit to death, and unite your death to his.'[83] The recognition of opportunity: this was the secret of the conjoined force and restraint of the two greatest (and, probably, most influential) works on death which the seventeenth century bequeathed to the eighteenth. Père Crasset refuses to denigrate earthly existence, even though he yearns for Paradise. We should welcome the chance to offer to God what in any case we owe him as a debt, to gain merit by bearing the burden of fear, to fortify our souls by exercising the virtue of hope. Caught up by the fiery chariot, Elijah escaped death, and this ultimate experience is now lacking to his happiness; that is why, at the end of all things, he will appear on earth again to complete his crown of glory by the surrender of his mortal life.[84] This view of death as a great opportunity is not just an example of Jesuit optimism. Contemporary Jansenists said the same. In Quesnel's *Le Bonheur de la mort chrétienne* (1688), a Jansenist work totally if austerely devoted to the virtue of hope, there is a sombre note: as a sinner, says Quesnel, I should desire to die to satisfy the judgement of God; but also, he says, with glowing expectation, I should wish to depart as a child of God awaiting perfection in sanctification, as a member of Christ seeking incorporation into his mystical Body, as a disciple learning to love more perfectly, and as a citizen of heaven going to my native country.[85]

But can a man be sure he is saved? God alone can weigh the thoughts of the heart and the opportunities of a lifetime; dare mere mortals presume to have penetrated the divine secret? The French Calvinists, according to their Catholic neighbours, claimed this sort of certainty for themselves, and though there is no logical reason why believers in a predestinarian theology should feel entitled to affirm their own election, it was true that Protestant writers spoke of justification in confident terms. There are wonderful passages of assurance in Drelincourt and Pierre du Moulin—death is God's messenger, and if we force open the fingers of his iron hand we find there the divine messages of love; Christ is our 'eternal friend' and 'it is a law of friendship that friends support one another'.[86] By contrast, Catholic writers were reticent and, sometimes, legalistic. A strange letter of the Jesuit Père de la Colombière to a dying man (published in 1727, half a century after it was written) is an exception to prove the rule. My confidence in rendering my final account, he says, will rest on the number and greatness of my sins, for they will show how God's mercy is infinite: 'Voilà une confiance vraiment digne de Dieu.'[87] He is exemplifying the scandal censured by St. Paul, 'Let us sin that grace may abound'—a curious example of the brinkmanship of some Jesuit moral teaching of the time. The opposite and equally dubious extreme was reached by some writers

who cheerfully exhorted their readers to take comfort in the good
works they performed; indeed, a canon of Reims described Heaven
as the wages paid to the labourers in the vineyard who had borne
the burden and heat of the day—a splendid, direct inversion of the
parable.[88] With greater finesse, Languet de Gergy specifies the signs
which are evidence of our predestination. You are a Catholic, you
are not a libertine, you are still alive having seen the sudden deaths
of the companions of your pleasures, you persevere, and—the
surest mark of all—you suffer tribulations; take courage, therefore, you must be one of the elect.[89] Similarly, Lafitau derives
assurance from the testimony of a good conscience. It cannot give
'metaphysical certainty' founded upon the knowledge that things
could not be otherwise (this could come only from a direct revelation); but it can give 'moral certainty', which humanly speaking is
all we can desire or deserve.[90] While Lafitau conveyed assurance by
analysing the two kinds of certainty, Père Vauge worked for the
same result by distinguishing true from false humility. A humility
which is not allied to hope, which creates a distrust of God's
promises, is merely a manifestation of human self-sufficiency and
pride. Virtues are tested by their fruits; a Christian who is truly
humble achieves thereby a new liberty to pray and to serve and,
even when confessing himself deserving of Hell fire, he never
supposes God will abandon him, never loses his interior peace.[91]

There is, however, a problem about assurance, for a mind set free
from fear of God's justice will fall into self-satisfaction and pride.
Assurance, therefore, should never be complete. There is a degree
of fear which is natural and inevitable, which afflicted Christ himself at Gethsemane. This fear is used by God and is one of his
gifts—he does not let us know our destiny, says Père Crasset,
because he wishes to keep us humble;[92] indeed, his providential
designs for the most prayerful of his followers may include the
torments of uncertainty.[93] By contrast, the courage which a few
worldlings and *esprits forts* manifest at the approach of death is a
mark of divine reprobation, lest they repent and are saved,[94] just as
the mingling of apprehension and confidence in the last hours of
many a Christian may be taken as the workings of grace through
the natural order.[95] We may regard a man who is just and who is
praying for perseverance as one of the predestinate, says the bishop

of Boulogne, though he himself must still 'work out his own salvation with fear and trembling.'[96] Dom Morel, a ruthless believer in predestination, urges Christians with a good conscience to consider themselves among the elect; yet he prays to have fear always in his heart; hope overcoming fear, but never entirely vanquishing it.[97] The necessary tension between fear and confidence is illustrated by the story of the death of Père Ambroise de Lombez, the Capuchin, in 1778, as related by a lay brother. Lombez had lived a life of ruthless asceticism, censuring even laughter as an 'imperfection' and examining himself for a quarter of an hour three times a day to keep his imagination pure. On his deathbed he showed signs of fear, and an insensitive friar exhorted him to have the confidence in God which his writings had instilled into so many others. '*Hé, Monsieur,*' Lombez replied, 'please do not reawake in me the power of *amour propre* which has always waged war on me, and do not expose me to the risk of losing, in a single moment, the fruit of all the vigils and tears with which I have striven to expiate my sins. I render a thousand thanks to the Lord for all the graces he has showered upon me, and I beseech him to continue them to me. I do not despair of his infinite mercy, but I am cast down by the thought of my nothingness, and by the idea of the rigorous account that I must render before his judgement; may it please heaven that this recollection will help me and incline him to show favour to me.' And his last words were, '*Mon Dieu,* I am deeply sorry that I have offended you. I ask your forgiveness. Have pity on me and spare me.'[98]

It was a question then of keeping a balance between confidence and fear. One way of doing this in practical spiritual direction, the common-sense way, as it were, is seen in the highly developed system of Père Grou, a Jesuit whose main writings come at the end of the century. In his intense and heavy-handed fashion he divided Christians into two distinct categories: those, the majority, who had chosen the 'active way' to serve God, and were to be exhorted 'to meditate upon death, its uncertainty, its terrors, in order that they may see how they live', and those who have chosen the 'passive way' and have thus attained to the 'interior life'. These 'need not dwell on that side of the question, God calls them rather to a perpetual mystical death, death to self in will, in thought and deed; so that when the actual moment of material death arrives, it is but the final passage to eternal joy for them.'[99] But the followers of the active way are not to remain under the lash of fear all their lives, for while fear is useful to help them to bridle the passions of youth and to stiffen their will to persevere in penitence, it is but the motivation of slaves, not of children of God.[100] 'Fear is a gift of the Holy Spirit: but it is a gift by which He wishes to prepare us for more excellent gifts . . . We must aspire to that perfect love which casts out fear, or rather, which so purifies and ennobles it, that it is changed into quite another sort of fear, the daughter of pure love.'[101] Yet, even in the state of pure love, we can never achieve an absolute certainty about our eternal destiny. We can, however, reach peace of mind, given 'a clear conscience, a fitting rule of life, and a steadfast purpose of obedience'. As we detach ourselves from earthly things, as we mortify ourselves to draw near to the Cross, so death will come to appear 'lovable and peaceful' to us. Timid souls will still feel the coldness of fear creeping over them, but let them remember that 'God loves them better than they love themselves', and would not wish the last narrow passage to the shores of his Kingdom to be a place of terror.[102] Indeed, the Christian does not cross that strait alone. The Eucharist, for Grou, is the heart of Christian practice, and the arrival of the *viaticum* is the point at which the loneliness of death is ended. True (for Grou never entirely forsakes his minatory style), those who have not sincerely and sacrificially received the sacrament in their lifetime will receive it now only to their condemnation; but for the true Christian, bound to his bed of suffering as his Master was nailed to the Cross, Christ will come to consummate the last act of sacrifice and offer the pledge of a happier life. This is no angelic visitation, but the coming of God himself, so that the heavenly life has begun already in our sublunary world of pain and illusion.[103]

Père Grou's picture of the progress of the 'active' soul—a lifelong process of love casting out fear, down to a final point of uncertainty, irreducible but small enough for confidence to cocoon it and pass over—was in accordance with common sense, but too brusque and unsubtle to set at rest all the scruples of sensitive, introspective, or sophisticated minds. The cycle of fear–confidence–complacency–pride, with pride, once recognized, leading back into apprehension, was still not broken. Saint François de Sales had categorized the religious emotions: fear was 'servile' if evoked only by the menace of damnation; hope was 'mercenary' if solely directed towards winning Paradise; and love was 'filial' only when the heart was responding directly to God without selfish motivation.[104] Yet, is it possible to exclude ideas of reward and punishment from the mind, more especially as death draws near? Can there be such a thing as totally disinterested love? There were good grounds for denying this possibility, whether psychological, seeing the human will as inevitably tending towards happiness, or theological, regarding eternal bliss as an idea automatically involved in the turning of the mind towards God, since he himself is the reward of those who seek him. On the other side, there was a tradition[105] descending from Abelard and Duns Scotus, through the Flemish mystics, the *Imitation*, St. John of the Cross, and, in early seventeenth-century France from Bérulle—a tradition which spoke of the 'nothingness', 'servitude', 'emptiness', 'annihilation' of the soul before God— which implied the possibility of reaching the state of 'pure love', *'pur amour'*, in which the soul, indifferent to its salvation or deliberately renouncing it, would love God alone and for his own sake. Saint François de Sales achieved this sort of love in the 'heroic act' of his youth when, having irrationally convinced himself of his own eternal reprobation, he decided to go on loving God without hope of reward: 'Il faut du moins pendant ma vie, aimer mon Dieu et le servir.' This experience lies behind his later speculation concerning a soul convinced that its damnation is more agreeable to God than its salvation. In this case, there is nothing to do but to choose voluntarily to go down to perdition—though all this, he admits, is 'imagining the impossible'. The Jesuit Père Guilloré, in his *Les Progrès de la vie spirituelle* (1675), went further, and ascribed to God himself the calculated implantation of this terrible conviction of eternal reprobation; it was the operation of the divine 'jealousy', a design to drive certain chosen vessels into a total surrender unmarred by any sort of hope or expectation.[106]

The doctrine of 'pur amour' as 'the key' to the spiritual life was proclaimed by Don Alexandre Piny in the early 1680s. Stumbling along the uncertain boundaries of secret mental complicity, I wander amid temptations; all my efforts fail because of my imperfections; sometimes the mysteries of the faith seem to me mere 'corrupt traditions'; I am afraid of death, and in some moods I convince myself that I am damned.[107] How can I find peace? Piny tells us to accept all these shadows on our lives and not to seek immunity. To every cross, say 'Fiat', 'Thy will be done'. We must be 'content never to be content',[108] to be forever uncertain. We accept our damnation,[109] and our only prayer is that we may *not* be admitted to eternal happiness unless it is God's pleasure.[110] Thus, we will come to the eleventh and final degree of disinterested love, 'l'amour désespéré', love without hope of recompense.[111] Yet, if the calculating penitent searches with self-interested diligence in the pages of Dom Piny's three volumes, he will find consolation of a less tragic kind. This intimation of reprobation is either a suggestion of the Devil,[112] and therefore invalid, or it is God's device to bring us, through especial sufferings, directly into glory, shortly after we die or even immediately,[113] and therefore to be welcomed. In what seems to us the utmost desolation, there is always a 'fine point de l'esprit' (the idea is from Saint François de Sales) by which God remains in contact with us, sustaining us by grace.[114] God is always holding on to us, so 'it is not possible nor believable' that he would allow a soul totally surrendered to him to go down to perdition.[115] Those who seek to lose their souls, say the Scriptures, shall save them: we are never more secure than at the moment when we accept our own damnation.[116] The paradox is explained when we ask what Hell and Heaven can possibly be like. Heaven, if gained against God's will, would become a little private Hell, while Hell, willingly accepted through love of God, becomes Paradise.[117] 'Quid ardet in inferno nisi propria voluntas?' asks St. Bernard:[118] if no self-will is left in us, there is nothing for the fires of eternal torment to burn away; we are immune. In short, the Hell we were willing to descend into turns out to lack the essential damning quality of every Hell men have imagined: the capacity to obsess and absorb the entire will of its inhabitants. The spirituality of despair turns out to have been a device, a manipulation of the emotions. We accept the idea of our own damnation as a mental discipline, as flagellation is a discipline of the body. By it, we defeat fear by assimilating it rather than fighting against it, and verify our love as disinterested by an imaginary excursion into a morally impossible universe.

The doctrine of 'pure love' came to its crisis and condemnation in the uncharitable clash of Bossuet and Fénelon and the papal brief *Cum alias* of 1699. Like Piny, but with infinitely more subtlety, Fénelon made an act of renunciation of salvation which had its ambiguities. It was 'conditional' upon God's will, and 'simple', involving neither despair nor deliberation: such were the arguments advanced before the Roman tribunal in its defence.[119] Although we have lost our way, our will still cleaves to God,[120] and while we see no sign of him, he is working in secret to help us; if we have no hope, this is only because hope has been burned out by the devotion of love. Even when we believe we are 'forsaken', we must continue to trust in God with childlike simplicity, and at the end, in our dying hour, if they ask us whether we are afraid of judgement, we reply with St. Ambrose that we serve a generous Master.[121]

Yet, when all these consoling qualifications are made, the renunciation of salvation remains a sombre reality for the great archbishop of Cambrai: for him it was no device of devotion, no manipulation of the emotions. He lacked the vision of a redeemed humanity striding forward, rich in individuality, but united and forgiven by the Son, into the kingdom of light. His faith was theocentric rather than Christocentric; he exalted God as Unity rather than Love, and looked forward, less to a final reconciliation of the whole groaning and travailing creation than to a consummation when the universe would dissolve like smoke and God would be all in all.[122] Our world is not the best of all possible worlds, but an approximation, gratuitously chosen, between being and non-being, and we live precariously on the edge of the void.[123] 'There are only two truths in the world, that God is all, and that the creature is nothing.'[124] In so far as we escape from emptiness and unreality, we are self-destructive creatures, for we are caught in the trap of *amour propre*, the selfishness which is the death of the soul. The shade of La Rochefoucauld haunted Fénelon: self-love enters into all our actions, and our virtues sully us as surely as our vices, for they are the mirror into which we gaze to stimulate our pride.[125] How can we escape from the underlying threat of the void and from the continual inner betrayal of *amour propre*? How can we find peace? From our side, there can only be uncertainty, even about the certain promises of God. There is one way. I must get out of the

whole complex of self-regard which is involved in the idea of
reward, even God's rewards. 'Religion in its entirety consists only
of escape from self and from love of self, so as to turn to God;' 'My
peace will come only from a love which binds me to God independently of all hope of reward.'[126] Such a love purified by renunciation
and 'indifference' does not fulfil or reinforce our individuality: it
destroys it. 'It is by the annihilation of my own limited being that I
will enter into your divine immensity.'[127] Fénelon's act of renunciation of eternal bliss was—as all such acts necessarily must be—a
mental construction of something that in the last resort was 'impossible'. But he was genuinely and totally renouncing something—
the strictly Christian Heaven. He did not seek individual survival.
By the way of 'indifference' he would be absorbed into the great
Unity of the divine love, the eternal cycle in which God possesses
his elect and is both the lover and the beloved, the beginning and the
end and the fulfilment of all things.

Writers on spirituality regard the Roman condemnation of Fénelon as a tragedy in the history of mysticism; for two centuries, says
Cognet, discredit was thrown on the idea of passive prayer.[128] But it
is difficult to regret the prohibition of the renunciation of personal
salvation, which could too easily become a fastidious psychological
manœuvre, an excessive gesture of baroque devotion or, more
dangerous still, a joyless journey towards a salvation which was too
Platonic, too intellectualized, to be entirely Christian. During the
time it had been allowable, however, the idea of 'indifference' had
produced a valuable psychological insight. The crude official theology of judgement, with its menace of Hell and its anxious concentration upon the last few moments of life, had fostered an
obsessive fear of death and damnation. Obsessions feed on the
concentration required to meet them in head-on combat; better to
evade the paralysis of apprehension and the cycle of fear–assurance–pride which was the alternative, and simply leave all in the
hands of God. Fear was swallowed up by being allowed to triumph
unopposed, by the acceptance of the worst possible outcome—but
that outcome was in the hands of God, and God is love.

Even without the papal condemnation, the devotion of *pur
amour* would have been only for the few. The deistic and, to some
extent, the Christian writers of the eighteenth century were to

make a cult of *bonheur*; in religion, happiness would be obtained
not only in heaven, but also on earth, in the mental contentmen
which the practice of virtue brings.[129] The idea of a love which
endures unrewarded and without response, acquiescing in the tota
loss of happiness, became unthinkable. 'It is not possible to love
unless one believes oneself to be loved,' said Père Vauge.[130] Toussaint the *philosophe* said the same: 'There is no disinterestec
love . . . Love is born only from the relationship between two
objects, of which one contributes to the happiness of the other.'[13]
On a realistic view, love would wither without reciprocity. Thus
exponents of 'enlightened devotion', like Mme Leprince de
Beaumont in 1779, while regarding the great archbishop of Cambrai with respect, dismissed his phraseology of disinterested love as,
simply, the hyperbole used by lovers the world over: 'l'amour divir
a son ivresse aussi bien que l'amour profane'.[132] Even so, the
insights of Fénelon's doctrine deserved to be preserved. In the early
1720s, the abbé de Brion tried—rejecting Quietism and, more
particularly, Mme Guyon's version of it, but retaining the 'way of
love' and praising 'indifference', though it was an indifference, no
to salvation, but only to the means by which it might be obtained.[133]
All this was suspect. Finally, Fénelon was rescued and reintegrated
into orthodox spirituality by the Jesuits Père Milley and Père de
Caussade, who replaced *pur amour* with 'abandonment to divine
providence'.

Milley speaks of 'la voie du pur abandon' as a sacred abyss into
which the soul can plunge in self-surrender; it means going blindly
where God leads, becoming 'a lifeless instrument' in his hands. By
following this path the soul becomes indifferent to every prompting
of self-will, including even the noble desire to suffer, achieving
ultimately a 'mystical death' in the midst of life, which is an
'anticipation of Paradise', since God rules there unchallenged. Père
de Caussade is more specific. Everything that happens is willed, or
at least permitted, by God. We must accept everything as coming
from his hand. We simply say, 'Fiat', "Thy will be done". Self must
be forgotten, for the merest attempt even to assess our progress in
the spiritual life can revive the hydra of self-love. We do not keep
going back over the past; we do not ask 'What will become of me?'
All we have is the 'sacrament of the present moment', where we

meet the gift or the duty or the cross which God is presenting to us. Whatever comes, hope, consolation, dryness, fear, or despair, we must accept. 'Souls that walk in light sing the canticles of light; those that walk in darkness sing the songs of darkness. Both must be allowed to sing to the end the part allotted to them by God in his motet. Nothing must be added to the score, nothing, left out; every drop of divinely ordained bitterness must be allowed to flow freely.' We must play our providential role: Thy will be done.[134]

What then of the fear of death and Hell? The acceptance of one's own damnation was now officially forbidden, and could only be thought of as an 'impossible' contingency for theoretical discussion[135] Milley, who was not without a wry sense of humour, found it difficult to sympathize with gloomy imaginings.[136] For himself, he asked little by way of consolation; having glimpsed the Promised Land, maybe like Moses he was destined to see no more of it in his lifetime.[137] To a timorous nun he said: think only of the in-dwelling Christ, not of yourself, and not of God's judgement. Once the soul is lost in God, death becomes an incident, like moving from one town to another, 'on trouve Dieu dans toutes les deux'. At Embrun in 1709 he saw two nuns dying as he would wish all to die who have found the secret of abandonment. 'Peaceful as the blessed ones [in Heaven], desiring neither life nor death, health nor illness, repose nor desolation, their hearts lost in the depths of God, without care, without fear, speaking of death as of a wedding—or rather, seeing no difference between life and death. I shall never forget what I saw'.[138] It is easy to misunderstand this attitude to dying, and in more than one fashion. It was unworldly yet did not reject practicalities; it was neither reserved for the few nor possible for the many. Milley regarded his discipline of spirituality as suitable only for chosen souls, and as presupposing a life of mortification. On the other hand, people of all conditions could enter it, including the married and those laden with worldly business—as the nuns he was directing struggled with the legal and administrative business of their convents, and as Fénelon had toiled amid the confusions of his war-torn diocese.[139] Milley's own death exemplified this truth. In the great plague of Marseille of 1720 he was civil commissioner for the rue de l'Escale, where the contagion had first shown itself. Isolated by barricades from the rest of the town, he organized alms, soup, disinfection, and burials as well as taking the last sacraments to the dying. 'Bénissons Dieu de ce qu'il daigne nous offrir pour quelques jours de souffrance sur la terre,' he said when his own turn came.[140] His was an inner peace in the midst of activity and squalor, and at his end he did not hesitate to speak of eternal felicity.

Like Milley, and in obedience to the papal ruling of 1699, Père de Caussade refused to separate our love of God from our reward. The question 'If God is not our eternal felicity, ought we then to love him for himself?' is illegitimate, for it puts forward the 'strange and pitiful supposition that God is not God at all'.[141] What we know of God can never be excluded from our minds, even in imagination; faithful servants of a king might appear before him wearing halters round their necks as a token of their unworthiness, but knowing him, they know that he will pardon.[142] Yet, keeping within boundaries of orthodoxy as prescribed in 1699, Caussade still remained very close to Fénelon's Christian Stoicism, drawing on writings of the archbishop of Cambrai which had not been condemned, and reinforcing controversial points with quotations from Saint François de Sales. In his picture of the Christian life there is never any certainty concerning our eternal destiny. God wills us to walk in darkness—to keep us humble and in dependence upon him, throughout our lives, and at our end.[143] Inevitably, we fear the divine judgement, and 'without an express revelation and assurance of eternal salvation, no one can be free from fear at the last moment'.[144] Fear is an imperfection and, sometimes, if it throws a devoted soul into disarray, it is a visitation from the Devil; but generally, there is a beneficent fear which is 'holy' and 'filial' and which necessarily and usefully comes to us all. We are neither to encourage it nor avoid it: everything must be accepted as coming from God.[145] And yet, we can have confidence. 'At the sight of death, fear should be united to confidence, but the latter ought to predominate.'[146] Assurance comes through considering the purposes of God, who put us into the world to love and serve him, so that in the end he can bring us, through suffering, to his eternity; we have hope when we look towards the Son, who is at once our Judge and our merciful Saviour.[147] However despairing or lonely we become, God is always in touch with us through the Salesian 'fine pointe de l'esprit', and while to us this contact may seem a barely perceptible thread of linkage, it is a thread as strong as a great cable, anchored in God, who will never let us go.[148]

How then do I prepare for death?—with fear and yet with confidence. There is one prerequisite: I am obliged to strive for perfection—from the moment the aspiration ceases, I am in danger of being lost.[149] And there is one continuing obligation: I must accept suffering, the crosses that are sent to me daily, which are instalments of Purgatory, and signs of God's favour towards me.[150] Nothing could be more simple, and nothing could be more difficult. There is no special preparation for death; it is a question of complete commitment to Christian living and to acceptance of God's will. 'The most solid preparation for death', says the Jesuit, 'is that which we make every day, by a regular life, a spirit of recollection, of annihilation, of abnegation, patience, charity and union with our Lord.'[151] It is the Pauline formula of dying daily spiritually, before we die naturally. Yet, while Christian living is the only preparation for our last hour, Père de Caussade does not reduce death (as Milley does) to an incident in our journey. We must allow our minds to dwell on it continually, overcoming our natural repugnance, accepting it as a necessity, and coming to see it as salutory and, finally, as welcome—like a bitter medicine.[152] On the other hand, while death is often in our minds, we must not think directly about our salvation. We did this at a particular point in our lives, when we decided to enter God's service; but it was for the last time. Thereafter we leave our destiny in the hands of God, like a retainer who has enlisted under a great king, who will surely make his fortune in the way that is best for him.[153]

As our lives draw to their end, we make no attempt to assess past years. 'Have I ever made a good confession?' 'Am I forgiven?' 'Am I in a state of grace?' 'Have I made progress in prayer?' We do not ask these questions. 'God has willed to hide all this from me to make me abandon myself blindly to his mercy. I submit and adore his judgements.' 'But I am so unprepared'—another irrelevant consideration. 'Am I ready to do the will of God?'—here is all that matters. And above all, there must be no looking backwards to make a tally of good works, for this comes from the prompting of *amour propre*, seeking to regain a footing within the soul from which it has been banished.[154] There is nothing to rely on but the mercy of God and the merits of Jesus Christ, with the intercessions of the saints and of good souls who love us.[155] When the last hour comes, the soul that has followed the discipline of abandonment should go on exactly as before. The last confession is not to be a voluminous rehearsal of all past sins: it should be 'sans trop de recherche'. The time is better spent in 'acts of faith, hope, contrition, confidence, and union with the merits of Christ'. Accept suffering, strive for perfection, yet forget self and never ask how you have progressed or where you are going; look only to God, fear his judgements but, above all, trust in his mercy: this is living, and this is dying.

Père de Caussade meant his way of 'eminent sanctity' to be open to all.[156] None were excluded but those who refused to make the necessary sacrifices. True, it might be dangerous to speak too clearly of the reassurances of the life of abandonment in books meant for every eye, as distinct from the comfort given to committed souls in private by their spiritual directors.[157] Père Grou, who succeeds Caussade in the chain of Jesuit spirituality, made this caution into a principle; as we have seen, he divides Christians into those who follow the 'active' and the 'passive' ways, and the active are subjected to the lifelong (though ideally ever diminishing) discipline of fear. The writers of the Enlightenment attempted to banish the fear of death and judgement altogether. They revalued human nature and justified it as inherently capable of goodness. They devalued the act of dying by putting the emphasis on living: a man would be judged by his life's achievements, not by his last dispositions, whether it was a judgement by posterity in this life, or by God in the life to come. They rejected Hell as incommensurate with human guilt and as incompatible with the love of God. By contrast, Père de Caussade does not take from death any of its solemnity or from Hell any of its terror. He does not join the Enlightenment to deny Original Sin, rehabilitate human nature, or to accept human pride with complacency. Yet, in a different psychological world and with a different inspiration, looking always towards God, rarely at man and never at self, he absorbs and sublimates the fear of death and judgement, and makes life and death into a unity. The colourful and tumultuous armies of the *philosophes* and Rousseauists were surging forward along the plain, while high on vertiginous mountain tracks, parallel to them and above them, were clambering the spiritual writers of the Fénelonian tradition. All were moving in the same general direction towards the sun, towards a fuller realization of the implications of the doctrine that God is love, and away from the darkness of the old theology of Hell and judgement. But from the plain it was not possible to see all the obstacles of pride, self-love, and self-deceit which haunted the spiritual writers on their painful odyssey, and were to bring to an exhausted halt the optimistic march of the humanitarians and deists of the Enlightenment.

IV

What part did preparation for death play in the devotions and mental outlook of ordinary people—the men and women of average conformist piety, those whom Père de Caussade would describe as being in danger through not striving for perfection? There was an extensive literature on the subject, and as a contribution to the history of spirituality we can construct a model of the recommended patterns of devotional observances. But what influence did the books have? Even if we found all the works which were published, when and where and how many copies, there would still be a long way to go before we could say who read them, let alone who was influenced by them.

We should beware of the assumption, especially where devotional books are concerned, that only those who have read a particular treatise have been influenced by it, or that printed books are the only sources of guidance. Pious individuals prepared—or had prepared for them—manuscript handbooks; the poet Ducis entitled his devotional diary 'Ma grande affaire', and Filassier's *Sentiments Chrétiens . . . pour . . . se préparer à une bonne mort* (1723) had circulated in manuscript until the pages began to disintegrate and its author drew near to his end.[158] The great rush of new books about death came in the last quarter of the seventeenth century; of 236 titles published between 1600 and 1800, 60 appear between 1675 and 1700. The renewal of titles continued at a slower pace in the first quarter of the eighteenth century (38). In 1705, a reviewer rejoiced in the almost 'daily' appearance of new essays on the spirituality of dying: 'Every day we see books of devotion on this subject: but there is no limit to the number of different ways in which we ought to strive to inspire Christians with the idea of putting themselves effectively into the right dispositions for a holy death.'[159] There were fewer new titles in the second quarter of the century (20) and in the fifty years from 1750 to 1800 there were only 13.[160] After 1775 there was an increase in the circulation of works of devotion, since the provincial presses were allowed after that date to print items which had previously been a monopoly of their Parisian rivals; in the flood of publication, the old favourites predominated, so far as the theme of death was concerned. The inference seems to be that theological writers were becoming less interested in, or less insistent on, the subject. On the other hand, there was a continuing substratum of popular demand—not expansive enough to keep pace with the general increase in book sales or even, until 1775, with the rise in the number of copies of theological works sold, but a solid and established demand all the same. Thus, the declining number of editions throughout the century is offset by the impressive showing of works on preparation for death in the provincial revival of devotional literature in the last decade before the Revolution—nearly a tenth of the total number of copies. Booksellers' catalogues in Paris and Rouen show the sales of such works increasing along with the increase in the sale of devotional books generally, and thereafter maintaining the level as other trends of devotion decline.[161] Intelligent scepticism was increasing in France, and so too, it would seem, was highly individual personal piety. Both were being promoted by widening intellectual horizons, increasing literacy and the expansion of the book trade. Within this generalization (as with most generalizations about eighteenth-century France) provincial qualifications have to be made. Piety, as judged by statistics, had sharp regional variations. The provincial printing-presses produced many more religious books per head of the population in Lorraine, Franche-Comté, Brittany, Picardy, Artois, and Flanders, than in Provence, Auvergne, the Limousin, Guyenne, and the Lyonnais.[162] Specialist works on death conform to this general pattern. In the provincial boom of 1775–89, the East (Lorraine and Franche-Comté) lead, in both numbers of copies and numbers of editions; the Norman and Breton West came next, and after that came the North, with Lille and Amiens as the printing centres. These are the traditionally religious areas of France. But the reluctance to print books on death in other parts of the country is not necessarily evidence of a secularization of attitudes. The printers of the Midi may not have been interested, but to what extent did southern France obtain its books from Paris? Were its extensive bilingual areas more particularly dependent on oral instruction in religious matters? Were the confraternities of Penitents of Provence and Languedoc the cadre within which most pious folk made their preparations for dying?[163] The Midi may have been less religious than other areas, or its religion may have had a different emphasis or different channels of expression.

According to the statistics of the booksellers, dying was not a fashionable theme, but there was a steady demand for guides on how to do it. Perhaps this is what might be expected. Every literate and reasonably pious person needed a handbook available to refer to when worried, just as a dictionary or a simple medical treatise was required for occasional use, but few would have wished to follow up the subject or keep abreast of the latest ideas. The writers of the manuals sometimes spoke of the comprehensive indispensability of their spiritual merchandise—all ranks of society and all ages should be familiar with their contents; give copies to the peasants rather than alms, which confer only earthly benefits; it is worthwhile to study various devotional methods; read extracts to the children and the servants at family prayers. But these observations, surely, are just the *clichés* of authorship, and do not constitute proof of the wide distribution of the product. Most of the writers were members of religious congregations, more especially Capuchins and Jesuits; the latter order alone accounted for half the publications in this field in the seventeenth and eighteenth centuries.[164] Although the more learned and literary-minded of the *curés* cheerfully rushed into print, very few ventured advice about dying; their interests were in local history, antiquities and archaeology, agricultural improvements, scientific curiosities, ecclesiastical controversy, or moralizing reflections on subjects set for prizes by local academies. Ordinary pastoral experience among simple folk is not evident in the manuals, though there is abundant evidence of the preoccupations and techniques of the Lenten preacher or the evangelistic

missioner. The unworldly severity of so many of the publications
betrays their monastic origin, so too does the inordinate length of
some of them. It is easy to understand how *Pensez-y bien* with its
anecdotes and the sombre refrain of its title hypnotized curious and
frightened readers; easy too to see why, with its dense prose and
500 pages, Dom Morel's *Entretiens spirituels en forme de prières
pour servir de préparation à la mort* would gather dust on a shelf.
On the other hand, the sort of readers who bought books on serious
subjects did not expect the writers to talk down to them, and the
developing sophistication of taste sharpened their eye for anything
exaggerated, superstitious, or ridiculous. Illustrations fade out of
the books on death in the course of the eighteenth century.[165]
Conventional ornaments like skulls, trailing thorns, candles, and
teardrops remained acceptable, but there were fewer pictures of
deathbed scenes, fewer angels, and hardly any devils. The arrangement of the text became more logical, the advice more comprehensive and encyclopaedic in scope. More editions appeared in
convenient pocket sizes.

We might infer—though not with certainty—that if books were
made for carrying round, more people would do so; but were they
acting on the advice contained within the covers? This is what we
cannot say. Certainly, there was a pious tradition which encouraged men or women, once active life was over, to dedicate their
remaining years to preparation for dying. After a career of dubious
escapades, some countess might take the veil[166]—or, more usually,
women of good family would rent apartments in nunneries for
their retirement, where they could share some of the devotions of
the monastic life without entirely going out of social circulation.[167]
Nobles of the Court might turn to religion; of the great names of
the Regency, the duc de Lauzun retired to a Parisian monastery in
1723 (though he was more concerned to avoid giving an account of
his spendthrift career to his relatives than with piety), the duc de
Villars retired to the abbey of Bec in 1721 (and moved to the
Oratory at Paris ten years later), and the maréchal de Noailles
exiled himself to his estates, where he attended all the parish offices,
and would lie under the *drap mortuaire* (the pall used for funerals)
to have the office of the dead read over him as a penitential
exercise.[168]

No doubt, among pious folk in the evening of their days—even if they did not retire from the world—the manuals of preparation for death were much used. And there were at least a few lay people who made the preparation for death central to their meditation, or who were driven into obsessive fear by ruthless clerical direction (at the Court of Louis XV we hear of the Queen meditating in the presence of a skull, supposedly that of the great courtesan Ninon de Lenclos, and of one of the King's daughters driven nearly to hysteria by the nuns of Fontevrault, who sent her to pray in the funeral vault of the abbey when she went there to make her confession).[169] No doubt too, during missions and at certain penitential seasons, most reasonably pious people would concentrate their meditations on themes concerning judgement and the great finalities. But the books on these themes were not the only or the most important guides to devotion, and their prescriptions would not be regarded as necessarily relevant to all persons and all seasons. Duguet, the Jansenist, devises a regime of prayer for 'a Christian lady' willing to live 'in saintly fashion in the world'. There are long intercessions in the morning, followed by half an hour's meditation, then psalms, mass, vespers, and prayers for the whole household about 9 a.m.; at night, a quarter of an hour's prayer and compline. There is little about death except at the point where practically all the devotional writers insist on it—when retiring for the night: 'try to go to bed with the sentiments you would have if you had to appear before God at your awakening'. (Significantly, however, when he recommends allowing any 'important truth' to intrude accidentally into the meditation, his example is, 'our uncertainty about the time when we must die and our certainty that this must happen'.[170]) In another work on preparation for receiving the sacrament, Duguet concentrates on death only when it is time for an examination of conscience: he asks for 'a shaft of that great light by which, at the moment of my death, I shall see precisely all the offences of my lifetime'.[171] Another writer's system of preparation for Sunday communion has each day of the week consecrated to a meditation on some particular role of Christ in our lives—as King, Husband, Shepherd, Redeemer, Physician of the soul, Brother, Friend, and Head; Sunday is reserved for Priest and Victim and Saturday for Judge—a pre-eminence, but not an undue one, for the apocalyptic theme.[172] A rigorist guide to conduct, published in 1750, lays down an exact pattern of pious reflections for daily observance, and almost excludes the theme of judgement altogether. At waking, think of God, 'near to you and who has been near all through the night', and make an act of thanksgiving and surrender. Then a prayer for forgiveness, followed by the Pater, Ave, Credo, Misereatur, and the recitation of the commandments of God and of the Church; then a recommendation of oneself to Guardian Angel and to Patron Saint, and intercessions for one's family and for all men, especially for the dying. When the church bell rings in the morning and at midday, say the Angelus, when it rings for mass say a Pater or other prayer with the intention of participating. Say Grace before and after meals, and make an act of thanksgiving for any fortunate occurrence, and of resignation when affairs turn out ill. At the end of the day, examine your conscience and ask pardon, offer thanks and recite the same prayers as in the morning. In all this programme, though the dying are specially prayed for, there is no concentration of the mind on death or on Hell.[173]

Pious souls were not necessarily obsessed with death, and average Christians might not have concerned themselves with it except when absolutely necessary. As the preachers complained, good health and worldly employment so often sufficed to exclude the shadow of death from the mind. Much of the eloquent and threatening exhortation of the eighteenth-century moralists passed unheeded. This is demonstrably the case where the conferment of ecclesiastical benefices or lending at interest is concerned, and in certain sexual matters.[174] It is unlikely that the full rigours of preparation for death as proposed in any one manual were practised except by the pious few. But such preparation was, nevertheless, regarded as a major and indispensable part of the devotional life and the duties of a Christian, and was, no doubt, often in the forefront of the mind of the average believer. He would be uncomfortably aware of the issues at stake and of the obligations he ought to be assuming—that one day he intended to assume—and as he grew older, or illness came, or rumours of the approach of pestilence were heard, or he received the sombrely ornamented *billet* inviting him to the requiem for a departed friend, he would search for his copy of

Père Crasset or Quesnel or *Pensez-y bien* and resolve to try, once again, to be ready for the end.

We have been considering the attitude of the literate minority. The mass of the population consisted of peasants, and of these, only a few, the more prosperous and better educated, would ever possess books of devotion of any sophistication. Most people in the countryside, even if they could read, would get no further than the little tracts hawked by the *colporteurs*.[175] These simple publications seized on the lurid or sentimental details of violent or tragic deaths—'The execution of six young criminals', 'The death of a rich miser', 'A circumstantial relation of the illness and death of Frederick I, King of Sweden', 'The gay yet tragic story of two Swiss soldiers', 'The peasant who by his death made his wife and children happy', 'A preacher dies in his pulpit', 'Abominable murder committed by an inhuman woman', 'The fatal wedding night'. The terrors of the afterlife were well advertised, and Hell was described in detail; the titles of the simple popular works of devotion reveal their central preoccupation—to emphasize the need for constant preparation, constant vigilance: *Il faut mourir, Pensez-y bien, Préparation à la mort, Sept trompettes pour réveiller les pécheurs.* More especially, the popular literature reflects the themes of death as a punishment for sin, and of death as the great leveller. The *danse macabre*, with its picture of the representatives of the hierarchies of society brought low, of crown and coronet, mitre and money-bags all confounded in the dust, is often evoked; so too was the idea that death comes more kindly to 'bonhomme Misère', the wretched and disinherited. In the less sophisticated of these writings the element of strictly Christian preparation for death was limited. More was said about indulgences than about prayer. The appeal to fear as a moral instrument and to the equality of the grave as a remedy for envy and a substitute for earthly justice were as much instinctive devices of social therapy as of spiritual instruction.

For simple folk, and for many who were not so simple, preparation for death came from the oral instruction given by the *curé* and his *vicaire*. By the early eighteenth century, the delivery of a sermon at mass and the catechizing of children and young people had become an established part of the duties of the parochial clergy, enforced by the inquiries of episcopal visitations. There were parishes where these obligations were strictly fulfilled, ones where they were neglected, and others—the most—where they were intermittently performed so far as harvest, weather, cattle-minding, and the recalcitrance of human nature permitted. There is some evidence that the themes of Hell and judgement were being preached in a more restrained fashion and less frequently as the century went on.[176] Even so, they were prominent enough. The foundation of fear was laid in the catechism; there were many and diverse diocesan versions, but they rarely seem to have made concessions to childish susceptibilities.

'Where do those who have done evil go?'
'To Hell, to burn with the devils'.
'Why must I love and serve God?'
'Because God will send those who do so to Heaven, and the others to Hell'.
'Why are the wicked inconsolable in Hell?'
'For three reasons. The first is that it pleases God to make them suffer; the second is that the demons study to invent new punishments to torment them; the third is that the gnawing of their conscience gives then no repose. The saints are pleased to watch them suffer.'[177]

A diocesan catechism falling short of these severities was likely to be denounced by Jansenist propagandists. Thus Paul-Albert de Luynes, translated from the bishopric of Bayeux to the archbishop-ric of Sens in 1753, began by introducing a new catechism which described unbaptized children as deprived of the vision of God—and was taken to task for failing to consign them to eternal damnation.[178] Sermons would carry on the grim instruction, some-times crudely, sometimes with some literary flair. 'You say *we have to die*, and you think of nothing less than of dying; you say, *we have to die*, and you think only of living, and you live as though you would not have to die'—this from a *curé* who published some of his sermons in the seventies.[179] Advent, Lent, All Souls' Day, and times of pestilence and famine gave the preacher special oppor-tunities; so too did the missions which, in many places, descended on a town or village at decennial intervals, with their processions, addresses, and canticles in which the theme of death so often reverberates. To the missioners, death was to be a matter of daily remembrance, connected with the everyday events which we all experience. 'Do you not sleep in the bed in which you will die? Do you not go to rest between the sheets which will form your shroud? Do you not hear the sound of bells which one day will tell the whole town that you have died?'[180]

Yet the mission preaching and, *a fortiori*, the less dramatic everyday sermons and catechizings, were not so obsessively centred on death as citation of lurid passages might suggest. The question is (as we saw with devotional literature) what part did death play in the total presentation of the Christian message? For preachers and teachers, the desire to inspire fear was balanced by more positive aims, or perhaps we should say, fear was a means to an end. The missioners, who gave such a disproportionate time to judgement, wished to renew affection for the suffering Christ—'my sins have crucified my Saviour'; they wished to bring about a change of conduct—to reconcile enemies, restore peace in troubled families, wind up lawsuits, enforce moral standards in the community, found a group dedicated to continuing the influence of the mission through prayer. A *curé*'s course of sermons throughout the year[181] would not necessarily harp on Hell: he might follow the Gospel for the day, or take themes like the Ten Commandments, the Lord's Prayer, or the Sacraments; he could progress through the full story of Salvation—Creation, 'the different hierarchies of angels', the making of man, the Fall, the promised Messiah, the Immaculate conception of Our Lady, the life of Christ, 'dialogues on the Passion', and, of course, the Last Judgement; there were also the 'precepts of the Church' to be expounded—fasting in Lent, Sunday observance, the wickedness of stage plays and of the pursuit of riches, the honest performance of daily work and the honour due to God's ministers; as circumstances required, there would be denunciation of the social and moral evils of the times and, in more fashionable churches, the eloquent psychological 'portraits' of various types of sinners and lukewarm Christians that made the sermon into a branch of literature owing more to La Bruyère than to Bossuet. Catechisms[182] would enumerate the theological virtues (and, by contrast, the hierarchy of possible sins), the sacraments, God's commandments, the precepts of the Church, the Creed, the essentials of prayer (more especially teaching the Pater, Ave, and intercessions for various hours of the day). Other catechisms, based on Fleury's famous model, would be designed within a historical framework, starting at Creation and ending with the sacramental life of the Church, a method which had the advantage of accommodating a homilitic pattern of the truths, the duties, and the means to enable us to perform them. Sensational threatening about death and specific instruction to prepare for it should be seen in the context of the routine teaching which was given in the parishes of France. The total effect would be to suggest that the basic preparation for the last hour was a love of God through devotion to the suffering of his Son, an obedience to the Church, and a serious effort at amendment of life. All the devices recommended by the specialists, from flagellation to the recitation of litanies, to meditation in the presence of a skull, were but psychological aids to these greater ends.

Inevitably, in that age of high morality and harsh theology, the ideas of death, Hell, and judgement were frequently present in people's minds. Yet frequency does not prove intensity: familiarity may make terrors somewhat ordinary as well as more pervasive. Towards the end of the *ancien régime*, preachers were complaining that the message of doom was provoking ridicule. 'We would not be pardoned the slightest mitigation of doctrine,' said one of them, 'but if we speak of hell-fire, then from that moment we are no longer worthy of attention, and we are regarded as playing on the gullibility of our listeners.'[183] It was not just a matter of theological misgivings encouraged by all the deistic writers who were recalling Christians to the implications of the doctrine that God is love; there was also the introverted process, described by Groethuysen, by which the rhetoric of the pulpit and pious literature—the insistence on describing the indescribable, the assault on the emotions explicit in every detail, the logical mapping-out of the details of the ultimate and infinite purpose—proved counter-productive. The excess of fear ran to curiosity and brinkmanship as well as to incredulity; Hell was not so much rejected as transformed into 'literary fashion', a stylistic and psychological device, a set theme for eloquence to be appreciated by connoisseurs. And whatever obsessions with morbidities historians may subsequently discover in the climate of ideas of a particular age, the fact remains that men will always be more concerned with living than with dying. Indeed, even the most austere and unworldly spiritual directors always put the business of living, the meticulous performance of duty at work and in the family, as the first priority of the Christian.[184] Even if the only point of life is to prepare for death, the concentration of the mind has to be upon the process of living. And when life is briefer and more hazardous, men instinctively live it more intensely: death cannot dominate the mind in proportion to its incidence.

By our modern view, preparation for death is a highly individual matter, a lonely preparation for the loneliest journey. Generally, the seventeenth- and eighteenth-century spiritual writers were operating in these individualistic terms, as spiritual writers normally do. But most people's minds were moulded by their attendance at the ceremonies of the Church, rather than by the books which they had not read, or which if they had read them, seemed unrealistic. In these ceremonies, the idea of a corporate salvation (which had become obscured since the Church became a comprehensive organization based on mass conformity) lived on. The procession to the graveyard on All Souls' Day and, in central France, on Palm Sunday also,[185] the masses for the dead, the concourse around the deathbed, and the prayer of commendation adjuring the Christian soul to depart in the company of the patriarchs, prophets, saints and martyrs and all the faithful departed, fortified by the prayers of the whole congregation—everything spoke of the unity of Christians in a common faith and a common hope. Not surprisingly then, to men who practised their religion but did not normally read about it, the best way to prepare for death was by corporate action, through membership of a confraternity. Some of these, like the *Pénitents* of Provence, were almost exclusively organized for mutual comfort in the face of death—for prayers in life, for attendance at deathbeds of *confrères*, and for marching in their funeral processions. Since representatives of the *Pénitents* also took on the tasks of accompanying the bodies of the poor to their graves out of charity, and of the rich for payment to the association's funds, in many places the sight of the long-robed figures (the robes generally white or grey, but occasionally red or violet), anonymous behind their hoods with eye-slits, became inseparable from the idea of death. These types of confraternity flourished only in certain areas—in Provence, Languedoc, Dauphiné, and around Limoges—and they were an urban phenomenon, with rank-and-file membership drawn chiefly from merchants, shopkeepers, and artisans.[186] All over France, however, there were other confraternities of varying kinds and with less dramatic costumes (or with no special costume at all) which had as their primary object the saying of prayers for dying and deceased members. Some walked in funeral processions, like the Guild of the Holy Sacrament in the Church of Ferrière, near Plantis; according to the regulations, forty members were to attend, taking with them the processional cross, the banner, two handbells, and fourteen big candles—the dress to be white robe, red cloak adorned with a symbol representing the sacrament of the altar, stiff black hat, and white stockings (the latter to be laundered every four months, a realistic provision).[187] More sober associations would eschew display and simply meet to pray for dead brethren and sisters: such was the confraternity of St. Sebastian in the Church of Saint-Nicolas at Maule, much favoured by widows.[188] Or the object might be, more specifically, to concentrate on preparing oneself for death, like the association founded at Rennes early in the century 'pour obtenir une bonne mort', whose devotions consisted of meditation upon the agonies of Jesus and his mother on Calvary.[189] There might be some special attachment to a saint whose assistance was supposed to be particularly efficacious at the end—more especially to St. Joseph (who died in the arms of Mary and Jesus) and the Blessed Virgin herself, 'la patronne de la bonne mort' because of her influence with her Son who holds the keys of Death and Hell.[190] Almost invariably, there would be a provision for making a levy to pay for masses for the souls of members, generally during the month after their death.[191] Confraternities with other objects as their chief aim—trade guilds, associations to forward particular devotions or connected with a particular religious order, or to support some chapel—often included in their rules the saying of prayers and the saying of masses for departed members. The Jesuit confraternities of better-class citizens, the so-called 'Messieurs', which met for instruction and meditation, also arranged obituary masses and attended funerals.[192] Around Avignon, pilgrims who had made the journey to St. James of Compostella attended the obsequies of others who had gained entrance to this exclusive spiritual club.[193] The trade guilds had decorations, such as a pall to spread over the coffin, which were available for the funerals of members, and a rule obliging each master (or his representative) to attend, as well as a levy of one or two sous for masses when a *confrère* died.[194]

There were signs, in the eighteenth century, of the decline of confraternities, more especially the *Pénitents*. It was unusual for a new group to be founded, and some of the old were wound up. Oddly enough (or was it, in fact, what would have been expected?), the pious organizations devoted to the sombre business of dying were those most subject to abuses—disputes about precedence, wasting funds on good cheer, and the scandals which enraged reforming bishops.[195] The upper-class members were drifting away from the *Pénitents* of Provence. At the beginning of the century, the officers included members of many leading families, but by the end of the *ancien régime* those places were occupied by shopkeepers and the like, while the leading families were represented in the masonic lodges.[196] No doubt the decline corresponds to changing patterns of sociability on a complex scale, but a contributory factor may be the beginning of a new attitude to death, a view of grief as an intense and intimate concern of the family, and of dying as a private individual tragedy emancipated from the rituals of a corporate, hierarchical society.[197] The heyday of the theology of judgement had also been the heyday of prayers and masses for the dead, and in the confraternities (picturesque abuses and confusions notwithstanding) had been expressed the idea of the corporate life and responsibility of Christians and their hope for a corporate salvation, in which the merits of the saints would help the frailer brethren and the union of all, in different degrees of sanctity, with Christ, would bring all into his kingdom. Yet this had been a different branch of theological speculation, hardly integrated into the grim pictures of judgement, in which the naked individual stood or fell alone, before his maker. By popular demand, as it were, through the confraternities the gap in technical theology had been bridged. Unfortunately, as Hell declined, so too did the idea of a corporate salvation, and with this decline began the loneliness of our modern way of dying.

8

Deathbeds

I

In seventeenth- and eighteenth-century France, deathbeds were a place of polite resort and public ceremony. When Pascal said 'on mourra seul', he meant that a man is alone in his last hour *in spite of* the throng. Today, we die alone in the strict meaning of the word. Since death is the unthinkable eventuality, and science has resources for alleviating its pains and concealing its imminence, our departure can be contrived as a quiet event in a hospital, with a minimum of fuss and embarrassment. We are thus deprived of our last chance of individual self-expression, says Philippe Ariès,[1] we cannot act our final gestures and bring others into a ritual pattern woven around our personal drama. But if our ancestors had rights and roles which we have lost, they could exercise them only within a tight social cadre, which had its exigencies and oppressiveness. They lived their lives on a stage, and their concept of the family was broader than ours, bringing in more relatives, and servants and dependants. They died fulfilling and seen to be fulfilling their obligations to family and connection, their station and its duties.

There were religious arguments to justify public dying. The sovereign remedy against despair, Erasmus had said, is the awareness of the presence of faithful believers, representatives of God's great household, offering their prayers. When a monk of La Trappe neared his end, the whole community would assemble; the dying man, lying on straw and ashes, would be consoled by their intercessions.[2] A pious Christian in secular life might also expect his friends to gather, less formally, to pray with him and for him. That was why confraternities of *Pénitents* had a duty to attend at the deathbed of one of their members. Even if my final agony lasts many hours, said a spiritual writer in 1729, I must insist that those who love me do not leave for a single moment—let them continue to inspire me to acts of confidence, love, and faith long after I have

234

ceased to be capable of making any audible or visible response.[3] This was the duty of the pious and the few—the close friends. But there was one moment in the rituals of dying when all the faithful without exception were summoned to demonstrate their unity with the dying man and offer their prayers for him: this was when the last communion, the viaticum, was brought. In the street, as the procession passed, cabs and carriages stopped and passers-by genuflected. Everyone was entitled to follow the sacrament into the house and into the room where the man was dying; indeed, there was an indulgence of forty days' remission of purgatorial pains which accompanied this pious work.

The wider community of Christians had a duty to the dying man; conversely, he had obligations to them. For a priest, here was the chance to deliver a final sermon. An archdeacon of Évreux, who had been a famous preacher, unable to make himself heard by all the assembly round his bed, asked an ecclesiastic near at hand to proclaim that he wished them 'to serve and love God with all their might' while they had time.[4] And for every Christian, even those whose lives had been lukewarm and conventional (perhaps, more especially for these), death provided an opportunity for a public display of repentance, submission to God's decrees, and confidence in his mercy. Here was the psychological moment when a good example had the utmost leverage to overturn complacent sinners. 'Point de Prédicateur plus éloquent que l'exemple. Aucun Apôtre plus persuasif qu'un moribond.'[5] The attendant clergy would ensure that the lesson was not wasted. A handbook for priests published in 1718 included specimen exhortations, ostensibly directed to the dying but clearly intended to be overheard; they were for the use of clergy 'unaccustomed to public speaking', lest by a repetitious and boring discourse they 'bring the ministry into contempt'.[6]

The crowded deathbed scene of the *ancien régime* is a convenient stereotype for the historian. But distinctions should be made. So many in those days were alone in the world, or living in misery; after the *curé* had been and gone, they died as best they could. And dying according to the rules had stages—the crowd was not always there. Nor, according to the best ecclesiastical authorities, ought it to have been, except for any announcement of public penance or reparation, and at the ceremony of the viaticum. In an essay on

Christian dying published in 1702, Mabillon held up St. Augustine
as an example; in his last fever he had allowed no one but his doctor
to approach him, so as to be undisturbed in prayer.[7] In the com-
pendia of 'belles morts' of the second half of the seventeenth
century, there are those who insist on excluding even their friends.
One is frère Benoist of La Trappe, who does not want the whole
community to gather: 'he had more need of their prayers than of
their presence'.[8] His abbot did not demur, for to him all intercession
pointed finally to a lonely relationship transcending the community
of the faithful and prayer itself; when leaving a dying monk to
attend to indispensable business he had a simple formula of parting—'I leave you with Jesus Christ', or 'I leave you with our Lord'.[9]
In a series of thirty-nine engravings published in 1700 to demonstrate the rules of Christian dying, the wife and children are present
on most occasions (they sleep on chairs in the room); two friars
acting as confessors are alone with the sick man twice; a number of
older folk are present once at a session of mutual reconciliation; and
the wife, children, and friars are the only ones there at the very end.
As for the traditional crowd, there is no sign of it except when the
curé brings the viaticum.[10] Certainly, it was axiomatic to spiritual
writers that a man must have peace and repose after receiving the
last sacraments, though they would expect the closest relatives to
remain. Once he realizes that there are only a few hours left, the
confessor (or in his absence, the best friend) has the duty of urging
the assembly to disperse, said the abbé Filassier in 1726; by all
means let them continue praying, but elsewhere, in churches or
other quiet places.[11]

The religious observances of eighteenth-century France were
part of the social order, and the price of universality was infiltration
by the world. The visitors crowding at a deathbed were seeing and
being seen, paying their respects to an individual and a family.
Moreau was pleased when the maréchale de Noailles took his wife
to the bedside of the princesse d'Armagnac, and went himself that
evening. 'All the family and friends were assembled,' he reported,
'these people came to adorn her tomb, though they cared little for
her during her life.'[12] There would be gossip about family concerns,
property and feuds, and the human interest of a spectacle of devotion, courage, or cowardice ('Je savoure la mort,' Moreau reports

the princess as saying, in the midst of great pain). There would be anecdotes to recount afterwards about incongruous incidents. Voltaire advised the failing comtesse de Ségur to take egg yolks in potato flour; 'Quel homme,' said someone fatuously, 'pas un mot sans un trait.'[13] Lamenting over one of her daughters, the maréchale de Noailles cried, 'Mon Dieu, rendez-la-moi, et prenez tous mes autres enfants', so that the duc de la Vallière, who had married one of them, asked, 'Madame, les gendres en sont-ils?'[14] The procession of the viaticum might be followed into courtyard and house by a crowd showing its respect for some distinguished local notable (as Restif remembered in his village), or by beggars seeking alms, collectors of indulgences, or merely by the curious—like the brazen *avocat* Barbier who followed some great ones of the Court when the *curé* of Saint-Eustache took the last sacrament to the duchesse d'Orléans.[15] The century was to see a reaction against the custom of dying in public. No doubt a major shift of human and cultural attitudes was involved, as well as a deistical reaction against Christian ceremonies, but there was also a Christian revolt against the infiltration of the world.

A dying man had special obligations, spiritual and material, to his family; the 'public' way of dying tended to formalize them, but also to ensure their fulfilment. From the seventeenth century came an ideal of a Christian end which included a solemn farewell and exhortation to wife and children. The Oratorian Jean Hanard in 1667 published numerous recent examples. The most complete was that of the soldier duc de Longueville in 1663, who gave a speech to his assembled children, then addressed them individually, and finally gave to each a document which he had dictated, signed with his dying hand. He spoke of the transience of greatness and the limitations of the ideal of honour; he urged them to respect their mother; to live in union, and to serve the King; always they should take good ecclesiastical advice concerning the conferment of benefices, be generous to the poor, and give servants fair wages, treating them 'according to Christian obligations' rather than according to their lowly status.[16] Sometimes, the servants would be noticed directly. The duchesse de Fronsac, another example of 'une belle mort', asked them collectively to forgive her, and thereafter spoke to individuals, more especially those who were younger and lowest in rank.[17] Chancelier d'Aguesseau describes the death of his father in 1719 in terms that might have come from Hanard's anthology.[18] Children and grandchildren gathered round the bed-side of the aged patriarch—eighty-one years of age; in tears, they implored his blessing. The dying man urged them to read a passage of Scripture daily, to meditate upon it and to reflect on eternity; then he gave them all his blessing and invoked God's grace upon them. Later he insisted on being helped out of his bed to his desk, to set his papers in order, and he gave his will to a friend of the family to read aloud to the assembled company. A small boy of three who had been absent from the general ceremony of benediction was brought in to receive an individual farewell, a servant who needed a testimonial was given one from the deathbed, and the sons of the family were again exhorted to follow the ways of scriptural re-ligion. Persons of average piety might not say their farewells with the fervour of Hanard's elect, but it was customary for them to give deathbed advice to their children. Restif de la Bretonne describes how a father ordered his son to marry immediately, and how a mother called in her daughters for a final exhortation about their domestic duties.[19] The heroes of eighteenth-century novels were aided in their misfortunes by memories of such dying admonitions: the abbé Prévost's Dean recollects how his father exhorted him to care for his brothers and sisters and ordered them to obey him, the abbé Gérard's Valmont remembers his mother's final benediction and her words, 'Adieu, my children, do not forget, before God, how greatly I have loved you'. Such were the 'derniers adieux'.[20] One of the less agreeable forms of spiritual writing of the century was the invention of 'derniers adieux' as a literary device to confer dramatic force on improving moralizing. Lasne d'Aiguebelle, after censuring such fictions on the part of the clergy (how can a 'froid célibataire' appreciate family relationships?), showed by his own invention how pedestrian the imaginings of the laity could be;[21] Caraccioli has 'la maréchale de —' going on for three weeks in nightly exhor-tations to her children, with everything taken down by a hidden secretary.[22] And while the clergy had no children of their own, they still had their duty to their spiritual family when dying. Priors would summon their monks, and abbesses their nuns, for words of farewell and encouragement; the Jansenist Quesnel called together his companions of exile to bless them and direct them to kiss his crucifix as a symbol of their unity.[23]

It was the duty of a confessor to bring a dying man to peace with his family. Equally, the confessor was obliged to encourage his penitent to leave his temporal affairs in order (that was why, in the case of the minority of people who had worldly goods worthy of legal attention, a notary generally attended after the visit of the priest).[24] The Church wished the faithful to make their wills calmly and at leisure, while in health, and the effect of ecclesiastical pressure can be seen in the statistical pattern of the last will and testament in Paris; in the first half of the seventeenth century, 68 per cent of these documents were drawn up *in articulo mortis*, while in the second half of the eighteenth century, only 40 per cent of the men and 45 per cent of the women left matters so late.[25] The duty of a priest to a dying man was to warn him not to disinherit any of his heirs without a reason which could be put before God; to avoid all occasion for subsequent litigation by ensuring that the requirements of law and custom had been observed; to give generously to the poor of the parish and the town; to provide suitably for faithful servants; and (such was the force of anticlerical suspicion) to divert proposals for legacies to churchmen which might be to the detriment of the decent maintenance of the family.[26] The emphasis of the religious handbooks on the duty of making a will and on the accompanying casuistry of distributive justice, which seems excessive to our modern taste, is easily understood in the circumstances of eighteenth-century France. Though the imagination lingers on a few romantic legacies (like Lally-Tollendal, a prisoner of the English in India, leaving 2,000 *livres* a year to his natural son, in the charge of a cloth merchant of the rue Saint-Honoré),[27] all sorts of routine injustices could arise from carelessness, more especially in the northern two-thirds of the country, where the various customary laws prevailed for commoners, and where the compulsorily divisible part of the inheritance, the 'propres', could be juggled into the categories of 'chattels' or 'acquisitions', or disposed of by carefully devised earlier settlements in favour of a single heir.[28]

A last will and testament began with religious phraseology. Up to the mid-eighteenth century, the preamble would normally consist of an invocation of the Trinity, a recommendation to God, the

Blessed Virgin, and the patron saint and guardian angel of the testator; there might also be a statement of resignation to the will of God, of the wish to live and die in the Catholic, Apostolic, and Roman religion, a prayer that despair and the demon would be kept at bay by the intercessions of the saints, and a prayer for enlightenment in the disposal of worldly goods.[29] In an unusually pious will for the date (1747), the testator 'recommends his soul to God, by the merits of the blood and the death of our Lord Jesus Christ, his God and his redeemer, imploring the powerful intercession of the most Holy Virgin, Mother of God, in whose protection he has always had a great confidence, having given her name to all his children, to impress on their minds a particular devotion towards her and trust in her mercy, imploring also the intercession of his Guardian Angel, of his patron saint, St. Louis, and of all the court of Heaven to obtain through their intercessions the grace to die as a faithful child of the Catholic, Apostolic, and Roman Church, and to attain to everlasting felicity.'[30]

By the mid-century, preambles of this kind were becoming less frequent. One Angevin notary gradually whittled down his pious phraseology until by 1774 he was using the simple form, '*Au nom de Dieu, Amen*'.[31] Vovelle describes how terms of devotion gradually disappear from the wills of notables everywhere in Provence except in Nice, an area of strong traditionalism. Marseille is an extreme case of a complete overthrow of the old conventions. At the beginning of the eighteenth century, 90 per cent of the wills used the rich, traditional Christian formulas, and only 5 per cent were limited to a simple invocation of the Deity. By the eve of the Revolution, the positions were reversed, only 5 per cent using the old formulas and 66 per cent using the simple invocation—with 22 per cent containing no religious reference at all.[32] Paris was like Marseille—indeed, the evolution of the preamble towards simplicity and brevity was swifter there.[33] In the process of abbreviation in Paris, Chaunu has noted[34] that the appeal to 'the merits and death of Jesus Christ' declined throughout the eighteenth century, as did the phrase 'the Son of God'—the invocation was becoming shorter in the direction of deism, by economizing in references to the claims of revelation. We are dealing, of course, with the stylistic changes of notaries. Some testators no doubt regarded the old ıvocations as 'les plus plates capucinades', as a journalist said of the vill of Louis XV;[35] but to many, the change to an abbreviated form vould signify little. To others, persons of scrupulous piety, baring ıe's soul before a lawyer's clerk might have come to seem a ompous exercise destructive of true religious feeling. It is a change lustrative both of the growing secularization of social *mores* and of ıe growing sophistication of religious attitudes. No doubt notar- ːs could not defy the wishes of their clients in matters where these vere formulated. But how often did the religious invocations of vills become an issue? Nearly half the wills of Paris were drawn up ı the shadow of death: would a man desperately addressing his few ːmaining days or hours to God think that it any longer mattered vhether the fears and hopes that filled his horizon were recorded by ıwyers? The clergy, so watchful against the encroachments of the ʲorld, and the handbooks of preparation for dying, so meticulous in ʰeir requirements, seem to have ignored the whole question of the iety of preambles.

More significantly, the content of legacies was changing. By the ɛginning of the eighteenth century, only rarely did a testator ɔund a mass in perpetuity. Religious institutions often refused to ɔcept such an obligation, and, as for past commitments, the pro- ress of inflation and other economic vicissitudes, or the sheer ʲeight of accumulated duties, sometimes led to episcopal ordi- ances consolidating the foundation masses on a lower tariff.[36] Vith such examples of 'spiritual bankruptcies'[37] before them, tes- ıtors preferred to specify a precise number of masses. Legacies for igh masses with full ceremonial also became rarer: a larger num- ɛr of low masses could be obtained for the same investment. This ʰange has been called 'une ruse naïve avec la Transcendance',[38] ʰough such a ruse was taking religion seriously, as well as elimi- ating worldly pride. The impact of the great surge of devotion of ʰe seventeenth century can be seen in the growing proportion of ʰe worldly possessions listed in wills which were being devoted to ıasses; the peak came late—the highest proportion in the wills of ıen in Paris being between the years 1680 and 1720, and in those of ʲomen between 1680 and 1730.[39] Thereafter came the decline. 'ovelle's masterly analysis of the testaments of Provence shows ʰe decreasing demand for masses from the mid-eighteenth

century. This was a change of custom which began with the educated classes—magistrates, office holders, merchants, and members
of the liberal professions. Here was another case where religious
scepticism coincided in its effects with the requirements of a refinement of the religious outlook. In this respect, as in the question of
prescribing funeral ceremonies, testators seem to have become
more inclined to trust their heirs—family affections were intensifying. Severe moralists, more especially the Jansenists, taught
that charitable donations in a will were preferable to legacies which
(however worthy the liturgical content) tended to encourage clerical comfort. 'If you give it[your legacy] to ecclesiastics, they will
spend it on good cheer. If you give it to the poor, they will pray for
you, and you will have merit in the sight of God.'[40] The point could
be made more sharply still, for it was a commonplace with spiritual
writers to say that charitable works during a man's lifetime were
more efficacious for his salvation than generous actions postponed
for his testamentary executor to perform. In the wills of nobles in
Brittany in the eighteenth century there is evidence of an increase
of charity to the poor to offset the declining numbers of masses;[41]
this does not seem to be the case, however, in Paris. But a basis of
calculation or comparison is hard to find. Were charitable works
performed during life increasing in number? The poor of towns
were largely 'institutionalized',[42] and the fashion of institutional
charity changed in the course of the century, from the multitude of
small legacies which ensured a dozen to thirteen poor marching in
the funeral procession, to the fewer but bigger legacies, given
unconditionally.[43] There is some gossipy evidence that public opinion was coming to judge the generosity of a will by the legacies to
servants. Voltaire, who in his youth had spent fruitless hours at the
deathbed of a friend pleading her servants' cause,[44] was to meet with
censure after his death in this respect,[45] and even Cardinal de la
Roche Aymon, who left everything else to the hospitals of his
diocese, was blamed because his domestic staff were left only a
year's wages.[46] The pious duc de Croy, with memories of his
mother's generosity to the poor to inspire him ('Vous ne trouverez
pas que c'est trop?', she asked as she showed him her will as she lay
dying, and he borrowed to be able to fulfil her wishes), left five
times as much in pensions to servants as he did for masses for

himself and his wife, and further sums for the poor of his lands in Hainault, 'both French and Austrian'. And he instructed his heir to find the officer who had been in charge of provisions at Cologne during the wars, to whom he still owed four or five hundred *livres*.[47] It was a nice balance of obligations, and the masses are not the most significant item.

Once the lawyers had departed, a dying man was supposed to be concerned exclusively with spiritual affairs. The deathbed rituals of the Church began with confession, made to the priest of the penitent's choice. Then followed the viaticum. This ceremony could be performed only by the *curé* of the parish or his representative. A monk, friar, canon, or other ecclesiastic might have heard the confession and given absolution, and have duly informed the *curé* he had done so; but he could not administer either the viaticum or extreme unction. This rule, designed to preserve the parochial clergy from monastic and capitular encroachments, was inflexible.[48] The King himself paid deference to it, for although he received the sacraments from one of the two great prelates who acted as his major chaplains (the *grand* or the *premier aumônier*), this was always in the presence of the diocesan bishop or the *curé* of Versailles.[49] Like all communions, the last one demanded the submission of the soul to God's will, in this case to death, and offered union with the life of Christ.[50] But, as its name implied, the viaticum was also the preparation for a journey from earth to Heaven, and it provided the great essential for this venture into the unknown, 'the hope of eternal life'.[51] In France, it was customary to give extreme unction after the viaticum. As Mabillon pointed out, this was a departure from the older tradition[52] (it was, in fact, the result of a ruling of Pope Paul V in 1614, one which has been reversed in the *Ordo* of 1972), and the logic of the old order of ceremonies was evident when spiritual writers listed the benefits conferred by extreme unction, some of which might have been more appropriately received before the communion. The anointings, as in all anointing of the sick, were for the healing of the body and in hope of recovery;[53] they were also a supplement to the last confession, providing an opportunity of penitence for the abuse of each of the bodily senses, and an indemnity for sins not confessed because honestly forgotten, as well as fortifying against fear.[54]

Finally, at the very end, the Church provided its *prières des agoni sants*, litanies and intercessions which came to their supreme mo ment in the prayer of commendation of the soul, *Proficiscere anima Christiana de hoc mundo*, which broke through the harsh systematizings of the theologians about the chronology of judge ment, and spoke as if the heavens were opened immediately, and Mount Sion glittered on the near horizon.

According to proverbial wisdom, the third time the doctor bled his patient was the moment to send for the sacraments of the Church.[55] But the rules of the State were stricter. By a Royal Declaration of March 1712, a physician was obliged to advise his patient, on the second day of a serious illness, to send for a con fessor, and to inform the *curé* if no action was taken. This Declara tion was repeating regulations issued by the Parlement of Paris in the early fifteenth century, and was itself renewed by the Royal Council on 14 May 1724.[56] The clergy were accustomed to de nouncing the 'shamefaced delicacy' and 'false compassion'[57] of relatives who tried to put off the dread moment when the confessor was summoned; but this was natural human frailty—for the vast majority, it was unthinkable to die unshriven. 'Absolution, miséri corde!' was the universal cry amid the victims trampled down on the steps of the cathedral of Mâcon when the roof began to crack on a July day in 1759.[58] Except in Protestant areas, or in cases of sudden death, there were few who died without the ministrations of the Church.

When the confessor arrived, he might begin with an exhortation of a semi-public kind, in the case of a virtuous penitent, for general edification, in the case of a dubious one, to bring him to serious frame of mind. 'I tremble for you, Monsieur, all the more because you do not tremble.'[59] But this sort of hectoring was unusual. Sermons and guides to long-range preparation often used the weapon of fear, but when a man was dying, the time for intimi dation was over. Perhaps, to bring an obstinate character to make a good confession, something could be said of eternal damnation, but that was all. ('It is good to frighten him a little before he has made his confession,' said the Jesuit Père Crasset, 'but after he has received the viaticum, you must speak to him only of the goodness of God.'[60] The historian does not have direct access to the dialogue between penitent and confessor, but we can be sure that a priest at a deathbed spoke essentially of consolation.[61] He urged resignation to death and the loss of earthly loves and friendships, and in return offered hope, pointing to Christ on the Cross, his blood giving assurance and 'fortifying against the last assaults of the Devil'. (Diderot put the confessor's consolations into reverse when he wrote the terrible death scene of the lesbian Mother Superior—the sanctifying blood streamed over her, but did not adhere, and it was then she knew she was lost.)[62] The message of the priest, as summarized by a poet, was of a meeting with the divine love—

> Mon frère, de la mort ne craignez point les coups;
> Vous remontez vers Dieu, Dieu s'avance vers vous.[63]

Ever since the bitter seventeenth-century disputes about the moral theology of the Jesuits, the manuals of the confessional had become more and more rigorous;[64] it is doubtful if the actual practice of confessors conformed to them. Yet, while they made ruthless recommendations for witholding absolution from habitual sinners, even the most severe theologians did not propose to refuse absolution if the penitent was in danger of dying. The terror of the shadow of death was taken as a guarantee of the sincerity of contrition—'Cum probabile sit poenitentem mortis timore perterritum vera contritione moveri'.[65] A man's last hour was not the time for inquisitional procedures; the last confession, one bishop ruled, was to be general, covering the whole of life, with not too many questions asked and no complaints or declamations; the priest would be 'praying for him and with him.'[66] A strict moralist (who prescribes no less than an hour's prayer and meditation every morning for 'une dame du monde') describes possible courses for a confessor dealing with a dying man who shows no sign of contrition. One is to refuse absolution, but to allow the administration of extreme unction; another is to give absolution if the person's life had been respectable; the third is to absolve anyone who could be described as belonging to the Roman faith, provided he had not been stricken down in the act of mortal sin—and the last, the most lenient course, was prescribed as the most reasonable.[67] *The Dictionnaire portatif des cas de conscience* (new ed. 1761) was more liberal still. All priests have power to absolve the dying and there are no *cas réservés*. The mere desire to confess should be taken as a guarantee of sincerity. Imagine a man of scandalous life who had lost the power of speech by the time the confessor arrives; he should be absolved if he asked for a priest in the first place, and granted conditional absolution if an assurance could be given, however vague, that he had wanted to do so. Nor was ignorance of the faith a bar to acceptance; all that was needed was a promise to seek instruction in the event of recovery.[68] It would appear that only the most notorious sinners were in danger of rejection and, in their cases, the desire to serve the Church by obtaining a public recantation helped to discourage confessors from excessive rigorism; according to an anteclerical lampoon, the alleged deathbed confession of Voltaire had been a hoax perpetrated by his secretary, who had impersonated the great man and related to the good abbé Gaultier a catalogue of crimes of which forty murders were the least sensational items—and he had been absolved without difficulty.[69]

A deathbed confession might be the occasion for the startling righting of some great wrong. In 1778, the lawyers rejoiced in an insoluble inheritance problem arising from the dying admission of a nurse who had substituted the infant of a pastry-cook for the dead child of a rich merchant.[70] In the following year, news of the death of Mme de Saint-Vincent in the convent where she had been incarcerated led to rumours, sinisterly inspired, of a last confession admitting her duplicity in a lawsuit involving the maréchal de Richelieu.[71] Her family got the abbess to give an assurance that throughout a long illness she had always denied her guilt, and had finally died with every sign of deep religious sentiments.[72] Righting an ancient wrong might, of course, have grievous consequences, presenting the confessor with a casuistical dilemma. There is a strange example in Marivaux where a confessor, in all sincerity, insists on concealing an injustice to avoid scandal.[73] A dying priest, who had abandoned his vocation and made a new life for himself as a married man, asked the *curé* of La Chevrette to publish the story of his crime and repentance and to have him carried off to die among the paupers in the common hospital. But the *curé* (who regaled Grimm and Diderot with the story) refused; 'Your wife would be dishonoured, your children will be declared illegitimate—where is the good of that?'—and he administered the last sacraments with-ut further ado.[74] This was a humane decision in defiance of the usual rule: generally, a public scandal called for public reparation. A notorious feud would require a formal reconciliation.[75] In 1727, the prince de Conti ordered his mistress out of the house, asked his wife's pardon for having set his valet to spy on her, and left entirely in her hands the allocation of legacies to his servants.[76] In 1736, the luc du Maine sent his confessor on a mission of reconciliation to his sister, and in 1742 the *curé* brought Mme de Mailly to the bedside of Mme de Mazarin.[77] The abbé de la Porte, an ex-Jesuit who in a long career on the fringes of literature and the theatre had accumulated enemies, sent for all of them, and since Fréron was dead, made a vicarious peace with his wife and son.[78] A notorious liaison would have to be brought manifestly to an end. In 1719, the duchesse de Berry, daughter of the Regent, who oscillated between debauchery and retreats with the Carmelite nuns, was denied the sacraments by the *curé* of Saint-Sulpice (and, on appeal as it were, by the archbishop of Paris) because her paramour was still living in the Luxembourg palace—the *curé* sat in her antechamber for four days ready to enforce the prohibition. Later in the year, when she did receive the sacraments, she was eloquent to the assembled throng about her wicked life, and when the doors were closed, asked her familiars if she had spoken well, 'and if they thought she was dying with nobility and courage'.[79] The prince de Carignan, dying in 1741, closed the gaming-house which he ran in the hôtel de Soissons;[80] a duke in 1751 had to make a bonfire of indecent pictures; Charles de Saint Albin, son of the Regent and an actress, who for long had held the archbishopric of Cambrai unworthily, made 'a kind of solemn reparation' before receiving the last sacraments in 1764.[81] Like Louis XIV before him, Louis XV authorized an announcement to the assembled courtiers that he asked pardon for the scandal he had caused.[82] The more elevated the rank of the sinner and the more public his transgression, the more solemn must be his official repentance.

This rule applied to writers, who might be required to disavow some of their publications. The abbé de la Porte, organizing his deathbed according to all the rules, after seeing his enemies, instructed the parish priest to publish, in church, a disavowal of anything in his writings which might be taken to be against religion, morals, or Christian charity.[83] La Fonatine, in the presence of representatives of the Sorbonne and the Academy, had expressed regret at writing his masterpieces; Montesquieu declared that he had never really doubted and had written against religion out of a desire for singularity; his Jesuit confessor required publicity, and reported these sentiments to Rome, whence a notice was sent to all the nuncios.[84] In his manœuvres to outwit the clergy as his end drew near, Voltaire's supreme achievement was to persuade the abbé Gaultier to give him absolution without raising the question of his writings. What should have happened was described by the Capuchin Père Lombez; Voltaire would have been welcomed into the fold by the clergy 'immediately he had expressed himself as totally contrite and humble, through the solemn disavowal of his impieties, and making authentic reparation for the scandal he had caused'.[85]

Absolution once given, there must be no looking back. The abbé de Mangin's *Science des confesseurs* (1752) told how a dying man lost his soul because his mistress looked in after he had been shriven, so that he recollected his past sins with pleasure. This was a tale from Gregory of Tours, but to the abbé de Mangin all deathbeds were contemporaneous; 'learn from this, O Christian, that no one has assurance of salvation . . . however holy his dispositions towards death may have been.'[86] Rigorism of this kind gave edge to the glee of anticlericals when a pious death diverged from protocol—the archbishop of Sens exulting over the exile of the Parlement in the words of Racine, 'Et mes derniers regards ont vu fuir les Romains';[87] Cardinal de la Roche Aymon slipping into dotage and singing a comic song about the marital infidelities of Mme de la Luzerne.[88] After Mme de Pompadour had received the last sacrament, Louis XV visited her no more;[89] by contrast, when the mistress of the comte de Clermont (who after a stormy youth had fallen into devotion) stayed by his bedside, it was proof that a *mariage de conscience* existed between them.[90] Louis XV, who spent his life in self-indulgence, haunted by fear of death but gambling on a last-minute reconciliation, nearly missed his chance because of the maréchal de Richelieu's plot to preserve Mme Dubarry in favour if he recovered. 'If you want to hear a confession,' the maréchal said to the archbishop of Paris, who was hurrying to be available, 'hear mine and you'll hear of such sins as you never heard of before.'[91] An actor who renounced the stage (as was necessary to receive absolution) could never return to it. Mme Favart was going to die unreconciled rather than risk her salary from the Comédie- Italienne, until her lover, the abbé de Voisenon, saved her by getting a promise from Versailles that her income would be continued in any case.[92]

After absolution, the viaticum:[93] 'Accipe frater viaticum Corporis Domini nostri Jesu Christi, qui te custodiat ab hoste maligno et perducat in vitam aeternam'. 'Brother'—all men are equal now. Yet the procession corresponded to the rank of the recipient—a hundred liveried lackeys with torches and resplendent clergy and courtiers marching to the Luxembourg palace; a dingy canopy carried by two urchins, the clerk with handbell and lantern, the hobbling beadle, and a single priest with the ciborium, stumbling down the meaner streets of Paris.[94] In the crowded room, an exhortation which might also be according to social distinction, from Mercier's 'banal discourse, the same for young and old, men, women, and girls, for all conditions and all ranks', to the abbé de Castrie's oration at the bedside of the duchesse de Berry, 'brief, polished, touching, and so apposite that it was admired by all who heard it'.[95] It was so in the country too: a vast and reverent throng in chamber and courtyard when some prosperous farmer received the ministrations of the clergy, and for some inconsiderable person, a hurried ceremony pushed into a gap in his daytime programme by a *curé* anxious to avoid being called out in the night.[96] Yet it is Mercier, who describes the viaticum of the poor in Paris with such disillusioned realism, who also speaks of a priest of dignity and zeal taking the last sacrament into the hovel of some poor woman as if it was a palace.[97] It is in the nature of a sacrament that the inward reality be concealed, only to be glimpsed by the eye of faith. The ceremony began at the door with 'Pax huic domui' and ended with 'A damnatione perpetua liberet Dominus', and the blessing. To those who believed it so, there was peace, and the lifting of the fear of damnation.

'Peace be upon this house.' This was again the formula when the priest arrived, in surplice and purple stole, with the consecrated oils for unction.[98] Once again the ceremony began with the sprinkling of holy water on the room and all assembled there. The priest presented the sick man with a crucifix to kiss. After an exhortation, prayers, and litanies, the seven anointings were given, beginning with the eyes. The sights and sounds and perfumes that had beguiled, the touchings and the travellings and the acts of physical love were recalled, for the last time. When the priest departed, he left the crucifix with the dying man. Now, it was all he possessed in the world.[99]

After the viaticum, Père Crasset had said, 'Speak to him only of the goodness of God.' Whatever you say to the dying, he added realistically, is soon forgotten, or overwhelmed by pain. Discourses are useless. Go through the words of Christ on the Cross—forgiveness, the offer of Paradise, the care of his mother, his thirst. Do not avoid the words of darkness: 'My God, my God, why hast thou forsaken me?' When all was finished, he yielded his soul to God: 'Into thy hands I commend my spirit.' As the end approaches, just murmur an occasional phrase, something familiar from Scripture that speaks of union with Christ—words from the Song of Solomon about yearning for the Beloved, words of the Psalmist who was glad to go to the house of the Lord, words of loyalty from the disciples, words of St. Paul who thought it 'better to depart and be with Christ'. The crucifix is there, something tangible to cling to, to kiss—the feet that sought you for thirty-three bitter years, the hands that made you and were pierced for love. 'My heart is ready', 'Thou knowest that I love thee', 'Into thy hands . . .'[100] And the *prières des agonisants* roll on, more for the benefit of the living than the dying—calling on Christ to deliver by his Passion, Death, and Resurrection, calling on the angels, patriarchs, prophets, martyrs, saints, and rising to the vision of the heavenly Jerusalem in the prayer of commendation: 'Proficiscere anima Christiana de hoc mundo'.[101]

II[102]

'Ce n'est pas contre la mort que nous nous préparons, c'est chose trop momentanée . . . nous nous préparons contre les préparations de la mort.' This sentiment of Montagne was re-echoed throughout the eighteenth century, and not always by those who followed Montaigne's rule of reflecting on death to take away its alien nature, to become familiar with it.[103] The Catholic ceremonies of dying, *l'appareil*, were a focal point for objectors: Protestants, deists, agnostics, atheists, anticlericals—all found offence here. Those who disliked the theologians' doctrines of Hell and Purgatory, of the confessional and the sacraments, here found the extreme case to illustrate their objection. Anticlericals resented the way in which the clergy achieved their moment of greatest power at the point where human resistance was at its lowest—'le moment . . . favorable pour les prêtres, toujours forts dans ce cas-là'.[104] With all its limitations, the deism of the century emphasized a truth which official religion so often obscured—the love of God directly flowing to those who seek him. At peace in the sunshine of this optimistic creed, men of reason and men of *sensibilité* alike had reservations about the sombre procedures of the *appareil* and the beliefs behind them.

The Church, so the accusation ran, was creating the fears which gave it domination. D'Holbach's atheism was supposedly the result of seeing how his first wife died, racked with fears of eternal damnation. Restif de la Bretonne complained of 'ce qu'on appelle les sacrements' driving country folk into terror and despair,[105] the sight of the clergy bringing reminders of their doctrine of judgement. 'Our religion has spoilt everything with its gloomy ceremonies,' said Mme de Sabran at Rousseau's tomb amid the undemanding beauty of Nature. Maine de Biran, at the deathbed of his sister during the Terror, experienced the consolation of religious feeling dispelling the gloom of 'philosophy', yet he complained of the arrival of the pastor—'He exercises a consoling ministry, why then does he bring fear in his train?'[106] Christian controversialists were fond of stories about unbelievers who panicked at the end; the *philosophes* countered by inventions about pious souls driven to final despair by their own doctrines—Pascal dying in a frenzy, Louis Racine dehumanized by 'drink and devotion'.[107] Was it true, however, that if the ceremonies of Catholicism were taken away, death would lose its terrors? Yes, indeed, d'Holbach argued, provided we succeed in restraining the vagaries of our imaginations. Logically, a man ought not to wish to prolong his life beyond a certain point, for old age is a burden; death is a sleep with no awakening, hence it is pointless to brood on a future which can have no meaning for us—our funeral procession, the grief of our friends, the world going on without us.[108] The *Encyclopédie* describes death as a gradual, inevitable, and natural process, and because natural, therefore not to be feared.[109] This was an optimistic *non sequitur*, but the argument from Nature could be improved. In a discourse published in London in 1732, a Piedmontese exile showed the way, using Locke's philosophy to categorize death as an acquired, not an innate idea—what the mind had invented, it could always erase.[110] Unbelieving doctors of medicine claimed, as a fact of observation, that death comes easily; patients who had lost consciousness and had then miraculously been revived, reported only peaceful sensations at the end. La Mettrie the materialist, who had been a surgeon in the campaigns in Flanders, had often seen life ebbing away in tranquil fashion, with a certain languorous pleasure, like falling asleep or relaxing after making love.[111] In Rousseau's system of thought, the natural man dies this way, scarcely knowing what happens to him. It is civilization which has created our fears: we anticipate our end and awake new anxieties by our 'raffinements insensés'.[112] To Jean-Jacques, the man according to nature, the ceremonies of churchmen are the final, intolerable invention of civilization; notaries, heirs, and physicians gather round our deathbed to conspire against our peace of mind, but worst of all are the 'barbarous priests', who use their arts to make us conscious of every nuance of the bitterness of dying.[113]

Another line of attack on the Catholic ceremonies of death was to equate them with superstitious practices the world over. Christians think a resounding *Peccavi* effaces their sins, said d'Holbach: the Hindus attribute the same virtue to the waters of the Ganges.[114] Voltaire has another Indian parallel: in some countries you have to be anointed, in others you must hold the tail of a cow; 'Forget the oil and the tail and serve the Master of the Universe.'[115] These were not just picturesque forays into comparative religion to discomfort the clergy. There was a serious theological point at issue. In strict theory, churchmen regarded the last moment as decisive. Their opponents cried injustice: surely God would weigh the whole life? *Philosophes* and deists did not accept the idea of a verdict depending, as it were, on one last final examination; they believed in continuous assessment. It did not matter how a man died, provided he had served 'the Master of the Universe', or whatever else he believed in. Rousseau's Julie has no special duty towards God to perform as she is dying. 'The preparation for death is a good life,' she says. She does not presume to offer to God a tardy repentance and her remaining, useless days. 'Are these remnants of a half-extinguished life, consumed by suffering, worthy of being offered to him?'[116] Julie is transfigured by her intense confidence in God: what if someone is dying who cannot believe? In a strange poem, *L'Homéiade* (1781), the marquis de Culant gave an answer, using for the purpose that stock figure for eighteenth-century psycho-logical experiment, a noble savage lost amidst the artificialities of European civilization. Unluckily, away from his native forests, the Red Indian falls fatally ill. A rabbi tells him there is just time to be circumcised, a Jansenist insists he must love God with a disin-terested love, a Jesuit says it will do to receive the last sacraments, give money to the Church, and show a little repentance, and an atheist consoles him with the reflection that the soul ends with the body anyway. But the marquis, as a sound Rousseauistic deist, tells him simply to trust in God, even if his mind cannot muster a firm conviction, for God knows all our difficulties—

> Eh bien, offrez à Dieu votre incrédulité,
> Il en sait les motifs, il est plein de bonté,
> Mettez en lui, mon cher, votre espérance unique,
> Il le fit, et mourut avec tranquillité.[117]

There is an epilogue to the story however. A doctor agrees with the marquis, but draws a further, and conservative, inference: since God is an indulgent Father who can be relied on not to misunder-stand us, there can be no harm in conforming to the laws of our country. It might be possible to send for the priest after all.

'A subitanea et improvisa morte, libera nos Domine!', said the litanies. If it was essential to make one's peace with God and man, to be shriven and receive the sacraments, a sudden death was to be feared; Père Crasset had even suggested that it was 'a certain sign of reprobation'.[118] Le Maître de Claville, who allied Christian spiri-tuality with the social graces, held that a last illness of from one to three weeks was much to be desired. 'Ha! how dear are these last moments! How important is my use of them!'[119] If, however, the

last moments of life had no decisive significance in settling a man'
eternal destiny—as, for different reasons, d'Holbach and Rousseau
atheists and deists, argued—there was no reason to hope for
preliminary warning; indeed, a swift and unexpected end migh
seem desirable. Of an acquaintance who dropped lifeless whil
ringing for his servants to bring his horses, Mme de Sabran said
'M. de Tingy has just died the most desirable death of all, that is t
say suddenly.'[120] A sentimental young woman asked why God di
not give this gift to everyone: 'This is a natural event, which we al
have to undergo—so why does not God, in his goodness, make i
easy for us?'[121] The Ancients had said that it was better to di
quickly, and it was a commonplace to say that death in the heat o
battle was easier than a slow and predictable end.[122] Even so, exce
for the very poor,[123] who lived and died with grim simplicity, th
idea of dying entirely without warning was not welcome to th
Frenchmen of the eighteenth century. It was a sociable age, pre
occupied with the formalities of personal relationships and wit
every detail of rank and precedence. To depart anonymously an
unsung would please no one. Those who saw no virtue in sendin
for the parish priest might still feel that they would like to settl
their accounts with 'the Master of the Universe', or possibly
simply to come to terms with themselves—to have 'le temps de s
connaître', in Saint-Simon's words (on the occasion of the startlin
death of the Regent from apoplexy).[124] And as family affection
intensified, the necessity of leave-taking moved from its Christia
and moralizing contest into a secular and sentimental one. In
specific instance which concerned her, the young lady who wishe
God to make dying easy was not so sure; they say a sudden death i
'assez douce', but what would the wife and children have given for
single word, a single look?[125]

Here was a debating ground where the gulf between Christian
and their opponents was narrower than might have been supposed
Deists and atheists were aware of the value of time for civilize
farewells and psychological adjustment; on the other hand, as w
have seen, the theologians' doctrine of the decisive importance o
the last hour was subject to interpretation.[126] Also, to qualification
for a very good man, Saint Augustine had said, it mattered littl
how the end came, whether from the angry waves, the daggers o

assassins, or the claws of wild beasts.[127] Indeed, Père Judde speculated on God's wish to spare his elect the terrors of dying, although
Judde's condition—an established state of innocence—would limit
the concession to the few.[128] But there was a concession—at least as
preached by the bishop of Lescar in the Cathedral of Auch in
1781—which would indeed admit all comers. A soldier in battle was
risking an unprepared end. (When the duchesse de Longueville
heard her son had been killed, Mme de Sévigné tells us, she did not
ask if he died painlessly. 'Ah! mon cher fils! Est-il mort sur-le-
champ? N'a-t-il pas eu un seul moment? Ah mon Dieu! quel
sacrifice!'[129]) The bishop, dedicating the standard of the Royal
Dragoons, reassured soldiers that even a single moment was not
necessary; the warrior can achieve instantaneously what others can
win only by years of penitence and austerity. 'There is also a
penance by which blood takes the place of the bitter waters of
reconciliation, and in a single moment washes away the stain of sin,
expiates its punishment, and restores the sinner (washed and re-
generated in his own blood) to his baptismal innocence.'[130] The
bishop did not say so, but attendance at the mass before the battle
and the taking of what opportunities there may have been for
making a confession might be assumed to be necessary pre-
requisites for the 'pénitence de sang' being totally efficacious.

According to Stendhal (writing in 1837), the polite convention
among worldly Parisians was to contrive to die alone. In the provinces, they send for a priest and there is great lamentation ('on ne
sait rien faire bien en province, pas même mourir'); in Paris, there
is gossip with a few intimate friends and, at the very last, a polite
excuse and death unobserved.[131] Hardly anyone in eighteenth-
century France seems to have wished for such a lonely and sophisticated end. Perhaps Mme de Custine, fortified by the sacraments and
the reading of the *Imitation*, had meant to avoid sad farewells when
she sent her friends off to hear mass—if so, it was a nice blend of
religion and the stoical tradition of Montaigne, of public and private
dying.[132] True, an unsociable deistic writer, in an essay of 1757, said
that leaving the world, unlike coming into it, required no assistance, from which he concluded, illogically, that none should be
encouraged.[133] This was not the deism of Rousseau. The famous
deathbed scene in the *Nouvelle Héloïse* is not a public ceremony of

the corporate and hierarchical society, but it is essentially social all the same—an intense, intimate family affair. Both Church and world are shut out—except for the pastor who comes on his own initiative and does nothing but express admiration for Julie's sentiments, and Fanchon's husband, who suddenly returns and is immediately absorbed into the little community of which Julie is the soul. This is not the death scene of the *grande dame* of Clarens, but of the woman who is the psychological centre of a family world which is unified by the love all bear to her and on which she imprints her commands and memory for ever. To Jean-Jacques, our last moments are left to us by God so that we can devote them to those we love. Julie will soon be concerned with God alone; in the meanwhile, her time is for her family—'c'est d'eux qu'il faut que je m'occupe, bientôt je m'occuperai de lui seul'. This is the very opposite of the teaching of the confessors, urging their penitents to forget all earthly affections as the end approaches.[134] A lady wrote to Rousseau in 1765, describing how her husband died: 'Throughout his last illness he continually manifested his affection for me and for my children'[135]—this was how to die according to the principles of the *Nouvelle Héloïse*.

To Diderot also, the cult of *sensibilité* focused on the family gathered round the deathbed, though being devoid of convictions about God and immortality, he concentrated on the moral and humanistic theme of family solidarity. In Greuze's picture, *Le Mauvais Fils puni*, the father has just died, with the eldest daughter still holding the crucifix she had offered him to kiss; the prodigal son is entering, too late to say 'adieu'. By contrast, in Greuze's *La Piété Filiale*, the whole family is gathered round a venerable dying man, including a grandchild presenting a pet bird for inspection. Of the first picture, Diderot observed, 'What a lesson for fathers, and for children!'; of the second, he said, it was a *genre* which pleased him—'la peinture morale', and the lesson was 'the recompense for giving a good education'.[136] The last farewell is the supreme reward of family solidarity. Perhaps both Rousseau and Diderot were, in different fashions, idealizing a way of dying which was becoming common among the more respectable middle classes. For in this stratum of society where families were becoming more closely integrated, once the acquaintances had paid their respects and the crowd that accompanied the viaticum had dispersed, the intimate family group would take over the vigil by the bedside. This is the picture given by Chertablon's engravings in 1700, by Greuze's pictures, and by Pierre-Alexandre Wille's *Les Derniers Moments d'une épouse chérie* (exhibited in 1785).[137] In Wille's picture, the husband supports his dying wife, two grandparents look on helplessly, the elder daughter weeps, the two younger children crouch at the foot of the bed, the older restraining the uncomprehending infant from beating his toy drum, while the dog looks on forlornly. There is no powerful moral lesson here, and none of Julie's radiant certainty, but simply family affection—and despair.

With his burning imagination, Rousseau produced—as was his wont—not only a criticism of traditional ways but an inspired alternative. A dying Catholic, says the pastor in the *Nouvelle Héloïse*, is 'surrounded by objects that make him afraid, and ceremonies that bury him alive'.[138] But Julie dies as one who has made her peace directly with her Maker and knows that, in her heavenly Father's bosom, she will be reunited to the lover she had relinquished out of social and family duty. She had prepared for death by living, and she lived to her last breath, trusting in God without intermediaries, and devoting her last hours to those she loved best on earth. She had no fear—'Qui s'endort dans le sein d'un père n'est pas en souci du réveil.'[139] Her deathbed scene is the supreme manifesto of sentimental and moralizing deism against hierarchical and sacramental Catholicism. By contrast, Voltaire, whose God is unlikely to concern himself with man, does not offer an imaginative picture of an alternative way of dying. He hated the ceremonies of the Church—extreme unction is barbarous; it is cruel to inform a man that his end is near; it is degrading to be treated like a puppet, to be passed through a standard ceremonial routine; it is absurd for an intelligent man to spend his last hours with a priest—if priest there must be, two minutes should suffice.[140] But what was the alternative? Julie's glowing confidence was impossible. Voltaire's description of the death of Mlle de Saint-Yves in *L'Ingénu* may be read as a criticism of Rousseau's heroine and her radiant insensitivity to her own fate. 'Let others strive to praise the ostentatious deaths of those who go down to destruction with indifference. Whosoever suffers so great a loss has great regrets; to suppress them is to cling to vanity even in the arms of death.'[141] As in other respects, Voltaire differs from Rousseau in being, as it were, the civilized man as against the natural. He is bitterly conscious of the blind forces uprooting the individual from the pleasures of the social nexus; for his part, he wishes to die fulfilling his obligations, not to religion, but to society and its hierarchies, in return hoping to achieve, both in life and in death, the recognition due to him. Voltaire had devoted his long life to warfare against the Catholic Church. As his years declined, the eyes of all Europe were upon him—would he seek refuge with the priests at the end? Frederick the Great thought so; 'he will disgrace us all', said his Prussian majesty.

III

'Ils meurent tout comme les autres, bien confessés et communiés,' said Bayle of the *esprits forts* who ridicule the ceremonies of the Church during their lives, then seek consolation in them when they are dying.[142] According to Christian apologists, there were few unbelievers who retained their sceptical composure to the end. Their apparent indifference was a pose, a 'prejudice', an 'imposture';[143] they were brave only when death was far away. Once they were in danger, they suddenly rediscovered their faith ('the mask falls, the Christian remains and the unbeliever vanishes')[144] or if they did not, they fell into panic and despair.[145] The very few who acted out their role to the final curtain were motivated essentially by pride. Gros de Besplas, a vicar general of Besançon, tells a story of a *philosophe* who is almost converted on his deathbed. Shaken out of complacency by a zealous *curé*, he prays that his flesh may suffer to atone for his sins, asks pardon from his lackey for the scandal he has caused, and orders him to burn his copies of Bayle, *De l'esprit* and the *Encyclopédie*. But during the bonfire, his philosophic friends arrive; they persuade him that he is making himself ridiculous, and having cancelled his application for the sacraments, they ensure him a quiet, irreligious finale. 'Que de traits mordants contre moi dans les cafés!' His pride, his fear of the wits in the coffee-houses, makes him an eternal castaway.[146]

To send away the *curé* left the unregenerate sinner liable to the penalties of God and the Church—Hell in the next life and the refusal of funeral ceremonies and of ecclesiastical burial in this. There were degrees of severity in the procedures for censuring a corpse. The liturgy might be withheld or truncated without the more extreme step of refusing decent interment. (The *curé* of Saint-Sulpice was blamed by some for exacting the full penalties in the case of the charming actress Adrienne Lecouvreur, so that her friends had to bury her in a garden.[147]) For unbaptized infants and vagabonds with no chaplet or pious image on them, a special area of unconsecrated ground was set aside within the walls of cemeteries; perhaps, if it was a tolerant locality, some reputable Protestant could finish up there.[148] Suicides were supposed to be ignominiously disposed of in some unconsecrated and unmarked spot—so too anyone else dying in mortal sin or in manifest alienation from the Church. But, given the temper of the century, it was becoming more and more difficult for the clergy to exclude anyone from Christian burial. The police of Paris put pressure on the *curés* to dispose of suicides with abbreviated rites at unfrequented times of day. The Church's ban against stage players—now wholly incompatible with the practices of society—was losing its force. In 1751, an actress was buried in the cemetery of Saint-Maurille at Angers.[149] When, two years later, at Le Havre, a troupe of itinerant actors was refused this amenity for one of its number, an appeal was made to the Chancellor (the body was pickled in brine while awaiting a ruling and the company was fined by the agents of the Ferme générale for using illegal salt).[150] Bristling with anticlerical zeal, the secular magistrates watched over the interests of the dying and the dead. For the dying, they made it their task to ensure that the sacraments were available—in fairness to the faithful who wanted them, to guarantee them against the 'public defamation' which a refusal implied, and to avoid disputes prejudicial to public order and decency.[151] The *curé*'s latitude to refuse the sacraments was very limited. A parishioner who had been duly shriven was entitled to receive them. Inquiry could not be made behind the fact of absolution, for the secret of the confessional was sacrosanct. And to the theologian, absolution was the narrow gate, the point at which the verdict of the Church was given. 'The act of giving Communion to those who are not worthy is not in itself intrinsically wrong,' says the standard handbook of casuistry. 'On the other hand, it can never be permissible to give absolution to a person who is not worthy, because that would be something wrong—essentially so.'[152] There were, however, a few seventeenth-century precedents[153] for bishops ordering their *cQés* to demand *billets de confession* signed by authorized confessors. A rule of this kind would not justify the refusal of communion publicly in church, for this would be defamation with a vengeance; it was argued, however (though the lawyers never accepted this), that a parish priest could refuse a request for a private communion, which would include the viaticum.[154] Thus, given sufficient ill will, it was marginally possible for a legal wrangle to take place over a deathbed. Through the folly of Christophe de Beaumont, archbishop of Paris, who attempted to deprive dying Jansenists of the consolations of religion, such disputes became an everyday occurrence in Paris in the mid-century, leading to a tremendous outburst of anticlerical rage and resistance to the Crown, the magistrates of the Parlement remorselessly pursuing *curés* who refused the last sacraments to parishioners. According to the wits, the Church was engaged in pressing the sacraments on unbelievers who did not want them, and in refusing them to Jansenists who did.

After a man had died, the courts were still watchful, this time to guarantee his rights to decent burial. The lawyers did not concede that failure to ask for the sacraments or, indeed, positive refusal to accept them was justification for exclusion from the cemetery. A surgeon had been refused burial because he had been absent from Easter Communion for years; the Parlement of Paris ordered exhumation, committal to consecrated ground, a requiem mass, and the payment of a heavy fine and costs by the *curé*.[155] Could ecclesiastical burial be refused to a public blasphemer and fornicator who had died in an alcoholic debauch? Certainly not—that is, unless, which was unlikely, he had been formally excommunicated by name beforehand.[156] Though the duchesse de Mazarin died 'philosophically' in 1781, sending away the *curé* of Saint-Sulpice, she was buried by the Church; indeed, the family pursued the *vicaire* at law and got him interdicted because he slipped a reference to her final impenitence into his harangue on her virtues.[157] A *grand seigneur* who died in 1785 had had his son buried in his garden and asked to be laid there himself; he had sent a formal *sommation* to his *curé* forbidding prayers for either of them, and during his last illness had sent the bishop of Amiens away twelve times. This would seem to constitute a clear case for leaving M. de Créqui in his flower-beds, and so the bishop ruled;—even so, the family went to law until the bishop agreed to exhumation and ecclesiastical burial.[158] Who then could be excluded? The clergy in search of an object lesson would have to find a specialist sinner, someone clearly under the ban of the Church; one example given is that of an apostate monk who had written a libel against his order and refused to retract it.[159] In 1746, an earlier bishop of Amiens had laid down a rule for his clergy concerning the treatment of dying Jansenists. A *curé* could refuse the viaticum (on the ground that the sacrament was being privately administered) but he should never refuse religious burial: 'on peut se flatter que le dernier soupir du défunt a été un acte de contrition parfaite'.[160]

There were a few *libertins* and *esprits forts* who died as they had lived, at war with the Church or totally indifferent to it—these could be omitted from the bishop of Amiens's optimistic assumption about the final sigh of penitence. Among the great was the duc de Vendôme (whose death was described by Saint-Simon in 1712): 'without a priest, without any question of mentioning one'. So too was his duchess, dying three years later, 'intestate and without sacraments'.[161] In 1751, when Jansenists were asking for the last sacrament in vain, Boindin died, spurning the ministrations of priests with outrageous jests.[162] In 1765, the bishop of Auxerre and other relatives gathered around the expiring comte de Caylus, hoping for an opportunity to bring this notorious sinner to think of his salvation. 'I can see that you want to talk to me for the good of my soul,' he said; 'everyone' we are told 'felt comforted at these words'. He went on: 'But I am going to let you into my secret, I haven't got one.'[163] Two years later the bishop of Valence and his cathedral clergy failed to convert the bishop's relative, the marquis de Maugiron. 'I'm going to cheat them' the marquis told his doctor, 'I'm off!', and so he died, leaving behind him verses ridiculing his unfortunate physician and calling, in pastoral vein, for shepherd-esses to lull him with their kisses into his final insensibility.[164]

Among the last jests of Caylus had been a pun at the expense of his parish priest, the *curé* of Saint-Germain l'Auxerrois, who had the vulnerable name of Chapeau. Duclos died in the same parish in 1772, having had seven years to work out an improved version—'Je suis venu au monde sans culotte, je le quitterai bien sans chapeau.'[165] And Duclos was the permanent secretary of the Academy—'There is no longer any religion, morals, or decency,' wrote a respectable lady.[166] Next year Piron died, after driving the clergy of Saint-Roche away with crude insults—a diarist, however, heard the story that, once he had lost consciousness, his friends had arranged for him to receive extreme unction.[167] The year after, La Condamine, dying with his doors locked against priests, sent to Mme Geoffrin to ask for the name of a confessor who did not believe in the Real Presence, and 'laughed like a madman' when she naïvely referred him to the Capuchins.[168] A year later still, in 1775, came the death of the abbé de Voisenon, who thanked the archbishop for sending his grand-vicar to him: 'Tell *Monseigneur* that. however great my sins, I would not exchange souls with him, even if he threw in yours for good measure.'[169] And, as if it was the breaking-off of a love-affair, he handed his breviary and crucifix to the priest who exhorted him—'*Rupture entière, Monsieur*, I hand back to you letters and portrait.' (According to stop-press news, however, in his very last breath he implored the divine mercy— 'quel exemple pour M. de Voltaire!'[170])

By many, these irreligious gestures were regarded as excessive. The unbeliever's death scene had its traditions as well as the Christian one, and up to the end of the previous generation, these traditions had been more restrained, as a comparison of the deaths of Boindin, Caylus, and Piron with those in André-François Deslandes's popular *Réflexions sur les grands hommes qui sont morts en plaisantant* (1712) reveals. From classical antiquity to Saint-Évremond, Deslandes could produce hardly a worthwhile jest, and only one forceful blasphemy (and this was wrung from Vanini, as he was burned at the stake). The aim, indeed, was to recommend, not a defiant death, but a stoical disposition 'à continuer en mourant le train ordinaire de notre vie'.[171] When the author (a distinguished naval administrator with a brother archdeacon of Metz) came to die himself in 1757, he contrived to avoid sceptical ostentation, so much so that Fréron and the *Mémoires de Trévoux* were able to run a story about a document drawn up by notaries which repudiated irreligious writings. It was appropriate and wryly amusing, perhaps, for the musician Rameau to complain of the *curé* hitting the wrong note and the painter Watteau to reject the crucifix because the artist's representation of Christ was unworthy,[172] but this did not mean that a man should cause a sensation by rejecting the representatives of the Church. To die in a blatantly godless fashion like Boindin was to say too much. In this century of humanitarian and sentimental deism, few wished to proclaim their disbelief in religion to the point of appearing in the same category as atheists and materialists. A description of the poet Barthe's death in 1785, written to propagate 'the principles of modern philosophy', tells how he refused confessor and sacraments, but made a point of mentioning God to show that he believed in his mercy.[173] Why should a civilized man disrupt his peace of mind at the end by over-emphatic gestures? The manner of dying proves nothing, Mme du Deffand wrote to Voltaire, 'un tour d'imagination en décide, et bien sot est celui qui se contraint dans ses derniers moments.'[174] It was possible to protest too much, to overact the parade of courage. The man of true bravery, said an essayist on death in 1774, is content to have courage within himself, rather than demonstrating it ostentatiously.[175] Defiance and singularity could slip into buffoonery, appropriate only for soldiers, footloose *abbés*, and *grands seigneurs*.[176] It was more civilized to face the end in the tradition of Montaigne, showing a need of conformity, tinged with irony, to the customs of one's country. Lully, the great musician of the court of Louis XIV, renounced his libertine past and accepted all the ceremonies of the Church, spending his last hours composing a canon for five voices on the theme of the death of a sinner. Meanwhile, the *curé* of the Madeleine burned the manuscript of his penitent's last opera. 'Hush,' said the dying Lully to an anxious musical friend, 'I have a second copy.' The aged and sceptical abbé de Chaulieu solemnly conformed in 1720; Voltaire celebrated his decision in a poem—how oil and Latin and 'ce que vous savez' provided a passport to eternity.[177] Montesquieu had done the same, fulfilling his promise to the *curé* of Saint-Sulpice to act as befitted an *honnête homme*—though making sure that his corrections to the *Lettres persanes* did not fall into the hands of his Jesuit confessor.[178] It was the fulfilment of a social duty and, perhaps, something more: 'Je veux bien m'y livrer et mourir du côté de l'espérance.'[179] This consolation meant nothing to the abbé de Saint-Pierre, but he chose to die with the sacraments, purely in the cause of social decorum—as he quietly confided to his *curé* when the ceremony was over.[180] The Fermier Général Jean Sénac, who died in 1783, consented to receive the viaticum to please his family, but asked the clergy to come without ceremony 'So as not to stir up gossip in the neighbourhood'.[181] Not everyone would approve of such clandestine conformity: a citizen has an obligation to set a good example. Two years later, the aged Buffon, then within three years of his end, put this point of duty to an atheistical visitor. The people must have a religion and must be encouraged to respect it; 'when I fall dangerously ill and I feel my end is approaching, I won't hesitate to urge them to send for the sacraments. One owes this to the established religion. Those who act otherwise are mad.'[182]

For the unbeliever who was unwilling to make concessions to society, the most sophisticated way to die was to evade the clergy rather than defy them. 'En voilà assez, M.l'abbé. Ce qui est le plus certain c'est que je meurs votre serviteur et votre ami'—if we may believe the story, this is how Mgr de Vintimille, archbishop of Paris, died in 1746.[183] Vauvenargues heard out the priest, but did nothing about his exhortations except to sum up his discomfiture in a quotation from Racine.[184] The abbé Terrasson regretted he could not offer a profession of faith to qualify for the sacraments, but he made his confession—an odd one, it is true, punctuated by references to his housekeeper for the verification of details.[185] In spite of the long-incubated pun about the abbé Chapeau, Duclos seems to have given some sort of satisfaction to his parish priest at the end.[186] Even the defiant La Condamine was given his 'passport' in the form of extreme unction by 'an accommodating priest'.[187] The prince de Conti got rid of the *curé* of the Temple, but practised polite evasion before his friend the archbishop of Paris, until death crept quietly upon him as he sat fishing by one of his ornamental pools.[188] D'Alembert in 1783[189] and Diderot[190] in the following year had courteous exchanges with their *curés* as their end drew near, though they always had friends present to head off the conversation if it threatened to become too serious.

How would Voltaire choose to die? It was a question which exercised the curiosity of the wits and gossips and the partisan zeal of churchmen and *philosophes*, as the aged Patriarch of Ferney neared his end. He was saddened by the futility of life: 'la vie n'est que de l'ennui ou de la crème fouettée.'[191] Yet he preached a gospel of work, and of pity. Above all else, we must console one another. Men generally are indifferent when others die; we close our ranks and forget them. By contrast, Voltaire weeps over each individual tragedy and strives to teach those who survive 'that they are, indeed, all victims of death and ought at least to console one another'.[192] He resented the brevity of life: eighty years are so little, barely time to write a mere 'two dozen plays'. Then, exasperatingly, the end. 'Je me meurs . . . et j'en enrage.'[193] At this last moment, how should we behave? The guilty fear death, the unhappy desire it, the brave defy it, and the wise accept it with resignation: this was the standard formula of the tragic playwright.[194] Perhaps we should strive to bring the heroism of the stage into our own lives; Voltaire would have been glad to be both brave and wise and to face his end with the serenity of Chaulieu's famous poem.[195] But he could not see how it was reasonable or possible to defy death in real, everyday circumstances. A great monarch, surrounded by many witnesses, might be inspired to put up a show of courage[196]—but this was at Versailles, a sort of extension of the theatre. Suspended between present pain and future annihilation, how is it possible to be light-hearted, or to retain a sense of pride when racked by a tertian fever?[197] We cannot console ourselves with the hope of a life beyond the grave. Sometimes Voltaire allowed his imagination to dwell on this possibility,[198] and there were Christian apologists who reluctantly conceded that they could not accuse him of the final blasphemy of disbelieving in immortality.[199] But more often he talked of death as annihilation and, in any case, there could be no certainty. We dare not look forward: it is painful to look back. The most we can do is to overcome our bitterness at being evicted and, like Epictetus, offer thanks for having been allowed a brief glimpse of the spectacle of the universe. Resignation is the nearest approach to defiance of death which a reasonable man can make.[200] Regrets are inevitable: it is 'vanity' to pretend otherwise. [201] Fear is inescapable, and we know from his doctor's outrageous and gloating predictions of a cowardly end that Voltaire was afraid. [202] (Why should Tronchin think this discreditable? There is no courage where fear has not gone before.)

In a moving correspondence with Mme du Deffand, Voltaire discussed the melancholy problem of dying—he was much concerned to conduct himself 'en philosophe' and not like a 'poule mouillée[203]'. He did not wish to finish up like La Fontaine, in subjugation to the Church, 'comme un sot', like Boureau-Deslandes giving instructions to burn his notorious book, like Maupertuis between two Capuchins, or like Montesquieu directed by the Jesuits. But what were the rules for philosophic dying? So notorious an opponent of the Church as Voltaire was not likely to be able to evade the clergy and depart with sophisticated ambiguity. Yet he did not wish to demonstrate the vulgar defiance of a professional *esprit fort*. During his last months, in remarks to friends of the philosophic persuasion, he spoke of the need to avoid 'scandal' and 'ridicule' and to ensure 'decorum'; [204] he shrank from the thought that his corpse might be denied civilized burial, [205] and he wanted the Academy to do honour to his memory by the usual service at the Cordeliers. [206] In justifying his sacrilegious communions of 1768 and 1769 he had shown the same preoccupations—to avoid 'disagreeable consequences for my family', to edify his vassals, to do his duty as a royal official and a member of the Academy and, indeed, as a citizen, with an obligation to die in 'la religion de sa patrie'. [207] As patriarch of the *philosophes*, he was also concerned to avoid a clash with authority which would imperil the great propaganda campaign; [208] that was why, while conforming to the fashionable philosophic jargon in praise of Socrates, he always had reservations about this injudicious martyr, this 'pitiless wrangler' who had brought down persecution on himself and his cause. [209] Long ago, in 1733, Voltaire had compelled his friend Mme de Fontane de Martel to send for the clergy to her deathbed: 'she didn't want to hear any talk about the ceremonies of departure; but I was obliged, as a matter of honour, to ensure she died within the rules.' [210] In Potsdam in 1751 he had laughed when the vast corpse of La Mettrie, the materialist, was borne off to church; even so, he had conceded that this was in accordance with 'the proprieties'[211] The defiant death of Boindin had not impressed him; it was 'very ridiculous' on his part to refuse to 'submit himself to the laws of his country'.[212] A *philosophe* ought to show a proper conformity to the customs of his country and the conventions of society. How far along the road of Catholicism should such a conformity go? D'Alembert, consulted by Voltaire shortly before the famous confession to the *abbé* Gaultier, advised going the whole way like Montesquieu, and specifically and irreverently mentioned the reception of the sacraments.[213]

D'Alembert was trying to make things easy; but his friend had more resources of craft and courage than he realized. A dying Catholic who made his confession would be asked for a statement of belief (in a comic piece on the 'death' of Père Berthier Voltaire had described how that good Jesuit used all the casuistry of his Order to answer the question, did he love God?[214]). He would also be asked to disavow anti-religious writings (great had been the rage of the bishop of Annecy in 1768 when he had been allowed communion without having to face this demand[215]). Then, at the viaticum, the priest would ask if the recipient believed in the presence of Christ in the Eucharist (when Mme de Fontane de Martel had said 'Ah oui!' at this point, Voltaire had found it difficult to suppress his laughter[216]). Among these procedures what was the essential minimum—to comply with the customs of society and to obtain civilized burial? Here, the great *philosophe*, descendant of lawyers, defender of Calas, successful capitalist and estate owner, was not likely to make a mistake. He always had good legal advice, to manage his fortune, to succour the oppressed, and, indeed, over the affair of the Communions of 1768 and 1769.[217] The events of his last illness did not just happen: they were monitored by one of his nephews, a legal expert, who collected the documentation that would be necessary if there was to be a lawsuit against the clergy. Voltaire would know that, to the theologians and lawyers, the giving of absolution was the crucial point: this proved membership of and reconciliation to the Church, and once this was established, the refusal of ecclesiastical burial was almost impossible. He would not disown his writings; he would not recognize the divinity of Christ or the efficacy of the sacraments. On the other hand, he had no objection to expressing his belief in God, or his penitence—both of which were genuine. It was a question of finding a confessor who would not ask for more.

Providentially (if the word is not thought inappropriate) the zealous abbé Gaultier presented his services.[218] The story of how the author of the *Dictionnaire philosophique* confessed to this naïve priest has often been told, but it has hardly been noticed how masterly was the penitent's manœuvring. On the one hand he tied up the details to leave an open-and-shut case for his lawyers if they had to go to the secular courts to demand ecclesiastical burial for him; on the other, he contrived to separate the duties of the citizen from the observances of the believer. Witnesses were invoked to testify that Gaultier had been sent for,[219] and two distinguished signatures witnessed Voltaire's declaration of faith; the abbé Gaultier was not allowed to call again to see his penitent once absolution was given, so he could not ask for additions or clarifications. The declaration itself includes the phrase 'n'ayant pu me traîner à l'église', which could be used as a proof of willingness to go to church, presumably to receive the sacrament; Gaultier is spoken of (incorrectly) as being sent by the *curé* of Saint-Sulpice, and in a flattering letter afterwards Voltaire assured his parish priest that he had believed this to be the case—you are a general from whom I asked the services of a soldier; I had not foreseen you'd have been willing to come yourself.[220] There was ample here to enable the lawyers to clinch the proof that Voltaire had been, in formal terms, a Catholic.[221]

But this wily penitent yielded nothing of principle: he did not disavow his writings, he did not acknowledge revelation. He was a Catholic, but not a Christian. Beforehand, he gave to his secretary a declaration—he died adoring God, loving his friends, not hating his enemies, and detesting superstition; this is what he really believed.[222] In his original letter to Gaultier, he promised no more; he would say what he had said to Franklin, 'Dieu et la liberté'. The abbé came armed with a ready-made profession of faith which Voltaire evaded, and rapidly produced his own. 'Je meurs', he said, 'dans la religion catholique où je suis né',—*in* the religion, not of it, that is, not necessarily believing a word of it; the religion in which he was born, part of the routine inheritance of every citizen. The nearest he came to disavowing his writings is: 'Si j'avais jamais scandalisé l'église, j'en demande pardon à Dieu et à elle', which is oblique and conditional. Gaultier was alarmed by the possibility that his penitent might have registered a secret protest against any concessions to the clergy; Voltaire denied this, though in ambiguous terms half suggesting that such a subterfuge was an attribute of superior minds. The abbé had thus been allowed to make a point and extract a concession—maybe his little triumph had been contrived to head him off from the issue of the disavowal of the writings, which he failed to raise. On a flimsy excuse, Gaultier's offer of the sacrament was refused. For a man of eighty-three coughing blood and tormented by a urinary constriction, with very little true friendship to sustain him and the eyes of the world upon him, it had been a masterly performance.

When death came three months later, Gaultier and the *curé* were sent for. Voltaire was no longer coherent enough to sign a more complete declaration or to receive the viaticum— there is reason to believe that he could have been coherent if he wished.[223] At this point, the clergy played the game and left the way open for ecclesiastical burial. Gaultier signed a *billet de confession* saying he had been summoned to hear the confession but had found his penitent unconscious, and the *curé*, after asking the decisive question concerning the divinity of Christ, ignored the reply and declared that Voltaire was no longer in possession of his faculties (a gesture which La Harpe, Grimm, and d'Alembert all applauded).[224] As he had so often, through devious shifts and deceptions, Voltaire had ended up by concentrating hearts and minds on the essential issue.

He paid tribute to the social decencies, the institutional framework of morality and the traditions of his nation. One thing remained.

'M. de Voltaire, you are at the end of your life: do you recognize the divinity of Jesus Christ?' I do not know from what depths of fear or loneliness or weariness the answer came, but it was unmistakable—

'Laissez-moi mourir en paix'; 'Let me die in peace.'

9

Funerals

When death was imminent, the relatives sent out to inform the parish bell-ringer—unless they were desperately poor and friendless and could not afford his modest fee. As the bell tolled, everyone in the village and its fields, or in the crowded streets around a church in town, knew that a fellow Christian was dying; by counting the strokes, they would know if it was a man, a woman, or a child.[1] When the last prayers had been said and the eyes of the dead man had been closed, it was time to send for the women, whether relatives or local professional experts, who washed the body and wrapped it in its shroud. They left it with face exposed, with candles burning at the bedside, and a stoup of holy water (for visitors to sprinkle on the corpse and on themselves).[2] Thus the lifeless body was ready to keep its last social engagements with the friends and neighbours who came to say farewells and prayers. In the house, the clocks were stopped at the hour of decease, mirrors were turned to the wall, and black cloth was thrown over pictures—and even over the beehives in the garden. If there was wine in the cellar, someone went down to strike three blows on each barrel—a mysterious ceremony, as if the casks needed warning that they had lost an appreciative customer. If the family owned a mill, its sails were stopped in the form of a cross.[3] The funeral was quickly organized. Mercier complains that there was a delay of only twenty-four hours—'on l'arrache chaud de son lit'. But even as he wrote, the custom was changing, thanks to the currency of alarming stories about people being buried alive; sometimes a last will and testament prescribed an extended period, sometimes local police authorities issued a general regulation against precipitate burials. In any case, the corpse would stay in the house for a night, and vigil would be kept over it. Among the richer classes, a cleric would be hired for the purpose. The fishmonger who organized the obsequies of a

270

canon of Soissons put a charge on his bill for 'une carpe pour souper avec le cordelier qui a gardé le corps'.[4] This was handsome fare; twenty sous and a bottle of wine were more usual rewards, and if the broken-down old clerk who performed this gloomy office so cheaply whiled away his vigil with some scandalous book, who could blame him?[5] The bottle sometimes had much to answer for—it accounted for the nocturnal conflagration in the church of Saint-Roch in 1739, when the corpse of the duc de Tresmes, which was lying there in state, had its feet burnt off.[6] In the countryside, the peasants themselves performed the *veillée*, eating toast soaked in sugared wine, singing litanies, telling stories of the dead man, and cracking jokes. It was a major social occasion: nothing like a good fireside and a death in the house, it was said, to bring folk together.[7] Or perhaps only the close relatives would be there. Restif tells a grim story of a husband and wife bringing down their little boy to look into two coffins they were watching over; here was Edmond killed in a carriage accident—'Regarde comme Dieu l'a tué. Il n'a qu'un œil, il n'a qu'un bras', he had gone to the wicked city and forgotten his God. And here was Ursule, all disfigured—Ce n'est pas ma tante Ursule, si belle, qui me caressait tant!'[8]

Meanwhile, relatives and friends had been invited to the funeral. In villages, messages were sent round informally; in most towns there were established officials who had bought their offices from the Crown and charged a fee for the services of a bellman to cry the news in the streets and to call at individual houses. In Angers, the municipality bought back this lucrative business in 1761, and gave it to the Hôpital Général.[9] From the thirteenth century, there had been *jurés-crieurs* in Paris who made announcements of wine for sale; they soon extended their scope to include lost property, and in the fourteenth century took on funerals. Early in the seventeenth century, they were printing placards announcing the obsequies of distinguished citizens, and fifty years later they were being commissioned to print and distribute smaller individual invitations. Very soon, the death of anyone of reputable social position was being announced by such *billets d'obsèques*. The courageous printer Gonichon who defied the monopoly of the corporation of the *jurés-crieurs* (and by 1752 had won his case before the Royal

Council) estimated that of the 18,000–20,000 deaths every year in Paris, 4,000 were commemorated with printed invitations.[10]

When the time for the burial drew near, the corpse was exposed at the entrance to the house, flanked by yellow candles.[11] If the family was reasonably well-off, the body would rest in a coffin (otherwise simply in its shroud) and there would be a black canopy and hangings at the doorway. Holy water would be sprinkled and candles and torches lit by those who were to carry them, and the procession to the church would begin; the *De profundis* and the *Miserere* would be sung on the way, their grimness relieved by the antiphon *Exultabunt Domino ossa humiliata* and the concluding *Requiem aeternam*. Members of confraternities bearing lights (if such were present) formed the vanguard, the exorcist with holy water and the cross-bearer followed, then the rest of the clergy, wearing hats and walking in pairs; next came the officiating priest, preceding the body; then came the relatives in long black mourning cloaks; if women were present (in many places this was not customary), they would follow the men.[12] Even if the church was two or three miles away, the coffin would be borne on men's shoulders, a demonstration of the idea of the solidarity of the dead and the living. When the municipality of Lille tried to enforce the use of a hearse, there was serious discontent; all the guilds of the town, the military Governor reported, have the duty of pallbearers written into their statutes 'for motives of charity, religion and confraternity'.[13] The pious brotherhoods which attended deathbeds and funerals did more than offer their prayers; as the parlement of Rouen in 1731 declared, they were indispensable in the country-side, for who else would join the *curé* in visiting those with infectious maladies, or volunteer to carry bodies for half a league or even a league over difficult roads?[14] However, if the distance made wheeled transport inevitable, as in a transfer to another parish, there would be a wagon got up as a hearse with sombre draperies. Diderot describes one pulled by four horses caparisoned in black, with two men in black with the coffin and two more on horseback alongside, and the coachman distinguished by a long black hatband which floated over his shoulder—as it happened, this macabre *décor* was serving as disguise for a band of smugglers.[15] In the South of France it was customary for the funeral procession to make a tour of the town, with the face of the corpse still exposed and as much accompanying pomp as could be mustered; but with the more respectable citizens, this baroque display was falling out of favour.[16] Everywhere, the composition of the procession depended on the wealth of the family and its distinction. For the great, there would be clergy and monks, candles and torches galore. By contrast, in the slums of Paris, there would be a few ragged people stumbling through the streets after perfunctory suffrages and a hurried *De profundis* had been said, with never more than four candles on show.[17] Worse still was the routine daily journey of the *emballeurs* of the Hôtel-Dieu, moving off every morning before the city was awake, with a whole cartload of corpses for the cemetery of Clamart. One December day in 1767, the officiating priest complained to a sergeant of the watch of their haste and indecency, and the sergeant called in an army detachment, leading to an affray when the drunken party returned.[18] A poor peasant in the Breton countryside might have only his wife and children, the *curé*, and the four bearers in his funeral procession—stopping at every roadside Calvary for silent prayer, the sombre pall on the coffin and the dark figures of the bearers contrasting harshly with the rippling gold of the barley field powdered with blue flowers.[19] In the early days of the Church, a funeral cortège went by triumphantly; the robes were white, palms were carried, incense burned, and there were cries of 'Alleluia'. It was different now. There was a parade displaying the wealth—or revealing the poverty—of the family, and conveying a dire warning, a dramatic reminder of the futility of worldly honours and of the brevity of our days. In 1776, Bordeu, the great physician, whose health was failing so that he only had a few months to live, went from Paris to the Pyrenees to take the waters. At Poitiers, he and his companions passed a funeral *convoi*. 'Ah!' he said, 'Pourquoi cherchez vous à fixer ainsi ma curiosité? Est-ce que vous ne voyez pas que c'est la mort qui me poursuit partout?'[20]

When the procession arrived at the church, the bier was carried through the doors to the singing of the response *Subvenite sancti Dei*. Within, the building would be decorated according to the rank of the family and the arrangements it could afford. It was common to have hangings on the walls, hired from the churchwardens and

273

vestry (*la fabrique*). These hangings were generally black, though for a virgin they could be white (the decision to take this colour sometimes invited indecent merriment—as when the unmarried old ballet dancer Carmago was buried in splendour at the expense of a former admirer, who insisted on the letter of the law).[21] For a nobleman, there would be further decorations on the walls, the *litres funéraires*, sheets of parchment adorned with his coat of arms. More splendid still, at the entrance to the choir there might be a catafalque, a bed of state with an ornate decorative structure about it, all ablaze with candles. And for the all but totally indigent, there would be candles on the altars; a patrician widow of Angers who left instructions for a funeral of the utmost simplicity, prescribed for her requiem six candles on the high altar, two on the lower candlesticks, seven on each minor altar, and seven torches around the coffin.[22] If the dead man had been an ecclesiastic, his body was taken into the choir, if a layman to the east end of the nave. The cross-bearer stood at the head, the celebrant at the feet, the other ecclesiastics gathered at each side, and the office of the dead began. Though there were some local variations, the observances were those laid down in the Ritual promulgated by Pope Paul V in 1614.[23] They began with the 'Dirge' of the medieval service (so called from the opening word, 'Dirige'), which consisted of two parts, Matins and Lauds. The Matins fell into three Nocturns, each with three psalms and their antiphons, responses, the *Pater*, and a Lesson (in every case from the Book of Job). Lauds had five psalms, the *Benedictus* with 'Ego sum resurrectio et vita' as the antiphon, *Kyries*, and the *Pater*. These were lengthy recitals, but the rubrics allowed for their abbreviation; indeed, everything except the first Nocturn of Matins could be omitted, and no doubt this was the case with many ordinary funerals.[24] But in any event, the office ended with the Lord's Prayer, responses, and the prayer *Absolve, quaesumus, Domine, animam famuli tui*. Then the requiem mass was celebrated. In cathedrals, collegiate churches, and monasteries the high altar was not used—a sort of recognition that death must not interrupt the ordinary liturgical round of the living. No one communicated, the proceedings were austere; the altar was not incensed, the subdeacon did not ask the celebrant's blessing after reading the Epistle, the priest did not kiss the Gospel before reading it, the Pax was not given.[25] At the end of mass, after the *Requiescat in pace*, the clergy gathered round the bier to say the prayer *Non intres in judicium* and the *Libera me Domine de morte aeterna*, the *Kyries*, and the *Pater*; there were aspersions with holy water and the prayer *Deus, cui proprium est misereri*. This was the prelude to the last procession, to the grave. Here, perhaps, a small wooden cross had been erected, with three candles burning on its arms.[26] The *Benedictus* with the antiphon of Resurrection was said again, followed by *Kyries*, the *Pater*, and other responses, ending with the *Requiescat in pace*. The congregation stood bareheaded now. The clergy aspersed the grave and the coffin within it with holy water. Others might throw in flowers, or the dead man's crucifix, or the stub of the candle which had been burning during his death throes, or a fragment of the *buis bénit* which had been kept at home since Palm Sunday;[27] the bearers might add their white gloves or the black bands from their hats. In some places, an earthenware cup, the *écuelle du mort* was added, no one was sure why—perhaps it was supposed to have held holy water.[28] Earth was thrown on the coffin. Before they departed, friends and acquaintances bowed to the close relatives, gathered round the grave. The clergy returned to the church, ending the ceremonies on the note of gloom with which they had begun at the house, by intoning the *De profundis* with the antiphon *Si iniquitates*.

The Catholic liturgy of death was a blend of hope and menace,[29] of trust in God's promises and fear of his judgement, a symphony in which the soaring aspirations of the anthems *In paradisum* and *Chorus angelorum* and the solid confidence of the *Pater* and the *Benedictus* competed with the deep penitential bass of the *De profundis* and the *Miserere*, and the thunders of the *Dies irae* and the *Libera*.

'Deliver me, O Lord', says the *Libera*, 'from eternal death in that great day, when heaven and earth are swept away, the day of wrath and desolation, the day of bitterest judgement.'

This was gloom, but gloom most logical. For a baptized infant, there was no *Libera*, and the mass would not be a requiem—the priest would say the mass of the Holy Trinity or more probably that of the Holy Angels. Sinless members of Christ are secure; but for the rest of us, sinful men, if we have not taken hold on the proffered salvation while there was time, the lake of fire and the lion's mouth of the *Libera* deservedly await us. The early Christian burial liturgies had scorned the black and red garments of the mourning pagans, the sackcloth and the ashes, and, even, the tears. Death came as the perfecting of our baptism, bringing us to full participation in the Paschal mystery; the faithful soul goes to refreshment, light, and peace in the confident hope of resurrection with Christ. But as the Church conquered the world and the world infiltrated the Church, and the sense of destiny became more and more concentrated on the isolated individual (and, to tell the truth, as the clergy became more insistent to assert their indispensability), the liturgy of death became concerned with judgement, rather than with Paradise, with prayers to preserve the departed from the jaws of Hell. Durandus of Mende in the thirteenth century said that the office of the dead ought not to contain any notes of rejoicing; its pattern was that of the last three days of Holy Week, without Glorias, Alleluias, blessings, or hopeful responses.[30] The Counter Reformation took up the solemnities of the Middle Ages with a new fervour, didactic in inspiration. That was why, in 1570, the *Dies irae*, the terrifying picture of the last judgement, became the official sequence of the requiem mass. All who heard it were driven to consider the salutary terrors of death, and apply the lesson to themselves. The Ritual of 1614 was doing a necessary task of codification, for the medieval burial rites were so long and complex that they were suited only for recital in monasteries (where, indeed, they had been evolved). But the architect of the 1614 revision had been Bellarmine, the author of the famous *De arte bene moriendi*; he was writing a further chapter in his manual of preparation for dying, addressing the survivors, leading them in a meditation upon death on the occasion of the obsequies of a particular individual. No doubt, the lesson was taken by many, and, often enough, quickly forgotten. It was customary, among the peasants, to adjourn from the graveside to a funeral repast, where the conversation was not always sorrowful or nostalgic—it was, indeed, an occasion for preliminary speculation about remarriage.[31] The *Rituel* of the diocese of Alet forbade ecclesiastics to go to such celebrations, for things contrary to the modesty that churchmen should observe would be heard. If there were no family social arrangements to round off the funeral there was always the tavern. 'Nothing is more common at Paris than to see the populace gathering at a tavern to amuse themselves after having walked in the funeral procession of their friends,' said a Parisian journalist in 1772; 'but there is no evidence that this is motivated by a principle of Philosophy.'[32]

A wake at its conclusion was not the only occasion for scandal at funerals. These were litigious days, when everyone was preoccupied with status and precedence; society, divided hierarchically into multitudinous strata was, nevertheless, ill-policed and lacking in the constraints of civilized reticence and inclinations to compromise; religion was so tied up with ordinary life that reverence at its ceremonies was an ideal of the monks who wrote its liturgical handbooks rather than an attitude of mind of the worshipping congregation. Stray dogs and children wandered into the most splendid and sombre of ceremonies, and the long prayers, responses, and anthems were taken as opportunities for gossip. Those who had inherited were sometimes openly jubilant; Mme de Sabran, watching the splendid procession for old Mme d'Argenton down the rue Saint-Honoré, could not help noticing the indecent joy of the duc de Luxembourg, the principal legatee.[33] Liturgiologists complained about the disputes for precedence which so often disturbed the peace of church services, but as a lawyer pointed out, churches were the principal places where men could display their rank, seeing that assemblies of a political complexion were not allowed in France.[34] Every provincial town had some running feud—say, between the canons of a collegiate church and the lawyers of the présidial—and funerals were as good an opportunity as any for challenging the rival organization. At the obsequies of Madame in 1722, Mlle de Charolais, a princess of the blood, outwitted the duchesse de Humières' designs to walk equal with her by flanking herself with grooms, but the duchess got her footstool insinuated into the front row, so the master of ceremonies had to be called in to arbitrate.[35] At the memorial service at Saint-Denis two months later, the bishops were not given their due precedence, so they retired immediately the church proceedings were over, refusing to dine as a mark of their displeasure.[36] The feud between the *premier gentilhomme de la Chambre* and the *gouverneur* of Fontainebleau over the right to arrange the funeral

ceremonies of the Dauphin in 1765 was so intractable that the King
had to intervene by issuing letters patent to the duc d'Orléans to
take over from both of them.[37] The ranks of poor, orphans, and
soldiers who marched in processions were difficult to discipline; the
musketeers who carried torches at the funeral of Mme Henriette in
1752 amused themselves during the service by singeing the wigs of
the spectators.[38] The rabble of minor clerics which attended at all
ecclesiastical ceremonies and lived on the proceeds was notoriously
irreverent. The widow who died in 1781, leaving a small legacy to
each of the clerks at her obsequies on condition they did not laugh,
ensured for herself the most hilarious funeral of the century. (The
attendant clergy, in fact, went to law and got their money—the will
deprived those who had laughed 'for no reason', and they argued
that the sight of the executor with his notebook taking a record of
every smile was reason good enough).[39] The ludicrous and the
lugubrious ran side by side in those days.

Some of the liveliest disputes (culminating occasionally in picturesque violence, swipes with incense boats and prods with
processional crosses, leading to broken crowns and torn surplices)
arose from the rivalries of the clergy among themselves, whether
curé versus *curé* or the parochial clergy versus some local monastic
foundation, over the custody of the corpse and the privilege of
burying it.[40] A man had the right to elect where he would be buried;
a woman, equally, had her independent choice, and was not necessarily laid alongside her husband. If no choice had been made, it was
the *curé* of the parish where the death took place who was entitled to
perform the obsequies—this was the common-law custom, contradicting the papal rule which favoured the parish of actual domicile.
There were complexities, however. What degree of formality was
needed to authenticate the decision of the individual? A direction in
the last will and testament was beyond argument, except the ordinary arguments about validity which testaments could provoke; a
deposition before witnesses had the same effect; the erection of a
tomb in readiness was strong presumptive evidence, and the existence of a family vault created a probability. But it was not enough
to have left the matter as a vague understanding with the family,
nor could the family hope to impose its own wishes, though the
Parlement of Paris, anxious to favour the laity as against the clergy,

tried to make 'élection par les défunts ou leurs héritiers et parents' a standard formula in the seventeenth century. One obvious occasion for clerical rivalry was when the precise boundaries of parishes were uncertain; there are stories of bodies smuggled over garden fences or through holes knocked in party-walls, and of pre-emptive ecclesiastical raids into disputed territory. In 1787, the abbé Lefèvre died at Rennes, in the parish of Saint-Aubin, though he had been living in that of Saint-Étienne. But neither parish buried him, for before his retirement, the abbé had been precentor of the Church of Saint-Sauveur, whose clergy wished to perform the last pious duties towards their erstwhile colleague. The family liked the idea and moved the corpse surreptitiously on to the parish boundary, where it was kidnapped by the priests of Saint-Sauveur, armed with cross, mortuary ornaments, and holy water.[41] The parochial clergy particularly resented the filching from them of so many burials by the religious orders, especially the Jesuits, Carmelites, and Cordeliers. The wills of nobles in Provence show that about half of those making a specific choice preferred monastic institutions, though the fashion was declining throughout the eighteenth century.[42] In 1682, the bishop of Rennes tried to rule that no one could be buried away from the parish church unless he had left specific directions in his will, a limitation of the customary right of the laity to choose which the Parlement of Brittany refused to accept. Occasionally, through some legal ambiguity or oversight in the arrangements, one side or other, seculars or regulars, would score a resounding victory. The entrails of Louis XIV went to the cathedral of Notre-Dame, not to the abbey of Saint-Denis (thanks to the influence of the archbishop of Paris); on the contrary, the great king's heart went to the Jesuits of the rue Saint-Antoine, and the local parish priest, the *curé* of Saint-Paul, was humiliated by not being allowed to act as intermediary.[43] At Caen in 1753, the *recteur* of the University was killed in a hunting accident; the *vice-recteur* arranged for a service at the Cordeliers, but the *curé* of Saint-Sauveur intervened at law to win for his parish a prestigious funeral, packed with dignitaries and adorned with a catafalque.[44] Even when the case for monastic burial was clear-cut, the *curé* still had his right to *la levée du corps*; he collected the body from the house, took it ceremonially to the chapel of the monastery, and certified that the

dead person had expired within the fold of the Roman Church. In
1664, the Parlement of Paris confirmed these procedures, though
existing 'transactions' were to continue to be observed. Nine years
later, the Royal Council cleared up a doubtful point: the *curé* was
entitled actually to enter the portals of the monastic church. But
ample occasions of contention remained to keep up the lawyers'
profits. Was the parish priest entitled to go as far as the choir, or
must he leave the coffin in the nave? Was he entitled to pronounce a
harangue on the dead person's virtues? Did he and his assistants
raise their voice in song? These were difficulties when the *curé*
wished to make parade of his status; what if he showed his contempt of the regulars by the opposite manœuvre, and bundled the
corpse in unceremoniously or at inconvenient hours—at night, or
during the saying of the monastic offices?

A different sort of scandal might arise when manifest heretics or
sinners were concerned.[45] As we have seen, it was not easy for the
clergy to refuse ecclesiastical burial if the dead man's family was
disposed to insist on it; Louis Recle of Cernon, who in 1729 was laid
to rest in his garden, bottle of wine at head and to the sound of
violins, presumably had friends who were as unbelieving as himself. Short of a formal excommunication the consecrated ground
was available to almost anyone except Jews, Protestants, and the
unbaptized. Attempts by zealots to keep out Jansenists generally
failed. The bishop of Laon's uncharitable pastoral letter of 1739,
ordering his clergy to refuse Jansenists a grave as well as the
sacraments, was repudiated by the Assembly General of the Clergy
of France. No doubt the Jansenists were excommunicate in the eyes
of God, said another ultra-orthodox bishop, but they had to be
given the benefit of the doubt, on the principle of 'economy'. Of 203
Jansenists whose deaths are recorded in the *Nouvelles ecclésiastiques* between 1749 and 1757, 72 were refused the sacraments, but
only 5 were denied Christian burial. What happened generally was
that the ceremonies were limited to bare essentials: the parish
would not make the pall available, only the minor clergy would
attend, and then without stoles, the bells would remain silent, there
would be no incense, no holy water, the prayers would be reduced
to a minimum, the cross-bearer might hold the cross upside down,
and the *curé* might insist that the burial take place at dusk or first

light. These inconvenient hours served to mark the displeasure of the clergy rather than to keep spectators away: at Orléans, at 5 p.m. on a November day in 1754, there were more present at the funeral of an aged Jansenist canon than had turned out for the fireworks for the entry of the new bishop.[46] Protestants and Jews, having no legal existence in France, buried their dead, on the authority of a police ordinance, in gardens or cellars. The Jews of Paris, who had been using the garden of an inn on the Senlis road, obtained permission to have their own cemetery in 1780, provided they made use of it only at night, and without any ceremonies. By the edict of 1787 Protestants were to be provided with cemeteries, though they were forbidden to have music or to say prayers aloud. The pervasive anticlericalism of nineteenth-century France owed much to family memories of these persistent humiliations inflicted at times of mourning and distress.

In the eighteenth century, however, it was the charges levied by the clergy for Catholic funerals, rather than their intolerance towards Jansenists, Protestants, and Jews, which aroused anticlerical ire.[47] Tithe, the argument went, was levied to pay for the services of the clergy to the laity. True, in gratitude for the sympathetic performance of the occasional offices, a pious family might wish to reward its parish priest with a gift: thus, a tradition of generosity had arisen, the 'louables coutumes'. But these praiseworthy customary offerings had been made into obligations towards the end of the sixteenth century, and in Louis XIV's edict of 1695 bishops were authorized to fix the tariffs, though they were exhorted to 'suitable moderation'. As a check on this moderation, the episcopal ordinances were to be supplemented by letters patent registered by the Parlements. For families which were prepared, or obliged, to accept a minimum of ceremony, the charges were not high, but in every diocese the tariff was a precise and unspiritual shopping list which underlined the humiliations of poverty. In Paris, the simplest burial cost 6 *livres*, and there was an extra charge of 4 *livres* to have the *curé* attend in person, 2 *livres* for a *vicaire*, 1 *livre* for any extra priest, 10 sous for each choirboy or cross-bearer, 5 sous for the exorcist with holy water. These sums were too much for the poor and too little for the rich. In 1763, the parish of Saint-Eustache went to the Parlement to get authorization for a higher tariff, for as

Mercier said, this *curé* was a *grand seigneur* who only buried people of distinction.[48] Some dioceses had differential scales for these payments for attendance. In the new table of fees published by the bishop of Amiens in 1744,[49] an ordinary funeral, of procession, high mass, and burial, cost 2 *livres* for the *curé* and 12 sous for a *vicaire;* but there were four higher tariffs, culminating in a 'service très solennel à neuf leçons, vigiles à neuf leçons, convoi, enterrement, grandes commendations', at which the presence of the *curé* cost 12 *livres* 15 sous and of a *vicaire* 3 *livres*. These were the figures for a country parish: it cost rather less in a town. No doubt those who wanted a 'service très solennel' deserved to have to pay for it, and occasionally we find evidence that the poor were content to see the rich having to do so—the *curé* of the diocese of Boulogne who tried to proclaim a decent spiritual equality and have the same service for all was accused of unfairness towards 'le petit peuple'.[50] Even so, the tragedy of poverty can be imagined from the differences in the tariff. An infant could be buried drably for a mere 12 sous, but to have a mass of Holy Angels, with the white stole and white candles, the Pax and the incense, and the message of assured salvation cost 2 *livres* 5 sous, the price of three days' labour amid the sheaves or the furrows. The rapacity of the clergy in exacting their burial fees was a routine subject of anticlerical jesting. 'He is sad even at funerals' was the appropriate *cliché* to describe a melancholy ecclesiastic,[51] and if some macabre drama with a crop of corpses was playing at the theatre, the wags wanted to know in which parish the scene was set: 'this must have brought in a lot of money for the *curé*.'[52] A journalist recalled the tale of the Duke of Milan who had a priest thrown into the grave alongside the corpse which he had refused to bury;[53] a *curé* himself recounted the comic anecdote of the gypsy women who were astonished to hear that they had to pay the clergy for 'singing' at their family funeral, and offered to settle the bill by taking out their tambourines and dancing.[54]

> Monsieur le mort, laissez-nous faire,
> Il ne s'agit que du salaire

was the motto of the clergy, said a Parisian jingle.[55] An example of this grasping attitude is pilloried in the *cahier* of the parishioners of Fougerolles in 1789; their *curé* draws substantial tithes, yet is not willing to collect his surplice fees at the lower rate which his fellow tithe owners accept as sufficient.[56] 'Is it not sufficiently distressing for us to lose our relatives?', asks another *cahier*. 'Must the memory of our sorrows be renewed by a bill for surplice fees which is even more burdensome to us than the crushing weight of official taxation?'[57] A pamphlet of 1789, *Le Rêve du pauvre moine*,[58] professes to reveal the 'sordid' secrets of the *clercs des convois*, the clerics who in the bigger Parisian parishes act as masters of ceremonies at funerals—how they persuade the weeping heads of families to choose the most expensive tariff as being 'le plus honnête', so that they even use up the money saved for their daughters' dowries; how the printed lists of prices which look so convincing, 'insolently' charge separate fees for functions which, often enough, are performed by the same person in different guises; how the cortège of minor clergy is recruited at the last moment from dingy attics and the back rooms of shops, sometimes including characters who have no clerical qualification beyond the cassocks loaned to them, and who rush from the graveside into taverns to spend their undeserved gains. Yet, the income of the parochial clergy proper—the *curé* and his *vicaires*—from funerals was modest enough. When there was ostentation, the *jurés-crieurs* got the lion's share of the profits, the *fabrique* of the parish a reasonable proportion, and the horde of minor ecclesiastics a good deal of the rest. At the comparatively modest obsequies of the wife of a farmer-general at Saint-Roch church in 1766, the *juré-crieur*, with his bills for three attendants, the hire of black hangings, and the printing and distribution of invitations, ran away with 336 *livres*, and 89 assistant priests received 1 *livre* each; this came to more than half of the total cost.[59] The *fabrique* generally collected payments for the burial space, whether in church, nave, or cemetery, the fees for the bells, for the hire of the *drap mortuaire* and ornaments, and the profits from the sale of the candle ends remaining after the service (though the *curé* was sometimes allowed a share of these). When a large amount of money was being spent on a funeral, there were many to share it: when a pauper died, the *curé* was left to see to the burial without hope of payment. Sometimes, a charitable individual or confraternity would intervene, but often enough, to preserve the decencies, the parish priest himself would provide the shroud or the coffin and the minimum of candles. In reply to a questionnaire from his bishop in the 1780s, one *curé* of the diocese of Comminges reported that it was impossible to collect burial fees: only 'a priest without heart or compassion' could do so. Another replied: 'Surplice fees are no longer customary . . . the dead are a surcharge on the *curé*.'[60] A monk who was locum tenens to a *curé* who had gone up to the Estates General in 1789, wrote to Versailles to ask what was the fee for a mass of the Holy Angels for a dead child. Clearly, *curé* Barbotin had never levied it, though he thought there must be a book in the presbytery somewhere which gave the figure: 'le règlement est quelque part dans un livre: mais où le trouver?'[61]

The expenses of a funeral were a privileged debt at law; like servants' wages, they were settled before the claims of ordinary creditors and, indeed, before the collection of arrears of taxes.[62] There was a presumption that such expenditure would be in accordance with status. Sometimes, with pessimistic exactitude, precise sums were stipulated in marriage contracts, so that if the bride was unlucky and had to mourn her husband, she would at least be able to do so in accordance with her rank.[63] In 1727, the heir to the maréchal de Montesquiou offered the widow, *la maréchale*, a sum of 4,000 *livres* for the funeral and mourning expenses, with a promise of extra payments against the production of receipts. *La maréchale* went to law before the Parlement of Paris and won; 4,000 *livres*, it was ruled, was too little for the widow of a marshal of France, nor was it suitable for one of her rank to have to justify such necessary expenditure.[64] Parisian diarists frequently commented on the splendour of the funeral processions of the great. There was always a troupe of paupers, recruited from institutions or confraternities, and bearing candles or torches and, maybe, a length of cloth slung over one arm, as evidence of the generosity of the testator. There were 40 such almsmen in the cortège of the prince de Conti in 1721, 200 in that of the duchesse d'Orléans in 1726, 100 in that of the duc de Tresmes in 1739, 60 in the day-long march from Versailles to Sens to escort the body of the Dauphin to its tomb.[65] Sometimes, more especially in the provinces, the place of the poor would be taken by orphan children from the *Enfants trouvés*, regimented through the streets in rain or snow or sunshine to earn some small legacy for the austere institution which boarded them. Always, there would be friars—Carmelites, Cordeliers, Capuchins—robed and cowled and bearing candles. For royalty and princes of the blood there would be a display of military pomp—the *Suisses* of the Royal Guard with lowered halberds, musketeers, dragoons, all bearing torches, together with heralds, trumpeters, and mounted pages. On these occasions the hearse would be huge and ornate. When the body of the young duchesse de Bourbon was taken to the Carmelites of the faubourg Saint-Jacques at night, by the light of 300 torches, the hearse was covered in black velvet with silver ornaments, and drawn by six horses caparisoned in ermine decorated with coats of arms, and the *cordons* at each corner of the coffin were carried by four chaplains mounted on horseback.[66] Having seen the procession, the curious diarist would adjourn to the church to assess the catafalque, some portentous structure adorned with allegorical figures and macabre emblems and blazing with candles. At the obsequies of the Queen in the abbey of Saint-Denis in 1768, the whole nave was engulfed in black hangings adorned with the arms of France and of the Queen herself, the choir forming a sort of amphitheatre surrounded by arcades, pillars, and black-carpeted steps, around a catafalque covered with golden lilies and silver tear-drops, flanked by life-sized figures of Piety, Wisdom, Meditation, and the Catholic Faith, and surmounted by a golden angel.[67] It was customary to leave the candles burning for an hour or so more after the service finished, so that the public could circulate and admire these theatrical marvels. 'The catafalque was left illuminated for more than an hour,' said Hardy of the requiem for the repose of the soul of the Dauphin in Notre-Dame, 'so that the public could enjoy this brilliant spectacle.'[68]

It was customary to spend more, rank for rank, than was reasonable by any provident standard. There were so many extras of furnishing or liturgy, so many gestures which ministered to pride yet which could be regarded as spiritual or charitable, so many local characters who would speak ill of the family if they were not allowed to play their customary role and draw their exorbitant fee. At Lille, early in July 1772, Placide Flamen, aged thirty-four, died.[69] The family was comfortably off: three doctors attended the dying man and duly presented their bills, one writing his on the back of a playing-card, the seven of hearts. But the payments to the doctors,

40 *livres* altogether, were vastly exceeded by the expense of the funeral. The dead man's mother took in hand the buying of black cloth to make the mourning clothes for the widow and children, together with the bonnets and black stockings. Including her carriage fare—'le carosse qui a servi à grand maman Flamen pour faire des différents achats', this cost nearly 200 *livres*. Almost as much went to the candle merchants. The churchwardens hired out their best pall, hangings for the choir, the six silver candlesticks, the 'twelve apostles', and the processional cross; they had straw spread on the church floor and charged for the use of the bells in a 'peal extraordinary'—altogether, rather more than 100 *livres* to the *fabrique*. The ringers, for half an hour on each of three successive days and tolling at the moment of death, shared 15 *livres*; the *prêtres habitués* and choral clerks shared 24 *livres*, the singers 6 *livres*, and smaller sums went to the Irish students (the *Hibernois*) who carried the coffin and to the orphans who processed with candles. The *curé* received 8 *livres*, and there were payments to a dozen friars of four different orders, the players of the *serpent*, the *Suisse* for his dignified presence, and to other clerks for decorating the altar and opening the coffers to display the relics, and for acting as messengers to deliver the *billets d'obsèques* to people's houses. The printer got nearly 40 *livres* for these *billets*, together with other notices distributed later to recommend the deceased to the prayers of various ecclesiastical institutions, and for visiting-cards with a message of thanks to those who had offered their condolences (these cards were an innovation; their use was not general in France until the mid-nineteenth century).[70] Two hundred masses were commissioned for the soul of the dead man, for which the parochial clergy received 125 *livres*. A rather larger sum was given to the poor, in the form of *plombs obituaires*, tokens which were exchanged for loaves at bakers' shops; eventually, seven bakers claimed 145 *livres* for 1,108 loaves, 58 of which had pieces of money concealed in them. The grand total, over 1,200 *livres*, was four times the annual amount which would have pensioned a wounded soldier, and seven times the annual income required as a 'title' for ordination, the barest minimum on which a priest could live.

The *billet d'obsèques*, or *billet d'enterrement*, was far from being a mere invitation to a funeral; it was a statement of rank, social class, and hierarchical precedence. 'Vous êtes priés d'assister au Convoi du Très-Haut et Très-Puissant Seigneur Mgr Louis-Cezar, Duc d'Estrées, premier baron du Boulonnais, baron de Montmirail, marquis de Cœuvres, et al., Maréchal de France, Ministre d'État, gouverneur des villes et citadelle de Metz, pays Messin et Verdunois, chevalier des Ordres du Roi et général de ses Armées . . .'[71] The sonorous phrases rolled on, recapitulating worldly honours and temporal distinctions in the face of the featureless equality of death. Grimm reports a *billet*—for the duc de Vauguiron—whose author could have been elected to the Académie des Inscriptions et Belles-Lettres on the strength of his heraldic expertise, and which would have needed the foundation of a special professorial chair if its antiquarian lore was to have been adequately expounded. In 1783, genealogists sought for their collections the *billet* of the marquis du Guesclin, bearer of the greatest name in chivalry and the last of his line,[72] just as the curious had sought copies of that for the duchesse de Chaulnes the year before for very different reasons (she had married beneath her, and her insensitive husband, a *maître des requêtes*, had recited his own titles instead of hers).[73] The bourgeoisie did its best with what titles it possessed—'former churchwarden' ('ancien marguillier') or honorary secretary of some confraternity, or member of guild. One splendid Parisian example proudly rehearsed the distinctions of 'Ancien Marchand de laine, Bourgeois de Paris, Officier-Inspecteur-Contrôleur de Porcs'.[74] The invitation did not often contain religious phraseology: 'R.I.P.' perhaps, occasionally a 'De profundis', and, very rarely, 'Priez Dieu, s'il vous plaît, pour le repos de son âme'.[75] For these sorts of pious requests, there were other *billets* which could be circulated, inviting to masses at the end of a month, or six weeks, or a year: 'Vous êtes prié d'assister au Service du Bout de l'An pour le repos de l'Âme de ——'.[76] The only change of emphasis in the wording of the eighteenth-century *billet d'obsèques* was the introduction of the names of the heirs, executors, or close relatives who were issuing the invitation; by the mid-century, women were being included.[77] Society was becoming more sophisticated and more conscious of family ties and affections. By the end of the seventeenth century, ornamentation was becoming customary.

Pour égayer la vue et servir d'agréments
Aux billets destinés pour les enterrements,

said a satirist in the *Mercure Galant* of 1683.[78] A skull crowned or
backed by bats' wings or underlined by the legend 'Hodie mihi, cras
tibi', reversed and extinguished torches, tear-drops, overturned
crowns and mitres, antique sepulchres, shrouds with black crosses
and grave-diggers' spades were common decorations—sombre,
though not religious in the high-serious sense. Occasionally, there
would be a scriptural quotation and illustration: the raising of
Lazarus on a *billet* of 1740; the angel telling the women that Jesus
has left his tomb; a rural scene of ploughing and sowing, with 'Si le
grain n'est mis en terre, il ne peut porter de fruit'. During the
Revolution, funeral invitations, now addressed to 'Citoyens et
Citoyennes', became plain again. When illustration revived after
the Restoration it was generally secular—drooping willows,
mourning beauties, melancholy dogs at the graves of their masters;
very soon, illustration was to be banished again and replaced by
black borders.[79]

As a family document, the *billet d'obsèques* suitably embodied
the pride of lineage and achievement. But, in theory at least,
religion was indifferent to these things, so the funeral sermon
presented the clergy with a problem of principle. It was customary,
and generally not too difficult, for a *curé* to say sympathetic words
at the requiem for a parishioner; it was not so easy for the preacher
of a formal sermon on some great man, and these discourses were
numerous, since various churches would hold commemorative services (for the King or Queen, there was one in every cathedral). By
the eighteenth century, the pattern of such solemn pulpit oratory
had become established after the manner of the famous preachers of
the reign of Louis XIV, more especially Bossuet. What had originally been an *éloge*, an essay in biography and praise, had become a
déploration, a lament, enriched by the baroque imagination with
devices of rhetoric and hyperbole, but counter-weighted towards
severity by the Counter Reformation's insistence on serious religious purpose. Public opinion, instructed by journalism and the
theatre, watched narrowly to see that the character portrayed was
correct in detail and convincing in totality, and savoured excursuses

into the problems of the day like duelling, the plight of the poor, and the duties of kings.[80] With Bossuet, the *éloge* remained as the apparent justification of the oration, but it led into a sweeping review of all earthly goods and greatness as an ephemeral pageant in which long life and civic honours, intelligent achievement. and even human kindliness, are trivialities compared to the fulfilment of the Christian duties of charity and piety.[81] It was difficult to combine this tremendous Christian world-view with praise of a transient mortal, and it became doubly so in the next century, when the inhibitions of the critics were removed by an increasing secularity of outlook, and their faculties sharpened by a heightened sense of the incongruous and a penchant for ridicule. Even the monumental performances of the great bishop of Meaux were not entirely approved of three generations later; in 1780, Turgot (who might be expected to be a competent judge, seeing he combined a seminary training with high birth and high office) described these famous funeral orations as a combination of sublimities and pious banalities ('plates capucinades').[82]

An expert on sacred oratory, who published many volumes of sermon hints and outlines in the 1730s, advised the clergy to refuse invitations to preach funeral sermons whenever they possibly could. While in an ordinary sermon mediocrity is supportable, even praiseworthy (presumably he meant that *naïveté* might carry conviction), here only the utmost distinction would be acceptable.[83] If it was only a question of learning a different style, that might not be too difficult, but what was required was the ordinary style, inspired throughout by subtlety of thought, elevation of sentiments, and graciousness of imagery. 'The great, the sublime, the touching, the pathetic, the marvellous, must all be there.'[84] Similarly, the aim of the funeral oration was the same as that of any other sermon: everything that was said must be with the aim of converting the congregation.[85] The editor of a collection of funeral sermons (delivered by a canon of Chartres who had died in 1735) described the overriding intention in similar terms: 'to prepare all hearts for the salutary sorrow of penitence'.[86] How could this be combined with the *éloge*, with the celebration of worldly achievements, and the satisfaction of family pride? 'A funeral oration is a blending of the sacred and the profane. What a deal of skill is needed to ally the one with the other!'[87] Even in ordinary human terms, it was always difficult to know what to say about the dead man's faults: it was almost as dangerous to refer to them as to conceal them. In spiritual terms, and by a strict interpretation of the preacher's duty, praise should be given only to what was praiseworthy in the eyes of God—a rule that left so little to say that it had to be broken. A funeral oration, said a Christian apologist, rarely recounts the life of the man: it describes more often the life he ought to have led.[88] Le Prévôt, the canon of Chartres, made it his rule not to pay tribute to birth or genius, but only to the use which had been made of them in the service of God and man; he would rehearse worldly successes, but only to portray their ultimate emptiness.[89]. In fact there was an accumulation of conventions about what could be said (in another type of sermon, for example, court preachers were expected to denounce Louis XV's sexual immoralities, but could get promotion or incur disgrace according to their grasp of the nuances of pulpit protocol).[90] A funeral orator needed to be skilled in the manipulation of words and up to date about the assumptions concerning the place of religious matters in polite society, before he indulged in the necessary apostolic brinkmanship. The bishop of Angers's sermon over the coffin of the debauched Regent prayed for 'a prodigy of mercy' from God;[91] the abbé de Boismont, reviewing Louis XV's wasted years, used the device of blaming Fleury for failing to teach the king not to separate himself from the nation, while simultaneously praising the Cardinal for his own exemplary rule, which could not alas, last for ever;[92] the bishop of Senez, in his oration over Louis XV in Saint-Denis, said that the people were not entitled to murmur against their king, but they had a right to be silent, 'et son silence est la leçon des rois'.[93]

With the critics sardonically assembled, it was easy to fail in the funeral genre of pulpit oratory. The archbishop of Sens, receiving the body of the Dauphin in his cathedral, pronounced 'un discours fort long, mais qui ne fut nullement goûté des connaisseurs en pièces de ce genre'.[94] At the commemorative service for the Empress Maria-Theresa, the bishop of Blois preached for one and a half hours, a sermon which, like the sword of Charlemagne, was 'long et plat'. 'Le pauvre évêque de Blois est tombé de manière à ne jamais se relever dans le genre d'oraison funèbre,' it was said.[95] In 1786, three major sermons were delivered in honour of the duc d'Orléans, and only one was found acceptable. The abbé Fauchet, who at Saint-Eustache lauded the duke's non-existent achievements, was declared ridiculous; the preacher at Notre-Dame, who tried the opposite tack and apologized for the lack of great deeds to inspire his eloquence, was censured as insolent, and the King forbade publication.[96]

The preacher of the funeral oration had an impossible task: he was attempting to produce a convincing discourse at the very point where the alliance of spiritual and secular into an accepted official religion was breaking down. Since God's judgements are inscrutable, it was impossible to offer praise to a dead man that was more than provisional. This was another instance where the processes of the refinement of religion on the one hand and of the secularization of social life on the other pointed towards the same conclusion; that was why the *éloge* in a purely secular context became one of the favourite literary exercises of the French eighteenth century. The Academy, the Academies of Medicine and of Science, and numerous provincial academies offered their prizes for orations in praise of great men, whether recently deceased or from earlier centuries, and in 1764 a specialist periodical, the *Nécrologe* was founded .[97] It is interesting to see how a new social idealism quickly took the place of religion as a criterion for criticizing and rejecting family pride, sometimes causing the secular orators problems resembling those of the ecclesiastical ones. Thomas, the specialist on *éloges* and the most successful prize-winner, went out of his way to deny the significance of high birth and long ancestry. 'Whenever the dead are praised,' he complains, 'the first thing is to praise their ancestry, as if the great man needs an origin.' Elsewhere he says that the 'least of all virtues' is to be of illustrious lineage, that he will leave the description of family descent to 'genealogists and slaves', that it is a favour of heaven to be born without ancestors, that 'true nobility' is to serve the State, and blood shed for the fatherland is always noble.[98] This was not the Christian egalitarianism: the thought of the Enlightenment was focused on the career open to the talents, not on the equal worth of every human person.

The funeral, says a modern sociologist, is 'a social rite par excellence. Its ostensible object is the dead person, but it benefits not the dead, but the living.'[99] In its simplest sense, and in a civilized context, the statement is obvious, for apart from some offering of prayer in the depths of the heart, what possible activity of man could be supposed to help the dead? Taken beyond its simplest sense, the observation is at once illuminating and on the way to becoming dangerous. To take an extreme formulation: Durkheim's view of mourning as a duty imposed by the social group and not the spontaneous expression of individual emotions, is unsubtle, missing all sorts of nuances of individuality and possibilities of self-expression, psychological release, and consolation that lie behind formalities and folk-ways. The men of the eighteenth century accepted what was, as we would think, an astonishing burden of ceremonial observances. Within them they found social satisfactions and psychological fulfilment, but they were under no illusions about the limited relevance of these expensive and cherished obligations. 'C'était pour les vivants qu'on honorait les morts,' said a minister of the Crown, attempting to persuade his son, the strict bishop of Amiens, to allow burial in consecrated ground to an unbelieving nobleman.[100] Splendid funeral processions, said a journalist in 1772, are devised merely to console the descendants or to flatter their vanity.[101] There is a touching example of such flattery in the diary of Marais in the year 1723.[102] He was deeply moved by the death of his sister, but could not help reflecting, when he saw so many 'gens de qualité' attending her obsequies, that his profession of *avocat au Parlement* was 'bien glorieuse'. If we smile at his vanity it should be tolerantly. He knew his satisfaction was trivial, but was grateful to his fellow citizens for offering it and was glad to accept it for what it was worth. There was no other consolation.

Though the graduated pomp of funerals reflected the hierarchical structure of society, the whole outward parade centred on the liturgical core and was, in theory at least, subordinate to it. When in 1389 the paladin du Guesclin had been given a magnificent funeral by his king, the celebrant had interrupted the mysteries to go in mitre and chasuble to the cathedral door to receive the sword, armour, and banner of the dead hero: Christian writers remembered the incident as an unworthy concession to worldly priorities.[103] Ideally, said Père Menestrier, the catafalque and other decorations should illustrate biblical stories, and he only regretfully admitted other allegorical symbols of mortality.[104] It was natural for Christians to weep, as Christ wept over Lazarus, said Girard de Villethierry, but excesses of grief should be avoided, as incompatible with the gospel of hope and the obligation of submission to God's will.[105] 'Il est peu de chemin du murmure au blasphème,' said a *curé* in a poem directed against excessive mourning.[106] A funeral, according to Christian writers, was a restrained, solemn occasion, to show fear of God and trust in his mercy, rather than to demonstrate personal feelings. Still less was it an occasion to manifest family pride. At the heart of the liturgy of death was the theme of equality. Funeral sermons for the great, said Bossuet, should not be 'vain eulogies', but a contemplation of 'the common condition of all mortals'. It was not easy, especially in the reign of Louis XIV, to combine this theoretical egalitarianism with the realities of the social scene; so far as the king was concerned, preachers and artists were glad to seize on a rhetorical device to bridge the contrast, depicting the nine saints of the royal house, led by Saint Louis, pointing their successor to a throne in a heaven where kings are more equal than others. But the underlying menace remained. 'Oh Dieu!' cried Bossuet, 'que cette place ne soit pas vacante!'[107] Death strikes arbitrarily in palace and hovel alike, it demolishes all trappings of wealth and glory, it reduces all bodies to a common corruption—these were the established themes of preachers, and the writers on preparation for dying gave yet another turn to the screw of egalitarian fear, for they told how even a well-spent life could be thrown away at the last hour, when all men are equidistant from eternity. All that mattered when a man came to his end was his relationship with God. Why therefore should we care how or where we are buried? It was customary on this point to cite Saint Augustine, who was indifferent as to whether his body sank beneath the waves or was eaten by wild beasts, and Monica his mother, who did not care where she was laid, since wherever we are, we are not far from God. It might be 'prudent', conceded one writer, to be buried alongside the saints, and 'laudable' to wish to be with one's family, though those desires were legitimate only when there was not the least admixture of 'vanity', that 'criminal' passion.[108]

What use, asked Caraccioli, are funeral orations over men who have lived like animals, or catafalques whose splendour merely provides new evidence of the transience of worldly things? The poor are the true friends of God, he says, and they alone deserve to have a show of pomp at their funerals.[109] The abbé Bergier ridiculed those who asked to be laid in their coffin dressed in the habit of a friar; it was useless to them, though perhaps it might serve a good purpose in demonstrating to the heirs how all the parade of the funeral is 'foolish vanity'.[110] Scripture gives us no warrant for mortuary pomp. With four exceptions, we do not know where the bodies of the Apostles were laid; Moses, Aaron, and Jeremiah found graves in forgotten places in foreign lands. Joseph of Arimathea was in charge of the burial of Jesus: he gave his Master nothing but a shroud.[111]

Since the generality enjoyed a free spectacle[112] put on by those who could afford it, the Christian ideal of funereal austerity was not popular. Even so, the public watched narrowly to see that the decencies of rank were not infringed by pushful families. France was not England, where a *vil artisan* could be pulled to his grave in a six-horse hearse and in a coffin of any colour.[113] The duchesse d'Olonne, whose will specified a funeral procession to far-off Navarre, six carriages, and an escort of almsmen travelling at five leagues a day, was an eccentric offending the social canons at one end of the scale by excessive expenditure;[114] the *avocat* who commissioned an ornate mausoleum for himself and his wife in the Church of the Carmelites of the Place Maubert,[115] and the joiner who had worked on the church of Ste Geneviève and invested his life-savings in being buried there 'with the pomp of a *grand seigneur*',[116] offended at the other by their pretensions. In the last resort, the magistrates might intervene to repress family presumptuousness, as in 1711, the Parlement of Paris banned the erection of the tomb which the Cardinal de Bouillon had ordered from a Roman sculptor for his father the *maréchal*, because of its unjustifiable genealogical emblems.[117] And woe betide the careless or ambitious family which boasted excessively on its *billet d'obsèques*. These collectors' pieces would perpetuate the memory of its folly for the amusement of future generations.[118]

The Christian theme of equality before death was reflected in the

secular writers of the century. 'Lorsque la mort a égalisé les fortunes', said Montesquieu, 'une pompe funèbre ne devrait pas les
différencier.' Noble souls, said a less illustrious contemporary, do
not seek for monuments, epitaphs, or funeral distinctions, for they
know that posterity will remember them, though higher still in the
scale of virtue are those who recognize the vanity even of a good
reputation, and prefer to come before God in total simplicity.[119]
Delisle de Salles appealed to natural equality; as a proposition in
life, its utility was arguable, but in death the principle reigned
supreme, and our ceremonies should recognize the fact.[120] Other
writers complained of the folly of wasting money on funerals, of
the 'simulated regrets' that thrive behind the façade of 'pompous
bagatelles', of the time wasted by young ecclesiastics in walking in
useless processions, and of the encouragment given to the thriftless
poor, who spend their funeral fees on drink.[121]

Though the funeral customs were subjected to tests of equality
and utility, the writers of the eighteenth century did not make a
fetish of abstract principle; where religion was concerned, the more
usual test was historical and comparative, treating Christianity as
one manifestation among others of deep-rooted inclinations and
convictions. From classical authors, a great deal was known about
the burial customs of antiquity; archaeology was beginning to
reveal those of the succeeding barbarian kingdoms—the intendant
of Poitou, in 1737, organized a large-scale 'dig' at Civaux on a site
containing 6,000 graves, supposedly of warriors who had fallen in a
battle between Clovis and the Visigoths.[122] Seventeenth-century
and contemporary travellers described the picturesque observances
of the whole world, from the philosophical Chinese to the North
American savages. The waxed corpses of Babylonia, Egyptian
mummies, Greek and Roman funeral pyres, dervishes who ate their
old men cooked alongside the mutton, the inhabitants of Colchis
who hung their dead in leather bags from trees, Ethiopians who
coated them with white plaster then embedded them in blocks of
glass—antiquity had left records of many strange burial customs,
to be compared, in modern times, with the Parsees of Persia who
expose their dead on towers to the birds of prey (if the right eye goes
first it is a sign of divine election), with the Red Indians who paint
the faces of corpses, the Brazilians who hang skeletons in their huts,

the natives of Virginia who stuff the skins of their kings with sand, the savages of the Orinoco who grind up the bones of their ancestors to fortify their drink, the Japanese who keep ashes piously in urns, and the savages of the Balearic islands who chop up bodies for storage in earthenware pots. Among the Red Indians the funeral is a time for singing and burning the dead man's possessions; in Florida, the widow of a tribesman cuts off her hair to hang on her husband's tomb (and cannot remarry until it has grown to shoulder length again); in Calicut, the mourners shave their heads and forswear the chewing of betel nut for thirteen days; Jews circle the coffin seven times, tear their garments, and leave their beards untrimmed for a month; Chinese families visit the temples of their ancestors every six months, and once a year, in springtime, go to their tombs in the hills for a picnic.[123] When a Chief of san Domingo dies, two of his wives are buried with him; in India, wives burn themselves on the funeral pyres of their husbands—pushed in by Brahmins in Bisnagar, tied to a stake in Gujrat, lying on a bed in Bengal, and jumping into the flames on the Coromandel coast; in Guinea, the favourite wife is buried with the chief and the heads of the others are put on poles around the grave.[124]

These picturesque details, much savoured by eighteenth-century writers, taught contradictory lessons. Christian observances had parallels among other peoples. Thus, the procession to the parish cemetery on All Souls' Day resembled the springtime festivals of the departed among the ancient Romans and the Chinese, and the 'Festin des Âmes' or 'Fête des Morts' of the Red Indians, when they reverently dig up the remains of their ancestors for celebrations which bring together many villages.[125] So Christianity was not unique. By the same token, however, the Christian belief in a life after death received confirmation from the experience of other peoples; indeed, it seemed that there must be a common substratum of belief in immortality inherited from the foundation of the world—who could believe that the Indians would dig up rotting corpses, unless the act had been ordained by 'the tradition that their Ancestors had received from our earliest forebears, that dead bodies must one day regain a new life, which will endure to all Eternity'.[126] Catholic apologists had no reason, then, to deny that their funeral rites had affinities with those of other peoples; all that was necess-

ary was to insist on their superior quality and inspiration. The
Jesuits compared the practices of classical antiquity with those of
the Red Indians, finding in forests of Canada institutions corresponding to the Roman professional mourners, the Spartan cymbal
players, the burning or burial of a warrior's weapons along with his
corpse, and beliefs of a common sort about the underworld, including even a fierce dog at the portals.[127] In spite of the gulf of
sophistication between them, the vaunted Greeks and Romans had
progressed spiritually little further than the heroic savages of the
New World. Christians shared with both the primitive revelation,
but embodied it in a liturgy illuminated by the hope and certainty
which sprang from the resurrection of Christ.

Granted that the funeral customs of so many peoples were
outlandish and barbarous, there was yet a lesson in them for
spiritually-minded men, whether Christians or deists. 'However
bizarre and ridiculous the different manners of mourning the
dead . . . may seem to us, it is certain that the principle is just,
reasonable, and natural.'[128] Indeed, savages, by their honesty in
facing the reality of death and their unselfconscious respect for
their dead kinsmen, have a certain superiority to civilized men.
Since they are not afraid to tell a friend that he is dying, they are
better able to console him, and their funerals are marked by forceful
and highly personal expressions of grief. 'They respect their dead,'
wrote Buffon; 'they adorn them, they speak to them; they recite
their great deeds, they praise their virtues: and we, who pride
ourselves on our sensitivity, we do not even show ordinary human
sympathy; we flee, we abandon them, we do not wish to see them,
we have neither the courage nor the will to speak of them; we even
avoid going to places which could recall their memory; we are
either too indifferent, or too weak-spirited.'[129]

Admirers of the demonstrative natural mourning of primitive
days could find examples of its survival on the fringes of the
Mediterranean world. In the Arab women of the Barbary Coast
who tear their hair and address all sorts of pleas and reproaches to
the corpse, the abbé Poiret saw 'une éloquence naturelle et
pathétique'.[130] In Greece, Madame Chénier reported, there were
similar lamentations from the women—'You are but sleeping',
they say, 'Do not abandon me', 'I will revive you in my embrace', 'I

am dragged down to the grave with you'.[131] One of the abbé Barthélemy's characters justifies this kind of mourning; what is this philosophy, he asks, which teaches me to love my wife yet forbids me to weep for her—you say my tears cannot bring her back, 'Eh! c'est ce qui les redouble encore'.[132] In one of Madame de Genlis's stories for children, a Greek beauty laments for her dead brother, causing astonishment, terror, and compassion in all who hear her. 'Among a people enslaved by the decencies of fashion', says Nicandre, 'sorrow has to be still and silent; but with us it is eloquent and sublime.' More sober writers doubted the superiority of this 'natural' and 'sublime' eloquence.[133] It was the result of a hot climate, said one, and he took the opportunity to score off his compatriots in Southern France; the inhabitants of Languedoc are exhibitionist, their women mourn in the Greek fashion: 'they weep because they see others weeping'.[134] They resemble the professional mourners of Ancient Rome, said another—we should give them leather aprons to collect the tears and lachrymatory urns to store them.[135] Alphonse, in Mme de Genlis's story, had doubts about Nicandre's enthusiasm for demonstrative lamentation, and was more impressed by the old gardener who went off quietly to cultivate the flowers his master had loved.[136] Barbarians have hard hearts, said another, so when death finally breaks through to afflict them they are drawn into exaggerated demonstrations of grief. By all means let us learn from them to feel deeply about the deaths of others; in this respect, we can listen to 'the voice of nature'.[137] But we do not need to adopt their outrageous means of self-expression.

By contrast to the idea of 'Nature' as manifested in the conduct of primitive people, the true ideal of the Enlightenment was to treat death as 'natural' in the sense that it should be met with calm acceptance. This is what Bernardin de Saint-Pierre would have us teach our children, as some tiny corpse, crowned with flowers, is buried among the shrubs in a corner of the school playground.[138] In one of the most satisfying utopias of the Age of Reason, the abbé Terrasson's Egypt, once the body of the good Queen had appeared before the Judges of the Dead and been ferried across the lake to the 'labyrinth', all mourning ceased; there was feasting, dancing, games, and the nobles and nymphs and satyrs from the sacred groves joined with the common people in rejoicing.[139] In an attrac-

ive civilization which had evolved outside the Christian revelation—Japan, as described by its Jesuit historian—the funeral
procession was an affair of calm and beauty: the chief Bonze in cloth
of gold and silks leading the way in an ornate litter, the other
Bonzes with placards mounted on sticks and inscribed with the
several names of God, attendants in pearl-grey robes scattering
paper roses among the spectators, the women in white, with multi-
coloured veils, the corpse dressed in white in a posture of prayer
borne on another litter, and accompanied by the youngest child
bearing the torch which was to light the funeral pyre.[140] What is
primitive and 'natural' quickly accumulates superstitious ac-
cretions; the highest point of civilized conduct is to move back,
through complexities, to the pure and primitive feelings as they
ought to be in their essential distillation, purged of all adulteration
of superstition or taint of crudeness. In the last resort, there was no
contradiction between feeling and reason, between Nature and
Enlightenment.

For not entirely congruous reasons, the theologians and the
thinkers of the Enlightenment converged in their attitude to
mourning: ideally, grief should be expressed with solemnity, restraint, and egalitarian simplicity. Pious folk in their last will and
testament might take the strictest Christian view and ask for a
pauper's funeral; even so, the question arose: how recognizably
pious must an individual's life have been, and what particular
elevation of rank must he have held, before such humility was
appropriate. Sometimes, the gesture was made within the context
of a confraternity; a member of the 'purple' Penitents of Limoges
(who specialized in burying executed criminals) might ask to be laid
to rest himself in the felons' graveyard.[141] Sometimes, it was an
aristocratic prelate leaving his fortune to the poor and asking to be
joined to his legatees in death. 'Je recommande et même ordonne
d'être enterré en vrai pauvre', was the direction of a La Rochefoucauld, bishop of Beauvais.[142] Cardinal de Saulx, archbishop of
Rouen, leaving all to a seminary for aged and infirm priests, made
himself equal to them and forbade incongruous armorial bearings
or decorations on his tomb.[143] In this way, a courtier would make
his gesture of severance from the gilded life of Versailles; thus the
duc de Beauvilliers left the court of Louis XIV without hangings,

coats of arms, or *billets* of invitation, lighted by only two dozen torches and an equal number of candles; thus the chancellor d'Aguesseau in the mid-eighteenth century joined the anonymous poor in the cemetery of Auteuil (though his family defied his wishes and marked the spot with a marble cross).[144] A king's mistress in this way could offer a final proof of her repentance—that was how Mme de Mailly came to rest in an unmarked plot in the cemetery of the Innocents. 'Is there not a touch of ostentation in this great humility?' asked the cynical Barbier.[145] Such simplicities were naturally admired by Jansenists, the supreme example in high society being that of Mme de Beauvau who died in 1752, leaving instructions that only the poor of the Hôpital Général were to follow her to her grave in the common cemetery where, if her family insisted on a commemorative stone, the sole inscription was to be 'Cy-gît Marie-Anne-Elisabeth-Thérèse de Beauvau, ci-devant Duchesse de Rochechouart, à présent poussière'.[146]

This pious insistence on joining the poor in death had its secular utilitarian counterpart in the offer of one's body for anatomical research. The practice was supposed to be common among the English, but few donors were found in France,[147] where medical students had to make do with corpses of paupers from the hospital or those they could filch from graveyards. But, on a less heroic level, the idea that funerals should be simple and mourning restrained was one which was progressively gaining acceptance among the upper classes. What had begun as a pious ideal for the few became a secular convention of good taste and sophistication. The magistrates of Lille in 1783, replying to a complaint of the parish priests that surplice fees were declining now that the new cemeteries were coming into use, argued that people had been spending less on funerals for some time. 'The display of our ancestors was concentrated entirely on religious ceremonies. In those days they were glad to make funerals occasions of lavish pomp, the only sort of acceptable expenditure by which private individuals were able to show off their position and fortune'. But now, they said, splendid processions had come to an end, and funerals were reduced to 'the majestic simplicity of their original form'.[148] Though it appears that the more flamboyant expenditures and baroque gestures were being eliminated, we cannot use wills to give straightforward chart of the progress of simplicity, since a testator's demand for austerity was not always observed by his heirs. Certainly, there was a prestigious display at Notre-Dame and at Saint-Denis for the Queen in 1768, and for the duc de Luynes at Saint-Sulpice in 1771, in defiance of their testamentary dispositions. Still less are we entitled to assume that the absence of directions in a testament implies that the family will exercise moderation; sometimes, indeed, what is left unsaid may imply a confidence that the usual pomp will ensue, rather than an indifference to it. What is certain, however, from the evidence of last wills and testaments, is that fewer and fewer people of the upper classes were interested in ensuring a pompous funeral for themselves. The examination of a large number of Parisian wills by the pupils of Chaunu[149] shows that in the second half of the seventeenth century, most testators were concerned about the place where they were to be buried; only 16 per cent of the men and 12 per cent of the women made no reference to this question, and only 12 per cent of the men and 10 per cent of the women left the choice to their executors. By contrast, in the first half of the eighteenth century, the figures were 32 per cent and 24 per cent and 13 per cent and $10\frac{1}{2}$ per cent, while in the second half of the century they were 59 per cent and 51 per cent and 23 per cent and 24 per cent—that is, between 1751 and 1800, 75 per cent of the women and 82 per cent of the men left no personal directions about the place of their burial. Throughout the eighteenth century too, the wills of the capital show a progressive decline of interest as to whether friars, almsmen, or orphans should march in the funeral procession, and whether or how many torches and candles should be carried. In the rich *quartier* of Saint-Honoré, from 1700 to 1740, just over half the wills repudiated the baroque splendours of the traditional funeral. One only gives a religious reason: 'ostentation being incompatible with the state of humiliation and annihilation of a body destined to be food for worms'. For many of the others, we may imagine there were secular or social reasons. By the reign of Louis XVI, most of the wills of the magistrates of the Parlement of Bordeaux stipulated a minimum of pomp.[150] Vovelle's analysis of the wills of Provence[151] shows that direct requests for simplicity did not increase significantly during the eighteenth century (at Marseille, they stood at

12 per cent), but that the formula asking for the accustomed cer
emonies died away; one-third of the notables of Marseille wer
asking for them early in the century, but only one-sixth on the ev
of the Revolution. Taking the figures in proportion to the number
of individuals in each social class, it was the clergy who wer
heading the movement for simplicity, followed by the nobles, ther
by the magistrates and members of the liberal professions. N
doubt aristocratic piety and Jansenism on the one hand, and scepti
cism and unbelief on the other, were combining to reject the hier
archical pomp of the traditional funeral observances. But for most
the turning towards simplicity was more likely to have been th
result of Rousseauistic sentimentality and egalitarianism, mani
fested in devotion to Nature as against the artificialities of civiliz
ation, and in an increasing consciousness of the bonds of affectior
between the members of the small family group. Grief was becom
ing more introverted and intense, more private, separated from th
formal observances of the corporate hierarchical society.

10

Graveyards: Patriotism, Poetry, and Grim Realities

I

At the beginning of the eighteenth century the cemetery was usually alongside the parish church: 'It is by way of death that we arrive at the presence of God,' wrote Chateaubriand,[1] who gloried in the arrangements of those days, when religion was the binding force of the community and men were continually reminded of their debt to their ancestors. For long, the faithful, anxious to enjoy the benefits of the prayers of those who came to worship, and believing there was virtue in physical proximity, had striven to ensure for themselves a burial place within the church building itself, or, failing that, a place in the graveyard as near to the church walls as possible. The parish priest, the patron, the *seigneur haut justicier*, and members of noble families which could prove immemorial privilege, were entitled to be buried in the sanctuary of the church; the laity generally (or, at least, those who could afford the fees) were put in the nave—in a family vault or the crypt of a confraternity, or simply under the paving stones, whether anonymously, or in a spot marked by an inscription on a slab or a plaque on the wall. As always in eighteenth-century France, there were privileges—the guild of fencing masters in Paris bought a corpse in 1772 to bury it in a particular monastic chapel lest their rights fell into abeyance.[2] In the same year, an official at Morlaix spoke of the madness—'une sorte de fureur'—of people to get their relatives buried as closely as possible to the church; soundings in the parish registers of Brittany show that, in some places, a third or even half of the population did manage to find a last resting-place within the actual building.[3] The graveyard was left for the common sort. As a dictionary said, cemeteries were only for 'le peuple'.[4]

How was it possible to accommodate so many corpses in what were, generally, exiguous quarters? In the cemetery, there would be only a limited number of separate graves. Most bodies—whether in a coffin, or merely in a shroud—were put in the *foss' commune*, the burial pit, and this stayed open—with just an inch o two of earth thrown over each new arrival—until the quota o corpses was complete. The day after a funeral, says Mercier of wha he observed in Paris, a coffin will be under four or five more, and th digger will not close up the pit until the bodies have reached th required level.[5] These *fosses* and whatever individual graves ther were, as well as most of those inside the churches, were reopene comparatively often, and the bones would be taken away for stack ing in a charnel-house (a *charnier*), possibly staging en route in a *ossuaire* for the completion of the process of drying out.[6] Thes were grim practicalities. Meditations among the tombs and spir itual and lyrical reflections in graveyards are not found before th second half of the eighteenth century; the stench of the *foss commune* and the utilitarian packaging of the *charniers* did no incline the soul to leisurely reverie.

There might well be other features to inhibit lofty thoughts. A canon of Reims described the cemetery of Saint-Symphorien in th seventies: the inhabitants used it as a short cut and rubbish dump hung out washing to dry, and trundled their carts through it animals came in and dug up the corpses, and wild dogs took refug there; old men foregathered for gambling and the choirboys t play, while 'disorders between the sexes' were not unknown; dur ing fairs, hard-pressed citizens relieved themselves in the shadow o its walls, and if this provided examples of 'nudité scandaleuse' t alarm the canons on their way to divine service, 'jugez quel scandal pour les enfants de chœur'.[7] This catalogue of outrages has only on standard item missing: there is no reference to the snatching o bodies for anatomy demonstrations, a crime common in cities wit an active Medical Faculty—nothing less than a fifteen-foot wall just as in all the Catholic cemeteries, would deter the medica students, said the Protestants of Montpellier when, in 1789, the were at last given an official burial-ground of their own.[8]

All these confusions were flatly contrary to royal edicts an episcopal ordinances. From the Edict of 1695, cemeteries wer supposed to be enclosed by solid walls and gates with locks, an from the mid-seventeenth century reforming bishops had pursue

1ose who danced there, bought and sold, threshed corn or grazed
attle, played boule or dice or tennis.[9] (As for those who had affrays
nd fights, this could be a serious matter, for any effusion of blood,
ven a bleeding nose, might necessitate the reconsecration of the
round, at great expense to the offenders.[10]) Also (oddly enough,
onsidering later romantic views of what a cemetery should be like)
he bishops tried to get rid of trees[11]—their roots hampered the
iggers, their branches kept out healthy breezes, and in their shade
chools of cards, or dice, or worse, could congregate. Episcopal
isitations, more frequent in the eighteenth century than was at
ne time supposed, always included a perambulation of the cem-
tery; orders would be given to repair the walls, to expel the cattle
r remove the stacked firewood; in 1766, the bishop of Saint-Papoul,
cting on purely hygienic grounds, closed one parish cemetery
ltogether, 'à cause de l'odeur'.[12] Sometimes, the agents of seign-
urial justice would lend a hand in maintaining the decencies; thus,
he affair of Michon's washing in the graveyard of Conflans Sainte-
Ionorine in 1781 got into the lawbooks, for the seigneur defended
is *procureur fiscal* right up to the Parlement, Michon having in the
nd to pay all the costs—an expensive way of doing the laundry.[13]
'his steady pressure from the bishops (aided by a parochial clergy
ising in intellectual status and corporate pride) was having its
ffect throughout the eighteenth century. Profane business and
leasure were being excluded from the enclosure of the dead. The
ictory of ecclesiastical reformers in imposing their austere concept
f the sacred was not all gain, even by their own presuppositions; in
utting off the dead from the living and separating death from
veryday reality, they were intensifying the harshness of a spiri-
uality which already insisted too much on the vanity of human
ndeavours and sited the Christian hope too exclusively in a king-
lom beyond the grave.

Austere theologians censured the superstitious rush to obtain
urial places near the altars. The early Church knew of no such
ractice, while St. Augustine, the Councils of the sixth century, and
he capitularies of Charlemagne had expressly forbidden it. Kings,
otably the Emperor Constantine, had been buried in the basilicas
hey founded, and worldly pride had led others to seek similar privi-
eges.[14] Such pushfulness was self-defeating, for it was calculated

to bring down divine punishment.[15] The argument from the use
fulness of the prayers of the faithful had been misconceived; th
places of honour should be reserved for the very pious, those wh
might work miracles from their tombs in answer to the inter
cessions of the worshipping congregation.[16] Alas! how incongruou
it would all appear on Judgement Day, when a horde of lost soul
would emerge from under the steps around the altars, boun
briskly for Hell.[17] Aesthetic considerations reinforced these theolo
gical arguments. The eighteenth century was an age of architec
tural improvement—or, depending on the point of view, of vandal
ism. In the interests of simplicity, light, and perspective, reformin
ecclesiastics were evicting Gothic shrines from cathedrals, for the
were, after all, 'the gilded tombs of frail and sinful mortals'.[18] Th
abbé Porée, a canon of Caen, who in 1745 published a powerfu
essay against burials in churches, or anywhere else near huma
habitations, wanted to adopt the principles of the aesthetic reforn
for a clear didactic purpose. Churches should speak of life and hope
by contrast, let the cemeteries, lined with cypresses and adorne
with a new and simple form of funereal architecture, speak only o
death—'tout y serait reduit à l'unité d'objet'.[19] Clean and unclut
tered, concentrated on a single object, they would be places o
haunting solemnity.

In Porée's *Lettres sur la sépulture dans les églises*, a good
looking young widow tells her *curé* she will no longer attend hi
church so long as burials take place there—she is not prepared t
risk the 'pestilential vapours'; another of Porée's characters, a
magistrate, wonders if the evil passions of the dead are also giver
off as infectious exhalations.[20] For long, the stench of bodily decay
had been regarded as a warning of a menace to health; this was ar
axiom laid down by the great physician Ambroise Paré at the end o
the sixteenth century, and in the church of Saint-Étienne du Mon
at Paris there was an undated Latin epitaph to Simon Pierre, a
medical practitioner, who had insisted on being buried outside, 'ne
mortuus cuiquam noceret, qui vivus omnibus profuerat'.[21] La
Reynie, the *lieutenant général de police* of the capital, who died ir
1709, had the same sentiments, leaving instructions that his body
should rest in the cemetery and not in the parish church of Saint
Eustache, since he did not wish to contribute to the infection of the

ir 'in the place where the Holy Mysteries are celebrated and where he ministers of the Lord pass the greater part of their lives'.[22] The ²arlement of Rouen backed its archbishop in 1721 in framing egulations to limit burials in churches,[23] and the Parlement of Paris n 1737 set up an inquiry by medical experts into the dangers of emeteries to public health.[24] In the following year, Voltaire took up he hygienic theme; he wrote of 'the war of the dead against the iving', and praised the customs of the ancient Greeks and Romans vho transported their dead outside their cities. Surely, we ought to trive to fulfil our duty to posterity—a man should look forward vith pleasure to the prospect of becoming manure on the barren ·lain of Sablons, to help the crops to grow.[25] And what of reverence owards God? 'Quoi! . . . ces peuples enterrent leurs morts dans es mêmes lieux où ils adorent la Divinité,' cries Babouc in 'Persépo-is'—in *Le Monde comme il va*, published the year after Canon ²orée's onslaught.

Meanwhile, a horror story from Montpellier began to circulate, is recounted by Haguenot, Dean of the Faculty of Medicine of that ·ity, in a lecture delivered before the Estates of Languedoc at the ·ehest of the intendant.[26] In mid-August 1744, the vault of the *²énitents blancs* of the church of Notre-Dame was opened to ·eceive the body of Guillaume Boudon, one of that confraternity. Overcome by poisonous vapours, the gravedigger collapsed. A ·esuit father, Joseph Sarrau, was lowered into the vault, with nembers of the congregation hanging on to his cowl and girdle. He ·ad to be pulled out, unconscious and in convulsions. One of the *²énitents* went down and collapsed, so too did the sexton's brother, vho made a rescue attempt with a ladder. In all, the vault claimed ·hree dead. When they were finally pulled out with ropes and ·ooks, their clothing stank and was covered with a greenish-yellow ·rust'. The heroic Jesuit recovered, but went around pale and hag-·ard; in town they called him 'le ressuscité'. Dr Haguenot was nclined to think that the lethal vapours in the vault were not ·ntirely concerned with the decay of corpses, but were related to ·hose found in a local cave, which killed caged birds in seconds, and ·ats and dogs within two minutes. In 1753, in a prize-winning essay ·or the Academy of Bordeaux, Boissier de Sauvages, also of the Medical Faculty of Montpellier, tried to fit Haguenot's empirical findings into a scientific theory.[27] The molecules of the air, the microscope shows, are one-tenth the size of those in the blood, so they can easily fit into the minute intervals in the bloodstream, getting there through the pores or through the delicate tissue of the lungs. A putrefying corpse releases a swarm of sulphurous mole cules, which have a two-fold detrimental action on living beings. Firstly, acting in their own right, they can nullify electric charges and as our 'fluide nerveux' is essentially electrical in nature, they weaken and diminish it. Secondly, these sulphurous molecules join with the harmful vapours exhaled from the earth and which gather in caves and tombs, greatly increasing their malignancy. That is why fresh air is so salutary, though even without this scien tific proof we ought to have known it, through our 'sentiment intérieur'.

In 1763, thanks to the unmasking of clandestine manœuvres by the churchwardens of Saint-Sulpice,[28] there was a great outcry about the overflowing cemeteries of Paris. The churchwardens finding their graveyard too small for the growing population of the parish and considering their auxiliary one too far distant for con venience, bought some extra land near the church, conspiratorially through a third party. The secret leaked out and, threatened with the dead as their new neighbours, local citizens complained. As one of them was the prince de Condé, the Parlement sprang into action. A report on the cemeteries of the capital was prepared in the astonishingly short time of twenty days.[29] It recited well-known facts, but the cumulative effect was alarming. In some places successive generations of the dead had contributed to lift the soil level above that of the surrounding houses, causing nauseous drainage problems. The cycle of burials–exhumations–new burials was generally about nine years. Charnel-houses were filling up; at Saint-Gervais, the bones were being stacked above the rafters of the aisles of the church, and these were heavy-laden. Statistics con cerning the pits for common burials were hair-raising, and few parishes seem to have used the device of Saint-Nicolas-des-Champs of a boarded cover and a padlocked trap door. At Saint-Séverin, the *fosse commune* was open all the year (250 corpses), being closed when the hot weather began; in Saint-Gervais it was filled in every four months (about 130 corpses); at Saint-Cosme, which registered

nly thirty deaths a year, the period of use was indeterminate; the
ew graveyard of Saint-Sauveur, opened in 1760, still had its first
osse commune open—three years of use with an accumulation of
o8 bodies; some inhabitants of neighbouring houses had fled,
thers signed angry petitions. But churchwardens, who would have
o levy a rate on the inhabitants if they were to buy extra land for
emeteries, were not squeamish. Dwellers near the church of Saint-
'aul were enraged, but the wardens, presiding thriftily over a *fosse*
ommune 63 metres long by 44 metres wide and 5 metres deep, said
hat their cemetery was 'le plus aéré de Paris et n'incommode
ersonne'.

The overwhelming evidence of this full inquiry determined the
'arlement of Paris to take action, and on 21 May 1765 its *procureur*
énéral issued an ordinance which was to become operative on the
ollowing first of January. Except for *curés* and founders' kin,
urials in church buildings would cease. Hospitals and religious
ommunities would be allowed to go on using their existing
emeteries, but the parish ones would be closed. Seven or eight
ew, large cemeteries would be established outside the city, and all
itizens would find their last resting-place in them, either in a *fosse*
ommune or, at the stiff price of 300 *livres*, in an individual plot.
ouis XV backed the magistrates by setting a good example at
'ersailles, presenting the church of Saint-Louis there with land in
he open country to replace the old graveyard. But in Paris, the new
'ear came and nothing happened. Apart from the enlightened
lergy and people of Saint-André-des-Arts and Saint-Germain
'Auxerrois, the parishes were in revolt against the new regu-
ations. Complex mutual negotiations would be required to set up
ew cemeteries, and the expense would be enormous. Nor did
nyone like the new funeral arrangements which the Parelement's
cheme would necessitate. The solemnities would end at a mortu-
ry chapel; coffins would accumulate here during the day, and
vould be ferried out at night (2 a.m. in summer, 4 a.m. in winter)
eyond the city boundaries. It sounded too much like the clandes-
ine procedures to which the Protestants had to resort.[30] So nothing
vas done. No doubt, the Parlement could have enforced its edict so
ar as burial in churches was concerned (the Parlement of Brittany,
vhich had issued a prohibition ten years before the magistrates of

Paris, in 1758 had been ordering exhumations in cases where it regulations had been flouted).[31] But there was no resort to draco nian measures. In 1772, a journalist notes how the 'mania' fo burials in churches continues in Paris: 'the most worthy project are devised. Edicts are published, and no one obeys them.'[32]

The medical profession carried on with its learned and siniste analyses of the effects of exhalations from graves. A few volatil and imperceptible atoms, said Leclerc in 1767, can have dispropor tionately widespread effects, just as leaven can transform a whol lump. And he warned against fat men, whose deaths menace so ciety, so swiftly and powerfully do they putrefy.[33] Olivier, a expert from the Faculty of Montpellier, after a massive display o learning about Greek, Roman, and Hebrew customs, tried to add explanatory detail to Boissier de Sauvages's theory of molecula absorption into the bloodstream. He agreed that this happened, bu had a different explanation of the deleterious effect. Some mol ecules consist of 'phlogiston', that inflammable, intangible stuff which may be assumed to be harmful; some may be bearers o unsavoury properties of the corpse from which they came. But th most dangerous, he thought, were caustic alkalis, which destroy th acids in the air we breathe. These acids are essential to our health for they renew the 'cement' of 'vitriolic' substances which hold together the fibres of our bodies, and which is continually bein destroyed by the alkalis produced by our 'humours'.[34] Anothe doctor of Montpellier, Maret, was invited by the Academy of Dijo to write a memoir of advice for the municipality, and this wa published in 1773. It put forward Boissier de Sauvages's theory o the molecules of putrefaction increasing the malignancy of th exhalations of the earth (and cited Buffon's view that these ar caused by 'the central fire'); it also publicized some new horrifi incidents: three dead at Marseille because they dug into an ol plague pit when planting fruit trees, a fat man's grave at Saulie prematurely opened resulting in the death of the *curé* and thirty others.[35] In the following year the *Gazette de Santé* published story from Nantes: a corpse was moved after three months, and no a single survivor from the fifteen people who were present at th exhumation.[36] Navier, a doctor of medicine writing for th Academy of Châlons-sur-Marne, added another warning story om thirty years ago: one-third of the inhabitants of a country own killed off by an epidemic when the old cemetery was dug up.[37] s for practical advice, the medical profession said the obvious— nove the cemeteries away from human habitations, dig very deep its, leave a balk of at least 2 feet between graves laterally, throw in uicklime (which was the common practice at mass burials in time f plague). There was support also for two old ideas which might ave seemed less useful, that is, removing all trees and firing unshots to clear the air. Burials in church buildings were con- emned, but as some were regarded as inevitable, ingenious pro- osals were made—embalming, filling the coffin with plaster, fur- ishing vaults with ventilating chimneys up to the roof, or keeping hem filled with cold water.[38]

In 1775, the Gallican Church threw its influence on to the side of he magistrates and the medical profession. Individual bishops had lready attempted to regulate burials in churches; in March 1775, oménie de Brienne, the reforming (and, possibly, unbelieving) rchbishop of Toulouse, published a pastoral letter prohibiting hem altogether in his diocese; even the archbishops would be xcluded from their cathedral. In July, the Assembly General of the lergy of France appealed to the new king to take comprehensive ction. The result was the Royal Declaration of 16 March 1776.[39] emeteries in built-up areas which endangered 'the salubrity of the ir' must be moved, 'insofar as circumstances permit' (there was a oophole here, and many parishes sought exemption this way). only parish priests (or bishops in cathedrals,) patrons, and seig- eurs could be interred in churches. It was still possible to be buried n cloisters, provided they were not closed to the open air. There vere to be no more tombs in the chapels of monasteries and aunneries. In every case where a burial was allowed within a building, whether it be a church or cloister or any other, the body nust be laid 6 feet below the interior soil level of a vault of spacious limensions, entirely lined with solid stonework. The Declaration pplied to the whole country, and was backed by the full weight of he royal officials and lawcourts. At last the great reform was under vay.

For the most part, the countryside was not disturbed by the royal egislation, since it seemed to be conceded that a cemetery in the middle of a rural village was not 'nuisible à la salubrité de l'air'. But in the towns there were confusions and tribulation as th ponderous legal procedures[41] rolled forward. The *procureur du ro* or a similar official would summon the local judges (seigneurial i royal ones were not available) to issue an ordinance for the inspec tion of the cemetery by experts. Generally, there would be four o these, including at least one medical practitioner, and one practica man capable of handling surveying and building problems. The would ask about the prevailing winds (southerly the most danger ous), the depth of the soil (6 feet considered to be the decen minimum), the area in relation to the expected number of corpse (taking decaying time as three to six years), the distance from houses, and the state of health of the nearest inhabitants. If th cemetery was unsatisfactory, a second ordinance would convok the *curé*, churchwardens, and parishioners before a legal official they would have to find a new site and the experts would have to approve it. When it had been walled and gated, the bishop would b asked to arrange for its consecration. As for the old cemetery, i would have to be left untouched by secular use for fifteen years (thi was the normal time specified by the lawcourts), with the parishioners obliged to maintain the walls and gates during tha period.

As the procedures dragged on, there were feuds and intrigue galore. Parishes had to negotiate to form combinations to buy nev cemeteries; at Angers, two joined with the Hôtel-Dieu, five with a fortunate parish which already had a spacious burial-ground, and the seven remaining ones struggled on until 1788 before they foun a suitable place.[42] There were clashes with bishops—as with th bishop of Luçon who short-circuited matters by laying an interdic on the cemetery of Noirmoutier. At Calais, the army garrison wanting the town made healthy—why not? the soldiers did no have to pay—met with a universal conspiracy, which included th medical profession, to maintain the inexpensive status quo.[43] A Caen, the garrison tried to manipulate things to obtain a site for a new barracks;[44] elsewhere, improving municipal authorities were darkly suspected of forcing the parishes to move their cemetery ou of town to leave room for projected new institutional buildings Within the parishes, there were disputes about who was entitled to attend the assemblies, disagreements between clergy and laity, manœuvres to hit on some cheap solution. Great bitterness was engendered when compulsory purchase was the only way in which a suitable plot of land could be obtained. This was especially so when ecclesiastical property was involved, since townsmen preferred to oppress religious institutions rather than private citizens, while churchmen had a good case for exemption since the mortmain legislation prevented them from acquiring new land to replace what was taken from them.[45] At Lyon, the town looked on with thrifty glee while there was a dispute of experts, the Collège de Médecine versus Dr Rast de Maupas. Thirteen years later, nothing had been done. In Marseille, some grudging action was taken, two cemeteries being replaced and one enlarged, but in An XII three of the old ones were still in use. At Lille, the improving municipality, alarmed by an epidemic of typhus, defied the parish clergy, the director of fortifications, and the public generally by acquiring a new cemetery in 1778, and closing the old one in August 1779. The churchwardens of Sainte-Catherine defiantly allowed a burial in theirs, and the magistrates had the body exhumed on 15 August; that night, there was a riot, the municipal hearses were smashed to bits, and one Gaussart, supposedly a ringleader, was promptly flogged and branded by order of the Parlement on the 21st. The winter rains began and the new graveyard flooded and proved useless.[46] The cemetery issue, affecting the feelings of all and the pockets of many, stirred up the towns of France as never before—it was a sort of psychological preparation for the intense municipal life which sprang up at the Revolution.

Progress was slow and disputes were universal essentially because money was at stake. The lawyers and experts required their fees, new land was expensive, and masons charged heavily for walls and gates. One parish in Angers paid out a total of 2,118 *livres*, another 1,436; in one country town the *curé* records an expenditure of no less than 12,000.[47] Anxious to avoid levying a rate, church-wardens racked their brains for reasons why their cemetery was an exception: the soil has the peculiar quality of reducing a corpse to a skeleton and 'impalpable dust' in eighteen months; a doctor of Montpellier has been to see it; there is a smell only when the wind is in the wrong quarter; those living near by are nearly all

octogenarians; our grave-digger has been in office for fifty years
and daily eats his lunch beside the open *fosse*; his predecessor died
at the age of sixty-one and he was unlucky in catching pleurisy. But
sentiment was involved as well as parsimony. The bishop of Luçon
spoke of the country folk as superstitiously attached to the place
where their ancestors rest; their 'respect outré pour les cendres de
leurs pères', says a royal official; 'l'attachment aveugle qu'ils ont
pour les sépultures de leurs ancêtres', says another. 'Leurs ancêtres
y étant inhumés,' says the petition of one parish in defence of its
graveyard, 'ils vouloient également y être et mêler leurs cendres
aux leurs.'[48] Ordinary folk, said a Parisian journalist, liked to point
to the place where their parents were buried—'C'est ici que mon
père, que ma mère sont enterrés', and with such a natural sentiment
he was obliged to sympathize: 'Ce préjugé, Monsieur, est d'ancienne date, tient à la nature, et on a de la peine à déraciner une
erreur qui prend sa source dans le sentiment.'[49] And what was naïve
feeling among the people shaded off into family pride among the
richer sort. *Curés* still occasionally buried someone important in
the church, whether in fear of the threats of the family, or encouraged by its offer to pay the fine and expenses if the matter was ever
brought before the lawcourts.[50] Indeed, though bishops had played
an active part in the hygienic reform, many of the clergy had
reservations. Some of the *curés* of Paris had combined to publish a
pamphlet hinting at a conspiracy of the *philosophes* against the
doctrine of prayers for souls in Purgatory: 'before long, piety
towards the dead will be annihilated'.[51] The campaign to move the
cemeteries, said the abbé Bergier, was being encouraged by the
libertines, who wished to get rid of all reminders of death so they
could enjoy their pleasures with complacency. While the places of
debauch stay open, we are busy removing the monuments which
tell of the brevity of life, the hope of heaven, and of the tenderness
of old friendships. Was it worth while to abandon an agency of
moral instruction in the interests of hygiene?—'If we gain in
respect of the purity of the atmosphere, it is to be feared that we lose
much so far as morality is concerned.' And for sober Christian
reasons—without, perhaps, a thought of Edward Young—Bergier
recommended his readers to visit the tombs of their friends and
relatives. 'Il est bon . . . que les morts ne soient pas sitôt oubliés,

ue l'on puisse aller encore de temps en temps s'attendrir et
'instruire sur leur tombeau.'[52] 'S'instruire'—that perhaps was the
ifference between the French theologian's attitude and the new
omantic cult of melancholy; death has stern lessons to teach us.

The will of enlightened administrators to press on with the
eform was stiffened by the continuing influx of macabre stories
rom the provinces—medical reports from La Rochelle in 1778
bout headaches, stomach upsets, and 'anxieties';[53] the canons of
·aint-Didier of Avignon assailed in their choir by a 'quantité de
rosses mouches noires et luisantes'; and in January 1780, at
ear-by Cavaillon, the death of a young grave-digger when open-
ig a tomb;[54] the Faculties of Medicine of Paris and Montpellier
ending advice to Malta on how to deal with disturbed graves and
racked vaults after the earthquake of the same year;[55] the dis-
overy of hundreds of half-rotted bodies when digging the foun-
ations of a new church porch at Dunkirk;[56] an epidemic at Beaune-
n-Gâtinais in 1781, and 32 dead and 300 suffering from tumours,
urple patches, and convulsions at Ceyrat three years later—all
lamed by doctors on the cemeteries.[57] Then came an incident,
ivestigated by the Faculty of Medicine and sensationally reported,
vhich gave the reformers their chance of a breakthrough against
he forces of obscurantism in Paris. The Cimetière des Saints-
nnocents[58] was a picturesque, macabre corner of the ancient city—
he high medieval walls with three gates, the church in the north-
vest corner, the three oratories over the vaults of the families
)rgemont, de Villeroy, and Pommereaux, the open-air pulpit sur-
nounted by a pyramidal roof with a cross at its summit, an obelisk,
nd a stone cross which had once marked the place where the house
f the Gastine brothers had stood before it had been razed for
arbouring a Protestant assembly. For eight centuries burials had
ontinued; here the dead of fifteen parishes were taken, as well as
ome of the poor who died in the Hôtel-Dieu and others from the
ospital of Sainte-Catherine (where the nuns gathered the bodies of
hose who died in gaol or in the streets or were fished out of the
iver). Places were also available for the rich who bought con-
·essionary plots from the landowner and seigneur, the Chapter of
·aint-Germain l'Auxerrois (absorbed into the Chapter of Notre-
)ame from 1744). The bones of a million dead, so it was said, were

stacked in the *charniers* above the fourteenth-century Gothic arcades which ran round the walls. At one point, houses of three storeys had been built above the arches, so that they had bones underneath their floor boards and windows looking out over the graves; during this reconstruction, the famous wall-painting of the *Danse macabre*, dating from 1424, had been destroyed. In the galleries, sellers of books, engravings, and second-hand clothing, and public letter-writers set up their stalls.[59] Prohibitions of burials in this venerable and unhygienic spot had been issued in the past, none of them effective for long. Then, at the end of 1779, 'méphitisme' from one of the immensely deep *fosses communes* began to penetrate laterally into the cellars of houses in the neighbouring rue de la Lingerie. The Chapter of Notre-Dame tried, unavailingly, to shut out the pestilential vapours; trenches dug around the *fosses* and filled with quicklime proved ineffective.[60] In February 1780, one of the cellar walls collapsed, and the organic debris of the ages rolled in. Sickness broke out in the *quartier*. The cemetery, lit by night by huge bonfires built to disperse the evil miasma while workmen walled and dug, became a resort for the curious (no doubt, they did not stay for long). The Faculty of Medicine set up an inquiry, and the Parlement closed the cemetery as from 1 November. Cadet de Vaux, the medical expert, informed the Academy of Sciences that samples of air from the cemetery were as contaminated as those from hospitals. There was urgency in his report, which he claimed took into account 'newly acquired knowledge of the nature of the atmosphere'.[61] By this he meant that the old idea of Boerhaave, that the particles of the air did not unite or cohere with other matter, was now invalidated: air engaged in chemical reactions and was not just a vehicle for dangerous particles from elsewhere. It made the neglect of any source of infection seem more dangerous, more likely to lead to unforeseen consequences. Now that the Parlement had closed the biggest cemetery of them all, the *lieutenant de police* of Paris proceeded to interdict another four graveyards. In 1783, Cadet de Vaux published an article in the *Journal de Physique* describing the Cimetière des Innocents as a continuing source of infection, and in November 1785, after taking further medical advice, the Royal Council ordered the deconsecration of the site and the removal of bodies, bones, and religious emblems, leaving an empty space which, in due course, would be made into a market.

The removals took place at night, in the cold weather from December to March of 1785 and the two following years.[62] Coffins and sacks of bones were ferried out in carts, each covered with purple draperies decorated with silver crosses, and pulled by four horses; police on horseback went ahead, together with two dozen almsmen carrying torches; two priests and two lawyers brought up the rear in a funeral carriage. All the while in the graveyard bonfires blazed, lighting a macabre scene recorded for posterity in the paintings of Hubert Robert, like a tableau from the outrageous sepulchral dramas which had become the fashion in the Parisian theatre of the time. When the buildings were demolished, the pyramidal pulpit was taken off to the château de Betz to adorn the *Vallée des tombeaux* there, a strange link between the haunted pre-romantic cult of tombs and death and the grim realities of the *fosse commune* and its insupportable odours. The bones went to the quarries of Montrouge, the labyrinth of excavations from which the building stone of Paris had been extracted over the centuries, and for long the haunt of bandits, smugglers, and mushroom growers. Here, in subterranean galleries newly consecrated, skulls and skeletons were arranged and festooned in decorative patterns, and further materials for the artistic enterprise of the custodians came in as other cemeteries were deconsecrated and emptied.[63] In 1787 the comte d'Artois and ladies of the Court went out to enjoy a collation in these novel surroundings, and in the following year another excursion was organized by Mme de Polignac.[64] Three years before the Terror made the guillotine a national institution, death was providing them with a *frisson* to enliven their picnics.

In sizeable towns, the suppression of existing cemeteries led groups of parishes to collaborate in finding new ones. The complexities of the Parisian situation made it logical to devise a master plan. In its abortive ordinance of May 1765, the Parlement had proposed seven or eight new burial-grounds with arrangements for collecting coffins in mortuary chapels and moving them out of the city at night. In 1768, the abbé Coyer, in a pamphlet with the splendid title of *A la vallée de Josaphat: étrennes aux morts at aux vivans, ou projet utile partout où l'on est mortel*, suggested a single vast necropolis in the open country, with something like a hundred coffins ferried out to it daily on a funeral barge. In the seventies and eighties, the office of the *procureur général* of the Parlement received new propositions from 'architects' or 'honest citizens' in the interests of public health and decency, though clearly they had behind them associations of business men with an interest in making burials into a commercial monopoly.[65] One group wanted a 20 per cent levy on funeral expenses; another the proceeds of a tax on all funeral processions in proportion to their ostentation, and the right to charge heavy fees for private burial plots and chapels; another wanted the cemetery contractors to have the best suit of clothes of the deceased, to be sold in monthly auctions, with surplus above profits to be given to the hospitals. In return, these projectors offered services which, presumably, they thought would be welcome to the Government and to public opinion. Their plans conform to the hierarchies of society. In the architect Delafosse's huge single cemetery there would be five zones—for ecclesiastics, the well-off ordinary folk, paupers, for the very big spenders who insisted on a private plot, and, most expensive of all, places in a colonnade for the plutocrats. Another scheme has the *fosses communes* in the centre, and five concentric circles around them, ending with the great, once again in a colonnade. Renou et Cie offer much the same—nobles in the centre circle around a temple, the middle class in the square which encloses the circle, and the rest in pits outside. Everyone assumes the participation of the clergy; Delafosse has twenty-one priests (nominated by the two senior *curés* of Paris) living in a hostel at his necropolis, and his nocturnal carts have a cab-like structure at the front to house the officiant. A respectable and necessary place for the clergy then in these schemes—but they have become public officials, stipendiary chaplains to the burial corporation. As yet, there is little interest in the idea of the solidarity of the family: the State, hierarchically organized, is burying its citizens. One project, that of Labrière, architect to the comte d'Artois, has at its centre a sort of national Panthéon, to be built from the stones of the abbey of Saint-Denis and to be the new repository of the royal tombs; there would be a gallery for *grands seigneurs*, and a place of honour for great men, adorned with their statues, 'ainsi que cela se pratique en Angleterre dans l'église de Westminster'. But this project does recognize the family, though only in so far as the very wealthy are concerned, for it offers 2,000 chapels to be bought by families 'in perpetuity'. Inevitably, the organization of a cemetery on a vast scale brought in ideas of landscaping, and thus, without any romatic ideas of reverie among the tombs, hard-headed contractors came to think of the English garden layout. There will be flowers and trees (trees now being supposed to improve the air) around the *fosses communes* say Renou et Cie; the setting will be a vast park, says Labrière, planted with cypress and poplar; here, those who have the fantasy to build 'un tombeau pittoresque' can do so, on payment of a substantial fee.

The reality of the new cemeteries of France, reluctantly bought and as cheaply as possible, was far from the commercial idyll of picturesque tombs amid trees and flower-beds, with temples, colonnades, and statues. The immediate effect of the reform, indeed, was to add a new scandal to the arrangements for burials. The mourners continued to process to the church, but no longer accompanied the body to the cemetery, and the last journey of all became an indecent, anonymous shamble. A priest splashed with mud from the foul byways, accompanied maybe by a muddy choirboy carrying a cross and a holy-water sprinkler, would precede the corpse (in a coffin or without one), borne by bearers who had been hired at street corners, and expended their wages as they went, stopping at wineshops for suitable restoratives.[66] Men were to be buried like dogs during the Revolution because religion was scorned; at the end of the *ancien régime* they were unceremoniously disposed of when the graveyards were moved out of walking distance.

II

By the eighteenth century, French churches of any size or distinction were filled with the funereal monuments of the great and rich, and their prestigious epitaphs. It was, and is, tempting to assume that these memorials constitute a record of the changing attitudes of successive generations to the grim fact of death, and the expression of the intensity of their loyalties and affections. But the assumption is dangerous, for in lapidary inscriptions a man is not on oath, and sculptors follow artistic fashions which change within a world of technical expertise whose relationships with the universe of general ideas are complex and ambiguous. On the other hand emotions are shaped and evolved by the very process of expressing them. Evidence of an artistic or ceremonial kind about patterns of thought and belief often means less than it seems to say, yet it can never be dismissed as purely formal and conventional.

Since the sixteenth century, the advance of civilization had improved the epitaph towards precision, simplicity, and decency.[67] The use of bizarre literary forms, of couplets, acrostics, and riddles, of incongruous reminiscences of pagan antiquity, had been abandoned. It was no longer customary to use the marble of tomb or plaque as a convenient place to engrave a list of the obligations of the parochial or monastic clergy by way of masses for the souls of the deceased, still less to add specifications of candles, holy water, ceremonies, reminders about sending annual circulars to descendants, and the name and address of the family lawyers—all of which had been common in the seventeenth century. (There is a nice example in 1736 of the recording of a very different sort of obligation: an *auditeur* of the Chambre des Comptes tells how his dead wife had longed for her infant son to become a priest, and he prays that the child will conform to her pious wishes.[68]) The typical epitaph of the eighteenth century was a historical document, drawn up, whether in French or in Latin, with a sense of style, with emphasis and economy. Piganiol de la Force speaks of the inscriptions on tombs as 'public archives' containing the secrets of the origins of families; he had collected many transcripts, but forbore to publish them in his description of Paris, to spare the vanity of those who had acquired pretensions superior to their ancestry.[69] When some famous man died, there would be open contests, officially ordained or spontaneous, to provide a suitable epitaph. When the sculptor Pigalle was commissioned in 1750 to devise a tomb for the maréchal de Saxe, the greatest soldier of the reign of Louis XV, the *directeur des bâtiments* called on Schoepflin, the historian of Alsace, to produce a legend for it; the Academy of Inscriptions was also consulted, while Marmontel, D'Alembert, and the abbé Pernetti volunteered suggestions. Even so, when a version was produced, the phrase 'Obiit Camboriti 30 Nov. anno salutis MDCCL' was suspect; it meant Maurice de Saxe died at Chambort, but could this be mistaken for Cambridge in England? The learned Fonce-magne was called in to establish the true Latin name for Chambort from twelfth-century charters. In the end, the problem was by-passed by abbreviation; no reference was made to the place of the marshal's death, and the words 'anno salutis' were omitted as well, ostensibly because there was insufficient room, though there may have been some deistical satisfaction in evicting a Christian formula.[70]

By the beginning of the eighteenth century, the standard form for a mausoleum was the dramatic group, a concept on which Bernini in Italy and Le Brun in France had set the seal of their genius. The dead man was represented in activity—reading, praying, descending to his tomb or rising from it, or involved in some stylized incident from his career, being supported or consoled the while by angels, virtues, or other allegorical figures (or, in his absence, being mourned by them), with Death or Time beckoning or grasping, amid floating drapery, books, crucifixes, armour, and bric-à-brac, against a background of columns or pyramids. True, the masterpiece of the reign of Louis XV, which unites the sophisti-cated pathos of the baroque with the solemnity of Versailles and the elegance of the eighteenth century, dispenses almost completely with allegory, and limits funereal paraphernalia to a smoking vase and a pyramid (of the French kind, with a narrow base like an obelisk). This is Michel-Ange Slodtz's tomb for the two arch-bishops of Vienne, commissioned by cardinal de la Tour d'Auvergne for himself (he died in 1745) and Mgr de Montmorin, whose vicar-general he had been. Montmorin, magnificent in embroid-ered cope and stole, is dying, handing over his cross and mitre to the cardinal, a haughty figure resplendent in lace; the white figures stand out against the sombre veined red marble of the sarcophagus, the lighter red of the pyramid, and the brown and yellow of the vase and funeral pall. There is a child with a book to the left of the group, but it is not one of the cherubs or *génies* commonly used to hold medallions, lift draperies, trail extinguished torches, or look sadly up from from pedestals— it is the spirit which has custody of the annals of the diocese, rushing off to record the death of its chief pastor.[71] By contrast, and conventionally, Pigalle's mausoleum for

321

Maurice de Saxe unites realistic portraiture with a group of allegorical figures. In contemporary dress, the imperturbable warrior marches proudly to the grave; a lion, a leopard, and an eagle represent the nations he has defeated; France and Hercules mourn, Love weeps, and a skeleton Death presides. A later national monument, the tomb of the Dauphin and his wife in the Cathedral of Sens, consists solely of allegorical figures, the dead pair being represented by urns, supposedly containing their ashes; around are Immortality, with the *génie* of the Arts and Sciences at her feet, Religion putting a crown of stars on the urns, Time drawing a veil over them, and Conjugal Love looking sadly at a broken flower chain held by the *génie* of Hymen.[72]

There were conventions regulating the ingenuity of monumental sculptors. A tomb was supposed to be appropriate for the rank of its occupant. In a straightforward case of misappropriation of genealogical emblems, the lawcourts might intervene. This was why the Parlement of Paris in 1711 banned the tomb Cardinal de Bouillon had commissioned in Italy for his father; for sixty-five years the whole package of marble and bronze remained under the seal of the magistrates—columned portico, statues, smoking vases, angels, the maréchal in Roman armour, and the wife who had converted him from Protestantism drawing his attention to some improving volume.[73] And for legitimate monuments, there was the sanction of ridicule, such as descended on the sons of the lawyer Louis Boullenois in 1786, when they invested in a statue of Justice, bearing a steel sword engraved with the title of their father's unreadable treatise, against a background of pyramid, eagle, urn, and sarcophagus—all much too sumptuous for 'un avocat peu connu'.[74] As for artistic conventions, they required verisimilitude. Firstly, ordinary historical details must be accurate: the tomb of that unpopular Controller General, the abbé Terray, was censured for showing the dead man kneeling to receive the seals of office, while wearing the robes of an Order which had not been conferred on him until after he became a minister.[75] Equally importantly, there must be some verisimilitude in the world of allegory, taking it seriously as a coherent social unit. Contemporary criticisms of Pigalle's mausoleum for the maréchal de Saxe are significant, more especially because, whatever reservations they made, the critics all regarded it as a masterpiece. As Hercules represents War, why had the child figure of Love been given a helmet? Death is supposed to be speaking, so surely some flesh upon the bones is needed? Is it natural for the maréchal to show no regret? Why does the stone of the grave open towards him, impeding his entry? Death is given a veil, which is inappropriate, and an hourglass, which is properly an attribute of time.[76] The tomb of the Dauphin at Sens came out well from this sort of searching, but myopic scrutiny. Dandré Bardon, himself a painter, regarded it as a masterpiece, proving the superiority of the Moderns to the Ancients, and of the French to other nations. This was partly because all the details were correct (Religion's cross; Immortality's laurel wreath; Time's scythe; maps, books, and musical instruments for the *génie* of the Arts and Sciences, and so on)—all these symbolic attributes were authorized by history, mythology, and religion; 'ils sont généralement connus et sont à l'abri de toute obscurité'. Similarly, the grouping of the figures made the theme of the allegory clear and harmonious. Given ordinary technical proficiency on the part of the sculptor, thought Dandré Bardon, such a logically satisfactory scheme was sure to attain to 'sublimity', by the sheer operation of the formula. 'Une allégorie aussi intelligible, aussi nécessaire et aussi juste n'avait besoin que de fidélité de la part de l'Artiste dans l'exécution qu'il en fait.'[77] The art critics of the eighteenth century left no room for the illogical and they distrusted the unexpected. If a painter wished to represent the family of Darius coming before Alexander, he must give to each member an expression suited to his or her age, condition, and situation; a representation of Andromeda is convincing only if she is showing due modesty before 'un homme qu'elle ne connoît pas'.[78] There must be no anachronism: Aeneas must be depicted with the features of a soldier of fortune, not of one of the rulers of the world—empire was for his successors.[79] These were the rules, and they applied with especial strictness to funereal monuments, since tombs were the most solemn form of sculpture, and sculpture was the most formal of the representational arts. Everything—whether historical details or symbolic ones—had to fit into a realm of sternly regimented fantasy.

A tomb in a church must conform to the presuppositions of the Christian religion.[80] But what were these presuppositions where questions of aesthetic taste were concerned? There was one tradition which disapproved of the pompous business of monumental commemoration altogether. From Pascal, and from Mme Deshoulières,[81] came the insistence on the present moment as the only time which is really ours, the time to serve God, indifferent to the possibilities of praise or blame from future generations. Tombs are like prisons, said Caraccioli; however we strive to adorn them, they will never be beautiful.[82] The abbé Bergier declaimed against the 'senseless luxury', 'depraved taste', and 'pagan mentality' of those who seek to minister to their pride by the elaboration of objects whose essential purpose is to humiliate us, and who hire engravers to inscribe on marble palpable lies which deceive no one.[83] A less puritanical tradition of Christian thought accepted the human desire for commemoration, but expected severe restraint on the part of the artist. Chateaubriand was to belong to this school of opinion, detesting the massed allegorical figures crushing the dust of the dead under their icy marble, and wishing to return to the medieval model of the tomb, where a bishop or abbot would lie peacefully, awaiting the resurrection.[84] The funereal artist, said the Jesuit Père Menestrier at the end of the seventeenth century, was to aim at a grandeur 'solemn, ingenious, agreeable to the eye, diversified and sad,' elevated above the noise and destructiveness of a 'drunken grief'. Ideally, his themes should be taken from the Bible, but Menestrier reluctantly conceded that the hourglass, torches, rainbows, the bird of paradise, the phoenix, Roman funeral pyres, temples, pyramids, figures of the Virtues, and worthy actions of kings could be used.[85] His concession was, in fact, the common practice. The figures on a tomb were subject always to severe critical scrutiny, but they were checked against their description in Cesare Ripa's *Iconologia*,[86] not against the evidence of the Scriptures.

In fact, the severities of Bergier and Mensestrier were not representative of ecclesiastical opinion generally, and the concept of the tomb as a dramatic group with a range of allegorical possibilities which had little necessary connection with the Christian revelation was accepted. This was not eighteenth-century complacency, but a realistic recognition of the inseparability of practical, secular, and religious inspirations. The evolution of sepulchral sculpture from the recumbent medieval figures which Chateaubriand admired to animation and diversity had been, in part, the prosaic outcome of necessity, the limitation of space in churches compelling sculptors to put monuments against the walls in vertical extension. It had also been inspired by a new and pagan zest for living—but not exclusively so, for there was also a desire to express, in stone and marble, a greater variety and intensity of religious feeling. The arrival in France of the kneeling figure (at the end of the fifteenth century), of the baroque gesture of self-offering, of the deathbed scene and the resurrection tableau, of the allegorical analysis of mourning and of the stylized biographical incident had provided opportunities for displays of artistic virtuosity, of family and civic pride, and also for some powerful expressions of religious emotion. These elements were often complementary; only artificially can they be considered in isolation. True, it may be easy to see that the theme of a tomb is more or less 'Christian', but the artistic conventions used will almost certainly be ambiguous. From Bernini's tomb of Pope Alexander VII, the skeleton Death had figured commonly among the allegorical figures. It was at once an echo of the spirituality which taught meditation in the presence of a skull, a reflection of the growing fascination of anatomical studies, and a response to an artistic challenge. In the eighteenth century, says Baudelaire, sculptors were haunted by the skeleton's abstract and mysterious beauty, the secret inner structure of the poem that is humanity.[87] And Christian attitudes were evolving. The tomb of Alexander VII, as described by the literary traveller the abbé Barthélemy in 1756, with its 'hideous' figure of Death over his 'gloomy lair', and the funeral pall about to fall like a great curtain to end the drama, was a scene of unrelieved terror—'tout cela imprime la terreur, tout cela montre le tombeau ouvert et ne montre que cet objet'.[88] In the same year that Barthélemy visited Rome, Michel-Ange Slodtz finished his tomb of Languet de Gergy, *curé* of Saint-Sulpice. Here again is the skeleton Death so commonly victorious in sepulchral art, but now collapsing, defeated. The winged angel of Immortality lifts the funeral veil from the kneeling priest, while the *curé* prays, hands outstretched, his otherwise commonplace face transfigured in the dawning recognition of the divine acceptance. Contemporaries seem to have been blind to this splendid, optimistic originality; they regarded the tomb of Languet de Gergy as a curiosity; Bouchardon even said that it was laughable, but he was a rival sculptor.[89]

While capable of becoming a vehicle for intense religious feeling, the dramatic group could easily be 'secularized'. The writer of an account of the Salon of 1743, referring to a project to build a mausoleum to Cardinal Fleury, blandly assumed that the purpose of funereal architecture was secular commemoration. 'Since the purpose of tombs is to make known to posterity the good qualities of those for whom they are erected, the sculptor should choose the most interesting moments in the life of his subject, those by which he has shown himself to best advantage.'[90] Drawing attention to the 'bonnes qualités' of the defunct was also a way, of course, of teaching a moral lesson. Diderot tried, more specifically, to transform the tomb into an agency of humanistic morality. His design for the mausoleum of the Dauphin at Sens was concerned with the theme of conjugal love alone; he only puts in more specifically Christian symbolism when he devises complexities to please those who do not see how 'la richesse est la mort du sublime'. And his inscription for the Galitzin tomb summarizes his humanistic faith in the face of death: this is the moment 'when the man of goodwill sees all the illusions of life fading, and when all that remains is virtue to console him and and friendship to regret his passing'.[91] The aim of Diderot was to have a tomb which could fit into a chapel in Amsterdam, a mosque in Constantinople, or a temple in Pekin as easily as into Notre-Dame at Paris; the sepulchral monuments of eighteenth-century France might be classified to show statistically how the dramatic group was tending towards this sort of secularization. But the results would be subject to qualifications. For one thing, from about 1760, the idea of the tomb as a dramatic composition within the cadre of a certain mythological symbolism began to wane. Under the influence of archaeological discoveries, sculptors turned to classical formulas; their marble figures became calm; floating draperies were suspect; often the effigy of the dead man was replaced by a medallion, bust, or urn. For another, Christian attitudes were becoming more sophisticated or, at least, more reticent. There was a new reluctance to attempt to depict the mysteries of salvation or the ecstasies of devotion, or to adorn the graves of manifestly worldly men with too ostentatiously Christian symbolism. And finally, in the second half of the century there arose a powerful tide of moralizing thought and fashion which carried both Christians and *philosophes* along, concealing their differences under its formulas, *clichés*, and imagery.

'Render virtue agreeable, vice odious.' Such must be the aim, said Diderot in 1765, of the artist whenever he takes up pen, brush, or chisel.[92] Falconet the sculptor defined the duty of his craft as being the perpetuation of the memory of illustrious men.[93] A commentator on the Salon of 1753 expected paintings of historical subjects to constitute 'une école des mœurs', a presentation of the virtuous and heroic acts of those who have served their country or its religion.[94] Antoine Thomas the rhetorician did not exempt the poet from these obligations: he was to 'transmit to posterity the record of virtues and of crimes for the instruction of mankind.'[95] One aspect of this 'moralizing fervour' which 'penetrated the arts'[96] from the middle of the century was the development of the idea of patriotism. The word *patriote* lost its original meaning of 'compatriot' to become, in the Academy dictionary of 1762, 'celui qui aime sa patrie et qui cherche à lui être utile'. The abbé Coyer, with his journalistic flair for hitting on the issue of the day, in 1754 published the *Discours sur le vieux mot de patrie*, denouncing the assumption that a man's fatherland was merely the place where he was born; it ought to be 'une divinité'.[97] President Hénault's *Abrégée chronologique de l'histoire de France* (1744) marked an improbable beginning of enthusiasm for the national history. In 1765 came de Belloy's *Le Siège de Calais*, a patriotic play appealing to the emotions which the Seven Years' War had inflamed; it was the most successful drama of the century, receiving the flattering tribute of numerous imitations.[98] The example of the proud English was often cited, more especially when Shakespeare's historical plays became generally known. So too were the examples, familiar from school-days, of the Greek city states and republican Rome. For too long the visual arts had dabbled in the frivolities of classical antiquity. In 1750 Rousseau complained of the choice of useless mythological figures for decorative statues, instead of 'the defenders of the Fatherland, and those men, greater still, who have enriched it by their virtues'. In the seventies, d'Holbach denounced 'lascivious' mythology, and asked for the portrayal of examples of magnanimity, Goodness, Justice, and 'amour de la patrie'.[99] The civic heroism of antiquity, for long studied in the *collèges* of France for improving reasons, was being rediscovered by artists just at the time of the archaeological finds at Pompeii and Herculaneum. The immoral gods and goddesses of the ancient world had been as much at home in the setting of the rococo as in their natural habitat. Now the civic heroes of antiquity took their place and the more austere artistic conventions of Greece, and more particularly, of Rome, accompanied them. David's *Oath of the Horatii* (1783) marked the victory of neoclassicism over rococo and the triumph of citizenship and patriotism over individualism and cynicism.

The painting of the second half of the century is dominated by the idea of the *exemplum virtutis*. Illustrations were taken chiefly from classical antiquity—Marcus Aurelius feeding the victims of the plague, Manlius Torquatus condemning his own son to death, the fidelity of a satrap of Darius, the continence of Scipio. There were examples from more recent history too, like Bayard's magnanimity, as well as imaginary parables, like *La Veuve inconsolable* by Greuze—reading the letters of her dead husband, crowning his bust with flowers, and casting the spell of her grief on the faithful dog. The favourite theme for a moralizing tableau was the death-bed. Poussin's *Death of Germanicus* and his *Testament of Eudamides* were influential models.[100] The Academy of Painting and Sculpture chose the death of Socrates and the death of Germanicus—the man of virtue condemned by a suspicious oligarchy, the glorious hero assassinated by a jealous tyrant—as the subjects for the prize competition of 1761; it was the first time incidents from classical history had been preferred to biblical ones. A multitude of paintings of death scenes followed, from Alexander the Great to du Guesclin, from Cleopatra to Leonardo da Vinci, all pointing a moral lesson, whether of patriotic devotion or of the futility of worldly greatness. These two lessons were complementary, not contradictory, for the rewards of those who served their country were thought of (ideally, at any rate) in the frugal terms of Sparta or the Roman Republic. 'Ci gît un citoyen' was praise enough for a good man, said a poet, honouring Rousseau.[101] Virtue does not need pompous marble or bronze, said another, in an ode to the heroes of the battlefield: 'Le temple de mémoire est dans le cœur des hommes.'[102]

Taken literally, this austere doctrine would simplify sepulchral architecture, but would have less effect upon the epitaph; indeed, here was a literary convention ideally suited for the formulation and transmission of moral judgements. With their human and antiquarian interest, the inscriptions on tombs are noted by every-one: 'nothing', says Piganiol de la Force, 'is less boring than the reading of epitaphs.'[103] Given their sombre implications, they also have force to edify as well as to interest. 'The variety of tombs and their inscriptions serve to entertain and instruct the traveller,' said a writer of 1787, recommending the siting of cemeteries on the borders of main highways, for purposes of edification.[104] The device of the epitaph was used by the prince de Ligne, Mably, and many others to defend Rousseau;[105] by Rousseau himself to defend the two lovers of Lyon; by Dorat and others in praise of Helvétius;[106] and by Moreau (in 43 lines of verse) as an encomium of the comte de Chastellux.[107] Voltaire wrote epitaphs for the abbé de Resnel and the abbé de Voisenon, two clergy who had worked with the *philosophes*, and another for a Protestant pastor, at the request of his widow.[108] Some revealing epitaphs were written by the subjects themselves; by Mme de Sabran, the Chevalier de Boufflers, Dom Calmet, the Chevalier d'Éon and (sardonic but savagely serious) by Piron.[109] It was more than an intellectual parlour game: as Marmontel said, every man should write his own epitaph early in his career, in as flattering terms as possible, then employ all his life in striving to live up to it.[110] Passing judgement on an individual might involve a judgement on society as well, and the epitaph is some-times deliberately used as an instrument of social criticism. Voltaire's on the actress Adrienne Lecouvreur is an implicit attack on the Church, which refused her burial; the verses of the *Année littéraire* on Le Tourneur censure the Academy which rejected him.[111] A masterpiece of this kind, combining the classical virtues of force and brevity with sentimental and reforming egalitarianism, dates from the early seventies—a tablet in the Church of Saint-Eustache at Paris reads,

Ci-gît François de Chevert, commandeur, grand croix, de l'ordre royal et militaire de S. Louis, chevalier de l'Aigle Blanc de Pologne, Gouverneur de Givet et Charlemont, Lt-Général des Armées du Roi. Sans aïeux, sans fortune et sans appui, orphelin dès l'enfance, il entra au service à l'âge de 11 ans. Il s'est élevé malgré l'envie à force de mérite. Chaque grade a été le prix d'une action d'éclat. Le seul titre de Maréchal de France a manqué, non pas à sa gloire, mais à l'exemple de ceux qui voudront le prendre pour modèle. Il était né à Verdun sur Meuse, le 2 février 1696. Il mourut à Paris, le 24 janvier 1769. Priez Dieu pour le repos de son âme.[112]

Taken together, this epitaph of François de Chevert and Diderot's inscription for the Galitzin tomb give a recital of the duties of friendship, the consolations of virtue, the right of merit to rise, and the obligations of patriotism—an epitome of all that is most elevated in the thought of the Enlightenment.

The reforming patriotism of the last generation before the Revolution was 'republican' in spirit: its ideals included, without derogating from the status of France as a monarchy, the achievement of a government founded on consent, at once preserving and being sustained by the spirit of citizenship and liberty. The King had occasionally paid for a public monument such as the tomb of the maréchal de Saxe (another had been planned for Cardinal Fleury), but the new patriotism required a national and systematic commemoration, extending to a wider range of civic devotion and founded on consensus. Together with the traditional glorification of the soldier, the Enlightenment exalted the intellectual; this had been the inspiration of Titon du Tillet's *Le Parnasse français* (1727); along with a Temple of Victory for the tombs of warriors, he proposed a Parnassus for those of writers and musicians, a pyramid for the interment of magistrates, and arcades to receive the scholars.[113] Frenchmen looked with envy on the proud and solemn English, who buried their great men splendidly in Westminster Abbey—they alone could have paid fitting honour to the genius of Newton.[114] There was, too, the example of republican Rome, where lists of meritorious servants of the State were inscribed on the walls of temples, an observance which Fénelon and Montesquieu admired. But what, above all in the ancient world, caught the eye of the writers of the Enlightenment, was the Egyptian custom of calling together a jury on the death of a Pharaoh to pass a verdict on his life and achievements, and to decide if he merited an honourable funeral. This was the theme of the abbé Terrasson's *Séthos* (1731). The novel begins with the 'judges of the dead' acclaiming the virtues of their queen who has just died; her body is then rowed across the lake to its tomb amidst popular rejoicing; the story continues with the history of the education of Séthos in the duties of rulers: he learns how love of mankind is a virtue superior to courage and how public utility is to be preferred before the personal glory of the sovereign.[115] It was understood, and sometimes explicity stated,[116] that there were 'judges of the dead' in the France of the Enlightenment: 'truth' was the tribunal, and even the greatest were subject to the verdict of educated public opinion.

From 1755, the Academy began to collaborate with the moralizing temper of the age by devoting its annual prize for eloquence to the *éloge* of some noble character. According to Antoine Thomas, who won on five successive occasions and was not inclined to belittle the achievement, these *éloges* were the French equivalent of 'the statues of ancient Rome, Chinese triumphal arches, and the tombs of Westminster Abbey'.[117] In January 1765, the year of *Le Siège de Calais*, the *Mercure* launched the idea of a Pantheon, where the mortal remains of the great men of the nation would be concentrated. None of the existing Parisian churches was regarded as suitable, but the new one, dedicated to Sainte-Geneviève, which was under construction, might be adapted. 'O vous qui avez éclairé la France et l'Univers . . . sortez de vos tombeaux Gothiques; un nouvel Elisée se prépare.'[118] Two years later, a 'disinterested citizen' published a pamphlet containing 'diverse patriotic ideas' for the embellishment of the capital, including the transformation of a wing of the Louvre into a 'gallery of illustrious Frenchmen'.[119] Within three years, the Royal Academy of Architecture awarded its prize for a design for a Temple of Fame for kings and other great servants of the nation.[120] Those whose distinction was rather less could have tombs allotted to them in squares and public places, instead of in churches, said the *Mercure* in 1772.[121] Under Louis XVI, success in a war for the cause of liberty—the American War of Independence—revived the claims of soldiers to national recognition. The bishop of Lescar, Marc-Antoine de Noé, in a sermon for the dedication of the standards of a regiment, asked for a monument for 'les cendres de nos guerriers'—a mountainous collection of the debris of war: cannon, weapons, wreckage of fortresses and warships, with a column rising above it inscribed with the deeds of the most courageous, and an altar below where masses would be offered for the souls of the fallen.[122]

After the Royal Declaration of 1776, ambitious contractors put forward their schemes for new cemeteries. In every case they proposed to zone burials in some sort of hierarchy, but, realistically, they thought more in terms of whose relatives could pay than of merit in the abstract. However, Labrière, the architect of the comte d'Artois, had a grandiose scheme of patriotic vandalism in mind; his intention was to transport the royal tombs from Saint-Denis to form the nucleus of a collection of national heroes, to demolish the abbey and use the stone to build a Pantheon in the centre of his new municipal cemetery.[123] The Government, laden with debt, could do nothing about any of these projects, though the *directeur des bâtiments* began to commission paintings of a 'moral or patriotic kind' on subjects of French history.[124] Meanwhile, the commemoration of great men was carried on by private initiative. The *décor* of the gardens of the comte d'Albon near Paris constituted a sort of Pantheon (was it to Liberty and Science?); there was an obelisk to his wife, a temple to the dying Christ, and statues (an idiosyncratic choice) of Haller, the elder Mirabeau, Court de Gébelin, Franklin, and William Tell.[125] In 1780, Cardinal Rohan, as befitted the bishop of the frontier see of Strasbourg, bought the site where Turenne, France's greatest general, had been killed on the battlefield, and designs were invited for a monument there. Boullée, the visionary architect, made a proposal on a sombre, gigantic scale—a truncated pyramid surrounded by a high colonnade with a few tiny loopholes in its harsh exterior walls, a frieze of battle scenes around its summit, and a single, dark, narrow entrance displaying the inscription borrowed from the defile of Thermopylae.[126] The more modest project which was accepted had a house for a wounded soldier who would act as caretaker, a pyramid surrounded by laurels, but nothing but thorns growing on the spot where the great general had been struck down.[127] Six years later, in a cemetery near Boulogne, a model of a shattered Montgolfière was set up between funeral urns to mark the grave of Pilâtre de Rozier and his fellow balloonist, martyrs to the cause of science;[128] and at the same time, a memorial was being planned in honour of the sailors who had lost their lives on La Pérouse's voyage of circumnavigation.[129]

Since there was so much talk of new cemeteries, patriotic monuments, and of a Pantheon, it became a fashion among architects to exercise their ingenuity in designing them. There were some bizarre imaginings, as if their inventors found insipid the cool neoclassical style which sculptors were preferring for tombs in place of allegories of baroque force or rococo delicacy. Delafosse, Neufforge, Le Canu, and, above all, Jean-Jacques Lequeu accumulated incongruities[130]—like Lequeu's vast quill pen upon a terrestrial globe and a figure of death with bat's wings for a tomb of Voltaire, and a sheep surmounted by a mermaid for a monument to Socrates.[131] These eclectic visions showed a particular interest in ancient Egypt. Pyramids, truncated or in steps, and obelisks figured in cemetery designs, like those of Louis-Jean Desprez (1766) and P.-F.-L. Fontaine (1785). The former had decorative motifs of sphinxes and owls, and a statue of Death wearing a Pharaonic head-dress, with skeleton feet protruding from under the flowing robes.[132] The greatest of these funereal architects was Étienne-Louis Boullée (1728–99),[133] who gained fame in the eighties by his design for a cenotaph for Newton (a vast hollow sphere half-buried in the earth, empty, lit only by pin-point apertures representing the stars). Like his colleagues, he felt the spell of Egyptian temples or, at least, he admired their colossal simplicities. From his master Blondel he inherited the ideal of imitating 'Nature', in the sense, not of devising organic complexities, but of adapting form to the material and creating effects by the arrangement of masses rather than by symbolic sculptural ornaments. From Nicolas Lecamus Mézière's *Le Génie de l'architecture, ou l'analogie de cet art avec nos sensations* (1780), he took the ideal of 'l'architecture parlante', moving the soul of the beholder by insistence on mood and by unified focus on meaning. Funereal architecture, he held, was a superior branch of the art with affinities with poetry; it must have solidity, to create the illusion of a memory that endures; it must shun the day and seek out the darkness, to convey an overwhelming impression of the harshness of death—to this end he used bare walls, underground spaces, and black masses silhouetted against pale light. It was 'l'architecture ensevelie', 'l'architecture des ombres'.[134] Vast, functional, fantastic in a grimly austere fashion, this was an architecture concentrated on the finality of death,

333

refusing to moralize with the humanists or to hope with the Christians, a funereal *décor* suited to some gigantic necropolis for the collectivist nationalism of the future. It was an odd, prophetic detour of the pre-romantic imagination. Perhaps Boullée and the architects had been studying the *Contrat social* while everyone else was weeping over the *Nouvelle Héloïse*.

III

Enfin mon deuil me plaît, et je trouve des charmes
A pousser des soupirs, à répandre des larmes.

So wrote a country *curé* in an elegy on the death of a friend, which he published in a collection of poems in 1750.[135] This inversion of common-sense mental processes caused him naïve bewilderment. Four years later, a professional author made the point sardonically; one of his characters is deeply moved when his wife dies—'Quel bonheur! Mon amour—propre en est ému.'[136] It is something to know that one is a man of feeling. A more congenial hero, in a novel of 1779, living in a desolate spot beside the grave of his mistress, strives (unsuccessfully) not to die of grief, for then he could not weep, and weeping is a pleasure.[137] And there is a religious variant of the satisfaction we obtain in reflecting on mortality; there are those, says Caraccioli, who find a thousand times more fulfilment in brooding on death than in theatres and parties—a sad pleasure, maybe, but a real one, 'une volupté véritable'.[138] The eighteenth century had invented a new pleasure—or rather, had brought secrets of the subconscious up to the conscious mind for aesthetic analysis. Sorrow was found to have a hypnotic attraction, and there were sophisticated delights to be discovered in melancholy. At one end of the scale was the *frisson* which comes over us at the sight of a terrifying landscape,[139] at the other the perverse savouring of tales of cruelty;[140] between are all the nuances of emotion which we feel at the thought of death and its exigencies, at the sight of its ceremonies and monuments.

It is not easy to explain this new venture in the ways of the imagination. One step towards understanding is to recognize that the novelty lies not so much in the venture itself as in the self-conscious awareness with which the exploration proceeded; it is the fall of the old inhibitions which has to be accounted for. Perhaps, as religious themes ceased to be the staple subjects of artistic inspiration, a place was left which had not been available before, for the 'gliding spectre and the groaning grave' and the harsh and haunting beauties of Nature.[141] Maybe, Starobinski suggests,[142] boredom drove men to seek for new inspirations on the sombre side of life, extending even to the 'exoticism of evil'. When Boucher's nymphs became insipid Fuseli's tormented dreamers drew the attention of the jaded epicure. Or, more likely, this sophisticated generation was probing and seeking for the complex and mysterious affinities linking beauty with ugliness as they move like complementary figures in a masquerade, each necessary to the other's piquancy, and in this quest found its imagination riveted on untoward subjects—like Velasquez preoccupied with the clowns and dwarfs of the court of Philip IV and the elder Brueghel with the dance of the epileptics at the gates of Brussels.[143] Whatever the explanation, the eighteenth century was conscious that it had discovered a new and paradoxical dimension of pleasure, and in his poem *Les Styles* (1761) the abbé Cournand invented a separate genre to cater for it—the 'sombre', only one step lower than the 'sublime'. Strong impressions of grief, the groanings of a soul wandering among the tombs, profound reflections on the misery of man, and the spectacle of savage landscapes are the examples he gives of the materials on which the mind works to build up the satisfactions which the new genre can offer, and he illustrates the charm of brooding on death in verses unsparingly describing the subterranean timetable of decay. But his argument fades away into platitudes. Far from being mysterious, the charm of the macabre has an unsubtle, soundly religious origin in our conviction that the tomb is a refuge from unhappiness and a lesson to us to be helpful to others.[144] Poets should never give explanations.

Since education in the *collèges* of France was based on Roman history and Latin literature, the literary cultivation of mortuary themes and melancholy from 1770 onwards naturally owed much, in a superficial way, to Seneca, Lucretius, and Ovid.[145] But Cournand, with a passing reference to the Ancients, concentrated his praise on Edward Young, whose *Complaint, or Night Thoughts on Life, Death and Immortality*, 'admirable in spite of its defects', was his consolation in disillusionment and his guide to true values.[146] The astonishingly successful career of the *Night Thoughts* in France began in 1760, when translated excerpts were published, followed by a translation of the first 'Night' by the comte de Bissy in 1762, and of the second, by the same great nobleman, two years later. Then in 1769 came Le Tourneur's two-volume version, one of the publishing triumphs of the century.[147] 'The nocuturnal Poems of Young are all the rage here,' says a letter from Paris. 'It is an incontrovertible proof of the change in French intellectual attitudes.'[148] Four years later Manon Philipon (the future Madame Roland) was yearning to find a copy, hoping to study those 'dark depths' ('ce profond ténébreux') which lead to the sublime truths.[149] Sophie Mounier read the *Nights* in her convent, as did her unsatisfactory husband, Mirabeau, in his dissipations; Robespierre had a copy in his pocket during his days of power, and his victim Camille Desmoulins read a page on the way to the guillotine—'Tu veux mourir donc deux fois?'

Translations were followed by imitations—'epistles' and 'meditations' on solitude, sadness, death, and graveyards. One inspiration of the Anglomania which became prevalent in French society towards the end of the *ancien régime* was an admiration of the gravity of the English, assumed to be connected with their solid constitutional arrangements in government. The tradition of versification on melancholy, which had continued north of the Channel since the age of Elizabeth, sustained, maybe, by Puritan influences,[150] arrived in France with the seal of a sober and dignified ancestry, but also with all the force of novelty. Apart from Feutry's *Le Temple de la mort* (1753), there had been no indigenous example in poetry of Cournand's 'sombre' genre, and in any case Feutry had been concerned with the wickedness of rulers rather than with the tragedy of human transience.[151] So far as France was concerned, Le Tourneur thought Young unequalled and likely to remain so: he had built the monument of his fame among the tombs, a place where his rivals would have difficulty in following him.[152] But there were other English writers on Young's themes who powerfully reinforced his influence: James Hervey, whose *Meditations among the Tombs* was translated into French by Le Tourneur in 1771, Gray, whose *Elegy* went into many French versions after that of

Madame Necker in 1765, and James Macpherson, the discoverer of *Ossian*, which was made available in France in parts from 1760 and completely by Le Tourneur in 1777. No doubt there were deep-seated social reasons, quite apart from patterns of cultural transmission and changes of literary fashion, to account for the triumph of sepulchral melancholy in France; whatever they were, the tide of 'Youngisme' could not be turned back. Voltaire deplored platitudes and obscurities; Diderot denied the possibility of reflecting the immediacy of grief in poetry ('on dit qu'on pleure, mais on ne pleure pas lorsqu'on s'occupe à rendre son vers harmonieux').[153] Delisle de Sales complained of Young's lack of psychological realism and of 'Le délire de son style oriental';[154] liberal churchmen rejected his 'maximes gothiques et folles' which undermined the serenity that the practice of virtue should bring into our lives[155]— all to no avail. The *Nights* had broken the old canons of sophisticated reserve, and even those who accused the author of bad taste conceded he was a genius: 'un homme de génie sans goût', was Delisle de Sales's formula.

> In human hearts what bolder thought can rise
> Than man's presumption on tomorrow's dawn?

Though Young was an ambitious publicist (he was ordained at fifty and became the man of his book rather than starting there), he was also, and essentially, a Christian apologist. In truth, he did not meditate on the tombs of those he loved or frequent his parish cemetery; he was conveying to careless men the eternal warnings of the preacher, that time is short and life precarious. The atmosphere of James Hervey's *Meditations* was the same. Gray was different; the *Elegy* has been described as one of the first European poems to express the pathos of human destiny without the intervention of religious ideas; even the afterlife receives but a perfunctory reference.[156] Significantly, Le Tourneur presented Young and Hervey to France as if they were deists rather than Christians.[157] Passages concerning revelation were collected at the end of each 'Night', leaving in the main text only 'what had more universal moral implications, like the existence of God and the immortality of the soul'. Biblical references and the parallel between the warrior and Christ were cut out of the *Meditations among the Tombs*. We have enough pious literature, said Le Tourneur in sly self-justification, without needing to borrow from the Protestant nations.[158] It was a question, said Madame Thiroux d'Arconville, of abridging Hervey's moralizing to highlight his ideas, images, and feelings, as well as omitting vague observations which were incompatible with the clarity of the French language.[159] In fact, the Enlightenment was taking over the emotions and fears which had accumulated around the concept of death. They became a subject of literary interest, the inspiration of a new genre, a source of lyrical reflections, and a device for the enrichment of the personality.

An extreme manifestation of the new 'sombre' genre, with its emotions debased and run to seed, was the 'black theatre' of Baculard d'Arnaud—tales of tortures, executions, rapes, wanderings in funeral vaults and graveyards, and sleeping alongside coffins and corpses. These melodramas, said the writer of a satirical comedy, *Le Manie des drames sombres* (1777), are 'sepulchral farces', puerile spectacles which have nothing to say to the soul.[160] Another critic, a lover of melancholy who claimed to meditate daily on tombs, skulls, and crucifixes, condemned Baculard for using these aids to sober reflection as stage decorations; to bribe the offending playwright into laying down his pen, he offered to get him the lucrative job, in one of the leading parishes of Paris, of *tapissier d'enterrement* (the functionary who puts up the black hangings in churches on the day of a funeral).[161] The terrors of the valley of the shadow were being annexed by the commercial theatre; to anyone who took these gloomy dramas seriously, dying—'exhaler le dernier soupir' was the *cliché*[162]—was being made both lurid and ludicrous. According to Baculard himself, his plays had a high serious purpose. The ancestry of the 'sombre', he said, included Rembrandt and Rubens in painting, Pergolese's *Stabat* in music, Dante, Milton, and Young in literature—to these he later added the Greek tragedians and Shakespeare. It was a literary genre which, above all others, could strike home to men's hearts—'les impressions qu'excite le *sombre* sont toujours plus profondes'—and these forceful impressions would encourage moral conduct.[163] (His point did not go unchallenged: Marmontel argued that the depiction of the excesses of evil raises up imitators.[164]) But neither Baculard's solemnities nor those of his opponents need to be taken too seriously. Before the technical term was invented, the 'sombre', or at least the macabre, had been a standard device of writers for more than a century. *Les Spectacles d'horreur* had been a device of a bishop for moralizing purposes—but the moralizing tended to become secondary. Oubliettes and graveyards under the moon abound in novels like Marie-Jeanne Lhéritier de Villaudon's *La Tour ténébreuse* (1703). Novels of the first half of the eighteenth century refined the tradition, making it dramatically relevant to the plot and to the psychological development of character, witness Mme de Tencin's use of the Trappist way of dying, Prévost's account of the conduct of the Duke of Monmouth at Cécile's deathbed, and of the vigils over Sélima's heart in the black-draped chamber in the woods.[165] And in the second half of the century the macabre remained as an acceptable dramatic ingredient in the love story—Lucile with burning eyes wandering in the twilight looking for her dead Doligny,[166] Lesbros de la Versane's hero restoring his friend's wife's desire to go on living by making love to her on her deathbed.[167] What had been accepted as a piquant flourish in the novel was taken over by Baculard and turned into an obsessive theme.

The sepulchral melodrama was also the final, exaggerated gesture in a dispute about the subjects which were appropriate for representation on the stage, the partisan manifesto of a literary faction which included Mercier, Ducis, and Le Tourneur, and had Shakespeare as its watchword as against Voltaire.[168] In fact, Voltaire himself had sought some relaxation of the convention which limited death scenes on the stage to the suicide of a tragic hero. Crébillon, a disreputable genius with a licence to outrage, had been able to break the rule,[169] but Voltaire's own modest attempt at innovation, in *Mariamne* in 1725, was stopped by ridicule; even so, he still believed that most of his audience would wish to see some combination of Shakespeare's vivid action with French elegance.[170] The first murder on the French stage, in 1740 (in Gresset's *Édouard III*), was condemned by the critics but welcomed by the public.[171] Yet, twenty years later, when the actress Mlle Clairon asked for a scaffold on the stage when she was playing in *Tancrède*, Voltaire was horrified.[172] Her proposal went too far even for Diderot, who three years earlier had been attacking the conservative conventions of the theatre. 'Ah! bienséances cruelles, que vous rendez les ouvrages délicats et petits!'[173] But he had been thinking then, not of high tragedy, but of the 'bourgeois' sentimental drama, and it was in the interests of sentimentality, not of horror, that the rules of the French stage were first breached.[174] Audiences became accustomed to weeping and pathos as the first step on their way to the acceptance of crude emotions. Baculard d'Arnaud exploited the new liberty; the descendants of the wits who had stopped a queen drinking a poisoned chalice in 1725 could ridicule his melodramas as a whole, but could hardly attack a particular incident, for the macabre procession of events formed a universe of horror which had to be accepted or rejected *en bloc*. Perhaps these sombre dramas should be considered simply as commercial successes, novelties transferred from the English theatre or the French novel to take advantage of the relaxation of the rules and the more eclectic public taste, rather than significant evidence about a change of attitudes to death. Ironically, the Revolution was soon to enact some of these horrors in earnest, shorn of their pseudo-religious paraphernalia of crucifixes, cowls, and coffins—a laicization of terror, as it were.

The sepulchral dramas of France borrowed little from the *Night Thoughts* or the *Meditations among the Tombs* beyond items for a gloomy scenario. Horror is associated with the cruelties of men or the harsh vagaries of chance: melancholy with the peaceful recognition of human transience. *Et in Arcadia ego*: Poussin's famous picture haunted the last generation of *ancien régime*. It stood at the point of transition, said the artist Dandré Bardon, where the 'sombre' rose into the highest artistic category of all, the 'sublime'.[175] Lezay-Marnésia in 1787 praised its 'douce mélancolie' and its 'sentiment tendre', in comparison with the ephemeral and excessive impressions created by cemeteries or evocations of the scaffold.[176] It was a masterly inspiration, said Watelet, one which makes the spectator reflect profoundly.[177] They were speaking of the artist's broad meaning, untroubled by the problems of interpretation which give concern to modern critics. The picture is in the line of a macabre tradition which was becoming progressively less grim: the fourteenth-century meeting of three huntsmen with the three skeletons, becoming transformed into three shepherds gazing at a skull, until in Poussin the evidence of mortality is reduced to a tomb with its brief inscription.[178] The words, 'Et in Arcadia ego' may be meant to be spoken by Death personified;[179] if so, though the trappings of mortality have been made more sophisticated, an edge of harshness remains to the message, the shadow of a threat. But there is another possibility: the words may be a statement concerning our common lot,[180] coming to us from the grave, from someone who has gone before us. The French eighteenth century chose this more sentimental view, and if the speaker was supposed to be a young girl cut off in the flower of her beauty,[181] the mystery of the tomb in the Arcadian landscape was rendered more poignant. Two critics offered a translation; Watelet—'J'ai aussi vécu dans l'Arcadie', and Dandré Bardon—'Je vivois cependant en l'Arcadie'.[182] There is a nuance of meaning between the two, the first being more resigned, yet more inclined to proffer a warning. What should our reaction be? According to Diderot, we should be afraid; Watelet expects 'profound reflections' to arise; Dandré Bardon assumes that like the shepherds and shepherdesses we too will reflect that death does not spare youth or beauty; Masson de Pezay talks of emotions of bitter-sweet melancholy; Jacques Delille draws hedonistic inferences—'hâtez–vous de jouir.'[183] Roucher, the poet of autumnal decline and harsh landscapes, and Hubert Robert, the highly successful painter of ruins, were in gaol together during the Terror—a significant possibility of collaboration for the development of the scenario of melancholy. The result was a sketch of the martyr Sainte-Pélagie with the tomb of a girl in the background—imitated from Poussin. But the inscription, taken from Malherbe, was very different:

> Rose, elle a vécu ce que vivent les roses,
> L'espace d'un matin.[184]

The victory of sentimentality was complete.

'D'où vient, à leur aspect, le plaisir que je sens?' asked the author of *Les Ruines: épître* in 1768. And he gave a comprehensive list of reasons for the paradoxical pleasure which the sight of ruins evokes.[185] It was not a question of the satisfaction of archaeological curiosity; it was, rather, the emotions aroused by reminders of a vanished splendour, by the reflection that our own pomp will go down to the same doom, and that all superiority of one man over another is ephemeral. And there was, above all, the aesthetic satisfaction derived from the sight of tragic and unexpected contrasts—trees growing out of domes, briars climbing marble columns, broken carvings half hidden in the grass. For this poem Jean-Baptiste Coeuilhe, an official of the Bibliothèque du Roi, received the laurels of the Academy, a recognition of his originality in pointing to a new departure in the poet's repertoire. For long, ruins had adorned paintings: Poussin and Claude Lorrain and lesser artists had used them to make a landscape 'heroic', or as a background to Nativities and Christian martyrdoms—as symbols of the old order which the new religion was to vanquish. From the Renaissance, moralists had reflected among the broken columns on the fall of empires. But it was the Enlightenment which discovered the aesthetic appeal of ruins, and created a cult of fallen grandeur, a 'sensibilité ruiniste'. A whole school of artists, French and Italian, arose to exploit the new fashion; Hubert Robert, who returned from his studies in Rome in 1765, being the most original and successful of them. Before Coeuilhe's poem, Watelet, an artist himself, had tried to give an explanation of the spell which ruins had cast over painters, starting from the proposition, more believable then than now, that civilization is artificial. City dwellers strive to conceal their emotions and to imitate their neighbours; art reacts against this dull uniformity. A tree deformed by the wind or uprooted by a gale, a vast overhanging rock threatening to crush the beholder—these sights lead us into the unpredictable and infinitely varied world of Nature. Ruins are on the borderline where the artificial is being absorbed into the natural; in themselves, they provide arbitrary and picturesque deformities, and remind us that Nature is always young, always renewing herself, while the proudest works of man are ephemeral.[186] Diderot, the most profound of the art critics (writing at about the time of Coeuilhe's poem), went further, for to him, even the works of Nature are not eternal—all perishes, all is fleeting, and time alone endures. At the sight of ruins, he would have us at once attracted and overwhelmed by the recognition of universal transience. 'Qu'il est vieux ce monde! Je marche entre deux éternités.' Though he had the utmost admiration for Robert as a draughtsman, he suspected him of being ignorant of this poetic and tragic inspiration of his subject. 'Monsieur Robert, vous ne savez pas pourquoi les ruines font tant de plaisir.' And he accused Robert of detracting from the atmosphere of solitude and silence by putting too many figures into his paintings.[187] For once, Diderot was being unperceptive and, not for the first time, was taking life too seriously. Robert was not like Volney,[188] whose solemn work *Les Ruines* (1791) was to be heavy with menacing platitudes about the fall of empires; he was a cheerful, irreverent character who liked to show a washing line tied to the arm of an antique statue, a shed propped up against a broken column, a circular temple of Venus used as a dovecote, and ordinary people going about ordinary business amid the ruins of forums and amphitheatres—a woman nursing a child, peasant girls filling their pitchers at decaying fountains, a horseman muffled againt the wind passing through the shattered columns. He was not concerned with the vertiginous edge of eternity, but with the ironies of life and its continuities. He was very near to the secret of the attraction of ruins to contemporary taste. Their lesson of the folly of grandeur was in tune with the new egalitarian spirit of the age; their picture of the nemesis of cities appealed to a generation which was discovering the charms of the countryside. Above all, they were welcome as an adjunct to the cult of melancholy, for amid the ruins a man could savour the sad emotions which arise from the brevity of our days without the intrusion of repellent thoughts of the corruptions of the grave or of the shadow of judgement.

The rise of the cult of melancholy coincided with the beginnings of organized archaeological investigation, so that ruins became sentimentally fashionable and technically interesting simultaneously. Something of the kind happened about cemeteries, the pleasure of brooding among the tombs being discovered just as practical men, for hygienic reasons, were proposing to clean up the graveyards. The repulsive economies of the *fosse commune* and the promiscuous packing of the *charniers* stood in the way of poetic reflection and nostaligic meditation. This was why Canon Porée in 1745 said that prayer at the tombs of one's ancestors was impossible. Yet he assumed that there would be visits to these tombs, inspiring appropriate emotions, once they were moved to his new cemeteries outside the towns—'Les visites que nous leur rendrions, deviendraient touchantes.'[189] Ordinary folk had an attachment to the place where their parents were buried: 'c'est ici que mon père, que ma mère sont enterrés'[190]—in some places, people put up little wooden crosses to mark the spot. In a poem on All Souls' Day,

Fontanes[191] describes how, when the procession goes from the parish church to the cemetery, each family halts beside the stone or plot of turf where its ancestors lie (the unromantic thought arises that these must have been the more prosperous households of the hamlet, which had been able to afford a 'fosse particulière'). But as a rule, individuals did not resort to the cemetery to pay their pious duties. Diderot in 1759 went to Langres to visit the tomb of a girl he had once loved[192]—but his sentimental journey is not evidence for the attitude of the generality. When graveyards were near the church and in the midst of habitations and people passed by and through them continually, familiarity must have inhibited them from making any particular visit into a special occasion; though no doubt, as they went by, old memories revived and, maybe, they performed their Christian duty of prayer. But in the generation before 'Youngisme', before melancholy became accepted as self-justifying, sentimental deism was moving into Christian territory and adding to the range of emotional attitudes which the sepulchres could evoke. Cleveland, the abbé Prévost's hero, lived in the grotto where he had buried his mother, regarding her as 'a witness of all his actions'.[193] Rousseau's Julie wondered if her soul could return after death to dwell near those she had loved—not to speak to them or see them, but simply to know what they thought and felt through the immediate communication of sympathy. When she dies, Claire feels her presence everywhere, and passing her tomb, hears once again the familiar voice: 'Claire, ô ma Claire, où est-tu? Que fais-tu loin de ton amie?'[194] Here is no question of the community of the faithful or even of the solidarity of the family: there is, rather, an individual, personal relationship, a friendship that reaches out across the barrier of death. Intense affections of this kind could only be expressed in loneliness. Four years after Rousseau's novel—in 1765—Diderot condemned a sketch by Deshays of Artemis visiting the tomb of her husband because she is depicted as surrounded by guards and companions. 'True sorrow needs solitude; it abhors display, it does not wish to be observed.'[195]

To mourn for someone deeply loved and forever lost, to mourn in solitude, far from the busy world which does not understand the secret magic of a unique love, to mourn religiously, yet without religion, to mourn and be in love with mourning—the concept, a stage in the development of human affections and individuality, was formed, but it required an appropriate setting. Where else should this be found but against the tremendous backdrop of Nature?—scenery changing from light to darkness and from colour to greyness as the days and the seasons revolve, ever beautiful to recall us to our memories of departed beauty, but with sombre moods conveying the charm of melancholy to purify and sustain our grief. The second half of the eighteenth century discovered the romantic concept of Nature.[196] Townsmen escaping to the country-side from the squalor of the expanding cities, the revival of pastoral literature under the influence of translations of Gessner and a reappraisal of Virgil and Theocritus, the fashionable craze for bota-nizing, the switch of aesthetic appreciation from 'mountain gloom to mountain glory', the sentimental impact of the *Nouvelle Héloïse*—whatever the reasons, a new way of the imagination opened. Roucher's *Les Mois* (1779) conveyed a sense of threatening awe with its hallucinatory vistas of torrents, glaciers, and volca-noes; Delille's *Les Jardins, ou l'art d'embellir les paysages* (1782) moved through the dreamlike calm of civilized landscapes in which art was used only to serve Nature rather than embellish or impose on it. 'Je sens donc j'existe,' said Bernardin de Saint-Pierre, giving a mystical extension to Locke's epistemology, and bringing the exotic magnificence of tropical landscapes to complete the world view of a natural order in which death becomes a picturesque and—almost—welcome incident. As early as 1749 the abbé Yart was contrasting the formal garden of Le Nôtre, divided into regular compartments and adorned with statues and avenues, with the English preference for wild scenery;[197] in 1764, Watelet complained of the walled, regular garden as 'feudal', much preferring the new idea of the English who, he said, had learnt it from the Chinese. A garden in 'the disorder of Nature' had the advantage of being capable of playing on the emotions of the beholder, creating sensa-tions of 'the Noble', 'the Rustic', 'the Agreeable', 'the Serious', and 'the Sad', more especially the latter two, for 'le sentiment que ces lieux inspirent est le plus ordinairement une rêverie série-use, et quelquefois triste'.[198] Alas! it was soon evident that the creators of gardens did not mind giving Nature a helping hand, and diversifying her 'disorders' with evocative artefacts: artificial ruins, tombs, and sepulchral monuments.

Grands seigneurs ostentatiously took the lead.[199]At Bagatelle in the Bois de Boulogne, the comte d'Artois, brother of Louis XVI, erected an antique tomb of black marble over a fictitious grave. At Monceau, the duc de Chartres had a 'bois des tombeaux' as a setting for an Egyptian sepulchre, with other exotic features all around, including a minaret and a Dutch windmill; servants in appropriate costumes stood by and camel rides were available. Méréville, near Étampes, a site diversified by a river with islands, was made into a garden by Hubert Robert for M. de Laborde, the court banker; its sepulchral ornaments were not merely a plutocratic fancy, for they led to the monument to Captain Cook in the form of a domed and colonnaded tomb, and on to a simple column on an island, erected in memory of Laborde's two sons, naval officers drowned in 1786 in a shipwreck off the coast of California. The most complete of these professionally devised sites of natural melancholy (again by Hubert Robert) was the 'vallée des tombeaux' in the gardens of the château of Betz, belonging to the princesse de Monaco. The entrance was by an avenue of trees symbolic of mourning—poplars, cypress, syca-mores, planes, and the *arbor-vitae* imported from China. Next came the open-air pulpit surmounted by dome and globe and cross, carted from Paris when the Cimetière des Saints-Innocents was closed. In the centre, flanked by four poplars, was a circular stone supporting an urn, with an inscription exhorting the worthy to pray and the profane to depart. Then, there were three tombs: one a genuine old grave slab with modern statues of the four theological virtues guarding it; a tomb by the contemporary sculptor Mézières, supposedly containing the remains of Thibaut de Nanteuil, killed in the Holy Land in 1182; and another, also by Mézières but in the Gothic style, in memory of the ill-fated crusader's wife, who was shown recumbent, dog at feet, on a sarcophagus upheld by legen-dary beasts. As the visitor left the valley of the tombs, he could continue to nourish his sombre fancies at the hermit's cell and the ruins of the castle of Gabrielle d'Estrées (genuine ruins, transported there) and, maybe, at the temple of the Druids, before finding matter for more cheerful thoughts at the temple of Friendship, the Chinese pagoda, and the obelisk commemorating American Independence.

This mania for 'English' gardens, abandoning formality to return to Nature, accompanied all the while by a baggage of picturesque artifices to manipulate the emotions, was an intellectual game played by the very rich and their landscape designers. The contemporary arbiters of aesthetic taste had reservations. The 'Triste', said Watelet, should be sparingly employed in gardens and only to provide contrasts, for a man cannot be permanently melancholy unles he has a defect in his make-up, an 'indisposition of the soul'.[200] Lezay-Marnésia warned of the dangers of slipping into the bizarre or the ridiculous.[201] The prince de Ligne denounced artificiality, more especially manufactured ruins.[202] Delille had no time for invented tombs, 'les urnes sans douleur', capriciously scattered in irrelevant places. Someone else complained of 'monuments of melancholy, sepulchral promenades and hideous surprises'.[203] Cérutti, the Jesuit who became a journalist and a revolutionary enthusiast, in a poem on the gardens of Betz written in 1785, censured 'cette foule de tombeaux factices dont on charge les jardins anglais'.[204] Yet, surprisingly, he praises the valley of the tombs at Betz as a civilized exception. It is important to note why: the ornamentation was simple, there were no bronzes, gilding, pomp, or curious inventions, while the epitaphs were brief, without literary finesse or insincere praises, having no reference to worldly greatness, but only to mutual love and the sadness of parting. All this restraint, however, Cérutti counted as a mere theatrical contrivance when compared to the noblest garden tomb of them all—the tomb of Jean-Jacques Rousseau on the isle of poplars at Ermenonville.

Though Ermenonville was the triumph of the natural, the marquis de Girardin had been at expense to ensure it. The isle of poplars had been laid down in the lake before Rousseau's death (there had been talk of putting an urn there containing the ashes of two faithful lovers).[205] To provide rugged effects, the countryside had been searched for picturesque rocks; these had been broken up, the pieces numbered, then reassembled by the lake, with the joins carefully covered by moss.[206] On the island there was a tomb for Rousseau, with *bas-reliefs* by Le Sueur of a woman holding her child by the hand as she read *Émile*, and of another offering flowers before a statue of Nature while an infant burns its *maillot*. There was an inscription 'Ici repose l'homme de la nature et de la vérité'.[207] It was the burial place of a real person, not the decorative mausoleum of a character invented by a landscape artist. And, once the original contrivance was forgotten, it was a tomb in simple natural surroundings. An abbé, visiting the isle, left a couplet (greatly praised subsequently in the Parisian press), a poetical rendering of Girardin's epitaph:

> Sous un simple feuillage, au milieu d'une eau pure,
> Ici repose en paix, l'ami de la nature.[208]

Here was the generation's ideal sepulchre—the trees, the clear water, the silence, a resting-place for one who had been Nature's closest friend, a shrine where his admirers could pay tribute to his memory, a solitary retreat in which they could cultivate the new and subtle delights of melancholy. The island tomb was the antithesis of the promiscuity of the *fosse commune*, of the oppressive vista of past generations stacked in the *charniers*, of the fetid breath of towns and of the crowded urban landscape; it was far from the interference of churchwardens and municipal officials, from the intrusion of alien families, from the hierarchical and dogmatic ministrations of the Church. Rousseau had never liked to pray in his room, for the walls and all the trivial works of men seemed to form a barrier to keep him from God, he said in the *Confessions*. It was in contemplating God in the glories of creation that he worshipped.[209] And now he slept in the shade of the poplars, with the infinity of the sky above him, Jean-Jacques the lay confessor of the pre-revolutionary generation, the 'maître des âmes sensibles', the high priest of natural religion, preacher of a relationship with God and a hope of immortality granted directly to the just. In death as in life—and in attitudes to death as in attitudes to living—Rousseau was at the inspirational centre of the transformation of the religious consciousness of Western Europe which took place in the eighteenth century.

Rousseau spoke to the heart, eliciting the complicity of his readers. A Frenchwoman touring Switzerland, moved by the thought of the unhappy love and untimely death of his Julie, betook herself to a cemetery, to sit on a tombstone in the shade of a tree, gazing at the portrait of the one she had once loved, while the sun went down and darkness closed over the vast mountain perspective.[210] Few could go to Switzerland, but Ermenonville was close to Paris, and pilgrims flocked to the isle of poplars, coming in crowds through the fields of barley rippled by the wind and down the avenue of cherry trees, or coming alone at night to cross the lake by moonlight. Some, no doubt, were merely tourists—the marquis de Girardin closed his park in 1788 because of vandalism.[211] But like Claire at Julie's tomb, elect souls felt the immediacy of the presence of the dead writer who had guided them in love and friendship, in care of children and in education, in praying and in preparation for dying. Here, said one of them, the soul is deeply moved yet not tormented: 'rien ne déchire l'âme, et tout vient l'émouvoir'.[212] At the sight of Ermenonville and its seductive peace, Mme de Sabran wished that she too could die, becoming an object of pleasurable, melancholy memory to those she held dear, not an object of horror. Christianity, she complained, had made death so terrible: 'Our religion has spoiled everything with its gloomy ceremonies; it has, so to speak, personified death.'[213] For some, the approach to Rousseau's tomb brought them to the highest point of sophistication and spirituality reached by the cult of melancholy. 'Dans ces lieux solitaires, rien ne peut vous distraire de l'objet de votre amour; vous le voyez, il est là. Laissez, laissez couler vos larmes, jamais vous n'en aurez versé de plus délicieuses.'[214]

'The two ferments of the mental life of the eighteenth century, *sensibilité* and religious scepticism, combined to ripen that original fruit which is the sentimental concept of the tomb.'[215] This is true, but the role of religious scepticism must be carefully defined. The sentimental concept—one might almost say 'religion'[216]—of the tomb was adopted by atheists as an amenity, for death and friendship alike must have their observances, and there is satisfaction in the idea of sacrificing one's individuality, proudly, to the march of the mysterious universe. To the vastly more numerous and growing company of deists of the Rousseauistic kind, here was the highest point of their religiosity, at which God was worshipped as the author of the beauties of Nature, as supremely generous and good, and as the guarantor of the continuance of human loves and friendships beyond the grave. Yet deists did not have the monopoly of the new concept of the tomb as an aid to devotion. Christians adopted it. As enlightened ideas spread, it was not difficult to think of orthodox arguments in favour of placing cemeteries among trees and shrubs instead of crowding them near the churches, and it was time for the theologians to remember that the God of redemption is also the God of Nature. Delille, the poet of gardens, imagines for himself a Rousseauistic grave on the banks of a clear stream in the shade of an old oak, or under the delicate drooping branches of the birches, and he calls on all who love 'the sad pleasures of melancholy' to visit this poetic spot; but his last resting-place, he says, must be blessed by religion, sprinkled with holy water and marked by a cross, the symbol of our glorious resurrection.[217] Sentimental visits to the sepulchres could be occasions for meditation of a Christian kind, as the theologian Bergier said in 1788.[218] Whether for these, or for more fashionable reasons, there were plenty of good Catholics, Louis XVI and Marie-Antoinette included, who made the pilgrimage to Ermenonville.

From the death of Rousseau to the Revolution, sentimental writers had to put their tombs into unspoilt natural landscapes. Restif de la Bretonne was the exception to prove the rule, for he would have no formal cemeteries at all, but would bury the dead haphazardly in the fields[219]—which was carrying the movement back to Nature recklessly far. Trees, which had been hacked and harried out of cemeteries at the behest of reforming bishops, were now indispensable to a sepulchral setting. Being longer-lived than man, they were mute witnesses of his pilgrimage.

> Beaux arbres qui m'avez vu naître,
> Bientôt vous me verrez mourir,

the abbé Chaulieu had written,[220] and Chateaubriand was to yearn for a tomb under the trees in the place where he was born. The foliage would afford shade to the visitors who took their reflective promenades beside the graves of their friends: this was Mme Necker's reason for wanting to be buried under the great trees of Saint-Ouen[221] (in fact, she ended up pickled in alcohol at Coppet, where she could be visited in indoor comfort). Besides, a lofty grove was in itself a superior monument to those devised by men, said the prince de Ligne: 'nature is majestic, . . . simple, noble, . . . primordial, older than art.'[222] But the cult of *sensibilité* required more than a monument—Nature itself must be in sympathy with human grief, and thus the drooping willow came to be considered a more appropriate symbol than the formal cypress or evergreen for those who had missed greatness but had loved and suffered and died—

> Il fut sensible et mourut malheureux,
> Chantez le saule et sa douce verdure.[223]

Under the willow trees the famous lovers of Lyon asked to be buried; the good *curé* ensured the fulfilment of their wishes by leading a torchlight procession to the spot they had chosen before they committed suicide.[224]

This was their story as told by Nicolas Germain Léonard in his epistolary novel, *Lettres de deux amants, habitants de Lyon* (1783). At the time he published this best seller Léonard, though still only thirty-nine years of age, had already become the poet of nostalgic commemoration, obsessed with paying tribute to his departed friends amidst the solitudes of Nature.

> Errant sur les tombeaux de ceux que j'ai perdus,
> Délaissé maintenant, et plein de leur image,
> Je traverse le monde, où je ne les vois plus,
> Et je confie aux bois mes regrets superflus
> Comme le tourtereau qui gémit sous l'ombrage.[225]

In the year his novel appeared, he made a voyage to the Antilles, and on his return published an account of his adventures. In the primeval forest he had found a wooden cross marking a few moss-grown tombstones. On a moonlight night he visited the spot and sat on one of the anonymous stones (they had no inscription: 'pride does not seek out such solitary places'); there he brooded on the years he had lost in the frantic search for happiness as his life went on to its inevitable end.[226] This theme of the hidden burial-ground in the tropical wilderness provided Bernardin de Saint-Pierre with the final tableau of *Paul et Virginie* (1787; additional details in 1806); the graves of the star-crossed lovers and the few who had loved them best (including the faithful dog) were in the shade of a great mountain and amid the gigantic reeds, whose rustling was orchestrated by the distant noise of the sea, the vast ocean which is

351

the image of eternity.[227] Another ill-fated pair buried amid wild scenery were the noble, though adulterous, hero and heroine of Loaisel de Tréogate's *La Comtesse d'Alibre* (1779). Milcourt and his servant dig up Lucile's coffin and take it, through serried pines and deep ravines, to the lonely sea coast, and here, at the foot of an ivy-covered ruin, they bury her again. Milcourt builds a hut near by where he will shortly end his days—and be buried by the indispensable servant.[228] But these were high tragic settings. For family mourning, from which he wished to eliminate all regret, Bernardin de Saint-Pierre would use Nature as an ally in homely surroundings; a dead child would be buried in a corner of the school garden, and the best friend would plant a sweet-smelling shrub there for remembrance.[229] Fleuriot de Langle had noted the valley of a stream near Madrid where he would wish to be buried amidst jasmine, roses, and apple trees; his children would come here one day to gather roses at his tomb, and eat apples—'et me manger dans une pomme'.[230] According to Mme Chénier's *Lettre sur les tombeaux grecs*, published in November 1778 in the *Mercure de France*, visits of this sort were joyful family events at the garden sepulchres of the Greek aristocracy. She tells of the block of white marble, with its epitaph, among cypress, poplars, elms, jasmine, roses, and honeysuckle in a walled garden overlooking the sea; of the oratory of resident priests, of the drinking fountain with massive brass cups (on chains long enough for riders to drink without dismounting); of the summer visits of relatives, who renew their alliances and end their feuds, dance, sing, and picnic (the menu being listed, including a whole roast chicken for each of them).[231] Nature in its multitudinous moods could be pressed into the service of sentiment, with ravines and seascapes for tragic tombs, and smiling gardens for happy family remembrance.

Moral purpose was never far from the minds of eighteenth-century sentimentalists. Nature must be conscripted to join, not only in our griefs, but also in a conspiracy for human betterment. Léonard borrowed a pastoral theme from Gessner: two shepherds gaze on the wreckage of the tomb of an empire-builder then on the rustic grave of their benefactor who planted trees and diverted a stream: 'Et voici son tombeau sous le riant ombrage'.[232] In a poem of the same title as Léonard's, *Les Tombeaux*, Le Franc de Pompignan sees a desolate beach with the ruins of triumphal arches; near by, a lyre and a lute hang on a laurel bush to mark the grave of a poet, and a simple net, the instrument of his trade, that of a fisherman; each was good at his craft, and both were superior to the now forgotten conqueror.[233] Loaisel de Tréogate tells of libertines who read Young and go off to brood in the forest of Fontainebleau and be converted,[234] and in his novel, *Ainsi finissent les grandes passions* (1788), by the side of an antique cenotaph amid yews and juniper trees, the lovers learn that even their love cannot endure— ironically enough, for it is Eugénie's treachery, and not death, that separates them eventually.[235] It was not far from the fashionable *frisson* over mortality to genuine unease and thoughts of moral reformation. The comte de Tilly, a *roué* of the Court, progressed from 'Youngisme' and the composition of pastoral poems haunted by the transience of Arcadia, to prayers in a moonlit graveyard: 'I arose less inclined to guilty passions and more disposed to virtue.'[236] The new religion of the tombs had its moral duties towards man and, through Nature, its links with eternity. As the individual escaped from the web of corporate custom, and grief became a lonely private business, Nature was taken as an associate and a reflection of man's deepest feelings.

> Eh! qui n'a pas pleuré quelque perte cruelle?
> Loin d'un monde léger, venez donc à vos pleurs,
> Venez associer les bois, les eaux, les fleurs,
> Tout devient un ami pour les âmes sensibles.[237]

So wrote Delille in 1782. The poetry of graveyards had far outrun the modest reform projects of the Royal Declaration of 1776 which moved the cemeteries out of built-up areas.

IV

On 6 August 1793, commissioners from the National Convention, representatives of the local municipality and of the Commission des Arts, and the *commissaire aux plombs* arrived at the abbey church of Saint-Denis. The lead-collector was the key man in this embassy to the royal tombs. In three days they destroyed fifty-one monuments, the work of twelve centuries. The lead coffins were sent to the Hôtel de Ville. Statues of stone or marble were, mostly, thanks to Lenoir of the Commission des Arts, preserved for the new national museum. Metal effigies, like those in brass of Charles the Bald and his accompanying angels and Doctors of the Church, were melted down for cannon, 'destinés à foudroyer les ennemis de la République'. The work began chronologically, the first monument to be wrecked being the chapel of Dagobert, founder of the abbey, buried in 638; but the *bas-relief* of the king being rescued from Hell by his three patron saints was kept, 'parce que ce morceau de sculpture pouvait servir à l'histoire de l'art et à celle de l'esprit humain'. After a rest, the exhuming expedition returned on 12 October to ransack the crypt of the Bourbons. Here, on rusting iron trestles lay two lines of coffins covered with funeral palls, dark red with crosses of silver braid. Henri IV was the first to be pulled out; he was well preserved, and a soldier trimmed a sliver from his beard and wore it as a false moustache. The royal corpses were put into a single *fosse*; Louis XV's pestilential remains (he had died of small-pox and never been embalmed) were tipped in at the very time Marie-Antoinette was executed. Turenne, the greatest of French generals, was spared the common pit; the caretaker of the abbey kept him in a box in the sacristy for eight months and exhibited him to visitors for a fee, and sold his teeth as souvenirs. Subsequently, the great marshal went to the museum and then, on Napoleon's orders, to the Invalides. Meanwhile, the Revolution was rendering homage to its own heroes. In the *ci-devant* church of Sainte-Geneviève, renamed the Panthéon, Mirabeau rested (though soon to be evicted when his treacheries were discovered), also Voltaire and Beaurepaire, the hero of Verdun. Rousseau was taken there on 10 October 1794. The procession stopped at the devastated abbey of Saint-Denis on the way to the Panthéon. A Mountain of Liberty had been made out of some of the debris of the tombs, and on it, between a statue of Carloman and another of Clovis II, citizen Pollart, the mayor of the commune, gave a patriotic oration.[238] Thereafter, the abbey remained desolate. Grass grew on the shattered altars; the only sound was the rain dripping from the broken roof, the fall of a stone from the crumbling walls, or the chime of the clock, reverberating over the empty tombs and plundered vaults. Children had played there with the bones of mighty kings—

to Chateaubriand,[239] it was the consummation of a contempt for the dead which had begun when reformers had moved the cemeteries away from the churches. Without religion, men forget their debt to the past and their duty to posterity.

The violators of the tombs of Saint-Denis were helping the war effort, and showing their contempt for monarchy, hereditary rank ('l'infection généalogique'), and religion.[240] They were also treating the ancient dead very much as they had begun to treat their own. The moving of cemeteries had degraded the last stage of the funeral journey, and in many places, as in Paris, the new arrangements were makeshift.[241] The suppression of many monastic houses, the reduction of the number of parishes, and the redrawing of their boundaries by the Civil Constitution of the Clergy added to the confusion. During the Terror, massacres and the working of the guillotine provided mass burials whose revolting details were re-corded by royalist propaganda and shocked even hardened revolutionaries.[242] And the churches were closed, so that the last semblance of religious observances through the streets and at the graveside vanished. Patriots put atheistical notices on the gates of cemeteries: 'C'est ici le séjour de la paix et du sommeil éternel.'[243] Attempts to devise revolutionary ceremonies for funerals were embarrassing. At Orléans, the *commissaire de police* for the section, *bonnet rouge* on head and black stick with ivory knob in hand, accompanied the coffin, which was draped in the national tricolour, and a consoling notice was carried, 'The just man never dies, he lives on in the memory of his fellow citizens'.[244] In fact, these fellow citizens were usually conspicuous by their absence or their ridicule. 'Laissez donc passer le mort' and 'Ah! voilà bien un heureux' said the jostling Parisians as Delamelle's mother was carried to the cemetery by whistling porters, on the evening of 6 February 1794. The *commissaire* did not enter the cemetery himself because it was deep in mud. The porters took off the bands keeping the planks of the coffin together and tipped the body of his mother into the mire, to be thrown into the common grave later.[245] Worse could happen: the bearers might get drunk, or there might only be one of them, slinging the corpse over his shoulder.[246] There were country places, villages in the mountains, where the old religious rites went on unchanged.[247] But in the towns and in anti-clerical areas of the countryside, funerals had become sordid, utilitarian affairs. 'No people, no epoch has ever shown such a cruel indifference to a man after his death,' said an official report of 1799.[248] 'Oh mon Dieu!' said the actor Brunet, as one of these revolutionary funerals went by, 'pour être enterré comme ça, j'aimerais autant ne pas mourir'— 'If I have to be buried like that, I'd rather not die.'[249]

The role of the French Revolution in the secularization of life was never more evident than in its impact on the observances of death. In many places, the old decencies, already in decline, were abandoned. By contrast, the new patriotic zeal for commemorating great citizens and heroes, which had been an intellectual fashion of the last decades of the *ancien régime*, now came to its positive and rather disillusioning fulfilment against a background of national reforming enthusiasm followed by a lurid war for survival.[250] Mirabeau became the first occupant of the national Panthéon, established under the unfinished dome of the new church of Sainte-Geneviève (he was evicted later when his treasons became known or, rather, when his peculiar balancing allegiances became anathema to a partisan monolithic Revolution). On 11 July 1791, the body of Voltaire was brought to join Mirabeau's in this temple of national devotion. David, whose *Oath of the Horatii* had typified the *ancien régime*'s enthusiasm for the civic virtues of classical antiquity, devised a Roman pageant for Voltaire's procession; it rained, and the cortège following the triumphal chariot drawn by twelve white horses was mud-bespattered and unheroic. The funeral festival of 3 June 1792 in honour of the mayor of Étampes, murdered by peasants protesting against the high price of grain, was imposed by the revolutionary *dirigeants* on an unwilling people; there were hymns to music by Gossec and a towering statue of the Law with sword and open book; the National Guard, the popular societies, and David himself would have nothing to do with this celebration of official repression. But the State funeral for Le Peletier de Saint-Fargeau, murdered because he had voted for the execution of the King, was David's work. The naked corpse was exhibited in pagan fashion in the Place Vendôme before the procession to the Panthéon, and the painting which David presented to the Convention made the corpse of the dead legislator look like that of Christ in a *pietà*, or that of Hector in one of the artist's own earlier scenes from classical antiquity. Lasowski's funeral on 28 April 1793, also stage-managed by David, was a partisan Jacobin ceremony directed against the Girondins and was redolent of the atmosphere of civil war, with pistols and cannon, and a tricolour flag over the bier; the body was buried in the very spot where Lazowski had given the signal for the assault on the Tuileries on 10 August. The culminating patriotic funeral, the greatest and most sinister of all, was that of Marat.[251] On 15 July 1793 his embalmed body lay in republican state in the chapel of the Cordeliers—no longer a chapel, of course, but an annexe of the Club. The crowds filing past were shown the bath in which the tribune of the people had expired; simple folk gaped at the books of the old convent library, stacked high in the side-chapels, and wondered at the indefatigable industry of the murdered journalist who had written so many volumes. On the following day the Convention and Sections joined in a funeral procession, and at midnight the body was placed in its tomb in the Cordeliers' garden—a cave in a mound of granite rocks, surmounted by a pyramid, with an inscription to 'the friend of the people'. On 17 July the women of a revolutionary society took an oath to bring up their children in the cult of Marat and to give them no other scripture but his works. A day later was celebrated the feast of the translation of the heart of Marat to the Cordeliers' Club room, where it was suspended in an urn from the roof, amidst applause. David's famous picture of the death of Marat confirmed the impression that the Revolution was accumulating saints for its calendar. The paper Marat has just signed concerns compensation for the widow of a soldier. The possessions of the tribune of the people are of the utmost simplicity; the sheet is patched, the bathroom walls crude (in fact, we know that they were covered with white patterned wallpaper). The face of the dead man is transfigured. The legend could have been, 'Ecce homo'.[252] We should beware, however, of talking too easily of a new cult of 'saints' and of a 'new religion'. 'O cor Marat, O cor Jesus' were the words of a single orator, who was humanizing Jesus, not divinizing Marat. The 'immortality' of the 'martyrs of liberty' was purely secular. The State funerals of the Revolution were a device of propaganda, an encouragement to national unity and patriotic pride. They had no message about death. It is significant that the republican calendar, which in so many places ousted the religious one (not only officially, but also in the popular mind), totally failed to take over or undermine the allied festival of All Saints and the commemoration of All Souls. Under the grey skies of early winter, such bells as had not been annexed to make guns, tolled out, re-echoing from commune to commune, and the revolutionary officials were helpless.[253] For death, real death, the death of someone ordinary and near at hand, there was no consolation but religion.

Delamelle, brooding over his mother's gruesome burial, put the blame on the revolutionary exaltation of reason. 'Few men have a superior reasoning power,' he said; 'all have a feeling heart, when they are moved. Man's reason is a source of errors; his feelings (*sa sensibilité*) are a source of generous actions.' Surely, concessions should be made to the generous promptings of our nature—a decent, simple ceremony, with allusions to God, immortality, virtue, fatherland; then a procession to a cemetery on some breezy upland 'planted with trees in pyramidal shapes, sweet-smelling shrubs and aromatic herbs'.[254] After the ending of the Terror, the more extreme manifestations of de-Christianization fell out of favour, and the 'eternal sleep' notices vanished from cemetery gates: the municipality of Saint-Dizier said that these gloomy announcements had been the work of certain tyrannical individuals, aiming 'to demoralize men and thereby to promote their own criminal designs'.[255] Even those who disbelieved in God and immortality wished to commemorate their dead with decency, and to be commemorated themselves. André Chénier, who perished in the Terror, was a hater of priests and all religion, but he wished his friends to bury him in some tranquil corner of the woods, near shade and flowers and clear water, to engrave a stone with an enumeration of his virtues so that the passing traveller would know of his integrity and courage, to visit his tomb and tell their children his story, and he asked the woman he loved to go there at the break of day and to think he lived again in the caresses of the breeze of dawn.[256] In 1794 Delille completed a poem which he had begun nine years earlier; it was a plea to the State to recognize the solidarity of the successive human generations and the duty of families to have religious ceremonies to honour their dead.

> Que dis-je? ces devoirs, ces cultes domestiques
> Sont-ils donc étrangers aux fortunes publiques?
> L'État n'est-il pour rien dans ces touchants regrets?[257]

At Orléans in June 1795, a masque was performed in honour of nine citizens of the town who had been executed by the Revolutionary Tribunal. The stage showed a black marble urn amid cypress trees and roses on a river bank, with choruses of women and children wearing garlands. In this celebration, the whole mystique of pre-romantic melancholy and Nature worship was evoked. In their lives, the martyred nine had loved to walk on the lonely banks of the Loiret, where every grotto seemed designed for a melancholy inscription and every poplar tree to shade a funeral urn. It is a cold heart that seeks forgetfulness to escape the memories of loss. Let us rather cherish our grief as we experience 'un plaisir mélancolique à pleurer sur leur cendre'. The noble dead would have wished us to do this. 'For the man of feeling heart (*un cœur sensible*), second only to the happiness of being loved in his lifetime, there is no more flattering satisfaction than the hope of being mourned when he has passed away.'[258] In this same year 1795, Fontanes's poem on All Souls' Day, written ten years earlier, was published:

> Malheur aux temps, aux nations profanes
> Chez qui, dans tous les cœurs, affaibli par degré
> Le culte des tombeaux cesse d'être sacré.

The author was soon to flee to England and there, deep in consultation with Chateaubriand, in country inns and in the shade of old elms, he was to be converted, if not to Christianity, at least to the belief that the Christian religion is necessary to society.[259]

'Aux grands hommes, la Patrie reconnaissante.' For its heroes, the Revolution had the Panthéon with a tomb beneath this proud inscription—for the rest of its citizens, an oafish shamble to the *fosse commune*. Yet they too were patriots, serving the great nation which was at war with the kings of Europe. Ordinary folk had shown regard for the place where their families were buried; about 1796, from this sentiment, and to fulfil the needs of the new democratic patriotism, the idea of 'la terre et les morts' was born. Pastoret in the Conseil des Cinq Cents praised the savages who weep when they pass the mounds which mark their ancestral burial-grounds: we too should respect 'the sacred soil, where our fathers repose'. Richer de Sérezy published a discourse on the value of funereal monuments: 'Amongst the funeral monuments man studies the lessons of his heart and draws tighter the bonds uniting him to his fatherland and to humanity.'[260] This was official patriotism, newly sentimental. With greater delicacy, the author of *Les Délices de la solitude* defined the love of fatherland to exclude ambition and heroic crimes. 'I give the name *patrie* to the places, much beloved, where we were first nurtured and preserved, and where our hearts felt the first stirrings of our most tender affections.' Therefore, let us scorn the monuments of worldly greatness, like the monstrous pyramids of Egypt, which commemorate the evils of despotism, and bury our dead in the bosom of Nature. In a lonely valley of tombs, amidst cypress and evergreen bushes, we will pay our tribute to past generations, shedding tears of gratitude—'les larmes délicieuses de la reconnaissance, de la tendresse'.[261] But independently of arguments from enlightened patriotism, the reaction against the Revolution's crude utilitarian attitude to death was universal. In exile, the émigrés were dreaming of a tomb under the trees in the place where they were born, and clandestine royalists at home were noting the burial places of their martyrs. One of them had already planted cypresses in the graveyard where Louis XVI lay,[262] and the *ci-devant* duchesse de Tourzel had erected a monument in her park to the royal children, whose graves were unknown: 'Quid sunt cineres? Heu! Cinis ipsa deest.'[263] Soon, royalists were to buy the garden of the old convent of Picpus, where so many of the victims of the guillotine had been thrown, and restart the monastic life in the old buildings. As religious persecution ceased, some of the churches cautiously reopened, and Christian ceremonies became possible again, though it was illegal for a religious procession to go to the graveside. Legouvé, in a poem read before the Institut in October 1797, appealed to families to fulfil the role of the clergy themselves and to walk in the funeral procession:

> La sensibilité n'est pas le fanatisme,
> De la religion gardons l'humanité.

There was a general concern to find a ceremonial basis for morality (the Institut's current essay competition was on this subject) and to provide decent observances to mark births, marriages, and deaths. New religions, such as Theophilanthropy, were being invented to fill the need without resorting to Christianity.[264]

It was thus that projects for a well-regulated necropolis, which had circulated in the seventies and eighties at the time of the cemetery reform, were remembered again. Citizen Cambry, in a report to the Department of the Seine in 1799, revived their complacent ingenuities. Like them, he envisaged a commercial company in charge, this time enjoying a thirty-year monopoly. The very rich should be allowed to do imaginative things independently. Given a chance, Cambry himself would wish to build his own tomb among woods and mountains; there would be a portico where the weary traveller could find shade, and a bubbling spring for his refreshment, while all around would be roses and lilacs and trees planted to the memory of Cambry's father and each of his children, and in honour of 'Justice', 'Science', and 'Persecuted innocence'. In this tomb, his wife would eventually join him, and then, perhaps, his ashes would stir like those of Abelard when Heloïse arrived. Alas! our author could not afford these amenities, but he urged the authorities to allow those who could to build interesting mausoleums for themselves—this would encourage artists, provide the public with edifying monuments, and, if unreasonably ostentatious, would bring excessive riches into ridicule. Either way, with good taste or with bad, they would be morally useful. For the rest of us, the burial company would take over. A hearse in the form of an 'antique tomb' would arrive; the body would be taken to one of four mortuary chapels and laid on a marble table flanked by candlesticks and a tripod for burning perfumes; as evening fell, there would be a procession to the cemetery, with an escort of soldiers, two men with 'trumpets or trombones', and the relatives in carriages, 'which would be available on payment of a fixed tariff. The 'Champ de Repos' would have four gates, entitled Childhood, Youth, Maturity, and Old Age, and roads would wind through trees and flowers to the central pyramid, at whose corners would be incineration machinery (chemical, as wood was in short supply). The ashes of great men would have a place of honour in the pyramid; those of the rest of us would be packed in individual urns. Let no one say he could not afford to collect his departed kinsman, since there would be a manufactory of urns on the premises, and the officials would be obliged to ensure that there were always cheap models available at the price of 80 centimes. A relative collecting ashes would, of course, have to sign for them: 'il en donnera un reçu au concierge du champ de repos'.[265]

While Cambry was drawing up his scheme for the Department of the Seine, architects were designing a model necropolis—to be called an 'Élysée'—in a competition organized by the Academy of Architecture. Two years later, in 1801, the Institut offered a prize for an essay on funeral ceremonies and cemetery organization. The competitors (so far as we know from their published entries) gener-ally accepted the possibility of Christian ceremonies, provided they were privately organized, and families paid extra for any trouble they caused to State officials.[266] Pommereul, the prefect of Indre-et-Loire, was an exception: he would exclude religion altogether.[267] Girard was an exception the other way, in that he looked back nostalgically to the days when 'venerable priests' had consoled the bereaved; 'par qui les remplacerons-nous? Car il nous faut des amis.' He lacked conviction in his official consolers chosen from reputable citizens. 'Materialism,' he says sadly, 'destroys all the magic of the social order.'[268] Another contributor, Dolivier, an ex-*curé*, solved Girard's problem with all the atavistic zeal of the inventors of revolutionary cults of Robespierre's day. He would have a temple to 'the common Father of mankind' at the cemetery, and a 'minister of morality' who would also be the 'caretaker of the cemetery' (with attractive terms of employment, and two curates to help him). The religion preached by this moral officer would be one of patriotism and social utility. A jury would pronounce over every dead man whether he had been useful in life. If found wicked, his corpse would be sent off in a 'voiture sinistre' to the 'fosse des réprouvés; if just harmless, to a quiet burial with no ceremony; if worthy of public esteem, a crown of flowers would be awarded, hymns sung, the bells rung, a panegyric pronounced, and a memo-rial urn provided. There would be no family tombs, for these encourage men to live in isolation from their fellows. The cemet-ery, an instrument of moral classification, would be a breeding ground for patriotism: 'l'amour de la patrie a toujours été lié et confondu avec la religion des tombeaux.'[269]

Dolivier's inquisitorial procedures apart, the funeral ceremonies prescribed by the essayists were much alike. Amaury Duval is unique in having his *magistrat des funérailles* award the deceased's best possession—a picture, a watch, or the like—to the person who looked after him at the end, and this worthy character, to be called '*le pieux consolateur*,' leads the procession, with the gift in his hand. Of all the palls on coffins, Détournelle has the most picturesque—blue and white, with gold stars; Mulot has the most impressive uniform for his *officier funéraire*—ample black cloak, hat with black feathers, a medallion engraved with a serpent eating its tail, a staff surmounted by a butterfly and inscribed with the legend, 'Nos jours sont mesurés'. Prefect Pommereul has, predictably, the most disheartening pronouncements. 'Adieu, nous te suivrons quand notre tour marqué par la nature arrivera,' say the mourners at the graveside, 'Adieu! Adieu!'; but the *maître des cérémonies funéraires* has the last word: 'La pompe funèbre est terminée.'[270]

The banality of these lay liturgies does not make them contemptible. They were designed to encourage family solidarity. The relations are all assumed to be present: in one project, the magistrate may compel them. The writers are in revolt against the crude anonymity of the *fosse commune*. 'Heureux qui peut venir pleurer sur le tombeau de l'être qu'il aime.'[271] The tomb is becoming the symbol and the centre of family loyalty; only ex-*curé* Dolivier thought that this would be a danger to patriotism. Those who can afford it are to be encouraged to buy individual plots. Packing up undifferentiated bones in *charniers* is no longer recommended. One writer would have them chemically treated to form a vitreous substance from which a bust or family medallion could be made; another would allow the family to take the earth away from the cemetery to their own garden once the body had decayed; another wishes the dead to remain inviolate in their graves for ever: 'I think that we must never disturb their repose; once consigned to the earth, the place becomes a sacred spot where they must rest eternally.'[272] A Napoleonic decree was soon to allow families to buy burial plots 'of which the ownership shall be assured to them in perpetuity, whatever may happen'.[273] It was a reaction against the Revolution's confusions and its grim, communal utilitarianism, a transfer to the open air and a secular locale of the privileged concept of a vault in the parish church, a recognition of the growing sense of family solidarity and of the rising tide of sentimentality, and of the bourgeois instinct for annexing everything possible into inalienable property.

Dolivier was alone in seeing a conflict between patriotic loyalty and family devotion. To the other essayists, the two are complementary. If the peasant is buried under the oak tree which had been his shade and shelter at midday, says Girard, his sons will not sell the land, and they will defend it against the enemy. 'Such are the elements of which the true love of fatherland is composed.' As for townsmen, an annual festival of remembrance would bring all families, under the orders of the magistrates, to the place of tombs, there to share their memories of grief and their sadness at human transience. These tender emotions are the bonds of society. 'Sadness and melancholy draw men together more powerfully than pleasure and self-interest.' These feelings also bind us to Nature: 'Douce sensibilité, c'est toi qui nous rattache encore à la nature, lorsqu'elle paraît nous abandonner.'[274] Men united to each other in family affections, in common humanity, and in harmony with the rich and beautiful land which sustains and inspires them—here is true patriotism.

The essayists (except, perhaps, the dour Pommereul with his alleys 'lined with dwarf yew trees') make their ideal cemetery into a romantic garden, and assume it is a place for reflective visits— walking, brooding, meditating. The architect Gasse describes his project of 1799 as providing terraces 'propres à la promenade et au recueillement'. Amaury Duval has a park of trees and flowers, with no monuments other than a tiny stone inscribed with a name marking each grave; if the *gardien* charges to go in, that is only to be expected. Mulot has symbolic statues amid formal trees, but concedes that the ideal is burial in a private garden; he would lay his wife to rest in the grove she had adorned with her presence, under the canopy of honeysuckle and lilac where she gave him her vows of love, and surrounded by dark trees, 'as sad as my memories'. Girard has cypresses and poplars and murmuring streams, with lonely walks 'où la mélancolie ira promener ses rêveries', and even Dolivier, the moral inquisitor, has groves, meadows, and trees, with contrived perspectives to encourage meditation, and inspire the soul with a 'douce mélancolie'. Grief demands loneliness, says Détournelle; for those who mourn, 'the most solitary and silent place charms away their weariness, and is best suited to their sad reflections'. And grief rejects all man-made splendours: 'Nature's splendour alone should form a setting for the simple, rustic places destined to become the sanctuary of the tombs.'[275]

In 1801, as the essayists were publishing, Préfontaine offered the public some verses on sepulchral piety. Under a régime of tyranny like that of Tiberius and Nero (now mercifully ended by the rise of a heroic general), Frenchmen had become cynical about their dead; they had given up funeral processions—'on n'accompagnait plus la dépouille mortelle'. But Préfontaine, steeped in the study of the Ancients, and of Young, Hervey, Gessner, and Ossian, weeps for those he loved, and under the quivering shade of a weeping willow, he crowns their funeral urns with flowers. He makes explicit what is often implied by others: mourning the dead is not only a civilized duty, but also a sophisticated pleasure.

> Du culte des tombeaux lugubre jouissance!
> Des vivans et des morts respectable alliance!
> Qu'il est doux ce besoin d'aimer, de s'attendrir!
> La douleur nous est chère et devient un plaisir!

Far from hurrying off the dead and trying to forget them, we should keep alive the memory of our loss—

> Cet état de langueur où notre âme se plonge,
> Nous afflige et nous plaît; on l'aime, on le prolonge![276]

Préfontaine is speaking of a new religion, the *culte des tombeaux*. Here were observances blending human affections, family loyalties, the mystique of Nature, and a new kind of introspective and sentimental self-awareness that found its fulfilment in melancholy, into an emotional substitute for Christianity. But the *culte des tombeaux* was Christian too. Chateaubriand romanticizes the burial customs of the North-American Indians—the groves where families lay their dead, 'les Bocages de la mort', the cradle coffins of

children in the trees, rocked by the zephyrs and where the nightin-
gale nests and sings her plaintive song; he even praises (on grounds
of tribal solidarity) the gruesome custom of digging up the bones of
ancestors for display at great ceremonies. For himself he chose, not
a cold marble tomb in the sanctuary of a church, but a grave on a
rocky promontory near the ocean, marked by a cross of iron on a
block of granite, and consecrated by the *curé* of Saint-Malo. He
speaks movingly of the rural cemetery where the sheep crop the
grass on the grave of their shepherd under the shade of the yew
trees—it is a churchyard, dominated by the church spire and dotted
with little wooden crosses of grace and consolation, and filled with
the inspiration of a single inscription that haunts him: 'Sinite
parvulos venire ad me'[277]

Meanwhile, architects were carrying on the well-established
game of designing a splendid necropolis for some dream world of
the future. They were parting company with the cult of Nature
now, and were refining introspectively the mysteries of their own
discipline, preoccupied with patterns of interpenetrating masses
and the austere symbolism in which Boullée had excelled. In 1802
Jean-Nicolas Sobre published a project for a Temple of Immortality—a vast dome with the Northern Hemisphere and signs of the
zodiac illustrated on its surface, and surrounded by still water
reflecting it into the appearance of a sphere.[278] Two years later,
Claude-Nicolas Ledoux devised a crematorium in a vast empty
space, treeless, featureless, 'l'image du néant'; in the centre would
be a subterranean spherical hall lit only by a shaft above, with a
gallery for those who came there to contemplate 'le noir séjour
où finit la grandeur'.[279] Practical men had no time for these ingenuities. In accordance with the decree of 23 Prairial An XII,
straightforward arrangements were being made for decent burials,
and citizens would be allowed as much of the *culte des tombeaux* as
they could pay for. In Paris, the new cemetery of Père la Chaise had
been opened. By bringing in the bones of the great (the bureaucrats
had the names of Molière, La Fontaine, Heloïse, and Abelard on
their files) it was hoped to arouse public interest in buying plots,
and by juggling with the tariff, to bring in the rich to give a lead to
others—'on ne saurait y offrir trop d'attraits à la vanité'.[280] In the
catacombs of Montrouge, the bone stackers were still pattern mak-

ng. In one bay, they made a classical tomb with the motto, 'Silence, êtres mortels: Néant!'; in another, a chapel with the text 'Qui dormiunt in terrae pulvere evigilabunt, alii in vitam aeternam, et alii in opprobium'.[281] Which of the two, nothingness or the resurrection to judgement, was to be believed? A *culte des tombeaux* was arising which was to be common to both Christians and unbelievers. Its ambiguities helped them to live together after the persecutions of the Revolution, and masked the great question of human destiny to which every man, in his heart, must one day give an answer.

Death as an Instrument: The Public Execution

'Malheur à la société renfermant les hommes qui en voient mourir d'autres sans frémir,' said Pierre Pastoret, a reforming lawyer, reflecting on the multitude of crimes for which the death penalty could be exacted.[1] This was in 1790, in the magic days before revolutionary enthusiasm had run into disillusionment, and when the Terror was still just a cloud no bigger than a man's hand upon the horizon of the future. According to Pastoret, the jurisprudence of the *ancien régime* had accumulated no less than 115 capital crimes, though some melancholy satisfaction of a patriotic kind could be derived from the consideration that the French total was half the English one, the sturdy and barbarous islanders being contemptuous of death, even their own.[2] In eighteenth-century France treason, murder, attempted murder, infanticide, robbery and smuggling under arms, were offences liable to the death penalty—so too were duelling, coining, false witness, forgery of legal documents, theft of property worth more than 3,000 *livres*, breaking and entering, more especially at night, fraudulent bankruptcy, the forcible abduction of an heiress, rape, bigamy if forgery was involved, sexual relations with a nun or of a manservant with his mistress and certain other flagrant kinds of adultery, breaches of the press censorship, sacrilege, sodomy, incest, and the exercise of the Protestant ministry. Executions were public and the painfulness of the manner of dying was adjusted to fit the crime. For an attack on the king's person there was a lurid ritual of savageries laid down by the Parlement of Paris, which was revived in all its gruesome details to provide a lingering end for Damiens in 1757 for the crime of lifting his hand against Louis XV; in addition, the close relatives of the traitor were deprived of their family name and banished, and the family house was razed to the ground. For most

apital offences, the penalty was hanging; for crimes of violence it
vas breaking on the wheel; for poisoning, sodomy, and bestiality
.nd some cases of sacrilege it was burning. Sometimes the punish-
nents were cumulative: in 1787 a parricide had his hand cut off,
vas broken on the wheel, then consigned to the flames. There was a
itual of torture too, which might be made a preliminary to execu-
ion—*la question préparatoire* to extract an avowal of guilt, and *la
question préalable* to obtain the names of accomplices, and these
grim methods of persuasion were divided into two grades of in-
ensity, *ordinaire* and *extraordinaire*. According to Diderot's guess,
here were something like 300 executions annually in France at the
·nd of the *ancien régime*.[3] Comparatively speaking, this is not a
great number: as Diderot himself crudely put it, as many were
cilled by carriages, a high wind, a diseased whore, or a bad—indeed
. good—doctor. Even so, it represents a harsh, imaginable total of
uuman agony, a rough edge of reality to nag and fray the com-
·lacency of our pattern-weaving in the history of ideas.

The French legal system was cruel, but it did not make light of
nen's lives. In theory, the death sentence could be passed only if
he evidence was conclusive. If it amounted to certainty but fell
·hort of complete demonstration, the magistrates ought to impose a
ighter penalty.[4] According to Serpillon's commentary, published
n 1767, for criminal cases a 'moral certainty' was not enough, a
physical certainty' was required, 'celle qui dépend des témoins qui
·nt vu commettre le crime'.[5] His examples of the sort of evidence
equired are demanding. In practice, however, high-flown language
ibout conclusive evidence must be set in the context of the standard
nethods of procedure, which were devised to supplement the in-
·fficient police methods rather than to protect the accused. The
nvestigation was conducted in secret; the accused was ignorant of
he charge until he was confronted by the witnesses, and as these
iad already made their depositions, he could not hope to persuade
hem to risk the penalties they would incur if they changed their
·estimony.[6] The defence advocate moved in an unreal world of
vritten submissions in which it was impossible to unpick the web of
he prosecution argument. Too much has been made (on the basis
·f Voltaire's savage ironies) of the fractional 'proofs' that could be
.dded together to make a whole one; this was legal jargon rather

than a fair description of the way the magistrates operated, though it is indicative of the way in which, in the last resort, the 'instinct' of the judges fed by prejudices of class or *milieu*, could take over the decision without conscious dishonesty.

In addition to the requirement, so often ineffective, of conclusive evidence, death sentences passed by inferior jurisdictions needed the confirmation of the 'Sovereign Courts', chiefly, the parlements. True, this was not a retrial, but simply a review of the existing documentation,[7] but it was a safeguard none the less. There were, however, three exceptions to this rule of parliamentary review—significantly, all were concerned with threats to law and order. The Army had its independent system of military justice. The penalty for desertion was death. But there were so many deserters (anything from 4,000 to 10,000 a year). Except in cases of treasonable flight in face of the enemy, the extreme penalty was exacted in only a limited number of cases; sometimes there was a drawing of lots, with the execution of one in three. Often, those who drew the 'lucky' straw would be sent to the galleys—in the earlier part of the century, with savage brandings and mutilations of the face, barbarities which ceased when it was discovered that they affected the breathing while rowing. Since hanging, clubbing to death, or the galleys awaited captured deserters, it was not surprising that the peasants favoured their escape—a clear instance, the marquis de Monteynard pointed out to the higher command in 1764, of severities which were defeating their own object.[8] Another exception to parliamentary review was the exercise of powers of life and death by the summary jurisdiction of the *prévôts des maréchaux* in the countryside, dealing with violence, riot, or crimes committed by soldiers; these *cas prévôtaux* had to be judged by seven magistrates (*officirs* or *gradués*, as the formula had it), and of these a majority of two was required for passing the death sentence. Capital sentences were frequent. While the Parlement of Paris would sentence about sixty persons to death in a year, the jurisdiction of the *prévôts* would condemn at least a hundred throughout France, sometimes many more. Few who appeared before these summary tribunals got off scot-free—out of 100 arrested, only 6 or 7 would be acquitted, while 17 or 18 would be executed and 20 eliminated from society by a life sentence to the galleys. This severity should be interpreted in

ne light of d'Aguesseau's definition of the peculiar duties of these
ribunals, which were 'not designed to punish every crime nor even
he most serious ones, but all those which directly threaten public
afety'.[9] Here was the point where the justice of the *ancien régime*
vas at its most ruthless.

The third exception to the review of death sentences by the
overeign courts was the emergency jurisdiction of *commissions
riminelles* set up to deal with particular crises of law enforcement.
n 1778, an ordinance of the Royal Council conferred extraordinary
owers on the intendants of four areas, authorizing them to sen-
ence smugglers (caught bearing arms and members of a band)
vithout appeal;[10] in 1733, a formal *commission criminelle*, con-
isting of a Commissioner and six assessors, was set up at Valence to
udge such crimes over the vast area of Dauphiné, the Lyonnais,
lourgogne, Provence, Languedoc, and Auvergne. Subsequently,
imilar extraordinary courts were set up at Reims (1740), Saumur
1742), Paris (1777), and Caen (1785). They acted ruthlessly. In
hirty-eight years the Commission de Valence condemned 57 men
o be broken on the wheel, 77 to be hanged, 631 to the galleys, and
cquitted only one. But the threat to law and order was grave. It was
ot so much the 'smuggling explosion' of the eighteenth century
vhich drove the government to measures outside the ordinary legal
rocess, as the rise of armed bands ferrying contraband widely and
errorizing the inhabitants (like Mandrin's gang, which in 1754
ccupied twenty towns, taking hostages and selling the goods by
orce).[11] Without specialist, permanent machinery of investigation
xtending over various provinces, it was unlikely that these
narauders would have been tracked down, and local courts, includ-
ng even the parlements, were suspected of laxity. The death sen-
ences of the Commission of Valence refer, not just to smugglers,
ut to 'assassins', to scoundrels 'attroupés et armés',[12] and there is
o reason to believe that its procedures were defective or its
everities excessive by the standards of the ordinary justice of the
ime. Even so, the lawyers showed the utmost suspicion of the royal
ommissions criminelles. The Cour des Aides of Paris only regis-
ered the letters patent establishing such an extraordinary jurisdic-
ion in the capital after striking out the right to pass death sen-
ences; the Cour des Aides of Normandy held up the registration

for the Commission at Caen;[13] and the parlements of Grenoble and Dijon pursued the Commission de Valence with accusations of bias and cruelty—'un tribunal de sang'.[14]

The parlements and other sovereign courts exercising final jurisdiction in cases involving the death sentence had a wide discretion concerning the degree of pain and ignominy with which a criminal had to die. Hanging (or, for nobles, decapitation) was the most merciful. Wretches who were condemned to the wheel or the fire might be spared the full agony (more especially if they revealed their accomplices), since the judges, by a *retentum* at the foot of the *arrêt* of execution (revealed only to the executioner), might order strangulation beforehand, or after a certain number of minutes or hours, or a specified number of blows. These gruesome calculations were regarded as a serious part of the duties of the magistrate: insofar as there was a science of criminology in the eighteenth century, it consisted in making the punishment fit the crime. Judicial torture was far from being an arbitrary proceeding, let alone a sadistic one. The lawyers had built up a code of rules to regulate its application.[15] The charge must concern a crime for which death was the penalty, the documentation must be complete, so that the admissions extracted were an addition to the structure of proof, not part of it, the resort to the *question* had to be confirmed by the court of final jurisdiction, even if the suspect had not made an appeal to it. Evidence of guilt must be compelling—'des preuves presque complètes et de violentes présomptions'. For example, a dying man's accusation was not enough; if the suspect was of good reputation one witness was insufficient; if he was of doubtful reputation one might do, but in this case it must be an actual eyewitness and a person of good moral standing (eyewitness being tightly defined—two people seeing the accused leaving the scene of a murder waving a blood-stained sword were not proof enough unless evidence of previous threats or feuding was forthcoming).[16] Youths under fourteen years of age were not subject to torture and men over seventy were allowed some relaxation of its rigours. Doctors had to be in attendance, perhaps to certify the point at which the grim ritual began to defeat its object, but also to offer the solace of bleeding. The amount of pain to be inflicted was prescribed; four wedges between the planks that compressed the legs for

he *question ordinaire* and another four for the *extraordinaire*; or if
t was the water torture, six measures of water exactly, down the
unnel. There was discussion, though no formal regulation was made,
bout precautions to avoid crippling the victim permanently; every
letail of iron rings, tightness of ropes, and height of trestles was
pecified and, astonishingly, by a regulation of the Parlement of
'aris dating from 1697, the water torture was to be applied only
vith warm water and in a comparatively warm dungeon.[17]

By the rules of legal procedure, extenuating circumstances were
aken into account only after the death sentence had been actually
ronounced. An offender who was very young or very old, or who
vas certified as mad, or who could claim to have acted in self-
lefence or under extreme pressure, might be pardoned by *lettres de
râce* issued from the Chancellery attached to the sovereign court
vhich had passed sentence; those who had committed their crime
under the influence of passion might be pardoned too, though their
ettres de grâce had to come from the Grande Chancellerie because
his was an exercise 'of the full plenitude of the power of the
sovereign, being the result, not so much of his justice, as of his
lemency'.[18] When grave and violent crimes were being judged,
pleas of mitigation arising from the disabilities of the criminal,
vhether youth, age, or mental deficiency, were only grudgingly
onsidered by the courts. The *bailliage* court of Alençon in 1718
allowed a youth of fifteen to escape the gallows for homicide
because of his 'extreme youth and drunkenness at the time', but the
sentence was to the galleys for life.[19] The Châtelet of Paris in 1788
ondemned two octogenarians to breaking on the wheel for
murder.[20] The Parlement in its latter days condemned two boys,
one fifteen and one sixteen years of age, to the same punishment,
and burned a sixteen-year-old girl who had poisoned her mother.[21]
Youth, indeed, in the sense of 'imbecility' and irresponsibility was
narrowly defined, ending at the age of seven; from seven to fourteen a minor was sentenced at the court's discretion, which did not
exclude the galleys for crimes of violence. As for madness, it was
not until the last decade before the Revolution that it became a
serious medical concept. The Châtelet rarely took account of the
mental state of the people it sentenced, unless, indeed, some startling character emerged, like Pierre Charenton, who murdered his

mistress because she distracted him from his religious duties, 'preferring to sacrifice [her] life rather than lose his soul before God'.[22] In 214 cases of arson before the Parlement of Paris from 1750 to 1789, an *information de démence* was asked for in only 27 cases; true, in five of these the culprit escaped death as a result of the medical verdict and was locked up for life in the Salpêtrière or Bicêtre.[23] For treason and parricide, madness was not taken into any sort of account, the necessity of making a fearful example being regarded as paramount over all other considerations.[24]

In an age when life was brief and precarious, it was not unnatural to consider adult responsibility as beginning early and, perhaps, to consider old age to have received all the favour it deserved through the mere achievement of survival; with no scientific study of medicine or psychology, it was difficult to find criteria for establishing a code of diminished responsibility. But things were otherwise when the courts considered specific acts against the background of their social implications—a subject on which the magistrates were well informed and proud of being so. In the reign of Louis XVI, the Châtelet[25] was ruthless with armed burglars (5 executions) and with servants who betrayed their trust (10 executed, 6 to the galleys, and 2 women to the Salpêtrière for life). The one condemnation to burning at the stake concerned a servant who broke open his mistress's desk then set the house on fire to conceal his depredations. In these cases, civilized life and the sanctity of property were endangered. By contrast, other offences subject to the death penalty, and morally no less scandalous, were treated leniently. Girls who murdered their illegitimate babies would be released for 'lack of evidence' (a judgement of 'plus amplement informé'); adulterers, abductors of minors, and, even, violators of very young girls generally escaped with fines and payment of damages. In certain cases, a seducer or rapist would be sentenced to hanging, but with the offer of commutation of the penalty if he married his victim[26]—there were jokes about fastidious Don Juans who refused the bargain, but no well-authenticated instances. The judges seemed aware of the conditions of promiscuity and untoward temptation which often lay behind offences of a sexual nature. They conceded, too, at least in theory, that hunger was an overriding excuse for thefts of provisions, provided the offender was not a

agabond, and that no violence to persons had been used. A diarist
otes a provincial case of 1740 in which a housebreaker was par-
oned because he had not eaten for three days; the difficulty, of
ourse, was to provide convincing evidence of this sort of
ecessity.[27] But one thing was clear: if ever the judges were dis-
osed to mercy, it was only when public order was not at risk.

This priority of the issue of public tranquillity is probably the
est clue to the interpretation of the sentencing policy of the
arious parlements, whose magistrates would act with hysterical
erocity, or with a mildness which undermined the force of royal
dicts. A murder by a servant, an ambush on the highway, an affair
f black magic with undertones of a conspiracy against morals[28]
ould lead to breakings and burnings. Yet, in spite of the strictness
f royal edicts, of the 44 duellists brought before the Parlement of
aris between 1700 and 1725, 12 were acquitted, 26 released under
he *plus amplement informé* formula, and 6 were sentenced—one
o pay expenses, one hanged in effigy, one banished for nine years,
ne to the galleys for nine years—none was executed.[29] Fraudulent
ankruptcy, since 1673 a capital crime, was not treated as such in
ractice; writers and publishers who evaded the censorship went in
ear of their freedom, but hardly of their lives (though one of the
anic measures taken after Damiens's attempt was a renewed ordi-
ance prescribing death for printing and selling books against
eligion and the tranquillity of the State). In cases of homicide,
etters of remission would normally be forthcoming if a proprietor
ad been repelling nocturnal thieves, a woman resisting rape, or a
oung man had been forced into a duel or a soldier insulted, or if a
usband had killed his wife caught in bed with her lover (though
his must be in the family home, and not elsewhere). Yet even if it
as obviously a case where letters of remission would be forth-
oming, the death sentence had to be passed—for no one was
ntitled to disturb the peace of society, France being a kingdom
where all acts of violence are absolutely forbidden'.[30]

How did the lawyers who manipulated this sophisticated and
arbarous criminal code justify the exaction of the death penalty?
o destroy a man, they conceded when they wrote of murder, was a
errible thing—the breaking of the image of God, taking away from
fellow human being his greatest possession, depriving a family of

its support and the State of a citizen.[31] Even so, they argued, the magistrates had the power of life and death, and they cited Old Testament texts prescribing death as the penalty for murder, selling a man into slavery, cursing father or mother, and blasphemy (Gen. 9:6; Exod. 21; 12, 24; Lev. 24:16). Less confidently, they cited the Pauline reference to the secular ruler who 'beareth not the sword in vain' (Rom. 13:4).[32] The final power over mens' lives rests in God's hands, and God has, under conditions, delegated his power to secular sovereigns, who in turn delegate it to their magistrates.[33] Muyart de Vouglans, the refuter of Beccaria, put this myth of a series of delegations into a more realistic form when he assimilated the divine commission to the sovereign with the 'consent of the people'; God is a God of order, the people need tranquillity, so the basis of the State is 'the necessity of the establishment of an authority which can rectify the injustices and [repress] the violence of those who dare to disturb the order of society'.[34] To the lawyer this is the single great utilitarian argument—the necessity for keeping order in society. The object of punishment, says Jousse, is to prevent the criminal repeating his crime and to make of him an example to restrain others. That is why executions are public with 'an impressive display including every circumstance which can strike fear into the people', why a cruel form of death is imposed in certain cases, and why the children of a traitor are punished as well as the offender himself—'to inspire a greater horror for certain crimes'.[35] In his legal dictionary, Ferrière speaks of the object of punishment as, quite simply, 'to serve as an example to others and divert them from committing crimes'; it is a matter of 'terror' and 'fear of punishment'. And he makes it clear that the legal system is defending the hierarchical society of the *ancien régime*. A crime is worse if it is committed against a person of distinction, and the punishment is always more severe for a criminal from the lower orders, a man of 'basse condition'.[36] To the lawyers, death is justified as an instrument of terror to keep order in society.

This, no doubt, was a doctrine appropriate to an age more familiar with death than we are, and inured to pain as an ineradicable evil. But the lawyers of eighteenth-century France were not unfeeling men; their minds, we may guess, were conditioned more by an ever-present fear which we are just beginning to rediscover—the awareness of the fragility of the foundations of order on which society is built. They were men of property, and must have been aware of the fact (which modern statistical studies are revealing) that there had been an enormous increase in robberies and other crimes against property from the middle of the century. For them, a whole twilight world of vagabonds and criminals lurked round every bend in country lanes and in the shadows beyond the pale gleam of rudimentary street lamps. The machinery for tracking down law-breakers was hopelessly inefficient. True, Paris was reasonably policed, as befitted the capital, but provincial towns were less secure: in Bordeaux there were only seventy policemen, thirty of them mounted. In the countryside, the tightly knit, suspicious, and defensive local communities had to see to their own safety to a remarkable degree. The *maréchaussée*, the rural police patrolling on horseback, totalled only 3,500 for the whole kingdom, and was inefficiently distributed—in one area, five men covered nearly two hundred parishes, and attended at 600 fairs and markets annually. Payment was at subsistence level, so officers of the law usually made ends meet by doing extra jobs as innkeepers, custodians of billiard halls, and shopkeepers. Some on the payroll did nothing but draw their erratically paid wages: one lieutenant is recorded as not having ventured out of doors for years lest he be arrested for debt, then for years more because this sedentary life had brought on the gout.[37] If it came to the risking of life and limb, the *maréchaussée* was wont to fade away, leaving the provincial governor to send in the army—not unreasonable conduct for a force which was forbidden to shoot first, even against armed criminals.[38] By contrast to these miserable policing arrangements, the financiers of the *Ferme générale* had no less than 23,000 'guards' covering the internal provincial boundaries to catch smugglers, a private army which, by its very presence, incited to violence and conspiracy. Here was the most effective law-enforcement agency in France (a quarter of the wretches sentenced to the galleys were smugglers); but the laws that were being enforced were solely concerned with extracting money.

The police of eighteenth-century France had no systematic, let alone scientific methods of crime detection, and, short of the barbarity of branding with the fleur de lis, no secure means of identification. Even when the perpetrators of major crimes were well known locally, it was difficult to find them, for insofar as all but the most outrageous crimes were concerned, public opinion had little sympathy with the forces of law and order. A *bailliage* court in Normandy might expect to have to try half its identified murderers *in absentia*.[39] In Languedoc, if an escaping robber threw down his loot, it was regarded as only fair play to let him go; no one would volunteer to be a witness, and those who were compelled to testify took the view that a lie was in order to save a man from the scaffold. At the end of the *ancien régime* reformers were declaiming against the 'inquisitorial' practice of the courts in examining witnesses in secret—but how else could anyone have been persuaded to say anything?[40] And if a criminal was apprehended, unless he was put in the dungeons of the State or of a major court, his chances of escape were good, for no one was anxious to spend money on him, whether to give him a fair trial or to lock him up securely. Often, the buildings of the gaol would be a ruin, and the gaoler would have paid a fee for the right to make an income from the prisoners, charging 1 sou a day for straw and bread, and up to 4 *livres* a day for a fire and soup with the gaoler's family.[41] The dark, dank cells of State or parliamentary prisons were horrible enough, but in those parsimonious days they were the only secure places of detention; it needs the expenditure of the taxpayer's money to have light, air, and freedom from lice and bedbugs allied to locks, bolts, and bars that work effectively.

No doubt the certainty of being caught is the most effective deterrent, and prevention is better than repression; but in those days, these were not viable alternatives to the existing brutal system. As a result, while the lawyers themselves had doubts about the *question préparatoire* (the commissioners of Louis XIV presiding over the codification of 1670 had wanted to abolish it), they were virtually unanimous in wishing to retain the *question préalable*. It was not just that the men of the *ancien régime* had a simple belief in the efficacy of pain as a sort of truth drug (it was the rule to ask the mother of an illegitimate child for the name of the father at the height of the birth pangs).[42] Evidence was hard to come by, a criminal already condemned to death was regarded as worthy of little consideration; he might have a sense of grievance against his associates who were escaping scot-free, he had nothing to fear from their vengeance, and, by revealing their names, he might qualify for merciful strangulation. The lawyers were not cynical when they spoke of torture in terms of strict control and economical use. 'Often, it is only by use of torture that the truth can be extracted from criminals,' wrote one of them in 1770, 'but how sad a spectacle this makes for a tender, feeling heart.'[43] This was fashionable sentimental jargon, but sincere enough. Diderot accepted the same grim deduction from the principle of social necessity: if a few minutes' pain inflicted on a rogue can save a hundred innocent people from being murdered by his accomplices, torture can be defended as a humane act.[44] The social order, the maintenance of peace which is the essential interest of the great majority, was the overriding consideration for the magistrate. This was the justification for the use of torture as an instrument of criminal investigation, and for the use of the death penalty in repulsive forms. Society was not safe without them.

In this context of fear, the nauseating business of adjusting agony to fit the menace of the crime becomes more understandable. The picking and choosing among the terrifying penalties attached to so many edicts, the choice of hanging, breaking, or burning, of torture ordinary or extraordinary, of *retentum* or no *retentum*, of three minutes on the wheel or two hours were part of a scientific process, the judiciary's contribution to the art of government. To rely on broad principles about punishment, as Beccaria did, was regarded by the jurisconsults as an abdication of responsibility: whole volumes in folio would be needed, said Muyart de Vouglans, to deal adequately with the issues Beccaria dismisses in 200 pages. With a basic inheritance from Greece and Rome, he goes on, and many centuries of experience in which kings have manipulated the weight of punishment according as crimes of different kinds became more or less frequent or menacing, France has at last achieved a sophisticated calculus of deterrence, which is the envy of the world. 'By means of these augmentations and moderations of Penalties, one can say, to the honour of France, that our jurisprudence has been elevated to a degree of perfection which gives it a rank of distinction among civilized nations.'[45]

The central argument of the lawyers was the necessity of

maintaining order. They also had a secondary argument—or, rather, it was a nuance, an extension of the first. Muyart de Vouglans spoke of the need to 'purge' society, to 'avenge' society for the scandal and damage caused to it.[46] Another legal writer in 1773 tells of the 'vengeance' which is forbidden to men, but which the king and his officers can exact by virtue of a delegation of authority from God. Another, four years later, speaks of the necessity 'to punish and avenge the crime by the public satisfaction imposed on the criminal'.[47] It was not enough for the magistrate to preside intelligently over the operation of a calculus of deterrence: he must also feel that he is an agent of divine vengeance, the vindicator of an outraged social order. It was not enough for the malefactor to appear as a horrifying example of the fate of transgressors: he must also make, and be seen to make, a public reparation, a recognition of the majesty of the law and of the sovereign he has flouted. There is a revealing sentence in Jousse when he speaks of the importance of fair and open procedures—'il faut encore que les accusés se jugent et se condamnent eux-mêmes en quelque sorte'[48]—the accused must condemn themselves. The *question préparatoire* was not, in theory, torture applied to complete the proof of guilt, for this proof was supposed to amount to a moral certainty already; rather, it was to extract the formal avowal which the process of reparation demanded. Immediately before his execution, a condemned man was encouraged to make a *testament de mort*. This was distinct from any record of admissions under the *question* and was not a last will and testament of the ordinary kind, for having incurred civil death (*la mort civile*), he was no longer capable of disposing of his property; it was, simply, a formal avowal of guilt 'par acquit de conscience'.[49] A magistrate of the court accompanied by a clerk and the executioner would interview the prisoner just before he was taken out to the scaffold, or at some staging point on the way;[50] they would interrogate him on oath, and if he volunteered a confession it would be formally recorded, ending with a formula recognizing the justice of the sentence and asking pardon of God. If he refused to make such a testament, there was still a chance on the scaffold itself, and the clerk in attendance was authorized to take the record without the presence of a magistrate. Often, the death sentence would include an injunction for the criminal to make the *amende honorable* on the way to the place of execution. Before the portals of the cathedral or other principal church of the town, on a cart, facing backwards, dressed only in a shirt, rope round neck and candle in hand, and bearing placards declaring the nature of his offence, the condemned man would kneel and ask pardon 'of God, the King and of Justice'. Any outrageous crime, even if it had not warranted the death sentence, might be the subject of such an act of reparation.[51] Sometimes, the ceremony would be supplemented by the inauguration of some more permanent memorial, paid for from the estate of the criminal—the foundation of a mass for the soul of the man he had murdered, or the engraving of an epitaph to commemorate the victim and the sentence of the court.[52]

In the *amende honorable* the condemned man was asking pardon, in the first place, from God. Thus, he was not only making an act of public reparation, he was also completing the act of reconciliation towards his Maker which—presumably—he had begun by making his confession to a priest in his cell. If he persisted in denying his guilt and refused to make the *amende honorable*, it was for his confessor, there with him on the cart, to exhort him. Reformers publicized the courageous reply of the baker of Saint-Omer wrongly convicted of murdering his drunken mother (in 1770): 'Are you prepared to take onto your own conscience before God the lie which you wish me to utter at the door of this church?'[53] Religion, of course, was not only concerned with the *amende honorable*, but with the whole execution, which was a lurid prefiguration of the death that comes equally to us all and makes us all equal when it comes, a reminder of the end of the sinner, of the necessity for confession, restitution, and reparation, and of the hope and assurance of forgiveness to the truly penitent. From the religious point of view, the central figure of the drama was not the executioner, but the confessor. In France, it was the custom to offer no other sacrament to the condemned but that of penitence, the confessor limiting himself to instructing and exhorting to the spiritual reception of the benefit of Communion and extreme unction.[54] Absolution was to be withheld if the names of accomplices were not forthcoming, though the Capuchins were said to err on the side of mercy in this respect.[55] The confessor (there were two for Damiens and for Calas, but one was usual) accompanied the victim to the scaffold and stayed with him to the end, offering the crucifix to kiss as the torments intensified. The handbooks of the confessional always emphasized the infinite extent of God's mercy: a sincere repentance, even at the very last breath, could reconcile the most depraved of sinners. Some of the clergy, however, wondered if, in practice, in the bitterness of an agony officially imposed, it was possible for a man to turn his mind towards his Maker,[56] and their voice was joined to those who wanted an end to the wheel and the faggots. Other clergy wished to have practice conform to the strict logic of the Christian doctrine of mercy: the repentant sinner, however odious his offence had been, should be given, not only absolution, but also the viaticum.[57] The eighteenth-century editions of the *Rituels* of various dioceses made it clear why communion was refused—it was solely because of the legal rule by which the death penalty was normally put into effect on the very day of the sentence, so that 'le corps adorable de Jésus Christ' would be united with a body soon to be exposed to the utmost indignities.[58] The case for withholding the sacrament was weak, and from the Edict of 1788 was non-existent, for a delay of a month was then prescribed to allow time for royal review and, possibly, pardon. But the rule remained unchanged: at least three of the *cahiers* of the clergy in 1789 complained of this unchristian severity.

Lay society, whether represented by critics of the Church or critics of the penal code, did not seek to deny the clergy their melancholy right to monopolize the last moments of the criminal on the scaffold—with the exception of Boucher d'Argis, who in 1781, on grounds of religion alone, wanted priests to absent themselves from such scenes of cruelty. The spectators, he said, curse them as if they are in league with the judges, while the dying criminal blasphemes against the God who has abandoned him.[59] In fact a more usual reaction was to admire the confessors who performed these sickening duties. Restif de la Bretonne tells of a priest escorting a livid figure, half-dead already from the tortures of the preliminary *question*, to the scaffold: 'I saw him embrace the wretch, devoured with fever, as infected as the dungeons from which he was taken, covered with vermin. And I said to myself— 'Oh religion, here is your triumph!'[60] In some towns, this 'triumph of religion' was emphasized by the presence at the execution of one

of the *Confréries des Agonisants*; there were those like the Pénitents de la Croix, of Autun, the Pénitents de la Miséricorde of Lyon
and the Pénitents Pourpres of Limoges who undertook the special
obligation to attend funerals and bury the dead. The Pourpres of
Limoges held an auction among themselves the night before an
execution for the grim honour of collecting the corpse from the
gibbet or wheel and wrapping it in its shroud. Then on the morrow,
in their blood-red robes, and cowls, with black girdles and rosaries
of black beads encircled with a crown of thorns, they processed with
candles to the place of execution, their two ecclesiastical members,
arrayed in black stoles, supporting the prisoner. They sang a *De
profundis* and litanies to Christ and the saints, and when all was
over, bore the shrouded body back to the Church of St. Cessateur.
There, they kept their vigil over it all night, then buried it in the
cemetery of that church—a cemetery which had been used only for
criminals since the great plague of 1632.[61] These sombre proceedings were a testimony to the Christian hope and to the solidarity of
all believers in the great drama of sin and redemption; to complete
the demonstration, a pious *confrère* would sometimes instruct his
heirs to have him buried alongside the outcasts he had accompanied
on their last journey of pain.

It is the historian's duty to go back, sympathetically, into the
minds of former generations. But there are areas of their thought
where we cannot penetrate except to record without comprehension, areas opaque to our understanding, where sympathy dies.
It is difficult to make the effort of the imagination and accompany
the men of the past on their way to a public execution—on the way
to the Place de Grève in Paris in 1757, for example, to see Damiens
slowly pulled to pieces by horses because he had lifted his hand
against the King. It is more difficult still to accompany the women
of quality who had hired strategic windows for the occasion and, we
are told, proved to be less squeamish than the men.[62] (One might,
perhaps doubt the anecdote of the day about the delicate young lady
who wept when the executioners whipped the horses: 'Ah! Jésus,
les pauvres bêtes, que je les plains').[63] Sensitive people were sickened by this ritual of terror. Louis XV himself was sunk in gloom
on the day of the execution, and spent the afternoon praying for his
would-be assassin. The comte Dufort de Cheverny spent the day

away from Paris with his wife and two friends (whose names he gives 'to pay tribute to their humanity'), with instructions that on his return that night no one should speak of what had happened. The pious duc de Luynes shuddered at the part he had had to play in the trial and condemnation. But not a voice was raised to say that Damiens should be executed in a less outrageous fashion.[64]

True, the crime of Damiens was unique, subversive of the whole social order. We are, perhaps, obliged to allow some element of patriotic duty as an excuse for the continuance of the terrifying traditional savageries and, even, for the sadistic behaviour of the onlookers. But the numerous routine executions also had their concourse of spectators. At Paris they would crowd into the Place de Grève in front of the *hôtel de ville* for all the major events of this kind (and it was here that the guillotine first began work in April 1792); there were less dramatic scenes—hangings and decapitations—at the *pilori* in the Halles; there were floggings and brandings in the courtyard of the Palais de Justice; for a military hanging in front of the whole regiment, enthusiasts would make the journey out to the Plaine de Sablons.[65] Barbier, the tough Parisian *avocat* who believed that 'one man hanged keeps ten thousand in order' and never missed these orderly occasions, tells of multitudes waiting in the rain, of men injured and horses stifled in the press.[66] It was the same with the less frequent opportunities for seeing executions in the provinces. There would be crowds pressing around the iron grilles which surrounded the scaffold in the Place Saint-Georges at Toulouse, spectators with money to spare taking refreshment at the near-by Cerf-Volant, which specialized in meals for days of executions. It was estimated that there were 40,000 people, including 2,000 children, gathered at Montpellier in 1746 to see a Protestant pastor hanged. When the notorious smuggler Mandrin was broken on the wheel at Valence in 1755 the crowd was estimated (more realistically) at 6,000; they had poured in from fifteen leagues radius all round, and paid 12 sous each for places on platforms around the square erected by enterprising householders.[67]

There were women in all these crowds as well as men. Perhaps ladies of quality would go only to executions with an interest of a political or a controversial sort (a poetaster reproached one of them for lamenting when her poodle was kicked but going off avidly to see Lally's head fall).[68] But women of the ordinary sort were found around the scaffold on every occasion. Restif de la Bretonne tells how a pretty girl on the arm of her lover laughed when three men were being broken on the wheel at a torchlight execution at the Grève. 'Mademoiselle,' he told her, 'you must have the heart of a monster; from what I see of you tonight, I think you would be capable of every crime. If I had the misfortune to be your lover, I would leave you for ever.'[69] The pair were reduced to silence and another girl in the concourse, says Restif, 'called me an *honnête homme*'. The Roman women who applauded at gladiatorial shows, said a writer in 1791, 'enjoyed them just as ours enjoy major executions'.[70] The *tricoteuses* of the Revolution had their ancestors in the *ancien régime*.

Ours is an age of statistical history, and it is worth pointing out that we do not have more than impressionistic evidence for the composition of the crowds around the scaffold. In particular, one would wish to know whether they were the same people every time, or were they different? According to a humanitarian writer in 1787, most spectators went there for the first and only time; they were sickened, repented, and never went again. Others, a minority, got over their revulsion; they had averted their faces at the crucial moments, but heard others relating the horrors on the way home; for a while, they ate little and slept little, but in the end came back again and became *habitués* of the scaffold, attending every time 'comme au retour d'une comédie'.[71] And some of these *habitués*, he says, were children. No doubt, the crowds at an execution contained unpleasant characters whose minds do not bear contemplation. But what of the others?

To be fair to these coarse and jostling multitudes, we must remember that they were there at the behest of constituted authority to see a ceremony of State—to see a ceremony of religion too, for which the great bell of the Cathedral of Angers tolled nine times (to warn the faithful to attend, as the naïve annalist of that great foundation tells us).[72] To the audience, it was not just a predictable display of cruelty to be sadistically savoured: at the scaffold, the verdict of the magistrates was, in some sense, exposed to the verification of public opinion. According to Madame du Deffand's account, in 1769, the people meanly showed their enthusiasm for the execution of Lally, rejoicing at the fetters and the gag and the base journey on the cart (because the black coach, suitable for an aristocrat, was not available).[73] By contrast, there were groans of disapproval in 1721 when the young brother of the bandit Cartouche died while undergoing the supposedly more lenient punishment of suspension by the armpits, and there were stirrings of revolt in 1725 when two men were hanged for taking part in a food riot. Voltaire describes how the mob at Lyon in 1772 showed its disapproval of the hanging of a pretty serving girl for a trivial theft: 'all the *canaille* which rush to these spectacles as they do to a sermon, because they get in without paying, burst into tears'.[74] Sometimes the condemned criminal might even be rescued by the force of popular disapproval. At Limoges in 1742, a popular conspiracy prevented a harsh sentence of hanging from being carried out; there was a tumult, the rope broke, and the *Pénitents* smuggled the victim away in an extra robe and cowl brought along for the occasion. In Paris in 1761, a serving girl condemned to the gallows for petty larceny was rescued by the crowd; her master's shop was pillaged and the tumult continued until letters of pardon arrived.[75] At Cahors in May 1779, one of two men who was due to be hanged for assassination, thefts, and sacrilege was rescued by the crowd, unwilling to see him suffer again after the rope had broken; the *maréchaussée* intervened and were driven off with showers of stones.[76] In the history of the struggle for religious toleration in France, some minor place must be found for the spectators who came, many no doubt with sadistic curiosity, but also with moral disapproval, to see the hanging of Protestant pastors. The vast throng at Montpellier in 1746 groaned as one when the executioner pushed his victim, the young pastor Desubas, from the fatal platform; the hordes of children present booed the attendant soldiers, and the ladies wept again when the coffin arrived too late, just after the corpse had been buried near the scaffold by a few faithful Protestants. All went away remembering how Desubas had refused the ministrations of the Jesuit confessors and rejected their crucifix, and had died 'un honnête homme et un héros'.[77] It is an invention of our century to do away with dissidents in whitewashed cellars with no witnesses to their martyrdom.

At the scaffold there was always a human drama of an elemental kind to be played out. The execution was, as it were, a real-life theatre production with the gallows as the stage set, and the executioner, the condemned man, the confessor and the escort as the *dramatis personae*. The crowd knew the cast and speculated keenly how well each would perform his role. More especially, they knew the executioner.[78] In Paris, leading his train of four or five assistants, a resplendent figure would mount the steps, with hair curled and powdered, gold braid on jacket, stockings of white silk, and polished dancing shoes, one of the great Sanson dynasty, with its family vault in the church of Saint-Laurent, its official residence by the *Pilori des Halles*, and substantial revenues from dues on grain and flour entering the city. In Rennes, the executioner was Jacques Gannier, who always communicated as an act of expiation, on the morning of days when he had to perform his professional duties, and who was regularly chosen as umpire by the magistrates of the parlement for their games of *boule*. At Dijon, there was a character equally well known for less reputable reasons (he kept a brothel as a sideline); in contrast to his colleague at Caen, a rival to the medical profession when it came to setting broken bones (the miller of Fontenay went to him after catching his arm in the wheel); at Tours, there was a dubious individual also known in medical circles for the embrocation of macabre ingredients which he furnished. Even small and unimportant towns (in the north of France at least) had their own *exécuteurs des arrêts criminels*, men of standing who bought their offices and would bring you before the courts for defamation if you called them *bourreaux*. These sinister local dignitaries were universally maligned: their wages, it was said, were thrown at their feet when they were paid, and popular legend had it that they advertised for husbands when they wished to marry off a daughter. The rising tide of sentimentality at the end of the *ancien régime* redoubled their unpopularity; the three Ferey brothers, executioners at Rouen, in 1781 complained that they were victims of a 'new prejudice', which like an 'epidemic' had turned the ordinary people, especially women and children, against them. How well could Sanson, or Gannier—or Desmorets or Jouenne and the others—perform their task? A display of clumsiness would be execrated; indeed, the executioner might find his own life in danger from the mob. By contrast, a display of dexterity might be applauded.

The criminal was likely to be well known, and there would be an established public opinion—or public controversy—about his crime. Everyone knew about his family and the *quartier* he came from, how he had behaved on trial (though this was always held in secret), what admissions he had made under torture. All sorts of reflections—about guilt or innocence, his character and motives—could arise from observing the way he died. The classic case was that of Damiens, who had wounded Louis XV. The gazettes reported his imperturbable demeanour under guard in the Montgomery Tower—his persiflage, his sound sleep and hearty meals, his comb and hair powder. The poet Robbé de Beauvest was fascinated: 'I am burning with curiosity to see if he will sustain this attitude to the very last, or if he'll change his tune when he sees the horses that are to give his hide such a painful stretching.'[79] Then came news that Damiens had burst into tears when the *curé* of Saint-Paul arrived to confess him, but how at the final session of condemnation before the Grande Chambre on 26 March he had regained all his original insolence. On the afternoon of the 28th, there was the opportunity to see this insouciance tested by the protracted ritual of pain traditionally prescribed in the national interest. At one level, these horrors could be seen as a sociological experiment; the scientist La Condamine was there with his notebook taking down everything Damiens said—the executioner told his assistants to let him come close: 'Laissez; monsieur est un amateur.' At the level of ordinary people, the same motivation, at a generous interpretation, could be called curiosity. For the first time since his arrest there was a chance to see the 'monster' who had lifted his hand against the King. Did he look like a madman (as some said he was)? Or a Jansenist convulsionary? Or the agent of a Jesuit conspiracy? Or was he just a dim-witted servant inflamed by anti-monarchical gossip he had heard in the houses of a couple of parliamentary magistrates? Was he—a subversive thought—a sort of lunatic champion of the oppressed people, or a symbol of the great, subconscious conspiracy of lackeys and servants everywhere (the idea is Michelet's) against the complacent possessing classes? Not that anyone, even those with telescopes and a place near the barriers, learned anything significant, though it was said that the victim exhorted his executioners not to curse and swear, but to pray for him. It was only in the case of less exalted criminals, who might be allowed a last speech from the scaffold, that significant revelations might occur—or the dying man might break out in imprecations against the magistrates and the great, shocking, but inviting the poor into a secret complicity.

As the drama unfolded, there might be a diversity of incident and, sometimes, an unexpected denouement. The routines of the scaffold were susceptible to variations: a man broken on the wheel might be strangled early in the proceedings. (There was a grim error when Cartouche was broken in 1721—the *greffier* forgot to tell the executioner about the merciful strangulation, and it was the confessor who ordered one of the guards to pull the rope tight.) A man burned might be strangled, or stabbed to the heart with a *croc de batelier* before the fire took hold; some of the prescribed horrors might be omitted—the tearing-out of La Barre's tongue was only simulated. Those assembled in the Place de Grève in December 1738 to see a provincial nobleman beheaded for murdering a woman could recount afterwards how the executioner struck early, at the start of the prayer *Salve Regina*, 'pour lui cacher le moment du coup';[80] those in the same square eleven years later to watch an abbé hanged for forging lottery tickets saw the almost unparalleled scandal of a dying criminal refusing the aid of a confessor;[81] more outrageous still was the affair of October 1784, when two murderers, to be broken on the wheel, turned their backs on the priest to address the executioner: 'C'est à vous que nous avons affaire.'[82] By contrast, the spectacle might turn out to be grimly edifying—an assassin at Caen in 1760 singing the *Veni Creator* on the wheel while the priests held up his head,[83] a double murderer at Paris in 1765 surviving for ten hours and manifesting 'very Christian sentiments'.[84] The crowd might wait for long hours around the scaffold uncertain of what the eventual outcome might be: would the Jew Joseph Levi escape the full rigmarole of torment because he had declared himself 'converted' and been baptized that very morning,[85] or, more genuinely pathetic, as the rain poured down throughout a long summer's day, would the young chevalier de la Barre receive a last-minute reprieve from the Parlement of Paris?[86]

Even when the criminal had taken to flight and was beyond the vengeance of the law, the spectacle would still be put on for the edification of the public, and executioner, lawyers' clerks, *huissiers*, *archers*, the town trumpeter, the furnishers of faggots and other gear, not forgetting the humble artist who made the effigy, would draw their appropriate remuneration.[87]

The view of the execution as a theatrical performance brings us as near as we can get to understanding the mind of the multitude (as for the folk of quality at their hired windows, perhaps we must abandon them in incomprehension). Marivaux's description of people rushing to see a street fight is as good an indication as any of the state of mind of those who thronged around the wheel and the gallows. They are not there, says Marivaux, to rejoice at cruelty or to mock at pain: they are, simply, in their stupid, cruel fashion, curious. They want to see the spectacle, to have something to talk about; they want to undergo the surge of powerful emotions, to weep with sympathy and tremble with alarm; they enjoy, not cruelty itself, but the shudder of fear that the sight of cruelty brings.[88] Voltaire, no lover of the populace, makes the same excuse for them. There is a universal, dominating human instinct of curiosity. Lucretius is being over-subtle in detecting the secret thrill of pleasure at our own immunity when others suffer; like the children who climbed trees at the battlefield of Fontenoy to see the fighting, we are not hard-hearted, we are simply anxious not to miss anything. The mob in *Tancrède* surge around the prison 'shamefully eager' to see the execution, but 'curious with compassion'.[89] People want to have something to talk about, says Diderot; they are not inhuman, they would rescue the criminal if they could; they probably avert their eyes at the most horrible moments, and they go home in tears. They attend, as they would attend any fête or sensational happening, to have something to recount to their neighbours.[90] The typical spectator is the fireside story-teller who wishes to maintain his reputation as 'the Demosthenes of the *quartier*'.[91] Mme Roland takes up the other aspect of Marivaux's explanation: the desire to experience the thrills and catharsis brought by powerful emotions. The crowd, swarming like ants, even on the rooftops, driven by a collective 'curiosité secrète et sanguinaire', are a fearful sight—she had seen them from the windows as a girl. But in each individual there is a driving force, for good as well as evil, which needs to be fuelled by 'powerful impressions' which give us 'a keener consciousness of our existence'. For people of sensibility, the theatre fills this need: for the populace, the place de Grève.[92]

And what of the lawyers' contention that these scenes of terror served to deter from crime those who came to witness them? Some of the *cahiers* of 1789[93] cited two—not entirely compatible—grounds for thinking otherwise. The people, they said, were brutalized and hardened by these atrocious spectacles. The Tiers État of Paris gave this warning, but added a rider which showed more confidence in the sentiments of the multitude: perhaps, instead of creating a horror of crime, public executions had the opposite effect and excited compassion for the criminal. Indeed, there was one execution of the eighteenth century which, through special circumstances, provided a startling exemplification of this. The smuggler Mandrin, with his thirty murders, his practice of taking hostages, and his armed rabble, was a ruffian, but his execution in 1755 led to an outburst of plays, pamphlets, and songs celebrating his career of violence—his gold-braided hat, his six double-barrelled pistols, the spy who betrayed him, his illegal seizure on foreign soil, his courage on the scaffold, how he had sent away the monk who was there to confess him (as being 'too fat for a man who preaches penitence'), how his last words had been a complaint about the poverty of the common people.[94] No doubt some, like Voltaire, thought that he might have been spared to serve in the king's armies against the American savages, but for most, Mandrin was a hero because he had plundered the hated *fermiers généraux*, and the eight blows of the iron bar which the Commission de Valence prescribed for him were regarded as eight blows of revenge by the oppressive tax-gatherers. 'They broke him on the wheel—a punishment for the modest contributions he had extracted from the richest men in the State.'[95]

The French criminal code was cruel. Its defenders did not deny this: they pleaded necessity. Its cruelty was under permanent challenge from two great traditions of thought, Christianity and Renaissance humanism. Two names epitomized these traditions and were continually cited by reformers. There was St. Augustine, who conceded to the magistrate the power of death (though only in accordance with a law which was 'the rule of justice and of reason'), but condemned torture—a device of the ignorance of judges which turned to the misery of prisoners.[96] And there was Montaigne: 'For my part, any judicial punishment which goes beyond straightforward death, seems to be pure cruelty.'[97] Various seventeenth-century writers, including La Bruyère, developed the humanitarian case,[98] but it was a French lawyer, Augustin Nicolas, a *maître des requêtes* of Louis XIV, who published the most comprehensive denunciation of judicial cruelties in 1681. Having systematized all there was to say about the uselessness of torture, he ended on a different note. Even if it was effective, it was always unjust. 'Neither the atrocity of the crime nor the difficulty of obtaining evidence can justify an unjust procedure.'[99] In adopting this ground of absolute principle, Nicolas had gone beyond the point where most of the writers of the Enlightenment would be willing to follow him; on the rare occasions when their two driving forces, humanitarian emotion and utilitarian logic, came into conflict, the logic tended to win.[100]

The famous manifesto of the Enlightenment against the cruelties and illogicalities of the penal code was Beccaria's *Trattato dei delitti e delle pene* (1764). In France, it had enormous influence, through the translation of 1766, through essays by Servan and Voltaire popularizing its ideas, and, as is the way with refutations, through the writings of the jurists who attacked it. Yet the Italian reformer and the French lawyers accepted the same basic utilitarian principle. To Beccaria, the argument from deterrence was everything. He accepted death as the appropriate fate for those who threatened the internal or external security of the State,[101] but for other crimes, he argued that perpetual slavery would be a more effective deterrent. A cruel execution arouses sympathy for the victim and thereafter is forgotten: a slave in fetters is an ever-present object-lesson. Beccaria, in fact, carried the utilitarian principle to its logical extreme. The *amende honorable* and all the ideas of 'vengeance' and 'reparation' played no part in his scheme; all that mattered was the damage to society. He took no account of the dignity of the person injured or of the status of the criminal[102] or of the offence to the majesty of God; by ignoring these considerations he was, by implication, defining society as essentially egalitarian and secular. He abolished the sombre *mystique* that had been woven around the concept of the official execution. Rousseau had just demonstrated how this mystique could be transferred from the law books of the parlements to the new egalitarian city of the General Will, where the power of life and death comes, not from delegation by God, but from delegation from every man who enjoys the benefits of the social order. 'So that I will not fall victim to an assassin, I agree to my own death if I become one.' More than this, criminal conduct carries the stigma of rebellion and treachery (and there is a further, more sinister extension of this idea in the chapter on the Civil Religion).[103] Beccaria rejects all this. No one ever gave another power over his own life. Death is just one evil more. Executing a man may be a utilitarian necessity, but it is not derived from any sort of consent: it is an act of war. Beccaria is not defending the Christian principle of the sacredness of human life; he is asking those who propose to destroy a life not to deceive themselves about what they are doing. There is a simple test of honesty in this matter: do you, in fact, accept the public executioner as a 'good citizen who is contributing to the general welfare' or do you shrink from him?[104]

Beccaria's famous principles of punishment—public, prompt, the least possible in the circumstances, proportionate to the crime, and fixed by the law—were accepted already by the French lawyers. The difference lay in the enormous discrepancy in their definition of what was 'necessary', 'least', 'proportionate', and 'fixed'. Montesquieu had already proposed to draw a line: the death penalty should not be exacted in matters of religion and morals or (in favoured states where fortunes were not too unequal) for offences against property.[105] Rousseau had taken a different criterion: it was wrong to execute a man who could be left alive without danger.[106] The application of these limitations would have transformed the jurisprudence of the *ancien régime*. Voltaire had denounced useless cruelties and wanted to force a reconsideration of all death sentences by having the warrant signed by the sovereign in person.[107] And in 1762 he had begun his campaign against the injustices of French criminal procedure, his first victory coming in March 1765 with the rehabilitation of the memory of Calas. 'Il est certain qu'on fait trop peu de cas en France de la vie des hommes,' he wrote on 26

September 1765, three weeks before he first opened the pages of Beccaria.[108]

'The least possible in the circumstances': it was easy to insist that there were circumstances where the death penalty was necessary, but difficult to defend specific obscenities like breaking on the wheel or burning. Aided by the upsurge of *sensibilité* in literature, which at the least provided the humanitarian *clichés* of discourse, protests against cruel punishments became insistent. In 1770 Voltaire was willing to retain painful methods of execution for parricides, traitors, and incendiaries: seven years later, he wanted 'simple death' alone.[109] Nothing should be added to the sentence of death, said Boucher d'Argis in 1781, ridiculing the idea that there ought to be 'nuances entre les supplices' when capital punishment was in question.[110] Brissot compares the civilized executions of ancient Egypt, when the criminal was drugged with a grain of incense, to the barbarous penalty of the wheel, an invention of northern Europe artificially introduced into the more civilized south.[111] If possible, he held, we ought to make it easy for the condemned man to die, yet at the same time make the execution appear terrible to the spectators—'rendez affreux l'appareil du supplice, mais que la mort soit douce,' said Marat, adopting the same formula.[112] This humanitarian propaganda began to have its effect. Before the Revolution torture was abolished—the *question préparatoire* in 1781 and the *question préalable* in 1788 (typically of the age, the magistrates had been abandoning the *question préparatoire* before authorized by the Edict of 1781, but did not entirely give it up afterwards).[113]

The supreme test case for cruel punishments was the treatment of regicides. The shadow of the fearful end of Damiens hung over the discussion. 'La sûreté publique' was the irrefutable argument. Toussaint, in 1762, said that he would simply ask if it was possible to provide for the security of the State by less extreme measures—if he was told there was no alternative, he would not inquire further.[114] According to the Capuchin P. Joseph Romain Joly, in a dictionary article on 'Cruelty' in 1771, even the mildest of philosophers would be content to watch an hour's torture with red-hot pincers applied to a 'monster' who had tried to assassinate his king.[115] Boucher d'Argis, campaigning for the swift and simple death penalty, made an exception for a regicide—his crime deserved 'special punishment that would be long remembered'.[116] By contrast to these conventional concessions to cruelty and royalty, Lacretelle's *Discours sur le préjugé des peines infamantes* (1784), crowned by the Academy of Metz, is as humane as it is courageous.[117] He takes the new reforming line that the apparatus of an execution should be 'sombre, gloomy, menacing', while the punishment itself should be characterized by a 'hallowed moderation'. True, no torture could be too severe for the assassin of a king, if we intended to demonstrate our full execration of his crime; but we ought not to attempt to do this by cruel actions—we must follow the dictates of reason. We do not wish posterity to shudder at the fearful vengeance we wreaked on the murderer of our king, or to imagine that this foul deed has been expiated. We wish to load the memory of the assassin with 'infamy', to bring out the contrast between his savagery and the civilized code against which he offended. A prince who reformed the existing law in France would not suffer thereby: his life would be the more sacrosanct because of his clemency. There will always be danger from fanatics, but these are never deterred by the atrocity of punishment; on the contrary, an atmosphere of cruelty exacerbates their lunatic exaltation. The case against the torture of Damiens was complete. But when the Revolution came, a new argument could be added. Such horrors, said Marat in 1790, were invented as a manifestation of the will to dominate, they were part of the terrifying panoply with which despots love to surround themselves.[118]

There was an overwhelming case against the crueller methods of execution, but few contemporaries made the further step towards doubting the necessity of the death penalty altogether. France did, however, contribute something new to Beccaria's utilitarian criticism of the old criminal law. Reactionary lawyers cited the Scriptures, more especially the Old Testament—but there had always been difficulties. Cain, the first murderer, had not been condemned to death by God, even though (as a theologian early in the century had pointed out) this was 'at the birth of the world when everything was of consequence for the future, since what happened was to serve as a rule for all posterity'.[119] The Mosaic law of an 'eye for an eye' was suited only to a barbarous people: it was neither the continuation of the instinctive precepts of natural law,[120] nor an adequate guide for the positive laws of later and more civilized peoples. The abbé Bergier insisted that this record of primitive ferocity should not weaken our respect for Christianity, the religion of charity—'there is no challenge here to the holiness of our religion which, indeed, exhorts us vehemently to show kindness, charity, and pity.'[121] Landreau de Maine-au-Picq put the idea of development more clearly; not only have we outgrown the Mosaic code, we have also progressed in our religion, as we have in our reasoning, since the coming of Christ.[122] Interpreting the Scriptures in this light, he brought the New Testament, and new texts in it, to bear on the old debate about capital punishment. The apostles' task was to preach the Gospel, not to agitate to reform the penal code, so we must look for guidance in the Bible, not to specific discussions of legal questions, but to the whole spirit of the Gospel which was preached. We are not to render evil for evil; God does not wish for the death of a sinner but rather that he turn from his wickedness and live. The Quakers, ridiculous in other respects, have in this matter seized on the true meaning of the Scriptures and the will of God.

One old argument against the death penalty had been its irreversibility: it made it impossible to compensate the victim if a mistake was made. France, thanks to the vigorous intervention of Voltaire and other reformers, began to afford some startling examples of these irremediable errors. The Calas affair was the first of a series of revelations in which the death sentences passed by various courts were shown to be miscarriages of justice. In some cases, the evidence had been inadequate—Sirven (like Calas, a Protestant before Catholic judges), the farmer Martin, the baker Montbailli, the three men who were the subject of President Dupaty's famous *Mémoire pour trois hommes condamnés à la roue* (1786), a *curé* mistakenly accused because the real criminal had dressed as a priest, a husband held responsible for his wife's absence when she had gone off with her lover. In other cases, the capital charge itself was an absurdity—the young chevalier La Barre dying for his blasphemies, and the luckless General Lally-Tollendal beheaded for treason in 1766 and exonerated by the Council twelve years later. Stories of this kind received wide publicity. From

François Gayot de Pitaval's *Causes célèbres et intéressantes* (20 vols., 1734–43), a new popular literary genre[123] began, a sort of 'Police Gazette' style of true story, drawn from the proceedings of the lawcourts. Nicolas-Toussaint Le Moyne des Essarts published no less than 100 volumes of this 'edifying criminology' between 1773 and the Revolution. The moving details of injustice done and the outrageous details of legal prejudice and inefficiency became well known—poor Montbailli's pathetic protestations of innocence, the obscure political persecution of Lally-Tollendal, his gag and the haste and mismanagement of his execution.[124] A lawyer could make his name in his own profession, among the *philosophes* and before the reading public, composing a memorandum on some victim of the legal process. President Dupaty's *Justification de sept hommes condamnés par le Parlement de Metz* (1787) is a masterpiece of the genre, combining this triple appeal with a dash of anti-Semitism. His story concerns four men hanged and three sent to the galleys by the Parlement of Metz on a charge of brigandage—all on the word of two 'rich and avaricious' Jews. Eighteen year later, two gypsies confessed to the crime. This miscarriage of justice is compared to the later case of the 'Ermite de Bourgogne' before the Parlement of Dijon in 1780 (one man executed and one to the galleys on the word of a single witness) and the affair, five years later still, of the wicked judges of the Comté de Comminges, who condemned an innocent girl to be burned alive, and in their turn were punished by the Parlement of Toulouse.[125] A result of the outcry raised by these scandals was the Edict of 1788, which made two major changes in criminal procedures. A majority of three out of seven judges (instead of two as formerly) was required for a death sentence, and such a sentence was not to be put into effect until a month had elapsed, thus allowing time for the intervention of a royal pardon. This reform reduced the chances of a miscarriage of justice; even so, the unjust executions which had already taken place remained as a powerful testimony against the use of the death penalty. Reforming lawyers did not fail to use this argument, and to cite these examples before the National Assembly in the early days of the Revolution.[126]

One practical way of applying Beccaria's principle of utility was to look at each capital crime individually—on its demerits, as it were—to see if the death penalty really constituted an efficient deterrent. This was done for desertion from the army by Merlet, an old professional officer, in an essay published in 1770.[127] He was cashing in on a growing public interest: Sedaine's opera *Le Déserteur* had some success in 1769, and Mercier was at work on a prose drama on the same theme. Merlet describes how the army enforced its punishments—deserters to the enemy were hanged; ordinary deserters were clubbed to death by an execution squad of fellow soldiers. Yet the crime was common. Some who fled had grievances about the way they had been enlisted—impressed, or bribed into signing on; most were peasants who did not regard loyalty to the colours as a virtue. It was always the young soldiers who ran away, those who had not had time to get over their grievances or to become inured to discipline—and who would be most useful to their country if their lives were spared. In future, Merlet suggests, deserters should continue to serve the State: they should be sent to the galleys, and on release take a new oath of fidelity and begin a new term of military service. Six years later, his argument of social utility was put forward by the abbé Jaubert[128] in support of a plea to spare the lives of girls convicted of infanticide; they deserved to die, but executing them meant the destruction of fully grown individuals, reared at the expense of society and capable of serving it, to avenge the death of undeveloped infants. It was equally wasteful and harsh, said Jaubert, to put smugglers to death, for men are more valuable than manufactures. The splendid principle of utility had its dangers, however—there would not always be a humanitarian outcome. Venereal disease, said the Swiss writer of a 'code of happiness', causes more damage to the State in a single year than the capital crimes of a whole century; this being so, he recommended the scaffold for the immoral characters who propagated it.[129]

Another way of applying the principle of utility—and allying it with the rising force of *sensibilité*—was to examine the impact of the rituals of the scaffold on society generally; even if individuals with criminal tendencies were restrained by fear, there might be others whose minds were corrupted and drawn to an unhealthy interest in violence by the savage repressive measures society itself employed. This is Landreau de Maine-au-Picq's contention. A sinister vortex of brutal instincts swirls around public executioners, their affairs, and their families: anatomy students are depraved by working on the corpses of criminals whose faces show evil and terror rather than the repose of death, the multitude is hardened by the sights and sounds of the scaffold. That is why, says Landreau, our police receive no co-operation from the public; if the criminal law was made clear and simple and its penalties moderate, the whole population would collaborate to enforce it—this should be our aim, 'de rendre tous les hommes maréchaussée'.[130] When the first massacres of the Revolution came, a legal pamphleteer took up Landreau's theme—we have seen the people bathing in human blood: 'where did it get the idea of this so-called right to massacre unless it is the same right that society is said to have?'[131]

This pamphleteer, Perreau, wanted the total abolition of capital punishment on the ground that it is wrong to kill a fellow human being under any circumstances; no writer before him, he complained and boasted, had had the courage to go to this logical extreme. With the possible exception of Landreau de Maine-au-Picq, he seems to be right in his contention. For even the most humane theorists, like Servan and Lacretelle, there are crimes so heinous that the criminal who commits them thereby proves he is no longer a human being—he is a 'monster', his 'soul is dead within him', he can be exterminated.[132] The main theme of reforming thought ran very much on the line of Beccaria: the death penalty would remain, but would rarely be exacted; it would be replaced generally, by perpetual slavery. The idea of reprieving sturdy rogues from the gallows and setting them to work for economic reasons had occurred to Frenchmen before Beccaria published. Faignet de Villeneuve had advocated the establishment of barracks for 'des galériens de terre', felons spared from execution, branded on the face to prevent them ever regaining normal society, and spending their lives repairing roads or working in the mines.[133] Beccaria made this thrifty scheme more respectable by adding humanitarian enthusiasm and a lawyer's calculation about its deterrent effect. Voltaire took up the idea with enthusiasm and for all the reasons, particularly the economical one—'un homme pendu n'est bon à rien'. From 1777 he was asking for the ending of the death penalty for murderers; they could become useful, as England had proved by sending gallows-birds to the colonies and Russia by sending convicts to Siberia.[134] Diderot, a realistic supporter of the death penalty, proposed to spare all but the most desperate murderers for employment of public works: 'because one man has been killed is no reason for killing another'.[135] And he put the calculation of the value of a human being in those days of high morality with harsh precision. 'When we put to death a man of thirty years of age, we do not know what we are doing. We have not made the calculation that this man is the sole survivor of twenty men. Our criminal legislation does not know the value of the life of a man of thirty.'[136] The idea of replacing the death penalty with perpetual penal servitude became generally accepted by the French reformers; Boucher d'Argis, Mirabeau, Pastoret, Brissot, and 'Moheau' all urge the acceptance ('Moheau' adding the sinister utilitarian variant of surgical experiments on criminals who might opt for vivisection, with a marginal chance of release, rather than life imprisonment). Landreau de Maine-au-Picq recommended imprisonment instead of execution, and in his overflowing Christian charity, stipulated kind treatment and release at the age of seventy, naïvely observing that these patriarchs of the prison out on parole would give good advice to young people.[137] In 1790, the *avocat* Vasselin drew the attention of the National Assembly to the pool of well-motivated labour which could be made available by rescinding the death penalty: 'Thus, the most crying abuse of despotism can become the most splendid institution of our new legislation.'[138] It seems odd than the thinkers of the eighteenth century should so easily have persuaded themselves of the potential value of a prison labour force; but colonial slavery was profitable, the doctrine of work was developing as against the Christian practice of almsgiving, populationists were making the multitude of toiling hands in a State the test of successful government, the more effective disciplinary methods being tried in military camps, schools, factories, and workhouses[139] seemed to offer hope of an effective penal regime, and there was an undue confidence in the possibilities of a rational reorganization of society.

To Brissot, the value of slave labour to the State is a secondary consideration: like Beccaria, he is convinced that the barbarities of the scaffold are unnecessary, since life imprisonment can be made into a much more effective deterrent. Condemned criminals would be obliged to appear publicly and on several occasions to be exposed to the view and indignation of their fellow citizens before being sent to the mines, where expeditions of young folk would call regularly to see their fate and scorn them.[140] Thus Brissot, one of the most advanced reformers, upholds the argument from deterrence with a vehemence akin to that of the reactionary lawyers. Idealists, pursuing logical reorganizations, can be blind to the new harshness which they introduce in place of the old. Servan, who vied with Brissot in his hatred of capital punishment, speaks of imprinting a precise picture of every punishment, indissolubly attached to the appropriate offence, on the brain of every citizen, on 'les molles fibres du cerveau'—one wonders what grim compulsions would have to operate to bring so many minds to order. Indeed, Mably asked if those who opposed the death penalty were, in fact, less humane than those who supported it,[141] and Lacretelle questioned the justice of keeping men alive solely to make them suffer.[142] Brissot's murderers doing hard labour under the gaze of patriotic youth—a cameo from a Spartan utopia or from More's—caught the imagination of the new legislators of France during the Revolution. In May 1791, Lepelletier de Saint-Fargeau, reporting to the National Assembly in favour of the abolition of the death penalty, reproduced Brissot's scheme almost to the letter. Criminals, laden with chains, and with their name and judgement affixed above the door of their dungeon, would be exhibited weekly to the people as a fearful example. Another speaker added the scriptural precedent, for when God forbade the slaying of the murderer Cain, he marked him on the forehead as a sign of perpetual reprobation.[143]

Death penalty or no, there was agreement that the fate of a criminal was to be made into a public spectacle: this followed from the view, common to both reactionaries and reformers, of punishment as a deterrent. If men are regarded as free agents, the deterrent view must be qualified by moral considerations, for motive will be the blameable element in criminal conduct, rather than its effects. Since the structure of order was so fragile, there was good reason to give priority to the effects—to the suppression of dangerous consequences—and this tendency was encouraged among reformers by a fashionable current of thought which cast doubt on human freedom.[144] There was Diderot, thinking chiefly of hereditary factors and inextricably entangled in all the problems concerning the freedom of the will; there was Helvétius, preoccupied with the conditioning force of education and *milieu*; and La Mettrie reducing men to predetermined products of seed and soil like vegetables, so that to him the notorious robber and murderer Cartouche was 'made to be Cartouche' and could be no other. There were writers on the fringe of determinism but clinging to moral responsibility like Voltaire, and others, like d'Holbach, who coolly accepted the end of moral responsibility altogether. In so far as these thinkers accepted any kind of determinism, their ideas of punishment were bound to be affected: d'Alembert put the case clearly—if men are free, punishment is both necessary and just; if they are not free, it is necessary only. In the last resort and, maybe, without any moral condemnation, there will have to be some amputation, some maladjusted individual will have to be removed from society. If men are what they are because of some mysterious predestination, then we say to them, when we are dissatisfied with their conduct, that they are also predestined to punishment. If, as is more likely, they are the product of conditioning factors subject to manipulation, the levers of punishment must be adjusted to produce the social type most useful to our common life. So we come back, albeit with a more humane and enlightened imagination, to the calculus of pain as operated by the lawyers of the *ancien régime*, who had believed that they were dealing with free agents. Whether man was free or psychologically determined, there were arguments to justify the crowds in the place de Grève, the weekly prison peepshow in Le Peletier's abolitionist utopia, and the *tricoteuses* at the foot of the guillotine.

Has the State the *right* to execute a murderer? No, said Beccaria: this is an act of warfare, for it is impossible to imagine anyone surrendering to society the right to dispose of his own life. This argument went further than its author realized, for it is equally impossible to imagine anyone accepting in advance a sentence to lifelong slavery—Beccaria's chosen deterrent. In logic, all severe punishment becomes an act of warfare, an unwelcome conclusion to the men of the eighteenth century, who were groping their way towards an understanding of the 'consent' behind all government.

Diderot and Muyart de Vouglans agree in preferring Rousseau to Beccaria at this point. 'It is because life is the greatest of all possessions that each person consents to society having the right to take it away from him who takes it away from others,' says Diderot.[145] Mably neatly redefined the original transfer which must be postulated as the foundation of society's right to use the death penalty: I have surrendered to the magistrate, not the right over my own life, but the right I have, in the state of nature, to kill anyone who tries to kill me.[146] Apart from Mirabeau,[147] that ambitious desperado of the reform movement, Beccaria found little support in France for his reduction of the execution of criminals to an act of warfare. True, Marat doubted the right of existing States to enforce the death penalty, in view of 'the unjust origin of all the governments of the earth', but given a free and egalitarian people, he was willing to keep the executioner at work for premeditated murder, parricide, and treason.[148]

Biographers point the contrast between Robespierre's opposition to the death penalty before the Revolution, and his advocacy of the Terror. But there is no inconsistency. Beccaria had accepted death as the appropriate punishment for those who threaten the security of the State, and virtually all the French abolitionists follow him. Like the jurists of the *ancien régime*, they thought of punishment as primarily deterrent, and thus it seemed axiomatic that rebels should be deprived of all hope of rescue by fellow conspirators. Treason would never prosper, not only for semantic reasons, but because the traitors would not be there to see it. The scaffold, said Servan, is our final weapon 'to rid us of those rare criminals whom we cannot keep in our midst without danger'.[149] Voltaire would use it if there was no other way of saving the lives of the greatest number; it would be like killing a mad dog.[150] Brissot and Pastoret make death the punishment for treason—for 'secret conspiracies . . . tumultuous uprisings', said Pastoret, 'which menace the fatherland so long as the agitators are not executed'.[151] He was writing at the dawn of a new era, and the earlier abolitionists had been looking forward to some great reform. When they wrote of treason they had in mind, not just the *salus populi suprema lex* of the Roman history which had been the staple of their studies in the *collèges*, still less of Diderot's cynical version of it: 'the supreme law is the . . . safety of those who govern the people'.[152] It was not just their country as it was, but as it would be, that they were protecting, and this gives a new edge to their hatred of conspiracy. On behalf of his utopia, his dream of a free and egalitarian nation, Marat goes to the verge of asking for the retention of the cruelties of the scaffold which had darkened the legal system of the *ancien régime*. For the man who would set fire to ships, arsenals, archives, or public edifices, he wanted death, and 'que l'appareil de son supplice soit effrayant, et qu'il en soit témoin lui-même'.[153] This sombre eloquence—though no one could have foreseen it—was one day to find an application to the monarch himself. The idea of the sacredness of the person of kings, which had justified the torments of Damiens, went on into the Revolution in the constitutional concept of 'inviolability', and Marat was to lead in demanding its redefinition by a trial and a sentence of death. 'How should the former monarch be judged? With pomp and with severity. Far from us those false ideas of clemency and generosity by which the national vanity is flattered!'[154] And it is sad to see how, in the debate on Louis's 'treason', the darker side of Beccaria and Brissot's theme of exemplary slavery in place of the death penalty was appropriated by the lunatic fringe of hatred in sansculotte rhetoric about tyrants exhibited in cages as object-lessons to the people of Europe.[155]

More and more, the writers of the Enlightenment showed an awareness of the need for social reform to remove the causes of crime. Beccaria had blamed excessive taxation, the paternalistic family, and the bias of the laws as the source of violence in society.[156] A government which made its people happy and prosperous, said d'Holbach, would not need to devise cruel punishments for murderers.[157] The rich who made the laws, said Voltaire, should study what to do to help the poor before calling in the executioner: if they set up discreet institutions for fallen girls, for example, there would be no infanticide.[158] Boucher d'Argis pointed out the injustice of making domestic theft by a servant a capital crime, such offences being most often the result of the contrast between the luxury of the master and the poor wages he pays to his employees.[159] Marat wanted an egalitarian, puritanical reform of society—the land shared out, education available to all, old people well cared for—thereafter the legislator would be able to return to the best traditions of classical antiquity, and to use the laws to reward virtue rather than to suppress vice.[160] 'Man is not born an enemy of society,' wrote Brissot, 'it is circumstances that make him such—poverty and misfortune.' Equalize fortunes, moderate taxation, give moral education to all, simplify the laws so they can all be put in a slim volume as cheap to buy as a catechism, and the vast majority of citizens will become worthy and law-abiding.[161] Some pages of Brissot came near to making criminology a social science, more especially when he sees that many criminals need re-education or medical assistance.[162] Some atrocious crimes, said La Mettrie (he was speaking of a woman who had killed and eaten her children), can only be the result of mental derangement; in these cases, the judges should not be lawyers, but experienced medical practitioners—such indeed, as La Mettrie was himself.[163] In this respect as in others, Landreau de Maine-au-Picq is the most generous of the humanitarian reformers, since he regards all criminals as mentally disturbed people: 'all criminals are really mad, and ought to be treated as such by those that are sane.'[164] Even so, to all these writers deterrence is the primary object of punishment, and to all except Landreau, the death penalty remains as the indispensable weapon to deal with conspiracies against the State.

To what extent was the sentencing policy of the magistrates of the parlements and the other great lawcourts influenced by the ideas of legal reformers? According to Roederer, an informed observer, the courts became more merciful during the last decade before 1789.[165] He was probably right, though it is difficult to confirm this impression with entirely convincing statistics. The policies of the magistrates cannot be analysed in isolation, for criminal conduct was evolving, presenting new problems and dangers. In the latter years of the *ancien régime*, more offenders were being brought to trial; there were twice the number of entries in the prison registers of Aix for an average year in the early seventies as there had been in 1750.[166] In Normandy, Languedoc, and within the jurisdiction of the parlements of Lille, Valenciennes, and Flanders, there is clear evidence of a switch from the predominant crimes of violence of the early century to crimes against property later on,[167] and there is also evidence of theft becoming

405

more professionally organized. Society was becoming more civilized, better policed, more property-conscious, while on their side, the criminal classes were developing their own brands of efficiency. Maybe there was a greater pressure towards dishonesty as the increasing population outran the resources of certain areas. Certainly, there was an increase of vagabondage, and a growing unease among the propertied classes. In face of a rising criminality of a new kind, the Parlement of Toulouse seems to have inclined towards severity, and the parlements of northern France towards leniency.[168] The Parlement of Flanders condemned 39 to death out of the 160 people convicted between 1721 and 1730, but between 1781 and 1790, out of 500 criminals, only 26 received capital sentences.[169] The Parlement of Paris increased its death sentences in 1760–2, but thereafter—perhaps because of a developing social awareness—greatly reduced them (there were 7 only in 1787). On the other hand, it sent many more convicted felons to the galleys.[170] Here, it might be supposed, is an intention to try the reforming schemes of exemplary penal servitude instead of capital punishment, though so grim was the existence of a *galérien* that it was more like an alternative way of giving effect to the death penalty than anything else.[171] Unless he was of an unusually strong constitution, a man sentenced for life to the galleys did not last long. Of the 4,000 convicts at the base of Marseille in 1748, barely 200 had been sentenced before 1720, and over 2,500 had been locked into their fetters within the last eight years (not all were serving life sentences of course, but most were serving long terms, and the end of a term was no guarantee of release).[172] The spectacle of the *galériens* being dragged on their 'chain' through the countryside and the stories of the living death that awaited them under the Mediterranean sunshine constituted, no doubt, a deterrent, but it would not be fair to Beccaria and his followers to suggest that they had anything so grim in mind. The truth was that the *ancien régime* had not reached the point of mental conviction at which there was a willingness to pay for, or a capacity to organize, penal establishments which would be both humane and effective. Things might have been different if Australia had fallen to the French and Brissot and Lafayette had been called in to organize a transportation system. There were prisons galore in France. Some of them were

pectacles of Piranesian horror—the underground dungeons of the
Citadel of Caen where, ankle deep in water, the fettered legs of the
inmates grew gangrenous; the iron cages of the Parlement of Paris
in which a man could not stand upright and could stay for years
without seeing sunshine, a fire, or a confessor;[173] *maisons de force*
where delinquent women and children and dubious characters
saved from a worse fate by family influence and a *lettre de cachet*,
rotted away among incorrigible vagabonds and debauchees. Other
prisons were symbolic ruins, furnished with doors with broken
hinges and windows without bars, and run by incompetent and
venal gaolers. But, apart from the galleys, where a technical necessity called for slave labour, the *ancien régime* had no prison
system directed to any other purpose than temporary incarceration,
no concept of an institution which could be used as an alternative to
the scaffold.

We have seen what life was worth to the reformers of the French
Enlightenment. To what extent did the legislation of the Revolution put their ideas into effect? The *cahiers* of 1789 give an impression of the extent to which these ideas had permeated society
—at least, among the literate classes. Some *cahiers* demand the
end of cruel punishments 'which revolt humanity', the reduction of
the number of capital crimes, and the equality of nobles and commoners on the scaffold. But only one asks for the abolition of the
death penalty, and that with the rider 'as far as may be possible'.[174]
The Code of 1791 went beyond the *cahiers* and was a fair reflection
of the lowest common denominator of reforming enthusiasm. A
new method of execution, the same for all classes was prescribed; it
was the least cruel method known to science (the good Doctor
Guillotin did not invent the fatal machine, but he conducted laborious experiments to refute the proposition that severed heads feel
pain).[175] Fairer procedures gave more guarantees to the innocent—
though, by contrast, there was no hope of pardon. Punishment no
longer extended to the family of a condemned man, whether by
confiscation, or through the concept of legal disgrace. Death was no
longer the penalty for offences against property, morals, or religion. But for murder and violence, capital punishment remained,
and executions were still to be public spectacles. And above all, the
new *régime* was as insistent as the old on the paramount necessity

of preserving the State, now made doubly sacred by the presumed consent of the people. The death penalty was retained for treason, for any attempt on the life of the prince, and also for attempts against the legislative assembly, the publication by a minister of a law which had not been voted, the illegal collection of taxation, and trafficking in parliamentary votes.[176] The legal highway to the Terror was being kept wide open.

Suicide

Suicide, an offence against God, was also a crime against society. Royal ordinances prescribed the bringing of the corpse before the secular judges for 'trial'; on conviction, it was to be dragged on a hurdle through the streets, exposed ignominiously hung up by the feet, then buried in an unmarked grave, or burned, and the ashes thrown to the winds. The judges of the *ancien régime* relished the observance of punctilio and the symbolic impressiveness of macabre ceremonies. The diarist Moreau has a story of a thief who hanged himself in prison during the law vacation; the body was pickled in brine until the magistrates returned, then, duly sentenced, was hanged again by the neck for the theft and once again by the feet for the suicide. There was an even more gruesome climax to the legal formalities when a pregnant girl killed herself. The executioner would rip out the infant for burial in the corner of the cemetery reserved for unbaptized children, before stringing up the mutilated body of the mother on the gallows. This is what happened at Château-Gontier in the spring of 1718 when Marie Jaquelin, six months gone with child, chose death rather than dishonour[1]—one would like to think that this is the last example of the kind.

A rational man, more particularly an unimaginative one, might not be deterred by the prospect of posthumous humiliations, though he might consider what would happen if his attempt was unsuccessful—maybe internment for a time in a madhouse or a monastery.[2] For would-be suicides who retained something of the spirit of family loyalty, there was, however, a more serious discouragement: on proof of the crime, all property was confiscated—there would be nothing for the heirs. This being so, when a person of substance was found dead in suspicious circumstances, pressure would be brought to prevent a verdict of suicide. When the corpse was 'tried'[3] before the royal judges (there were disputes as to whether the ecclesiastical courts should also be concerned), the heirs had the right to appoint a defence representative, and if they failed to do so, the magistrate would name a *curateur* to look after their interests. One trial was not necessarily the end: there could always be an appeal. And the presumptions of the lawyers would be on the side of the defence. We assume, said the jurist Rousseaud de la Combe, that a man must have wished to preserve his life, save his soul, avoid bringing dishonour on his family and ensure their inheritance.[4] As for the deaths of the poor, the laborious formalities necessary to establish the fact of suicide—inspection of the corpse by surgeons, the seal of the magistrates set on the brow, interrogation of possible witnesses, the drawing-up of a formal *procès-verbal*—might well be omitted, and the affair never come to the notice of the courts at all. Thus, suicides officially recognized as such were rare. Lebrun has found only two cases of dragging on the hurdle in all the Angevin parish registers of the seventeenth century, and only one in the eighteenth—this was in 1761.[5] Sometimes the attempt to hush up a scandal would arouse suspicions. In Paris, in 1726, Charles de la Fresnaye shot himself at the house of his mistress, the notorious Mme de Tencin; his fellow-magistrates of the Grand Conseil had the body spirited away for burial under cover of darkness, and this surreptitious proceeding led to sinister rumours, culminating in Mme de Tencin being sent to the Bastille, in spite of the influence of her brother, the bishop.[6] But later in the century, the police of the capital, as a matter of routine, exercised pressure on the *curés* to bury suspected suicides without question, to avoid scandal. A young priest of la Rochelle, who came to Paris, got into debt, then shot himself, 'was buried the next day at seven in the morning, by an order of the *lieutenant criminel* in the church of Saint-Côme, his parish', a diarist records in March 1767; a defaulting banker who blew his brains out two years later was given a funeral in the church of Saint-Gervais with some splendour—the ceremonial tapestries on the walls and no less than forty priests in the procession—though again, it was at an early hour to avoid publicity.[7] 'La police a soin de dérober au public la connaissance des suicides,' said Mercier in 1782; the *commissaire* comes in civilian dress ('sans robe') to make his investigation, and he instructs the *curé* to bury the corpse quietly.[8] Properly, the clergy ought to have denied their ceremonies to M. Deslon, the mesmerist (this was in 1786), for he died in a mesmeric trance and was technically a suicide from having risked his life in improper experiments, but the lieutenant of police sent a *lettre de cachet* to the *curé* of Saint-Eustache and the obsequies took place with unobtrusive decorum.[9] No doubt, in these cases, the ecclesiastical ceremonies were truncated formalities; the essential thing was that the obscene business of dragging the corpse on a hurdle and its shameful disposal were abandoned. Even when a man had killed himself to escape criminal proceedings, there was no question of reviving these odious observances. There was a dispute over such an affair at Versailles in 1772, but it concerned only the place where the body should be buried; one court ruled in favour of the corner of the cemetery of the church of Saint-Louis reserved for still-born children, another changed this to a wood away from the church, and a royal ordinance finally settled for the parish cemetery proper, though in a spot behind the gates.[10]

In a century of progressive refinement in the arts of civilization, the abandonment of the ceremony of dragging on the hurdle, which, on any showing, was of little use, does not require an explanation from the history of ideas. Even so, such an explanation can easily be given. The writers of the Enlightenment inherited a tradition, coming to them from classical antiquity through Montaigne and Charron,[11] which argued that man's dignity, his ability to evaluate himself in the scale of nature, made suicide justifiable. It was no disadvantage in their eyes if humanistic reflections of this kind provided opportunity to cast doubts on the teachings of the Church. This could be done by cautious manœuvre, as in Maupertuis's *Essai de philosophie morale* (1750). Clearly, he was principally concerned to praise the ideals of the ancient Stoics and, in the last resort, to defend the proposition: 'As soon as the total of evils surpasses the total of goods, nothingness is to be preferred to existence.'[12] Yet he claims to be saying this solely from the point of view of the 'natural man'. Christianity, with its threat of eternal punishment and its overwhelming insistence on duty, has a different scheme to take care of our ultimate happiness; unenthusiastically and formally, this is taken to be superior. With d'Alembert, Maupertuis's trick of manœuvre becomes an end in itself; his discussion of suicide in his essay on the duties of the citizen[13] is not a serious philosophical argument, but simply an excuse for ridiculing revealed religion by relentlessly plastering it with ironical deference. As it happens, he says, the only people which have unequivocally condemned self-destruction are those who have 'had the happiness to embrace the Christian religion'. 'Purely human legislators' do not try to interfere with a man's freedom once he has given to the fatherland all that his talents can offer; they think it pointless to invoke the laws to prohibit an action which Nature has made sufficiently difficult already, and which surely must be the result of madness or, in rarer cases, of supreme courage. While on the subject, d'Alembert drags in the question of monastic austerities, those 'macérations indiscrètes' which inevitably abbreviate the life span. For reasons which we must accept with humble adoration but which are incomprehensible to us, the Supreme Being has 'chosen certain of his created beings as victims who must sacrifice themselves in his service'—thus, a few anchorites may have to go off, uselessly, into the desert. But only a few; generally speaking, Christianity properly understood will join with Reason in condemning this lingering form of suicide.

In contrast to d'Alembert's clumsy sarcasm, Montesquieu's defence of suicide in the *Lettres persanes*[14] is wholly serious. Unlike d'Alembert, he was a professional ironist, but deliberately refrained from using this gift in the interest of sober argument. As an aristocrat, a magistrate, and a *philosophe* he was concerned to proclaim the pre-eminent right of the individual. It is absurd, he says, to tie ourselves to the 'order of Providence'; nor should we regard ourselves as bound by the terms of a convention with society from which we no longer draw advantage. Do other people really wish to profit from 'ce partage inique de leur utilité et de mon désespoir?' The book ends with a practical illustration of the theme, for Roxane kills herself, in despair, but achieving heroic stature by her courage, and revenging herself on Usbek, who receives her message of defiance from beyond the grave. Paradoxically, though we can affirm ourselves by such acts of self-destruction, the real reason we forbid suicide, says Montesquieu, is because of our overwhelming pride, our unwillingness to admit our insignificance

412

in a vast universe where a hundred million worlds like ours sweep on with their myriad populations—'we imagine that the annihilation of a being as perfect as ourselves would degrade the whole of Nature'.

Voltaire's defence of suicide, like Montesquieu's, implies the recognition of our humble, insignificant place in the universe. Lost in the infinities of space and time, we should not boast of our place in the divine economy: we are rats on a ship bound for an unknown destination, mice scuttling in the cracks of a castle built for a mysterious purpose beyond our understanding. God does not need to keep a strict account of what men do; he will not notice if a soldier deserts his post.[15] It is tempting to go on from this position to a contrasting one of Promethean defiance, elevating the stature of man as he exercises his power of self-determination. Yet, even in his tragedies, Voltaire stops short of this antithesis. His heroines, proudly demanding the right to decide their own fate, are not, in reality, acting through pride—they are demanding a reasonable freedom to make a decent escape from intolerable circumstances. By death, Idamé would avoid the embrace of the tyrant, emulating the Japanese who live in freedom and choose the hour of their death ('vivent libres chez eux et meurent à leur choix'). Alzire regrets having deserted the kindly, undemanding pagan gods who would have allowed her to put an end to her days—what crime can it be to hasten the inevitable moment which God prepares for us all?—'Faut-il boire à longs traits la lie insupportable?'[16] Indeed, there is an element in Voltaire's defence of suicide which is rare among his free-thinking contemporaries. Philosophers may show lofty defiance in face of God's indifference, the Stoic elect may go proudly to their doom, but most men and women die sadly, defeated, and we can but show them pity. *Candide* is full of sardonic special pleading, but there is sincerity and force in the reversal of the common-sense judgement that it is cowardly to give up when life is unbearable; on the contrary, our clinging to life in these circumstances is ridiculous: the outcome of 'one of our most baneful tendencies'.[17] When l'Ingénu, in despair at the death of Mlle Saint-Yves, asks Gordon if anyone has a right to prevent him killing himself, the good Jansenist priest avoids inflicting on his friend 'ces lieux communs fastidieux' about the providential order and sentries who are not allowed to desert their post.[18] In fact, in his heart, Gordon always believed that suffering serves some higher purpose, and to the end of his life he remained in this conviction. Alas! says Voltaire in conclusion, how many good folk have proved the contrary! The truth is, suffering is useless: 'Malheur n'est bon à rien!' At this point, Voltaire rejects not only the Christianity of his day, but also all possible reinterpretations of it; he was the prince of ironists, but his unbelief arose, not from his scepticism, but from his despair.

There are, of course, suicides and suicides: the Enlightenment's defence of the right to self-destruction was not absolute; a man exalts himself by acting as a free agent, but only if he is acting rationally. At the highest point of the scale of rationality, or very near it, comes the argument of patriotism. Christian martyrs courted death and refused to save themselves—the same right, perhaps, should be allowed to citizens passionate for the honour of their fatherland. The *collèges* of France founded the education of youth on the study of Latin literature and the history of ancient Rome. During the century, there was some turning to French literature, more especially of the age of Racine, and to the national story of France; even so, from the repetitions of the class-room, from prize-essay competitions, from exercises in rhetoric, and from institutional theatrical performances,[19] the Frenchmen of the future were indoctrinated with the heroic standards of classical antiquity. From an early age they became familiar with the stories of the famous men who had put an end to their own lives with magnanimous or ostentatious gestures—Curtius, Decius, Mark Antony, Cato—and the heroic women—Dido, Cleopatra, Lucrece, Portia the wife of Brutus, and Arria who showed her husband how easy it was to drive home the sacrificial blade; they knew too of the mass suicides of the defeated—how German women slew their children and themselves because Marius refused to spare their honour, how Philip of Macedon, after taking Abydos, left its inhabitants three days' freedom to kill themselves.[20] Of course, familiarity does not always breed approval, and the portentous doings of antiquity could easily appear (as Diderot said of the classical tragedies staged in the *collèges*) ridiculous or boring.[21] The vague but general approval which the *philosophes* showed for the Roman way of suicide was essentially an inspiration which came to them from Montesquieu, the inaugurator of the comparative study of social ends and motivation. In his *Grandeur et décadence des Romains* (1734), Montesquieu lauded the proud spirit of the city on the banks of the Tiber, and the 'natural and obscure instinct' which made the ancient Romans love what was worthy in themselves more than mere life. They had civilized laws: they did not refuse burial to suicides, nor did they confiscate their inheritances. Citizens would kill themselves to escape the degradation of slavery, to avoid being dragged in the triumphal procession of the victor, to maintain their family honour, and, above all, to defy tyrants and serve the fatherland. On the vast stage of the Roman world they acted out their parts, enjoying the advantage of being able to call an end to the drama at the moment which suited them—a supreme privilege for the artist in living. Men have become less free, says Montesquieu, less courageous, less inclined to great actions than in the days when they were conscious of their power to control their own destinies to the exclusion of all external authority.[22]

As the century went on, a leaven of political liberty stirred in France, and the word 'republic', if not the thing, was becoming associated with public spirit and liberal feelings. For the republican ideal, Rome provided one obvious great hero whose career was fully and authentically documented—Cato, who killed himself in protest against Caesarean tyranny. 'The situation of a man who, jealous of liberty, prefers a glorious death to a shameful slavery can excite in the soul no other sensations but astonishment and admiration,' said the writer of a tragedy on the death of Cato in his preface of 1768.[23] In the same year Grimm, who was campaigning to ban suicide from the stage, made one exception: 'If you wish to interest me [in this theme],' he said, 'let it be Cato disembowelling himself because he sees his destiny as bound up with that of his country.'[24] Such reckless patriotism was universally applauded, but it was unreasonable to expect anyone to fall upon his sword as a protest against the mild and hesitant despotism of Louis XV and Louis XVI. Admirers of the ancient Stoics had to search on the exotic and violent fringes of civilization for conditions which suited the patriotic suicide. Red Indian stoicism and the Japanese code of honour drew attention, but the only convincing contemporary example was the case of the

African slaves who killed themselves (by the trick of stifling themselves with their tongue) on the journey across the Atlantic—'a ship which leaves Guinea is full of Catos, who prefer to die rather than to survive the loss of their liberty'.[25]

In spite of the shadow of the *donjon* of Vincennes, the *philosophes* faced none of the rigours or threats to liberty of the Atlantic passage; to them, Cato's heroism was a theoretical talking point, a rhetorical device, a *cliché* from *collège* days. But to writers radical in thought yet submissive to authority, attempting to convert power to their way of thinking, not to subvert it, there was another heroic figure of antiquity worthy of attention, and his case seemed to resemble their own. Our position, Diderot told Grimm in 1762, is that of Socrates.[26] The Athenian philosopher had taught what he believed to be true, regardless of charges of impiety; he had refused to escape or resist, and drank the fatal hemlock in obedience to the laws. The parallel with Socrates was welcome; in the second half of the century his death became a favourite subject for painters; the earlier tendency to find his family affairs comic was forgotten. Diderot made him his hero, his lay saint. Even Rousseau, aloof from the *philosophes* and regarding Christ as superior to the Athenian philosopher in the universality of his human sympathy and the divine intensity of his forgiveness, nevertheless identified himself with Socrates—a misunderstood and persecuted genius. Significantly, Voltaire had reservations. Admittedly, here was an archetypal victim of intolerance to be exalted, and a religious genius to challenge the uniqueness of Jesus of Nazareth, 'le Socrate de la Galilée'. Yet Voltaire was never taken in by resounding phrases, even his own, and he had doubts about this 'Athenian babbler' and found a hint of 'charlatanism' in his reliance on his inner 'demon'. Besides unlike the sophisticated Sage of Ferney, Socrates had refused to conform, and had brought gratuitous trouble to his friends and to his cause by his obstinacy and relentless arguing. Voltaire had more sympathy with the suicide of despair than with serenely accepted martydom, and no sympathy at all (except for polemical purposes) with martyrdom that was unnecessary.

When the Revolution came, and its hopes were engulfed by war and the Terror, the example of Socrates gave way to the example of Cato, and the neo-Stoic doctrine of patriotic suicide became a refuge for leaders who were rejected by the faction in power yet remained true to revolutionary principles. Of the outlawed Girondins, Clavière and Condorcet killed themselves in prison, Barbaroux wounded himself but was carried off to the guillotine, and Pétion, Buzot, Ledon, Roland, and Valazé ended their own lives. Later, Jacques Roux the *enragé* stabbed himself in prison, succeeding at the second attempt; as a priest and an egalitarian reformer, he looked forward to immortality, to the 'happy destiny reserved for the friends of liberty'. At Thermidor, when the Government forces burst into the Hôtel de Ville, they found Lebas with a bullet through his head and Robespierre with his jaw shattered by a pistol shot, though Saint-Just stood there calmly waiting to be taken. Of the 'martyrs of Prairial', the Montagnards sent by the Thermidorian Convention before the Military Tribunal, Rühle stabbed himself before trial and the six others did so after conviction, so that Bourbotte, Goujou, and Romme died together, Soubrany expired on the way to the guillotine, and the wounded Duquesnoy and Duvary remained alive to be dragged up the steps of the scaffold. Later still, Babeuf and Darthé, the egalitarian conspirators, killed themselves in prison to escape public execution. What part did Stoic ideology play in their deaths? Pétion and Buzot starving in a lonely wood, Roland tramping in the rain after hearing the news of his wife's execution—these are deaths from sheer misery; perhaps others were. We know most about the martyrs of Prairial and their collective decision.[27] They were too proud to argue in self-justification; like Scipio, they would point to the nation as they had found it and as they had left it, or like Socrates, they would simply say they had done their duty—'j'ai travaillé pendant tout le cours de la Révolution; je n'ai rien à ajouter' (Soubrany). It was against their conscience to denounce the present regime: they merely wished to have different, honest men put in charge of it. The processes of revolutionary justice, which they had applauded, ought not to be sullied by proceedings against the true heroes of freedom—'cela fait frémir la nature et la liberté' (Goujon). In her last letter to her father, Charlotte Corday had accepted the guillotine because she knew that, in her own eyes, she was innocent: 'it is crime, not the scaffold that dishonours'. By contrast, the Montagnards, conditioned to regard the fatal machine as a peculiar national institution to eliminate traitors, did not accept it lest posterity confound them with the guilty. 'La palme immortelle due aux amis de la patrie morts en la défendant' would be more secure if posterity looked back on their deaths as battlefield casualites associated with specific incidents of warfare, rather than an addition to the statistics of the Terror, extra heads in the basket. They were legislators, and a legislator was not an ordinary citizen who took his place in the senate of the Republic by virtue of the electoral process; he was a being endowed with Rousseauistic 'virtue', an embodiment of the ideals of the nation. Romme, exact and puritanical, the fervent advocate of the simple life and of a civic and patriotic education, killed himself as an object-lesson: 'his suicide was the last action of a great member of the *Comité d'Instruction publique*'.[28] Cato was not far from all their thoughts. Their example, said Bourbotte, would be added to his to show how 'free men ought to make their escape from the scaffold of tyranny'. The 'martyrs of Prairial', were making a collective decision, and this circumstance tended to bring out the 'heroic' motives that can be openly avowed. Babeuf, who had never sat in the seats of the mighty, and had simply wanted equality to be taken seriously, killed himself without senatorial posturing. Like the rest of us, he merely sought the easiest way out, and was sad to find that it was so painful. 'Je ne croyais pas qu'il m'en coûterait autant pour voir la dissolution de mon être,' he complained.

Strictly speaking, the death of a patriot was not a decisive test case for the legitimacy of suicide: those who cited examples of this kind never knew quite how to separate them from instances of gallant soldiers leading forlorn hopes, like Leonidas at Thermopylae. A more instructive case would be one in which the motivation was strictly personal, directed to self-satisfaction. Alone, and with the bitter memory that of the two women he had truly loved, one was dead and the other married to a rival, Restif de la Bretonne put the issue clearly. 'Ah! Suicide is natural to a thinking being when the balance of misfortune has sunk too low and made pain prevail over the pleasure of existence.'[29] Yet he waited, lived on, and love came again—disastrously as it happened—for mathematical calculations of probability are not everything; who knew what unexpected healing, what unlikely new hope the passage of the years might bring? But this optimistic argument would wear out; sooner or later, the incurable illness would come, whether in some specialist form or simply as the irreversible decline of life itself. The arguments against anticipating the inevitable lost their force progressively as the inevitable drew nearer. There were more ways of dealing with old age than eighteenth-century France recognized. Travellers' tales and anthropological curiosities fascinated the eighteenth century, and were useful to the opponents of Christianity as providing embarrassing comparisons in the field of social morality. What was one to make[30] of Pliny's stories of the old men of northern barbarian tribes who jump into the sea from overhanging rocks, 'having no pleasures left to look forward to', of aged Ethiopians who allow themselves to be tied to wild bulls, of the natives of Amboyna who eat their tired and failing relatives out of charity, and the Congolese who jump on them until life is extinct, of the Formosans who, with a more genial ingenuity, choke them with strong drink, the Hottentots who give a sumptuous feast in honour of a declining senior citizen before abandoning him in a hut in the wilderness, and the legendary islanders who have special officials called 'Caritans' to perform the noble duty of stifling the aged 'to prevent them suffering'. Was Nature, under repulsive outward forms, conveying a message to the over-civilized eighteenth century? The abbé de Chaulieu, who expressed so many religious, pagan, and sceptical sentiments in coldly elegant verse, warmed into sad sincerity when he wrote of the sufferings which advancing years imposed on him, and of his vain yearnings for release:

> Pourquoi n'osé-je rompre une cruelle chaîne
> Qui m'attache à la vie, et m'éloigne du port?
> Il faudrait au moins que le sage,
> Quand il le veut, eût l'avantage,
> D'être le maître de son sort.[31]

In 1756, Rousseau had been tempted by Chaulieu's idea, and reflected that the wise man—'le sage'—would voluntarily relinquish his earthly tabernacle 'without murmuring or despair', once he felt that 'Nature and Fortune' had given him clear directions. (One may speculate about this emphasis on 'le sage'—did the writers of the Enlightenment who justified suicide really regard every man as competent to choose the moment of departure?) But in the *Nouvelle Héloïse*, milord Edouard's argument to Saint-Preux is a powerful refutation of the right of self-disposal. Suicide is defensible only if a man has become useless to his fellow citizens and to humanity. The extreme example of his uselessness is when persistent and incurable pain has taken over the bodily existence, so that a man is no longer a man; he is dehumanized, the soul is no longer present, death is a merciful release, and suicide a laudable act. Between 1761 and 1763, there are three references in Rousseau's correspondence to his own sufferings as bringing him very nearly into the exceptional category allowed by milord Edouard, so that it would soon become 'virtuous' to commit suicide, 'être rien, ou être bien'. But from 1764, Rousseau no longer thought of the possibility of suicide; he is ill, and does not wish to resort to medicines to prolong life, but he will not take any action to shorten it—he will leave all to Nature: 'laissons faire jusqu'au bout la nature, elle fera tout pour le mieux'.[32]

In practice, the formal way of dying imposed by religion and society put every obstacle in the way of an easy escape from life. There was an easy way, if the doctors dared to use it, but the story of the death of Mirabeau,[33] an unbelieving patient with an unbelieving doctor, shows how rarely it was taken. Cabanis, from meeting Mirabeau in July 1789, had been his friend and physician, treating the manifold infirmities of his massive frame with bleedings, purgatives, mustard plasters, musk pills, and Spanish fly. When he knew death was certain, the great tribune sent for all his friends, and spent his last hours in feverish conversation, as if to cram the affections of a lifetime into a brief and hurried compass. At sunrise on his last day Mirabeau said, 'We must crown ourselves with flowers and listen to music playing as we enter into the sleep from which there is no awakening.' There were no flowers or music, but he begged not to be allowed to suffer useless pain. Spasms of agony came and went throughout the day; they told him opium was on the way from the apothecary's, but it never came. 'On me trompe!' he cried, and his last words were a reproach: 'Have you not promised me to spare me the agony of such a death? Do you wish me to go regretting that I ever gave you my confidence?'

It is easy for casuists to accommodate the natural wish of the dying to escape unnecessary pain, but even the most unorthodox of moralists must hesitate before proposing to defend suicide over disappointment in love. According to one of Crébillon's characters (in 1732), the time was past when even a sympathetic tear would be shed over the destructive folly of star-crossed lovers: 'Vous savez aussi bien que moi que la plus sotte preuve d'amour qu'on puisse donner est de se tuer.'[34] After all, this was an age and country where there was a satisfactory alternative—in literature at any rate—masochistic, ostentatious, and calculated to wound the heart of ruthless parents and unresponsive or unfaithful lovers. The austere cloisters of Trappist monasteries or closed orders of nuns were a refuge where a life-in-death could be lived as a protest against family tyranny, a proof of sincerity to drive the unfeeling to remorse. If, at the end, the lovers were momentarily reunited as one of them lay dying on straw and ashes, amidst lugubrious religious chants,[35] this was a more dramatic denouement than an ordinary deathbed scene. But claustral tragedy was psychologically unrealistic, since it betokened a long-drawn-out will to self-immolation which was either improbable or truly religious in inspiration; for love-stories, gestures more immediately spontaneous and passionate were needed, so suicide could come into its own again. Besides, the great tide of *sensibilité* was rising. As in many other respects, the *Nouvelle Héloïse*, brilliant and moving in its ambiguities, reflected and inspired a change in attitude towards the theme of suicide for love. Saint-Preux dreams of the pleasure of thwarted lovers dying in each other's arms, but milord Edouard persuades him to stay alive. In his second preface to the novel, Rousseau seems to imply that his hero ought to have been less dramatically sensation-seeking in the first place, or less easily dissuaded in the second.[36] Yet though Saint-Preux talks of dying for love, it is really someone else who does so. Julie, in a sense, allows herself to die after rescuing her son from drowning. She has done her duty to her husband, and now looks forward to the home of her heavenly Father, where she will be reunited to the only man for whom she had ever had passionate affection. 'N'ai-je pas assez vécu pour le bonheur et la vertu?' She had lived for duty: when death came it was the release of love.

Seven years after the publication of the *Nouvelle Héloïse* a double suicide of the kind Saint-Preux had dreamed of took place, sensationally, at Lyon.[37] Thérèse and her Italian lover Faldoni shot themselves in a chapel, in front of the altar, with a pair of pistols adorned with pink ribbons. Jean-Jacques Rousseau tried to obtain a piece of the ribbon and wrote an epitaph for the unhappy pair: they lived for each other, and died for each other, the laws condemn them, and unreflective piety notes their transgression, but men of feeling admire them and men of reason remain silent ('le sentiment admire et la raison se tait'). It was a nine days' wonder, of course. In 1777 a comic dramatist wrily lamented the degenerate age in which he lived, where husbands were no longer jealous and lovers no longer killed themselves because their passion was not reciprocated.[38] Even so, four years afterwards the lovers of Lyon became famous again in Nicolas-Germain Léonard's novel, cast in the form of their 'letters', reflecting the admiration of sentiment which Rousseau had invoked, but ending reason's silence by an eloquent defence of their transgression. According to Léonard's invention, Thérèse was not only forbidden to marry Faldoni because of his poor health (as in reality), she was also escaping from her father's orders to marry a scoundrel who was already responsible for the deaths of two women; she promised to watch over her friends in the afterlife and to seek pardon for her father; Faldoni, who was dying anyway, proclaims his fervent belief in God and immortality, and borrows from *Werther* (available in French translation from 1776) the idea that God will not upbraid a son for coming home unexpectedly; the *curé*, who had given the two lovers decent burial, is sure that a single moment of weakness will not efface a lifetime of virtue.

There were those who believed that Rousseau had condoned suicide (Mme de Staël was one of them), and after his death there was a rumour that he had killed himself. One wretched man, self-described as a 'victim of love', came in 1791 to Rousseau's tomb at Ermenonville to brood, and finally, in a near-by grotto, shot himself. A month later, in June, the municipal officer found the body; it was buried unidentified, and for the next decade an unknown woman came every year to visit the anonymous grave.[39] But Jean-Jacques's true place in the history of dying for love lies, not in the escape from living, but in the hope of reunion in the world beyond—the inspiration of the lovers of Lyon in the novelist's version of their fate. The Rousseauist Bernardin de Saint-Pierre's hero, Paul, wishes to live no longer once the cruel sea has claimed Virginie: 'since death is good, and Virginie is happy, I too wish to die'.[40] When, in the Revolution, the Girondins were proscribed, Mme Roland allowed herself to be arrested, and self-consciously died like Rousseau's Julie,[41] writing to Buzot (as to Saint-Preux) of their meeting again in a refuge where 'we can love each other without crime' and to her husband (as to Wolmar) asking pardon for deserting him. (Roland in his turn, going outside the pages of the *Nouvelle Héloïse*, on the news of her death burned his notes for a history of his political career, and stabbed himself by the roadside.) Most deaths for love (whether suicide or not) were indeed, like Roland's, acts of misery and despair, without benefit of literature. 'Que le funeste moment qui vous a entraîné vers moi,' wrote Julie de Lespinasse, ugly, emaciated, racked by tuberculosis and opium poisoning, to the comte de Guibert who had deserted her, 'm'a coûté de larmes, de douleur; enfin ma vie y succombe.'[42] It was a far cry from the deathbed of Julie de Lespinasse and her reproaches to that of the fictional Julie of the *Nouvelle Héloïse*, dying so radiantly.

Whatever currents swirled under the surface of Rousseau's writings—yearnings for escape and for new meetings in another world where hearts would be open, transparent to the gaze of understanding and love—he nevertheless gave to the Enlightenment its key argument against suicide. Milord Edouard advised Saint-Preux to wait, do a good action, then another, then another. This appeal to benevolence, to generous practical action as the way out of the trap of despair, was immediately applauded. How could anyone claim to have exhausted all pleasures or to have outlived all usefulness? It was always possible to find enjoyment and serve some purpose by helping a fellow creature. In 1770, the year of the two lovers of Lyon, Paris rejoiced in the story of the two Englishmen, one rich and one poor, who had been going to jump off Westminster Bridge; the poor man changed his mind when the rich man gave him money, and the rich man went cheerfully home in a glow of self-satisfaction.[43] The two-Englishmen story went on; by

1777 the prosperous one was trying to shoot himself in the 'forêt de Hydpark', and the pauper gathering sticks who seized the pistol from him was rewarded with a purse of gold.[44] Some writers put the idea of the primacy of duty to others in the formal terms of a contract with society. The theologian Bergier made the social pact his principal argument, bringing in God as the guarantor of reciprocity.[45] True, we may imagine circumstances in which the contract is broken by our countrymen deserting or injuring us, but, according to Delisle de Sales, we are still under an obligation, since we can always flee elsewhere and carry on fulfilling our duty to the whole human race.[46] To kill oneself is 'un larcin fait à la Société, et un attentat contre la Nature'. A dutiful citizen would also weigh some subsidiary considerations. By suicide he would cause embarrassment to his neighbours, might even leave them open to a mistaken accusation of murder—as had happened to the old Protestant Calas, broken on the wheel by the Parlement of Toulouse after his ne'er-do-well son had hanged himself.[47] A man who killed himself devalued human life, and taught others to be reckless with the lives of their contemporaries.[48] Even those glorious heroes of classical antiquity might have found a more useful way to serve the State and defy the tyrant—they might, for example, have turned their weapons against his guards.[49] When the theoretical postulates of the Enlightenment ran into contradictions, it was usually the argument from social utility, in one form or another, which tended to prevail. Thus, in practical circumstances, when there was no dramatic or literary necessity for lofty sentiments, Voltaire always advised delay. Given time for reflection, a sensible man would, he was sure, prefer living in an uncomfortable house to sleeping under the stars. Starving paupers and bankrupts apart, only unsociable characters (like Cato or Brutus, he added mischievously) ever do away with themselves. Activity is the antidote to suicidal tendencies—music, theatre-going, hunting or agreeable feminine company, and—best of all—work: 'd'avoir toujours quelque chose à faire'. Diderot, with his strong sense of family duty and solidarity to reinforce his civic zeal, was an uncompromising opponent of the spurious 'right' of the individual to abandon his responsibilities. Only those whose minds have been warped by idleness, luxury, superstition, or melancholia ever contemplate suicide. And the damage a man can inflict on his fellows by ending his life to please himself is incalculable. 'Il est rare qu'on ne fasse du mal qu'à soi': no one lives to himself alone.[50] The abbé Bergier's emphasis on the social argument against suicide is significant. God came in because, as Creator, he had ordained a system of mutual obligations: 'il a formé l'homme pour la société', therefore man cannot be an independent judge of the extent and duration of his duties. Nonnotte, another theologian, takes the same line, defining suicide as 'un vol fait au genre humain'.[51] Here was common ground—man's duty to society— where religious apologists and *philosophes* could meet. The theologians, of course, could not accept Voltaire's picture of an aloof deity who would not notice if a soldier left his post, nor could they be happy with the variant by which a sentry stricken with colic would be stood down by his officer—for where would we find God's officer in such a case?[52] They experienced some difficulty, however, in this particular argument from the story of the death of Samson,[53] crushed when he pulled down the pillars of the house of Dagon. Here, it had to be conceded, God *had* stood down one of his sentries, had allowed and encouraged (indeed, according to St. Augustine, inspired) him to slay himself—'c'était lui donner son congé'.[54] All this was true, but Samson was, after all, called to be a liberator of Israel, and his death was the indirect consequence of fulfilling his vocation, like that of a soldier in battle. As for the other Old Testament suicides, our accounts come from historians who had no obligation to comment on the facts they recorded: an entry in a chronicle does not imply moral approval. The theologians were unable to cite a specific prohibition of suicide in the Bible—Rousseau had pointed this out. But God has 'made man in his own image', and the only exceptions he has authorized to his general commandment, 'Thou shalt not kill' concern the execution of criminals for the sake of preserving the social order; the general spirit of the Scriptures, from Job to Jesus Christ himself, is one of resignation to God's will. There is a general assumption in the Bible that God has foreordained the time and place of our dying, from the foolish rich man who built new barns to Moses, God's chosen servant; in the book of Revelation, Christ holds the keys, not only of Hell, but also of Death.[55]

There was still a further difficulty, however, one which would occur more particularly to readers of Rousseau. We can hope for reunion with our friends in heaven, so if I am in despair in this life, why should I not yearn to join them there? And from yearning, is it not possible to go one step further—must I strive to postpone that moment, am I allowed no complicity in hastening it? Jean Dumas, whose *Traité du suicide* (1773) is the most effective defence of the Christian position, invents an ingenious reply.[56] It is a question of God's total design for the Universe. He has willed everything that happens. For this world, he has arranged for a balanced population, and we have no right to upset the divine calculations. More important still, God is building up a new society in heaven. Differing life spans, differing experience, differing pressures of suffering are producing a vast population of attractively varied characters to people the world to come. Children who die early will be there as examples of purity and responsive feeling free from intellectual complexities; those who have lived long will bring depth of maturity and experience; those who have been crushed by suffering, until at last they can be satisfied with the sole pleasure of the song of a bird or the sight of a passer-by at the window, will bring their intensity of concentration, their blend of humility and wonder. Dumas is at the opposite pole of reflection to Voltaire; the rats on the ship, the mice in the castle, the sentry at his post, all play their parts in a vast design enduring through all eternity.

Patriotic suicides, Dumas realized, were the strongest examples that could be urged against him, and Montesquieu, the advocate of Roman Stoicism, was his most dangerous antagonist; he therefore did his best to circumscribe the evidence from classical antiquity.[57] Virgil puts suicides in Hell, Plutarch disapproves of them, the Stoics were just a 'sect', and in the last analysis the only genuine heroes who killed themselves were Brutus and Cato. Dumas might have gone further. Other writers were more scathing about the Romans[58]—they used Pliny as evidence for faint-hearted imperial citizens who departed this life to escape stomach ache or migraine; from Greek history they dragged out the example of Zeno, who hanged himself at the age of ninety to avoid a painful operation on a broken finger; they cast doubt on the virtue of Lucrece ('un homme seul avec une femme ne la viole pas'), and declared Curtius ridiculous for jumping into the abyss (what does a crack in the ground matter?); they preferred Regulus to Cato and asked why the latter had not used his sword against the tyrant. Maybe the suicides of the ancient world, which only began after Caesar had made all men into his slaves, were proof of the general corruption of society—this was to be Chateaubriand's argument.[59] Maybe the whole parade of civic virtue was a sham; Lefebvre de Beauvry said outright that the Greek and Roman heroes were victims of their pride, and not of patriotism—'martyrs plus tôt de leur amour-propre, que de leur patrie'.[60]

Paradoxical support for sober moralizing of this kind came from two unexpected quarters—from La Mettrie's atheistic materialism and from the comic stage. La Mettrie[61] poured ridicule on the ancient Stoics, those professional exponents of refined unhappiness who defended suicide with 'captious sophisms' and 'poetic enthusiasm'. The world is full of ignorant fools who are happy; indeed, an animal finds more contentment in food and exercise, and a dose of opium can create more joy, than all the treatises of philosophers. We should not fear death, we should not long for it—we should live out our natural span, unthinkingly, with as much enjoyment as we can muster. La Mettrie's flat-footed hedonism was no threat to the presentation of Stoic doctrines in the theatre, for Parisian audiences loved elevated sentiments; however, they also had an acute instinct for detecting when the hair-line boundary between the tragic and the ridiculous had been infringed. The first production of *Mariamne* (1724) was wrecked by the cry 'La Reine boit' when the queen lifted the fatal chalice, so that Voltaire had to write out the suicide scene and have his heroine murdered. Burlesque playwrights liked a holocaust as a finale, as in *Lamentine* (1779) when, after a murder and three suicides, the guards all kill themselves; or better still, an anticlimax, as in *Criardus* (1780) where Trotas drops the fatal dagger and decides not to join his friends in death—he will learn to spell correctly, so he can write a suitable epitaph for them:

> Je ne me tuerai point, j'apprendrai l'orthographe
> Pour leur faire en beaux vers une belle épitaphe.[62]

Had not the Revolution come with its proscriptions to create a neo-Roman situation, the eighteenth century would hardly have been associated in our minds with the classical theme of patriotic suicide.

If the best precedent for self-destruction was the example of the ancient Romans, the best preservative against it was the spectacle of the melancholic and pathological conduct of the contemporary English. How is it, asked a writer of 1759, that the people which passes for 'the most intelligent, the most humorous, and the most philosophical of all the nations of the world' is subject to these mysterious seizures?—they cut their throats, hang themselves, blow out their brains and jump into rivers with perfect composure, with gaiety even.[63] To Frenchmen, the *sang-froid* of suicidal Englishmen was almost incomprehensible. 'Ils se tuent', said Montesquieu, 'au sein même du bonheur', without despair or other overwhelming motive to drive them. A triviality can bring them to the fatal decision—their country is ill-spoken of in the gazettes (a new variant of the patriotic suicide?), or the duty on spirits is raised. Or, like the famous 'comte de Peterborough', they just become bored with living.[64] A mid-century novel depicts a cynical English-woman, 'Miss Otwai', who deliberately exhausts all pleasures (true, she tries hard to extend the range, offering a prize of a thousand guineas to anyone who can invent a new one), then decides to end everything—'I have lived enough, M. le comte,' she writes to her French lover; 'consult your heart, and act like the English. Adieu!'[65] Other islanders kill themselves for no reason at all—cheerful one day and gone the next;[66] always accept a prop-osition to postpone a duel with an Englishman, for his recklessness may have arisen from sheer indifference, and twenty-four hours is a long time for him to remain available.[67]

How could one account for the lethal inconsequentiality preva-lent north of the Channel? It does not seem as if the French had statistical evidence to work on, though we know in retrospect that the suicide rate in Greater London in 1700–6 was double what it had been thirty years earlier, and by 1750 had doubled again.[68] What was available, however, was literary and anecdotal evidence. The English themselves admitted their own suicidal tendencies, and the gazettes from time to time produced startling examples; in 1732, there was the story of the fate of Richard Smith and his wife, who killed themselves and their child because of their 'inveterate hatred' of 'Poverty and Rags'. More significantly, the English press freely published defences of the right of self-destruction—true, mostly by libertines or dubious figures like the Italian exile Radicati, but one by a Dean of St. Paul's, John Donne, whose *Biathanatos* had a second edition in 1700. For the most part, French commentators did not examine the arguments of these writings or the implications of specific examples; taking for granted that England was 'le pays natal' of suicide, they sought for broad general explanations. Of his two basic explanations of human conduct, the pressure of the laws and *mores* of society, and the influence of climate, Montesquieu chose the latter, with a 'scientific' and medical elaboration.[69] The English climate led to 'un défaut de filtration du suc nerveux', that is, of the supposed liquid in the invisible channels of the nervous system which acts hydraulically, transmitting sensations to the brain and sending back responses. This is a painless affliction, for pain would arouse alertness and resentment, not a death wish. The *suc nerveux* ceases to percolate effectively, the 'driving force' of the 'machine' declines, and with it the will to live. By contrast, a writer of 1772 tried to move to a theory which Montesquieu, with his sociological bent of mind might well have thought of; the Reformation, he suggested, had been a disaster for the English, since the abolition of the confessional left no easy means of release for minds sunk in despair: 'le cœur, surchargé du poids de son amertume secrète, a besoin de se répandre'.[70] Another idea was that marriage provides the best alleviation of mental tensions, and there were too many bachelors in England.[71] And more light-hearted explanations could be given. The abbé Prévost cited (or invented) a medical expert who suspected the ill effects of coal fires, of eating half-cooked beef, or excessive indulgence in sexual intercourse; whatever the explanation, Prévost says, the result is 'a sort of frenzied delirium which is more common among the English than among the other peoples of Europe'.[72]

Complacently, the French had reflected on the tendency of the English to destroy themselves. Then, in the late sixties, a suicide wave began in Paris. This time, there was no great economic crisis, no onrush of bankruptcies, as during Law's Scheme forty years ago, to explain the phenomenon. The English word 'suicide' had already

429

been taken into the French language; Prévost had introduced it
as an 'anglicism' in 1734; J.-B. Racine had protested against it in
1741 (it sounded appropriate for a butcher killing a pig); but by
1762 the *Dictionnaire de l'Académie Française* had naturalized it.
(Previously, the French had used 's'homicider', 'se défaire', the latter
euphemism being favoured by the police and the lawcourts).[73] But
now, it was not just the English word, but the sinister English
fashion which was afflicting France. The men of the Enlightenment, who had been to anxious to proclaim the rights of the
individual, became discouraged. In 1768, Grimm had proposed to
banish the theme of suicide from the stage: 'il n'est ni moral ni
pathétique en réalité' (though he was willing to make an exception
for Cato). A perceptive journalist, he was moving ahead of public
opinion, for 1769 was the notorious year of the 147 officially
recognized suicides in the capital. According to Delisle de Sales, the
explanation had to be sought in defects of reasoning and follies of
fashion: 'the sophisms of some clever men and the example of some
great ones'.[74] In his private correspondence, Voltaire has nothing to
say of God's indifference or the individual's independence. Informed of the circumstances of a particular case—a logical young
man who shot himself after a calculation of good and evil—he
refused to draw serious inferences: suicide, said the Sage of Ferney,
with his usual common sense, is generally the consequence of a
hereditary disposition, a mental illness.[75] The next year, 1770, was
the year of the famous suicide of two lovers of Lyon, and the year in
which Paris took refuge in the story of the rich and poor Englishmen and the duty of benevolence. But giving away money and,
even, receiving it, did not prove to be effective deterrents. On 5
February 1772, a Parisian diarist noted, 'Examples of suicide multiply daily in our capital, where it seems that the peculiar character
and genius of the English in this matter is being adopted', and he
told specifically of the apprentice who shot himself because his
master refused him the certificate of good conduct which he needed
to emigrate to Prussia.[76] In 1773, the diarist recorded the suicide of
eight women in Paris within the space of a fortnight.[77] Then came
the great Christmas Day scandal.

On the evening of Christ's Nativity, two young dragoons[78] put
up at an inn at Saint-Denis. On Christmas Day they paid the bill in

advance, took a walk, and after a meal with two bottles of wine (the second one ordered as an afterthought), they shot themselves, leaving behind a 'philosophic testament'. There was nothing in this document about giving themselves over to 'the infinite mercy of the Sovereign Arbiter of our destinies', as had figured not so long ago in a much-talked-of farewell letter of a compulsive gambler;[79] the two soldiers said they had exhausted all pleasures, including those of doing good to their fellow men, so, tired of everything, they were renouncing everything. If there is a punishment for leaving life without permission, they would try to get a message of warning back: otherwise they advised all who were unhappy (and they suspected that this included almost everyone) to follow their example. They bequeathed their neckcloths to the serving girl, and left extra money for the second bottle of wine. So their account was settled. This unseasonable Christmastide message caused great alarm. Moralists had a fund of curious stories about eccentrics who had trivialized both life and death by killing themselves for punctilious or experimental reasons—Creech, who hanged himself because of a mistake in the footnotes to his commentary, and Robek, who had published a book in defence of suicide then pushed out to sea in an open boat to give a practical demonstration.[80] But now the insouciance and black complacency generally associated with the melancholic English had found a supreme example in Paris. The devout blamed the *philosophes* and the *philosophes* blamed the Government.[81] Louis XV, who was hypnotized by the idea of death, so that he continually tried to pass on to others the fears that haunted him, as if he were the bearer of some virus of despair, refused to accept the comforting hypothesis that the two dragoons must have been deranged, and turned his back on the courtier who proposed it.[82] From afar, prosaically, Voltaire said that if they had asked his advice he would have suggested postponement. To Mme du Deffand, the arguments of the Christmas Day testament appeared logically unassailable; nature alone could refute them, she said, and stop others from following their advice.[83] Her forebodings seemed to be confirmed in January of the New Year, when a young lawyer of the Châtelet blew out his brains for no apparent reason; a journalist regarded his death as a consequence of the example of the two dragoons, and foresaw more deaths to come: 'no week passes without a suicide'.[84]

In 1775, there were new apprehensions. A courtesan who had taken a lethal dose of opium but had been revived by the doctors, declared the moment of final departure to be one of 'delicious sensations'.[85] Two Englishmen left their country, the classical land of suicide, to kill themselves in Paris, where they would be encouraged in their resolution by the numerous examples France afforded.[86] In the next two years, other suicides with irrational or absurdly rational motivation were noted—men who were bored or disgusted with life, or who left behind comic verses or lengthy philosophical justifications.[87] More conventionally, in August 1778, the brother of the Holstein envoy shot himself after setting fire to the house in three places in an attempt to conceal his guilt.[88] 'Suicides,' said a journalist in March 1779, 'executed with an astonishing presence of mind, have been not infrequent in the last few years.'[89] A year before this, Rodolphe Louis d'Erlach used much more sensational language; there was, he said, an epidemic malady of self-destruction in France, a phenomenon which fitted awkwardly into the massive scheme of his *Code du bonheur*.[90]

The progress, in France, of the English vogue for self-destruction had coincided with the increase in the number of publications of an anti-religious and sceptical nature; Christian apologists did not fail to notice the fact. In a solid treatise of 1779, *Les Moyens propres à garantir les hommes du suicide*, Père Laliman, a Dominican, summarized the geographical, climatic, dietary, and medical explanations of previous writers and dismissed them as comparatively unimportant. The suicide wave, he held, must be due to 'an infinite number of moral causes'.[91] It had begun in England among a people excessively jealous of their liberty, resentful of authority, and prone to irreligious speculation; it had swept into France because Frenchmen had been foolishly enamoured of the fashions of the English and had absorbed their ideas from books and theatrical performances.[92] He did not deny the existence of a melancholic temperament causing groundless fears and magnifying all difficulties, but apart from exercise and baths he saw no medical way of treating it. The best we can do is to discourage violent passions, possessive love affairs, gambling, and the reading of dangerous ooks (children, for example, should read La Fontaine's fables, and ot *Cleveland*).[93] And, above all, we must confute the immoral octrine that the soul dies with the body. Even the crude barbarity vith which the corpse of a suicide is treated can be justified if it erves to remind us of the 'penalties of eternity'.[94] The Dominican's rgument was more complicated than most. To theologians—for xample, to Nonnotte in 1785[95]—the progress of unbelief necesarily leads to an increase in the suicide rate. Here was a crime gainst society which only God could punish—so how could things e otherwise?

The *philosophes*, obsessed as they were with the social conseuences of ideology, were bound to feel vulnerable before such harges. The pseudo-logical nature of the 'English' type of suicide vas also worrying; the men of the Enlightenment worshipped eason, and were unwilling to accept the existence of a sort of reasoning' which would justify the premature departure from fe's responsibilities. No doubt, with Chaulieu, they had been ending to think of 'le sage', the wise man taking a considered view f his duties and destiny, rather than offering the key of escape rom misery to all and sundry; but clearly, the multitude had verheard the debates of the intellectuals and had drawn simple onclusions dangerous to the social order. In this context, the iagnosis of heredity and mental illness as the explanation for uicide was welcome. In the year after Voltaire proposed it d'Holbach dopted it in his *Système de la Nature* (1770)—it enabled him at nce to defend suicides in principle yet to escape the blame for those vhich actually took place. After demolishing the whole idea of a act with society ('the bond is happiness: once this is severed, man free'), he asked if he was justified in preaching these apparently angerous maxims of freedom. Yes: 'It is not maxims which deternine men to take such a violent resolution. It is a temperament mbittered by sorrows, a constitutional defect, a breakdown of the nachine; it is necessity. Oppressed virtue must not be deprived of ne right to die—its last expedient.'[96] The last sentence, tacked on nconsequentially, is revealing. The maxims of freedom are necesary to preserve to the virtuous their right of escape from opression, to make their gesture against tyranny, but the great najority of suicides are cases of the breakdown of the physical and

mental machine—the theories of the *philosophes* have nothing to
do with them.

It was difficult to carry the argument further, as medical knowledge had not yet achieved a degree of scientific insight which could
verify or accommodate the explanation of suicide as a hereditary
disposition or some other form of mental illness. Throughout the
century, mental illnesses were classified and reclassified in logical
hierarchies based on their most elementary external manifestations; in the *Encyclopédie*, according to whether fever, coolness,
melancholy, or complete mental incapacity predominated (*frénésie,
manie, mélancolie, démence*); in the *Nosologie* of Boissier de Sauvages (1763), according to whether imagination, the appetites, the
judgement, or the total rationality seemed to be under attack
(*hallucinations, bizarreries, délires, folies anormales*).[97] The explanation for suicide was sought in the unprofitable domain of
frénésie, manie, mélancolie—the first connected with feverishness,
the second with the tensions and dryness of the nervous fibres,
especially those of the brain, and the last with the adulteration of
the liquids of the brain and the nervous system. From this theoretical basis an explanation (though, maybe, a tautologous one) could
be given of the more dramatic cases of suicidal madness. Thus, the
painter Le Moine, laden with honours by Louis XV for his decor-
ation of the Salon d'Hercule at Versailles, brooded constantly on his
imaginary unhappiness and finally ran himself through nine times
with his sword—this was defined as 'un accès de frénésie causé par
une noire mélancolie'.[98] Presumably, the deficiencies of the liquids
had touched off the desperate final fever, the transition from
melancholy to frenzy. But what caused the adulteration of the
liquids of the nervous system which brought on the original melancholy? A report to the Royal Society of Medicine in the 1780s, no
doubt taking into account the prevalence of suicide in France as well
as England, suggested alternative possibilities: either a hot climate
or excessive exercise (including sexual activity and masturbation)
might evaporate the volatile elements of the blood or, conversely,
cold and fog might block the pores and thicken the heavier
elements.[99] Here was a system to explain suicide the world over, in
any sort of climate, but it was so conveniently elastic that it was not
likely to carry conviction. The medical profession remained im-

prisoned in the old world of humours, fibres, nerves, bile, and assorted liquids. There was, in fact, a vague adumbration of the way ahead towards the psychiactric treatment of the future in the eighteenth-century attitude to *maux de nerfs* and *hystéries*, which were accepted as arising from purely mental causes, but the connection with suicide was not pressed home, and the growing awareness of the subtleties of the mental processes, which was characteristic of the age, was the achievement of the novelists, correspondents, and memoir-writers and not the medical schools.

The Enlightenment's defence of suicide was set in a literary and philosophical context. The thinkers of the eighteenth century were too much in love with life to applaud the unhappy souls who, in a frenzy, or with cold-blooded and pathological calm, exercised their theoretical right to call an end to the drama. It was amusing to challenge the Christian prohibition of self-destruction in the abstract, and edifying even when a small number of peculiarly harsh cases were in consideration. But everyday practice was a different matter. Even the most cynical world-weariness ought not, logically, to lead to suicide. 'Life is too short to kill oneself', Mlle de Scudéry had said, 'it is not worth the trouble to get impatient.' If life is futile, it is because it is brief, not because it is empty. Men are but grains of sand before God, reflected Loaisel de Tréogate's hero, proposing to jump off the tower of the château of Vincennes because Eugénie had been unfaithful. But he saw all Paris spread out below him and felt the fresh breeze touch his face—'le plaisir d'exister coulait dans toutes mes veines'.[100] To live at all, to be self-consciously oneself, was a pleasure, and the attractions of death were specious. As Grimm had said, suicide was 'neither moral nor pathetic in reality'. The writers of the Enlightenment affirmed the rights of the individual, yet at the same time they reaffirmed, with a new vigour and original arguments, the duty of the individual to the community. The Rousseau of the *Nouvelle Héloïse* is also the Rousseau of the *Contrat social*, and in any case the novel does not stand for the unfettered rights of the individual. 'Je veux mourir, je veux mourir . . . une âme grande peut avoir quelquefois cette fantaisie,' wrote Joubert in his notebooks.[101] The age wanted to free the mind, so that every imaginable possibility, good or evil, could be pursued to its logical conclusion—to get rid of the concept of the

'unthinkable'. This is what Sade did in one respect. But wher
suicide was concerned, the logical conclusion was confined—
almost—to the intellectual sphere. After claiming the right t
cherish the fantasy of self-destruction, Joubert added, 'il faut s'e
distraire'. The defence of suicide as the final glorification of in
dividuality was balanced by its virtual prohibition in the context c
the duties arising from the social compact and the manifold obli
gations of benevolence. Those who had the courage to deny th
binding force of the social pact were assuming intelligence an
public spirit in their readers. The 'English' type of suicide and th
contagion or fashion of self-destruction spreading in Paris i
defiance of rationality had to be put down to mental and physic
derangement, unconnected with the influence of libertarian argu
ments, which thus remained respectably available to 'oppresse
virtue'. The Revolution, with its stern doctrines of patriotism an
citizenship tightening up to fever pitch in an emergency of surviva
drew on these arguments, out-flanking the social pact with a
alternative, intensified version of civic righteousness. The heroes c
classical antiquity were briefly rehabilitated, or rather, thei
speeches and examples, over-familiar and dehumanized, were use
to gild the necessities imposed by defeat and to give consolation an
some common formulas for mutual encouragement to men whos
cause had failed on earth and who were not always sure abou
heaven. Meanwhile, there carried on, underground, a traditio
arising partly from the 'English' fashion of suicide (what the Frenc
said was English), which through *ennui* almost reached the Gidea
idea of the *acte gratuit*, the unmotivated gesture, meaningles
except as an act of self-affirmation. Allied to *sensibilité* and th
maudlin sentiment that could gather round the theme of unhapp
lovers who chose to die, and to the feeling of man's insignificanc
before the universe which haunted Voltaire as it had haunte
Pascal, this underground tradition led to Senancour's *Oberman*.[1]
There are no echoes of Bernardin de Saint-Pierre's 'plaisir de
tombeaux' in *Oberman*; there is *ennui*, a sense of life's unim
portance, and a sense of the vast, oppressive cadre of space and tim
derived from Lucretius, and Buffon's immense fresco of hu
manity's long pilgrimage. Everything will end; the earth wi
become a dead star and darkness and coldness will reign to the en

of space and the far end of time; there will be no awakenings, no reunions, no assimilation to the universe, even. Yet the defence of suicide in *Oberman* does not lead to the act itself, but to intensified mental endeavour with a clear-eyed recognition of its futility. 'To come here, to grow up, to make much ado, to be anxious about everything, to measure the orbit of the comets and, after a few days, to find one's rest under the grass of a cemetery'—the scientific and sceptical intelligence had too much to do and too little time to do it. Even as it faded into the irrationalities of romantic despair, the Enlightenment was less than half sincere in its defence of suicide.

13

Living, Loving, and Dying

JOHNSON. 'No rational man can die without un-
easy apprehension. . . .'
BOSWELL. 'In prospect death is dreadful; but in
fact we find that people die easy.'
JOHNSON. 'Why, Sir, most people have not
thought much of the matter, so cannot *say* much,
and it is supposed they die easy.'[1]

One is tempted to side with the great lexicographer on the point of
fact, without necessarily agreeing with his implied criticism of
popular attitudes. Most people did not think of the matter. If there
is a general inference to be drawn from a study of attitudes to death
in eighteenth-century France, it is that people are concerned essentially with living, and not with dying. This was true even of the
gloomy spiritual writers who were obsessed with man's latter end,
for it was a way of life which they were advocating in the first place,
a life of charity, prayer, and austerity daily offered to God as a
preparation for the last self-offering of all. With death so heavy in
its incidence, so unpredictable, the people of the eighteenth century
were more inured to pain and loss than we are. Though the poor
fatalistically relinquished hope as the cycle of ill health and malnutrition closed in on them, most people clung to life with more
determination than we can easily understand. Their loves and
friendships were doomed to be more fragile, less assured, than
those we cherish, but it would be presumptuous to say their grief
was easier to bear. They were callous about the deaths of young
children, but could they have endured such losses without hardening their hearts? Besides, they believed that infants were saved, a
powerful consolation in an age that still feared damnation. They
were unsentimental about marriage, quickly finding a new partner
when the first one died; no doubt this was because time was short

but also because economic circumstances usually made marriage both possible and advisable. Indeed, the pace at which life was lived was dictated by economic pressures and by the exigencies and opportunities of the hierarchical social structure, rather than by the uncertainty of the future and the brevity of time available. Though the underprivileged began work early in life, they married late; the privileged few married (with some deference to social convention) when they pleased, and moved at a youthful age into the distinguished offices reserved for them, though the Crown would impose a longer apprenticeship to administrative business for those who aspired to intendancies and bishoprics. Financiers building up a fortune would wait until its foundations were secure before they took a wife and set up a household. Most men lived as if they expected to reach the Psalmist's allotted span. Contingency made their ambition more insistent, their desires more reckless, without shortening the time-scale of their plans. Yet they knew how heavily the dice were loaded against them. In this century, for the first time, it became possible to make mathematical calculations of the odds. The dream of a vast prolongation of the human span was a subject of utopian or pseudo-scientific speculation, but—except for simple propositions about living on mountain slopes and being moderate in bed and at board—little was said of the realistic hope of gaining a few extra years. Yet these extra years were, in fact, being gained. Men were living longer, and the effects of the improvement were felt before the evidence for it was certainly interpreted. And within the Psalmist's span and independently of any hopes of extending it, men were beginning to live fuller lives. Early in the century, a concept of 'social death' preceding the physical demise was accepted—the labouring man worn out at fifty, sexual passion fading early, widows withdrawing from circulation, older wives turning to devotion, older husbands deciding to 'put an interval between life and death'. But as the century progressed, the conventional span of active life was extended, at least for the upper classes, a result of improvements in the comforts and conveniences of living and travelling, of advances in surgery and medical treatment, of the growing sophistication of pleasures and recreations, of the breaking of old inhibitions and the rise of a new respect for old age as an aspect of the cult of *sensibilité*. Even so, medical and popular opinion continued to regard the aged with suspicion and reserve. Praise of the venerable patriarch was a sort of compensation; it was also evidence of a new enthusiasm for family life which we are coming to regard as the greatest contribution of the eighteenth century to the advance of civilization.

A study of attitudes to death in eighteenth-century France reveals changes which, at first glance, might be summed up by Michel Vovelle's controversial formula of 'de-christianization'.[2] The truncation of religious phraseology in wills, the reduction in the number of masses for the testator's soul, the decline in the number of books of devotional preparation for dying and the stereotyping of the contents of so many of them, the rise of the lay confessor (the supreme example being Rousseau) teaching men and women in deistic or humanistic terms how to live and how to die, the insinuation of lay, humanistic moralizing into the allegorical message of funereal sculpture and the wording of epitaphs, the rejection of the sombre and demanding Catholic deathbed rituals by blatant defiance or sophisticated evasion, or their devaluation by manifestly ironical acceptance, the ridiculing of eternal punishment and Hell by statistical, geographical, and moral arguments, the removal of cemeteries from proximity to churches, the usurpation of the emotions aroused by Christian liturgical observances by the sentimental and literary fashion of lonely grief, the cult of the tomb as a substitute religion, with the awesome beauty of Nature as its ideal environment—all these can be taken as pointers towards the decline of a Christian outlook and a Christian style of living.

There are difficulties, however, about de-christianization; firstly, with the appropriateness of the formula itself. Since Bishop Dupanloup spoke of the France of 1869 as 'une société déchristianisée', the word has been in use to describe the process of the secularization of modern life.[3] But originally and properly, the term referred to the anti-religious manifestations of the French Revolution, and these were neither homogenous in character nor unambiguous in meaning.[4] The transfer to the secular authorities of the registration of births, marriages, and deaths, and the institution of divorce marked the overthrow of the concept of a 'Christian civilization', of the hope that the Republic would be as 'Christian' as the Monarchy had been. The profanation of churches and tombs, the changing of religious personal names and place-names, the anticlerical masquerades, the forced abdication of priests,[5] the celebration of the festivals of Reason and of the Être Suprême were, in their different ways, attacks on Christianity itself. The Napoleonic Concordat 'restored the altars', but it did not restore the Gallican Church to its property, its position as first Order in the nation, or to its exclusive relationship with the State; nor could it revive among the mass of the people the habits of social deference towards the clergy and their ceremonies, or convert the lost generation of the wars (all the French soldiers in the hospitals of Moscow during the Russian Campaign refused the sacraments).

This revolutionary de-christianization, so traumatic in its impact, had roots in the life of the *ancien régime*; it marks a sudden intensification and focusing of the tendencies towards deism, scepticism, irreligion, and anticlericalism implicit in the thought of the Enlightenment and in the old social order. In the space of a couple of generations before 1789, there had been, says Vovelle, a cooling of religious fervour, a 'profound modification of collective feelings and attitudes towards life and towards death'[6]—witness the fall in the number of Easter communions in Paris and Bordeaux, the rising figures for illegitimacy, the spread of contraceptive practices, the decline in monastic vocations, the dwindling proportion of religious books issuing from the printing-presses, and the waning popularity of traditional saints in paintings in churches. But the word 'de-christianization', with its revolutionary overtones, is, surely, too sweeping a term to sum up these tendencies of the *ancien régime*. The *cahiers* of 1789 suggest that, in practice, nothing more radical than a reform of the Gallican Church was required—a partial confiscation of its wealth, the suppression of numerous monasteries, and the opening of careers in the ecclesiastical hierarchy to merit would have been enough for most and too much for many.[7] To explain how reforming practicalities and theoretical scepticism became the lurid de-christianization of the Terror, we must have recourse to some version of the 'thesis of circumstances'—foreign and civil war, the identification of the clergy with the invaders and the federalist rebels, the struggle for control of the harvests which set town against countryside, the cracking of the fabric of order which allowed scope for the leadership of fanatics and the eccentricities of buffoons. We are still a long way from a complete explanation of the revolutionary de-christianization, but it is clear that there is a radical discontinuity between manifestations of opposition to Catholicism under the *ancien régime* and in the febrile days of the high Revolution. That is why Bernard Plongeron[8] has suggested confining the word 'de-christianization' to the revolutionary epoch, and using 'desacralization' for what comes after, and 'laicization' for what happened before. Compared with 'de-christianization', 'laicization' is a neutral word, suggesting the erosion of the Church's alliance with power rather than a threat to the essence of revealed religion—indeed, constituting a step towards the balance approved by Aquinas: civil and religious society each being autonomous, going their own independent ways and seeking their own particular perfection.[9]

According to Gabriel Le Bras, 'de-christianization' is a 'fallacious' term anyway, since it improperly assumes the existence of a Christian order in the first place.[10] A Church which exercises power and monopolizes culture draws all men to itself—for nonreligious reasons. It takes more than 2,000 years, sixty generations, to convert the world. Jean Delumeau[11] asks (perhaps with excessive severi   wards unthinking loyalties) what would be left of eighteenth-century Catholicism if we took away routine conformity, official observances, the unhealthy religiosity which turns its back on the problems of society, the magical and superstitious undertones, Manicheism, and fear? The contrast usually drawn between the fervour of the seventeenth century and the complaisance of the eighteenth is misleading; the work of conversion to a deeper, interior piety was proceeding all the while. There are two graphs whose curves intersect: the graph of qualitative devotion and that of quantitative practice. Both indicators concern 'Christian' developments, but in different senses. The first refers to the conversion of individuals and the intensification of their religious awareness, the second to the working-out of the ideal of a Church as 'a community which serves the world, if necessary at the risk of losing its own soul', passing on to the secular social order the moral ideals and culture rescued from the shipwrecks of the past. In this quantitative context, decline is inevitable, 'failure is the true destiny of the great historic Churches',[12] and laicization is the process by which, in a mutual relationship, civilization has progressed and 'Christianity' has declined. Looked at in another way, however, Christianity has withdrawn to work at its original and fundamental task of bringing men to their meeting with God, as recorded on the imaginary qualitative graph—a graph which in fact can never be constructed, for the registers in which the statistics are recorded are not accessible to the terrestrial historian.

That there never was a Christian social order in the strict sense does not mean that Christianity should be regarded as some pure, unchanging essence. The qualitative graph is not a conspectus of the progress of a set of unchanging beliefs and permanent attitudes. The inspiration of 2,000 years ago is subject to reinterpretation and is the continual source of new insights. This process of rediscovery and renewal takes place within (but not exclusively within) Churches which are themselves complicated institutions, partly social and partly spiritual, and entangled and embedded in a multifarious social order. Christianity has played its part in the creation of this social order, and its ideas float everywhere within it, not least in the minds of critics and unbelievers. Certain changes taking place in this complex may be grouped together for convenient study under the heading of 'laicization'. Even so, a particular change which we are recording may be social rather than religious in nature, or, if religious, may represent some mutation of ecclesiastical conventions or spiritual emotions rather than another victory for secularism—an example, perhaps, of the Church learning from the world, or rediscovering a forgotten aspect of its own inspiration. The abandonment of Christian formulas in the preambles of wills is a matter of fashion and protocol, the demise of a pious practice, but not an issue which churchmen seem to have worried about. The replacement of masses for the testator's soul by charitable bequests marks the rediscovery of a Christian truth (we may suppose that it was not those whose religious beliefs were waning who turned to charity, but those whose religious beliefs were becoming more enlightened). The devaluation of Hell was a rediscovery of the Christian doctrine of love made by deists and sceptics; on Hell, Rousseau and Voltaire were better theologians than the apologists. Indeed, the preaching of eternal torment is the point at which

443

Catholic intellectual evolution lagged grievously behind the enlightened conscience of the century, thus casting doubts on the validity of the whole structure of spirituality which had been built around the business of dying. The deists of the Enlightenment took over from Christianity the hope of personal immortality (and with it, often enough, the idea of a limited punishment to redress the injustices of this life), and made it an element of a new religion centring on the tomb, with its liturgy of sentimental melancholy. Yet if this was the unbeliever's substitute for the Church's consolations in the face of death, it was a cult which Christians annexed to their own. The bizarre forest of monuments in the cemetery of Père Lachaise is testimony to a pattern of interaction and syncretism in which neither side is anxious to recognize its borrowings.

Confrontations between Catholicism and the Enlightenment were, for the most part, confined to words—polemical attacks, replies, counter-attacks. Sometimes, as in the defence of suicide or the ascription of souls to animals, sceptical theorists were more concerned to embarrass the clergy than to express their own convictions. Once in every lifetime, however, there came the unavoidable confrontation involving personal belief and commitment: all who wrote critically of revealed religion had to decide how they would die. It was not a question of challenging the public, set-piece deathbed scene (this was being challenged, but the issue was not essentially religious); the challenge was to the Catholic ceremonies and the confession of faith which they required. The more militant *philosophes* were as anxious to have a propaganda demonstration on their side as the less sensitive of the ecclesiastics were to have one on theirs. Voltaire, conscious that the world of scepticism and anticlericalism looked to him for leadership, craftily steered a middle course which, indeed, represented his own true opinions. The vast majority, however, conformed, and the issue remained— even late in the nineteenth century unbelievers were still haunted by the choice that lay before them at the end.[13]

The evidence for changing attitudes to death in eighteenth-century France can be fitted into the laicization theme, but with three provisos. Firstly, Christianity must be seen, not only passively, being ousted from its dominant role in the social and ideological complex, but also as developing and renewing itself. Secondly, the revolutionary de-christianization must be seen as a strange and violent phenomenon; in particular, the crudity of revolutionary burials was a contradiction of the ideals of both Christianity and the Enlightenment, a breach in the continuity of the development of ideas, sentiments, and social practices. Thirdly, the baroque 'pedagogy of death', 'la mort prédicateur'[14] of the post-Tridentine Roman Church, which was being challenged in the eighteenth century, must be seen as operating within a social structure which was changing—the old coherence was breaking down and new nuclei were forming. On the universal scale, there was the rise of the omnicompetent modern State; on the minute scale, there was a revolutionary change in the nature of the family and of personal relationships. Lawrence Stone, in tracing the latter development in English history, has invented a descriptive terminology for it.[15] He describes how personal relationships move from 'distance, deference and patriarchy' to 'Affective Individualism'; the individual is recognized as unique and independent, entitled to his own ideas and to a degree of physical privacy; the child becomes the centre of family affection, and grows up with the right to choose a marriage partner. The milieu in which this affective individualism flourishes is the new type of family which arises from about the mid-seventeenth century among the upper middle class and squirearchy. The 'open lineage' type of family was dominated by loyalty to ancestors and living kin and was under the surveillance of the local community; the new 'Closed, Domesticated Nuclear Family' is bound together by ties of affection between husband and wife, parents and children, and recognizes the rights of its members to their individual pursuit of happiness. This type of family is united in introspective intensity, and excludes kinsfolk and neighbours from its intimacies.

In broad terms, the French experience ran parallel to the English; indeed, Stone's analysis is, in some respects, an adaptation to English conditions of the generalizations of French historians about their own country. There were differences, the chief one being that, in the South of France, there were numerous examples of the 'polynuclear family', with brothers or cousins, married or unmarried, agreeing to live together, whether contractually or informally.[16] Even so, in the seventeenth and continuing into the eighteenth century, the pattern of relationships conforms to a norm: husband, wife, and four to five children constituting the 'nuclear' or 'conjugal' family group,[17] characterized by the arranged marriage which was its foundation, the despotism of the man, the inferiority of the woman, and the subjection of the children. The authority of the husband and father,[18] enshrined in custom and fortified by the laws of inheritance in various parts of the country, was backed up by the power of the State—for the upper classes, by use of the royal *lettre de cachet*. An adulterous wife could be incarcerated in a convent, while there was no such redress against an unfaithful husband. In the Midi, the wife controlled her own property, but her husband administered her dowry and used the revenues; in the North and Centre, the *pays de droit coutumier*, where there was community of goods, the husband controlled everything (though everywhere, on the death of the husband, the widow had rights upon the heritage).[19] In Normandy, Brittany, and Burgundy, the wife could not even make a will without her husband's permission. Churchmen who cited St. Paul on the duty of women to keep silent, who speculated on 'the curse of Eve', or complained of the demonic force of sexual attraction,[20] and medical men who pontificated on the weakness of the fibres of the feminine brain or the susceptibility of the fair sex to excesses of the imagination,[21] helped to provide theoretical justification for male domination.

Montaigne had held it 'a kind of incest' to employ the 'efforts and extravagances of amorous licence' within the 'venerable and sacred marriage bond'.[22] This view of sexual activity found support in the handbooks of the confessional—condemnations of visual satisfactions, unusual positions, imaginative enjoyment in anticipation or retrospect, recommendations to abstinence balanced by crude instructions to wives to satisfy their husbands to keep them from debauchery, the insistence on procreation as the first and indispensable object, and the prohibition of contraceptive practices—as one writer summed up, marriage is a 'cross' to be borne, a miserable state chiefly valuable in creating monastic vocations among the beholders.[23] These severities helped to confirm the impression that man and wife were bonded together by duty and economic necessity rather than by affection. Paradoxically, this unromantic view was reinforced by the cynical irreligious tradition which devalued sex in a different fashion, whether as an animal or mechanical activity, or as one marginal to personal fulfilment—Chamfort's 'l'échange de deux fantaisies et le contact de deux épidermes'. Earlier in this same tradition, Crébillon had specialized in demonstrating how everything ends in bed, whether from desire, curiosity, indolence, avarice, boredom, or vanity; this was a justification of the immorality of the Regency period, and of the graceless living of the great who 'married one woman, lived with another, and loved only themselves'. For them, marriage was but a convenient social arrangement.[24]

In vain the Church taught that mutual consent makes a marriage valid in spite of the opposition of parents, for the decrees of the Council of Trent did not run in France (they did in the papal enclave of Avignon, which became a sort of Gretna Green for runaway lovers). By French law,[25] a man under thirty years of age was disinherited if he married without parental permission (the age for a woman was twenty-five), and since inequality of fortunes was held to establish a presumption of abduction, one of the partners to an elopement might be in danger of the death penalty. The aim of the legislator, said a jurist in 1781, was to ensure freedom from the tyranny of passion: it was, of course, to protect the interests of families, and more especially their property. In every rank of society down to the very poor, material possessions dominated the institution of marriage—for the richer classes, the dowry, among the poorer, it was the number of sheep that the woman possessed that mattered, or the tools of the dead husband's trade inherited by the widow, or the serving girl's meagre hoard of savings. And in any case, children were brought up to obey. There was little recognition of their innocence and charm, though it is an exaggeration to say that they were regarded as stunted adults who as yet were good for nothing. During the *Grand siècle*, churchmen spoke of infancy as a vile and animal state, and literary men spoke of it as a time of greediness and laziness. Many great aristocrats neglected their children (in the eighteenth century, their heartlessness was denounced by Montesquieu, the prince de Ligne, and Talleyrand). The poor often had no alternative but to neglect theirs, and they necessarily sent them out to work at an early age. By modern psychological criteria, the young, packed off to wet-nurses in infancy, sent away to *collège* or to apprenticeship so soon, ruthlessly disciplined in the home, and suffering the loss, like as not, of one or both parents at an early age, must have been rendered hard, suspicious, and insecure. Marriage, so often imposed or mercenary, did not always bring affection or openness to them, and the years of family companionship were usually brief before death intervened. This gloomy picture is not, of course, the complete story. So far, what we have offered is a compressed and schematic account, confounding into one all social classes, all geographical areas, and cramming the diversity of reality and the uniqueness of individuals into averages—an arbitrary creation, a historian's model for the purposes of broad comparision. But one thing about it is clear—it is a picture of a society where there was little opportunity for affection to show itself, to develop and deepen; a harsh and loveless world.

The eighteenth century saw a change in attitudes to the institution of marriage and the family, to children, to women, and to sexual relationships—or, more exactly, there was a growth of new attitudes within the hard and empty shell of the old ideological carapace. The transformation is easy to document in a general way, but difficult to describe precisely or to explain. That women are as good as men had been a debating point since the sixteenth century, and the rational case for the proposition had been put definitively and unimaginatively in the 1670s by Poulain de la Barre. 'L'esprit n'a pas de sexe,' he had said, following the mind–body dichotomy of Descartes to a feminist conclusion.[26] It is society and custom that have brought women to subordination; in themselves they have the intelligence to exercise any profession and to rule as well as men. The argument carried on into the eighteenth century, fortified from time to time by examples of the heroines of classical antiquity, more relevant than the female martyrs of Christianity, because of their role in the family and their civic preoccupations. The implications of Christian teaching were a significant help, however. The central message of catechisms and confessionals was not that of Augustinian gloom about sexual temptations or Pauline moralizing about ecclesiastical leadership; it was, rather, one concerning companionship in a relationship of 'one flesh'. A handbook for confessors of 1713 states the theoretical principle that the husband rules, but asks the wife, anxiously, if she listens to his 'advice' and 'remonstrances'.[27] According to the Church, the essence of marriage was the free consent of both parties, and in the ecclesiastical courts (unlike the secular tribunals) husband and wife were treated equally when a complaint of adultery was put forward by either of them.[28] The medical profession was not always obsessed with feminine 'vapeurs'. In obstetrical practice, the surgeons took the side of women, rejecting the arguments of certain theologians that the life of the child should be preferred to that of the mother; this was before the growing sophistication of instruments made the dilemma less common.[29] Perhaps some physicians also helped women by making known the importance of the female orgasm; it was a subject on which little was said publicly, except by La Mettrie, who proclaimed the rights of women.[30] The eighteenth century also saw the medical experts rejecting the old theory that the male semen furnishes the foetus in human generation; perhaps it provided nothing more than a stimulus, so that an electric shock might replace it. Those who did not go so far as to accept the exclusive role of the woman in generation ascribed an equal part to husband and wife in the creation of their children.[31] Even so, everyone agreed that the unborn child was affected by the emotions of the mother, perhaps even to the point of acquiring her virtues and vices. In the womb, the infant received its basic 'education'.[32] An age that became enamoured of the idea of progress was obliged to grant a new respect to women: the future of the race depended on them.

There were few eighteenth-century campaigners for strict feminine equality. There was Riballier, whose *Éducation physique et morale des femmes* (1779) called on women to 'break their chains' and do everything, including competing in Olympics.[33] Condorcet in 1787 demanded educational equality in mixed schools and full political rights for women; one extremist pamphlet in 1789 asked for female representation in the Estates General, and another proposed female generals, magistrates, and preachers.[34] The following year saw the rise of women's clubs and newspapers, and during the Terror, Olympe de Gouges posed the famous question, asking why women were not entitled to mount the rostrum in legislative assemblies when no one challenged their obligation to mount the steps of the scaffold.[35] In Brumaire An II and Prairial An III the Convention gave short shrift to these subversive novelties. By their *pudeur* (modesty) and *exaltation* (proneness to excitement) women were deemed disqualified from interfering in affairs of state; their clubs were suppressed and they were excluded from political assemblies.[36] This illiberal legislation of the Convention was not so far removed from the ideas of the *philosophes* as might be assumed, for to them equality had been the starting-point of the argument, not its conclusion. All are equal at birth, but (and Locke's sensationalist philosophy helped here) the emergent personality can be moulded. In the theorizing of Morelly, Helvétius, and d'Holbach, women gain by being deemed equal to men and worthy of a scientific education free from the prejudices which belittle them, but they lose by being conditioned for service in a stern utopia—giving up their children to the State (Morelly), taught to award their favours to men of achievement (Helvétius), or educated especially for maternity (d'Holbach).[37] Indeed, at the heart of the revolution in personal relationships which began in the eighteenth century there was a flash of insight and sympathy much more significant than Poulain de la Barre's rational egalitarianism, or the belief in malleability and education which made the *philosophes* impatient with the injustices of the old family structure. This 'decisive mutation in the history of civilization'[38] was the discovery of 'femininity'.

If absolute equality between the sexes is to be the criterion, the most perceptive analysts of human emotions and motivation among the eighteenth-century writers were traitors to the cause of women's rights. In the *Esprit des lois*, Montesquieu seems to have forgotten his sympathy with Roxane in the *Lettres persanes*. Marivaux's women in *La Colonie* break all the male monopolies of employment until the enemy march and there is fighting to be done. The fair sex, in Diderot's *Essai sur les femmes*, 'as beautiful as Klopstock's seraphim and as terrible as Milton's devils', are agents of a universal conspiracy of sexual manipulation. 'La femme est faite pour plaire à l'homme,' said Rousseau. Yet these are the writers who discovered feminity,[39] and found women equal in a different sense, perfect in their own fashion, fulfilling their own vocation, and constituting the inspiration in human history which has created civilization out of barbarism. Montesquieu is a curious example of a divided mind. So much of the *Esprit des lois* is ungenerous, in political and legislative terms, towards women. There is a populationist insistence on the importance of procreation that ignores human affections, an unquestioned assumption (the matriarchal institutions of the ancient Scythians apart) that the father rules every aspect of the life of the family, and that male children inherit more than female. Yet this great magistrate was not blindly accepting the illiberal prescriptions of the current law books; he was ill-at-ease, continually conscious of the power of femininity as a force in society and history. If his outlook is a reflection of the 'pessimism of the Enlightenment concerning women', as Jeannette Geffriaud Rosso has said, this may be because his view of the destiny of so many variants of the social order was equally gloomy. At least, in monarchy, his ideal form of government, women give existence its charm, inspire to great deeds the men who desire to please them, and foster the atmosphere of liberty which preserves the State from despotism. In his pseudo-historical imaginings and political theorizing, Rousseau sees women as transmitting the traditions of the race and the love of liberty to their children, and inspiring their husbands to perform their civic duties. Not only are men incomplete without women, but the coherence of the social order is impossible without their influence. Buffon put the idea in simple terms when he described savages as isolated and suspicious in temper because they did not love their womenfolk—' the first and indispensable step on the way to sociability.[40] Whether in the free love of Tahiti or in the affectionate bourgeois marriage, his two contrasting ideals, woman is the heart of Diderot's universe, entitled to sexual gratification and to live as an equal partner, in spite of her biological handicap. For Marivaux, men rule the world and women rule the men. The most sophisticated psychological insights of the age are invoked in his theme of 'coquetterie'. Throughout the century, from libertinism to *sensibilité*, literature records a subtilizing and refining of the relationship between the sexes. Women frankly desire intercourse; 'je n'ai point cédé,' says one of Mme Riccoboni's heroines, 'je me suis donnée.'[41] Yet the preliminaries are delicate because of their susceptibilities: 'leur imagination aime à se promener à l'ombre'. There was an external impassivity to be preserved—one could pretend to ascribe all to moonlight or to circumstances, or hide behind raillery, divining secrets yet allowing the masked dancers to think their incognito was unbroken; one learnt to speak of love by routine, as in learning to dance, and yet one loved indeed; by coquetterie, the imagination was stimulated and the sincerity of motives tested. And behind coquetterie and the affirmation of independence which it implies, only women are capable of total self-giving. Charmingly in Marivaux and in a sinister fashion in Diderot and Choderlos de Laclos, the affinities between religious devotion and sexual desire in women are explored.[42] Marivaux is the century's witness to the boundless passion and devotion hidden behind the calm respectability of bourgeois wives and the frivolous charm of the girls of Fragonard. To this sort of ironical and sympathetic insight, Rousseau added moral fervour, and his Julie captured the imagination of the age as the ideal of womanhood, with her establishment at Clarens as the ideal of family relationships. The ruthless feminist Riballier condemned Rousseau for restricting women to domestic duties, yet the ladies who read the *Nouvelle Héloïse* did not complain. It was a novel dominated by a woman. Julie was the centre of the web of family affections; her self-sacrifice created the happiness and achieved the moral reform of the others; without her radiance, Wolmar's judicious insight would have made Clarens nothing better than a comfortable prison. Her femininity is not an inferior mode of being: it is perfection of its kind. And even Julie's secret, interior unhappiness points toward the great ideal, as yet unrealized, when lovers reach total unity; when, as the Rousseauist author of the *Nouvel ami des femmes* (1779) observed, 'les deux sexes ne forment qu'un tout moral'.[43]

The 'discovery' of women, whether in the manner of Riballier or in the manner of Rousseau, created an enthusiasm (largely theoretical) for the education of girls. For Riballier and Condorcet they were to be trained for full and equal citizenship. For Mme de Puisieux, they were at least to be educated out of the 'prejudice' of their own inferiority, so they could believe in the title of her book, *La Femme n'est pas inférieure à l'homme* (1750).[44] But the main current of reforming pedagogical thought came from Fénelon: a girl should receive as good an education as a boy, but religious and moral, and centred in the home—not the convent. Rousseau reinforced the Fénelonian tradition. The details—some illiberal—of the education of Sophie in *Émile* were forgotten; what was remembered was the need to train girls as wives and mothers and as the educators of the next generation of citizens.

Another consequence of the new view of women was a rising protest against the arranged marriage. The writers of the Enlightenment confuted the gloomy view of certain theologians making marriage a school of hardship to condition spiritual athletes—that was why a few voices were raised in favour of divorce.[45] Their main contention, however, was precisely that of the Church: marriage is the full, mutual self-giving of a man and a woman. This ecclesiastical definition was reaffirmed and pushed to its extreme conclusion against the laws of the land and the customs of society. The message of the *Nouvelle Héloïse* is that free choice is the only moral way in personal relationships. A 'voluntary union' says the *Encyclopédie*. 'Rien ne peut suppléer à l'union des âmes,' says d'Holbach. Two lovers, says Chamfort, belong to each other by nature, by divine right, in spite of all human conventions, including that of marriage itself.[46] By 1759, even the Government was beginning to have doubts about the issue of *lettres de cachet* in affairs of the heart: 'the disproportion of rank and fortune is not a sufficient reason to persuade His Majesty to limit the freedom of marriage'.[47] True, in the eighteenth century a free choice based on affection alone remained the less usual course—chiefly taken by odd, rich individuals indifferent to social status, the younger sons of richer peasants, and artisans and merchants whose wives shared in the work of shop, counting-house, or loom. In such a rigidly hierarchical society, there was hardly any means of rising out of one's station except by marriage and its material advantages; children, concerned to maintain and improve their lot, were rarely in revolt against negotiations to this end. Even so, the arranged marriage was being reformed and civilized from within. Parents would consult their children and allow them the power of veto (as Mme Roland records about the negotiations for her own marriage).[48] As for the couples themselves, they took refuge in Montaigne's principle and lived in friendship where they could not say they loved. It was common to say that friendship is more enduring, that 'passion' is dangerous, and a 'blind guide' when it comes to ordering a household.[49] Even those who chose their partner freely would agree sometimes; at thirty-nine years of age, an employee of the Ferme générale married a girl of twenty-five with no fortune—their union, he said, was based on 'l'amitié raisonnée, plus constante et aussi forte que l'amour'.[50] The eighteenth century clung to distinctions of rank even when it proclaimed the primacy of love. Marivaux's young people resort to disguise to find out about the partner they have not chosen, but they rarely finish up marrying outside their predestined circle; Voltaire's Nanine turns out to be high-born after all. 'Amitié' reconciled the contradictions. 'Quel est donc cet étranger dont je suis la femme?', cries one of Marivaux's heroines, yet she continues to live with him on genial terms, just as Julie in the *Nouvelle Héloïse* fulfils her duties towards Wolmar and her station; it was wrong that she should have this obligation, but it was right to accept it. With his insight into the affairs of the heart, Marivaux defines the true meaning of the vows we take at the altar. They cannot mean what they seem to say, for no one can promise to love for ever; but we are masters of our actions, so what we intend is that we will act *as if* we love, and that for always.[51] To act 'as if we love'; this, maybe, was the true sentiment of the Enlightenment for personal relationships.

About the middle of the century, it became respectable, in high society, to be in love with one's wife, though not, of course, to show it. Nivelle de la Chaussée made his fortune as a dramatist by satirizing the subterfuges necessary to disguise conjugal affection. As Montaigne's advice was forgotten, and the 'efforts and extravagances of amorous licence' came into marriage, so too did contraception—the transfer of attitudes and precautions used in love affairs into the marriage bed.[52] The change from a pre-Malthusian society to one in which family limitation is the established convention coincides, in long-term perspective, with a change in attitudes to Nature—a refusal to accept accidents as the decrees of Providence, and a willingness to isolate elements of experience for modification by technical interventions, an outlook necessary for the rise of medical science. But while inoculation against smallpox was advocated by scientific propaganda and was accepted only by an intelligent minority, contraception, with virtually no propaganda in its favour (thanks to the populationists), was adopted, by the educated in the first place, and very soon, here and there, in all ranks of society. It was not a question of a 'scientific' view of life, but of a deep human need. In another long-term perspective, the change to family limitation is allied to the revolution in human attitudes caused by the conquest of death. This conquest began in the eighteenth century, and one might guess that the significant figures are those of the decline in infant mortality in certain areas. But as yet, the advent of contraception, as distinct from its long-term victory, has not been tied to the decline of infant mortality as effect following cause.[53] So far, a less precise generalization fits the case: both phenomena are the result of a more fundamental change, the slow rise of civilized living, for the many, not just the few, above the subsistence level. For the educated classes, we have seen the evidence from literary sources of a new consideration for women and a new refinement in the relations of the sexes, and this, we may suppose, is at the root of the mental readjustment which leads to the adoption of contraception. This literary evidence is not directly relevant to the peasants who, in certain areas, were resorting to family limitation in the last generation before the Revolution. Even so, a guess at an explanation along the same lines for all classes of society may be made. The mental inhibitions were less than has been supposed. The laity would not allow the clergy to pry into their sexual conduct, and the outcry against 'l'art de tromper la nature' by some clerical casuists was not a fair representation of the subtleties and ambiguities of the moral theologians.[54] Maybe, the prohibitions of the Catholic Church had less effect than its teachings of self-restraint which could be transferred to the practice of *coitus interruptus*.[55] The sexual practices of the youth of rural France may have provided an initiation which would make the transition to contraceptive manipulation within marriage easier.[56] In the countryside, there was a conscious limitation of births in time of famine—a contraception of despair.[57] This desperate turning to Malthusian practices in misery became, I would guess, the beginning of a new way of life for some peasant families under exactly the opposite inspiration—the inspiration of improving standards of living, the chance of escape from the trap of grinding poverty, the glimpse of new possibilities of more generous human relationships. In human nature there was a great fund of affection and consideration seeking a chance to express itself whenever and wherever the struggle for bare existence was transcended, a mute but not inglorious potentiality for selfless devotion bound up with the sex drive, of the same kind as the literary sources reveal for the literate classes, but inarticulate and unrecorded. The Revolution, opening new avenues of aspiration and, as war and the Terror came, creating new apprehensions, forced on the development of contraceptive practice in the areas where it had already started, by the pressures of alternating hopes and fears. Men and women were beginning to control their living and to give a deeper content to their loving.

Contraception was adopted out of a new consideration for women—and also because of the rise of a more affectionate relationship between parents and children. The family began to focus on the child: it became necessary to have fewer children in order to care for them better. However the precepts of religion were employed to inculcate obedience to paternal authority or to encourage monastic vows, the central demand of Christian teaching was clear: it was sinful to oblige a child to marry where there was no affection or to undertake a career where there was no vocation, and there was an obligation to provide nurture, education, and comfort. The seventeenth-century cult of the Infant Jesus alongside that of Our Lady was a reminder that the world was not a masculine preserve, and that the devotion of a woman and the innocence of a child had been the beginning of our salvation. The medical profession, turning to the ideal of 'Nature', took up Locke's enthusiasm for giving freedom to the very young—let them run in the rain and dress comfortably. Nicolas Andry in 1741 denounced the swaddling of infants and imprisoning them in the *maillot* and the confining of girls in corsets; his advocacy of Freedom was taken up later by other medical writers—'Rendez la liberté à l'enfant'. Nature, the physicians were saying in the second half of the century, requires mothers to breast-feed their own babies.[58] It was a medical expert, albeit a Jansenist one, who in 1708 proved the argument from scriptural precedents from Eve onwards, and a churchman who in 1738 provided a medical reason: the temperament of the nurse was passed on with her milk. More serious medical arguments came later, based on the comparative statistics of infant mortality. Then Rousseau brought in the decisive, emotive appeal to the natural affections. If the affinity between mother and child 'is not fortified by habitual and continual caring, it vanishes in the first years of life.'[59] Less concerned about the suckling, the seventeenth century had been fascinated by the emerging personality; in contrast to the literary tradition about the greed and waywardness of children, we find affectionate diminutive terms coming into use, fairy-tales and sympathetic school-books are published. Most significant of all, children push into the family portrait, sometimes becoming the centre of attraction.[60] In the eighteenth century, they take over many pictures entirely.[61] Chardin shows them saying grace, playing with a top, learning sums or the alphabet—touching scenes of the family life the painter had lost when his wife and little daughter died. Greuze shows the baby taken off to nurse amidst the tears of all the family, and returning amid universal rejoicing, and children gathered round the sick-bed to reciprocate the affection which had been bestowed on them. Other painters show young people on swings, with sticks or toys, as Boucher depicts the duc de Montpensier holding the bridle of a wooden horse; others take pleasure in the early lessons in the social graces, as Fragonard with *Dîtes donc: s'il vous plaît*. Children were established as beings in their own right, and not as deficient adults. Parents had to try to see the world from their level. 'Il faut en général se faire petit,'wrote Diderot, 'pour encourager peu à peu les petits à se faire grands.'[62] Rousseau laid the foundation of a new educational psychology when he showed that children cannot picture distant scenes or abstract ideas, or understand and fear death— they look out on the world with a naïve immediacy. The demand for maternal care of infants and the new educational theories tie in with the key ideas of the Enlightenment: the rejection of the concept of Original Sin (giving confidence in education and environment to mould the personality for good), the recognition of the diversity of civilizations and admiration of the noble savage (another being in his own right), the idea of progress (with the future belonging to the new generation), and the wave of *sensibilité* at the end of the *ancien régime* (which made it fashionable to talk of simple emotions and in description to intensify them).

The conjugal family—husband, wife, and children—was a subject for universal enthusiasm in the eighteenth century;[63] sometimes, indeed, it was praised with saccharine *clichés* bordering on the ludicrous. Churchmen at least warned of the dangers of excessively introverted affections leading to dishonest partiality and neglect of obligations to the poor. In the family, said Diderot (in a play written in 1758 and performed in 1761), the human capacity for loving reaches fulfilment—where else do we find such sympathy, such certainty of support, such sharing of joy and sorrows? Voltaire (with a sidelong glance at polygamy to vex the clergy), Rousseau, the *Encyclopédie*, and Marmontel say similar things. Necker, in a practical description of the poor whose intimate story was not told in literature, reflects that their lives are made bearable in misery by companionship. Even Mercier (who believed that occasional wife-beating strengthened mutual devotion) and Restif (the only systematic theorist of male chauvinism in the Enlightenment)[64] were devoted to family life as the environment for achieving happiness. The family, said Jean-Jacques Rousseau, is 'la première et la plus sainte institution de la nature'. It was natural, though Rousseau (and Diderot and Laclos in unpublished writings) did not take this to mean a historical and chronological priority. Even so, 'natural' did not mean a distant ideal or a Platonic principle. Family life as it should be existed in a favoured stratum of the bourgeoisie, at least when seen through the golden haze of recollection—Diderot's father in his dressing-gown telling improving stories in the family circle, tearful goodbyes from mother and sisters as young Marmontel waited to mount behind his father to go to *collège*,[65] the firelight flickering round the farmhouse kitchen on the faces of Restif and the other children—all the happy life together that Rousseau never knew and never managed to make for himself, a failure for which he atoned in literary masterpieces devoted to the ideal of togetherness at the hearth with children or in the senate house with fellow citizens.

Why was the eighteenth century the crucial period for the discovery of the child and of femininity, and for the concentration of affection in the nuclear family? The explanation becomes less difficult when we remember the systematization and simplification by which our two contrasting models were created as an assessment of the pattern of change, and the predominant role played in both of them by literary evidence. The change we are concerned with is not, strictly speaking, something new; we are describing how a possible way of living which had already been exemplified among certain sensitive individuals in favourable environments became accepted as a general ideal, even though it was still practised only by a minority. In the institution of late marriage which developed in Latin Christianity from the fourteenth century (unlike Japan and Eastern Europe where young people married ten years earlier) there were, implicitly, tendencies towards individual freedom to choose. In France, the average age of marriage (the aristocracy excepted) was twenty-five for women and twenty-eight for men; by then, parents might be dead, and in any case the power of the father would be much less over children as old as this than over the brides and bridegrooms of seventeen and eighteen of Japan or Russia.[66] Women came to their husbands mature in mind, capable of helping with business, and, maybe, having amassed a dowry by a decade of hard work. The power of kin and local community over the family worked against parental and male domination as well as for it. Young people might appeal to a family 'council' to try to get permission to marry. In villages and in the artisan *quartiers* of towns public opinion supported the decencies; only on isolated farms and in tiny hamlets in *bocage* country could husbands fool around with serving girls or beat their wives with impunity. In Languedoc, women were subject indeed to their husbands, but could exercise remarkable rights on behalf of their family. They were 'entitled' to steal food for their starving infants, to demonstrate riotously against food shortages, to conceal their young people who might be fugitives from justice, to do battle royal in the streets to protect their children.[67]

When, from literary sources, we describe a certain attitude to family, women, or children as 'new', this does not necessarily mean that it had not existed before, but only that it had not been formulated or documented. Perhaps the novelty emerges because inhibitions against self-expression had broken down, or changes in the practical circumstances of living had provided new opportunities for expressing affection. Nor does innovation come solely as a refinement within a closed universe of ideas. The discovery of femininity implies that men were becoming more civilized; more importantly, it implies that social and economic developments were such that women were becoming more useful and more attractive. Men began to think of them as equal because they were, in fact, making an 'equal' contribution, one going far beyond biological necessities. Though France did not have female rulers, like the sinister empresses at St. Petersburg or the pious Maria Theresa at Vienna, and though the influence of political whores and royal mistresses (even Pompadour) was limited, foreign visitors to Paris affirmed that this was the capital where the power of women was greatest. The Goncourts exaggerate when they ascribe to them an occult political domination as 'the universal and fatal cause of everything',[68] but women did set the tone of society, manipulate the popularity of ministers, and make the reputation of writers. They presided over the *salons* where political reforms, literary theories, and religious beliefs were debated; they pulled the strings for elections to the French Academy; in the last decade before the Revolution they obtained entry to some of the masonic lodges.[69] There were women intellectuals, writers, and artists. Mme du Châtelet translated Newton; in 1783 Mme Vigée-Lebrun and Mme Labille-Guiard were received together into the Academy of Painting and Sculpture; Mme de Tencin, Mme de Graffigny, and Mme Riccoboni were the most successful of the women novelists. Their romances were calculated to prove the courage and generosity of their sex, thus helping to ensure that the debates of the critics about the propriety of the novel became involved in controversies about the status of women. Lenglet-Defresnoy praised fiction and the abbé Jacquin denounced it for the identical reason: it revealed the power of women to sway the affairs of the world (a truth, says Lenglet-Dufresnoy, which historians ignore).[70] Choderlos de Laclos cynically inverted this feminist theme; his *Liaisons dangereuses* is a study of a female monster who refuses to be a 'machine à plaisir' and uses sex to dominate and destroy. In spite of the lamentations about the deficiencies of convent education, the nuns do not seem to have made their charges colourless or sedate; stories of ink in the holy water and muffles on the bells, of painting the teachers' faces while they were asleep, and dressing up as devils at night to scare the novices are reassuring evidence that the court aristocracy married spirited wives.[71] Aristocratic ladies of great families ruled as abbesses over wealthy monasteries, ordering round their estate managers and minor clergy with despotic sway.[72] Merchants of Bordeaux tended to marry young women in their early twenties, but they made them their associates and in their wills they assume that the widows will carry on the trade.[73] Mercier describes 'the air of equality' which reigns between husband and wife in bourgeois families in Paris—'the wife is consulted on all affairs'.[74] There are many examples of single women running their estates (or their children's if they are widows) and directing industrial enterprises, even mines.[75] In Paris the guilds of dressmakers, drapers, and florists were feminine preserves, and in other trades, such as bookselling, wives were entitled to carry on when their husbands died. Among the artisans of towns, wives brought in their share of the family income; at Lyon they would work alongside their husbands on the silk machinery; in Le Puy and the near-by villages, the women were lace workers, earning—if skilled—more than the men: in this case they were the decision makers. The farmer's wife ran the *basse-cour* with its eggs and dairy produce, and among the poorer, had to toil to bring in the harvest. In Auvergne, where the men went off in spring to do casual labour in the North , the women tilled the holding single-handed, brought up the children, and organized them to beg when necessary.[76] One might conclude that women achieved recognition by earning it. As civilization became less crude and more diversified, they rose in status, the agitation in favour of their rights being as much a demand for recognition of the increasing value of their contribution as an expression of egalitarian theory.

We can hardly relate social transformation to the movement of ideas in this particular way when we consider changing attitudes to children. Unlike women, who were pushing their way to recognition, children could not impose themselves by achievement. True, their status improved along with that of the mothers whose principal concern was to look after them, and family life became more manifestly sympathetic and affectionate as material circumstances became more comfortable—warm rooms, and furnishing for ease and not for splendour, privacy, fabrics of greater delicacy to wear and baths and mirrors as aids to personal appearance, safer travel, books, more leisure for conversation. But at the risk of stating the obvious, I would suggest a more precise statement to describe what was happening.[77] When we read Mme de Sévigné's doting reflections about the quaint affectionate ways of her baby granddaughter, or Racine's comic letter about little Lionval's panic when the elephant put its trunk into the keeper's pocket, or the duc de Croÿ's reminiscences about chatting with his grandsons in their tent about his life under canvas in the wars, or Diderot's sophisticated and touching analysis of how to encourage Angélique to moral understanding,[78] we are not documenting the advent of a new attitude to children; we are collecting samples of an overflow from a vast reservoir of interest and affection stored up in human nature, and awaiting only the lessening of the rigours of social conditions to manifest itself. The unremitting sacrificial effort of the human race lying behind the interdependence of men and women and the rearing of children needs only a beginning of leisure, a degree of ease and comfort and assurance for the future, an opportunity of education towards finesse, self-awareness, and literate expression, and it breaks out in a thousand imaginative expressions of affection and concern. The historian does not have to account for the rise of the marriage of free choice, the improving status of women, the centring of family life on the children, so much as to account for the delay and distortion of these manifestations of devotion under the pressure of adverse social conditions.

The rise of the small nuclear family as the emotional centre of existence coincides with the beginning of the conquest of death. Husband, wife, and children were to have a longer time together and a new assurance that this will be so, the inherent desire for emotional enrichment antedating, or at least coinciding with, the means of obtaining it. With a longer time together, the affections could more often deepen and diversify. At the same time, the old community and neighbourhood life was beginning to disintegrate; guilds, the village youth organizations, kinship groups, the nexus of conformity around the parish church would exercise less power over young people's minds. (With the rise of the factory and urban concentration, the family became, more than ever before, a refuge against the loneliness that is worst of all in the midst of a crowd.) As the boundaries of death's empire were pushed back, the small

nuclear family became more stable—it became the essential edu-
cative unit for the children.

With this new focusing of the emotions, attitudes to death
changed. Death was seen, not as a public event with the whole
community taking part, not as a religious crisis in which all the
faithful share, but as an intense, introverted family affair. The last
will and testament became a family document, rather than a public
and religious manifesto: the details of funeral ceremonies and,
even, of masses can be left to the affection of the heirs—the
important question is, has generosity and fairness been shown
within the family circle? The deathbed becomes the centre of family
loyalties, a scene of sorrowful leave-taking unsuited for the
curious, or, even, for the pious onlooker from outside the close
circle. Religious writers had wanted a public demonstration of
Christian faith by the dying, but once this religious gesture had
been made, had preferred that the throng be excluded. Of these two
principles, it was the second that was adopted, while the first
became optional. The duty to edify could be confined to the family
circle. As a woman, wife, and mother, and as an example of how to
die, Julie became the idol of the generation of *sensibilité* on the eve
of the Revolution. In Christian thought, the concept of the solidarity of the faithful had been forced into a subordinate place by the
concentration on the judgement which brooded over the lonely
individual. The new religiosity annexed the hope of immortality
and transformed it into the comforting conviction that 'we must
meet again'. There will be a reunion with those we have loved best
and loved exclusively. And those who could not convince themselves, could not achieve this certainty, would at least promise
always to remember, and make the tomb a place of melancholy
pilgrimage. The old graveyards were beside the parish church (and
intruding into it); the plans for new cemeteries outside the boundaries of habitation, which were drawn up in the seventies and
eighties, devised layouts according to the hierarchies of society; the
plans of 1801 were concerned rather with family solidarity and the
cult of melancholy and memory. The new 'religion' of the tomb
provided common ground (if the word is acceptable in the context)
for both deists and agnostics, and it also became a constituent
element of popular Christianity.

But in contrast to the pre-romantic *sensibilité* of the second half of the eighteenth century, there was a very different current in the thought of the Enlightenment—a fervent, moralizing enthusiasm which insisted on secular immortality as the reward of virtue, and which ran on into a new brand of patriotism, solemn and humanistic. The Pantheon it dreamed of was set up, crudely, in the midst of a war for survival, during the Revolution, and there were innovating architects who gave sombre, monolithic, expression to a concept of commemoration which seems to look ahead to totalitarian nationalism. Significantly, amidst all the enthusiasm for getting rid of the cruelties of the scaffold, an exception was made—almost universally—for the punishment of crimes against the State. The age was divided between the belief in the rights of the individual and the overwhelming obligation to social solidarity; the theoretical right of suicide, granted under the one heading was taken away under the other. The eighteenth century, indeed, saw a bifurcation of the ways of the imagination. For all, there is the lonely, inconsolable yet cherished mourning of the tightly-knit, small family group with—ideally—no *décor* other than the sad, eternal beauty of Nature. They hope that they will meet again; they swear that they will always remember. For great servants of the State, there are splendid monuments and ceremonies of public commemoration. The old hierarchical society of numerous exclusive corporations, of neighbourhood and kin, is disintegrating, and in its place is arising, on the one hand the small nuclear family, and on the other, the omnicompetent State. Rousseau glimpsed both worlds, the world of the *Nouvelle Héloïse* and the world of the *Contrat social*. Are they, as Jean-Jacques saw them, mutually exclusive, or are they compatible and complementary? We may answer, perhaps, by looking at ourselves. Do we not live, uneasily, in these two worlds, finding our fulfilment in our intimate circle, and owing a vague, but enforced obligation to the great collectivity, with nothing much in the way of allegiance to anything between? And is not this why the bonds of neighbourhood, community, trade, and vocation are so weak among us, and why the quality of our social life declines even as its material content improves—and why, except for the few who are closest to us and the medical technologists, we die alone?

As the multi-cellular society of the *ancien régime* has declined, Christianity—in the democratic West at least—has remained as the intensely personal religion of the individual who chooses it, while still retaining some of the aspects of the official *cultus* of the nation-state. But it is hard to see how it can become a community religion again. Perhaps its task for the future is to rediscover a spirit of community free from the inequalities and exclusivity of the *ancien régime*. As it does so, it may teach more confidently the doctrine of the community of the saints to alleviate the loneliness of our modern way of dying.

References

A PERSONAL VIEW

1. *Maximes* 26, *Œuvres* (Pléiade, 1957), p. 410.
2. J. Pieper, *Death and Immortality*, E. T. by R. S. C. Winston (1965), p. 21.
3. Cit. Pieper, p. 130.
4. D. E. Stannard, *The Puritan Way of Death: a Study in Religion, Culture and Social Change* (1979), p. 3.
5. For the view that only as we die do we finally become a true person, see Ladislas Boros, *The Moment of Truth: Mysterium Mortis* (1965), p. 62.
6. F. Borkenau, 'The Concept of Death', in *Death and Identity* ed. R. Fulton (1965), p. 42.
7. The following two paragraphs are taken largely from my article, 'The Historians of Death', in *The Times Literary Supplement*, 14 Dec. 1979, pp. 111–13. I am grateful to the editor for his permission.
8. M. Vovelle, 'La mort apprivoisée: de la mise en bière à la mise en livres', *Nouvelles littéraires*, 15 Apr. 1976.
9. P. Ariès, *L'Homme devant la mort* (1977).
10. F. Lebrun, *Les Hommes et la mort en Anjou au 17e et 18e siècles* (1971).
11. M. Vovelle, *Piété baroque et déchristianisation en Provence au XVIIIe siècle* (1973).
12. R. Favre, *La Mort dans la littérature et la pensée françaises au siècle des lumières* (1979).
13. Freud's views utilized by J. Morin, *L'Homme et la mort dans l'histoire* (1952), pp. 51–2.
14. R. E. Neale, *The Art of Dying* (1941), p. 9.
15. See below, p. 208.
16. André Malraux, *La Voie royale* (1930). The dying words of Perken at the end of the novel: 'Claude se souvint, haineusement, de la phrase de son enfance, "Seigneur, assistez-nous dans notre agonie . . ." Exprimer par les mains et les yeux, sinon par les paroles, cette fraternité désespérée qui le jetait hors de lui-même!. . . . Perken regardait ce témoin, étranger comme un être d'un autre monde.'

467

CHAPTER 1

Death's Arbitrary Empire

1. J. Fourastie, 'De la vie traditionnelle à la vie tertiaire' *Population* (1959), p. 415.

2. J. P. Peter, 'Disease and the Sick at the end of the 18th Century', in *Biology of Man in History*, ed. R. Forster and O. Ranum (1967), p. 114.

3. B. Luckin, 'The Decline of Smallpox and the Demographic revolution of the 18th Century', *Social History*, 6 (1977), pp. 793–7.

4. F. Granel, *Pages médico-historiques montpelliéraines* (1964), p. 66.

5. 'Réflexions philosophiques et mathématiques sur l'application du calcul des probabilités à l'inoculation de la petite vérole', in *Mélanges de littérature, d'histoire et de philosophie* (Amst. 1767), cit. M. Florkin, *Un prince, deux préfets et le mouvement scientifique et médico-social au Pays de Liège, 1771–1830* (1957), pp. 49, 52.

6. A. Corvisier, *L'Armée française de la fin du XVIIᵉ siècle au ministère de Choiseul. Le Soldat* (2 v. 1964), ii. 667.

7. Choderlos de Laclos, *Les Liaisons dangereuses*.

8. Prévost, *Mémoires pour servir à l'histoire de Malte* (2 v. 1741), i. 107–8.

9. Montesquieu to the duchesse d'Aiguillon, 3 Dec. 1753, *Œuvres compl.* (ed. A. Masson, 3 v. 1955), iii. 1481.

10. P. Goubert, 'Environnement et épidémies: Brest au XVIIIᵉ siècle', *Ann. de Bretagne* (1974), pp. 734–8.

11. J. P. Peter, pp. 114–15.

12. Messance, *Recherches sur la population des généralités d'Auvergne, de Lyon, de Rouen . . .* (1766), p. 181.

13. For winter the peak of mortality with autumn secondary, J. Dupâquier, 'Villages et petites villes de la généralité de Paris', *Ann. démog. hist.* (1969), 68–70; J. Beaud and G. Bouchart, 'Le dépôt des pauvres de Saint-Denis', ibid. (1974), pp. 127–31; A. Le Goff, 'Auray au XVIIIᵉ siècle', ibid, pp. 199–220. For the maximum in September, secondary peak in winter, see Y. Blayo, 'Trois paroisses de l'Ille et Vilaine', ibid. (1969), p. 195; M. Lachiver, 'En Touraine et en Berry', ibid., p. 218.

14. A. Poitrineau, *La Vie rurale en Basse-Auvergne au XVIIIᵉ siècle* (1969), p. 114; Y. Castan, *Honnêteté et relations sociales en Languedoc, 1715–80* (1974), p. 277. For the cast-off clothing in cities see Richard Cobb's remarkable essay in *Death in Paris, 1795–1801* (1978).

15. N. Pluche, *Histoire du ciel considérée selon les idées des poètes, des philosophes et de Moïse* (2 v. 1739), i. 15.

16. R. Mercier, *Le Monde médical de Touraine sous la Révolution* (1936), p. 234.
17. For the unusual case, the highest mortality of babies in winter, see M. Indré, 'Démographie de la paroisse Saint-Michel à Bordeaux', *Ann, démog. hist.* (1974), p. 235; J. Dupâquier, ibid. (1969), p. 49; Ph. Wiel, 'Une grosse paroisse du Cotentin', ibid., p. 188.
18. 15 Apr. 1672.
19. M. Laget, 'Pratique des accouchements en France au XVIIe et XVIIIe siècles', *Annales* (1977), p. 959; J. Gélis, 'Sages-femmes et accoucheurs', ibid., p. 927.
20. A. Dupuy, 'Les épidémies en Bretagne au XVIIIe siècle', *Ann. de Bretagne*, 3. (1886–7), 194–5.
21. A. Playoust-Chaussis, *La Vie religieuse dans le diocèse de Boulogne au XVIIIe siècle (1725–1790)* (1976), pp. 215–16.
22. J. Gélis, p. 986.
23. R. Pillorget, *La Tige et le rameau: familles anglaise et française, 16e–18e siècle* (1979), p. 152.
24. P. Delaunay, *Le Monde médical parisien au 18e siècle* (2nd ed. 1906), p. 442.
25. Laget, pp. 986–7; Delaunay, p. 443.
26. Gélis, p. 931. Cf. a curé in 1785 in M. Bouvet et P.-M. Bourdon, *A Travers la Normandie, XVIIe et XVIIIe siècles (Cahiers des Annales de Normandie*, 1968), p. 313. At the draw for the militia in one place in 1780, of 1,123 appearing, 873 were rejected. Of these, 560 were too short of stature, and 56 were 'mal tourné'. In 1781, 53 were 'mal tourné', in 1782, 35, in 1787, 14. Had government attempts to improve midwifery succeeded? (R. Molis, 'L'armée de l'ancien régime: la milice provinciale dans la subdélégation de Saint-Gaudens', *Rev. d'hist. écon. et soc.* 49 (1971) 44–5.)
27. Gélis, pp. 952–5.
28. See C. Morazé, *La France bourgeoise* (1940), p. 37.
29. P. Goubert, *Beauvais et le Beauvaisis de 1600 à 1730* (2 v. 1960), i. 39–40.
30. A. Molinier, 'Une paroisse de Bas-Languedoc, 1650–1792', *Méms. Soc. archéol. de Montpellier*, 12 (1961), cit. *Ann. démog. hist.* (1970), pp. 421–7. For the general figures W. C. Jonchleare, 'La table de mortalité de Duvillard', *Population* (1965), pp. 865–74.
31. P. Galliano, 'La Mort infantile dans la banlieue de Paris', *Ann. démog. hist.* (1966), pp. 139 ff.
32. M. Lachiver, *La Population de Meulan du XVIIe au XXe siècle* (1969), pp. 128–9.
33. D. Hunt, *Parents and Children in History* (1970), pp. 119–22.

34. Foucroy de Guillerville, *Les Enfans élevés dans l'ordre de la Nature* (*1774*), cit. Morel, in *Ann. démog. hist.* (1976), p. 410.
35. And had no more children than others, because breast-feeding delayed conception (J. Tarrande, in *Hist. du Poitou, du Limousin et des pays Charentais*, ed. E.-R. Labande (1976), p. 291).
36. Loc. cit., pp. 173–4; A. Chamoux, 'L'Enfance abandonnée à Reims à la fin du 18ᵉ siècle', *Ann. démog. hist.* (1973), 274–5.
37. Lallemand, *Un chapitre de l'histoire des Enfants trouvés: la Maison de la Couche à Paris* (17ᵉ et 18ᵉ siècles) (1885), p. 31; C. Delassalle, 'Abandons d'enfants à Paris au 18ᵉ siècle', *Annales* (1975), 188–191.
38. F. G. Pariset (ed.), *Hist. de Bordeaux*, Vol. 5: *Bordeaux au XVIIIᵉ siècle* (1968), pp. 365–6; H. Bergues et al., *La Prévention des naissances dans la famille* . . ., I.N.E.D., *Cahier* 35 (1960), p. 173.
39. Olwen Hufton, *The Poor of Eighteenth-Century France, 1750–1789* (1974), pp. 335–40.
40. Ballexsert, *Dissertation sur l'éducation physique des enfants* (1762), cit. Mercier, *L'Enfant dans la société française* (1961), p. 58.
41. See Hufton, pp. 332–4; Delassalle, p. 201; Lallemand, p. 37.
42. Cf. the figures for stillborn children: illegitimate, 6.4 per cent; legitimate, 2.2 per cent (S. Dreyer-Roos, *La Population strasbourgeoise sous l'ancien régime* (1969), p. 191).
43. P. F. Aleil, 'Enfants illégitimes et enfants abandonnés à Clermont dans la seconde moitié du XVIIIᵉ siècle', *Cahiers d'histoire*, 21 (1976), 327.
44. Hufton, pp. 345–8: Delassalle, p. 193.
45. P. Galliano, 'Le Fonctionnement du Bureau parisien des nourrices à la fin du 18ᵉ siècle', *Actes du 93ᵉ Congrès des socs. savantes, Tours, 1968; Sect. d'hist. mod. et contemp.* 2 (1917), p. 67.
46. As at Alençon (François de la Rochefoucauld, *Voyages en France*, ed. J. Marchand (1933), p. 98); at the Salpêtrière in Paris (Bergues, p. 188).
47. C. Bloch, *L'Assistance et l'État en France à la veille de la Révolution* (1908), pp. 116–17; A. Durand, *Etat religieux des trois diocèses de Nîmes, d'Uzès et d'Alais à la fin de l'ancien régime* (1909), pp. 319–21; E. Lavaquery, *Le Cardinal de Boisgelin* (2 v. 1920) i. 205.
48. Lallemand, pp. 139–40; J.-P. Gutton, *La Société et les pauvres: l'exemple de la généralité de Lyon, 1534–1789* (1971), p. 138.
49. In fact, without his father's oversight of the hospital arrangements, d'Alembert would probably have vanished from history too.
50. J. Delumeau, *La Mort des pays de Cocagne: comportement collectif de la Renaissance à l'âge classique* (1976), pp. 139–43.

51. A. Chamoux, *Ann. démog. hist.* (1933), p. 285.

52. R. Philip, 'Women and Family Breakdown in 18th-century France: Rouen, 1780–1800', *Journal of Social History* (1976), pp. 209–10.

53. O. Hufton, 'Attitudes towards authority in 18th-century Languedoc', *Social History*, 3 (1978), 285–7.

54. M. Hours, 'Émeutes dans le Lyonnais au XVIIIᵉ siècle', *Cahiers d'histoire*, 9 (1964), 144–7.

55. R. Favre, *La Mort dans la littérature et la pensée françaises au siècle des lumières* (1978), i. 53–5.

56. J. Meyer, *Hist. de Rennes* (1972), pp. 213–15; for the Capuchins of Paris see E.-J.-F. Barbier, *Chronique de la Régence et du règne de Louis XV, 1718–63* (8 v. 1857–8), iii. 93, 103.

57. Floods at Grenoble, 1733, 1737, 1759, 1764, and especially 1740, B. Bonnin in *Hist. de Grenoble*, ed. V. Chomel (1974), p. 130.

58. F. Lebrun, *Les Hommes et la mort en Anjou aux 17ᵉ et 18ᵉ siècles* (1971), p. 291.

59. Lachiver, *Meulan*, p. 202.

60. A. Farge, 'Les artisans malades de leur travail', *Annales* (1977), p. 999.

61. 'Réfutation de l'ouvrage d'Helvétius intitulé l'Homme' (unpub., 1773–4), ed. J. Assézat, *Diderot et l'interprétation de la Nature* (n.d.), p. 130.

62. E. Grar, *Histoire de la recherche et de l'exploitation de la houille dans le Hainault français, dans la Flandre française et dans l'Artois, 1716–1791* (3 v. 1847–50), ii. 136, 189–99, 205–10.

63. A. Farge, pp. 996–1001.

64. A. Carré, 'Notes sur l'historique de la médecine du travail et de l'ergomanie dans la marine', *Rev. d'hist. écon. et soc.* 97 (1969), 271–3. Other information in A. Cabantous and J. Messiaen, *Gens de mer à Dunkerque aux XVIIᵉ et XVIIIᵉ siècles* (1977), pp. 31–8.

65. A. Corvisier, *L'Armée française de la fin du XVIIᵉ siècle au ministère de Choiseul. Le Soldat* (2 v. 1964), ii. 684–7.

66. M. Spivak, 'L'hygiène des troupes à la fin de l'ancien régime', *Dix-huitième Siècle*, 9 (1977), 117, 121.

67. T. Adams, 'Mœurs et hygiène publique au XVIIIᵉ siècle: quelques aspects des dépôts de mendicité', *Ann. démog. hist.* (1975) pp. 93–5; J. Beaud and G. Bouchert, 'Le dépôt des pauvres de Saint-Denis, 1768–92', *ibid.* (1974), pp. 127–43.

68. C. M. Cipolla and D. E. Zanetti, 'Peste et mortalité différentiale', *Ann. démog. hist.* (1972), pp. 199–201.

69. These are the figures for Geneva, in A. Perrenoud, 'L'inégalité sociale devant la mort à Genève au XVIIIᵉ siècle', *Population* (1975), Numéro Spécial, p. 283. The Lutherans at Strasbourg had an advan-

tage over Catholics, no doubt because more prosperous (deaths 30. per 1,000 as against 33.5). See S. Dreyer-Roos, p. 203.

70. P. Goubert, in *Médecins, climat et épidémies à la fin du XVIIIe siècl* (1972), p. 240.

71. J. N. Biraben, *Les Hommes et la peste en France et dans les pay européens et méditerranéens* (2 v. 1975), i. 250 n.

72. A. Lottin, 'Les morts chassés de la cité', *Rev. du Nord*, 60 (1978), 76

73. R. Favre, 'Du Médico-topographie à Lyon en 1783', *Dix-huitièm Siècle*, 9 (1977), 152.

74. 'Dissertation sur la nature des richesses' (1704, publ. 1707), publ. by the I.N.E.D. in *Pierre de Boisguilbert ou la naissance de l'économi politique* (2 v. 1960), ii. 1000.

75. M. Morineau, 'Budgets populaires en France au XVIIIe siècle', *Rev d'hist. écon. et soc.* (1972), pp. 203–29.

76. Olwen H. Hufton, *The Poor of 18th century France*, pp. 67–8.

77. C.-E. Labrousse, *Esquisse du mouvement des prix et des revenus er France au XVIIIe siècle* (1932), pp. 582–97.

78. J.-C. Toutain, *Histoire quantitative de l'économie française*, ed. J Marczewski (3 v. I.S.E.A. 1961–3), i. 80–5; Morineau, p. 456.

79. Moheau, pp. 58–60.

80. M.-J. Villeman, 'L'alimentation du pauvre à l'hôpital général d Caen au début du XVIIIe siècle', *Ann. de Normandie*, 21 (1971) 235–60; J.-P. Filippini, 'Le régime des soldats et miliciens pris er charge par la marine française au XVIIIe siècle', *Cahiers des Annales* 28 (1970), 96–9. (It was generally said that people lived better nea the coast because of the fish and shellfish, and the accessibility o imported grain in time of crisis—see J. Delumeau, 'Démographi d'un port français sous l'ancien régime: Saint-Malo, 1651–1750' *Dix-huitième Siècle* (1970), p. 15; R. Beaudry, 'Alimentation e population rurale en Périgord', *Ann. démog. hist.* (1979), pp. 50 ff A. Poitrineau, p. 105.)

81. Poitrineau, loc. cit.

82. Moheau, pp. 117–18. He also insists on the good food.

83. J.-J. Hémardinguer, 'Pour une histoire de l'alimentation', *Cahier des Annales*, 28 (1970), 24–8.

84. M. Jacquin, 'Le ravitaillement de Saint-Jean-de-Losne au XVIII siècle', *Ann. de Bourgogne*, 46 (1974), 134.

85. J. Vedel, 'La consommation alimentaire dans le Haut-Languedoc au: XVIIe et XVIIIe siècles', and J. Bennasar and J. Goya, 'Consommatio alimentaire (XIVe–XIXe siècle)', *Annales* (1975), pp. 478–89 402–27.

86. A.-G. Manny, *Hist. de Clermont-Ferrand* (1975), p. 296.

87. Poitrineau, p. 103.

88. S. L. Kaplan, *Bread, Politics and Political Economy in the Reign of Louis XV* (2 v. 1976), i. 339.

89. A. Babeau, *Les Artisans et domestiques d'autrefois* (1886), pp. 24, 30–1.

90. Y. Castan, p. 279.

91. F. Lebrun, pp. 350, 376, 385.

92. Voltaire, *Dictionnaire philosophique*, 'Guerre'.

93. Goubert, in *Médecins, climat et épidémies*, pp. 235–6, 231.

94. G. Poitou, 'Ergotisme, ergot de seigle et épidémies en Sologne au XVIIIᵉ siècle', *Rev. d'hist. mod et contemp.* 23 (1976), 356–61.

95. Goubert, pp. 238–9; A.-M. Cocula and J. P. Pousson, *Hist. de l'Aquitaine: Documents* (ed. Ch. Higounet, 1973), pp. 277–8.

96. All subsequent discussion starts from J. Meuvret, 'Les crises de subsistance et la démographie de la France de l'ancien régime', *Population* (1946), pp. 643–50.

97. Theses of J. M. Boehler reported by J. P. Kintz, *Ann. démog. hist.* (1969), p. 268.

98. J. Toutain, 'Démographie d'un village normand, Saint-Maurice du Désert, 1668–1770', *Ann. de Normandie*, 26 (1976), 71; Ph. Wiel, 'Une grosse paroisse du Cotentin', *Ann. démog. hist.* (1969), pp. 164–8; J. River, 'L'évolution démographique de Toulouse', *Bull. d'hist. écon. et soc. de la Révolution française* (1968), pp. 85 ff.; R. Cobb, 'Disette et mortalité: la crise de l'an III et de l'an IV à Rouen', *Ann. de Normandie*, 6 (1956), 267–91—see also his *Terreur et subsistances, 1793–95* (1964), pp. 308.

99. L. Blin, 'La face administrative d'une crise frumentaire en Bourgogne (1747–49)', *Ann. de Bourgogne*, 58 (1976), 41.

100. M. Bricourt and J. Queruel, 'La crise de subsistance des années 1740 dans le ressort du Parlement de Paris', *Ann. démog. hist.* (1974), p. 322.

101. M. Lachiver, *Hist. de Meulan et de sa région par les textes* (1967), p. 81.

102. S. Dreyer-Roos, pp. 217–33.

103. A. B. Appleby, 'Nutrition and Disease: the case of London, 1550–1750', *Journal of Interdisciplinary History*, 6 (1975), 1–22; L. Clarkson, *Death, Disease, Famine in pre-Industrial England* (1975), p. 58.

104. Walsh McDermott, 'Infection and Malnutrition', in *Health Care for Remote Areas*, ed. J. P. Hughes (Kaiser Foundation, 1972), p. 137.

105. E. Leroy Ladurie, *Les Paysans de Languedoc* (1966), p. 552.

106. Cit. Favre, pp. 48–9.

107. Favre, thesis version, i. 29.

108. p. 386.

CHAPTER 2

Defences against Death: Eighteenth-century Medicine

1. For what follows, C. P. O'Malley, 'Medical History of Louis XIV', in *Louis XIV and the Craft of Kingship*, ed. J. C. Rule (1969), pp. 133–52.
2. E. Lavisse, *Hist. de France . . . jusqu'à la Révolution* (9 v. 1902–10) viii. 475 (for earlier deaths at Court, pp. 463–4).
3. Dr A. Corlieu, *La Mort des rois de France* (1873), pp. 113–21.
4. *Émile*, I.
5. F. Granel, *Pages médico-historiques montpelliéraines*, pp. 75–6.
6. L. Dulieu, 'Le mouvement scientifique montpelliérain an XVIIIᵉ siècle', *Rev. d'hist. des sciences*, 11 (1958), 227–49.
7. A. Dupuy, 'Les épidémies en Bretagne au XVIIIᵉ siècle', *Ann. de Bretagne*, 2 (1886–7), 190–1.
8. A. Boguel, *La Faculté de Médecine de l'Université d'Angers, 1433–1792* (1951), p. 88.
9. L. Dermigny, 'De Montpellier à La Rochelle, route du commerce, route de la médecine au XVIIIᵉ siècle', *Ann. du Midi*, 67 (1955), 56–7.
10. A. S. C. M. Dufresne, *Notes sur la vie et des œuvres de Vicq d'Azyr, 1748–94* (*Thèse*, Bordeaux, 1906), pp. 47–9.
11. P. Huard, 'L'Enseignement médico-chirurgical', in *L'Enseignement et la diffusion des sciences en France au XVIIIᵉ siècle*, ed. R. Taton (1964), pp. 180–96.
12. J. P. Goubert, 'The Extent of Medical Practice in France around 1780', *Journal of Social History*, 10 (1977), 412–14.
13. J. Meyer, 'Le Personnel médical en Bretagne à la fin du XVIIIᵉ siècle,' in *Médecins, climat et épidémies à la fin du XVIIIᵉ siècle* (1972), ed. Meyer et al., pp. 173–9.
14. Goubert, p. 413. Cf. F. Lebrun, *Les Hommes et la mort en Anjou aux 17ᵉ et 18ᵉ siècles*, p. 228.
15. 1786 report in P.-D. Bernier, *Essai sur le Tiers État rural ou les paysans de Basse-Normandie au XVIIIᵉ siècle* (1891), pp. 146–7.
16. J. Salvini, 'Le Clergé rural en Haut-Poitou', *Bull. Soc. antiquaires de l'Ouest*, 4ᵉ S (1957–8), pp. 259, 238.
17. R. P. Nepveu de la Manoulière, *Mémoires* (ed. G. Esnault, 3 v. 1877–9), i. 223.
18. A. Brette, 'Les dépenses des assemblées électorales en 1789', *Révolution française*, 23 (1897), 113.
19. P.-D. Bernier, loc. cit.
20. A. Dupuy, *Ann. de Bretagne*, 2 (1886–7), p. 199.
21. Harvey Mitchell, 'Rationality and Control in 18th-Century Medicine: Views of the Peasantry', *Comparative Studies in Society and History*, 21 (1979), 98.

22. Lebrun, p. 232; J.-P. Goubert, 'Médecine savante et médecine populaire dans la France de 1790', *Annales* (1977), pp. 913–19. Cf. in the time of Napoleon I, G. Thuillier, 'Pour une histoire des médicaments en Nivernais au XIXe siècle', *Rev. d'hist. écon, et soc.* 53 (1975), 75.
23. A. Franklin, *La Vie privée d'autrefois: Les médicaments* (1891), pp. 212–31. For orviétan see Franklin's next volume, *Les Médecins* (1892), pp. 133–4.
24. Lebrun, p. 231.
25. W. Coleman, 'The People's Health: Medical themes in 18th-Century French Popular Literature', *Bull. Hist. Med.* 51 (1977), 65–8.
26. M. Bouteiller, *Médecine populaire d'hier et aujourd'hui* (1966), pp. 229–36.
27. Franklin, *Les Médecins*, pp. 200, 225, 237; M. Le Pesant, 'Traditions populaires de la Normandie', *Ann. de Normandie*, 3 (1953), 332, 329.
28. For the following, M. Georges, 'La Structure hospitalière de France sous l'ancien régime', *Annales* (1977), pp. 1027–40.
29. Lebrun, p. 287.
30. See generally, Bloch, *L'Assistance et l'État en France à la veille de la Révolution* (1908).
31. T. J. Schmitt, *L'Assistance dans l'archidiaconé d'Autun au XVIIe et XVIIIe siècles* (1952), pp. 304–7. The situation was entirely different at the Hôtel-Dieu of Moulins.
32. L. S. Greenbaum, 'Nurses and Doctors in Conflict: Piety and Medicine in the Paris Hôtel-Dieu on the eve of the French Revolution', *Clio Medica*, 13 (1979), 247–8.
33. A. Chevalier, *L'Hôtel-Dieu de Paris et les sœurs augustines, 1650– 1810* (1901), pp. 442–9.
34. E. Laurès, *La Municipalité de Béziers à la fin de l'ancien régime* (1926), pp. 217–18; Bloch, pp. 64, 71–4, G.-J. Sumeire, *La Communauté de Trets à la veille de la Révolution* (1960), pp. 127–9.
35. Greenbaum, pp. 252–3.
36. C. C. Fairchilds, *Poverty and Charity in Aix-en-Provence, 1640– 1789* (1976), pp. 131–47.
37. J. Imbert, *Le Droit hospitalier de la Révolution française* (1954), p. 41.
38. E. Lequay, *Étude historique de l'Ordre de la Charité de Saint-Jean de Dieu et de ses établissements en France* (1854), p. 54.
39. G. Armigon, *Banquiers des pauvres* (n.d.), p. 135.
40. François de la Rochefoucauld, *Voyages en France, 1781–83*, ed. J. Marchand, p. 13, gives 14 sous a day. Bloch, p. 70, for the accusation.
41. Schmitt, p.. 310–11.
42. Lequay, pp. 43–53, 71–4.
43. O. H. Hufton, *The Poor of Eighteenth-Century France*, p. 154.

44. Robin, *Nouvelles de Médecine et de chirurgie* (1787), cit. W. Bromberg, *Man above Humanity: a History of Psycho-Therapy* (1954), pp. 76–7.

45. A. Guillemot, 'L'Hôpital de Malestroit', *Rev. d'hist. écon. et soc.* 48 (1970), 515.

46. J.-F.-H. de Richeprey, *Journal des voyages en Haute-Guienne*, ed. H. Guilhamon, *Arch. hist. du Rouergue*, 19 (1952), 367.

47. A. Corvisier, *L'Armée française de la fin du XVIIᵉ siècle au ministère de Choiseul. Le Soldat* (2 v. 1964), ii. 655–60.

48. J. C. White, 'Un exemple des réformes humanitaires dans la marine française: l'hôpital maritime de Toulon (1782–7)', *Ann. du Midi*, 83 (1971), 381–93.

49. ii. 304.

50. *Mémoires du Prince de Ligne* (ed. A. Lacroix, 1869), p. 198.

51. Mme de Sabran, *Corresp. inéd. de la comtesse de Sabran et du chevalier de Boufflers, 1778–88*, ed. E. de Magnieu and H. Prat (1875), p. 212.

52. *Fables de M. de Florian* (Lille 1810; first ed. 1792), pp. 38–9.

53. Franklin, *Les Médicaments*, pp. 98, 101, 125, 149, 129.

54. A. Delage, *Hist. de la thèse du doctorat en médecine d'après les thèses soutenues devant la Faculté de Médecine de Paris* (1913), pp. 312–13; P. F. Cranefeld, 'The discovery of Cretinism', *Bull. Hist. Med.* 36 (1962), 501; L. Dulieu, 'François Boissier de Sauvages', *Rev. d'hist. des sciences*, 22 (1969) p. 302.

55. J. Génévrier, *La Vie et les œuvres de Nicolas Chambon de Montaux, 1748–1826* (*Thèse méd.* Paris, 1906), pp. 80, 99. Cf. Delage, pp. 64, 89.

56. P. Lejeune, 'Rousseau et l'onanisme', *Annales* (1974), pp. 1015 ff. Tissot did further harm with his *Traité de l'épilepsie* (1770), ascribing this affliction to sexual excesses.

57. P. Huard and M. J. Imbault-Huert, 'Jean Astruc', *Clio Medica*, 4 (1969), 89.

58. L. Dulieu, 'Jean Astruc', *Rev. d'hist. des sciences* 26 (1973), 122–8.

59. 1770–3, cit. F. Granel, p. 109.

60. J.-P. Desaive and E. Le Roy Ladurie, in *Médecins, climat et épidémies à la fin du 18ᵉ siècle* (1972), p. 24.

61. 'Documents', ed. J.-P. Kintz, 'Une épidémie en Basse-Alsace en 1786', *Ann. démog. hist.* (1968), pp. 386–7.

62. D. Dinet, 'Mourir en religion', *Rev. historique* (1978), p. 44.

63. O. Temkin, *Galenism: rise and decline of a Medical Philosophy* (1973), p. 165. See also for this para. pp. 140 ff.

64. L. S. King, 'Medicine in 1695. Friedrich Hofmann's *Fundamenta Medicinae*', *Bull. Hist. Med.*, 43 (1969), 17–26.

65. E. Haigh, 'The Roots of the Vitalism of Xavier Bichet', ibid. 49 (1979), 72–84.

66. O. Temkin, p. 179.

67. *Méthode abrégée pour traiter la dissenterie* (Lille, 1750), p. 14; *Maladie épidémique à Seulin en 1756* (Lille, 1756), pp. 4–8; both reproduced in J. Veber's typewritten thesis, 'Malades et maladies à Lille, 1750–89' (Lille, 1971).

68. For Hecquet, see A. Juillard and L. Perrier in *Presse et histoire au XVIIIᵉ siècle: l'anneé 1734* (ed. P. Rétat, 1978), p. 313.

69. R. Darquenne, 'Théorie de la santé et de la maladie à la fin du XVIIIᵉ siècle', *Études sur le XVIIIᵉ siècle*, 2 (1975), 111–28.

70. R. M. Shryock, *A History of Nursing* (1959), p. 144; Harvey Mitchell, 'Rationality and Control in 18th-century Medical Views of the Peasantry', *Comparative Studies in Society and History*, 21 (1979), 85–7.

71. J. Meyer, in *Médecins, climat et épidémies* (1972), pp. 188–91.

72. F. Berg, 'Linné et Sauvages: les rapports entre leurs systèmes nosologiques', *Lychnos* (1956), pp. 32–54; L. S. King, 'Boissier de Sauvages and 18th-Century Nosology', *Bull. Hist. Med.*, 40 (1966), 43–7.

73. Comment in O. Temkin, *The Falling Sickness: a history of Epilepsy* (1945), p. 241; I. Veith, *Hysteria: the history of a Disease* (1965), pp. 166–7.

74. J. N. Biraben, 'La médecine et l'enfant au 18ᵉ siècle', *Ann. démog. hist.* (1973), pp. 218–21; J. Théodorides, 'Quelques aspects de la rage au 18ᵉ siècle', *Clio Medica*, 11 (1976), 95–7.

75. R. M. Shyrock, 'Social and Internal Factors in Modern Medicine', *Centaurus*, 3 (1953), 107–22. Important for this paragraph generally.

76. W. D. Foster, *A History of Medical Bacteriology and Immunology* (1970), p. 4.

77. J. Raulin, *Traité des affections vaporeuses* (1785), cit. I. Veith, p. 168; Corvisier, ii. 876–8; G. Rose, 'Nostalgia: a "forgotten" psychological Disorder', *Clio Medica*, 10 (1975), 29–51; M. Reinhard, 'Nostalgie et service militaire pendant la Révolution', *Ann. hist. de la Rév. française* (1958), pp. 1–15.

78. Le Clerc, *Histoire naturelle de l'homme considéré dans l'état de la maladie* (2 v. 1767), i. 244–59, 54, ii. 102–12, 390–3, 408, 439, 111.

79. Boileau, *Satire X*; J. Gélis, 'La formation des accoucheurs et des sages-femmes au XVIIᵉ et XVIIIᵉ siècles', *Ann. démog. hist.* (1977), pp. 156–7.

80. For a curiosity, Marat's letter of 23 August 1781 refusing to dissect a friend: 'Ma sensibilité, mon cher Comte, ne me permettant pas

d'assister à l'ouverture d'un ami' (Sabatier, *Dictionnaire de la mort* (1967), p. 41).

81. A particularly good one at 3 a.m. 29 December 1791 in Paris in A. Dupic, *Antoine Dubois, chirurgien et accoucheur* (Thèse méd. Paris, 1907).

82. J.-G. Perrot, *Genèse d'une ville moderne: Caen au XVIIIᵉ siècle* (2 v. 1974), ii. 1171.

83. Denisart (corrected by Camus and Bayard), *Collection . . . de décisions nouvelles . . . relatives à la jurisprudence* (9 v. 1783), iv. 33.

84. [Lefebvre de Beauvry], *Dictionnaire social et patriotique* (1770), pp. 17–19.

85. M.-A. Le Maître, *Recherches sur les procédés chirurgicaux de l'école Bordelaise* (1905), pp. 49–59.

86. E. Desnos, *L'Histoire de l'Urologie*, in J. T. Murphy, *The History of Urology* (1972), pp. 111–20.

87. M. Mevel, *Chirurgiens dijonnais au XVIIIᵉ siècle* (1902), p. 39.

88. Ch. Singer and E. A. Underwood, *A Short History of Medicine* (1962), p. 174.

89. Modern dentistry begins in Fauchard's *Le Chirurgien dentiste* (1728). See G. Gysel, 'Pierre Fauchard', *Janus*, 9 (1973), 75–86.

90. For the brilliant inventiveness of Jacques Davie in the operation for cataract see M. Florkin, *Médecine et médecins au Pays de Liège*, pp. 117–19.

91. Daret, *Traité de la peste* (1606) and P. Jaquelot, *L'Art de vivre longuement* (1639), in A. Franklin, *La Vie privée d'autrefois. L'Hygiène* (1890), pp. 96, 91. For what follows, pp. 134, 161–2, 174, and P. Sadd, 'Le Cycle des immondices', *Dix-huitième Siècle*, 9 (1977), 206; R. Eflin, 'L'Air dans l'urbanisme des lumières', ibid., p. 123.

92. See J. Bouchary, *Les Compagnies financières à Paris à la fin du XVIIIᵉ siècle* (3 v. 1940).

93. For next paragraph, J.-N. Biraben, *Les Hommes et la peste en France et dans les pays européens et méditerranéens* (2 v. 1975), i. 230–5.

94. Ibid. ii. 27, 39; i. 290, 303.

95. Ibid. i. 251; ii. 878, 90, 109, 143, 177.

96. Ibid. ii. 247.

97. J. C. Gaussent, 'Agde pendant la peste de Marseille', *Ann. du Midi*, 89 (1977), 225–6.

98. Biraben, i. 249; P. Chauvet, *La lutte contre une épidémie au 18ᵉ siècle: la peste du Gévaudan, 1720–3* (Thèse méd. Paris, 1939), p. 38.

99. Chauvet, p. 13.

100. The Chevalier d'Antrechaus, *Relation de la peste dont la ville de Toulon fut affligée en 1721* (Paris, 1756), pp. xii, 5–6.

101. P. Lunel, 'Pouvoir royal et santé publique à la veille de la Révolution: l'exemple du Roussillon', *Ann. du Midi*, 86 (1974), 365–7.

102. La Coste reviewed in the *Mémoirs de Trévoux*, cit., Favre, *La Mort . . . au siècle des lumières*, pp. 261–2. See Favre for what follows. For the arguments against churchmen see M. D. T. de Bienville, *Le Pour et le Contre de l'inoculation* (Rotterdam, n.d.), p. 85.

103. Vallery-Radot, M. *Un administrateur ecclésiastique . . . Le Cardinal de Luynes, archevêque de Sens 1753–84* (1966), p. 206.

104. F. Granel, *Pages médico-historiques montpelliéraines*, pp. 66–7.

105. See B. Luckin, 'The Decline of smallpox and the demographic revolution of the eighteenth century', *Journal of Social History* (1977), pp. 793 ff., commenting on the views of McKeown and P. Razzell's opposition in *Edward Jenner's Cowpox Vaccine: the history of a Medical Myth* (1977).

106. Favre, i. 279.

107. G. Francière, *Théophile de Bordeu (1722–1776)* (*Thèse méd.* Toulouse, 1907), p. 31.

108. The prince de Ligne, *Œuvres choisies* (ed. G. Charlier, 1944), pp. 30–1.

109. A. Franklin, *Les Médicaments*, pp. 187, 193.

110. By J. B. Winslow, transl. by J. J. Bruhier. For rescues from funeral pyres in classical antiquity, see B. de Montfaucon, *L'Antiquité expliquée et représentée* (9 v. 1719), v (1). 6–7.

111. Thomassin, *Mémoire sur l'abus de l'ensevelissement des morts, par M. Durande, précédé de réflexions sur le danger des inhumations précipitées* (Strasbourg, 1789), pp. 6, 72–3; *Corresp. Mme de Sabran*, p. 116; Lebrun, p. 460; Restif de la Bretonne, *Les Nuits de Paris* (ed. M. Bachelin, n.d.), pp. 63–4.

112. *Des inhumations précipitées* (1790), pp. 10–14; Thomassin, loc. cit.; [Dinouart], *Abrégé de l'embryologie sacrée* (1762), pp. 65–6.

113. M. Vovelle, *Piété baroque et déchristianisation en Provence au XVIIIe siècle*, p. 81. Favre, i. 443–4; Lebrun, pp. 331–6; Ariès, p. 392.

114. Delauney, *Le Monde médical Parisien*, pp. 284–93.

115. G. Chaussinand-Nogaret, 'Nobles médecins et médecins de cour au 18e siècle', *Annales* (1977), pp. 852–4.

116. G. Francière, pp. 74–82.

117. M. Florkin, *Médecine et médecins au Pays de Liège*, pp. 122–3.

118. Y. Morand, '"La Faculté Vengée" de La Mettrie', *Ann. de Bretagne*, 83 (1970), 814.

119. Cit. Dufresne, *Vicq d'Azyr*, p. 53.

120. J. Meyer, pp. 181–6, 152–4, 196–7.

121. Acad. Royale de Chirurgie, pref. by Girodat, *Recherches critiques et historiques sur . . . les progrès de la chirurgie en France* (Paris, 1744), p. 13.

122. La Mettrie, *La politique du médecin de Machiavel ou le chemin de la fortune ouvert aux médecins*, by 'Dr Fum-Ho-Han' (La Mettrie). Amsterdam, 1746, p. xx.

123. D. Roche, 'Talents, raison et sacrifice: l'image du médecin d'après des Éloges de la Société Royale de Médecine, 1776–89', *Annales* (1977), pp. 874–82.

124. M. Foucault, *Naissance de la clinique* (1972), 32, 34–5.

125. Chaussinand-Nogaret, pp. 850–1.

126. P. Huard and M. D. Grmek, *Science, médecine, pharmacie, de la Révolution à l'Empire, 1789–1815* (1970), pp. 117–19.

127. Cit. C. Salomon-Bayet, 'L'institution de la science', *Annales* (1975), p. 1032.

128. *Recherches critiques*, etc., pp. 13, 302–6.

129. R. Rappaport, 'G. F. Rouelle', *Chymia*, 6 (1960), 69–100; Ch. Badel, 'L'Enseignement des sciences pharmaceutiques', in Taton, pp. 237–247; M. Berman, 'Conflict and anarchy in the scientific orientation of French Pharmacy, 1800–1873', *Bull. Hist. Med.* 37 (1963), 442–3.

130. J. Meyer, 'L'Enquête de l'Académie de Médecine sur les épidémies, 1774–94', in *Médecins, climat et épidémies*, p. 12, and J. Desaive and E. Le Roy Ladurie, ibid., p. 23. For inquiries by intendants see J. N. Biraben, 'Essai sur la statistique des causes de decès en France sous la Révolution et le premier Empire', *Hommage à Marcel Reinhard: sur la population française au 18ᵉ et 19ᵉ siècles* (1973), pp. 60–1.

131. P. Huard in *Enseignement des sciences*, ed. Taton, p. 209.

132. C. C. Hannaway, 'Veterinary Medicine in pre-revolutionary France', *Bull. Hist. Med.* 50 (1976), 441–3.

133. P. Huard, pp. 216–17.

134. For all this conclusion see R. M. Shryock, 'Social and internal patterns in modern medicine', *Centaurus*, 3 (1953), 110–11.

135. See the path-finding article of P. Huard, 'L'émergence de la médecine sociale au XVIIIᵉ siècle', in *Concours Médical* (1958).

136. D. B. Weiner, 'Le droit de l'homme à la santé—une belle idée devant l'Assemblée Constituante, 1790–1', *Clio Medica*, 5 (1970), 209–15.

137. Lebrun, p. 295. For their contents at the end of the reign of Louis XV see P. Lunel, *Ann. du Midi*, 86 (1974), 353.

138, e.g. at Caen; Perrot, ii. 1175, 1179.

139. A. Farge, 'Les artisans malades de leur travail', *Annales* (1977), p. 1000; Favre p. 316.

140. 'Moheau', *Recherches et considérations sur la population de la France* (1778), ii. 35–41.

141. M. F. Morel, 'Théories et pratiques de l'allaitement en France au XVIIIᵉ siècle', *Ann. démog. hist.* (1976), p. 406.
142. P Huard and P. M. D. Grmek, op. cit., pp. 443–4.
143. Full bibliography in D. B. Weiner, 'Les Handicapés et la Révolution française, aspects de médecine sociale', *Clio Medica*, 12 (1977), 97–109. See also her 'The Blind Man and the French Revolution', *Bull. Hist. Med.* 48 (1974), 60–9, and R. Heller, 'Educating the Blind in the Age of the Enlightenment', *Medical History*, 23 (1979), 393 ff.
144. C. Bloch, pp. 313–14, 140–1.
145. For what follows, L. S. Greenbaum's three articles: 'Jean-Sylvain de Bailly, the Baron de Breteuil and the Four New Hospitals of Paris', *Clio Medica*, 8 (1977), 261–84; 'Tempest in Academy; Jean-Baptiste Le Roy, the Paris Academy of Sciences and the project of a new Hôtel-Dieu', *Archives internationales d'histoire des sciences*, 24 (1974), 122–37; 'The Hospital Thought of Jacques Tenon on the Eve of the French Revolution', *Bull. Hist. Med.* 49 (1975), 43–55, and J. D. Thompson and G. Goldin, *The Hospital: a Social and Architectural History* (1975), pp. 126, 142, 178.
146. A. Tzonis (ed.), 'Un Mémoire sur les hôpitaux de Condorcet', *Dix-huitième Siècle*, 9 (1977), 110–13.
147. J. Imbert, *Le Droit hospitalier de la Révolution et de l'Empire* (1954), pp. 13–20. There was, of course, the idea that the monastic lands should be confiscated to pay.
148. Favre, p. 337.
149. *Sur les altérations qui arrivent à l'air dans plusieurs circonstances où se trouvent les hommes réunis en société* (to the Royal Soc. of Medicine, 1782–5), cit. J. C. Perrot, *Caen*, ii. 1166.
150. Mercier is an example of the fixation on this hopeless quest; he wished the anatomists to give place to the 'generalizing genius' who would find 'the single truth' from which all springs. *Tableau de Paris*, i. 261.
151. S. Moravia, 'Philosophie et médecine en France à la fin du XVIIIᵉ siècle', *Studies on Voltaire and the 18th Century*, 89 (1972), 1090–1101.
152. For the development of this point see L. J. Jordanova, 'Earth, science and environmental medicine: the synthesis of the late Enlightenment', in *Images of the Earth*, ed. L. J. Jordanova and R. Porter (1979), pp. 119–46.
153. Cabanis, *Du degré de certitude en médecine*, was written in 1789, published in 1798.
154. E. H. Ackerknecht, *Medicine at the Paris Hospital, 1794–1848*, (1967), p. xi.
155. E. Wickersheimer, 'La clinique de l'Hôpital de Strasbourg au XVIIIᵉ

siècle', *Archives internationales d'histoire des sciences*, 64 (1963), 261; J. Gelfand, 'The Hospice of the Paris College of Surgery, 1774–93', *Bull. Hist. Med.* 47 (1973), 19; Foucault, pp. 56, 61; Ackerknecht, p. 31.

156. Dufresne, p. 39.
157. Foucault, pp. 199, 148. For the idea of team work in morbid anatomy (1802) see P. Huard and M. J. Imbault-Huert, 'La Clinique Parisienne avant et après 1802', *Clio Medica*, 10 (1975), 178, 182.
158. Diderot, *Corresp.*, ed. G. Roth and Varloot (16 v. 1955–70), v. 197.

CHAPTER 3

The Shadow of Death and the Art of Living

1. Favre, p. 143.
2. Saint-Simon, *Mémoires* (1829 ed.) xvii. 319–24.
3. Thomas Bentley, *Journal of a Visit to Paris, 1776*, ed. Peter France (1977), pp. 56–7.
4. P. Ariès, *L'Homme devant la mort*, p. 505.
5. Caraccioli, *Tableau de la mort* (1761), p. 34.
6. *Les Historiettes de Tallement des Réaux* ed. MM. de Momergué and Paulin, 5 v. 1862), v. 275.
7. M. de Lescure, *Les Maîtresses du Régent* (1861), pp. 280–2.
8. Ch. Robert, *Urbain de Hercé* (1900), pp. 45–9.
9. *Corresp. littéraire et anecdotique entre M. de Saint Fonds et le président Dugas, 1711–39* (ed. W. Poidebad, 2 v. 1900), ii. 231 (27 Aug. 1735).
10. L. Versini, *Laclos et la tradition: essai sur les sources et la technique des 'Liaisons Dangereuses'* (1968), pp. 443, 452–3.
11. E.g. Caraccioli, pp. 162–5; P. Crasset, S. J., *La Douce et la sainte mort* (1708), pp. 142–7. For a problem of casuistry facing a *curé* over a will, see Diderot, *Entretiens d'un père avec ses enfants* (Pléiade), pp. 760–78.
12. Interesting procession of the Chapter of Sens in J.-B. Thiers, *Superstitions anciennes et nouvelles* (2 v. 1733), ii. 129–30.
13. Dom Claude Vert, *Explication des cérémonies de l'Eglise* (2nd ed. 4 v. 1709), iv. 443–4.
14. A. Le Braz, *La Légende de la mort en Basse-Bretagne* (1883), pp. 4–7.
15. Favre, pp. 177–9.
16. Marc-Antoine de Gérard, sieur de Saint-Amant, 'La Nuict', *Œuvres complètes*, ed. C-L. Livet (2 v. 1855), i. 97. He died in 1661.
17. J. McManners, *French Ecclesiastical Society at the end of the ancien régime: a study of Angers . . .* (1960), p. 308.

18. Lebrun, *Les Hommes et la mort en Anjou*, pp. 430 ff.

19. *Mémoires et aventures d'un homme de qualité* (*Œuvres choisies*, 39 v. 1810), i. 36–7.

20. M. Meiss, *Painting in Florence and Vienna after the Black Death* (1951), p. 65.

21. Mercier, *Tableau de Paris*, iii. 178.

22. Favre, pp. 16–19.

23. Chateaubriand, *Atala* (1801) and the 1805 preface (ed. F. Letessier, Classiques Garnier, 1958), pp. 134, 223.

24. Vasselin, *Théorie des peines capitales ou abus et danger de la peine de mort . . .* (1790), pp. 29–30.

25. *Journal intime de Maine de Biran* (ed. A. de la Valette-Monbrun, 2 v. 1927), i. 10.

26. *Cit.* Favre, p. 3.

27. *Ibid.*, p. 14.

28. A. Piron, *Recueil de poésies* (1773), cit. Favre, p. 14.

29. A. de la Borderie (ed.), *Corresp. historique des Bénédictins Bretons* (1880), p. 173.

30. M. Garden, *Lyon et les lyonnais au XVIIIe siècle* (n.d.), pp. 432–3.

31. *Mes Souvenirs*, ed. C. Hamelin (2 v. 1898–1901), i. 251–2.

32. Antoine-Léonard Thomas, *Ode sur le temps* (*Œuvres*, 1822–3, v. 341). Thomas died in 1785.

33. [Alix], *Les Quatre Âges de l'homme: poème* (1782).

34. Cabanis, *Rapports du physique et du moral de l'homme* (2 v. 1802), i. 27.

35. La Curne de Sainte-Palaye, *Mémoires sur l'ancienne chevalerie* (2 v. 1759), i. 62–4.

36. M.-G. Daignan, *Tableau des variétés de la vie humaine* (2 v. 1788), ii. 259–61.

37. Buffon, cit. C. Morazé, *La France bourgeoise* p. 37.

38. P. Goubert, *Beauvais et le Beauvaisis de 1600 à 1730*, i. 39–40 for a hamlet where 54 per cent died in the first two years.

39. This was the custom at the end of the seventeenth century. J. Ferté, *La Vie religieuse dans les campagnes parisiennes, 1622–1695* (1962), p. 300. A royal declaration of 1690 ordered baptism within 24 hours. In Meulan this order was 90 per cent effective, though a few families waited until the first Sunday after the birth. M. Lachiver, *La Population de Meulan du XVIIe au XXe siècle*, p. 70.

40. *Mémoires du duc de Luynes sur la cour de Louis XV* (ed. L. Dussieux and E. Soulié (15 v. 1860–5), xiii. 154.

41. Anne Zink, *Azereix: la vie d'une communauté rurale à la fin du XVIIIe siècle* (1969), pp. 243–5.

42. A. de Gannier, 'Lazare Carnot', *Rev. des quest. hist.* 54 (1893), 448.

43. E. Regnault, *Christophe de Beaumont* . . . (2 v. 1882), i. 6; *Journal du duc de Croÿ, 1718–84* (ed. Vicomte de Grouchy and P. Cottin, 4 v. 1906), i. 1–2. According to Simone Poignant, *L'Abbaye de Fontevrault et les filles de Louis XV* (1966), pp. 180, 186, two of Louis XV's daughters were baptized at the ages of eleven and twelve respectively.

44. F. Lebrun, pp. 423–4.

45. J. Mathorez, *Les Étrangers en France sous l'ancien régime* (2 v. 1919), i. 24–5.

46. Lebrun, p. 422.

47. G. Le Bras, *Introduction à l'histoire de la pratique religieuse en France* (2 v. 1942), i. 45 n. When the duc de Bourgogne died, aged ten, in 1761, he was confirmed and received First Communion, before being given Extreme Unction (P. Girault de Coursac, *L'Éducation d'un Roi. Louis XVI* (1972), pp. 47, 59).

48. T. J. Schmitt, *L'Organisation ecclésiastique et la pratique religieuse dans l'archidiaconé d'Autun de 1650 à 1750* (1957), p. lxxxvii; Mme Roland, *Mémoires* (ed. Perroud, 2 v. 1905), ii. 44 (age eleven).

49. Going to a *collège* at seven. J. Leflon, *Eugène de Mazenod, évêque de Marseille, 1782–1801* (3 v. 1957–65), i. 68; A. Monglond, *Le Préromantisme français* (2 v. 1930), ii. 275; Ariès, *L'Enfant et la vie familiale sous l'ancien régime* (1960), p. 234; to a *pension*, Georges Bouchard, *Prieur de la Côte d'Or* (1946), p. 21. Girls to Saint-Cyr at seven (D. Roche, 'Éducation et société dans la France du XVIIIᵉ siècle: l'exemple de la maison royale de Saint-Cyr', *Cahiers d'hist.* 23 (1978), 16). Entry to Louis-le-Grand at eight (M. Chisick, 'Bourses et boursiers du collège Louis-le-Grand, 1762–88', *Annales* (1975), pp. 1562–74).

50. A. Babeau, 'L'Intervention de l'État en l'instruction primaire en Provence sous la Régence', *Rev. hist.* 46 (1891), 304.

51. F. Lebrun, *La Vie conjugale sous l'ancien régime* (1975), pp. 135–6; R. Pillorget, *La Tige et le rameau*, p. 272.

52. P. Chevallier, *Loménie de Brienne et l'Ordre monastique, 1766–89* (2 v. 1959–60), i. 63–4, 69–70, 280.

53. A. Corvisier, 'La société militaire et l'enfant', *Ann. démog. hist.* (1973), p. 332. For Flanders, E. Vilquin, 'Vauban, inventeur des recensements', ibid. (1975), pp. 242—3.

54. Daignan, ii. 66.

55. L. H. Henry and Cl. Lévy, 'Ducs et pairs sous l'ancien régime: caractéristiques démographiques d'un caste', *Population* (1960), pp. 806–27.

56. Y. Durand, *Les Fermiers généraux au XVIIIᵉ siècle* (1971), p. 305;

P. Butel, 'Comportements familiaux dans le négoce Bordelais au XVIIIᵉ siècle', *Ann. du Midi*, 88 (1976), 139–40.

57. J. McManners, 'Living and Loving: Changing attitudes to sexual relationships in 18th century France', *British Soc. for 18-Century Studies*, 12 (June 1977), 1–19. I am quoting extensively from this article in this section on marriage.

58. [Le Maître de Claville], *Traité du vrai mérite de l'homme* (1734), p. 372.

59. J. Ghestin, 'L'Action des Parlements contre les mésalliances au XVIIᵉ et XVIIIᵉ siècles', *Rev. hist. de droit fr. et étranger*, Sér. IV, 34 (1956), 74–109, 196 ff.

60. Lebrun, *Les Hommes et la mort en Anjou*, p. 429; M. Lachiver, 'En Touraine et en Berry', *Ann. démog. hist.* (1969), p. 229; M. Garden, *Lyon et les lyonnais au XVIIIᵉ siècle*, p. 92; Lebrun, *La Vie conjugale* etc., p. 50; Lachiver, p. 133. For married people regarding themselves 'not as if united for eternity, but as destined to pass some years together', see M. Bailant, 'La famille en miettes: sur un aspect de la démographie du XVIIIᵉ siècle', *Annales*, 27 (1972), 966.

61. A. Lottin, *La Désunion du couple sous l'ancien régime: l'exemple du Nord* (1975), p. 190.

62. Lachiver, p. 73; A. Poitrineau, *La Vie rurale en Basse-Auvergne*, p. 77; B. Lepetit, 'Démographie d'une ville en gestation: Versailles sous Louis XIV', *Ann. démog. hist.* (1972), pp. 49–83; P. Valmary, *Familles paysannes au XVIIIᵉ siècle en Bas-Quercy* (I.N.E.D. *Cahier* 45, 1965), p. 103.

63. Ch. Carrière, M. Courdurié, F. Rebuffat, *Marseille, ville mort: la peste de 1720* (1968), p. 118.

64. M. Terisse, 'Le rattrapage de nuptualité d'après-peste à Marseille, 1720–24', in *Hommage à Marcel Reinhard*, ed. Dupâquier *et al.* pp. 565–78. For a general discussion of the controversy concerning the relationship between mortality rates and the age of marriage see D. Scott Smith, 'A homeostatic Demographic Régime' in *Population Patterns in the Past*, ed. R. Demos Lee (1977).

65. *Nouvelle Héloïse*, V (2), Pléiade ed., ii. 542. For commentary see R. Glasser, *Time in French Life and Thought* (E.T. from the German of 1936 by C. G. Pearson, 1972), pp. 244–6.

66. Lebrun, *La Vie conjugale*, p. 48; Zink, *Azereix*, p. 75; Poitrineau, p. 97.

67. For all this paragraph see J.-L. Flandrin, *Famille, parenté, maison, sexualité dans l'ancienne société* (1976), pp. 44–52.

68. See Gérard Bouchard, *Le Village immobile: Sennely-en-Sologne au XVIIIᵉ siècle* (1972), esp. pp. 51, 73, 82–3, 232–3.

69. M. C. Peronnet, *Les Évêques de l'ancienne France* (2 v. 1977), i. p. 59. For the joke, Marmontel, 'La Mauvaise mère', *Contes moraux* (3 v. 1765), ii. 101. For what follows, A. Babeau, *La Vie militaire sous l'ancien régime* (2 v. 1890), II: *Les Officiers*, pp. 99–100; P. 'Chalmin, 'La Formation des officiers des armes savantes sous l'ancien régime', *Actes Congrès Soc. Sav.* (1951), p. 167; C. W. Wrong, 'The Officers of Fortune in the French Infantry', *French Historical Studies*, 9 (1976), 407.

70. McManners, in *The European Nobility in the 18th Century* (ed. A. Goodwin, 1967 ed.), p. 42.

71. W. Doyle, *The Parlement of Bordeaux at the End of the Old Régime*, *1771–90* (1976), p. 24; M. Virieux, 'Une enquête sur le parlement de Toulouse en 1718', *Ann. du Midi*, 87 (1975), 40–1.

72. F. Bluche, *Les Magistrats du Parlement de Paris au 18ᵉ siècle* (1960), pp. 58 ff.

73. R. Goulard, *Une lignée d'exécuteurs des jugements criminels; les Sanson, 1688–1847* (1968), p. 32.

74. V. R. Gruder, *The Royal Provincial Intendants: a governing élite in 18th-century France* (1968), pp. 34–94.

75. Y. Durand, pp. 118–19.

76. Peronnet, i. 334 ff.

77. Dying at forty-three—'C'est mourir à la fleur de son âge' (*Mémoires de Trévoux*, Feb. 1704, p. 27).

78. Daignan, ii. 257.

79. [Le Maître de Claville], p. 50.

80. Buffon, *De l'homme* (ed. Duchet, 1972), pp. 111, 142, 147–8.

81. Cabanis, i. 283.

82. Senancour, *Oberman*, Lettre XLVII (ed. Monglond), ii. 16–17.

83. D'Argenson, 'Pensées sur la vie et sur la mort', *Journal et Mémoires* (ed. E. J. B. Rathery, 9 v. 1859–67), v. 214–15.

84. J.-C. Perrot, *Genèse d'une ville moderne: Caen au XVIIIᵉ siècle*, ii. 1084, citing L. Lébecq de la Cloture, *Observations sur les maladies épidémiques* (1776).

85. Mercier, *Tableau de Paris*, iii. 191.

86. M. Courdurié, *La Dette des collectivités publiques de Marseille . . .* (1975), p. 193.

87. Perrot, *Caen*, ii. 1085. The working class grow old more quickly than the well-fed servants of the *château*, says a writer on cookery in 1782 (cit. A. Girard in *Rev. d'hist. mod. et contemp.* 24 (1977), 509).

88. Restif de la Bretonne, *Le Nouvel Émile*, *Œuvres* (ed. M. Bachelin, 1931), iii. 257. For his view that it is impossible to fall in love without degradation after the age of forty, see P. Testud, *Rétif de la Bretonne et la création littéraire* (1977), p. 433.

89. [Le Maitre de Claville], loc cit.
90. Restif de la Bretonne, M. Nicolas, Œuvres, viii. 305.
91. Choderlos de Laclos.
92. Diderot, Essai sur la peinture (Pléiade), p. 1166.
93. Buffon, p. 170.
94. Daignan, ii. 267.
95. Cit. M. A. Legrand, La Longévité à travers les âges (1911), p. 31.
96. Senancour, Oberman, ed. cit. ii. 63.
97. P. Huard and M. J. Imbault-Huert, 'La vie et l'œuvre de Jean Astruc', Clio Medica, 4 (1969), 86. For Hippocrates' age ladder, see P. N. Stearns, Old Age in European Society: the case of France (1977), p. 24.
98. Caraccioli, Dict. critique, pittoresque et sentencieux (3 v. 1768), iii. 309, 144.
99. ii. 262.
100. J.-H. Meister, Lettres sur la vieillesse (1810), p. 100.
101. Saint-Lambert, Chagrins de la vieillesse, cap. III.
102. Daignan, loc. cit.
103. X. Bichat, Recherches physiologiques sur la vie et la mort (An VIII), pp. 181–2.
104. Cabanis, p. 297.
105. Essai sur la peinture, p. 1145.
106. Sénac de Meilhan (1787), cit. A. Monglond, Le Préromantisme français, i. 58.
107. Joannet, De la connoissance de l'homme dans son être et dans ses rapports (2 v. 1775), i. 283.
108. ii. 268–9.
109. M. Ferri, Les Portraits ou caractères et mœurs du XVIIIe siècle (1781), pp. 9, 54, 15, 31.
110. [Alix], p. 45.
111. [Dom Pernety], Observations sur les maladies de l'âme (1777), p. 285.
112. Diderot, Éléments de physiologie (Œuvres compl. ed. Assézat, ix. 276), cit. Faure, p. 15.
113. [Chomel], Aménités littéraires . . . (2 v. 1773), pp. 168–71.
114. P. Joseph Roman Joly (Capuchin), Dict. de morale philosophique (2 v. 1771), i. 39.
115. [Chomel], loc cit.
116. La Trompette du ciel qui réveille les pécheurs (recueilli par V. P. A. Yvan, Caen, 1711), p. 322.
117. Duguet, Explication de . . . Deutéronome . . . d'Habacuc et de Jonas (1734), pp. 491–9.
118. Caraccioli, Tableau de la mort.

119. Cabanis, i. 306–7.
120. Delisle de Sales, *Essai philosophique sur le corps humain* (3 v. 1773), iii. 319.
121. Mme du Châtelet, *Discours sur le Bonheur* (ed. R. Mauzi, 1961), pp. 38–9.
122. L. Versini, p. 437.
123. La Fontaine, *La Mort et le malheureux, Œuvres* (ed. L. Moland 7 v. 1872–6), i. 70.
124. Le Bret, cit. Favre, p. 169; M.-A. Hersan, *Pensées édifiantes sur la mort tirées des propres paroles de l'Écriture sainte et des Pères* (1722), Préf.
125. A. Le Breton, *La 'Comédie humaine' de Saint-Simon* (1914), p. 238.
126. See B. Pocquet de Haut-Jussé, 'La vie temporelle des communautés de femmes à Rennes', *Ann. de Bretagne*, 32 (1917), 77–8; Dom E. Lecroq, *Les Annonciades de Fécamp (1648–1792)* (1947), p. 171; E. and J. de Goncourt, *La Femme au 18ᵉ siècle* (1862), pp. 8–9.
127. *Éclaircissement sur les 'Mœurs'* (1762), p. lviii.
128. A. Guillois, *Pendant la Terreur, le poète Roucher, 1745–94* (1890), pp. 111–12.
129. Mme de Lambert, *Traité de la vieillesse*, cit. Favre (thesis), i. 165.
130. M. C. Peronnet, *Les Évêques de l'ancienne France*, i. 454.
131. L. S. Greenbaum, 'Ten Priests in search of a mitre: How Talleyrand became a Bishop', *Catholic Historical Review*, 50 (1964), 307–331.
132. A. Playoust-Chaussis, *La Vie religieuse ... diocèse de Boulogne*, pp. 136–8.
133. Peronnet, ii. 837–8.
134. G. Arbellot, 'Les routes de France au XVIIIᵉ siècle', *Annales* (1973), pp. 786–90.
135. Mme de Sévigné, 26 Apr. 1671.
136. A. Franklin, *La Vie privée d'autrefois*, (1888), *La Cuisine*, pp. 200–6; A. Girard, 'Le triomphe de la cuisine bourgeoise: livres culinaires, cuisine et société en France, XVIIᵉ et XVIIIᵉ siècles, *Rev. d'hist. mod. et contemp.* (1977), pp. 497–512.
137. Diderot, *Réfutation ... de l'ouvrage, d'Helvétius intitulé 'l'Homme'*, 1773–4, unpubl., ed. J. Assézat, *Diderot et l'interprétation de la nature* (n.d.), p. 436.
138. Buffon, *De l'Homme (ed. cit.)*, pp. 167–70. For the 'Climacteric' see *Dict. historique des mœurs* (3 v. 1767), i. 502; [Chomel], *Aménités littéraires*, i. 171–3; Louis de Beausobre, *Nouvelles considérations sur les années climactériques* (1757), p. 4.
139. J. H. Meister, *Lettres sur la vieillesse*, p. 3.
140. *Encyclopédie*, xvii (1765), p. 267.

141. A. Niderst, *Fontenelle à la recherche de lui-même, 1657–1702* (1972), p. 607.
142. Chamfort, *Caractères, Œuvres* (6 v. 1824–5, reissued by Slatkine, 1968), ii. 23–4.
143. Robert, *De l'influence de la Révolution française sur la population* (2 v. 1802), i. 151–4. For a libertine of eighty, a nobleman entertaining a shopgirl in his prison, see C. Quetel, 'Lettres de cachet . . .', *Ann. de Normandie*, 28 (1978), 151.
144. For all this paragraph, P. Sage, *Le Bon Prêtre dans la littérature française d'Amadis de Gaule au Génie du Christianisme* (1951).
145. H. de Broc, 'Une famille de province au XVIIIe siècle', *Bull. Soc. Hist. arch. de l'Orne*, 10 (1890), 195–7.
146. Lesbros de la Versane, *Caractères des femmes ou aventures du chevalier de Miran* (1769).
147. Cit. Sage, p. 415.

CHAPTER 4

Statistics, Hopes, and Fears

1. J. Dupâquier, 'Les caractères originaux de l'histoire démographique française au XVIIIe siècle', *Rev. d'hist. mod. et contemp.* 23 (1976), 187–8, 190. See also I.N.E.D. *6e Rapport* in *Population*, 32 (1977), 253 ff., and Dupâquier and C. Berg-Hanon, 'Voies nouvelles pour l'histoire démographique de la Révolution française', *Ann. hist. Rév. fr.* 47. (1975), 28–9.
2. Y. Blayo and L. Henry, 'Données démographiques sur la Bretagne et l'Anjou', *Ann. démog. hist.* (1967), p. 100; F. Lebrun, 'Les épidémies en Haute-Bretagne à la fin de l'ancien régime', ibid. (1977), pp. 181–93.
3. P. Goubert, 'Le phénomène épidémique en Bretagne à la fin du 18e siècle', *Médecins, climat et épidémies* (ed. Goubert *et al.*), p. 225.
4. P. Chaunu, 'Réflexions sur la démographie normande', in *Hommage à Marcel Reinhard*, ed. Dupâquier *et al.*, p. 105.
5. E. Leroy Ladurie, *Les Paysans de Languedoc*, pp. 556–60.
6. M. Vovelle, in *Hist. de la Provence*, ed. R. Baratier (1969), pp. 353–5 (commenting especially on R. Baehrel, *Une croissance: la Basse Provence rurale* (1961)).
7. M. Crubellier, *Hist. de la Champagne* (1975), p. 250.
8. F. Lebrun, *Hist. d'Angers* (1975), p. 92; F. Dornic, *Hist. du Mans* (1975), p. 185.
9. P. Chaunu, *La Mort à Paris . . .* (1978), pp. 190–200.
10. J. Meyer, *Hist. de Rennes* (1972), pp. 238–9, 256.
11. Y. Durand, in *Hist. de Nantes*, ed. P. Bois (1977), pp. 173–8.

12. J. Rivès in *Ann. démog. hist.* (1969), p. 407.
13. M. Crubellier, p. 250.
14. J. Combes-Monier, 'L'origine géographique des Versaillais', *Ann. démog. hist.* (1970), pp. 238–9; B. Lepetit, 'Démographie d'une ville en gestation: Versailles sous Louis XIV', ibid. (1977), pp. 49–83; J. Jacquart and M. François, in *Hist. de l'Île de France et de Paris*, ed. Mollet (1971), p. 321.
15. Yves Le Moigne, in *Hist. de la Lorraine*, ed. M. Parisse (1978), pp. 343–51.
16. G. Livet, in *Hist. d'Alsace*, ed. Ph. Dollinger (1970), pp. 306, 310–11.
17. G. Frêche, *Toulouse et la région Midi-Pyrénées au siècle des lumières* (1974), pp. 95, 99, 116; also 'La population de la région Toulousaine sous l'ancien régime', in *Hommage à Marcel Reinhard*, ed. Dupâquier *et al*, pp. 268–9.
18. J. Dupâquier, 'Croissance démographique régionale dans le bassin Parisien au XVIIIᵉ siècle', ibid., pp. 230–50.
19. A. Poitrineau, in *Hist. de l'Auvergne*, ed. A.-G. Mann (1974), pp. 342–7.
20. M. Garden, *Lyon et les Lyonnais au XVIIIᵉ siècle* (1970), pp. 141–2.
21. J.-F. Soulat and J.-B. Laffa, *Hist. de Tarbes* (1975), p. 154; Anne Lefebvre-Teilhard, 'La population de Dole au XVIIIᵉ siècle', *Ann. démog. hist.* (1970), p. 422; Ch. Higounet, *Hist. de l'Aquitaine* (1971), p. 538; M. Lachiver, *La Population de Meulan du XVIIᵉ au XXᵉ siècle* (1969), p. 5.
22. M. M. Jouan, 'Les originalités démographiques d'un bourg normand au 18ᵉ siècle', *Ann. démog. hist.* (1969), p. 92.
23. M. Lachiver, 'En Touraine et en Berry', *Ann. démog. hist.* (1969), p. 217; J. Lelong and P. Chaunu, 'Saint-Pierre-Église, 1657–1790', ibid. (1969), p. 127.
24. Dupâquier in *Rev. d'hist. mod. et contemp.* (1976), p. 194; S. Dreyer-Roos, *La Population Strasbourgeoise sous l'ancien régime*, pp. 107–8; Lachiver, p. 4; M. Terisse, *La Population de Marseille, 1654–1830* (3 v. 1971), i. 365–7; Garden, *Lyon*, pp. 142–3.
25. J. Jacquart and M. François, p. 321. According to A. Armengaud, *La Famille et l'enfant en France et en Angleterre du XVIᵉ au XVIIIᵉ siècle: aspects démographiques* (1979), the essential cause of the fall of mortality was the reduction in the deaths of children (a fall from the second half of the seventeenth century to the second half of the eighteenth from 250–330 per 1,000 to 180–260 per 1,000). According to Dupâquier, the significant fall in infant mortality came after 1790.
26. Dupâquier, loc. cit. I have not been able to fit Y. Blayo's argument ('La mortalité en France de 1740 à 1829', *Population* (1975),

pp. 123–37) into this picture. He makes 1740–89 a period of high mortality, with a fall after 1790.

27. Dreyer-Roos, p. 213.
28. D. Dinet, 'Mourir en religion au XVIIᵉ et XVIIIᵉ siècles', *Rev. hist.* 259 (1978), 29–39.
29. De Félice, *Code de l'humanité* (13 v. 1778), i. 512.
30. For all the above para., P. Buck, 'Seventeenth-century Political Arithmetic; civil strife and vital statistics', *Isis*, 68 (1977), 70–83.
31. S. Dreyer-Roos, p. 24.
32. G. Frêche, *Toulouse*, p. 24.
33. B. Gille, *Les Sources statistiques de l'histoire de France: des enquêtes du XVIIIᵉ siècle à 1870* (1964), pp. 24–5.
34. E. Vilquin, in *Population* (1978), p. 421.
35. E. Vilquin, 'Vauban, inventeur des recensements', *Ann. démog. hist.* (1975), pp. 207 ff.
36. Ibid., p. 236; Frêche, *Toulouse*, p. 21; Frêche, 'Dénombrements de feux et d'habitants . . . de la région toulousaine', *Ann. démog. hist.* (1968), pp. 393–4; other examples in Poitrineau, *La Vie rurale en Basse-Auvergne*, p. 47.
37. B. Gille, p. 30.
38. p. 51.
39. J.-N. Biraben, *Les Hommes et la peste en France et dans les pays européens et méditerranéens* i. 251.
40. Poitrineau, *La Vie rurale*, p. 53.
41. A. Schaer, *Le Clergé paroissial catholique en haute Alsace sous l'ancien régime, 1648–1789* (1960), p. 91; H. M. Legros, 'Le Fessier et "son Bérus"', 1764–91', *Rev. de l'Anjou*, 72 (1916), 26; J. Boyrea, *Le Village en France au 18ᵉ siècle* (1955), p. 122.
42. Poitrineau, *La Vie rurale*, p. 54.
43. A. Corvisier, 'Le Chevalier des Pommelles', in *Hommage à Marcel Reinhard*, ed. Dupâquier *et al.*, pp. 161–72.
44. Condorcet, *Tableau général de la science, qui a pour objet l'application du calcul aux sciences politiques et morales*, *Œuvres*, xxi (1804), 243–55.
45. R. Pillorget, *La Tige et le rameau*, pp. 91–2.
46. R. Mols, *Introduction sommaire à la démographie historique des villes de l'Europe du XIVᵉ au XVIIIᵉ siècle* (2 v. 1954), i. 14.
47. J. Dupâquier, *Statistiques démographiques du bassin parisien, 1630–1720* (1977), pp. 7–8.
48. See also Expilly, *Tableau de la population de la France* (1780), p. 30.
49. R. Moulinas, 'Les tribulations du *Dictionnaire* . . . de l'abbé Expilly', *Provence historique*, 21 (1971), 128–46.

50. His own story in *Nouvelles recherches sur la population de la France* (1788), pp, 2, 4.
51. *Recherches sur la population des généralités d'Auvergne etc.* (1768), pp. 148, 9, 179, 124, 180, 262–75.
52. *Nouvelles recherches* (1788), pp. 6, 24–7.
53. J. Lecuir, 'Statistiques du mouvement de la population en France de 1770 à 1780', *Ann. démog. hist.* (1970), pp. 403–4.
54. Lecuir, 'Moheau, statisticien du Parlement de Paris', *Rev. d'hist. mod. et contemp.* 21 (1974), 445–8.
55. There was a real Moheau in a minor bureaucratic office (M. Reinhard, 'Notes sur la démographie française au 18ᵉ siècle', *Ann. démog. hist.* (1968), p. 21).
56. Messance, *Recherches* (1766), pp. 150–6.
57. 'Moheau', p. 156.
58. Messance, *Nouvelles recherches* (1788), pp. 13, 70; 'Moheau', pp. 179, 191–2, 200–1, 230.
59. [Chomel], *Les Nuits parisiennes* (2 v. 1772), i. 156–7; De Félice, *Code de l'humanité*, i. 29–30.
60. Deparcieux, *Essai sur les probabilités de la durée de la vie humaine* (1746), p. 124.
61. Ibid., pp. 43–4, 120–3.
62. J.-N. Moreau, *Mes souvenirs*, i. 82–3.
63. M. Coudurié, *La Dette des collectivités publiques de Marseille*, p. 192.
64. H. Lüthy, *La Banque protestante en France* (2 v. 1959–61), i. 467–71.
65. In appendices to Deparcieux.
66. pp. 61–2, 83–4.
67. L. Beler, 'Des tables de mortalité au XVIIᵉ et XVIIIᵉ siècles', *Ann. démog. hist.* (1976), pp. 173–91.
68. pp. 82, 27, 69–71.
69. e.g. in *Manuel de l'homme du monde ou connoissance générale des principaux états de la société* (anon. 1761), p. 631.
70. Buffon, *De l'homme* (ed. cit.), p. 164.
71. A. Lottin, 'Les morts chassés de la cité', *Rev. du Nord* (1978), p. 78.
72. Daignan, ii. 273–93, 318–51.
73. G. Rosen, *From Medical Police to Social Medicine* (1974), pp. 211–12, 224.
74. *Avantages des caisses établies en faveur des veuves dans plusieurs gouvernemens, et démonstrations de leurs calculs* (anon., Bruxelles, 1787), pp. 2–25; M. Du Villard, *Plan d'une association de prévoyance* (n.d. 1790), p. 5.

75. See Courtépée's challenge to Buffon in 1774, cit. D. Dinet, *Rev. hist.* 259 (1978), 37.

76. J. Dupâquier, *Statistiques démographiques du bassin parisien*, pp. 62, 105, 137, 210, 319, 369, 405, 562, 598, 680–1.

77. Robert, *De l'influence de la Révolution française sur la population*, i. 18–19, 98, 162.

78. A. Armengaud, *La Famille et l'enfant en France et en Angleterre du XVIIe au XVIIIe siècle: aspects démographiques* (1979), p. 65.

79. The view of Dupâquier ('La France de Louis XIV était-elle surpeuplée?', *Ann. démog. hist.* (1974), pp. 31–43) and E. Le Roy Ladurie ('L'histoire immobile', *Annales* (1971), p. 689).

80. A. Morineau, 'Révolution agraire, révolution alimentaire, révolution démographique', *Ann. démog. hist.* (1974), pp. 349–67. See also G. W. Grantham, 'The Diffusion of the New Husbandry in France, 1815–40', *Journal of Economic Hist.*, 38 (1978), 312.

81. A. Armengaud, 'Agriculture et démographie au XVIIIe siècle', *Rev. hist. écon. et soc.* 49 (1971), 408–10.

82. J.-P. Bardet, P. Chaunu, J. M. Gouesse, *Hist. de la Normandie* (1970), pp. 327–8.

83. For the effect of the 'Canal des Deux-Mers' see G. Frêche, 'Études statistiques sur le commerce céréalier de la France méridionale au XVIIIe siècle', *Rev. d'hist. écon. et soc.* 49 (1971), 5–43, 150–224.

84. R. Cobb, *Les Armées révolutionnaires: instrument de la Terreur dans les départements* (2 v. 1961–3), ii. 371–81.

85. J. J. Spengler, *Économie et Population: les doctrines françaises avant 1800* (1964), p. 83.

86. *Lettres persanes*, CXIII.

87. See A. Landry (p. 28) and J. Conan (p. 51), in *François Quesnay et la Physiocratie* (2 v. I.N.E.D., 1958).

88. Jaubert, *Des causes de la dépopulation et les moyens d'y remédier* (1767), pp. 89, 60, 101 ff.

89. 1757, cit. A. Sauvy, 'Quelques démographes ignorés du XVIIIe siècle', in Spengler, pp. 365 ff.

90. Favre, pp. 346–7, 350.

91. Élie de Beaumont, *Discours de réception à l'Académie de Caen* (1762).

92. [J. M. Dufour de Saint Pathias], *Diogène à Paris* (1787), p. 30.

93. *L'Esprit des journalistes de Trévoux* (2 v. 1771), i. 468–70.

94. De Félice, i. 527–37.

95. [Faignet de Villeneuve], *L'Économie politique: projet pour enrichir et perfectionner l'espèce humaine* (London 1763), pp. 1–3.

96. For this para., H. Hasquin, 'Voltaire démographe', *Études sur le 18e siècle*, 3 (1976), 133–40.

97. R. Chartier and D. Roche, 'Démographie historique à l'Académie', in *Hommage à Marcel Reinhard*, ed. Dupâquier *et al.*, pp. 91–6.

98. E. Esmonin, 'Statistiques du mouvement de la population en France de 1770 à 1789', *Études de chronologie et de démographie historique* (1964), pp. 94–129.

99. M. Reinhard and A. Armengaud, *Hist. générale de la population mondiale* (1961), p. 193.

100. Cit. S. Champroux, *Le Vrai Moyen de vivre longtemps* (1885), p. 459.

101. Introductory 'Avis'.

102. In Champroux, p. 438. . . .

103. Lacroix, *Observations sur le nécrologe*, in Garden, *Lyon*, p. 141.

104. Buffon, *De l'homme* (ed. cit.), pp. 165–8.

105. Claude Chevalier, *Le Triomphe de la vieillesse, avec les moyens de faire paroitre les vieillards tel qu'ils étoient dans leur jeunesse* (1787), p. 37.

106. Mercier, *Tableau de Paris*, xi. 104.

107. Longeville, Harcouet de, *Histoire des personnes qui ont vécu plusieurs siècles* . . . , pp. 274, 298–9.

108. *Mémoires de Trévoux*, April 1703, pp. 597–600.

109. [Lottin], *L'Almanach de la vieillesse* . . . (1761), p. x. For proverbs concerning moderation as the secret of longevity see F. Loux and P. Richard, *Sagesse du corps: la santé et la maladie dans les proverbes français* (1978), pp. 53–6.

110. [Chomel], *Les Nuits parisiennes*, i. 159.

111. Claude Chevalier, *Le Triomphe de la vieillesse*. pp. iv, vii.

112. J. Tuot, *Le 'Plan Social' de Jean-Claude Chappuis: une utopie socialiste au XVIIIᵉ siècle* (*Thèse*, Paris, 1942, p. 31).

113. Lathenas, cit. Foucault, *Naissance de la clinique*, p. 33. For the revival of the old counsels of moderation—avoid cold baths and kissing babies, see la veuve Miaczynski, *Essai de l'influence des mœurs du premier âge sur la longévité* (1803).

114. For Descartes's rejection of them see M. D. Grmek, 'Les idées de Descartes sur le prolongement de la vie', *Rev. d'hist. des sciences*, 25 (1963), 285–3.

115. R.-L. d'Erlach, *Code du bonheur* (7 v. 1788), ii. 33.

116. X. Bichat, *Recherches physiologiques sur la vie et la mort*, pp. 183–4.

117. Delisle de Sales, *Essai philosophique sur le corps humain*, pp. 273–4.

118. Lecat, *Traité des sensations et des passions, Œuvres physiologiques* (2 v. 1767), i. 103–7.

119. A. Riguez, *Le Docteur Marat, 1743–83: son système physiologique* (*Thèse*, Paris, 1908), p. 55.

120. Buffon, *De l'homme* (ed. cit.), pp. 142–51.

121. Caraccioli, *Tableau*, pp. 112, 113–14.
122. Le Pileur d'Apligny, *Essais historiques sur la morale des anciens et des modernes* (1772), p. 54.
123. Père Joseph-Romain Joly (Capuchin), *Dict. de morale philosophique*, pp. 89–90.
124. Bossuet, 'Sermon sur la mort', 1662 (*Œuvres oratoires*, ed. J. Lebarq, 1921), iv. 267–8.
125. Letter 20 Feb. 1775, in Messance, *Nouvelles recherches*, p. 81.
126. Jean Dumas, *Traité du suicide* (1773), pp. 82–4. (Cf. J.-H. Meister, *Lettres sur le vieillesse*, pp. 97–100.)
127. Démeunier, *L'Esprit des usages et des coutumes des différens peuples* (3 v. 1776), i. 66, 266–7.
128. For what follows, except where otherwise stated, see C. J. Gruman, 'A History of Ideas about the Prolongation of Life: the Evolution of the Prolongevity Hypothesis to 1800', *Trans. American Philos. Soc.* 56 (1966), 6–89.
129. Longeville, Harcouet de, pp. 218–19.
130. Ibid., pp. 29–39, 41, 3–10, 25–7, 37. See also F. N. Egerton, 'The longevity of the Patriarchs: a topic in the history of demography', *Journal of the History of Ideas*, 27 (1966), 575–9.
131. Le Pileur d'Apligny, pp. 63–4.
132. Anon., *L'Esprit des Journalistes de Trévoux*, i. 463–5.
133. J. B. Bury, *The Idea of Progress* (1955), p. 139.
134. Cabanis, *Coup d'œil sur les révolutions et sur la réforme de la médecine* (An XII, 1804), pp. 24–6, 34—the work is said to have been written in An III. For the older view, 'le plus grand malheur qui pourrait arriver à l'homme, serait l'immortalité physique', see J.-A. Millot, *L'Art d'améliorer et de perfectionner les hommes* (2 v. 1801), ii. 211.
135. Diderot, *Entretien entre d'Alembert et D.*, *Œuvres philosophiques*, pp. 283–4.

CHAPTER 5
The Soul, Heaven, and Hell

1. Père Hubert Hayer, *La Spiritualité et l'immortalité de l'âme* (3 v. 1757), ii. 1; Bergier, *Examen du matérialisme ou réfutation du Système de la Nature* (1771) in *Œuvres* (8 v. 1855), i. col. 71; Joannet, *De la connoissance de l'homme dans son être et dans ses rapports*, ii. 618.
2. Ch. Bonnet, *Essai analytique sur les facultés de l'âme* (1760), pp. 80–1.
3. Joannet, i. xxxiii.

4. J.-A. Lelarge de Lignac, *Élémens de métaphysique . . . ou Lettres à un matérialiste sur la nature de l'âme* (1753), pp. 22, 30, 37.
5. Gérard, *Le Comte de Valmont, ou les égaremens de la raison* (3 v. 1776), i. 552.
6. Para du Phanjas, *Les Principes de la saine philosophie conciliés avec ceux de la religion* (2 v. 1774), i. 201. Cf. de Félice, *Code de l'humanité*, i. 246.
7. L. Versini, *Laclos et la tradition*, pp. 443, 452–3.
8. J.-B. Rose, *Traité élémentaire de morale* (1767), pp. 104–5.
9. Watelet, *Dict. des arts de peinture, sculpture et gravure* (5 v. 1792), i. 66–8.
10. Dom A. Calmet, *Dict. historique, critique . . . etc. de la Bible* (6 v. Toulouse, 1783), i. 185–6.
11. Para du Phanjas, i. 157; Père Joseph-Romain Joly, *Dict. de morale philosophique*, i. 43; [Chomel], *Aménités littéraires*, i. 312–13.
12. See cases of 1741 and 1773 in P. Cavard, 'Les enfants morts sans baptême', *Évocations*, 21 (Oct, 1964), 100–2.
13. [The abbé Dinouart], *Abrégé de l'embryologie sacrée*, pp. 186–91.
14. *Conjectures sur l'union de l'âme et du corps* (1703), reviewed in *Mémoires pour l'histoire des sciences et des beaux-arts* (Trévoux), vii. 1084–5 (May 1703).
15. [Nonnotte], *Anti-Dictionnaire philosophique* (4th ed., 2 v. 1785), ii. 151–4.
16. Joannet, i. 135–6.
17. Hayer, iii. 5–6.
18. Gros de Besplas (vicaire général of Besançon), *Le Rituel des esprits-forts, ou le tableau des incrédules modernes au lit de la mort* (2nd ed. 1762), pp. 121–4.
19. Bonnet, pp. 475–7.
20. Lelarge de Lignac, pp. 22–30, 121–3; Hayer, i. 12, iii. 3; Joannet, i. 83; [Astruc], *Dissertation sur l'immatérialité, l'immortalité et la liberté de l'âme* (1755), pp. 111–15.
21. L.-A. de Caraccioli, *Le Tableau de la mort*, p. 130; Bergier, op. cit., *Œuvres*, i. col. 147; Bergier, *Suite de l'apologie de la religion chrétienne*, *Œuvres*, viii, col. 618.
22. Bergier, *Dict. de théologie dogmatique* (1788), *Œuvres*, ii, cols. 176–84.
23. Bergier, *Examen*, *Œuvres*, i, cols. 148–9; *Principes de métaphysique*, ibid. ii, col. 1320.
24. Delisle de Sales, *De la philosophie de la nature* (3 v. 1770), ii. 315.
25. Père Griffet, *L'Année du Chrétien . . .* (new ed. 18 v. Lyon, 1811), i. 41; Père Hardouin, *Paraphrase de l'Ecclésiaste* (1729), Préf.; [Duguet], *Explication du mystère de la Passion . . .* (1731), pp. 125–6.

26. Bergier, *Traité de la vraie religion*, *Œuvres*, vii, vols. 1288–9.
27. M. Bullet, *Réponses critiques à plusieurs difficultés proposées par les nouveaux incrédules sur divers endroits des livres saints* (2 v. 1774), ii. 396–7.
28. Griffet, xii. 27–31; *Pensez-y bien* . . . (anon., 1737), p. 83.
29. Père Cl. Judde, *Retraite de trente jours* (1746), *Œuvres* ed. Le Noir-Duparc, 3 v. 1825), i. 163.
30. Le Maître de Claville, *Traité du vrai mérite de l'homme*, p. 511. For wills, see P. Chaunu, 'Mourir à Paris (XVIᵉ–XVIIᵉ–XVIIIᵉ siècle)', *Annales*, 31 (1976), 29–50.
31. G. F. Berthier and J. B. Lausausse, *La Science de l'oraison mentale* . . . *la Doctrine spirituelle du Père Berthier* (1791), p. 460.
32. *Sermons du Père Brydaine* (5 v. Avignon, 1823), i. 250.
33. Duguet, *Manuel de piété* (new ed. 1786), p. 233. Cf. *La Science de bien mourir enseignée dans trente considérations* (anon., 1696), pp. 210–11.
34. *Mandement de Mgr l'évêque d'Alais, qui ordonne des prières publiques pour le repos de l'âme du feu Roi* (1774), p. 7.
35. [Aubert de la Chênay Desbois], *Dict. historique* (3 v. 1767), iii. 224.
36. Bergier, *Dict. de théologie dogmatique* (1788), *Œuvres*, iv, cols. 934–8, 1689–97.
37. *Avis d'une mère à son fils sur la sanctification des fêtes* (anon., 1747), pp. 186–8.
38. Picart, *Cérémonies et coutumes religieuses de tous les peuples du monde* (11 v. 1723–43), ii (1733), p. 135.
39. 'S'il en étoit ainsi, on pourroit accuser Dieu de trop de cruauté' (J.-B. Thiers, *Traité des superstitions qui regardent tous les sacremens*, iii. 154).
40. Collet (prêtre de la Congrégation de la Mission), *Traité historique, dogmatique et pratique des indulgences et du Jubilé* (2 v. 1770), i. 321–8.
41. Yes, according to *Pensez-y bien*, pp. 166–7.
42. Caraccioli, *Tableau*, pp. 213–14.
43. *La Science de bien mourir*, p. 254.
44. Calmet, *Dict* . . . *de la Bible*, i. 249–56 (Antéchrist).
45. Bergier, *Traité de la vraie religion*, *Œuvres*, vii, cols. 481–3.
46. Thomas, *Ode sur le temps*, cit. M. J. de Pinto, *Précis des arguments contre les matérialistes* (1774), p. 124.
47. Emphasis on the duties of the angels, Griffet, i. 511; x. 131–2.
48. Bergier, *Œuvres*, vii, cols, 1277, 1273.
49. Dom A. Calmet, *Commentaire littéral sur tous les livres de l'ancien et du nouveau testament* (28 v. 1712–21), ii (*Les Épîtres de Saint Paul*, 1716), pp. xcvii–cvii.

50. Caraccioli, *Tableau*, p. 181.
51. [J. Chevassu], *Missionnaire paroissial* (3 v. 1753), ii. 243–4.
52. *Sermons du Père Brydaine*, i. 258–9.
53. *Pensez-y bien*, p. 106.
54. Judde, i. 181–2.
55. Collet, *Traité des devoirs des gens du monde* . . . (1764), p. 266.
56. *Pensez-y bien*, p. 104; Chevalier de Lasne d'Aiguebelle, *La Religion du cœur* (1768), p. 44.
57. Caraccioli, *La Grandeur d'âme* (1761), p. 287; *Sermons du Père Brydaine*, i. 307.
58. Bergier, *Dict. de théologie*, *Œuvres*, ii, col. 898; *Traité*, ibid., col. 1279.
59. Caraccioli, *Tableau*, p. 182.
60. Rapin, *La Vie des prédestinez dans la bienheureuse éternité* (1684), p. 81.
61. Brydaine, loc. cit.
62. See R. Favre, *La Mort dans la littérature* . . . i. 152–6, ii. 86 for this paragraph. I have given the evidence a different significance and, more especially, given a different interpretation of Nicole.
63. Clément, *Élévations de l'âme à Dieu, ou prières tirées de la Sainte Écriture* (new ed. 1755, approbation dated 1754), p. 110.
64. Caraccioli, *Tableau*, p. 125.
65. *Conjectures concerning the Nature of Future Happiness* transl. from the French of Mons. Bonnet of Geneva (York, 1785), p. 41.
66. Chateaubriand, *Génie du Christianisme* (ed. L. Louvet, n.d.), p. 255.
67. Calmet, *Commentaire, Tome second des Psaumes*, p. 159.
68. J. Gillet, *Le Paradis perdu dans la littérature française de Voltaire à Chateaubriand* (1975), p. 315.
69. Azais, *Bridaine et ses missions* (1882), p. 141.
70. J. de Viguerie, 'Les missions intérieures des Doctrinaires Toulousains au début du XVIIIe siècle', *Rev. hist.* 242 (1969), 51.
71. Bridaine, *Instructions sur le mariage* (1827), pp. 24–5.
72. Père V. Houdry, S. J., *La Bibliothèque des prédicateurs* (3rd ed. Lyon 1724–43), vi (1733), pp. 24–5.
73. J. Gaiches, *L'Art de la prédication ou maximes sur le ministère de la chaire* (1712), p. 245.
74. [Duguet], *Institution d'un prince* (1739), p. 15.
75. A. Bernard, *Le Sermon au XVIIIe siècle, 1715–89* (1901), p. 433.
76. Bion, *Recherches sur la nature du feu de l'Enfer par Mr Swinden, traduit de l'Anglais* (1728), pp. 52–6.
77. Lasne d'Aiguebelle, p. 43.
78. Bergier, *Œuvres*, iii, cols. 543–4.

79. J. Gillet, pp. 289, 305, 291–3. (Boesnier, *La Mexique conquise*, 2 v. 1752.)

80. Dom Calmet wavers and inclines to the view that there are devils at large destined for Hell, but not yet sent there (*Dict. de la Bible*, ii. 266). The devils insult the sinners sent to Hell (Sevoy, *Devoirs ecclésiastiques*, 3 v. 1770, ii. 56).

81. Bergier, loc. cit.

82. Calmet, *Tome second des Psaumes*, p. 489; Romain-Joly, i. 298; Bergier, loc. cit.

83. Caraccioli, *La Grandeur d'âme* p. 394; *Tableau*, p. 108.

84. *Sermons du P. Brydaine*, i. 252–4.

85. Griffet, vi. 266.

86. Or, repentance was not allowed: 'elles ne peuvent concevoir que des aversions violentes pour le Souverain bien qu'elles sçavent pourtant infiniment aimable, et ces aversions mêmes leur sont un supplice' (*Les Œuvres spirituelles de Mme de Bellefont* (1688), p. 229).

87. Bridaine, pp. 237–40.

88. Bernard, pp. 327–9; J. McManners, *French Ecclesiastical Society . . . Angers*, p. 146.

89. Lanse d'Aiguebelle, p. 44.

90. Bergier, *Œuvres*, iii. 545.

91. Dom B. Sinsart, *Défense du dogme catholique de l'éternité des peines* (1748), pp. xxi–ii, 43–9, 156, 130, x.

92. Sinsart, *Recueil des pensées diverses sur l'immatérialité de l'âme* (1761), p. 278.

93. Judde, pp. 265, 277.

94. Chevassu, i. 2–11.

95. Caraccioli, *Tableau*, p. 222.

96. Gros de Besplas, p. xiii.

97. *Œuvres très complètes de Mgr F.-J. de Partz de Pressy* (Migne, 2 v. 1842), i. col. 456; Griffet, *Exercice de piété pour la communion* (new ed. 1752), p. 126.

98. Bergier, *Œuvres*, iii, col. 540.

99. R. Bottereau, 'Histoire des écrits du P. Claude Judde, S. J., 1661–1735', *Rev. d'hist. de la Spiritualité*. 49 (1973), 162.

100. Abbé de la Baume, *La Christiade*, v. 405, 480, cit. J. Gillet, pp. 327–8.

101. See Frank Bowman, *Le Christ romantique* (1973).

102. Sinsart, *Défense*, p. 175.

103. Nonnotte, i. 336–7; Troya d'Assigny, *La Fin du chrétien, ou traité . . . sur le petit nombre des Élus* (3 v. 1751), ii. 419–23. For the small number of the elect, see *Pensez-y bien*, p. 200; Duguet, *Manuel de piété* (ed. 1786), p. 238. Against the idea, Bergier, vii, col. 1287; Caraccioli, *Tableau*, p. 219 and, especially, Para du Phanjas.

104. Bergier, ii. cols. 495–9.
105. Dom O. Rousseau, 'La descente aux Enfers dans le cadre des liturgies chrétiennes', *La Maison-Dieu*, 43 (1955), 118.
106. Bourdaloue, *Exhortations et instructions* (2 v. 1721), ii. 61–2.
107. *Œuvres complètes du P. Ambroise de Lombez* (ed. F. de Bénéjac, 3 v. 1881), iii. 67–72.
108. List of theologians who said pagans could be saved in d'Argens, *Lettres juives* (6 v. 1738), i. 321. For Saint François de Sales see Julien Eymard, 'Les degrés de perfection d'après Saint François de Sales', *Rev. d'ascét. et de myst.* 44 (1968), 20.
109. For Baudrand (died 1787), *Œuvres* (Migne, 2 v. 1855), i. cols. 530–1. For the rest of this para. see Favre, i. 109–26, ii. 72. The Para du Phanjas reference is to his *Principes de la saine philosophie . . .*, ii. 116–19.
110. J. Ehrard, *L'Idée de Nature en France dans la première moitié du XVIIIᵉ siècle* (2 v. 1963), ii. 636–8.
111. *Pensez-y bien*, p. 134; Judde i. 193; Sinsart, *Défense*, p. xvi.
112. Griffet, v. 16, 318–19.
113. [Dom Robert Morel], *Entretiens spirituels en forme de prières pour servir de préparation à la mort* (new ed. 1730), p. 73.
114. See P.-J. Carlé's ed. of Emery's *Du dogme catholique de l'enfer* (1842), pp. 381, 427, 442, 453. Discussion—how is it that, in the office of the dead, prayers are offered for all, to preserve them from Hell? Picart, *Cérémonies*, ii. 135–44). He concludes that the reference is limited to the souls in Purgatory to remove their residual fear of Hell. Another answer was that prayer must be offered for all who died in the communion of the Church, but it is not for us to judge if these prayers will be effective (Gaudron, *Instructions et pratiques pour passer saintement tous les temps de l'année* (2 v. 1763), ii. 243, 255).
115. Mgr F.-J. de Partz de Pressy, *Œuvres*, i, cols. 500–1, 641–54.
116. Lenglet-Dufresnoy, *Recueil de dissertations anciennes et nouvelles sur les apparitions, les visions et les songes* (2 v. 1752), i, pp. vii, xiii, xxxv, lxxiii–iv, lxxix, lxxxi. For its effect, Caraccioli, *Tableau*, pp. 191–3. Note: the Devil vanishes from the decorations of churches (J. Levron, *Le Diable dans l'art* (1935), pp. 92–6).
117. A. Bernard, p. 279.
118. B. Groethuysen, *Origines de l'esprit bourgeois en France: l'Église et la Bourgeoisie* (1927), pp. 81–6.
119. Grou, *A Little Book of the Love of God* (E. T. 1894, French original 1769), p. 72.
120. J. Candel, *Les Prédicateurs français dans la première moitié du XVIIIᵉ siècle* (1904), pp. 357–8.

121. J.-J. Gautier (curé), *Essai sur les mœurs champêtres* (1787), ed. X. Rousseau 1935), p. 20.
122. E.-G. Léonard, *Mon village sous Louis XV* (1941), p. 87.
123. E. Lavaquery, *Le Cardinal de Boisgelin, 1732–1804* (2 v. 1920), i. 189–90; Groethuysen, pp. 84, 89.
124. Le Pelletier; *Traitez des récompenses et des peines éternelles tirez des livres saints* (1738), p. iii.
125. Gaudron, ii. 233.
126. For what follows: *Lettres de consolation faites par MM. du Moulins . . . et plusieurs autres Pasteurs* (1632), pp. 187–8, 77, 63; and Ch. Drelincourt, *Les Consolations de l'âme fidèle contre les frayeurs de la mort* (2 v. 1760), i. 74–9, 195, 320.
127. Collet, *Traité des indulgences etc.* i. 25, 30–1, 38, 178, 277.
128. G. and M. Vovelle, 'Vision de la mort et de l'au-delà en Provence d'après les autels des âmes du purgatoire', *Cahiers des Annales*, 29 (1970), 27–41.
129. Diderot, *Salons* (ed. J. Seznec and J. Adhémar, (4 v. 1957–67), i. 139.
130. The fanatic wishes to make himself the object of 'an odious vengeance' (Delisle de Sales, i. 349).

CHAPTER 6

The Afterlife: Doubts and Reconsiderations

1. J. Macquarrie, *Principles of Christian Theology* (2nd ed. 1977), pp. 74–8. For the biblical view of resurrection see O. Cullmann, *Immortality of the Soul or Resurrection from the Dead?* (1958), p. 6.
2. J. Roger, *Les Sciences de la vie dans la pensée française du XVIIIe siècle* (1971), pp. 333, 364, 372–82, 397, 405–13.
3. O. E. Fellows and S. F. Milliken, *Buffon* (1972), p. 42.
4. Ibid, p. 134.
5. L. J. Rather, *Mind and Body in 18th-Century Medicine: a study based on Jerome Gaub's 'De regimine mentis'* (1965), pp. 12–16.
6. A. Le Camus, *Médecine de l'esprit* (1769), cit. A. Vartanian, *La Mettrie's 'L'Homme Machine': a Study of the Origins of an Idea* (1960), pp. 92–3.
7. J. Pernetti, *Lettres philosophiques sur les physionomies* (1746); see Vartanian, p. 70.
8. E. L. Haigh, 'Vitalism, the Soul and Sensibility: the Physiology of Théophile de Bordeu', *Journal of the History of Medicine and Allied Sciences*, 31 (1976), 30–42.
9. Joannet, *De la connaissance de l'homme dans son être et dans ses rapports*, i. 135–6.
10. Best discussion, Para du Phanjas, *Les Principes de la saine*

philosophie conciliés avec ceux de la religion, i. 159. Cf. Lelarge de Lignac, *Élémens de métaphysique*, p. 197.

11. Sauri, *Physique du corps humain, ou physiologie moderne* (2 v. 1778), ii. 4–5 (citing Bordeu).

12. Culant, *Opinion d'un Mandarin ou discours sur la nature de l'âme* (1784), pp. 14–16, 29; *L'Homéide* (1781), Chant 4, p. 68.

13. *Éloge* by M. de Ratte in Boissier de Sauvages, *Nosologia methodica* (2 v. 1768), p. 12. For his discussion of the 'moteur' or 'principle of movement' animating the body see *Dissertation dans laquelle on recherche s'il y a des Médicamens qui affectent certaines parties du corps . . . plutôt que d'autres* (1751), pp. 7–8.

14. Lecat, *Traité des sensations et des passions, Œuvres physiologiques*, i. 147–8, xxxi–xxxvii.

15. Marat, *De l'homme, ou . . . l'influence de l'âme sur le corps* (1775), cit. A. Riguez, *Le Docteur Marat, 1743–1793, son système physiologique*, pp. 53–4.

16. J. Ehrard, *L'Idée de Nature en France dans la première moitié du XVIIIᵉ siècle*, ii. 679.

17. *Mémoires pour l'histoire des sciences et des beaux arts* (Trévoux), vii. 866–1071, 1661–2.

18. Saint-Aubin, *Traité de l'opinion* (1733), cit. P. Tedeschi, *Saint-Aubin et son œuvre* (1968), p. 157.

19. Ch. Bonnet, *Essai analytique sur les facultés de l'âme*, p. xiv.

20. Para du Phanjas, i. 156–7.

21. Delisle de Sales, *De la philosophie de la nature*, ii. 231–53.

22. R. R. Palmer, *Catholics and Unbelievers in 18th-Century France* (1939), p. 131. For the importance of Locke's remarks about thinking matter see D. W. Smith, *Helvétius: a Study in Persecution* (1965), pp. 105–6.

23. J. Proust, *Diderot et l'Encyclopédie* (1962), p. 259.

24. H. Hayer, *La Spiritualité et l'immortalité de l'âme*, i. pp. xii, 42–3, 61.

25. [D'Argens], *Thérèse philosophe* (2 v. 1760), ii. 76.

26. Palmer, pp. 132–5.

27. Jean A. Perkins, *The Concept of Self in the French Enlightenment* (1969), pp. 49–64.

28. Joannet, i, pp. xxxvi–vii, lxxxii, xc.

29. Ehrard, ii. 680. Except where otherwise indicated, what follows is from Hester Hastings, *Man and Beast in French Thought of the 18th Century* (1936), and L. C. Rosenfeld, *From Beast-Machine to Man-Machine. Animal Soul in French Letters from Descartes to La Mettrie* (2nd ed. 1968).

30. M. de Keranflech, *L'Ame des bêtes* (Rennes, 1767), p.3.

31. Sinner, *Essai sur les dogmes de la métempsychose et du purgatoire enseignés par les Bramines de l'Indostan* (2 v. 1771), i. 135–6. Sinner was Swiss and published at Berne. Picart, *Cérémonies et coutumes religieuses* (1728), vi. 156–85. *Dict. historique des cultes religieux* (5 v. 1772), iv. 83–8.
32. *Corresp. inéd. de Condorcet et de Turgot, 1770–79* (ed. Cl. Henry, 1883, p. 89; H. Grange, *Les Idées de Necker* (1974), p. 613. For the Montesquieu, Voltaire, Diderot, and d'Holbach references see Favre, i. 613–17.
33. Barthélemy, *Voyage du jeune Anacharsis en Grèce* (7 v. 1799), i. 69.
34. Dom Calmet, 'Dissertation sur la nature de l'âme' in *Nouvelles dissertations* (1720), pp. 55–6. Also, *Dict. de la Bible*, i. 186–7. The abbé Porée is tempted by this explanation of ghosts (*Lettres sur la sépulture dans les églises*, 1745, p. 16).
35. Hastings, pp. 35–6.
36. Joannet, *Les Bêtes mieux connues*, ii. 105–6, 211, 305, 330–6.
37. Para du Phanjas, i. 164.
38. Joannet, ii. 95.
39. *Œuvres très complètes de Mgr F.-J. de Partz de Pressy*, i. col. 581.
40. P. Joseph-Romain Joly (Capuchin), *Dict. de morale philosophique*, i. 82.
41. Hastings, pp. 56–8.
42. Caraccioli, *La Grandeur d'âme*, p. xii.
43. 'Entretien entre d'Alembert et Diderot', Diderot, *Œuvres philosophiques*, ed. Vernière, 275–6.
44. H. Busson, *La Pensée religieuse française de Charon à Pascal* (1933), pp. 126–43; *La Religion des classiques, 1660–88* (1948), pp. 320–5.
45. *L'Âme matérielle* (ed. A. Niderst, 1973), pp. 66, 50, 232. For other manuscript treatises with similar views, Vernière, *Spinoza et la pensée française avant la Révolution*, pp. 207–9, and P. Naville, *D'Holbach et la philosophie scientifique au XVIIIᵉ siècle* (new ed. 1967), pp. 131–2, 159–60, 162–4; and R. Mortier, 'Les Dialogues sur l'Âme et la diffusion du matérialisme au XVIIIᵉ siècle', *Rev. d'hist. litt. de la France*, 61 (1961), pp. 342–58.
46. (Amsterdam, 1743), pp. 9, 82, 159.
47. Naville, p. 269.
48. [La Mettrie], *Histoire naturelle de l'âme* (1747), pp. 272–3, 281–3.
49. Vartanian, pp. 40–55.
50. Voltaire to Marie-Louise Denis, 14 Nov. 1751 (Besterman, no. 2958).
51. N. Willard, *Le Génie et la folie au 18ᵉ siècle* (1963), p. 119.
52. Hastings, p. 99.
53. Helvétius, *De l'esprit* (ed. G. Besse, 1959), p. 72.

54. The *mot* is Méri's cited by Fontenelle in his *éloge* (J.-J. Sue, *Recherches physiologiques, et expériences sur la vitalité et le Galvanisme* (3rd ed. 1803), Avert.
55. 'Fréret', *Lettres à Eugénie*, *Œuvres* (4 v. 1785), ii. 89.
56. Ehrard, i. 142, ii. 678.
57. A. O. Lovejoy, *The Great Chain of Being* (1936), pp. 188, 198, 215, 231, 252.
58. Ehrard, i. 196.
59. Ibid. 223–5.
60. For what follows see L.-G. Crocker, *Diderot's Chaotic Order* (1974), pp. 5–40.
61. *Œuvres* (Assézat), ii. 279.
62. *Élém. de physiologie*, *Œuvres*, ix. 275.
63. 15 Oct. 1759, *Corresp.* (ed. G. Roth, 1956), ii. 282–4.
64. *Œuvres* (ed. Assézat) ii. 84.
65. J. Proust, pp. 325–32.
66. Diderot and Falconet, *Le Pour et le contre* (ed. Y. Benot, 1958), pp. 77–8.
67. R. Mauzi, *L'Idée du bonheur dans la littérature et la pensée françaises au XVIIIe siècle* (1960), pp. 684–5.
68. 4 Dec 1765, *Le Pour et le contre*, p. 50.
69. D'Holbach, *Système de la Nature* (pirated London ed. 2 v. 1770), i. 257, 278–9, 296–9 (Cap. I, xiii).
70. Diderot and Falconet, *Corresp.* (ed. H. Dieckmann and J. Seznec, 1959), p. 70.
71. [Cérutti], *Notice mortuaire sur M. de Mirabeau*, (n.d.), p. 8; J. Trahard, *La Sensibilité révolutionnaire, 1789–1794* (1936), p. 17.
72. *Réflexions morales de Mme Deshoulières sur l'envie immodérée qu'on a de faire passer son nom à la postérité* (Paris 1693), pp. 3–4, 7.
73. Favre, i. 492–8 for full discussion.
74. Ibid. 656.
75. Anne Betty Weinshenker, 'Diderot's use of the Ruin-Image', *Diderot Studies*, 15 (1973), 311–15.
76. *Œuvres de M. Thomas* (new ed. Amsterdam, 4 v. 1773), iii. 2 ('Éloge du comte de Saxe').
77. Favre, i. 644–5.
78. Sabatier, *Poème sur la bataille de Lutzelberg* (1758), p. 4.
79. Favre, i. 626, citing Rémi, *Les Jours, pour servir de correctif et de supplément aux Nuits de Young* (1770), p. 7.
80. Favre, i. 412.
81. Caraccioli, *Tableau de la mort*, pp. 140–6.
82. P. Laugier, S. J., *Observations sur l'architecture* (1756), p. 150.

83. Judde, *Œuvres*, i. 141.

84. It is possible, of course, to believe in God but to have doubts about his interest in mankind. According to *L'Âme matérielle*, some deists said God alone was immortal, and that there was no distinction between vice and virtue (Niderst, p. 18). Lefranc de Pompignan in his *Questions diverses sur l'incrédulité* (1751) says the name *théistes* is given to those who believe in the existence of God, free will, the immortality of the soul, and the necessity of worship, while the *déistes* are those who believe only in the existence of God, leaving the rest as either 'errors or problems' (Ehrard, i. 456). On this terminology I should have said that most thinkers of the Enlightenment were 'théistes'.

85. A. Guillois, *Pendant la Terreur: le poète Roucher, 1745–96*, p. 98.

86. Parny, cit. Potez, *L'Élégie en France* (1898), pp. 116–17.

87. The marquis de Culant, *Morale enjouée, ou recueil de Fables* (2nd ed. Cologne, 1783), pp. 85–8.

88. *Dict. philosophique*, 'Âme', 'Enfer'—see I. O. Wade, *The Intellectual Development of Voltaire* (1973), p. 143. Voltaire, *Notebooks* (ed. Besterman), ii. 357; Ehrard, i. 242–5.

89. See J. McManners, *The Social Contract and Rousseau's Revolt against Society* (1968).

90. *Émile*, IV (*Œuvres*, Gallimard, 1969, iv. 589–90, 604–5).

91. D'Haussonville, *Le Salon de Mme Necker* (2 v. 1882), i. 252, 351–4, ii. 51.

92. N. Hampson, *The Life and Opinions of Maximilien Robespierre* (1974), p. 181.

93. M. Wallon, *Hist. du Tribunal révolutionnaire* (6 v. 1880–2), iii. 516.

94. J. McManners, *The French Revolution and the Church* (1969), p. 136.

95. Trahard, pp. 158–9 (Barbaroux, Brissot, Buzot, Louvet, Hoche).

96. Wallon, ii. 324.

97. For what follows, P. D. Walker, *The Decline of Hell: 17th-Century Discussions of Eternal Torment* (1964).

98. J. Locke, *The Reasonableness of Christianity* (ed. I. A. Ramsey, 1958), pp. 25–7, 52–3, 55.

99. For the French translation, P.-M. Conlon, *Jean-François Bion* (1966), p. 52.

100. Walker, p. 262.

101. E. R. Briggs, 'Pierre Cuppé's debts to England and Holland', *Studies on Voltaire and the 18th Century*, 6 (1958), 41–60; 'Mysticism and Rationalism in the debate upon eternal punishment', ibid. 24 (1963), 241–53.

102. Tobias Swinden, *Recherches sur la nature du feu de l'Enfer* . . . *traduit de l'Anglais* (transl. by Bion, 1728), pp. 52–6.

103. Voltaire, *Corresp.* (ed. Besterman), xlv. 68 (Jan. 1761). For below, *Dict. philosophique* (ed. R. Naves, 1967), pp. 178–80.

104. Diderot, *Entretien d'un philosophe avec Mme la Maréchale de* ——, *Œuvres* (ed. R. Lewinter, 15 v. 1969–73), xi. 138.

105. Marie Huber, *Le Système des anciens et des modernes concilié par l'exposition des* . . . *théologiens sur l'état des âmes séparées des corps* (1731). Subsequent editions in 1733, 1738, 1757, also translations into English and German. Rochet, a professor of theology of Lausanne, replied in his *Examen de l'Origénisme* (R. A. Metzger, *Marie Huber: sa vie, ses œuvres, sa théologie*, Geneva, 1887, pp. 41–6).

106. D'Holbach, *Le Bon Sens*, 1772 (ed. J. Deprun, n.d.), pp. 40–56.

107. R. Mandrou, *Magistrats et sorciers au XVIIe siècle* (1968); P. Chaunu, 'Sur la fin des sorciers au XVIIe siècle', *Annales*, 24 (1969), 895–910.

108. Barbier, *Chronique de la Régence et du règne de Louis XV, 1718–63* (8 v. 1857–8), ii. 89; P. Chevallier, *Les Ducs sous l'acacia, ou les premiers pas de la franc-maçonnerie française, 1725–43* (1964), pp. 168–9, 171.

109. G. Maugras, *Lauzun and the Court of Marie-Antoinette* (E.T. 1896), pp. 307–9.

110. Told, in 1752, with differing names, in *Lettres de Piron* (ed. E. Lavaquary, 1920), p. 64 (25 Feb.) and d'Argenson, *Journal et mémoires* (ed. E. J. B. Rathery), vii. 91–2. Repeated in 1777 by Métra, *Corresp. Secrète, politique et littéraire* (18 v. 1787–90), iv. 234–5.

111. G. de Closmadeuc, 'Les Sorciers de Lorient: procès criminel devant la sénéchaussée d'Hennebout', *Bull. Soc. Polymathique du Morbihan* (1885), pp. 11–33.

112. Churchmen who attacked superstitions were tempted to make an exception here and accept this affliction (no doubt frequent because of the late age of marriage) as a diabolical manifestation—e.g. see J.-B. Thiers, *Traité des superstitions qui regardent tous les sacramens* (3 v. 1704, first ed. 1696), iii. 567–84; [Daon] *Conduite des âmes dans la voie du salut* (1750), pp. 111–12. For the story of the attempt to use Marie-Antoinette's wedding-ring to cast a spell to prevent her having children, Mme de Campan, *Mémoires sur la vie de Marie-Antoinette* (ed. F. Barrière, 1886), p. 162.

113. Milner, *Le Diable dans la littérature française, 1772–1861* (2 v. 1960), i. 52–5; C. Bila, *La Croyance à la magie au XVIIIe siècle en France dans les contes, romans et traités* (1925), pp. 62–3, 71; Mandrou, p. 490.

114. J. Palou, *La Sorcellerie* (1957), p. 80.
115. New ed. 2 v. 1751.
116. Milner, i. 35–6.
117. Diderot, *Dorval et moi*, 3ᵉ entr., *Œuvres* (Assézat), vii. 155.
118. Watelet, *L'Art de peindre* (1761), p. 261. See also disapproval of Rubens's *Last Judgement* as frivolous in d'Argens, *Réflexions critiques sur les différentes écoles de peinture* (1752), p. 202.
119. Malebranche, *Recherche de la vérité*, (ed. G. Lewis, 2 v. 1946), ii. 205–11.
120. Th. de Cauzons, *La Magie et la sorcellerie en France* (3 v. 1861), iii. 363 (1720), 365 (1735); M. Beaune, 'Les Sorciers de Lyon: épisode judiciaire du XVIIIᵉ siècle', *Méms. Acad. impériale . . . de Dijon*, 2ᵉ Sér. 4 (1868), 65–151.
121. Hecquet, *La Cause des convulsions*, in Milner, ii. 50.
122. See J. Gillet, *Le Paradis perdu dans la littérature française de Voltaire à Chateaubriand*.
123. Guitton, 'A propos du mythe d'Orphée et de la crise du lyrisme au XVIIIᵉ siécle', *Approches des Lumières* (ed. Lecercle *et al.*, 1974), pp. 246–54.
124. *Éloge de l'Enfer: ouvrage critique, historique et moral* (2 v. anon., 1759), pp. 39, 57, 150–1.
125. *Dict. des cultes religieux*, ii. 295–300 (l'Enfer); Delandine, *L'Enfer des peuples anciens, ou histoire des dieux infernaux* (1784), pp. iv–v, 2–21, 292–3, 323.
126. Toussaint, *Les Mœurs* (1748), p. 223.
127. Delisle de Sales, *De la philosophie de la Nature*, i. 349.
128. Buffon, *Les Époques de la Nature* (ed. G. Gohau, 1973), p. 201.
129. *Henriade* vii, *Œuvres complètes* (ed. Moland, 52 v. 1877–85), viii. 171.
130. Toussaint, p. 42.
131. *Lettres à Eugénie*, *Œuvres*, ii. 29, 73–5, 82, 92.
132. D'Holbach, *Le Bon Sens* (ed. cit.), pp. 52–5.
133. Diderot, *Addition aux Pensées philosophiques*, *Œuvres philosophiques* (ed. Vernière), pp. 57–72; *La promenade d'un sceptique*, *Œuvres* (Assézat), i. 213–14.
134. Diderot, *Corresp.* xix. 111–13.
135. *Addition aux Pensées philosophiques*, loc. cit.
136. Marie Huber, *Le Système . . . sur l'état des âmes* (1738 ed.), p. 38.
137. Rousseau, *Lettre à d'Alembert*, in *Religious Writings* (ed. R. Grimsley, 1970), p. 76.
138. Toussaint, *Éclaircissements sur 'Les Mœurs'*, p. 177.
139. *Émile*, in Grimsley, pp. 184–6.
140. Mme Roland, *Lettres* (ed. Cl. Perroud, N.S. 1913), i. 102.

141. A discussion of Morelly's observation in Favre, i. 241–4.
142. Pierre Poiret, *L'Œconomie de la providence universelle pour le salut de tous les hommes* (7 v. 1682), ii. 59, 389–90, iv. 56, vi. 302, vii. 202, 213, 297.
143. Marie Huber, pp. 34, 106, 109, 111–14, 129, 238.
144. D'Argens, *Lettres juives*, i. 321, ii. 19–27.
145. [Dom Louis], *Le Ciel ouvert à tout l'univers* (1782), pp. 142, 144, 149–50.
146. *Émile, Œuvres* (Gallimard, 1969), p. 592; R. Grimsley, *Rousseau and the Religious Quest* (1968), p. 123. There is an interesting attempt to conciliate Rousseauism and Catholicism in the abbé Lamourette's *Les Délices de la Religion ou le pouvoir de l'évangile pour nous rendre heureux* (1788). Hell is an essential part of the Catholic doctrinal structure and the inevitable consequence of man's free-will and of his divine status (which makes his fall into an infinite degradation). Yet Hell is something which only the wicked need to think about; for the truly religious man it is just 'a speculation', a powerful expression of the truth that God desires to be loved by every soul (presumably he means that the rejection of God has to be expressed in terms of an almost unthinkable tragedy).

CHAPTER 7

Preparation for Death

1. Catechism of 1676, F. Lebrun, *Les Hommes et la mort en Anjou au 17ᵉ et 18ᵉ siècles*, p. 437; [Tribolet], *Réflexions sur Jésus-Christ mourant pour se préparer . . . à une mort chrétienne* (1729), p. 7.
2. J. Crasset, S. J., *La Douce et la sainte mort* (1708 ed.), p. 283.
3. *Corresp. littéraire et anecdotique entre M. de Saint Fonds et le président Dugas, 1711–39* (ed. W. Poidebad, 2 v. Lyon, 1900), ii. 25 (22 May 1730).
4. H. Bremond, *Hist. littéraire du sentiment religieux en France . . .* (11 v. 1916–32), ix. 375.
5. Ch. Gobinet, *Instruction de la jeunesse en la piété chrétienne* (new ed. 1719), pp. 38–44.
6. [Dom R. Morel], *Entretiens spirituels en forme de prières, pour servir de préparation à la mort* (new ed. 1730), p. vi; Gaudron, *Instructions et pratiques pour passer saintement tous les temps de l'année*, ii. 255.
7. Drexelius, *Considerations upon Death* (E. T. 1699), pp. 264, 270. He is much quoted in the 18th century.
8. Girard de Villethierry, *L'Homme du monde confondu dans le délai de sa conversion* (1700), p. 71.

9. Griffet, *L'Année du chrétien*, i. 69.
10. F. Nepveu, S. J., *La Manière de se préparer à la mort pendant la vie* (1713), pp. 22–37.
11. P.-F. Lafitau (bishop of Sisteron), *Avis de direction pour les personnes qui veulent se sauver* (1751), p. 32.
12. [Tribolet], p. 251.
13. G.-F. Berthier and J.-B. Lausausse, *La Science de l'oraison mentale . . . suivi de la Doctrine spirituelle du Père Berthier* (1791), p. 464.
14. Griffet, i. 75–6; *Pensez-y bien* (1737 ed.), p. 76.
15. M. de Chertablon, *La Manière de se bien préparer à la mort* (1700), p. 7.
16. Dom Morel, *Traité de l'espérance chrétienne* (1732), pp. 9, 24. For a modern working-out of the theme of despair when dying see the novels of Bernanos (G. Gauchet, *Le Thème de la mort dans les romans de Bernanos* (1953), pp. 51–2).
17. *Pensez-y bien*, pp. 61–4.
18. C. Judde, 'Retraite de trente jours' (1746), in *Œuvres spirituelles* (ed. Le Noir-Duparc), i. 150.
19. Chertablon, loc. cit.
20. Bremond, ix. 333–4.
21. *Mandement de Mgr l'évêque d'Alais qui ordonne . . . des prières pour le repos de l'âme du feu Roi* (1774), pp. 8–9.
22. p. 69.
23. Grou, *A Little Book on the Love of God*, p. 45; *The Hidden Life of the Soul* (ed. 1870), p. 200.
24. Collet, *Traité des devoirs des gens du monde et surtout des chefs de famille*, pp. 395–6.
25. P. Chaunu, 'Mourir à Paris', *Annales*, (1976), p. 40.
26. Père d'Avril, S. J., *Saints et heureux retours sur soi-mesme* (2 v. 1711), i. 120.
27. *Pensez-y bien*, pp. 149–54; [Nonnotte]*Anti-Dictionnaire philosophique*, ii. 124.
28. Griffet, ii. 181.
29. Crasset, pp. 22–3.
30. Jude, pp. 191–3.
31. [Duguet], *Manuel de piété*, p. 118.
32. The abbé de Boismont, *Sermon pour l'assemblée . . . de Charité . . . à l'occasion de l'établissement d'une maison royale de santé*, 13 Mar. 1783, p. 51.
33. Chertablon, p. 12.
34. L. Durand-Vaugaron, 'L'inventaire d'un fonds de librairie à Rennes en 1725', *Ann. de Bretagne*, (1957), 337.
35. D. Roche, '*La Mémoire de la mort*: recherche sur la place des arts de

mourir dans la librairie et la lecture en France au XVIIe et XVIIIe siècles', *Annales* (1976), pp. 76–7. See also R. Chartier, 'Les Arts de Mourir, 1450–1600', ibid., pp. 55–7. For editions of the *Imitation*, see Favre, ii. 107 n. 262.

36. J. Brancolini and Marie-Thérèse Bouyssy, 'La vie provinciale du livre à la fin de l'ancien régime', in F. Furet (ed.), *Livre et société dans la France du XVIIIe siècle* (2 v. 1970), ii. 11.

37. Roche, pp. 81–3.

38. F. Furet and A. Fontana, 'Histoire et linguistique', in Furet, i. 188.

39. Collet, *Conversations sur plusiers sujets de morale propres à former les jeunes demoiselles à la pieté* (1769), pp. 441–64; *Instruction chrétienne des jeunes filles tirée . . . du livre de l'instruction de la jeunesse, fait par M. Gobinet* (1782); Caraccioli, *Les Derniers Adieux*.

40. [Coret], *L'Ange conducteur . . .* (1746), pp. 31, 38; Le Chevalier de Lasne d'Aiguebelle, *Sentiments affectueux de l'âme envers Dieu* (new ed. Avignon, 1777), p. 229.

41. [Marie-Madeleine d'Aguesseau le Guerchoix], *Pratiques pour se disposer à la mort* (1747), pp. 2–4, 42, 83–4.

42. Ibid., p. 34.

43. *Pensez-y bien.*

44. C. de Sainte-Marthe, *Considérations chrétiennes sur la mort* (ed. 1713); comment in D. Roche, '*La mémoire de la mort*: recherche sur la place des arts de mourir . . .', *Annales* (1976), p. 107.

45. Sevoy, *Devoirs ecclésiastiques*, ii. 51.

46. Caraccioli, *Le Tableau de la mort*, p. 78.

47. J. Lovie, 'La vie paroissiale dans le diocèse de Die à la fin de l'ancien régime', *Bull. Soc. arch. hist. de la Drôme*, 63 (1931), 180–1. Lasne d'Aiguebelle (p. 235) ascribes these words to Père Rosemberg of La Trappe, substituting 'poudre' for 'cendre'. The words are found, however, in P. Calabre in 1711 (cit. Favre, ii. 95). The bishop of Boulogne quotes this prayer in the 1780s with both 'poudre' and 'cendre' (*Exercices de Piété*, in Partz de Pressy, *Œuvres*, Migne, 2 v. 1842, ii. 257).

48. Pierre de Clorivière, *Considérations sur l'exercice de la prière et de l'oraison* (1778, publ. 1802, ed. A. Rayez, 1961), p. 112.

49. P. Pourrat, *La Spiritualité chrétienne* (4 v. 1918–28), iv. 417.

50. Bremond, ix. 371.

51. Griffet, *L'Année du chrétien*, xvii. 398–402; Judde, *Œuvres*, i. 157–63.

52. Dom Masson, *Directoire des mourants à l'usage de l'Ordre des Chartreux* (Bremond, ix. 355–6).

53. *Dict. de spiritualité*, ed. A. Rayez, viii (1974), p. 142.

54. Bremond, ix. 375.
55. Ibid. 378.
56. *Traité de la joie de l'âme chrétienne* (1779), *Œuvres*, iii. 99.
57. Languet de Gergy, *Traité de la confiance en la miséricorde de Dieu* (3rd ed. Avignon, 1760), p. 13.
58. Bergier, *Tableau de la miséricorde divine*, *Œuvres*, viii, col. 1003. For the bishop of Boulogne in 1762, see A. Playoust-Chaussis, *La Vie religieuse dans le diocèse de Boulogne au XVIIIe siècle*, p. 124.
59. A. Rayez, *Formes modernes de vie consacrée: Adélaïde de Cicé et P. de Clorivière* (1966), pp. 99, 125, 19–20.
60. A. Rayez, 'Le curé d'Ars et l'abbé Boursoul', *Rev. d'ascétique et de mystique*, 43 (1967), 195–6.
61. pp. 81, 101, 111, 115, 118.
62. Du Bos, *Réflexions critiques sur la poésie et la peinture* (3 v. 1755), i. 232–6 (chap. XXVI (i)).
63. *Émile*, IV (*Œuvres*, Pléiade, 1969, iv. 626).
64. Crasset, p. 32.
65. Duguet, *La Croix de N.-S. Jésus Christ ou réflexions sur Jésus Christ crucifié* (1727), p. 114.
66. Ibid., pp. 78–9, and idem, *Explication du mystère de la Passion de Notre Seigneur Jésus Christ*, p. 14.
67. Watelet, *Dict. des arts de peinture, sculpture et gravure*, iii. 96; i. 477 (articles by Levesque).
68. [Tribolet], pp. 72–115, 319–23.
69. Ibid., pp. 9, 23, 16, 49, 64, 250–1, 295; Dame Marie-Madeleine d'Aguesseau le Guerchoix, *Pratiques pour se disposer à la mort*, pp. 34–9.
70. Chertablon, *passim*.
71. [Duguet], *Continuation de l'explication de la Passion de Jésus-Christ: ou réflexions sur la sépulture de N.-S.* (new ed. Bruxelles, 1735), pp. 128–30.
72. R. Darricau, 'De la cour de Louis XIV à l'ermitage de Lormont—l'abbé de Brion', *Rev. hist. de Bordeaux et du département de la Gironde*, N.S. 4 (1955), 106.
73. A. Rayez, *Formes modernes de vie consacrée: Adélaïde de Cicé et P. de Clorivière*, p. 111.
74. *Critique de l'histoire des Flagellans (1703) et justification de l'usage des disciplines volontaires* (n.d.).
75. T. Poulet and J. Roubert, 'Les assemblées secrètes des XVIIe et XVIIIe siècles en relation avec l'Aa de Lyon', *Divus Thomas* (1967), p. 159; Cl. Tournier, *Le Chanoine Maurice Garrigou. 1766–1852* (1945), pp. 33–4.
76. L. Tronson, *Corresp.* (ed. L. Bertrand, 3 v. 1904), i. 9–10, ii. 406. For

a seminarist at Saint-Sulpice being diverted from extreme courses, *Mémoires et lettres de François-Joachim de Pierre, Cardinal de Bernis, 1715–1758* (ed. F. Masson, 2 v. 1878), ii. 23–5.

77. Duguet, cit. Bremond, ix. 17.

78. Baudrand, cit. Favre, i. 183. An important discussion follows. Favre suggests that seventeenth-century writers had reservations about the idea of desiring death, but that the Christian literature of the eighteenth century abandoned them—'Désormais voici que se développe une pure spiritualité de l'évasion'. I have not found the evidence convincing.

79. [Girard de Villethierry], *Le Chrétien étranger sur la terre* (1696), pp. 28, 154; *Le Chrétien dans la tribulation . . . malade et mourant* (1706), p. 330.

80. *La Science de bien mourir* (1696), pp. 15–94; Caraccioli, *Tableau*, pp. 112, 127; Pierre-François Lafitau, bishop of Sisteron, *Avis de direction pour les personnes qui veulent se sauver*, p. 229.

81. Cit. Favre, i. 185.

82. 'Aucun Apôtre plus persuasif qu'un moribond' (Roissard, *La Consolation du chrétien* (2 v. 1775), ii. 328–9).

83. [P. Bernardin de Picquigny], *Pratique efficace pour bien vivre et pour bien mourir* (1701), p. 188; cf. p. 261 and Girard de Villethierry (1704), p. 480 and Mgr de Pressy, ii, cols. 1256–7.

84. Crasset, pp. 4, 25, 27, 50.

85. 1688 ed. Paris, pp. 108, 30, 37, 23, 41, 67, 88, 156.

86. Ch. Drelincourt, *Les Consolations de l'âme fidèle contre les frayeurs de la mort*, ii. 6; Pierre du Moulin, *Traité de la paix de l'âme . . .* (1695, La Haye), p. 42. For the influence of the sombre Roman Catholic tradition on Protestant writers see T. C. Cave, 'The Protestant devotional tradition: Goulart's *Trente tableaux de la mort*,' *French Studies*, 21 (1967), 1–10.

87. Cit. Pourrat, iv. 423.

88. Le Pelletier, *Traité des récompenses et des peines éternelles*, p. 42. (Cf. Roissard, *La Consolation du chrétien*, p. 333.)

89. Languet de Gergy, *Traité de la confiance en la miséricorde de Dieu*, pp. 200–3, 209–50.

90. Lafitau, pp. 268–77.

91. [Vauge], *Traité de l'espérance chrétienne* (1732 ed.), pp. 147–50.

92. Crasset, p. 27.

93. B. Baudrand, S. J., *L'Âme sur le Calvaire*, *Œuvres*, ii, col. 91.

94. [Girard de Villethierry], *Le Chrétien dans la tribulation . . . malade et mourant*, p. 486.

95. Letter on the death of the duchesse de Luynes, 1684, in [Boileau], *Lettres de M.B. . . . sur différens sujets de morale et de piété*, i. 9–11.

96. Mgr. Partz de Pressey, *Œuvres*, i, col. 857 (June 1779).
97. Dom R. Morel, *Entretiens spirituels en forme de prières pour servir de préparation à la mort*, p. 407. For predestination, *De l'espérance chrétienne*, p. 94.
98. Louis Antoine, 'Le Père Ambroise de Lombez par un témoin de sa vie', *Rev. d'ascétique et de mystique*, 44 (1968), 54–7.
99. *The Hidden Life of the Soul*, p. 254. Cf. *The Spiritual Maxims* (E.T. 1874, original French ed. 1789), pp. 16–19.
100. Grou, *De la paix de l'âme*, ed. A. Rayez, *Rev. ascétique et mystique*, 45. (1969), 280. Cf. *A Little Book on the Love of God*, pp. 73–8.
101. *Manual for Interior Souls* (E.T. 1889), p. 57.
102. *The Hidden Life of the Soul*, pp. 140–1, 252–4.
103. *The Practical Science of the Cross in the use of the Sacraments of Penitence and the Eucharist* (E.T. n.d., first ed. in French 1789), Meditation XXXI, pp. 201–6.
104. *Traité de l'amour de Dieu*, XI (xii, xviii), *Œuvres* (Pléiade, 1969), pp. 926–33.
105. Madeleine Huillet d'Istria, *Le Père de Caussade et la querelle du pur amour* (1964), pp. 147–55, 116–17, 191–2.
106. Ibid., pp. 120–1.
107. Piny, *La Clef du pur amour* (1680; ed. P. Noël, n.d., 1918?), pp. 25, 65, 49–51, 38, 130.
108. *État du pur amour ou conduite pour arriver à la perfection par le seul 'fiat' dit et réitéré en toutes sortes d'occasion* (1682, ed. P. Noël, n.d., 1921?), p. 153.
109. *La Clef*, p. 98.
110. *La plus parfait, ou des voyes intérieures la plus glorifiante pour Dieu, et la plus sanctifiante pour l'âme* (1682; Paris 1691), p. 307.
111. *La Clef*, pp. 156, 211.
112. *La Clef*, pp. 152–3.
113. *État*, p. 141.
114. *État*, p. 134.
115. *La Clef*, p. 154.
116. *La Clef*, p. 98.
117. *La Clef*, p. 21; *Le Plus parfait*, p. 310; *État*, p. 41.
118. *État*, p. 40.
119. G. Joppin, *Fénelon et la mystique du pur amour* (1938), pp. 256–7.
120. To Mme Guyon, 11 Aug. 1689, in *Correspondance* (ed. J. Orcibal, 1972), ii. 125.
121. M. Raymond, *Fénelon* (1967), pp. 81, 63.
122. J.-L. Goré, *L'Itinéraire de Fénelon: humanisme et spiritualité* (1957), pp. 720, 729; *La Notion d'indifférence chez Fénelon et ses sources* (1956), pp. 179, 181.

123. Goré, *L'Itinéraire*, p. 228.
124. Fénelon, *Œuvres*, vi. 90.
125. Ibid. 92.
126. Ibid. 130; ii. 190
127. Ibid. vi. 54.
128. L. Cognet, *Crépuscule des mystiques* (1958), p. 6.
129. See R. Mauzi, *L'Idée du bonheur dans la littérature et la pensée françaises au XVIIIᵉ siècle*.
130. [Vauge], *Traité de l'espérance chrétienne*, p. 9.
131. [Toussaint], *Les Mœurs*, p. 39.
132. Mme Le Prince de Beaumont, *La Dévotion éclairee, ou magasin des dévotes* (1779), p. 206.
133. See Brion's *La Vie de la très-sublime contemplative sœur Marie de Sainte Thérèse* (1720); *Lettres de la sœur Marie de Sainte Thérèse* (2 v. 1720); *Traité de la vraie et de la fausse spiritualité* (1728); also the *Examen des fautes de M. l'abbé de Brion* (1725) and Brion's *Réponse* (n.d.)
134. J. Bremond, *Le Courant mystique au XVIIIᵉ siècle: l'abandon dans les lettres du P. Milley* (1943), (this is an edition of Milley's letters), pp. 212, 213, 104, 182–3, 107–8, 250. J.-P. de Caussade, *L'Abandon à la Providence divine*, ed. M. Olphe-Galliard (1966), p. 134.
135. Milley, p. 142.
136. Ibid., pp. 142–3.
137. Ibid., p. 270
138. Ibid., p. 196.
139. For the chosen, pp. 87–8, 177, 44, 212, 346. For all conditions, pp. 181, 188.
140. pp. 70–2.
141. M. Huillet d'Istria, *Le Père de Caussade et la question du pur amour*, p. 101.
142. J.-P. de Caussade, *Lettres spirituelles*, ed. M. Olphe-Galliard, S.J. (2 v. 1960), i. 373–4.
143. Ibid. ii. 91.
144. Ibid. 59 (cf. i. 74).
145. Ibid. ii. 146, 60; i. 74, 259–60, 365, 370, 340.
146. Ibid. ii. 88.
147. J. Le Brun, 'Textes inédits du Père de Caussade', *Rev. d'ascétique et mystique*, 46 (1970), 229–30.
148. *Lettres* (ed. cit.), i. 102, 121, 277; ii. 19, 28.
149. Ibid. ii. 219.
150. Ibid. i. 177, 209, 99.
151. Ibid. 318 (cf. 131).
152. Ibid. ii. 103.

153. Ibid. 61–3.
154. Ibid. 87
155. Ibid. i. 93; ii. 26.
156. M. Huillet d'Istria, pp. 204–5; *Lettres* (ed. cit.), ii. 153–4.
157. *Lettres*, ii. p. 87.
158. Favre, i. 177–9.
159. *Mémoires de Trévoux* (Sept. 1705), p. 1603.
160. The essential authority for the statistical study of the question is D. Roche, '*La Mémoire de la mort*: Recherche sur la place des arts de mourir dans la librairie et la lecture en France au XVIIᵉ et XVIIIᵉ siècles', *Annales* (1976), pp. 76 ff.
161. Ibid., pp. 85–8.
162. J. Brancolin and Marie-Thérèse Bouyssy, 'La vie provinciale du livre à la fin de l'ancien régime' in F. Furet (ed.), *Livre et société dans la France du XVIIIᵉ siècle*, ii. 24–6.
163. D. Roche, art. cit., pp. 88–90.
164. Ibid., pp. 94–5.
165. Ibid., p. 78.
166. Mme de Genlis, *Mémoires inédits* (2 v. 1825), ii. 220–2.
167. J. McManners, *French Ecclesiastical Society . . . Angers*, p. 95.
168. E. Harrisse, *L'Abbé Prévost, histoire de sa vie et de ses œuvres* (1896), pp. 109–10; d'Argenson, iv. 183–4; M. Marais, *Journal et mémoires*, ed. M. de Lescure (4 v. 1863), iii. 39.
169. Favre, i. 93; ii. 52.
170. [Duguet], *Conduite d'une dame chrétienne pour vivre saintement dans le monde* (1725), pp. 52, 11.
171. [Duguet], *Manuel de piété . . . des maximes et des prières pour la réception des Sacremens*, pp. 26–30, 69, 74–7.
172. [Desprez], *Instructions sur les dispositions . . . des sacremens* (1753), pp. 478–9.
173. [Daon], *Conduite des âmes dans la voie du salut*, pp. 33–40.
174. For interest see M. Courdurie, *La Dette des collectivités publiques de Marseille au XVIIIᵉ siècle*; for sex, J. McManners, 'Living and Loving: changing attitudes to sexual relationships in 18th-Century France', *British Soc. for 18th-Century Studies*, 12 (June 1977), 1–19.
175. Geneviève Bollême, *Les Almanachs populaires aux XVIIᵉ et XVIIIᵉ siècles* (1969), pp. 63–72. R. Mandrou, *De la culture populaire au 17ᵉ et 18ᵉ siècles* (1964), pp. 88–9, 118, 83.
176. E. Lavaquery, *Le Cardinal de Boisgelin* i. 189–90; see also above, p. 144.
177. Two catechisms in *Conduite des âmes dans la voie du salut*, pp. 48–50, 84–5, and a catechism in J. McManners, *French Ecclesiastical Society*, p. 146.

178. M. Vallery-Radot, *Le Cardinal de Luynes, archevêque de Sens, 1753–88*. p. 46.

179. Régius, *curé* of Gap, *La Voix du Pasteur* (1773), cit. B. Groethuysen, *The Bourgeois: Catholicism versus Capitalism in Eighteenth-Century France* (E.T. 1968), p. 57.

180. M. Bruyère, 'Le P. Jacques Bridaine, 1701–1769', *Bull. du Comité de l'art Chrétien de Nîmes* (1939), p. 18.

181. McManners, *French Ecclesiastical Society* p. 145.

182. J. Pandellé, 'Une grande figure épiscopale du xviiie siècle: Jean-François de Montillet, archevêque d'Auch', *Rev. de Gascogne*, 32 (1933) 129–31; L. Pérouas, *Le Diocèse de la Rochelle de 1648 à 1724: sociologie et pastorale* (1964), pp. 378–86.

183. Groethuysen, pp. 70–1.

184. See e.g. Mgr Martial Levé, *Louis-Francois-Gabriel d'Orléans de la Motte, évêque d'Amiens, 1683–1774* (1962), p. 177.

185. Pierre Jounel, 'La semaine sainte en France au 17e et 18e siècles', *La Maison Dieu*, 4 (1955), 137.

186. M. Agulhon, *La Sociabilité méridionale. Confréries et associations dans la vie collective en Provence orientale à la fin du xviiie siècle* (2 v. 1966), ii. 174–80, 200–1, 213, 285.

187. Ch. Vérel, 'Le Plantis', *Bull. Soc. hist. arch. de l'Orne*, 15 (1895), 172–4.

188. Lorin, 'La confrérie de Saint-Sébastien à Saint-Nicolas de Maule', *Méms. Soc. arch. de Rambouillet*, 22 (1913), 438–9.

189. A. Rayez, *Formes modernes de vie consacrée: Adélaïde de Cicé et P. de Clorivière*, p. 63 n.

190. P. François Poire, S.J., *La Sauvegarde des mourants, ou Marie patronne de la bonne mort* (1861—original edition 18th century), pp. 145–50.

191. See e.g. J. Déchelette, 'Visites pastorales des archiprêtres de Charlieu par Mgr de Lort de Sérignan de Valras, évêque de Mâcon, 1745–64', *Ann. de l'acad. de Mâcon*, 3e Sér. 3 (1898), 558–60; 4 (1899), 574–5, 447.

192. L. Blond, *La Maison professe des Jésuites de la rue Saint-Antoine à Paris* (1965), p. 134; J. Pra, *Les Jésuites à Grenoble, 1587–1763* (1901), pp. 302–15.

193. M. A. Coulondres, 'Journal de Bernard-Laurent Soumille . . .', *Méms. Soc. Sci. litt. d'Alais*, 10 (1879), 179.

194. A. Rébillon, 'Recherches sur les anciennes corporations ouvrières et marchandes de la ville de Rennes', *Ann. de Bretagne*, 19 (1903–4), 54–5.

195. R. Suadeau, *L'Évêque inspecteur administratif sous la monarchie absolue* (2 v. 1940), i. 77.

196. Agulhon, i. 358, 274, 288.
197. For the beginning of opposition among nobles and magistrates to the funeral procession with the face of the corpse exposed see Vovelle, *Piété baroque et déchristianisation en Provence*, pp. 83–6.

CHAPTER 8
Deathbeds

1. 'La mort inversée: le changement des attitudes devant la mort dans les sociétés occidentales', *Archives européennes de Sociologie*, 8 (1967), 171–80.
2. See [Rancé] *Relation de la vie et de la mort de quelques religieux de l'abbaye de la Trappe* (new ed. 5 v. 1755). For Rancé's own death, iii. 41–5.
3. Tribolet, *Réflexions sur Jésus-Christ mourant*, pp. 260, 267.
4. *Œuvres compl. de Boudon* (ed. Migne, 3 v. 1856), i. col. 160.
5. Roissard, *La Consolation du chrétien*, ii. 328–9.
6. Cit. H. Bremond, *Hist. littéraire du sentiment religieux en France*, ix. 365–7.
7. [Mabillon], *La Mort chrétienne sur le modèle de celle de Notre Seigneur Jésus-Christ* (1702), pp. 148–9.
8. Rancé, i. 5–6. Cf. Marie Billiot in R. P. Jean Hanard, *Les Belles Morts de plusieurs séculiers* (1667), p. 349, and *Les Œuvres spirituelles de Mme de Bellefont*, Introd.
9. Rancé, i. 60, 382.
10. Chertablon, *La Manière de se bien préparer . . .*, pp. 41–2, 57, 63.
11. [Marin Fillassier], *Sentimens chrétiens propres aux personnes malades et infirmes* (1726), pp. xix, 375–6.
12. *Mes souvenirs*, ii. 244–5 (23 Jan. 1776).
13. Comte de Ségur, *Mémoires* (3 v. Stuttgart, 1829), i. 184–6.
14. Voltaire, *Œuvres* (Moland), iii. 443 n.
15. Barbier, *Chronique . . . 1718–63*, i. 437 (5 Aug. 1726).
16. R. P. Jean Hanard, pp. 77–80.
17. Ibid., pp. 217–20.
18. Ch. de Ribbe, *La Vie domestique: ses modèles et ses règles d'après les documents originaux* (2 v. 1877), i. 352–68.
19. Restif de la Bretonne, *La vie de mon père, Œuvres* (ed. H. Bachelin), iv. 117–19.
20. Prévost, *The Dean of Coleraine* (E.T. 3 v. London, 1742), i. 21; [Gérard], *Le Comte de Valmont* (3 v. 1776), i. 374–6.
21. [Chevalier de Lasne d'Aiguebelle], *Testament spirituel, ou derniers adieux d'un père mourant à ses enfants* (1776), p. vi.

22. Caraccioli, *Les Derniers Adieux de la maréchale de——à ses enfants*, p. viii.

23. *Relation abrégée de la maladie et de la mort du R. P. Pasquier Quesnel* (1719), p. 3.

24. B. Picart, *Cérémonies*, ii. 91. Cf. Mme d'Épinay to Duclos, Sept. 1750, *Corresp. de Charles Duclos* (ed. J. Brengues, 1970), p. 23.

25. P. Chaunu, *La Mort à Paris*, pp. 371–2, 394.

26. Chertablon, p. 33; Picart, loc. cit. In 1774, the *curé* of Saint-Eustache, at the deathbed of a courtesan, refused her offer of her fortune for the poor: she was to use most of it to provide for her parents (Bachaumont, *Mémoires secrets* ... (36 v. 1779–89), vii 150–1, 29 Mar. 1774).

27. R. Pillorget, *La Tige et le rameau*, p. 237.

28. See R. E. Giesay, 'Rules of inheritance and strategies of mobility in pre-revolutionary France', *American Hist. Rev.* 82 (1977), 271–6.

29. M. Vovelle, 'Entre baroque et Jansénisme: mentalités collectives dans la Provence au temps de la peste', *La Régence* (Centre Aixois d'études sur le 18ᵉ siècle, 1970), p. 216.

30. Will of a noble of Dijon, in M. Garden, 'Niveaux de fortune à Dijon au milieu du XVIIIᵉ siècle', *Cahiers d'histoire*, 9 (1964), 241. This will puts the weight on intercession; similar formulas could be used in a declaratory sense, 'I declare that I die in the sentiments with which a Catholic, Apostolic, and Roman Christian ought to be inspired'. (P. Delaunay, *Le Monde médical parisien au 18ᵉ siècle*, p. 372.)

31. Lebrun, *Les Hommes et la mort en Anjou*, p. 463.

32. M. Vovelle, *Piété baroque et déchristianisation en Provence*.

33. Chaunu, p. 432.

34. Ibid., pp. 448–51.

35. Métra (*et al.*) *Corresp. secrète, politique et littéraire*, x. 6–7.

36. Vovelle, pp. 116–19. For severe reductions at Angers in 1769 and 1774 see McManners, *French Ecclesiastical Society*, p. 123. For the great burden of foundation masses in a Parisian parish—3,856 annually, see M. Brongniart, *La Paroisse Saint-Médard* (1951), p. 99.

37. Vovelle's phrase.

38. Chaunu, p. 413.

39. Ibid., pp. 434–5.

40. Pavillon, bishop of Alet, cit. J.-B. Thiers, *Dissertation sur la clôture des chœurs des Églises* (1688), p. 27.

41. J. Meyer, *La Noblesse bretonne au XVIIIᵉ siècle*, ii. 1148–50.

42. J. P. Guiton, *La Société et les pauvres: l'exemple de ... Lyon, 1534–1789*, pp. 299–441.

43. Vovelle, pp. 257–60. One would imagine that concern for the poor is a better method of assessing true 'Christian' sentiments than other indications referring to personal salvation or institutional loyalty— or at least, the two should be compared. Vovelle's many statistical breakdowns do not attempt such a correlation—e.g. between numbers of masses asked and charitable bequests. But the complexities of analysis would be baffling. Account would need to be taken of fashions in generosity. Early in the eighteenth century there was founding a bed in a hospital (for about 10,000 *livres*—see the examples in M. Vimont, *Hist. de l'église et de la paroisse Saint-Léo-Saint-Gilles à Paris* (1932), pp. 96–7). Later in the century, there were dowries for poor girls or buying ploughs for peasants (Meyer, loc. cit.). On the change from *charité* to *bienfaisance* see J. Imbert, *Le Droit hospitalier de la Révolution et de l'Empire*, p. 12.

Also, in individual cases one would need to set charitable bequests against total fortune and make allowance for family obligations— numbers of children, daughters needing dowries, etc. A poor man leaving all to his son except for 800 *livres* devoted to the dowries of four daughters, not surprisingly can give only 12 *livres* for masses for his soul and none for charity (J. Donat, *Une communauté rurale à la fin de l'ancien régime* (1926), p. 260). One would also need to discover the extent of charitable gifts in the testators' lifetime, and the norm of bequests within the particular social class and geographical area. Indeed, the actual character of the heir would enter into the reckoning, since a charitable man might leave all to someone of the same mind as himself, knowing the fortune would continue to be used responsibly. True, a noble with a large income and savings of 280,000 *livres* in his coffers who leaves only 2,000 *livres* for his funeral expenses and for charity is mean (the marquis de Tessé, died 1766; see R. Forster, *The House of Saulx-Tavannes* (1971)). On the other hand, a country veterinary surgeon who leaves as much grain as constitutes half the crop of a small tenant farm is generous (P. Massé, *Varennes et ses maîtres, 1779–1842* (1956), p. 13). But few cases are as obvious as these.

44. Voltaire, *Corresp.* (Besterman), iii. 9, 21–2. This was at the deathbed of Mme Fontane de Martel in 1733. Her last words were interesting. 'What time is it?' 'Two o'clock, Madame.' 'Ah! it's consoling to think that whatever time it may be there's always someone working to ensure that the human race doesn't die out.' (Voltaire, *Notebooks*, ii. 355.)

45. Bachaumont, xii. 12–13 (June 1778).

46. Métra, v. 215–16 (28 Oct. 1777). The eccentric duchesse d'Olonne was generous to her servants, but only on condition that they lived

away from Paris in different places so they could not gossip about her (Bachaumont, ix. 285, Dec. 1776).

47. The duc de Croÿ, *Journal 1718–1784* (ed. the vicomte de Grouchy and P. Cottin), ii, 338–44, iv. 360–1, and R. Dauvergne, *Les Résidences du maréchal de Croÿ, 1718–84* (1950), p. 30.

48. P.-J. Guyot, *Répertoire universel et raisonné de jurisprudence* (64 v. 1775–83 and 14 v. additionally, 1786), xvi. 605–6. Cf. Barbier, ii. 286–7.

49. Luynes, ii. 255; ix. 301.

50. Bernardin de Picquigny, *Pratique efficace pour bien vivre et pour bien mourir*, p. 188.

51. Dom Claude de Vert, *Explication des cérémonies de l'église*, i. 54. Cf. the *Rituel* of Paris of 1735, cit. Lebrun, p. 455.

52. Mabillon, *La Mort chrétienne sur le modèle de celle de N. S. Jésus-Christ, Avert.*

53. Dom Claude de Vert, ii. 67. Cf. Diderot, *Jacques le fataliste* (Pléiade), p. 660, and Dom Guéranger, *Institutions liturgiques* (3 v. 1851), ii. 241.

54. Fillassier, pp. 257–62.

55. A. Corlieu, *La Mort des rois de France*, p. 125.

56. P. Delaunay, *La Vie médicale au XVIᵉ, XVIIᵉ et XVIIIᵉ siècles* (1935), p. 353.

57. These phrases in P. Lafitau, S. J., *Mœurs des sauvages amériquains comparées aux mœurs des premiers temps* (2 v. 1724), ii. 408.

58. Ch. Joathan, 'Le Journal inédit d'un curé de Saint-Vincent de Mâcon au XVIIIᵉ siècle', *Ann. de l'Acad. de Mâcon*, 3ᵉ sér. 42 (1954–5), 104.

59. A. Blanchard, *Nouvel essay d'exhortations pour les états différens des malades* (2 v. 1718), ii. 28, 31.

60. Crasset, p. 186.

61. Bremond, ix. 354.

62. 'Il ne faut qu'une goutte de ce sang pour me purifier . . . Son sang coule sur moi, et ne s'y attache pas . . . Je suis perdue!' (*La Religieuse*, ed. J. Parish, 1963, pp. 198–9.) By contrast, a pious death— 'La joie sainte qu'il a de se voir comme inondé du sang et des mérites de son Rédempteur', fortifying against 'les derniers assauts du tentateur' (Collet, *Traité historique, dogmatique et pratique des indulgences et du Jubilé*, i. 336).

63. Fontanes, 'Le Jour des morts dans une campagne', 1785–6, *Œuvres* (2 v. 1839), i. 35–6.

64. J. Guerber, S. J., *Le Ralliement du clergé français à la morale liguorienne: l'abbé Gousset et ses précurseurs, 1785–1832*, Analecta Gregoriana, 193 (1973).

65. Louis Bailly, *Theologia dogmatica et moralis* (1789), cit, Guerber, pp. 61, 63.
66. Lebrun, p. 454.
67. Daon, *Conduite des confesseurs dans le tribunal de la pénitence* . . . (6th ed. 1778; the first was 1738), pp. 438, 396 ff.
68. *Dict. portatif des cas de conscience* (2 v. 1761), ii. 13–24, 241, 248.
69. *Voltaire triomphant, ou les prêtres déçus, tragi-comédie* in Métra, *Corresp. secrète, politique et littéraire*, vi. 388–99.
70. Métra, vii. 139 (Nov. 1778).
71. Mme de Saint-Vincent, wife of a *président à mortier* of the Parlement of Aix, was shut up for libertinage. She was in communication with her relative, the maréchal de Richelieu (he said he had never slept with her because she was so ugly), and she claimed that Richelieu had given her two *billets* for large sums of money. He said these were forgeries (Moreau, *Mes souvenirs*, ii 279–80; Bachaumont, xiii. 238).
72. Bachaumont, xiii. 254, 260 (letter of 7 Jan. 1779).
73. Marivaux, *Vie de Marianne* (*Romans*, Pléiade, ed. M. Arland, 1949), pp. 275–7.
74. Diderot, *Corresp.* (ed. G. Roth, 1958–), iii. 111 (Sept. 1760).
75. F. Nepveu, S.J., *La Manière de se préparer à la mort pendant la vie*, p. 169.
76. *Lettres de Mlle Aissé* . . . (ed. A. Piedagnel, 1878), p. 24 (5 May 1727). Saint-Simon has an odd story about evading his Jesuit confessor on this last occasion (A. G. Y. Coirault, *L'Optique de Saint-Simon* (1965), p. 72).
77. Luynes, i. 75–6; iv. 224.
78. Bachaumont, xiv. 309 (Dec. 1779). For the abbé's facility as a compiler, see Grimm, *Corresp. littéraire, philosophique et politique*, ed. M. Tourneux (16 v. 1871–80), viii. 274.
79. Saint-Simon (1829 ed.), xvii. 379–86. She took the sacrament a third time with genuine piety, then, just as she was making an unexpected recovery, was killed by purges administered by her doctor.
80. Luynes, iii. 363.
81. Hardy, *Mes loisirs*, ed. M. Tourneaux and M. Vitrac (1912), p. 3.
82. The duc de Croÿ, *Journal*, iii. 101.
83. Bachaumont, xiv. 309.
84. R. Shackleton, *Montesquieu* (1961), pp. 394–8.
85. P. Ambroise de Lombez, *Œuvres complètes* (ed F. de Bénéjac), iii. 141 (the date is 1779—Lombez died soon after).
86. Mangin, *Science des confesseurs* (1752), pp. 369–70.
87. Grimm, *Corresp. littéraire*, ii. 260 (July 1753).
88. Métra, iv. 393–3 (1777).

89. The duc de Croÿ, *Journal*, ii. 137.
90. Bachaumont, v. 273 (1771).
91. E. and J. de Goncourt, *La Du Barry* (1880), pp. 1–2; De Nolhac, *Marie-Antoinette Dauphine* (1947), pp. 324–5.
92. Bachaumont, vi. 132 (25 Apr. 1772).
93. Helpful for the detail of the ceremonies, M. A. Hersan, *Pensées édifiantes sur la mort tirées des propres paroles de l'Écriture sainte et des saints pères* (1722). A conscientious *curé* would note in his registers when the illness was such that the communion could not be received. See extracts published by A. Lottier, *Ann. de Bourgogne*, 41 (1959), 79.
94. L. S. Mercier, *Tableau de Paris* (1782–8), v. 76–7.
95. Saint-Simon, xvii. 385.
96. J.-J. Gautier, *Essai sur les mœurs champêtres* (1787) (ed. X. Rousseau, 1935), p. 51.
97. *Tableau*, xi. 119–21.
98. Clear description of what happened in B. Picart, *Cérémonies*, ii. 90–2. Discussion in F. A. Isambert, 'Les transformations du rituel catholique des morts', *Archives des Sciences sociales des religions* (1975), pp. 90 ff.
99. Bernardin de Picquigny, p. 229.
100. Crasset, pp. 251, 229, 202–21, 237, 251–9, 269.
101. This prayer is the most ancient part of the final prayers (A. G. Martimort, 'Comment meurt un chrétien', *La Maison Dieu*, 44 (1955), 21).
102. I am grateful to Oxford University Press for allowing me to incorporate most of my Lecture, *Reflections at the Death Bed of Voltaire* (1975) in this and the following section.
103. Montaigne, *Essais*, III, xii (ed. P. Villey, 3 v. 1922, iii. 360). Cf. i. 71–2. The passages are quoted in the *Dict. des gens du monde* (5 v. 1770), iii. 512. See also M. Dreano, *La Renommée de Montaigne en France au XVIIIe* (1952), p. 105.
104. Bachaumont, ix. 275 (29 Nov. 1776).
105. Epilogue to *M. Nicolas* (1797), *Œuvres* (1932), ix. 237.
106. *Journal intime de Maine de Biran* (ed. A. de la Valette-Monbrun), i. 10–12.
107. Favre, i. 201–2.
108. Ibid. 231–2.
109. *Encyclopédie*. x (1765), 716–27.
110. By Radicati (Favre, p. 227).
111. Favre, i. 253–6; ii. 172 n. 307.
112. R. Grimsley, *Jean-Jacques Rousseau: Religious Writings* (1970), pp. 389, 145–6.

113. Rousseau, *Corresp.* (ed. R. A. Leigh), iv. 40.
114. Favre, i. 224.
115. *Entretiens chinois*, cit. R. Pomeau, *La Religion de Voltaire* (1956), pp. 383–4.
116. *Nouvelle Héloïse* (Grimsley, pp. 93–4).
117. René-Alexandre, marquis de Culant, *L'Homéide: poème*, pp. 75–6.
118. *La Douce et la sainte mort*, p. 2.
119. Le Maître de Claville, *Traité du vrai mérite de l'homme*, pp. 508–9.
120. Mme de Sabran, *Corresp. inédit* . . ., p. 217 (24 Apr. 1787).
121. [Mme de Charrière] *Lettres de Belle de Zuylen . . . 1760–75* (ed. Ph. Godel, 1909), p. 29 (18 Dec. 1762). In 1751, the idea is found even in a strict nunnery—a nun kept in ignorance of her approaching end because of her 'frayeur extrême de la mort' (D. Dinet, 'Mourir en religion', *Rev. historique* (1978), p. 46).
122. Duclos, *Histoire de Mme de Luz* (ed. J. Brengues, 1972), p. 22; [J. Deny de Verteuil], *Derniers sentiments des plus illustres personnages condamnés à mort* (2 v. 1775), ii. ii. For the Ancients, [Dionis]. *Dissertation sur la mort subite et sur la catalepsie* (1748).
123. For the peasants, van Gennep, *Manual of Folklore*, I (2) (1943), p. 665.
124. Saint-Simon, xx. 460 ff., 420.
125. Belle de Zuylen, loc. cit.
126. See above, pp. 195–7.
127. Girard de Villethierry, *Le Chrétien . . . malade et mourant*, pp. 547, 549–50.
128. Judde, *Œuvres* (ed. Le Noir-Duparc), i. 153–4.
129. *Lettres de Mme de Sévigné* (3 v. Pléiade, 1963), i. 573 (20 June 1672).
130. *Œuvres de Marc-Antoine de Noé* (1816), p. 92.
131. Stendhal, *Mémoires d'un touriste* (ed. Y. Gandon, 2 v. 1927), ii. 55–6.
132. See the memoirs of Mme de Genlis, cit. Favre, p. 121.
133. Gienet, *Contre les craintes de la mort* (La Haye, 1757).
134. 'Les retours que vous feriez sur tout ce que vous avez le plus tendrement aimé et le plus estimé, ne serviront qu'à vous mettre en danger de perdre l'héritage du Père céleste. C'est à Dieu seul qu'il faut vous attacher' (A. Blanchard, *Nouvel essay d'exhortations*, i. 192).
135. Rousseau, *Corresp.* (ed. Dufour), x. 286.
136. *Salons* (ed. J. Seznec), ii. 157–8; i. 233. Diderot was always sorry that he had not been present at the death of his father and his mother.
137. R. Rosenblum, *Transformations in late 18-Century Art* (1967), pp. 37–8. Important discussion in Anita Brookner, *Greuze* (1972), pp. 51–66, 90, 108. Wille's picture is in the museum in Cambrai.

138. *La Nouvelle Héloïse, Œuvres* (Pléiade), ii. 718.
139. 'La mort n'est pour elle que l'achèvement de la dialectique du bonheur' (R. Mauzi, 'Le problème religieux dans la *Nouvelle Héloïse'*, in *Jean-Jacques Rousseau et son œuvre*, (Comité National pour la Commémoration de J.-J. R. 1964), p. 165).
140. *Corresp.* lv. 22 (9 May 1764), 245–6 (31 Aug. 1764); lvi. 39–40 (21 Sept. 1764).
141. R. S. Ridgeway, *Voltaire and Sensibility* (1973), p. 245, takes this as an almost certain reference to Rousseau.
142. Bayle, 'Bion Borysthénite (E)', *Dict.* (cit. Favre, p. 94).
143. F. Nepveu, S. J., *La Manière de se préparer*, pp. 276–7; [The abbé Jacquin], *Les Préjugés* (1760), p. 289; P. Joseph-Romain Joly (Capuchin), *Dict. de morale philosophique*, ii. 92.
144. Nonnotte, *Anti-dictionnaire philosophique*, i. 495.
145. This was the allegation about Voltaire.
146. Gros de Besplas, *Le Rituel des esprits-forts ou le tableau des incrédules modernes au lit de la mort*, p. 73.
147. C. Rivollet, *Adrienne Lecouvreur* (1925), pp. 115–16. Guyot (xii. 261) points out that in England an actress could be buried in Westminster Abbey. Cf. Voltaire, *Lettres anglaises*, 23 ('Sur la considération qu'on doit aux gens de lettres').

For the procedures when burial in the cemetery was allowed but not the liturgical observances see the case of a Jansenist in 1738—the clergy in surplices but not stoles, no holy water, no cross, no prayers (L. M. Raison, 'Le Jansénisme à Rennes', *Ann. de Bretagne*, 48 (1941), 277). Cf. case of 1741 in A. Degert, *Hist. des évêques de Dax* (1903), pp. 391–2. The question still remained—which part of the cemetery to be buried in, and whether face up or face down (see the macabre incident at Douai in 1734 in J. Parguez, *La Bulle Unigenitus et le Jansénisme politique* (1936), p. 110).
148. In 1770 a Calvinist banker was buried in the cemetery of Saint-Eustache: he had left money for the poor of the parish (Bachaumont, xix. 221). The clergy of Lyon made no such gesture for the daughter of Edward Young—

> Denied the charity of dust, to spread
> O'er dust! a charity their dogs enjoy.
> (*Night Third, Narcissa*, lines 160–92.)

149. Lebrun, *L'Homme et la mort en Anjou*, p. 471.
150. H. Marion, *Dict. des institutions de la France au XVIIᵉ et XVIIIᵉ siècle* (2 v. 1923), i. 113.
151. Guyot, *Répertoire . . . de jurisprudence*, lvii. 131, 126–7.
152. *Dict. portatif des cas de conscience*, i. 209.

153. Barbier, iii. 370; E. Regnault, *Christophe de Beaumont*, i. 159–60; M. Vallery-Radot, *Un administrateur ecclésiastique . . . le cardinal de Luynes, archevêque de Sens*, pp. 56–8.

154. Mgr Martial Levé, *Louis-François-Gabriel d'Orléans de la Motte*, pp. 102–3.

155. Guyot, lviii. 208–9. But for the evidence of clerical strictness see A. Zinck, *Azereix*, p. 246.

156. *Dict. des cas de conscience*, ii. 393–6.

157. Métra, x. 205, 177.

158. Bachaumont, xxix. 4 (May 1785).

159. *Dict. des cas de conscience*, ii. 394.

160. Martial Levé, p. 103.

161. Saint-Simon (ed. 1829), iv. 34–6; xv. 456.

162. Grimm, *Corresp, littéraire*, ii. 127 (27 Dec. 1751).

163. Ibid. vi. 365–6 (Sept. 1765).

164. Ibid. iii. 155; Bachaumont, iii. 177; Voltaire, *Corresp*. lxv. 97.

165. J. Brengues, *Duclos* (1971), p. 214.

166. Mlle de Lubart, 5 Apr. 1772, cit. D. Gorce, *Le Grand Siècle devant la mort* (1950), p. 36.

167. Bachaumont, v. 260–7 (Jan. 1773).

168. Grimm, *Corresp. littéraire*, x. 368–70 (Feb. 1774).

169. Ibid. xi. 150–1 (Nov. 1775).

170. Métra, ii. 307. Voisenon's successor at the Academy found it hard to praise him for respectable reasons until he discovered that he had supported certain poor families (E. Lavaquary, *Le Cardinal de Boisgelin*, i. 259).

171. [A.-F. Boureau-Deslandes], *Réflexions sur les grands hommes qui sont morts en plaisantant* (Amst. 1732, 1st ed. 1712), pp. 2, 130; for Vanini p. 115. For what follows see J. Macary, *Masque et lumières au XVIIIe siècle: André-François Deslandes, citoyen et philosophe (1689–1757)* (1975), pp. 43–6.

172. C. Aveline, *Les Mots de la fin* (1957), p. 237; Sabatier, *Dict. de la mort*, p. 136.

173. Bachaumont, xxix. 218 (Sept. 1785).

174. Voltaire, *Corresp*. lvi. 14 (10 Sept. 1764).

175. *Encyclopédie . . . mis en ordre par M. de Félice*, xxix. 374.

176. There was a story about an old soldier who asked to have extreme unction with brandy and gunpowder (d'Argens, *Lettres juives* (1738 ed.), ii. 69). In 1769, the duc de Chartres invented the mock funeral supper to console the mistresses of great nobles who were contemplating matrimony (Bachaumont, iv. 217–18, Mar. 1769), a gesture of bad taste emulated by the son of a *Fermier général* in 1783 with a dinner for wealthy commoners, with *billets d'enterrement* for

invitations (Métra, xiv. 137–8). For the nadir of bad taste in anticlerical dying see the marquis de Sade, *Dialogue entre un prêtre et un moribond* (1782, publ. 1795, ed. M. Heine, 1926).

177. *Œuvres de l'abbé de Chaulieu* (2 v. ed. M. de Saint Marc, 1757), i. xcviii.
178. R. Shackleton, *Montesquieu*, pp. 393, 397.
179. The phrase is from the *Lettres persanes*, xxv. It seems appropriate to apply the words to Montesquieu himself.
180. D'Argenson, *Journal*, iv. 65 (May 1743).
181. Y. Durand, *Les Fermiers généraux au XVIIIe siècle*, p. 585.
182. 'Le voyage à Montbard par Hérault de Séchelles', *Révolution française*, 17 (1899), 58–9.
183. The anecdote is often told, e.g. by P. Lafu, *Le Prêtre ancien et les commencements du nouveau prêtre* (1967), p. 117. Professor Plongeron tells me that the source is the *Nouvelles ecclésiastiques*.
184. F. Vial, *Une philosophie et une morale de sentiment: Luc de Clapiers, marquis de Vauvenargues* (1938), p. 265. The words, 'Cet esclave est venu: Il a montré son ordre et n'a rien obtenu' are from Racine's *Bajazet*, Act I, sc. 1. The evidence for this story, alas, goes back no further than 1806. Voltaire said he died 'as a hero' and Marmontel said he died as a 'chrétien philosophe'. See A. Hof, 'État présent des "incertitudes" sur Vauvenargues', *Rev. d'hist. litt. de la France* (1969), p. 940.
185. Grim, *Corresp. littéraire*, ii. 453 (Dec. 1754). Terrasson died in 1750.
186. J. Brengues, p. 214.
187. Bachaumont, vii. 139–40.
188. Métra, iii. 222–3 (Aug. 1770).
189. 'Il y a toujours quelqu'un auprès du malade qui reçoit très bien le pasteur mais détourne la conversation lorsqu'il veut entrer en matière' (Bachaumont, xxiii. 226, Oct. 1763). Later, the *curé* was told his condition was too grave for anyone to see him (R. Grimsley, *D'Alembert* (1963), p. 289).
190. The *curé* of Saint-Sulpice came two or three times a week and talked about masses, good works, and so on. Diderot's wife and son-in-law ensured there was no tête-à-tête (Diderot, *Corresp.* xv. 322, 329, 332). Then death came unexpectedly.
191. Cit. Royer, *Voltaire malade: étude historique et médicale* (1883), pp. 147–52—over-emphasizing the despair.
192. Favre, i. 486; ii. 482. Ridgeway, *Voltaire and Sensibility*, pp. 166–187, 480.
193. Favre, ii. 349.
194. *Œuvres* (Moland), xxxviii. 500. (Cf. v. 309–10; iii. 322, 357, 46.)

195. *Corresp.* lxx. 238 (21 Dec. 1768). Cf. I. O. Wade, *The Intellectual Development of Voltaire*, pp. 60–2.

196. *Siècle de Louis XIV* (Moland), xiv. 481.

197. Favre, ii. 348.

198. *Notebooks* (ed. Besterman), ii. 357.

199. Nonnotte, *Les Erreurs de Voltaire* (3rd ed. Lyon, 2 v. 1767), ii. 89, 93. M. E. Gilbert, *Observations sur les écrits de M. de Voltaire* (London, 2 v. 1783), ii. 136, 160.

200. *Sophronime et Adélos* (1766), in Moland, xxv. 459, 465–8.

201. See above, p. 257.

202. *Corresp.* lxxxiv. 189; xcviii. 160. For Tronchin's cynical attitude to death, G. Desnoiresterres, *Voltaire et la société française au XVIIIe siècle* (2nd ed., 8 v. 1876), viii. 354. For the relations with Voltaire, R. Waldinger, 'Voltaire and Medicine', *Studies on Voltaire and the 18th century*, ed. T. Besterman, 58 (1967), 1791–8.

203. Voltaire, *Corresp.* lv. 245–6 (Aug. 1764).

204. Ibid. xcviii. 115–16. (Mme du Deffand to Walpole, 22 Feb. 1778). R. Pomeau, 'La confession et la mort de Voltaire', *Rev. d'hist. littéraire de la France* (1955), p. 302 (citing Voltaire's remark to Wagnière).

205. Voltaire's observations to Dr Lorry (Desnoiresterres, viii. 246) and to d'Alembert (whose letter to Frederick the Great, 1 July 1778, is printed in E. Damilaville, *Voltaire à Paris* (1876), p. 94).

206. On the day of his confession Voltaire told La Harpe of his motives: 'afin d'être enterré en terre sainte, et d'avoir un service aux Cordeliers' (Desnoiresterres, viii. 245).

207. *Corresp.* lxix. 45–6, 75; lxxi. 219, 223, 233.

208. The Academy, which was dominated by the *philosophes*, was in disgrace with the King: there were rumours in 1777 that it would be suppressed (L. Brunel, *Les Philosophes et l'Académie française au 18e siècle* (1884), p. 315). To obtain a respectable grave for Voltaire would, on the other hand, be a victory for the propaganda campaign of the *philosophes*. See Grimm's apostrophe to the clergy afterwards—'Avez-vous craint que ce tombeau ne devînt un autel et le lieu qui le renfermerait un temple?' (Damilaville, p. 69).

209. Voltaire, *Corresp.* lxx. 232 (Dec. 1768). See R. Trousson, *Socrate devant Voltaire, Diderot et Rousseau* (1967), pp. 31–4. For the admiration of Diderot and the painters of the second half of the century for Socrates see J. Seznec, *Essais sur Diderot et l'antiquité* (1957), pp. 11 ff.

210. *Corresp.* iii. 9 (Jan. 1733).

211. Ibid. xx. 81 (Nov. 1751).

212. Ibid. lxxi. 241–2 (Apr. 1769).

213. D'Alembert tells Frederick the Great (1 July 1778) that he advised

Voltaire to do 'comme tous les philosophes qui l'avaient précédé, entre autres comme Fontenelle et Montesquieu, qui avaient suivi l'usage.

> Et reçu ce que vous savez
> Avec beaucoup de révérence!'
> (Damilaville, pp. 93–4.)

214. *Relation de la maladie, de la confession, de la mort et de l'apparition du Jésuite Berthier* . . . (1759–60), *Œuvres* (ed. Moland, 1879), xxiv. 95–104. In fact Berthier did not die until 23 years later.

215. Voltaire, *Corresp.* lxix. 85 (25 Apr. 1768).

216. Ibid. iii. 9.

217. Ibid. lxxii. 16 (8 May 1769)—everything done by the counsel of an *avocat* who knows the province; p. 135 (7 July 1769)—the advice of two *avocats*; lxxi. 174 (Mar. 1769)—use of legal arguments to scare the *curé*; p. 219 (Apr. 1769)—legal certificate to be sent to the Academy.

218. The details that follow are in Pomeau's article and in Desnoiresterres's eighth volume (as cited above).

219. Damilaville, p. 22.

220. Voltaire, *Corresp.* xcviii. 130–1 (4 Mar. 1778).

221. Condorcet and d'Alembert say that the legal case was watertight and was certain to have won before the Parlement. All the friends of Voltaire, said d'Alembert, wanted the family to have recourse to the courts. The prior of Scellières, who eventually buried Voltaire, put the legal position clearly in defending himself to his bishop: 'je ne savais pas qu'on pût refuser la sépulture à un homme quelconque, mort dans le corps de l'Église . . . je sais d'après les canons qu'on ne refuse la sépulture qu'aux excommuniés, *lata sententia*' (in Damilaville, pp. 143–4).

222. The content of this declaration is precisely anticipated in the letter to Villevieille, of 20 Dec. 1768 (*Corresp.* lxx. 232). 'Je mourrai consolé en voyant la véritable religion, c'est-à-dire celle du cœur, établie sur *la ruine des simagrées. Je n'ai jamais prêché que l'adoration d'un Dieu, de la bienfaisance et l'indulgence.* Avec ces sentiments je brave le diable qui n'existe point, et les vrais diables, fanatiques qui n'existent que trop' (my italics).

223. D'Alembert was certain of this.

224. Desnoiresterres, p. 300.

CHAPTER 9

Funerals

1. Ch. Langlois, *Le Diocèse de Vannes au XIXe siècle, 1800–30* (1974), pp. 517–18.

2. B. Picart, *Cérémonies et coutumes religieuses de tous les peuples du monde* (9 v. Amsterdam, 1723–43), ii (1723), p. 93. For a local custom of taking the body to the river for washing, with ecclesiastical ceremonies, see Moléon, *Voyages liturgiques de France* . . . (1718), p. 152.

3. A. van Gennep, *Manuel de Folklore français contemporain* (4 v. 1946), i (2). 647, 676, 710–11; Lebrun, *Les Hommes et la mort en Anjou au 17e et 18e siècles*, pp. 459–60. For local variants see the review of A. Demard's study in *Ann. de Bourgogne*, 42 (1970), 209–10. For neighbourly co-operation in the Pyrenees, J.-L. Flandrin, *Familles, parentés, maison, sexualité dans l'ancienne société*, p. 41.

4. A. Delahante, *Une famille de finance au XVIIIe siècle* (2 v. 1881), i. 20.

5. Mercier, *Tableau de Paris*, iii. 183.

6. Barbier, *Chronique de la Régence et du règne de Louis XV, 1718–63*, iii. 170.

7. A. van Gennep, i(2). 704–8.

8. Restif de la Bretonne, *Le Paysan et la paysanne pervertis* (1775), in *Œuvres*, vi. 439–42.

9. Lebrun, *Les Hommes et la mort* . . ., pp. 461–2.

10. P. Clauer (= P. Sommervogel), 'Les Billets d'enterrement au XVIIIe siècle', *Études religieuses, philosophiques et littéraires*, 5e Sér. 12 (1877), 375.

11. Picart, ii. 99. Cf. 'Le matin, on exposa le corps devant la porte' (Restif de la Bretonne, *Le Mauvais Riche*, in *Les Contemporains, Œuvres*, x. 329–34).

12. Picart, ii. 95–100.

13. A. Lottin, 'Les morts chassés de la cité—les émeutes à Lille, 1779', *Rev. du Nord*, 60 (1978), 96–7.

14. M. Bée, 'La société traditionnelle et la mort', *Dix-huitième siècle* (1975), p. 85.

15. *Jacques le Fataliste* (ed. A. Billy, Pléiade, 1951), p. 542.

16. M. Vovelle, *Piété baroque et déchristianisation en Provence*, pp. 87 ff.

17. Mercier, iii. 181.

18. S.-P. Hardy, *Mes loisirs* (ed. M. Tourneaux and M. Vitrac), pp. 82–3 (11 Dec. 1767).

19. Chateaubriand, *Génie du Christianisme* (ed. L. Louvet), p. 394.
20. G. Francière, *Théophile de Bordeu (1722–1776)*, p. 88.
21. Grimm, *Corresp. littéraire* (ed. M. Tourneux), ix. 19 (May 1770).
22. Lebrun, *Les Hommes et la mort*, p. 469.
23. Discussion in G. Rowell, *The Liturgy of Christian Burial* (Alcuin Club, 1977), esp. pp. 70–3.
24. Picart, ii. 101.
25. Dom Claude de Vert, *Explication des cérémonies de l'Église*, iii. 367–8, 76, 215, 121, 319, 365, 418.
26. Picart, ii. 96.
27. H. Marlot, 'Rites et usages funéraires', *Rev. des traditions populaires*, 10 (1895), 108–9.
28. A. van Gennep, i (2). 760, 767–8. At a military funeral, the pick and shovel were laid in the form of a cross, there was a volley of musket fire, and roll of drums (A. Babeau, *La Vie militaire sous l'ancien régime, les soldats*, (p. 223).
29. Discussion in P.-M. Gy, O.P., 'Les Funérailles d'après le Rituel de 1614', *La Maison Dieu*, 44 (1955), 70–81. For the contrast with the French Protestants see F. Andrieux, 'L'image de la mort dans les liturgies des églises protestantes', *Archives de sc. soc. relig.* 39 (1975), 119 ff.
30. Rowell, pp. 65–7.
31. Picart, ii. 104; van Gennep, i (2). 782.
32. Le Pileur d'Apligny, *Essais historiques sur la morale des anciens et des modernes*, p. 264.
33. *Corresp. inéd. de la comtesse de Sabran et du chevalier de Boufflers, 1778–1788* (ed. E. de Magnieu and H. Prat), p. 48.
34. P.-J. Guyot, *Répertoire universel et raisonné de jurisprudence*, xxi. 264–5.
35. *Journal et mémoires de Mathieu Marais* (ed. M. de Lescure, 4 v. 1863), ii. 380–1.
36. Ibid., pp. 407–8. Cf. the withdrawal of the bishops from the anniversary service in memory of Louis XIV in 1717 (Saint-Simon (ed. 1829), xv. 179).
37. Hardy, i. 29.
38. H. Carré, *La Noblesse de France et l'opinion publique au XVIIIe siècle* (1920), p. 172.
39. Métra, *Corresp. secrète, politique et littéraire*, xii. 134 (Nov. 1781).
40. For what follows, see Jacqueline Thibaut-Payen, *Les Morts, l'Église et l'État dans le ressort du parlement de Paris aux XVIIe et XVIIIe siècles* (1977), pp. 20–8.
41. A. Dupuy, 'L'Administration municipale de Bretagne au 18e siècle', *Ann. de Bretagne*, 5 (1889–90), 175–7.

42. Vovelle, pp. 186–8.
43. Saint-Simon, viii. 131; Marais, i. 187.
44. P. D. Bernier, *Essai sur . . . les Paysans de Basse-Normandie au XVIIIe siècle*, p. 260.
45. For this para. see Thibaut-Payen, pp. 94–204.
46. *Relation circonstanciée de ce qui s'est passé au sujet du refus des sacremens . . . à M. de Cougnion* (1754), p. 137. For a Jansenist *curé* buried without tolling of the bell, and another with no ceremonies at all, and another put in the area of the cemetery reserved for unbaptized children, with no more than a *De Profundis* see A. Playoust-Chaussis, *La Vie religieuse dans le diocèse de Boulogne au XVIIIe siècle* (1725–90), p. 119.
47. For this para., Thibaut-Payen, pp. 58–68.
48. Mercier, ii. 183.
49. *Actes de l'Église d'Amiens: recueil de tous les documents relatifs à la discipline du diocèse, 811–1849* (ed. J.-M. Mioland, 2 v. 1849), i. 367–72. Cf. the arrangements in the diocese of Autun (T. J. Schmitt, *L'Organisation ecclésiastique et la pratique religieuse dans l'archi-diaconé d'Autun de 1650 à 1750*, p. 146).
50. A. Playoust-Chaussis, p. 279.
51. Cited by Lescure in introd. to Marais, i. 21.
52. Chamfort, *Petits dialogues philosophiques, Œuvres* (ed. P. R. Augis, 6 v. 1824–5; reissued by Slatkine, 1968), i. 332.
53. [Chomel], *Aménités littéraires*, i. 322.
54. Cottereau, *Poésies* (1750), p. 58.
55. Mercier, iii. 183.
56. A. Durand, *Une paroisse mayennaise: Fougerolles sous la Révol-ution, 1789–1800* (1960).
57. G. Hardy, 'L'anticléricalisme paysan', *Ann. révolutionnaires*, 5 (1912), 607–8.
58. [Mulot], *Le Rêve du pauvre moine* (1789), pp. 14–15. For the many clerical officials who could be hired, see Baloche, *L'Église Saint-Merry de Paris* (1911), pp. 445–6.
59. A. Delahante, i. 393–7, 381–8.
60. A. Sarramon (ed.), *Les Paroisses du diocèse de Comminges en 1786* (1968), p. 21. Other examples pp. 60, 90, 126, 128, 138, 302, 307, 330, 332.
61. *Lettres de l'abbé Barbotin* (ed. A. Aulard, 1910), p. 60.
62. J. Villain, *Le Recouvrement des impôts directs sous l'ancien régime* (1932), p. 60.
63. Denisart, *Collection de décisions*, vi. 362.
64. Ibid.
65. Barbier, ii. 5; i. 439; iii. 170. Hardy, i. 69–70.

66. Barbier, iii. 285–6.
67. Hardy, i. 105 (17 Aug. 1768). For catafalques generally see F. Souchal, *Les Slodtz, sculpteurs et décorateurs du Roi, 1685–1764* (1975).
68. Hardy, i. 35 (cf. p. 108).
69. L. Lefebvre, 'Le deuil d'un bourgeois de Lille en 1772', *Société d'études de la province de Cambrai: Bulletin*, 6 (1904), 262–76. The accounts are in florins; one florin = 1 *livre* 5 *sous*.
70. P. Flobert, 'Billets d'enterrement et pièces funéraires', *Bull. de la Soc. archéologique, historique et artistique: Le Vieux Papier (Lille)*, 5 (1907), 31.
71. Vicomte Oscar de Poli, 'Billets d'obsèques et lettres de faire-part', *Annuaire du Conseil héraldique de France*, 10 (1897), 119–20.
72. Bachaumont, xxii. 171 (24 Mar. 1783).
73. Ibid. xxi. 217 (5 Dec. 1782).
74. Vicomte de Poli, pp. 202–4.
75. Ibid., p. 126.
76. Clauer, p. 381.
77. Vicomte de Poli, p. 189.
78. Flobert, p. 24.
79. Clauer, pp. 382–5; Flobert, p. 26.
80. J. Truchet (ed.), *Bossuet: oraisons funèbres* (1961), pp. vii–xix.
81. J. Truchet, *La Prédication de Bossuet* (2 v. 1960), ii. 189.
82. *Lettres de Turgot à la duchesse d'Enville, 1764–74 et 1777–80* (ed. J. Ruwet *et al.*, Trav. Fac. Philos. Lettres Univ. Cath. Louvain, Histoire I, 1976), p. 138 (25 May 1780).
83. P. V. Houdry, S. J., *La Bibliothèque des prédicateurs* (22 v., 1724–43) xxii. 241. (By contrast, preaching on the subject of death is easy, v. 418–94.)
84. Ibid. xxii. 242–3.
85. Ibid. 43.
86. Pierre-Robert Le Prévôt, *Recueil des Oraisons funèbres* (1765), pp. xxv–xxvi.
87. Houdry, xxii. 240.
88. Caraccioli, *Dictionnaire*, i. 230.
89. Le Prévôt, loc. cit.
90. See my discussion in 'the Bishops of France in the 18th Century', in *Religious Motivation* (Studies in Church History XV, 1978), pp. 318–19.
91. Favre, i. 108.
92. Grimm, *Corresp. littéraire*, x. 477–8 (Aug. 1774).
93. Ibid. 68.
94. Hardy, i. 30 (28 Dec. 1765).

95. *Corresp. . . . comtesse de Sabran*, p. 39.
96. Grimm, *Corresp. littéraire*, xiv. 457–8 (Feb. 1786).
97. Favre, i. 638.
98. Thomas, *Œuvres* (4 v. 1773), iii. 2, 3, 63, 130, 213.
99. Raymond Firth, *Elements of Social Organisation* (1951), p. 64—cit. D. G. Mandelbaum, 'The Social Use of Funeral Rites', in *The Meaning of Death* (ed. M. Feipel, 1959), p. 338. See also D. Sudnow, *Passing On: the Social Organization of Dying* (1967), pp. 138–9.
100. Bachaumont, xxix, 4.
101. Le Pileur d'Apligny, p. 26.
102. 'C'est tout ce qui peut rester à un honnête homme et qui peut le consoler dans les maux de cette vie' (Marais, 22 Nov. 1723—see Favre, i. 445–6).
103. [Aubert de la Chesnaye Desbois], *Dict. historique des mœurs, usages et coutumes des François* (3 v. 1767), ii. 255.
104. C. F. Menestrier, S. J., *Des décorations funèbres* (1684).
105. Girard de Villethierry, *Le Chrétien dans la tribulation . . . malade et mourant*, pp. 576–89.
106. Cottereau, loc. cit.
107. J. Truchet, *La Politique de Bossuet* (1960), p. 133.
108. Girard de Villethierry, p. 581.
109. Caraccioli, *Le Tableau de la mort*, pp. 22, 172, 174–5.
110. Bergier, *Dict. de théologie dogmatique* (1788), *Œuvres*, iii. 936.
111. Girard de Villethierry, pp. 579, 585.
112. 'On mène les enfants à une inhumation comme à un spectacle' (Le Maître de Claville, *Traité du vrai mérite de l'homme*, p. 492).
113. *Dict. des gens du monde*, ii. 445.
114. Bachaumont, ix. 281–2 (5 Dec. 1776).
115. Ibid. xxxii. 247–8 (16 Aug. 1786).
116. Ibid. xxvi. 87 (9 July 1784).
117. See below, p. 322.
118. Another example of criticism—a *billet* boasting about its subjects' work on biblical languages (Bachaumont, xxviii. 252–3, 11 Apr. 1785).
119. Picart, iii. 379.
120. *De la philosophie de la Nature*, i. 347.
121. [Chomel], *Les Nuits parisiennes*, i. 9; *Dict. historique des cultes religieux*, ii. 420, 426; Restif de la Bretonne, *Les Nuits de Paris*, *Œuvres* (Bachelin), i. 40.
122. B. R. Routh, S. J., *Recherches sur la manière d'inhumer des anciens à l'occasion des tombeaux de Civaux* (1738).
123. Le Pileur d'Apligny, pp. 237, 256; Picart, i. 146–8; vi. 70, 72, 96, 107, 119, 122, 132; vii. 19, 23, 106–7, 211, 343–4; viii. 54. See also

Dom Calmet, *Les Épitres de S. Paul* (*Commentaire littéral sur tous les livres de l'ancien et du nouveau testament*), pp. xv–xvii—very severe on the barbarity of some non-Christian customs.

124. F. X. de Charlevoix, S. J., *Hist. de l'île de Saint-Domingue* (2 v. 1730), i. 45; Picart, vi. 280; vii. 5, 13; viii. 19, 34–9, 50.

125. Picart, viii. 69, 107, iii. 232, vii. 211–12; [Chomel], *Les Nuits parisiennes*, ii. 109–10.

126. P. Lafitau, *Mœurs des sauvages amériquains comparées aux mœurs des premiers temps*, ii. 458.

127. Ibid. i. 401; ii. 391–7.

128. Picart, vi. 69. (Cf. the comment on Mahomet's tomb, v. 62.)

129. Buffon, *De l'homme* (ed. Duchet), p. 160.

130. Poiret, *Voyage en Barbarie, ou lettres écrites de l'ancienne Numidie* (1789), pp. 108–9.

131. R. de Bonnières, *Lettres grecques de Mme Chénier* (1879), pp. 164–5.

132. *Voyage du jeune Anacharsis en Grèce* (2nd ed.), ii. 167–8.

133. Mme de Genlis, *Les Veillées du Château ou cours de morale à l'usage des enfants* (3 v. 1782), ii. 182 ('Alphonse et Dalinde').

134. Picart, vii. 71 (cf. iii. 125).

135. Watelet, *Dict. des arts de peinture, sculpture et gravure*, v. 130.

136. Mme de Genlis, p. 187.

137. Démeunier, *L'Esprit des usages et des coutumes des différens peuples*, iii. 268–300.

138. See below, p. 352.

139. *Séthos* (3 v. 1731), i. 173–6.

140. F. X. de Charlevoix, S. J., *Histoire et description générale du Japon* (9 v. 1736), i. 379–83.

141. See L. Guibert, *Les Confréries de Pénitents en France et notamment dans le diocèse de Limoges* (1879).

142. A. Sicard, *L'Ancien Clergé de France: les évêques avant la Révolution* (5th ed. 1912), pp. 405–15.

143. L. Pingaud, *Les Saulx Tavannes* (1876), pp. 268–9.

144. Thomas, 'Éloge de Henri-François Daguesseau', *Œuvres* (1773), iii. 122.

145. Barbier, v. 35.

146. Thibaut-Payen, p. 37; *Relation de ce qui s'est passé pendant la maladie de Madame la duchesse de Rochechouart* (anon., 1752). Examples of the choice of simple funerals because of austere devotion are the maréchal de Muy, 1775, and the comte de Clermont, 1771 (Bachaumont, viii. 204; v. 273).

147. On England, Le Pileur d'Apligny, p. 266. An isolated case in France, in [Lefebvre de Beauvry] *Dict. soc. et patriotique*, pp. 17–18. For the

poor in the hospital detesting the practice, J.-C. Perrot, *Genèse d'une ville moderne: Caen au XVIIIe siècle*, ii. 1171.

148. A. Lottin, *Rev. du Nord* (1978), p. 99.

149. P. Chaunu, *La Mort à Paris*, pp. 435–40.

150. W. Doyle, *The Parlement of Bordeaux at the end of the Old Régime, 1771–90* (1976), p. 135. Dr Doyle believes this was paying homage to the Christian spirit of humility.

151. Vovelle, pp. 93–8.

CHAPTER 10

Graveyards and Tombs: Patriotism, Poetry, and Grim Realities

1. *Mémoires d'outre-tombe* I. 1 (4) (Pléiade, 2 v. 1955), i. 25.

2. Hardy, *Mes loisirs*, i. 360 (8 Oct. 1772).

3. A. Dupuy, 'Administration municipale', *Ann. de Bretagne*, 5 (1889–90), 168; 'Les épidémies en Bretagne', ibid. 1 (1886), 124.

4. M. Foisil, 'Les attitudes devant la mort au XVIIIe siècle: le cimetière parisien des Saints-Innocents', *Rev. Hist.* 510 (1974), 303.

5. *Tableau de Paris*, ii. 185.

6. V, Dufour, *Les Charniers des églises de Paris* (1884), p. 3; [Chomel], *Les Nuits parisiennes*, i. 10.

7. Thibaut-Payen, *Les Morts, l'Église et l'État dans le ressort du parlement de Paris au XVIIe et XVIIIe siècles*, p. 242.

8. Ch. Delormeau, *Le Cimetière protestant de Montpellier* (1963), pp. 12–13.

9. See e.g. Lebrun, *Les Ho⋯ ⋯s et la mort . . .*, pp. 478–9. In country places, cemeteries ofter ⋯ere enclosed only by drystone walls or hedges, and people made gaps to take short cuts (A. Playoust-Chaussis, *La Vie religieuse dans le diocèse de Boulogne*, pp. 62–3).

10. Journal of A.-F. Dubois, *curé* of Rumegies, diocese of Tournai, ed. H. Platelle (1965), pp. 119–20.

11. A famous case; M. Bourde de la Rogerie, *Le Parlement de Bretagne, l'évêque de Rennes et les ifs plantés dans les cimetières, 1636–7* (1931).

12. R. Suadeau, *L'Évêque inspecteur administratif sous la monarchie absolue* (2 v. 1940), i. 37–43.

13. Denisart, *Collection de décisions*, iv. 550.

14. Historical summary in Scipione Piattoli's Italian work (Modena, 1774) almost immediately translated into French with a commentary by Vicq-d'Azyr (see his *Œuvres*, 6 v. 1805, vi. 257–313).

15. [Girard de Villethierry], *Des églises et des temples des chrétiens* (1706), p. 195.

16. Bourdoise, *Sentences chrétiennes* . . . (1714), cit. Thibaut-Payen, *Les Morts, l'Église et l'État*. pp. 77–8.
17. [Porée], *Lettres sur la sépulture dans les églises*, pp. 40–3.
18. P. Laugier, S. J., *Observations sur l'architecture*, p. 150.
19. Porée, loc. cit. For a plea for more land for cemeteries, since digging up the bones of the dead was a scandal, see [Duguet], *Le Tombeau de Jésus-Christ ou explication du mystère de la sépulture (1731)*, p. 187, and *Continuation* (1735), pp. 142–3.
20. Porée, pp. 5–8, 30.
21. Le Pileur d'Apligny, *Essais historiques sur la morale des anciens et des modernes*, p. 269.
22. Thibaut-Payen, p. 36.
23. Ibid., p. 32.
24. Foisil, pp. 317–18.
25. *Préface de Catherine Vadé* (Moland, x. 5).
26. See *Essai sur les lieux et les dangers des sépultures* in *Œuvres de Vicq-d'Azyr*, vi. 310–43. According to Maret (see below), Haguenot's account was published in 1747 (p. 19).
27. Boissier de Sauvages, *Dissertation où l'on recherche comment l'air . . . agit sur le corps humain*, pp. 37–43, 45, 47–8, 31.
28. Thibaut-Payen, p. 210.
29. Summaries in J. Hillairet, *Les 200 cimetières du vieux Paris* (1958). My quotations are from pp. 61, 65, 81, 84, 97, 110, 122, 211.
30. Ibid., pp. 217–18.
31. P.-J. Guyot, *Répertoire universel et raisonné de jurisprudence*, x. 28. From 1750, there were no burials in Angevin churches other than *curés* and *seigneurs* (Lebrun, *Les Hommes et la mort* . . ., p. 482).
32. [Chomel], *Les Nuits parisiennes*, ii. 207–8.
33. Le Clerc, *Histoire de l'homme considéré dans l'état de maladie*, i. 310–11.
34. Olivier, *Sépultures des anciens, où l'on démontre qu'elles étoient hors des villes* (1771), pp. 71–136.
35. Maret, *Mémoire sur l'usage où l'on est d'enterrer les morts dans les églises et dans l'enceinte des villes* (1773).
36. Vicq-d'Azyr, vi. 354–5.
37. P.-T. Navier, *Sur les dangers des exhumations précipitées et sur les abus des inhumations dans les églises* (1775), p. 11.
38. Chimneys: Boissier de Sauvages, p. 50, Olivier, p. 64; cold water: Olivier, p. 64; balks: Maret, p. 46; embalm or plaster: 'Embaumements', *Encyclopédie*, v. 562–5; no trees: Maret, p. 52; Navier, p. 64.
39. Text in Thibaut-Payen, Annexe I.
40. Lebrun, p. 486.

41. Thibaut-Payen, pp. 263–96.
42. J. McManners, *French Ecclesiastical Society* . . . *Angers*, pp. 120–1.
43. Thibaut-Payen, pp. 271, 302–3.
44. J.-C. Perrot, *Genèse d'une ville moderne: Caen au XVIIIe siècle*, ii. 732.
45. Towns tried to get ecclesiastical property (see McManners, *French Ecclesiastical Soc.*, p. 121) but the lawyers held that, as ecclesiastical institutions were not allowed to buy land, they ought not to be forced to sell it (Denisart, iv. 55).
46. R. Favre, 'Du *médico–topographie* à Lyon en 1783', *Dix-huitième Siècle* (1977), p. 157; R. Bertrand, 'Cimetières marseillais au XVIIIe et XIXe siècle', *Provence historique*, 22 (1973), 217–40; A. Lottin, 'Les morts chassés de la cité', *Rev. du Nord*, 60 (1978), 75–85.
47. F. Pichon (ed.), *Vie de M. Marquis-Ducastel, curé de Sainte-Suzanne* (1873), i. 118–19.
48. Thibaut-Payen, pp. 413–16.
49. Métra, *Corresp. secrète, politique et littéraire* ii. 154.
50. Thibaut-Payen, pp. 248–59.
51. Chaunu, *La Mort à Paris*, p. 444.
52. Bergier, 'Tombeau', 'Sépulture', *Dict. de théologie dogmatique* (1788), iii. 955; v. 703, 928.
53. Thibaut-Payen, pp. 228–30.
54. S. Gagnière, *Les Cimetières d'Avignon au XVIIIe et XIXe siècles* (1948), pp. 8, 33–4.
55. Bachaumont, xvii. 36–7 (22 Jan. 1781).
56. Gannal, *Les Cimetières depuis la fondation de la monarchie française jusqu'à nos jours* (1884), p. 43.
57. Thibaut-Payen, pp. 231–2.
58. The following details from Hillairet, pp. 23–32.
59. E. Raunié, *Épitaphier du vieux Paris* (5 v. 1890), i, p. xxx.
60. Ph. Ariès, *L'Homme devant la mort*, pp. 488–9; see also Bachaumont, xv. 243–4 (3 Aug. 1780); Thibaut-Payen, p. 222.
61. For this para. see M. Fichman, 'French Stahlism and Chemical Studies of Air, 1750–1770', *Ambix: the Journal of the Soc. for the Study of Alchemy and Early Chemistry*, 18 (1971), 94–122; J. Guillerme, 'Le malsain et l'économie de la nature', *Dix-huitième Siècle*, 9 (1977), 63–71; O. and C. Hannaway, 'La fermeture du cimetière des Innocents', Ibid. 181–7.
62. Hillairet, p. 303; Foisil, p. 329.
63. P. Fossy, *Les Catacombes de Paris* (1862), pp. 37–9.
64. Hillairet, p. 308.
65. All the following details from Gannal, pp. 80–94, 173–81, 186–94, 197–225.

66. [Mulot], *Le Rêve du pauvre moine*, p. 16. Similar account in Mercier, *Tableau de Paris*, x. 190, and in a letter to the *procureur général* of the Parlement (Thibaut-Payen, p. 491).
67. E. Raunié, i, pp. vi-vii.
68. Ibid. ii. 518.
69. Piganiol de la Force, *Description de Paris, de Versailles, etc.* (new ed. 8 v. 1742), iii. 137.
70. Marc Furcy-Raymond, *Inventaire des sculptures exécutées au XVIIIe siècle pour la direction des bâtiments du Roi* (1927), pp. 281, 326–36.
71. F. Souchal, *Les Slodtz*, pp. 306–7.
72. See the descriptions in 'Éloge du comte de Saxe', *Œuvres de M. Thomas* (new ed. 1773), iii. 1–2, and in [Dandré Bardon], *Mausolée de feu Mgr Le Dauphin* (1777), pp. 11–25.
73. F. Ingersoll-Smousse, *La Sculpture funéraire en France au XVIIIe siècle* (1912), pp. 92–5.
74. Raunié ii. 210–13.
75. Bachaumont, xv. 133–5 (27 Apr. 1780).
76. Diderot to Pigalle, *Corresp. littéraire*, iii. 298–330 (Oct. 1756); Bachaumont, v. 142–4 (31 July 1770). See also Pigalle's consultation of Voltaire concerning a monument to Louis XV (*Corresp. Voltaire*, lii. 183)—problems of getting the attributes of allegorical figures right, avoiding devices (in this case, the wolf and the lamb) which might encourage the wits, pleasing Voltaire himself (he did not like slaves in chains), and giving Pigalle a chance to display his skills (he liked doing nudes).
77. Dandré Bardon, pp. 4–6, 10.
78. Bachaumont, *Essai sur la peinture, la sculpture et l'architecture* (1751), pp. 10–18, 45.
79. D'Argens, *Réflexions critiques sur les différentes écoles de peinture*, pp. 196–7. For Diderot on the importance of context. *Traité du beau, Œuvres* (Pléiade), pp. 1129–30. Cf. Diderot's insistence that the face of Lazarus rising from the dead must be dominated by the simple pleasure of breathing the air again (to Grimm, Sept. 1763, *Corresp.* iv. 266–7), and that a corpse be blotchy, not uniformly livid (*Salons 1767*, ed. J. Seznec and J. Adhémar, iii. 186).
80. Cf. Bachaumont, *Mémoires*, xxxii. 248 (16 Aug. 1786)—'que la composition n'en est point assez religieuse pour une église'.
81. *Réflexions morales de Mme Deshoulières sur l'envie immodérée qu'on a de faire passer son nom à la postérité*, p. 3.
82. Caraccioli, *Dict. critique*, iii. 219–20; *Le Tableau de la mort*, pp. 141–2, 171–2.
83. Bergier, *Dict. de théologie dogmatique* (1788), *Œuvres*, v. 800.
84. *Génie du Christianisme*, (Pléiade, 1928), p. 935.

85. C. F. Menestrier, S. J., *Des décorations funèbres*, pp. 282–6.
86. Henriette s'Jacob, *Idealism and Realism: a Study of Sepulchral Symbolism* (1954), p. 214.
87. *Salon de 1859*, cit. A. Chastel, 'Le Baroque et la Mort', *Congrès . . . études humanistes*, Rome 1954 (1955), pp. 34–5.
88. *Voyage en Italie*, 6 Oct. 1756, cit. F. Souchal, p. 330.
89. Souchal, pp. 323–6, 335, 341.
90. S'Jacob, p. 223. One project showed Fleury taking over control of the kingdom, But there was another showing Virtue presenting him with a crown of rays of light and fleurs de lis. (Ingersoll-Smousse, p. 113.)
91. G. Bonno (ed.), *Corresp. littéraire de Suard*. (Univ. California Publ. Mod. Philol. XVIII, 1934), p. 213 (30 Mar. 1775).
92. Diderot, *Essai sur la peinture* (1765, not publ. until 1795), Chap. V, cit. R. Rosenblum, *Transformations in Late 18th-Century Art*, p. 52.
93. Cit. J. A. Leith, *The Idea of Art as Propaganda in France, 1750–99* (1965), p. 56. See also, generally, Leith's 'Nationalism and the Fine Arts, 1750–89', *Studies in Voltaire and the 18 Century*, 89 (1972), 919 ff.
94. La Font de Saint-Yenne, cit. J. Locquin, *La Peinture d'histoire en France de 1747 à 1785* (1912), p. 163.
95. Cit. E. Guitton, *Jacques Delille, 1731–1813, et la poésie de la nature* (1976), p. 332.
96. Rosenblum, p. 50.
97. Cit. D. J. Fletcher, 'The Civic Vocabulary in the XVIIIth Century', dupl. contribution to Conference of University Teachers of French, Oxford, Easter 1959. For poems entitled 'Le Citoyen' and 'Le Patriotisme' see D. Mornet, *Les Origines intellectuelles de la Révolution Française, 1715–87* (1954), p. 264.
98. C. D. Brenner, *L'Histoire nationale dans la tragédie française au XVIIIᵉ siècle* (Univ. California Publ. Mod. Phil, 14 (3), 1929), pp. 246, 310.
99. Cit. Leith, pp. 10–12.
100. P. Rosenberg and N. Butor, *'La Mort de Germanicus' de Poussin*, Catalogue (1973), pp. 31–8.
101. [Alix], *Les quatre âges de l'homme*, p. 64.
102. Sabatier, *Poème sur la bataille de Lutzelberg*, p. 4.
103. Cit. Raunié, i. liii.
104. [Thiery], *La Vie de l'homme respectée et défendue dans ses derniers momens* (1787), Préf.
105. De La Place, *Recueil d'épitaphes* (3 v. 1782). ii. 18; Métra, vii. 129; xv. 68; Bachaumont, *Mémoires*, xxix, 72–3.

106. De La Place, i. 334–5.
107. Moreau, *Mes souvenirs*, i. 32–4.
108. Métra, ii. 306; Voltaire, *Corresp.* xlvi. 99.
109. *Corresp. de la comtesse de Sabran et du chevalier de Boufflers*, p. xvii; Anon., *La Vie du très révérend Père Dom Augustin Calmet* (1767), pp. 147, 518; R. Sabatier, *Dict. de la mort*, p. 23; De La Place, i. 213.
110. De La Place, i. ix, 220.
111. M. G. Cushing, *Pierre Le Tourneur* (1907), p. 15. The comic epitaph ridiculing kings, physicians, *curés*, etc. was an old institution in France—De La Place has many examples.
112. Still in Saint-Eustache. Bachaumont printed it in 1771, 11 July (*Mémoires*, v. 279).
113. Favre, p. 634.
114. De La Place, i. ix.
115. [Terrasson], *Séthos*, i. 60–71, 275–6, 313–14.
116. Le Tourneur, *Éloge de Charles V, roi de France* (1767), cit. Cushing, p. 29.
117. Cit. Brenner, p. 249.
118. A. Chérel, *Fénelon au XVIIIe siècle, 1715–1820* (1917), p. 367.
119. Cit. Locquin, p. 159.
120. *Corresp. littéraire*, ix. 98 (Aug. 1770).
121. Chérel, p. 413.
122. *Œuvres de Marc-Antoine de Noé*, pp. 116–19.
123. See above p. 318.
124. Locquin, pp. 50–1.
125. Dulaure, *Nouvelle description de Paris* (2 v. 1787), i. 260–75.
126. H. Rosenau (ed.), *Boullée's Treatise on Architecture* (1953), pp. 1–11.
127. Bachaumont, *Mémoires*, xvi. 83–4 (2 Dec. 1780).
128. Ibid. xxxiii. 62 (30 Sept. 1786).
129. *Visionary Architects: Boullée, Ledoux, Lequeu*, Catalogue (Univ. of St. Thomas, Houston, 1968), pp. 220–1, referring to Vien, 1785.
130. E. Kaufmann, *Architecture in the Age of Reason* (1968 ed.), pp. 154–7.
131. Reproduced in *Visionary Architects*, pp. 154, 206–7.
132. Ibid. pp. 108–9; 210–12; 232–3; Kaufmann, p. 183.
133. See generally, E. Kaufmann, 'Three Revolutionary Architects: Boullée, Ledoux, Lequeu', *Trans. American Philos. Soc.* (1952), pp. 436–43, 447, 454–524.
134. Boullée, *Essai sur l'architecture*, ed. H. Rosenau (n. 60, above), pp. 80–3.
135. Cottereau, *Poésies*, p. 24.

136. Cit. R. Mauzi, *L'Idée du bonheur dans la littérature et la pensée françaises au XVIIIe siècle*, p. 55 n.
137. Loaisel de Tréogate, *La Comtesse d'Alibre, ou le cri du sentiment* (1779), p. 143.
138. Caraccioli, *Tableau de la Mort*, p. 177.
139. Barthe (1762), cit. E. Guitton, *Jacques Delille, 1731–1813, et la poésie de la nature*, p. 332. There is an essay to be written on how the cult of melancholy annexed landscapes. In M. de Piles, *Cours de peinture par principes* (1708), p. 219, rocks are described as 'melancholy' only by themselves; they become a refreshment to the eye when accompanied by trees, and when accompanied by water they are 'un agrément infini'.
140. See Mercier on 'la volupté des larmes', cit. G. van de Louw, *Baculard d'Arnaud* (1972), p. 22.
141. P. M. Spacks, *The Insistence of Horror: Aspects of the Supernatural in 18th-Century Poetry* (1962), p. 82.
142. J. Starobinski, *L'Invention de la liberté, 1700–89* (1964), 72–4.
143. L. Krestovsky, *Le Problème spirituel de la beauté et de la laideur* (1948), pp. 63, 75, 91.
144. Cournand, *Les Styles: poème en quatre chants* (1761), pp. xxvi–viii, 135–6, 155–6.
145. R. Michéa, 'Le Tombeau dans la pensée du 18e siècle', *Ann. de l'Université de Grenoble*, N.S. (*Lettres, Droit*), 14 (1937), 81–6.
146. Cournand, p. xxviii.
147. W. Thomas, *Le Poète Edward Young* (1901), pp. 522–7.
148. P. Van Tieghem, 'La Poésie de la nuit et des tombeaux en Europe au XVIIIe siècle', *Acad. roy. de Belgique, Classe des Lettres et des Sciences morales et politiques, Mémoires*, 2 Ser., 16 (1923), 81.
149. *Lettres*, N.S., ed. Cl. Perroud, 1913–15. i. 128.
150. C. V. Wicker, *Edward Young and the Fear of Death: a Study of Romantic Melancholy* (1952), p. 23. For the importance of Young's novelty, R. Birley, *Sunk without Trace* (1962), p. 107.
151. Van Tieghem, p. 135.
152. Cushing, *Pierre Le Tourneur*, p. 49.
153. Diderot, *Paradoxe sur le comédien, Œuvres esthétiques*, p, 333.
154. [Delisle de Sales], *Essai sur la Tragédie* (1772), pp. 56–7.
155. The abbé Remy, *Les Jours, pour servir de correctif . . . aux 'Nuits' de Young*, cit. Van Tieghem, p. 106. The *Journal de Trévoux* approved of the attack on Young.
156. Van Tieghem, p. 37.
157. Ibid., pp. 43–50, 67.
158. Cushing, pp. 79–80.

159. Mme Thiroux d'Arconville, *Mélanges de littérature, de morale et de physique* (7 v. 1775), i. xiv.
160. [Cubière de Palmezeaux], *La Manie des drames sombres; comédie* (1777), pp. 2–3.
161. *Corresp. littéraire*, viii. 44–5.
162. J.-L. Lecercle, 'Baculard, où l'embonpoint du sentiment', *Approches des Lumières* . . .(1974), pp. 301–4.
163. Disc. prélim. of *Le comte de Comminge* and of *Coligny, Œuvres dramatiques de M. D'Arnaud* (2 v. 1782), i, ix–x, xxvii–viii.
164 Marmontel, *Essai sur les romans considérés du côté moral* (1778). See J. Decottigniès, 'Entre la fiction et la fable: l'expérience du roman gothique', in Lecercle, *Approches des Lumières*, pp. 110–15.
165. Mme de Tencin, *Le Comte de Comminges* (1735). Prévost, *Cleveland; Mémoires d'un homme de qualité*. For the earlier writers see Th. Godenne, 'Les Spectacles d'horreur de J.-P. Camus, *Dix-septième Siècle* (1971), pp. 26–35; J. Fabre, 'L'abbé Prévost et la tradition du roman noir', in *L'Abbé Prévost, Colloque d'Aix en-Provence 1963* (1965), pp. 39–46.
166. M. de Laguerrie, *Les Amours de Lucile et de Doligny* (2 v. 1769), pp. 224, 231.
167. [Lesbros de la Versane], *Les Soirées d'un honnête homme, ou mémoires pour servir à l'histoire du cœur* (1773), pp. 70–2.
168. J. H. Tisch, 'Irregular genius: some aspects of Milton and Shakespeare on the Continent at the end of the Eighteenth Century', *Studies in 18th-Century Literature*, ed. J. Seznec et al. (1974), pp. 315–18.
169. H. Carrington Lancaster, *Sunset, a History of Parisian Drama in the last years of Louis XIV* (1941), pp. 100–3.
170. *Préface de Mariamne, Œuvres* (Moland), ii. 163–4; *Discours sur la tragédie* (1730), ibid. 315–21; *Obs. sur le Jules César de Shakespeare* (1764), ibid. vii. 484.
171. H. Lagrave, *Le Théâtre et le public à Paris de 1715 à 1750* (1972), p. 640.
172. *Œuvres* (Moland), vi. 269.
173. *Entretiens sur le Fils naturel* (1757), *Œuvres esthétiques*, p. 117.
174. Lagrave, p. 637; F. Gaiffe, *Le Drame en France au XVIIIe siècle* (1910), pp. 302–3.
175. Dandré Bardon, *Traité de peinture suivi d'un essai sur la sculpture* (2 v. 1765), p. 158.
176. [Cl.-Fr. Lezay-Marnésia], *Essai sur la nature champêtre* (1787), p. 35.
177. M. Watelet, *Dict. des arts de peinture, sculpture et gravure*, v. 3–4 ('Pensée').

178. L. Guerry, *Le Thème du 'Triomphe de la mort' dans la peinture italienne* (1950), pp. 38–40, 52, 81–2.
179. Panofsky's view as against Weisbach (*Gazette des Beaux Arts* (1937), p. 287, (1938), p. 305), *Philosophy and History: Essays presented to E. Cassirer* (1963), p. 223.
180. M. Guomar, *Principes d'une esthétique de la mort* (1967), p. 80.
181. Dandré Bardon, loc. cit.
182. Ibid.
183. Delille, *Les Jardins, ou l'art d'embellir les paysages* (1782), Chant IV, p. 85. For Diderot and Masson de Pezay see Favre, ii. 400 (notes).
184. Gabillot, *Hubert Robert et son temps* (1895), p. 187; A. Guillois, *Pendant la Terreur: le poète Roucher*, pp. 207–9. Watelet cites Malherbe's lines and recommends the rose as a emblem of a young life cut short *Dictionnaire*, iii. 75).
185. R. Mortier, 'Deux poètes des ruines au XVIIIe siècle', *Études sur le XVIIIe Siècle* (Univ. Libre de Bruxelles), 1 (1974), 42–7.
186. Watelet, *L'Art de peindre*, p. 138; *Dictionnaire*, v. 73–6, iv. 23, 28.
187. Diderot, *Salons 1767* (ed. cit), iii. 228.
188. Volney (C. F. Chassebœuf), *Les Ruines ou méditations sur les révolutions des empires* (1791).
189. Porée, *Lettres sur la sépulture dans les églises*, p. 24.
190. See above, p. 314. For the crosses, Ariès, pp. 268–70.
191. Fontanes, *Le Jour des morts dans une campagne* (1785–6), in *Œuvres*, i. 35–6. The regulations drafted by the Parlement of Paris in 1765 prescribed 300 *livres* as the charge for a 'fosse particulière' (Denisart, iv. 551).
192. Diderot, 3 Aug. 1759, *Lettres à Sophie Volland*, ed. A. Babelon (2 v. 1948), i. 40.
193. Cit. Favre, ii. 401.
194. *Nouvelle Héloïse, ad fin.*, discussed in R. Vivier, 'André Chénier, Rousseau et Foscolo', *Mélanges d'histoire et de littérature offerts à Henri Mauvette* (1934), p. 523.
195. *Salons 1767*. (ed. cit.), ii. 102.
196. D. Mornet, *Le Sentiment de la Nature en France de J.-J. Rousseau à Bernardin de Saint-Pierre* (1907), pp. 21–41, 153, 120–30, 217, 230, 259–62, 307; Marjorie Hope Nicholson, *Mountain Gloom and Mountain Glory, the development of the aesthetics of the Infinite* (1959).
197. Yart, *La Poésie angloise* (2 v. 1749), ii. 6–7.
198. Watelet, *Essai sur les jardins* (1764), pp. 47–60, esp. p. 47.
199. For what follows, E. de Ganay, *Les Jardins de France et leur décor* (1949), pp. 231, 206, 237–8, 232–4.
200. Watelet, p. 77.

201. Lezay-Marnésia, p. 34.
202. The prince de Ligne, *Coup d'œil sur Belœil* . . . (1781).
203. Mornet, *Le Sentiment de la Nature*, p. 254.
204. Cérutti, *Les Jardins de Betz, poème* . . . *fait en 1785* (1792), pp. 21–3. (Note 22)
205. René de Girardin, *De la composition des paysages* . . . (1777), discussed in Mornet, *Vies préromantiques* (1925), p. 49, and *Le Sentiment de la Nature*, p. 241.
208. [Girardin], *Promenade ou itinéraire des jardins d'Ermenonville* (1788), pp. 18–19.
207. Ibid., p. 26.
208. Métra, X. 26–7 (1780).
209. Discussion, R. Grimsley, *Rousseau and the Religious Quest*, p. 7.
210. Mme Gauthier, *Voyage d'une Française en Suisse et en Franche Comté depuis la Révolution* (2 v. 1790), cit. Mornet, *Le Sentiment de la Nature*, p. 262.
211. Girardin, p. 25.
212. [Alix], *Les quatre âges de l'homme: poème*, p. 62.
213. *Corresp. de la comtesse de Sabran et du Chevalier de Boufflers, 1778–88*, p. 18.
214. A. Monglond, *Le Préromantisme français*, ii. 47.
215. R. Vivier, p. 524.
216. R. Michéa, p. 75; for what follows, p. 80 and R. Mortier, 'Sensibilité neo-classique ou préromantique?', *Le Préromantisme, hypothèque où hypothèse*, ed. P. Viallaneix (1975), p. 315; Monglond, i. 155.
217. Delille, *Les Jardins* (1782), pp. 69–71.
218. Bergier, *Dict. de théologie dogmatique* (1788), viii, col. 928.
219. Restif de la Bretonne, *La Thesmographie* (1789), *Œuvres*, iii. 140–1.
220. Cit. Potez, *L'Élégie en France*, p. 6.
221. R. Favre, *La Mort dans la littérature et la pensée françaises au siècle des lumières*, p. 518.
222. The prince de Ligne, *Coup d'œil sur Belœil*, n.p.
223. J.-F. Ducis, *Œuvres* (1839), p. 312 ('Le Saule du malheureux').
224. L. W. M. Kerby, *The Life of Nicolas Germain Léonard* (1925), pp. 299–301.
225. Léonard, *Les Saisons* (1782), cit. Guitton, p. 345.
226. *Lettre sur un voyage aux Antilles* in Kerby, 330–2.
227. Ed. Trahard, 1959, pp. 41–2, 210–11, 277–8.
228. pp. 138–43.
229. *Les Harmonies de la Nature de Bernardin de Saint-Pierre*, ed. F. Baridon (Studi di Filogia e di Critica Testuale, 2 v. 1958), ii. 340–2.
230. *Voyage de Figaro en Espagne* (1784), cit. Favre, i. 551.
231. Ed. R. de Bonnières, *Lettres grecques de Mme Chénier*, pp. 187–99.

232. Léonard, *Idylles et poèmes champêtres* (1782), ii. 7, cit. Kerby, p. 35.
233. Le Franc de Pompignan, *Les Tombeaux* in De La Place, *Recueil d'épitaphes* (3 v. 1782), iii. 333.
234. *La Comtesse d'Alibre*, p. x.
235. *Ainsi finissent les grandes passions* (2 v. in one, 1788), pp. 167–8.
236. M. A. Stavary, *Jacques Pierre Alexandre, comte de Tilly* (1965), pp. 65, 112, 115–17. See also his *Mémoires*, ed. C. Melchior Bonnet (1965).
237. Delille, *Les Jardins*, pp. 85–6.
238. M. Billard, *Les Tombeaux des rois sous la Terreur* (1905), p. 18.
239. *Génie du Christianisme*, p. 409.
240. D. Hermant, 'Destruction et vandalisme pendant la Révolution française', *Annales* (1978), p. 712.
241. In May 1791, all Parisian cemeteries *intra muros* were suppressed, and four new ones nominated, two for the left bank, two for the right. In fact, these were close to the town, so in 1794 the municipality ordered the creation of new cemeteries further out, but no action followed. Clandestine burials in old cemeteries went on. At Saint-Médard, the old verger still held the keys (to wind up the clock) and he connived. The *commissaire de police* of the *quartier* complained (in 1795) of this 'manie de perpétuer l'ancien régime'. (Hillairet, pp. 15, 84, 90.)
242. Hillairet, pp. 294–7; Amaury Duval, *Des sépultures* (An IX), pp. 63–4.
243. C. Petit, *Les Cimetières de Saint-Dizier* (1937), pp. 12–13. Fouché's notice at Nevers is more notorious.
244. V. Pelletier, *Essai historique et critique sur les billets d'enterrement orléanais* (1861), p. 10.
245. G.-G. Delamelle, *L'Enterrement de ma mère, ou réflexions sur les cérémonies des funérailles* (17–18 Pluviôse, An III), pp. 2–8.
246. C. Détournelle, *Des funérailles* (An IX), p. 4.
247. Robert, *De l'influence de la Révolution française sur la population*, ii. 152.
248. Cambry, *Rapport sur les sépultures* (to central administration of the Department of the Seine, An VII), p. 2.
249. Ariès, p. 498.
250. For this para. see D. L. Dowd, *Pageant-Master of the Republic. Jacques-Louis David and the French Revolution* (1948), pp. 48, 67–9, 99, 103, 106. For David's turning to the cult of Sparta and his *Léonidas* of 1814 (exhibited after the Russian *débâcle*—the defence of Thermopylae had been, as it were, a failure), see Elizabeth Rawson, *The Spartan Tradition in European Thought* (1969), p. 291.

251. I am quoting in this para. from my *French Revolution and the Church* (1970 ed.), p. 98, with the permission of the publisher.

252. Anita Brookner, *Jacques-Louis David: a personal interpretation* (1974), p. 13.

253. Mona Ozouf, *La Fête révolutionnaire, 1789–1799* (1976), p. 320. See pp. 318–19 for a criticism of Soboul on the religious cult of Marat in *Ann. hist. de la Rév. fr.* 1957.

254. Delamelle, pp. 11–15.

255. Petit, pp. 12–13.

256. André Chénier, *Œuvres complètes* (Pléiade, 1940), pp. 76–7, 501 ('Clytie', 'Fragments de Bucoliques').

257. Delille, *L'Imagination*, Chant VII, *Œuvres* (1825), ix. 146.

258. [Aignan], *Aux mânes des neuf victimes d'Orléans: chants funèbres* (29 Prairial, An III), n.p.

259. G. Collas, *La Vieillesse douloureuse de Mme de Chateaubriand* (2 v. 1961), ii. 661.

260. Olga Longi, *La Terre et les morts dans l'œuvre de Chateaubriand* (Johns Hopkins Studies in Romance Literature and Languages, XXIII, 1934), pp. 85–7.

261. A.-J. Canolle, *Les Délices de la solitude* (2nd ed., 2 v. An VII), ii. 192–3; i. 39–41.

262. Hillairet, pp. 291–7.

263. *Mémoires de Mme la duchesse de Tourzel, 1789–1795*, ed. le duc des Cars (2 v. 1883), i. pp. xv–xvi.

264. McManners, *The French Revolution and the Church* pp. 133–7.

265. Cambry, pp. 9–10, 11–22, 65–82.

266. Amaury Duval, *Des sépultures*, p. 19; F.-V. Mulot, *Discours sur cette question: Quelles sont les cérémonies à faire pour les funérailles, et le règlement à adopter pour le lieu de la sépulture* (An IX), pp. 45–6, 59–60 (Duval and Mulot were the joint prize winners); C. Détournelle, *Des funérailles*, pp. 38, 43.

267. F.-R.-J. Pommereul, *Mémoire sur les funérailles et les sépultures. Question . . . jugée par l'Institut* (An IX).

268. J. Girard, *Des tombeaux, ou de l'influence des institutions funèbres sur les mœurs* (An IX), pp. 56, 38.

269. Pierre Dolivier, *Essai sur les funérailles* (An IX), pp. 59, 52, 65, 26. The architectural project of Granjean in 1799 provides an amphitheatre where the people congregate to vote on candidates for memorials in the Temple of Virtues—'Ici repose au sein de la gloire le petit nombre de ceux qui ont vécu pour la Postérité.' Allais, Détournelle, and Vaudryer, *Grands prix d'architecture:projets couronnés par l'Académie d'architecture et l'Institut de France* (1806), pp. 64–5.

270. Amaury Duval, pp. 24–5, 30; Détournelle, p. 16; Mulot, pp. 50–1; Pommereul, p. 7.
271. Amaury Duval, p. 16.
272. Mulot, p. 47; Pommereul, p. 39; Amaury Duval, p. 42: Détournelle, p. 7. For the vitreous substance, Ariès, p. 507.
273. 25 Ventôse, An XIII (N. Paul-Albert, Histoire du cimetière du Père la Chaise (1937), p. 37).
274. Girard, pp. 130, 147–8, 54, 10.
275. Pommereul, p. 32 (but see the trees on p. 28); Allais etc., Grands prix d'architecture, p. 66; Duval, pp. 41–4; Mulot, pp. 80–5, 42–3; Girard, p. 111; Dolivier, p. 59; Détournelle, p. 7.
276. P.-A. Préfontaine, Discours sur la vénération due aux tombeaux (An IX, 1801), p.3.
277. Chateaubriand, Atala, (Œuvres romanesques, ed. M. Regard, 1969), pp. 47, 51, 69, 94; Mémoires d'outre-tombe, p. lxiv; Génie, p. 404.
278. Visionary Architects, Boullée, Ledoux, Lequeu, Catalogue, pp. 228–9.
279. E. Kaufmann, Three Revolutionary Architects, pp. 476, 509, 519–24.
280. N. Paul–Albert, pp. 38–9.
281. T. D. [the abbé Th. Destruissart], Essai sur les catacombes de Paris (1812), pp. 11–12.

CHAPTER 11

Death as an Instrument: the Public Execution

1. Des lois pénales (1790), cit. J. Imbert, La Peine de mort: histoire-actualité (1967), p. 121.
2. The French did not know how few death sentences were carried out: 33 a year from 1749 to 1799 in London and Middlesex (D. Hay et al., Albion's Fatal Tree: Crime and Society in 18th-Century England (1975), p. 20). For what follows see P. Savey-Casard, La Peine de mort (1968), pp. 52–3.
3. Diderot, 'Des recherches sur le style de Beccaria' (1771), Œuvres (ed. Assézat), iv. 62.
4. C.-J. de Ferrière, Dict. de droit et de pratique (4 v., Paris, 1771), i. 359–60.
5. F. Serpillon, Code criminel, ou commentaire sur l'ordonnance de 1670 (4 v., Lyon, 1767), iii. 911–13.
6. D. Vidal-Hennequin, 'Le procès de maître Mazel', in J. Imbert (ed.), Quelques procès criminels des XVIIᵉ et XVIIIᵉ siècles (1964), pp. 183–4. For procedures generally, D. Bien, The Calas Affair: Persecution, Toleration and Heresy in 18th-Century Toulouse (1960), pp. 96–7.

7. J. Imbert, 'Principes généraux de la procédure pénale (XVIIe–XVIIIe siècles)', in id., *Quelques procès*, p. 4. The *cours souveraines* were the parlements and the corresponding *conseils souverains* of Roussillon, Artois, and Alsace, the *cours des aides*, the *cours des monnaies*, and the *chambre des eaux et forêts*.

8. A. Corvisier, *L'Armée française de la fin du XVIIe siècle au ministère de Choiseul: le soldat* (2 v. 1964), i. 701–24.

9. N. Castan, 'La Justice expéditive', *Annales* (1976), pp. 331–49.

10. E. Hepp, 'La contrebande du tabac au 18e siècle', in Hepp *et al.*, *Aspects de la contrebande au XVIIIe siècle* (Fac. Droit Sc. écon. Paris, 1969), p. 70.

11. M.-H. Bourquin, 'Le Procès de Mandrin', in Hepp *et al.*, *Aspects*, p. 2.

12. Hepp, p. 89.

13. Bourquin, p. 28; Hepp, p. 79.

14. Égret, *Le Parlement de Dauphiné et les affaires publiques dans la deuxième moitié du XVIIIe siècle* (2 v. 1941), i. 226–7.

15. M. Jousse, *Traité de la justice criminelle de France* (4 v. 1771), i. 816–20; Muyart de Vouglans, *Réfutation du Traité des délits et peines. Lettre à Monsieur* * * * (1767), published at the end of *Les Loix criminelles de France* (1780), p. 817.

16. Serpillon, iii. 912.

17. Ibid. ii. 933.

18. Imbert, *La Peine de mort: histoire, actualité*, p. 89.

19. Marie-Madeleine Champin, 'La criminalité dans le bailliage d'Alençon de 1715 à 1789', *Ann. de Normandie*, 22 (1972), 53.

20. G. Aubry, *La Jurisprudence criminelle du Châtelet de Paris sous le règne de Louis XVI* (1971), p. 231.

21. Y. Bongert, 'Délinquence juvenile et responsabilité pénale du mineur', in Bongert *et al.*, *Crimes et criminalité en France au 17e–18e siècles* (*Cahiers des Annales*, XXXIII, 1971), p. 87.

22. Aubry, pp. 223–4.

23. A. Abbiateci, 'Les incendiaires devant le Parlement de Paris: essai de typologie criminelle, XVIIIe siècle', in Bongert *et al.*, *Crimes et criminalité en France*, pp. 13–18.

24. Jousse, *Traité*, i, p. v.

25. Aubry, pp. 59, 83, 87. In theory the death sentence was obligatory for *rapt de séduction* (N. Rateau, 'Les peines capitales et corporelles en France sous l'ancien régime', *Ann. internationales de criminologie* (1963), p. 276). For a case of hanging for the violation of a child, Hardy, *Mes loisirs*, i. 71–2 (9 Apr. 1767). For another, together with one for which the penalty was merely banishment from Versailles, see J. Combes-Monier, 'Population mouvante et criminalité à

Versailles à la fin de l'ancien régime', in Dupâquier *et al.*, *Sur la population française au XVIIIe et au XIXe siècles: hommage à Marcel Reinhard*, p. 141.

26. R. Pillorget, *La Tige et le rameau*, pp. 227–8.

27. A. Farge, *Le Vol des aliments à Paris au XVIIIe siècle* (1973), pp. 52–3.

28. In 1742 the Parlement of Dijon executed 4 laymen and 3 priests (the charge being sacrilege as, since the Edict of 1682, 'magic' did not exist as a crime in its own right). The ecclesiastical court had sentenced the priests to imprisonment—for life, for 10 years, and for 3 years; the Parlement changed this to burning for the first two and hanging for the third (H. Beaune, 'Les sorciers de Lyon: épisode judiciaire du XVIIIe siècle', *Mémoires de l'Académie impériale . . . de Dijon*, 2nd Ser. 4 (1868), 65–151).

29. F. Billacois, 'Le Parlement de Paris et les duels au XVIIIe siècle,' in Bongert *et al.*, *Crimes et criminalité*, pp. 41–4.

30. Aubry, pp. 240, 244, 233.

31. Muyart de Vouglans, *Les Loix criminelles de France*, p. 166.

32. Ibid., p. 93; also p. 824 (*Réfutation*).

33. Savey-Casard, p. 48.

34. Muyart de Vouglans, p. xxx.

35. Jousse, *Traité*, i. pp. i–v. A sad case of the working of shame—an orphan girl asks the church courts to end her engagement because she has discovered that her fiancé is the grandson of a man hanged twenty years ago (A. Lottin, *La Désunion du couple sous l'ancien régime: l'exemple du Nord* (1975), p. 193).

36. Cl.-J. de Ferrière, *Dict. de droit et de pratique*, ii. 343–4.

37. I. A. Cameron, 'The Police of 18th-Century France', *European Studies Review*, 7 (1977), 47–75.

38. V. Boucheron, 'La montée du flot des errants de 1760 à 1789, dans la généralité d'Alençon', *Ann. de Normandie*, 21 (1971), 59. (A nice example of the *maréchaussée* keeping out of trouble in *Ann. de Bourgogne*, 32 (1960), 60–1.)

39. A. Margot, 'La criminalité dans le bailliage de Mamers (1695–1750)', *Ann. de Normandie*, 22 (1975), 205, 207. Cf. Champin, 'Alençon,' *Ann. de Normandie*, vol. cit. 53, 69, 70.

40. Y. Castan, *Honnêteté et relations sociales en Languedoc*, pp. 70, 76, 79, 93.

41. P. Deyon, *Le Temps des prisons* (1975), p. 33; D. Martin, 'Le milieu carcéral au XVIIIe siècle: l'exemple de l'Auvergne', *Cahiers d'hist.* 23 (1978), 157–62.

42. A. Lottin, 'Naissances illégitimes et filles mères à Lille au XVIIIe siècle,' *Rev. d'hist. mod. et contemp.* 17 (1970), 280–1. For a village

where the method worked in the seventeenth century but not in the eighteenth, see A. Zink, *Azereix*, p. 245.

43. Cit. A. Mellor, *La Torture, son histoire, son abolition; sa réapparition au XXe siècle* (1961), p. 184. Notice the remark of the most humane of contemporary experts on French history: 'Without torture the puny police force of the *ancien régime* would have got nowhere' (Olwen M. Hufton, *The Poor of Eighteenth-Century France, 1750–1789*, p. 283).

44. Diderot, 'Notes sur le Traité des délits et des peines', *Œuvres*, iv. 66.

45. Muyart de Vouglans, *Réfutation* in *Les Loix criminelles de France*, p. 814. Here, one may think, are facile and dithyrambic terms to justify cruelty, and a lawyer exalting the dignity of his own profession. But the *Encyclopédie* itself, hostile to torture and cruelty, speaks in terms of a calculus of deterrence: punishment is 'pour réprimer avec efficace l'audace la plus déterminée, et balancer ainsi les différents degrés de la malice humaine par un contrepoids assez puissant' (xxx. (1778). 515).

46. *Les Loix criminelles de France*, pp. 54, 38.

47. Savey-Casard, p. 48.

48. Jousse, i, p. viii. For the *aveu* 'pour la satisfaction publique' and denunciation of the use of torture to obtain it see [Seigneaux de Correvou], *Essai sur l'abus . . . de la torture dans la procédure criminelle* (Lausanne, 1768), pp. 40–1.

49. Aubry, pp. 41–2 and copy of a *testament de mort* of 1785 on p. 46.

50. Serpillon, iii. 126. A woman on her way to be hanged for directing a gang of highwaymen, asks to say something 'for discharge of her conscience', is taken to a house near by and here she names an associate of her crimes (J. Lorédan, *La Grande Misère et les voleurs au XVIIIe siècle: Marion de Faouët* (1933), p. 302).

51. Generally accompanying a condemnation to the galleys or banishment (M. Rateau, art. cit., p. 306). In a rare case, the *amende honorable* might be the only penalty—e.g. the Parlement of Paris dealing with three men on a charge of exorcism (Aubry, pp. 53–4).

52. Cases of 1736 and 1755 in Muyart de Vouglans, *Les Loix criminelles de France*, p. 174. As capital punishment involved civil death, confiscation of property was involved. But the *coutume* of various provinces modified the rule (it was the *coutume* of the province where the property lay, not where the crime was committed, that applied). For duelling, in 1711 a special regulation was made to overcome provincial modifications and confiscate two-thirds of the property as a fine (Jousse, i. 99–101). For the special case of an offender dying before the actual sentence was passed see Ferrière, i. 242–3.

53. *Causes célèbres, curieuses et intéressantes de toutes les cours souveraines du royaume* (12 v., Paris, 1773), i. 43.

54. Daon, *Conduite des âmes* (1750), p. 323.

55. *Journal et mémoires de Mathieu Marais* (ed. M. de Lescure), ii. 313.

56. *Cahier* of the clergy of Vic (cf. the nobles of Dourdon) in A. Desjardins, *Les Cahiers des États Généraux en 1789 et la législation criminelle* (1883), p. 55. They were making Montaigne's point— 'nous qui devrions avoir respect d'en envoyer les âmes en bon estat, ce qui ne se peut, les ayant agitées at désespérées par tourmens insupportables' ('De la cruauté', *Essais*; Pléiade 1950, p. 475).

57. Desjardins, loc. cit.

58. *Lettre de Mgr Gousset, archevêque de Reims, sur la communion des condamnés à mort* (Reims, 1841), pp. 6–10.

59. Boucher d'Argis, *Observations sur les loix criminelles de France* (1781), pp. 87–9.

60. Restif de la Bretonne, *Les Nuits de Paris*, *Œuvres* (Bachelin), i. 2–3, 171.

61. See L. Guibert, *Les Confréries de Pénitents en France et notamment dans le diocèse de Limoges* (1879).

62. E. J. F. Barbier, *Chronique de la Régence et du règne de Louis XV, 1718–63*, vi. 507–8.

63. J. Hillairet, *Gibets, piloris et cachots du vieux Paris* (1956), p. 19.

64. *Mémoires du duc de Luynes sur la cour de Louis XV*, ed. L. Dussieux and E. Soulié, xv. 477. For the other details see P. Rétat (ed.), *L'Attentat de Damiens: discours sur l'événement au XVIIIᵉ siècle* (1979), pp. 301, 258.

65. Hardy, *Mes loisirs*, pp. 393–4 (30 Mar. 1773).

66. Barbier, iii. 86–7; v. 247.

67. Bourquin, p. 29. For Toulouse, J.-M. Augustin, 'Les Capitouls, juges des causes criminelles . . . 1780–90; *Ann. du Midi*, 84 (1972), 192.

68. Gilbert, cit. *Lettre de M. François de Neufchâteau à M . . . Pankouke . . . au sujet de son 'Essai sur la peine de mort'* (1807), p. 13; E. Laffay, *Le Poète Gilbert* (1898), p. 133.

69. Restif de la Bretonne, *Les Nuits de Paris*, ed. H. Bachelin, n.d., p. 126.

70. M. de Cressy, *Discours sur l'abolition de la peine de mort, lu aux Amis de la Vérité* (1791), p. 4.

71. Landreau de Maine-au-Picq, *Législation philosophique, politique et morale* (3 v. Geneva, 1787), i. 70–2.

72. R. Lehoreau, *Cérémonial de l'Église d'Angers*, cit. F. Lebrun, *Les Hommes et la mort en Anjou*, p. 420.

73. *Lettres de la marquise du Deffand à Horace Walpole* (4 v. 1824), i. 31–2. The next two examples are from Barbier.

74. Voltaire, *Prix de la justice et de l'humanité* (1777), *Œuvres*, xxx. 335–6. Cf. *Dict. philosophique*, 'Supplices', *Œuvres*, xx. 463–4.

75. Guibert, pp. 128–30. For Paris, M. Foucault, *Surveiller et punir: naissance de la prison* (1975), p. 65.

76. N. Castan, in *Annales* (1976), p. 347.

77. M. Fletcher, 'Deux lettres inédites de Théophile de Bordeu', in *Recherches nouvelles sur quelques écrivains des lumières*, ed. J. Proust (1972), pp. 25–8.

78. G. Lenotre, *La Guillotine et les exécuteurs des arrêts criminels pendant la Révolution* (1927), pp. 8, 13, 119, 124, 330–1, 333. Dr R. Goulard, *Une lignée d'exécuteurs des jugements criminels, les Sanson (1688–1847)*, pp. 6–43. G. Bouchard, *La Famille du conventionnel Basire* (1952), pp. 53–4; J.-C. Perrot, *Genèse d'une ville moderne: Caen au XVIIIᵉ siècle*, ii. 1170; R. Mercier, *Le Monde médical de Touraine sous la Révolution*, pp. 205–6. There were at least 160 executioners in France, but in the South it was hard to find takers. For the Ferey brothers at Rouen, see M. Bée 'La société traditionnelle et la mort', *XVIIᵉ Siècle* (1975), pp. 101–9.

79. Cit. Rétat, *L'Attentat de Damiens*, p. 203. Other details at pp. 201, 322, 436, 207–10, 261.

80. Barbier, iii. 147. For Cartouche, Goulard p. 13.

81. D'Argenson, *Journal et mémoires* (ed. E. J. B. Rathery), vi. 95.

82. Bachaumont, *Mémoires*, xxvi. 225–9.

83. Perrot, *Caen*, ii. 1196.

84. Hardy, i. 16 (20 Mar. 1765); cf. p. 49.

85. Barbier, i. 87 (Nov. 1720).

86. M. Chassaigne, *Le Procès du chevalier de la Barre* (1920), pp. 204–5.

87. H. Pensa, *Sorcellerie et religion au XVIIᵉ et XVIIIᵉ siècles* (1933), pp. 186–7. The execution in effigy served a legal purpose, as it fixed the beginning of the five-year term within which the criminal who had fled could surrender to justice and thus avoid the definitive seizure of his property (D. Vidal-Hennequin, pp. 188–9).

88. *La Vie de Marianne* (*Romans*, Pléiade, 1949), p. 152. For a less sympathetic view—the people at the execution of two highwaymen showing a machine-like compassion allied to an equally mechanical curiosity—see Marivaux, *Journaux et œuvres diverses*, ed. F. Deloffre and M. Gilot (1969), from the *Mercure*, 1717–18.

89. On Voltaire, Rétat, p. 321.

90. *Jacques le Fataliste Œuvres romanesques*, p. 670.

91. Cit. G. van Louw, *Baculard d'Arnaud*, p, 153.

92. *Lettres* (N.S., ed. Cl. Perroud), i. 240–1. For the idea, in Rousseau and d'Holbach, that the people, like children, need strong emotions, see H. C. Payne, *The Philosophes and the People* (1976), p. 24.

93. Desjardins, *Les Cahiers* . . ., pp. 25, 55.
94. L. S. Gordon, 'Le Thème de Mandrin, le "brigand noble" ', in *Au siècle des lumières* (S.E.V.P.E.N., 1970), pp. 189–207.
95. Servan, *Discours sur l'administration de la justice criminelle* (1767), cit. Égret, i. 86–7.
96. St. Augustine, *The City of God*, i. 20. xix. 6 (trans. J. Healey, ed. R. V. G. Tasker (2 v. 1962), i. 26; ii. 242).
97. Montaigne, *loc. cit.*
98. Clivensis the Dutch theologian, von Spee the German Jesuit, Grevius the Arminian minister, Bekker, and Bayle included. La Bruyère, *Les Caractères: de quelques usages*, No. 51, *Œuvres*, ed. J. Benda (Pléiade 1951), p. 441.
99. Augustin Nicolas, *Si la torture est un moyen seur à vérifier les crimes secrets* (Amsterdam, 1681), p. 131.
100. Voltaire, passionately moved at the thought of cruelty of any kind, in 1752 still allowed torture for cases 'où il s'agirait évidemment du salut de l'État' and in 1777 reduced this to one example in history where the necessity was clear: the murderer of Henri IV (*Fragment des instructions pour le prince* . . . (1752), *Œuvres*, xxvi (1879), 445; *Prix de la Justice* . . . (1777), ibid. xxx (1880), 582).
101. Beccaria, *Traité des délits et des peines* (Lausanne, 1766—French trans. from the 3rd Italian ed.), pp. 115–16. A discussion of this point in P. Savey-Casard, 'Le deuxième centenaire du *Traité des délits et des peines*', *Rev. de science criminelle et de droit pénal comparé*, N.S. 19 (1964), 303 ff.
102. Beccaria, *Traité*, pp. 190–4. In later life Beccaria changed his mind— nobles should escape certain punishments because they feel them more keenly (M. Maestro, *Cesare Beccaria and the Origins of Penal Reform* (1973), p. 145).
103. Rousseau, *Contrat social*, Bk. II, ch. 5.
104. Beccaria, *Traité*, p. 131.
105. Montesquieu, *L'Esprit des lois*, xii. 4 (*Œuvres*, Pléiade, 2 v. 1949, ii. 435). Cruel punishments were a sign of despotism, frequent ones an indication that revolution was near, ii. 318–19). Cf. *Lettres persanes*, 80 (Pléiade, i. 252–3).
106. Rousseau, *Contrat social*, Bk. II, ch. 5.
107. Voltaire, *Fragment des instructions pour le prince* . . . (1752), *Œuvres*, xxvi (1879), 444. This is the wise rule of the English (*Histoire d'Élisabeth Canning*, 1762, *Œuvres*, xxiv. 401).
108. Letter D12902, Besterman, vol. 113 (1973), p. 315.
109. M. Maestro, *Voltaire and Beccaria as Reformers of Criminal Law* (1942), pp. 73–117.

110. Boucher d'Argis, *Observations sur les loix criminelles de France* (1781), p. 76.
111. J.-P. Brissot, *De la suppression de la peine de mort* (repr. A. Brissot, Lille, 1849), p. 24.
112. Marat, 'Ami du Peuple', *Plan de législation criminelle* (1790; ed. D. Hamiche, 1974), pp. 60, 64.
113. Aubry, p. 190.
114. Toussaint, *Éclaircissements sur les 'Mœurs'*, p. 407.
115. P. J. Romain Joly, *Dict. de morale philosophique*, i. 217.
116. Boucher d'Argis, pp. 76, 84.
117. M. Lacretelle, *Discours sur le préjugé des peines infamantes* (1784), pp. 125–33.
118. Marat, p. 47.
119. J. Crasset, *La Douce et la sainte mort*, p. 59.
120. Toussaint, pp. 407–8; Démeunier, *L'Esprit des usages et des coutumes des différens peuples*, iii. 69.
121. Bergier, *Traité de la vraie religion*, *Œuvres*, vi. 319.
122. Landreau de Maine-au-Picq, *Législation philosophique, politique et morale*, i. 125–6 (whole argument pp. 84–137).
123. J. Sgard, 'La Littérature des causes célèbres', in Lecercle *et. al.*, *Approches des lumières* (1974), pp. 459–70.
124. [Baudouin de Guemadeuc], *L'Espion dévalisé* (1783), pp. 191, 194–7.
125. Dupaty, *Justification* (1787), pp. 3 ff., 100–1. The original sentence by the magistrate, which the Parlement of Metz confirmed, was inspired by obstinacy—'il faut justifier mon arrêt' (p. 12, 14).
126. M. Vasselin, *Théorie des peines capitales ou abus et danger de la peine de mort et des tourmens*, pp. 174–8.
127. M. Merlet, *Lettre sur la Désertion* (1770), pp. 6, 9, 12–13, 17.
128. Jaubert, *Des causes de la dépopulation*, p. 249.
129. M. Rodolphe-Louis d'Erlach, *Code du Bonheur*, ii. 75.
130. Landreau de Maine-au-Picq, i, p. ix.
131. M. Perreau, *Sur l'abolition de la peine de mort* (n.d.), p. 20.
132. [Servan], *Discours sur le progrès des connoissances humaines . . . de la morale et de la législation en particulier* (1781), p. 96; Lacretelle, p. 363.
133. Faignet de Villeneuve, *L'Économie politique; projet pour enrichir et perfectionner l'espèce humaine*, p. 114.
134. *Commentaire sur le livre 'Des délits et des peines'* (1766), *Œuvres*, xxv. 555; *Dict. philosophique*, ibid. xx. 456.
135. Diderot says dangerous men should be got rid of—see the argument of 'moi' against the doctor who wishes to cure a notorious assassin (*Entretien d'un père avec ses enfants* (1770–3), *Œuvres philosophiques*, ed. P. Vernière, pp. 415–18). But we should spare a

man who might amend and become useful on public works (*Observa-tions sur the Nakaz, Œuvres politiques* (1963), pp. 374–5). By contrast to his harshness as a philosopher. Diderot the sentimental writer is generous towards reptentance: 'Vous êtes un brave homme qui a eu son malheureux moment; et qui est-ce qui n'a pas eu?' (*Les Pères malheureux*, 1770, Œuvres (Assézat), viii. 53).

136. *Notes sur le 'Traité des délits et des peines'*, Œuvres (Assézat), iv. 69.

137. Landreau de Maine-au-Picq, ii. 369–70. For 'Moheau's' view, see his *Recherches et considérations sur la population de la France*, Bk. II, p. 97.

138. Vasselin, p. 64.

139. In these disciplinary methods Foucault sees the origin of the modern idea of the prison (pp. 137–97).

140. Brissot, *Théorie des lois criminelles* (1781), cit. Imbert, *La Peine de mort: histoire, actualité*, p. 114.

141. G. Bonnet de Mably, *De la législation, ou principes des loix* (1776), in *Œuvres complètes de l'abbé Mably* (12 v., London, 1789), ix. 279. Mably regarded death as necessary for murder and treason, but there was to be no cruelty (pp. 273, 286).

142. Lacretelle, p. 364.

143. Imbert, p. 129.

144. For all this para., see the chapter 'Freedom and Determinism: the Moral Consequences' in Lester G. Crocker, *An Age of Crisis. Man and World in Eighteenth-Century French Thought* (1959), pp. 161–76.

145. Diderot, *Notes sur le 'Traité des délits et des peines'*, Œuvres, iv. 67.

146. Mably, Œuvres, ix. 278.

147. Mirabeau says, in a footnote, that he agrees with Beccaria 'que la société n'a point le droit de vie et de mort' and that the prince who arrogates this power commits '*un crime de lèse-majesté divine*'. But the rest of the footnote should be cited: 'Le but de toute association humaine est de garantir, par la réunion des forces, la sûreté publique et particulière, et son premier effet doit être . . . d'anéantir, autant qu'il est possible, le droit que la nature a donné à chaque homme d'arracher la vie à celui qui attaque la sienne s'il ne peut la conserver autrement, en le sauvant de cette cruelle nécessité.' (*Des lettres de cachet et des prisons d'État*, Œuvres (9 v. 1827), i. 88–9.) Men associate, not contractually, but in families, then confederations, with the aim of resisting 'despotism', co-operating in common tasks, and receiving protection (*Essai sur le despotisme*, ibid. ii. 272; *Des lettres de cachet*, ibid. i. 42, 44, 87, 88). The monarch is merely 'le salarié de l'état' with the special duty of protecting each individual's property (*Despotisme*, i. 301). How exactly does society act to

protect my life as well as my property, and to save me from the 'cruel necessity' of exercising my right to kill those who try to kill me?

148. Marat, *Plan de législation criminelle*. For premeditated murder, painless death; for poisoning, death preceded by the *amende honorable* and the pillory (p. 96); for parricide, painless death, but the *appareil* to be fearsome; for conspiracy 'ignominious' death; for destruction of ships, arsenals, etc., 'que l'appareil de son supplice soit effrayant, et qu'il en soit témoin lui-même' (p. 92).

149. Imbert, 'La peine de mort et l'opinion au XVIIIe siècle', *Rev. de Science criminelle et de droit pénal comparé*, N.S., 19 (1964), 516.

150. Voltaire, *Prix de la justice* . . ., *Œuvres*, xxx. 535.

151. Imbert, art. cit., pp. 519–20, 524.

152. Diderot, 'Des recherches sur le style de Beccaria', *Œuvres* (Assézat), iv. 61.

153. Marat, p. 92.

154. 3 Dec. 1792 (E. T. in M. Walzer and M. Rothstein, *Regicide and Revolution: Speeches at the Trial of Louis XVI* (1974), p. 166).

155. e.g. Sylvain Maréchal, *Le Jugement dernier des rois*, played the day after Marie-Antoinette was executed (M. Lumière, *Le Théâtre français pendant la Révolution*, n.d., p. 216). Cf.a royalist picture of Lequinio saying 'Qui'il vive, pour l'opprobre, en contemplant son bras, Enchaîné pour jamais aux travaux des forçats' (E. Aignan and J. Berthevin, *La Mort de Louis XVI, tragédie* (1793), p. 8).

156. Beccaria, *Traité*, pp. 3, 232, 242–73.

157. D'Holbach, *Système de la Nature*, cap. XIV, i. 294). He wanted the death penalty to be rare, limited to crimes 'dont l'exemple est si funeste' (*La Politique naturelle*, Disc. VII (XLII), vol. ii. 170).

158. Voltaire, *Prix de la justice* . . ., *Œuvres*, xxx. 535.

159. Boucher d'Argis, pp. 91–4.

160. Marat, *Plan de législation criminelle*, p. 69.

161. Brissot, *De la suppression de la peine de mort*, pp. 11, 13, 26.

162. President Dupaty praises Brissot's originality in seeing the criminal as 'un malade ou un ignorant qu'il faut guérir ou éclairer' and in adjusting his penal system to take account of 'le triste sort du peuple dans tous les coins de l'univers, en voyant que partout la balance est contre lui' (3 July 1781, in J.-P. Brissot, *Corresp. et papiers*, ed. Cl. Perroud (1912), pp. 22–4). Favre (ii. 295) notes that Cabanis connected vindictive crimes with a 'melancholy' temperament. Mercier observed that poisoners were short of stature, while Bernardin de Saint-Pierre suspected that criminals had usually had an unhappy childhood.

163. N. Willard, *Le Génie et la folie au 18e siècle*, pp. 127–8.

164. Landreau de Maine-au-Picq, i. 74.

165. Cit. Maestro, (1973), p. 143.

166. M. Vovelle, 'Le tournant des mentalités en France, 1750–89', *Social History* (1977), p. 7.

167. B. Boutelet, 'Étude par sondage de la criminalité dans le bailliage du Pont-de-l'Arche (XVIIᵉ–XVIIIᵉ siècle)', *Ann. de Normandie*, 12 (1962), 234–8; J.-C. Gégot, 'La criminalité dans le bailliage de Falaise (XVIIᵉ–XVIIIᵉ siècle)', ibid. 16 (1966), 103–32; Y. Castan, *Honnêteté et relations sociales en Languedoc, 1715–80*, p. 113; P. Deyon, *Le Temps des prisons: essai sur l'histoire de la délinquence et les origines du système pénitentiaire* (1975), pp. 76 ff. See also A. Farge, *Le Vol des aliments à Paris au XVIIIᵉ siècle*, pp. 64–6.

168. Y. Caston, 'Délinquence traditionnelle et répression . . . à la fin de l'ancien régime dans les pays de Languedoc', *Ann. hist. de la Rév. française*, 49 (1977), 186; Deyon, p. 85.

169. P. Dautricourt, *La Criminalité et répression au parlement de Flandre* (1912), cit. Foucault, *Surveiller et punir*, p. 37.

170. D. Muller, 'Magistrats français et peine de mort au 18ᵉ siècle', *Dix-huitième siècle*, 4 (1972), 79–107.

171. For life on the galleys see Oliver Goldsmith's translation of Jean Marteille, *The Memoirs of a Protestant Condemned to the Galleys of France for his Religion* (1758; ed. A. Dobson, 2 v. 1895).

172. A. Zysberg, 'La société des galériens au milieu du XVIIIᵉ siècle', *Annales* (1975), p. 44.

173. A. Farge, p. 89 (description of 1783).

174. Desjardins, *Les Cahiers* . . ., pp. 54–5, 258–63; Imbert, in *Rev. de Science criminelle et de droit pénal comparé*, N.S. 19 (1964), 522.

175. Studies of the guillotine by A. Kershaw (1958) and A. Soubiran (1962). The dispute about pain went on—e.g. the guillotine is condemned by J.-J. Sue, *Recherches physiologiques et expériences sur la vitalité et le Galvanisme* (3rd ed. 1803), pp. 30–2, 61, while R. Castellier denies the pain but disapproves on aesthetic grounds in *Que penser enfin du supplice de la guillotine?* (An IV), p. 10.

176. J. Viaud, *La Peine de mort en matière politique* (1902), p. 121.

CHAPTER 12

Suicide

1. J.-N. Moreau, *Mes souvenirs*, ii. 475–6; F. Lebrun, *Les Hommes et la mort en Anjou*, p. 422.

2. The lawyers held that a merciful view should be taken (Guy du Rousseaud de la Combe, *Traité des matières criminelles* (2 v. 1751), i. 558).

3. Procedures in Denisart, *Collection de décisions*, vi. 32–8.

4. Rousseaud de la Combe, i. 557.
5. Lebrun, p. 418.
6. J. Sareil, *Les Tencin: histoire d'une famille au dix-huitième siècle* (1969), pp. 139–41.
7. S.-P. Hardy, *Mes loisirs*, i. 68–9 (18 Mar. 1767); 160 (28 Nov. 1769); cf. pp. 305–6 (13 Dec. 1771).
8. Mercier, *Tableau de Paris*, ii. 195.
9. Grimm, *Corresp. littéraire*, xv. 55–6 (Aug. 1786); cf. R. Darnton, *Mesmerism and the End of the Enlightenment in France* (1968), p. 50.
10. Hardy, i. 324 (11 Feb. 1772).
11. Montaigne, *Essais*, ii. 3; Charron, *De la sagesse*, ii. 11. See Lester G. Crocker, 'The Discussion of Suicide in the 18th Century', *Journal of the History of Ideas*, 13 (1952), 47–72, also his *An Age of Crisis; Man and the World in 18th-Century French Thought*, pp. 13–14.
12. Maupertuis, *Essai de philosophie morale*, p. 43.
13. D'Alembert, *Essai sur les élémens de philosophie*, XI (*Œuvres complètes*, 5 v. 1821), i. 227–8.
14. Lettre LXXVI in *Œuvres* (Pléiade, 1951), i. 246–7. Lettre LXXVII, written later, puts the other point of view, feebly and in a Muslim context.
15. R. Mauzi, *L'Idée du bonheur dans la littérature et la pensée françaises au XVIIIᵉ siècle*, pp. 64–8; R. Pomeau, *La Religion de Voltaire*, pp. 306–7.
16. *L'Orphelin de la Chine*, V. 5 (Moland, v. 353); *Alzire*, V. 4 (ibid. iii. 379). Cf. *Œdipe*, i. 2 (ibid. ii. 65–6).
17. *Candide*, XII (Moland, xxi. 162).
18. *L'Ingénu*, XX (Moland, xxi. 302). The famous sentry who is not allowed to leave his post comes from Cicero, *De senectute*, citing Pythagoras.
19. E. Boysse, *Le Théâtre des Jésuites* (1880), pp. 239–40, shows how these performances were organized to be specially edifying.
20. Erlach, *Code du bonheur* (1788), ii. 155–6; Démeunier, *L'Esprit des usages et des coutumes des différens peuples*, iii. 225; *Éloge de l'Enfer*, i. 95.
21. *Œuvres*, xii. 19.
22. *Œuvres* (Pléiade, 2 v. 1951), ii. 135–6. Cf. *De l'esprit de lois*, XXIX. 9 (ibid. ii. 870) and *Réponses . . . à la Faculté de Théologie*, X (ibid. ii. 1179–80), and generally, J.-M. Goulemot, 'Montesquieu: du suicide légitime à l'apologie du suicide héroïque', in *Gilbert Romme et son temps*, ed. Goulemot et. al. (Inst. d'Études du Massif Central, Fac. Lettres Sci. hum., Univ. Clermont-Ferrand, 1966), pp. 163 ff.
23. [H. Panckoucke], *La Mort de Caton: tragédie* (1768), Préf., p. iii.

24. Grimm, *Corresp. litt.* viii. 79 (May 1768).
25. Maupertuis, *Essai de philosophie morale*, p. 40.
26. R. Trousson, *Socrate devant Voltaire, Diderot et Rousseau*, pp. 19, 45–64, 71, 95–9, 32, 36, 43; J. Seznec, *Diderot et l'antiquité*, pp. 11 ff.
27. M. Eude, 'Le Suicide heroïque d'un Montagnard, Jacques-Philippe Rühl'; R. Andrews, 'Le Néo-Stoicisme . . . le suicide de . . . Romme'; J. Dautry, 'Réflexions sur les martyrs de Prairial . . .' —all in *Gilbert Romme et son temps*, ed. Goulemot *et al.*, pp. 186–208.
28. R. Andrews, p. 200.
29. M. Nicolas in *Œuvres*, viii. 35.
30. *Dict. hist. des cultes religieux*, i. 84; iii. 34–9; iv. 139–40; Delisle de Sales, *Essai . . . sur le corps humain*, iii. 291, 333; Lesbros de la Versane, *Caractères des femmes*, ii. 34–7. For interest in other kinds of suicide, F.-L.-Cl. Marin, *Hist. de Saladin* (2 v. 1758), i. 296–300 (the 'Assassins') and F.-X. de Charlevoix, *Hist. de . . . Saint-Domingue*, i. 45.
31. 'Sur la mort de M. le marquis de la Fare en 1718', *Œuvres de l'abbé de Chaulieu* (2 v. 1757), ii. 45.
32. M. Launay, 'Contribution à l'étude du suicide vertueux selon Rousseau', in *Gilbert Romme et son temps*, ed. Goulemot *et al.*, pp. 175–82.
33. Cabanis, *Journal de la maladie et de la mort de Mirabeau l'aîné* (1791), pp. 45–62. Different version, with a reproachful letter, in [Cerutti], *Notice mortuaire sur M. de Mirabeau* (n.d.).
34. P. Stewart, *Le Masque et la parole: le langage de l'amour au 18ᵉ siècle* (1973), p. 25.
35. See Mme de Tencin, *Mémoires du comte de Comminges* (1735).
36. *Œuvres* (Pléiade, ii. 28, 393); J.-L. Lecercle, 'Baculard ou l'embonpoint du sentiment', in *Approaches des lumières*, ed. Lecercle *et al.*, p. 380.
37. L. W. M. Kerby, *The Life of Nicolas-Germain Léonard*, pp. 241, 259–93, 304; A. Monglond, *Le Préromantisme français* (2 v., new ed. 1965), i. 190.
38. [Cubière de Palmezeaux], *La Manie des drames sombres: comédie* (1777), Act I (4), p. 37.
39. A. Monglond, *Le Journal intime d'Oberman* (n.d.), pp. 153–4. For Mme de Staël see J.-A. Bédé, 'Mme de Staël, Rousseau et le suicide', *Rev. d'hist. litt. de la France* (1960), pp. 52 ff.
40. *Paul et Virginie* (ed. P. Dubois, 1970), p. 136. Note that Paul, correctly, describes Virginie's death as a sort of suicide ('j'ai mieux aimé perdre la vie que de violer la pudeur' he depicts her as saying.

She drowned because she refused to take her dress off). He then goes on to imagine her describing their happiness together in heaven.

41. G. May, *De J.-J. Rousseau à Mme Roland* (1964), pp. 213–16.
42. *Corresp. entre Mlle de Lespinasse et le comte de Guibert* in Monglond, *Le Préromantisme français* (1965), ii. 31–5.
43. Grimm, *Corresp. litt.* ix. 231–2 (15 Jan. 1771).
44. Chomel, *Aménités littéraires*, i. 165–6.
45. Bergier, *Examen du matérialisme ou réfutation du 'Systéme de la Nature'* (1771), *Œuvres compl.* i. cols. 173–2.
46. Delisle de Sales, *Essai . . . sur le corps humain*, iii. 307–9.
47. Erlach, *Code du bonheur*, ii. 166.
48. Ibid. 167; cf. D'Argens, *Lettres juives*, iv. 232.
49. Delisle de Sales, iii. 314.
50. On Voltaire and Diderot, see Favre, i. 581–5.
51. *Anti-dictionnaire philosophique*, ii. 400–1. Toussaint puts the claims of God as strongly as the theologians (*Les Mœurs*, pp. 375–7).
52. Erlach, ii. 171–5.
53. Dom Calmet, *Commentaire littéral: Josué, les Juges et Ruth* (1726), pp. 256–7.
54. J. Dumas, *Traité du suicide*, pp. 404–5. The rest from pp. 390–402.
55. [Girard de Villethierry], *Le Chrétien dans la tribulation . . . malade et mourant*, pp. 527–33.
56. Dumas, pp. 31–2, 77, 85–6.
57. pp. 143–55.
58. Erlach, iii. 155–9; Delisle de Sales, iii. 282–314; Chomel, *Aménités littéraires*, i. 173–4.
59. Delisle de Sales, iii. 258. Chateaubriand, *Génie du Christianisme* (*Œuvres compl.*, Garnier), ii. 529.
60. *Dict. social et patriotique*, p. 510.
61. La Mettrie, *Anti-Sénèque, ou discours sur le bonheur; Œuvres philosophiques* (Berlin, 2 v. 1764), i. 123, 128, 172, 173–4.
62. Valleria Belt Grannis, *Dramatic Parody in 18th-Century France* (1931), pp. 51–2, 54.
63. *Éloge de l'Enfer*, i. 89.
64. Delisle de Sales, iii. 295. 'Gazettes' etc, in Erlach, ii. 168.
65. F.-A. Chevrier, *Mémoires d'une honnête femme* (1753), cit. L. Versini, *Laclos et la tradition*, p. 465.
66. D'Argens, *Lettres juives*, iv. 227.
67. Lefebvre de Beauvry, p. 124.
68. S. E. Sprott, *The English Debate on Suicide from Donne to Hume* (1961), pp. 70–2.
69. *L'Esprit des lois*, XIV. 12 (Pléiade, ii. 486).
70. [Chomel], *Les Nuits parisiennes*, i. 47.

71. Delisle de Sales, iii. 322.
72. *Le Philosophe anglais ou histoire de M. Cleveland*, iv. 202. Prévost's earlier points from *Le Pour et contre* (5 v. 1734), iv. 87–4; v. 77–8.
73. Favre, i. 573–4; ii. 421–7. For 'euthanasia' reaching its modern meaning in the eighteenth century see P. Villard, 'Réflexions sur un mot . . . L'euthanasie est-elle l'euthanasia?', *Provence historique*, 25 (1975), 167.
74. Delisle de Sales, iii. 280; Dumas, p. 2. For the idea of suicide as 'infectious' see A. M. Meerloo, *Suicide* (1962), p. 8.
75. *Corresp.* (Besterman), lxxiii. 155 (1 Nov. 1769).
76. Hardy, i. 323.
77. Ibid. i. 427.
78. Grimm, *Corresp. litt.* x. 341–5 (Jan. 1774).
79. Lefebvre de Beauvry, p. 511.
80. Robek's adventure took place in Sweden in 1736. Thomas Creech, Fellow of All Souls, and translator of Lucretius, hanged himself in 1700. The explanations current in Oxford were unrequited love, melancholia and lack of money.
81. *Corresp. littéraire de Suard* (ed. G. Bonno), p. 183.
82. Bachaumont, *Mémoires*, xxvii. 142 (1 Jan. 1774).
83. Voltaire, *Corresp.* lxxxvii. 5, 10 (Jan. 1774).
84. Bachaumont, *Mémoires*, xxvii. 158 (25 Jan. 1774).
85. Ibid. viii. 79–80.
86. Ibid.
87. Ibid. v. 171–2; x. 86; Métra, iv. 360.
88. *Lettres de Mlle Aïssée à Mme Calandrini* (ed. A. Piedagnel, 1878), p. 72 (13 Aug. 1778).
89. Métra, iv. 255.
90. Erlach, ii. 152.
91. P. Laliman, *Moyens propres à garantir les hommes du suicide* (1779), p. 14.
92. Ibid, pp. 16–37.
93. Ibid, p. 55.
94. Ibid, p. 115.
95. Nonnotte, i. 333.
96. *Système de la Nature*, ii. 449.
97. M. Foucault, *Histoire de la folie à l'âge classique* (n. ed. 1972), pp. 210–20, 315.
98. D'Argens, *Réflexions critiques sur les différentes écoles de peinture*, pp. 205, 270–1.
99. M. Andry, *Recherches sur la mélancolie: extrait des Registres de la Soc. royale de Médecine, 1782–3* (1785), pp. 26–8.
100. Loaisel de Tréogate, *Ainsi finissent les grandes passions*, pp. 223–4.

101. *Les Carnets de Joseph Joubert* (ed. A. Beaunier, 2 v. 1938), i. 54 (1779–83).

102. Béatrice Le Gall, *L'Imagination chez Senancour* (1966), pp. 72–3, 410, 412–17.

CHAPTER 13

Living, Loving, and Dying

1. Boswell, *Life of Johnson*, ed. G. B. Hill, rev. L. F. Powell (6 v. 1964 ed.), iii. 294–5. Omitting Mrs Knowles's interventions.

2. Cf. the title of Vovelle's *Piété baroque et déchristianisation èn Provence au XVIIIe siècle* (1973).

3. B. Plongeron, *Conscience religieuse en révolution: regards sur l'historiographie religieuse de la révolution française* (1969), p. 103. For its use today, R. Rémond, 'The Problem of Dechristianisation: the present position and some recent French studies', *Concilium*, 7 (1), (1965), 77.

4. For all this paragraph see Plongeron, 'Entre XVIIIe et XIXe siècles: "Civilisation chrétienne" et déchristianisation' (typescript, Colloque Internat. d'hist. ecclés., Oxford 1974). For 'civilisation chrétienne' see also *Cahiers d'histoire* (1972), pp. 369–72.

5. For powerful statistical studies of this and other evidence, see M. Vovelle, *Religion et Révolution: la déchristianisation de l'an II* (1976).

6. M. Vovelle, 'Étude quantitative de la déchristianisation au 18e siècle', *Dix-huitième Siècle* (1973), p. 172.

7. See J. McManners, *The French Revolution and the Church*, pp. 12–14.

8. *Colloque*, 1974, p. 7.

9. Plongeron emphasizes Thomism, see his *Théologie et politique au siècle des lumières, 1770–1820* (1973), pp. 84 ff.

10. G. Le Bras, 'Déchristianisation: mot fallacieux', *Social Compass* (1963), pp. 445–52.

11. J. Delumeau, *Le Catholicisme entre Luther et Voltaire* (1971), p. 330. See also his 'Déchristianisation ou nouveau modèle de Christianisme', *Archives des sciences sociales des religions*, 40 (1975), 3–20.

12. Discussion in J. M. McManners, 'Believers and Worshippers', in *Faces of Europe*, ed. A. Bullock (1980), p. 198.

13. See the literary examples in my *Church and State in France, 1870–1914* (1972), p. 60.

14. Phrases of Vovelle ('Les attitudes devant la mort, problèmes de méthode', *Annales* (1976), p. 127) and Chaunu ('Mourir à Paris', ibid. p. 30).

15. L. Stone, *The Family, Sex and Marriage in England, 1500–1800* (1977). For the present state of family studies see also T. K. Rabb and R. T. Rotberg (eds.), *The Family and History: an Interdisciplinary Enquiry* (1973) and C. E. Rosenberg (ed.), *The Family in History* (1975).
16. J.-L. Flandrin, *Famille, parenté, maison, sexualité dans l'ancienne société*, pp. 77–83; A. Armengaud, *La Famille et l'enfant en France et en Angleterre du 16ᵉ au 18ᵉ siècle: aspects démographiques* (1979), pp. 20–1; R. Pillorget, *La Tige et le rameau: familles anglaise et française 16ᵉ—18ᵉ siècle*, p. 182.
17. F. Lebrun, *La Vie conjugale sous l'ancien régime*, p. 108.
18. G. Snyders, *La Pédagogie en France aux XVIIᵉ et XVIIIᵉ siècles* (1965), p. 265.
19. L. Abensoir, *La Femme et le féminisme avant la Révolution* (1923), pp. 21–7.
20. P. Hoffmann, *La Femme dans la pensée des lumières* (1978), pp. 36–7, 96.
21. M. D. T. de Bienville, *La Nymphomanie, ou l'excès du tempérament chez les femmes* (Bruxelles, n.d. 1777). pp. 72–6.
22. Cit. Lebrun, *La Vie conjugale*, p. 88.
23. H. Bergues, P. Ariès et al., *La Prévention des naissances dans la famille: ses origines dans les temps modernes* (I.N.E.D. *Cahier* 35, 1960), pp. 203, 212–14, 222; J.-L. Flandrin, 'Contraception, mariage, et relations amoureuses dans l'Occident chrétien', *Annales* (1969), pp. 1373 ff; R. Mercier, *La Réhabilitation de la nature humaine, 1700–1750* (1960), p. 84.
24. See P. Stewart, *Le Masque et la parole: le langage de l'amour au 18ᵉ siècle*, 149 ff.
25. J. Ghestin, 'L'action des Parlements contre les mésalliances au XVIIᵉ et XVIIIᵉ siècle', *Rev. hist. de droit fr. et étranger*, Ser. IV, année 34, pp. 74–189, 196 ff.
26. For the Cartesian background, G. Ascoli, 'Essai sur l'histoire des idées féministes en France du XVIᵉ siècle à la Révolution', *Rev. de synthèse historique* (1906), p. 170.
27. Flandrin, pp. 125–8.
28. A. Lottin, *La Désunion du couple sous l'ancien régime: l'exemple du Nord*, pp. 183–5.
29. Hoffmann, pp. 207, 213–31.
30. J. Falvey, 'Women and Sexuality in the thought of La Mettrie', in *Women and Society in 18th-Century France* ed. E. Jacobs et al. (1979), pp. 63–8, abbreviated henceforth as *Women and Soc.*
31. Hoffmann, pp. 89–104.
32. Ibid., p. 116.

33. Discussion in Jean H. Bloch, 'Women and the Reform of the Nation', in *Women and Soc.*, p. 11.

34. Condorcet, 'Lettres d'un bourgeois de New-Haven à un citoyen de Virginie' (1787), in *Œuvres*, xii; *Cahier des doléances et réclamations des femmes par Mme B.B.*, cit. J. Abray, 'Feminism in the French Revolution', *American Hist. Rev.* 86 (1975), 46; *Requête des dames à l'Assemblée nationale*, cit. A. Dessens, *Les Revendications des droits de la femme . . . pendant la Révolution française (Thèse*, Toulouse, 1905), p. 129. For other feminist manifestos in 1787, see J. F. Tetu, in *La Femme au XIXᵉ siècle: littérature et idéologie*, ed. R. Bellet *et al.* (1979), p. 17.

35. The point had been made by the heroine of Voltaire's *Tancrède*—'L'injustice, à la fin, produit l'indépendance'.

36. M. Ostrogorski, *La Femme au point de vue du droit public* (1893), pp. 169–70.

37. Elizabeth J. Gardner, 'The Philosophes and Women', in *Women and Soc.*, pp. 19–23; Hoffmann, pp. 447, 470.

38. Gusdorf in preface to Hoffmann, p. 12.

39. For what follows see J. G. Rosso, *Montesquieu et la féminité* (1977), esp. pp. 464–8, 481–3, 513, 521, 576, 581; and, in *Women and Soc.*, see Sheila Mason, 'the Riddle of Roxane', T. H. Mason, 'Women and Marivaux', P. D. Jimak, 'The Paradox of Sophie and Julie', R. Niklaus, 'Diderot and Women', Eva Jacobs, 'Diderot and the Education of Girls'. See also Hoffmann, pp. 52, 536 (Marivaux), 309, 385, 563–7 (Rousseau), 487–503, 532 (Diderot), and R. A. Brooks, 'Rousseau's Antifeminism', in *Literature and History in the Age of Ideas: essays presented to George R. Havens*, ed. C. G. Williams (1975), pp. 209–37. For the quotation from Diderot's *Sur les femmes*, *Œuvres complètes* (Club français du Livre 1971), x. 38.

40. *Animaux communs aux deux continents* (1761), cit. Hoffmann, pp. 353–6.

41. For this para., P. Stewart, pp. 46–7, 104, 107–8, 111–12; and L. Versini, *Laclos et la tradition*, pp. 432–6, 599.

42. 'Pour aimer comme elle, il faut avoir été trente ans dévote' (Marivaux, *Le Paysan parvenu*, Pléiade, *Romans*, p. 702). Diderot to Sophie, 5 Sept. 1762: 'Il faut qu'elle marche, pour ainsi dire, sur son Dieu.' Valmont in *Les Liaisons dangereuses*: 'Qu'elle croie à la vertu, mais qu'elle me la sacrifie'. Duclos: 'Une dévote emploie pour son amant tous les termes tendres et onctueux de l'Écriture.'

43. Boudier de Villemart, *Le Nouvel ami des femmes* (1779), p. 24.

44. Abray, *American Hist. Rev.* 86. (1975), 43. Generally, see Jean H. Bloch, 'Women and the Reform of the Nation', in *Women and Soc.*, pp. 3 ff.

45. Voltaire and Helvétius principally. The *Encylopédie* supports divorce only when the children are grown up.

46. Chamfort, *Maximes et Pensées, Œuvres*, i. 413. See generally, X. Lannes, 'Le XVIIIᵉ siècle: l'évolution des idées', in *Renouveau des idées sur la famille*, ed. R. Prigent (I.N.E.D. *Cahier* 18, 1934), pp. 35 ff.

47. Cit. Pillorget, *La Tige et le rameau*, p. 85.

48. *Mémoires*, (ed. Cl. Perroud (2 v. 1905), ii. 152–70, 200–8, 247–51.

49. Lesbros de la Versane, *Caractères des femmes ou aventures du chevalier de Miron*, p. 4; Le Pileur d'Apligny, *Essais historiques sur la morale des anciens et des modernes*, p. 88; J.-C. Perrot, *Genèse d'une ville moderne: Caen au XVIIIᵉ siècle* ii. 1091. There is a discussion of the theme of *amitié* versus *amour* in R. Mauzi, *L'Idée du bonheur dans la littérature et la pensée françaises au XVIIIᵉ siècle*, p. 360.

50. Y. Durand, *Les Fermiers généraux au XVIIIᵉ siècle*, p. 307.

51. *Spectateur français* (1733), no. 16, cit. E. H. Greene, *Marivaux* (1965), p. 69. For the other references, Greene, pp. 127–8 and Larroumet, *Marivaux* (1882), p. 480.

52. J.-L. Flandrin, 'Contraception, mariage et relations amoureuses dans l'Occident chrétien', *Annales*, 24 (1969), 1390. For controversy about the beginnings of contraception see J. Dupâquier, 'Sur la population française au 17ᵉ et 18ᵉ siècles', *Rev. hist.* 239 (1968), 43 ff; Dupâquier and M. Lachiver, 'Sur les débuts de la contraception en France', *Annales*, 24 (1969); M. Morineau, *Les Faux-semblants d'un démarrage économique; agriculture et démographie en France au 18ᵉ siècle* (*Cahiers des Annales* XXX, 1971); A. Burgière, 'L'ancien régime démographique; un modèle? une stratégie', in *Mélanges en l'honneur de F. Braudel II (Méthodologie de l'histoire et des sciences humaines*, 1973) ed. Burgière *et al.*; Burgière, 'La Démographie', in *Faire de l'histoire* (3 v. 1974) i. 74 ff; and articles by P. Chaunu, Dupâquier, Frêche, etc., in *Sur la population française au XVIIIᵉ et au XIXᵉ siècles: hommage à Marcel Reinhard*, ed. Dupâquier (Soc. démog. hist. 1973). See also Flandrin's *Les Amours paysannes, XVIᵉ—XIXᵉ siècles* (1975).

53. The connection can be shown at Geneva over the whole century (Perrenoud, 'Malthusianisme à Genève', *Annales* (1974), pp. 980–8). Can it be shown that contraception arrives in France in the areas where infant mortality was falling as distinct from others?

54. See my 'Living and Loving: Changing attitudes to sexual relationships in 18-Century France', *British Soc. 18-Century Studies*, 12 (1977), 5–6. I quote a good deal verbatim from this essay here.

55. Did Jansenism help? (A. Burgière, 'De Malthus à Max Weber', *Annales* (1972), p. 1132.)

56. See my 'Living and Loving', p. 4.

57. See the testimony of a *curé* in Dec. 1774 (O. Hufton, *The Poor of 18ᵗʰ-Century France*, pp. 329–30). For family limitation among persecuted Protestants, Lebrun, *La Vie conjugale*. p. 166. Chaunu suggests that contraception among the very poor in the countryside is a sign of backwardness (*La Civilisation de l'Euopre classique* (1970), p. 240). It is hard to see why consideration for women under pressure of starvation is not true affection. We must admit that everything is guesswork—'en matière de contraception, tout reste à l'état d'hypothèse' (G. Frêche, *Toulouse et la région Midi-Pyrénées au siècle des lumières*, p. 90). It has not been possible to find space here to discuss illegitimate births, a subject full of pointers towards an explanation of the rise of contraception. Were the rising figures for illegitimate births caused by ventures into sexual relations relying on *coitus interruptus*, with the inevitable mistakes? Or were young people living together rather than having casual relations? (J. Depauw, 'Amour illégitime et société à Nantes au XVIIIᵉ siècle', *Annales* (1972), pp. 1155–82.) The desire to have fewer children, but to look after them better, may be illustrated, perhaps, by recent works on abandoned infants at the end of the *ancien régime*. There was an increase in their numbers, and some of the families concerned were not poor (Lebrun, *La Vie conjugale*, p. 159). But there is evidence of the increasing regret with which people let their children go (J.-C. Perrot, *Caen*, ii. 1120; J. Bardet, 'Les enfants abandonnés . . . à Rouen dans la seconde moitié du XVIIᵉ siècle', in Dupâquier (ed.), *Sur la population française au XVIIIᵉ et au XIXᵉ siècles: hommage à Marcel Reinhard*, pp. 37–9).

58. R. Mercier, *L'Enfant dans la société française*, pp. 78–94. For the concept of 'Nature', Jean H. Bloch, 'Rousseau's reputation as an authority, on childhood . . . before the Revolution', *Paedagogica Historica*, 14 (1) (1974), 9–33.

59. *Émile*, Bk. I (*Œuvres*, Pléiade, iv. 259).

60. Ph. Ariès, *L'Enfant et la vie familiale sous l'ancien régime*, pp. 16–38. As against Ariès, Snyders argues that the eighteenth rather than the seventeenth century was the decisive epoch (*La Pédagogie*, p. 9).

61. Pillorget, pp. 142, 278.

62. Cit. J. Calvet, *L'Enfant dans la littérature française* (2 v. 1930), i. 49.

63. X. Lannes, pp. 35–8.

64. J. Lough, 'Women in Mercier's *Tableau de Paris*' and D. Fletcher, 'Restif de la Bretonne and Women's Estate', in *Women and Soc.*, pp. 110–21, 98–102.

65. Snyders, pp. 59–60.

66. P. Chanu, *Histoire, science sociale* (1974), pp. 321–2, 329. Also

J. Hajnal, 'European marriage, patterns and perspective', in *Population in History*, ed. D. V. Glas and D. E. C. Eversley (1968), pp. 101–48.

67. Castan, *Honnêteté et relations sociales en Languedoc, 1715–1780*, pp. 176, 199, 243.
68. E. and J. de Goncourt, *La Femme au 18ᵉ siècle*, p. 372.
69. Abensoir, p. 300.
70. P. M. Hall, 'Duclos' *Histoire de Mme de Luz*', in *Women and Soc.*, pp. 139–44.
71. The comte de Luppé, *Les Jeunes Filles à la fin du XVIIIᵉ siècle* (1925), pp. 85–9, 103.
72. One example, the abbess of Ronceray in Angers (McManners, *French Ecclesiastical Society* . . . pp. 90–2).
73. P. Butel, 'Comportements familiaux dans le négoce bordelais au XVIIIᵉ siècle', *Ann. du Midi*, 88 (1976), 144–5.
74. Cit. Abensoir, pp. 162–6.
75. Abensoir, pp. 141–8, 177–80, 196. For the rule of a great lady in her château of La Roche-Guyon, see *Lettres de Turgot à la duchesse d'Enville (1764–74, 1777–80)*, ed. J. Ruwet *et al.*
76. O. Hufton, 'Women and the Family Economy in 18th-Century France', *French Historical Studies*, 9 (1975), 1–21.
77. The rest of this paragraph is quoted from my essay in *British Soc. for 18ᵗʰ-Century Studies*.
78. Mme de Sévigné, *Lettres*, i. 552 (20 May 1672); J. Calvet, i. 49–50; *Journal du duc de Croÿ, 1718–84* (ed. le vicomte de Grouchy and P. Cottin), iv. 281.

Bibliography

A. Eighteenth-century Works

Titles not in the Bibliothèque Nationale have been read in the Bodleian Library at Oxford or in the library of the Jesuit house at Chantilly (noted as 'Bodl.' or 'Chantilly'). Where I had difficulty in tracing a work I have given a shelfmark. Anonymous works are given first.

Anon., *L'Âme matérielle* (c.1730). ed. A. Niderst (1973).

Anon., *La Science de bien mourir enseignée dans trente considérations* (1696; B.Nat. D. 20702).

Anon., *Relation abrégée de la maladie et de la mort du R.P. Pasquier Quesnel* (1719; Bodl. Mason GG 120).

Anon., *Examen des fautes de M. l'abbé de Brion* (1725; B.Nat 17795).

Anon., [By Père Paul de Barry, S. J. ?], *Pensez-y bien, ou réflexions sur les quatre fins dernières* (1737, approbation dated 1721. Orig. ed. 1645; B.Nat. D. 20371).

Anon., *Avis d'une mère à son fils sur la sanctification des fêtes* (1747; B.Nat. D. 13959).

Anon., *Relation de ce qui s'est passé pendant la maladie de Madame la duchesse de Rochechouart* (1752; Bodl. Mason DD. 156).

Anon., *Relation de ce qui s'est passé au sujet du refus de sacremens, fait par le chapitre d'Orléans* (1754; Bodl. Mason DD. 201).

——, *Relation circonstanciée de ce qui s'est passé au sujet du refus des sacremens . . . à M. de Cougnion* (1754; Bodl. Mason DD. 202).

Anon., [By 'M. Dxxx'?], *Voyage pittoresque de Paris* (3rd ed. 1757; B.Nat. 8⁰ Lk⁷ 6018 B).

Anon., *Éloge de l'Enfer: ouvrage critique, historique et moral* (2 v. 1759).

Anon., *Dictionnaire portatif des cas de conscience* (new ed. augmented and corrected, 2 v. Lyon, 1761).

Anon., *Manuel de l'homme du monde ou connoissance générale des principaux états de la société* (1761; B.Nat. Z 20470).

Anon., *Nécessité de penser à la mort, ou instructions chrétiennes pour le tems de la maladie* (Senlis, 1764; Chantilly, A 966).

Anon., *La Vie du très révérend Père Dom Augustin Calmet* (1767).

Anon., *Dictionnaire des gens du monde* (5 v. Paris, 1770; Bodl. Douce S. 692).

Anon., *L'Esprit des journalistes de Trévoux* (2 v. 1771; B.Nat. Z 22913).

Bibliography

Anon., *Dictionnaire historique des cultes religieux* (5 v. 1772; Bodl.).

Anon., *Mandement de Mgr l'évêque d'Alais, qui ordonne des prières publiques pour le repos de l'âme du feu Roi* (1774; Bodl. Mason 11. 125).

Anon., *Avantages des caisses établies en feveur des veuves dans plusieurs gouvernemens, et démonstrations de leurs calculs* (Bruxelles, 1787; B.Nat. Rp. 3831–3860).

Anon., [By Suzanne Curchod, Mme Necker?], *Des inhumations précipitées* (1790; B.Nat. T 54.14).

Académie Royale de Chirurgie (pref. by Girodat), *Recherches critiques et historiques sur . . . les progrès de la chirurgie en France* (Paris, 1744; Bodl. Vet. E.4. d.3).

Actes de l'Église d'Amiens: recueil de tous les documents relatifs à la discipline du diocèse, 811–1849, ed. J.-M. Mioland (2 v. 1849).

Aguesseau le Guerchoix, Marie-Madeleine d', *Pratiques pour se disposer à la mort* (new ed. Avignon, 1777).

[Aignan], *Aux mânes des neuf victimes d'Orléans: chants funèbres* (Orléans, 29 Prairial, An III).

Aignan, E., and Berthevin, J., *La Mort de Louis XVI, tragédie* (1793).

Aïssée, Mlle (= Charlotte-Elisabeth Aïcha), *Lettres de Mlle Aïssée à Mme Calandrini*, ed. A. Piedagnel (1878. Orig. ed. 1787).

Alembert, Jean Le Rond d', *Œuvres complètes* (5 v. 1821).

[Alix], *Les quatre âges de l'homme: poème* (1782; B.Nat. Ye 30857).

Allais, Détournelle, and Vaudryer, *Grands prix d'architecture: projets couronnés par l'Académie d'architecture et l'Institut de France* (1806; B.Nat. V. 145).

Amaury Duval, *Des sépultures*, (An IX, B.Nat. R. 26413).

Andry, C., *Recherches sur la mélancolie: extrait des Registres de la Soc. royale de Médecine, 1782–3* (1785; B.Nat. Td. 86 40).

Antrechaus, the chevalier de, *Relation de la peste dont la ville de Toulon fut affligée en 1721* (Paris, 1756; B.Nat. LK 79687).

Argens, Jean-Baptiste de Boyer, marquis d', *Lettres juives* (6 v. 1738).

——, *Réflexions critiques sur les différentes écoles de peinture* (1752).

——, *Thérèse philosophe* (2 v. 1760).

Argenson, R.-L. de Voyer, marquis de, *Journal et mémoires*, ed. E. J. B. Rathery (9 v. 1859–67).

Arnaud, F.-T.-M. de Baculard d', *Œuvres dramatiques de M. D'Arnaud* (2 v. 1782).

[Astruc, J.], *Dissertation sur l'immatérialité, l'immortalité, et la liberté de l'âme* (1755).

[Aubert de la Chênaye Desbois], *Dictionnaire historique des mœurs, usages et coutumes des François* (3 v. 1767; Bodl.).

Avril, Père d', S. J., *Saints et heureux retours sur soi-mesme* (2 v. 1711).

Bibliography

Bachaumont, Louis Petit de, *Essai sur la peinture, la sculpture et l'architecture* (1751).

——, *Mémoires secrets pour servir à l'histoire de la République des lettres en France* (by Bachaumont, Pidanset de Mairobert, and Mouffle d'Angerville, 36 v. 1779–89).

Barbier, E.-J.-F., *Chronique de la Régence et du règne de Louis XV, 1718–63* (8 v. 1857–8).

Barbotin, the abbé, *Lettres*, ed. A. Aulard (1910).

Barthélemy, the abbé Jean-Jacques, *Voyage du jeune Anacharsis en Grèce* (7 v. 1799. First ed. 4 v. 1788).

[Baudouin de Guemadeuc, maître des requêtes], *L'Espion dévalisé* (1783).

Baudrand, the abbé Barthélemi, S. J., *Œuvres* (Migne, 2 v. 1855).

Beaumont, Élie de, *Discours de réception a l'Académie de Caen* (1762; B.Nat. Z. 28466).

Beausobre, L. de, *Nouvelles considérations sur les années climactériques* (1757, Bodl. 24762 e. 314).

Beccaria, the marquis Cesare, *Traité des délits et des peines* (Lausanne, 1766—French trans. from the 3rd Italian ed.).

Bellefont, Mme de, *Les Œuvres spirituelles de Mme de Bellefont* (1688; B.Nat. D. 17738).

Bentley, Thomas, *Journal of a Visit to Paris (1776)*, ed. Peter France (1977).

Bergier, the abbé Nicolas-Sylvestre, *Œuvres* (8 v. 1855).

——, *Dict. de théologie dogmatique* (8 v. 1788).

[Bernardin de Picquigny, Père], *Pratique efficace pour bien vivre et pour bien mourir* (1701).

Bernardin de Saint-Pierre, J.-H., *Les Harmonies de la Nature*, ed. F. Baridon (Studi di Filogia e di Critica Testuale, 2 v. 1958).

——, *Paul et Virginie*, ed. P. Dubois (1970). ed. Trahard (1959).

Bernis, F.-J. de Pierre, Cardinal de, *Mémoires et lettres de François-Joachim de Pierre, Cardinal de Bernis, 1715–1758*, ed. F. Masson (2 v. 1878).

Berthier, G.-F., and Lausausse, J. B., *La Science de l'oraison mentale . . . suivi de la doctrine spirituelle du Père Berthier* (1791; B.Nat. D. 51776).

Bichat, X., *Recherches physiologiques sur la vie et la mort* (An VIII).

Bienville, M. D. T. de, *Le Pour et le contre de l'inoculation* (Rotterdam, n.d.; B.Nat. Td⁶⁴ 174).

——, *La Nymphomanie, ou l'excès du tempérament chez les femmes* (Bruxelles, n.d. 1777; B.Nat. Td 86.36).

Bion, J.-F., *Recherches sur la nature du feu de l'Enfer par Mr Swinden, traduit de l'Anglais* (Amsterdam, 1728).

Bibliography

Blanchard, the abbé A., *Nouvel essay d'exhortations pour les états dif-férens des malades* (2 v. 1718).

[Boileau, the abbé J.-J.], *Lettres de M. B. . . . sur différens sujets de morale et de piété* (2 v. 1737).

Boileau-Despréaux, N., *Œuvres complètes*, ed. A. Adam (Pléiade, 1966).

Boismont, the abbé N. Thyrel de, *Sermon pour l'assemblée . . . de Charité . . . à l'occasion de l'établissement d'une maison royale de santé* (1783; Bodl.).

Boissier de Sauvages, François, *Dissertation où l'on recherche comment l'air . . . agit sur le corps humain* (1753).

——, *Dissertation dans laquelle on recherche s'il y a des Médicamens qui affectent certaines parties du corps . . . plutôt que d'autres* (1751).

——, *Nosologia methodica* (2 v. 1768).

Bonnet, Ch., *Essai analytique sur les facultés de l'âme* (1760).

——, *Conjectures concerning the Nature of Future Happiness transl. from the French of Mons. Bonnet of Geneva* (York, 1785; Bodl.).

Borderie, A. de la (ed.), *Correspondance historique des Bénédictins Bretons* (1880).

Bossuet, *Œuvres oratoires*, ed. J. Lebarq (5 v. 1921).

——, *Oraisons funèbres*, ed. J. Truchet (1961).

Boswell, *Life of Johnson*, ed. G. B. Hill, revised L. F. Powell (6 v. 1964 ed.).

Boucher d'Argis, *Observations sur les loix criminelles de France* (1781).

Boudier de Villemert, M., *Le Nouvel ami des femmes* (1779; B.Nat. R. 23990).

Boudon, the abbé H.-M., *Œuvres complètes de Boudon*, ed. Migne (3 v. 1856).

Bourdaloue, L., *Exhortations et instructions* (2 v. 1721).

[Boureau-Deslandes, A.-F.], *Réflexions sur les grands hommes qui sont morts en plaisantant* (Amsterdam 1732. First ed. 1712).

Brion, the abbé, *La Vie de la très-sublime contemplative sœur Marie de Sainte Thérèse* (1720).

——, *Lettres spirituelles de la sœur Marie de Sainte, Thérèse* (2 v. 1720).

——, *Traité de la vraie et de la fausse spiritualité* (1728).

——, *Réponse* (to the *Examen des fautes de M. l'abbé de Brion*) (1725; B.Nat. D. 5557111).

Brissot, J.-P., *De la suppression de la peine de mort* (reprinted by A. Brissot, Lille, 1849).

——, *Correspondance et papiers*, ed. Cl. Perroud (1912).

Brydaine (or Bridaine), Père Jacques, *Sermons du Père Brydaine* (5 v. Avignon, 1823).

——, *Instructions sur le mariage* (1827).

Buffon, G.-L. Leclerc, comte de, *De l'homme*, ed. Duchet (1972).

——, *Les Époques de la Nature*, ed. G. Gohau (1973).

Bullet, M., *Réponses critiques à plusieurs difficultés proposées par les nouveaux incrédules sur divers endroits des livres saints* (2 v. 1774).

Cabanis, P.-J.-G., *Journal de la maladie et de la mort de Mirabeau l'aîné* (1791; B.Nat. Lb.³⁹ 4764).

——, *Rapports du physique et du moral de l'homme* (2 v. 1802).

——, *Coup d'œil sur les révolutions et sur la réforme de la médecine* (An XII, 1804).

Calmet, Dom Augustin, *Commentaire littéral sur tous les livres de l'ancien et du nouveau testament* (28 v. 1712–21).

——, *Nouvelles dissertations* (1720).

——, *Dictionnaire historique, critique . . . etc. de la Bible* (6 v. Toulouse, 1783).

——, *Traité sur les apparitions des esprits et sur les vampires* (new ed. 2 v. 1751).

Cambry, *Rapport sur les sépultures* An VII; B.Nat. L⁴K.35)—to the Central Administration of the Department of the Seine.

Campan, Jeanne-Louise-M. Genest de, *Mémoires sur la vie de Marie-Antoinette*, ed. F. Barrière (1886).

Canolle, A.-J., *Les Délices de la solitude* (2nd ed. 2 v., An VII).

Caraccioli, Louis-Antoine de, *Le Tableau de la mort* (1761).

——, *La Grandeur d'âme* (1761).

——, *Dictionnaire critique, pittoresque et sentencieux* (3 v. 1768).

——, *Les Derniers Adieux de la maréchale de *** à ses enfants* (1769).

Castellier, R., *Que penser enfin du supplice de la guillotine?* (An IV).

Caussade, Père J.-P., S. J., *Lettres spirituelles*, ed. M. Olphe-Galliard, S. J. (2 v. 1960).

——, *L'Abandon à la Providence divine*, ed. M. Olphe-Galliard (1966).

——, 'Textes inédits du Père de Caussade', ed. J. Le Brun, in *Rev. d'ascétique et mystique*, 46 (1970).

Cérutti, J.-A.-J., *Les Jardins de Betz, poème . . . fait en 1785* (1792).

——, *Notice mortuaire sur M. de Mirabeau* (n.d.; B.Nat. Lp 39.4799).

Chamfort, Sebastian-Roch-Nicolas, *Œuvres*, ed. P. R. Augis (6 v. 1824–5; reissued by Slatkine, 1968).

Charlevoix, F.-X., S. J., *Histoire de l'île de Saint-Domingue* (2 v. 1730).

——, *Histoire et description générale du Japon* (9 v. 1736).

Charrière, Mme de (= Belle de Zuylen), *Lettres de Belle de Z à Constant d'Hermenches 1760–75*, ed. Ph. Godel (1909).

Chateaubriand, François-René, vicomte de, *Œuvres complètes* (12 v., Garnier, n.d.).

——, *Atala*, ed. F. Letessier (Classiques Garnier, 1958).

——, *Génie du Christianisme*, ed. M. Regard (Pléiade, 1978).

——, *Œuvres romanesques*, ed. M. Regard (1969).

——, *Mémoires d'outre-tombe* (Pléiade, 2 v. 1955).

Chaulieu, the abbé Guillaume Amfrye de, *Œuvres*, ed. M. de Saint Marc (2 v. 1757).

Chénier, André, *Œuvres complètes* (Pléiade, 1940).

Chénier, Mme, *Lettres grecques de Mme Chénier*, ed. R. de Bonnières (1879).

Chertablon, M. de, *La Manière de se bien préparer à la mort* (Anvers, 1700). Orig. ed. 1694.

Chevalier, Claude, *Le Triomphe de la vieillesse, avec les moyens de faire paroitre les vieillards tel qu'ils étoient dans leur jeunesse* (1787).

Chevassu, curé J., *Missionnaire paroissial* (3 v. Lyon, 1753, B.Nat. D. 5239).

Chevrier, F.-A., *Mémoires d'une honnête femme* (1753).

[Chomel, Antoine-Angélique], *Les Nuits parisiennes* (2 v. 1772. First ed. 1769).

——, *Aménités littéraires et recueil d'anecdotes* (2 v. 1773).

Clément, the abbé Denis-Xavier, *Élévations de l'âme à Dieu, ou prières tirées de la Sainte Ecriture* (new ed. 1755, approbation dated 1754).

Clorivière, Pierre de, *Considérations sur l'exercice de la prière et de l'oraison* (1778, publ. 1802, ed. 1961 by A. Rayez).

Collet, P. (prêtre de la Congrégation de la Mission), *Traité des devoirs des gens du monde et surtout des chefs de famille* (1764).

——, *Conversations sur plusieurs sujets de morale propres à former les jeunes demoiselles à la piété* (1769).

——, *Traité historique, dogmatique et pratique des indulgences et du Jubilé* (2 v. 1770).

Condorcet, M.-J.-A.-N. Caritat, marquis de, *Œuvres* (21 v. 1804).

[Coret, Père], *L'Ange conducteur dans la dévotion chrétienne* (Liège, 1746; B.Nat. BS 103).

Cottereau du Coudray, curé J.-B.-A., *Poésies de M. C. curé de la ville de Donnemarie, imprimées par les soins de M. C. . . . neveu de l'auteur* (Paris, 1750; B.Nat. Ye 10302).

Cournand, Antoine de, *Les Styles: poème en quatre chants* (1761).

Crasset, Jean, S. J., *La Douce et la sainte mort* (1708. First ed. 1681).

Cressy, M. de, *Discours sur l'abolition de la peine de mort lu aux Amis de la Vérité (1791); B.Nat. L6⁴⁰ 2351).*

Croÿ, the maréchal duc de, *Journal, 1718–1784*, ed. the vicomte de Grouchy and P. Cottin (4 v. 1906).

[Cubière de Palmezeaux (or Cubières-Palmezeaux = Michel de Cubières)], *La Manie des drames sombres: comédie* (1777; B.Nat. 8oYᵗʰ 1080).

Culant, René-Alexandre, marquis de, *L'Homéide: poème* (1781).

——, *Opinion d'un Mandarin ou discours sur la nature de l'âme* (1784).

——, *Morale enjouée, ou recueil de Fables* (2nd ed. Cologne, 1783).

Daignan, M.-G., *Tableau des variétés de la vie humaine* (2 v. 1788; B.Nat. Tb⁷⁷ 8).

Dandré Bardon, M.-F., *Traité de peinture suivi d'un essai sur la sculpture* (2 v. 1765).

——, *Mausolée de Feu Mgr le Dauphin* (1777; B.Nat. Lk⁷ 9301).

[Daon, Père Roger], *Conduite des âmes dans la voie du salut* (1750).

——, *Conduite des confesseurs dans le tribunal de la pénitence selon les instructions de S. Charles Borromée* (6th ed. 1778. First ed. 1738).

Delamelle, G.-G., *L'Enterrement de ma mère, ou réflexions sur les cérémonies des funérailles* (17–18 Pluviôse, An III; B.Nat. Li¹⁸ 2).

Delandine, Antoine-François, *L'Enfer des peuples anciens, ou histoire des dieux infernaux* (1784).

Delille, J., *Les Jardins, ou l'art d'embellir les paysages* (1782).

——, *Œuvres* (9 v. 1825).

[Delisle de Sales (Jean-Baptiste-Claude Isoard, called)] *Essai sur la Tragédie* (1772).

——, *De la philosophie de la nature* (3 v. 1770).

——, *Essai philosophique sur le corps humain* (3 v. 1773).

Démeunier, Jean-Nicolas, *L'Esprit des usages et des coutumes des différens peuples* (3 v. 1776; B.Nat. G22590).

Denisart, J.-B. (corrected by Camus and Bayard), *Collection de décisions nouvelles et de notions relatives à la jurisprudence* (9 v. 1783. First ed. 1754–6).

[Deny de Verteuil, J.], *Derniers sentiments des plus illustres personnages condamnés à mort* (2 v. 1775).

Deparcieux, A., *Essai sur les probabilités de la durée de la vie humaine* (1746).

Deshoulières, Mme Antoinette du Ligier de la Garde, *Réflexions morales de Mme Deshoulières sur l'envie immodérée qu'on a de faire passer son nom à la postérité* (Paris, 1693).

[Desprez], *Instructions sur les dispositions . . . des sacremens* (1753).

[Destruissart, the abbé Th.], *Essai sur les catacombes de Paris* (1812; B.Nat. Lk⁷ 7750).

Détournelle, C., *Des funérailles* (An IX).

Diderot, D., *Lettres à Sophie Volland*, ed. A. Babelon (2 v. 1948).

——, *Œuvres complètes*, ed. J. Assézat (20 v. 1875–7).

——, *Œuvres complètes*, introd. R. Lewinter, Club français du Livre (15 v. 1969–73).

——, *Œuvres philosophiques*, ed. P. Vernière (Garnier, 1956).

——, *Œuvres romanesques*, ed. H. Bènac (1951).

——, *Œuvres*, ed. A. Billy (Pléiade, 1951).

——, *Œuvres politiques* (1963).

——, *Correspondance*, ed. G. Roth and J. Varloot (16 v. 1955–70).

——, *La Religieuse*, ed. J. Parrish (1963).

——, *Œuvres esthétiques*, ed, Vernière (1968).

——, *Salons, 1767*, ed. J. Seznec and J. Adhémar (4 v. 1957–67).

——, and Falconet, *Le Pour et le contre*, ed. Y. Benot (1958).

——, *Correspondance*, ed. M. Dieckmann and J. Seznec (1959).

[Dinouart, the abbé J.-A.-T.], *Abrégé de l'embryologie sacrée* (1762).

[Dionis, P.], *Dissertation sur la mort subite et sur la catalepsie* (1748; B.Nat. Td⁸⁵ d. 39. First ed. 1718).

Dolivier, Pierre, *Essai sur les funérailles* (An IX).

Drelincourt, Ch., *Les Consolations de l'âme fidèle contre les frayeurs de la mort* (2 v. Berlin, 1760. First ed. 1651).

Drexelius, *Considerations upon Death* (E. T. 1699, from the Latin of the 1630s; Bodl.).

Dubois, the abbé Alexandre, *Journal d'un curé de campagne au XVIIᵉ siècle*, ed. H. Platelle (1965).

Du Bos, the abbé J.-B., *Réflexions critiques sur la poésie et la peinture* (3 v. 1755). First ed. 2 v., 1719).

Du Châtelet, Gabrielle Émilie le Tonnelier de Breteuil, marquise, *Discours sur le Bonheur*, ed. R. Mauzi (1961).

Ducis, Jean-François, *Œuvres* (1839).

Duclos, Ch., *Correspondance*, ed. J. Brengues (1970).

——, *Histoire de Mme de Luz*, ed. J. Brengues (1972).

Du Deffand, M. de Vichy-Chamrond, marquise, *Lettres de la marquise du Deffand à Horace Walpole* (4 v. 1824).

——, *Correspondance complète de la marquise du Deffand*, ed. M. de Lescure (Paris, 1865).

[Dufour de Saint Pathias, J.-M.], *Diogène à Paris* (1787).

[Duguet, J.-J.], *Conduite d'une dame chrétienne pour vivre saintement dans le monde* (1725).

——, *La Croix de N.-S. Jésus Christ ou réflexions sur Jésus Christ crucifié* (1727).

——, *Explication du mystère de la Passion de Notre Seigneur Jésus Christ* (1731).

——, *Le Tombeau de Jésus Christ ou explication du mystère de la sépulture* (1731).

——, *Continuation de l'explication de la Passion de Jésus Christ: ou réflexions sur la sépulture de N.-S.* (new ed. Bruxelles, 1735).

——, *Explication de . . . Deutéronome . . . d'Habacuc et de Jonas* (1734).

——, *Institution d'un Prince* (1739).

Bibliography

——, *Manuel de piété . . . des maximes et des prières pour la réception des Sacremens* (new ed. 1786).

Dulaure, J.-A., *Nouvelle description de Paris* (2 v. 1787).

Dumas, J., *Traité du suicide* (1773).

Dupaty, *Justification de sept hommes condamnés par le Parlement de Metz* (1767).

Du Villard, M., *Plan d'une association de prévoyance* (n.d., 1790; B.Nat. V. 6767).

Emery, J., *Du dogme catholique de l'enfer*, ed. P.-J. Carlé (1842).

Erlach, Rodolphe-Louis d', *Code du bonheur* (7 v. Gèneve, 1788).

Expilly, the abbé J.-J., *Dict. géographique, historique et politique des Gaules et de la France* (6 v. 1762–70).

——, *Tableau de la population de la France* (1780).

[Faignet de Villeneuve, J.], *L'Économie politique: projet pour enrichir et perfectionner l'espèce humaine* (London, 1763; B.Nat. R 20884).

Fauchard, Pierre, *Le Chirurgien dentiste, ou traité des dents* (2 v. 1728, B.Nat. 8⁰ Td¹⁰⁷ 13).

Félice, Fortunato-Bartholomeo de, *Encyclopédie . . . mise en ordre par M. de Félice* (30 v. 1776).

——, *Code de l'humanité, ou la législation universelle, naturelle, civile et politique* (13 v. Yverdon, 1778).

Fénelon, *Œuvres* (10 v. 1848–52).

——, *Correspondance*, ed. J. Orcibal (2 v. 1972).

Ferri, M., *Les Portraits ou caractères et mœurs du XVIIIᵉ siècle* (1781).

Ferrière, C.-J. de, *Dictionnaire de droit et de pratique* (4 v. Paris, 1771).

[Fillassier, Père Marin], *Sentimens Chrétiens propres aux personnes malades et infirmes* (1726; Chantilly A 92⁶. First ed. 1723).

Florian, J.-P. Claris de, *Fables de M. de Florian* (Lille, 1810).

Fontanes, L.-J.-P., marquis de, *Œuvres* (2 v. 1839).

François de Neufchâteau, *Lettre . . . à M . . . Pankouke . . . au sujet de son 'Essai sur la peine de mort'* (1807).

Fréret, N., *Œuvres* (4 v. 1785).

Gaiches, J., *L'Art de la prédication ou maximes sur le ministère de la chaire* (1712).

Gastellier, R., *Que penser enfin du supplice du la guillotine?* (An IV; B.Nat. 8⁰ Tb¹¹ 7).

Gaudron, *Instructions et pratiques pour passer saintement tous les temps de l'année* (2 v. 1763; B.Nat. A92ᵇ).

Gautier, J.-J., *Essai sur les mœurs champêtres*, ed. X. Rousseau (1935. Original publication, 1787).

Genlis, Caroline-Stéphanie-F. Ducrest de Mézières, comtesse de, *Les Veillées du château ou cours de morale à l'usage des enfants* (3 v. 1782).
——, *Mémoires inédits* (2 v. 1825).
Gérard, Sieur de Saint-Amant, Marc-Antoine de, *Œuvres complètes*, ed. C.-L. Livet (2 v. 1855).
Gérard, the abbé L.-P., *Le Comte de Valmont, ou les égaremens de la raison* (3 v. 1776).
Gienet, *Contre les craintes de la mort* (La Haye, 1757; B.Nat. R.32351).
Gilbert, M. E., *Observations sur les écrits de M. de Voltaire* (London, 2 v. 1783).
Gilibert, J.-E., *L'Anarchie médecinale ou la médecine considerée comme nuisible à la société* (3 v. 1772; B.Nat. T21.159).
Girard, J., *Des tombeaux, ou de l'influence des institutions funèbres sur les mœurs* (An IX).
[Girard de Villethierry, the abbé J.], *Le Chrétien étranger sur la terre* (1696).
——, *L'Homme du monde confondu dans le délai de sa conversion* (1700).
——, *Le Chrétien dans la tribulation . . . malade et mourant* (1706).
——, *Des églises et des temples des chrétiens* (1706).
Girardin, R.-L. marquis de, *De la composition des paysages, ou des moyens d'embellir la nature autour des habitations* (1777).
——, *Promenade ou itinéraire des jardins d'Ermenonville* (1788).
Gobinet, Ch., *Instruction de la jeunesse en la piété chrétienne* (new ed. 1719).
——, *Instruction chrétienne des jeunes filles tirée . . . du livre de l'instruction de la jeunesse, fait par M. Gobinet* (1782); Chantilly, A 926).
Griffet, Père Henri, *Exercice de piété pour la communion* (new ed. 1752).
——, *L'Année du chrétien contenant des instructions pour tous les jours de l'année* (new ed. 18 v. Lyon, 1811; Bodl. l.c.377).
Grimm, Frédéric-Melchior, *Correspondance littéraire, philosophique et politique*, ed. M. Tourneux (16 v. 1871–80).
Gros de Besplas, the abbé J.-M.-A. (*vicaire général* of Besançon), *Le Rituel des esprits-forts, ou le tableau des incrédules modernes au lit de la mort* (2nd ed. 1762; B.Nat. D21645).
Grou, Père J.-N., S. J., *A Little Book of the Love of God* (E. T. 1894, French original 1769).
——, *The Hidden Life of the Soul* (E. T. 1870).
——, *The Practical Science of the Cross in the use of the Sacraments of Penitence and the Eucharist* (E. T. n.d.; first ed. in French 1789).
——, *The Spiritual Maxims* (E. T. 1874, original French ed. 1789).
——, *De la paix de l'âme*, ed. A. Rayez, in *Rev. ascétique et mystique*, 45 (1969).
——, *Manual for Interior Souls* (E. T. 1889).

Guyot, P.-J., *Répertoire universel et raisonné de jurisprudence, civile, criminelle, canonique et bénéficiale* (64 v. 1775–83 and 14 v. additionally, 1786).

Hanard, Père Jean, *Les Belles Morts de plusieurs séculiers* (1667).
Hardouin, Père J., S. J., *Paraphrase de l'Ecclésiaste* (1729; Bodl. 8° B494 Linc).
Hardy, S.-P., *Mes loisirs*, ed. M. Tourneaux and M. Vitrac (1912).
Hayer, Père Hubert, *La Spiritualité et l'immortalité de l'âme* (3 v. 1757).
Helvétius, Cl.-A. *De l'esprit*, ed. G. Besse (1959).
Hersan, M.-A., *Pensées édifiantes sur la mort tirées des propres paroles de l'Écriture sainte et des saints pères* (1722).
Holbach, P.-H.-D., baron d', *Système de la Nature* (pirated London ed. 2 v. 1770; Bodl.).
——, *La Politique naturelle* (2 v. 1773).
——, *Le Bon Sens* (1772), ed. J. Deprun (n.d., 1971).
Houdry, Père V., S. J., *La Bibliothèque des prédicateurs* (22 v. Lyon, 1724–43; B.Nat D 8132). The first ed. was 1712–24).
Huber, Marie, *Le Système des anciens et des modernes concilié par l'exposition des sentimens différens de quelques théologiens sur l'état des âmes séparées des corps* (1731 and 1738).

Jacquin, the abbé A.-P., *Les Préjugés* (1760).
Jaubert, the abbé Pierre, *Des causes de la dépopulation et des moyens d'y remédier* (1767).
Joannet, the abbé J.-B.-Cl., *Les Bêtes mieux connues* (2 v. 1770).
——, *De la connaissance de l'homme dans son être et dans ses rapports* (2 v. 1775).
Joly, Joseph-Romain (Capuchin), *Dictionnaire de morale philosophique* (2 v. 1771).
Joubert, J., *Les Carnets de Joseph Joubert*, ed. A. Beaunier (2 v. 1938).
Jousse, M., *Traité de la justice criminelle de France* (4 v. 1771).
Judde, Père Cl., *Œuvres spirituelles*, ed. Le Noir-Duparc (3 v. 1825).

Keranflech, Charles-Hercule de, *L'Âme des bêtes* (Rennes, 1767 bound with *Suite de l'essai sur la raison* (1768, in B.Nat. 11320).

La Baume-Desdossat, the abbé J.-F., *La Christiade, ou le Paradis reconquis, pour servir de suite au Paradis perdu de Milton* (6 v. Bruxelles, 1753).
La Bruyère, *Œuvres*, ed. J. Benda (Pléiade 1951).
Lacretelle, Pierre-Louis, l'aîné, *Discours sur le préjugé des peines infamantes* (1784, Paris. Crowned by the Academy of Metz).

Lafitau, Père, S. J., *Mœurs des sauvages amériquains comparées aux mœurs des premiers temps* (2 v. 1724).

Lafitau, P.-F., bishop of Sisteron, *Avis de direction pour les personnes qui veulent se sauver* (1751).

La Fontaine, Jean de, *Œuvres*, ed. L. Moland (7 v. 1872–6).

Laguerrie, *see* Tesson de la Guéri.

Laliman, P., *Moyens propres à garantir les hommes du suicide* (1779).

[La Mettrie, J.-J. Offray de], *La Politique du médecin de Machiavel ou le chemin de la fortune ouvert aux médecins* (by 'Dr Fum-Ho-Han', Amsterdam, 1746).

——, *Histoire naturelle de l'âme* (1747).

——, *Œuvres philosophiques* (2 v. Berlin, 1764).

Lamourette, the abbé Antoine Adrien, *Les Délices de la religion ou le pouvoir de l'évangile pour nous rendre heureux* (1788).

Landreau de Maine-au-Picq, *Législation philosophique, politique et morale* (3 v. Geneva, 1787).

Languet de Gergy, J.-J., *Traité de la confiance en la miséricorde de Dieu* (3rd ed. Avignon, 1760. First ed. 1715).

Lasne d'Aiguebelle, the chevalier de, *La Religion du cœur* (1768).

——, *Testament spirituel, ou derniers adieux d'un père mourant à ses enfants* (1776).

——, *Sentimens affectueux de l'âme envers Dieu* (new ed. Avignon, 1777).

La Place, P.-A. de, *Recueil d'épitaphes* (3 v. Bruxelles, 1782; B.Nat. Ye 12177).

La Rochefoucauld, François, duc de, *Œuvres* (Pléiade, 1957).

La Rochefoucauld, François de, *Voyages en France*, ed. J. Marchand (1933).

Laugier, P, S. J., *Observations sur l'architecture* (1755).

Lecat, Claude-Nicolas, *Œuvres physiologiques* (2 v. 1767; B.Nat. 8° Tb 54 2. First ed. 1739).

Le Clerc, (Nicolas-Gabriel Clerc), *Histoire naturelle de l'homme considéré dans l'état de la maladie, ou la médecine rappelée à sa première simplicité* (2 v. 1767; B.Nat. Td30 196).

[Lefebvre de Beauvry, Cl.-R. avocat au Parlement de Paris], *Dictionnaire social et patriotique* (1770).

Lefranc de Pompignan, J.-G., *Questions diverses sur l'incrédulité* (1751).

Lelarge de Lignac, J.-A., *Élémens de métaphysique . . . ou Lettres à un matérialiste sur la nature de l'âme* (1753).

[Le Maître de Claville, C.-F.-N.], *Traité du vrai mérite de l'homme* (1734).

Lenglet-Dufresnoy, N., *Recueil de dissertations anciennes et nouvelles sur les apparitions, les visions et les songes* (2 v. 1752).

Le Pelletier, Claude, canon of Reims, *Traité des récompenses et des peines éternelles tirez des livres saints* (1738; B.Nat. D 12671).

LePileur d'Apligny, *Essais historiques sur la morale des anciens et des modernes* (1772; B.Nat. 20447).

Le Prévôt, Pierre-Robert, *Recueil des oraisons funèbres* (1765).

Leprince de Beaumont, Marie, *La Dévotion éclairée, ou magasin des dévotes* (Lyon, 1779; B.Nat. D 41451).

Lesbros de la Versane, Louis, *Caractères des femmes ou aventures du chevalier de Miran* (1769).

——, *Les Soirées d'un honnête homme ou mémoires pour servir à l'histoire du cœur* (1773).

Lezay-Marnésia, Cl.-Fr.-A., *Essai sur la nature champêtre* (1787).

Ligne, Charles-Joseph, prince de, *Coup d'œil sur Belœil et sur une grande partie des jardins de l'Europe* (1781).

——, *Mémoires du prince de Ligne* (ed. A. Lacroix, 1869).

——, *Œuvres choisies* (ed. G. Charlier, 1944).

Loaisel de Tréogate, J.-M., *Dolbreuse, ou l'homme du siècle* (1777).

——, *Ainsi finissent les grandes passions* (2 v. in one, 1778).

——, *La Comtesse d'Alibre ou le cri du sentiment* (1779).

Locke, John, *The Reasonableness of Christianity*, ed. I. A. Ramsey (1958).

Lombez, Père Ambroise, *Œuvres complètes*, ed. F. de Bénéjac (3 v. 1881).

Longeville, Harcouet de, *Histoire des personnes qui ont vécu plusieurs siècles . . . avec le secret du rajeunissement tiré d'Arnauld Villeneuve* (1715; B.Nat. Tc^{11} 158).

[Lottin], *L'Almanach de la vieillesse, ou notice de tous ceux qui ont vécu cent ans et plus* (1761; B.Nat. G 18294-5-6).

[Louis, Dom], *Le Ciel ouvert à tout l'univers* (1782).

Luynes, Charles-Philippe, duc de, *Mémoires sur la cour de Louis XV*, ed . L. Dussieux and E. Soulié (15 v. 1860–5).

[Mabillon, Dom Jean], *La Mort chrétienne sur le modèle de celle de Notre Seigneur Jésus-Christ et de plusieurs saints* (1702).

Mably, G. Bonnet de, *Œuvres complètes* (12 v. London, 1789).

Maine de Biran, *Journal intime*, ed. A. de la Valette-Monbrun (2 v. 1927).

Malebranche, Père Nicolas, *Recherche de la vérité*, ed. G. Lewis (2 v. 1946).

Mangin, the abbé, *Science des confesseurs* (1752).

Marais, Mathieu, *Journal et mémoires*, ed. M. de Lescure (4 v. 1863).

Marat, J.-P., *Plan de législation criminelle* (1790, written 1779; ed. D. Hamiche, 1974).

Maret, H., *Mémoire sur l'usage où l'on est d'enterrer les morts dans les églises et dans l'enceinte des villes* (1773).

Marin, F.-L.-Cl., *Histoire de Saladin, sulthan d'Égypte et de Syrie* (2 v. 1758).

Marivaux, Pierre Carlet de Chamblain de, *Romans*, ed. M. Arland (Pléiade, 1949).

——, *Journaux et œuvres diverses*, ed. F. Deloffre and M. Gilot (1969).

Marmontel, J.-F., *Contes moraux* (3 v. 1765).

——, *Essai sur les romans considérés du côté moral* (1778).

Marquis-Ducastel, curé (autobiography), *Vie de M. Marquis-Ducastel, curé de Sainte-Suzanne*, ed. F. Pichon (1873).

Marteille, Jean, *The Memoirs of a Protestant condemned to the galleys of France for his Religion* (Eng. trans. by Oliver Goldsmith, 1758; ed. A. Dobson, 2 v. 1895).

Maupertuis, P.-L. Moreau de, *Essai de philosophie morale* (1750).

Meister, J.-H., *Lettres sur la vieillesse* (1810).

Mémoires de Trévoux (*Mémoires pour l'histoire des sciences et des beaux-arts*) (265 v. 1701–67).

Menestrier. C.-F., S. J., *Des décorations funèbres* (1684).

Mercier, L.-S., *Tableau de Paris. Nouvelle édition, corrigée et augmentée* (Amsterdam, 12 v. 1782–8. First ed. 1781).

Merlet, M., *Lettre sur la Désertion* (1770).

Messance, *Recherches sur la population des généralités d'Auvergne, de Lyon, de Rouen et de quelques provinces et villes . . .* (1768).

——, *Nouvelles recherches sur la population de la France* (1788).

Métra, L.-F., (et al.), *Correspondance secrète, politique et littéraire* (18 v. 1781–90).

Miaczynski, la veuve, *Essai de l'influence des mœurs du premier âge sur la longévité* (1803).

Milley, Père, corresp. ed. J. Bremond, *Le Courant mystique au XVIIIe siècle: l'abandon dans les lettres du P. Milley*, (1943).

Millot, J.-A., *L'Art d'améliorer et de perfectionner les hommes* (2 v. 1801).

Mirabaud, J.-B., *Nouvelles libertés de penser* (1743).

Mirabeau, G.-H. comte de, *Œuvres* (9 v. 1827).

'Moheau', *Recherches et considérations sur la population de la France* (2 v. 1778).

Moléon (= Le Brun des Marettes, Père J.-B.), *Voyages liturgiques de France, ou Recherches faites en diverses villes . . .* (1718; B.Nat. Rés. B. 4519 bis).

Montaigne, M. E. de, *Essais*, ed. P. Villey (3 v. 1922).

——, *Essais* (Pléiade, 1950).

Montesquieu, Ch. L. de Secondat, baron de, *Œuvres* (Pléiade, 2 v. 1949).

——, *Œuvres complètes* (ed. A. Masson, 3 v. 1950–5).

——, *Œuvres* (Pléiade. 2 v. 1949–51).

Montfaucon, B de, *L'Antiquité expliquée et représentée* (9 v. 1719).
Moreau, J.-N., *Mes souvenirs par J.-N. M., historiographe de France*, ed. C. Hamelin (2 v. 1898–1901).
[Morel, Dom R.], *Entretiens spirituels en forme de prières, pour servir de préparation à la mort* (new ed. 1730. First ed. 1728).
——, *Traité de l'espérance chrétienne* (1732).
[Moulin, Pierre du], *Lettres de consolation faites par MM. du Moulin . . . et plusieurs autres pasteurs* (1632; B.Nat.Z. 14317).
——, *Traité de la paix de l'âme et du contentement de l'esprit* (La Haye, 1695; B.Nat. 15103).
[Mulot, the abbé F.-V.], *Le Rêve du pauvre moine* (1789; B.Nat. Lb³⁹ 6991).
——, *Discours sur cette question: Quelles sont les cérémonies à faire pour les funérailles, et le règlement à adopter pour le lieu de la sépulture?* (An IX).
Muyart de Vouglans, P.-F., *Les Loix criminelles de France dans leur ordre naturel* (1780) (contains *Réfutation du Traité des délits et peines. Lettre à Monsieur XX* (1767).)

Navier, P.-T., *Sur les dangers des exhumations précipitées et sur les abus des inhumations dans les églises* (1775).
Nepveu, Père F., S. J., *La Manière de se préparer à la mort pendant la vie* (1713. First ed. 1697).
Nepveu de la Manoulière, R. P., *Mémoires* (ed. G. Esnault, 3 v. 1877–9).
Nicolas, Augustin, *Si la torture est un moyen seur à vérifier les crimes secrets* (Amsterdam, 1681).
Noé, Marc-Antoine de, Bishop of Lescar, *Œuvres* (1816).
[Nonnotte, Cl.], *Anti-Dictionnaire philosophique* (4th ed. 2 v. Avignon, 1785; Bodl.).
——, *Les Erreurs de Voltaire* (3rd ed. Lyon, 2 v. 1767).

Olivier, *Sépultures des anciens, où l'on démontre qu'elles étoient hors des villes* (1771).

[Panckoucke, H.], *La Mort de Caton: tragédie* (1768).
Para du Phanjas, the abbé François, *Les Principes de la saine philosophie conciliés avec ceux de la religion* (2 v. 1774).
Partz de Pressy, Mgr. F.-J., bishop of Boulogne, *Œuvres très complètes* (Migne, 2 v. 1842).
[Pernety, Dom], *Observations sur les maladies de l'âme* (Berlin, 1777; B.Nat. R13386).
Perreau, M., *Sur l'abolition de la peine de mort* (n.d.; B.Nat. Fp2695).

Picart, Bernard, *Cérémonies et coutumes religieuses de tous les peuples du monde* (9 v. Amsterdam, 1723–43). Tomes I and II are in two parts, making 11 vols. in all. The illustrations are by Picart. Bodl.).

Piganiol de la Force, J.-A., *Description de Paris, de Versailles, etc.* (new ed. 8 v. 1742).

Piles, Roger de, *Cours de peinture par principes* (1708).

Pinto, M. J. de, *Précis des arguments contre les matérialistes* (1774).

Piny, Dom Alexandre, *La Clef du pur amour* (1680, ed. P. Noël, n.d., 1918?).

——, *État du pur amour ou conduite pour arriver à la perfection par le seul 'fiat' dit et réitéré en toutes sortes d'occasion* (1682, ed. P. Noël, n.d., 1921?).

——, *Le plus parfait, ou des voyes intérieures la plus glorifiante pour Dieu, et la plus sanctifiante pour l'âme* (Paris 1691. First ed. 1682).

Piron, A., *Lettres de Piron*, ed. E. Lavaquary (1920).

Pluche, the abbé N., *Histoire du ciel considéré selon les idées des poètes, des philosophes et de Moïse* (2 v. 1739).

Poire, Père François, S. J., *La Sauvegarde des mourants, ou Marie patronne de la bonne mort* (1861. First publ. in 18th century).

Poiret, the abbé J.-L.-M., *Voyage en Barbarie, ou lettres écrites de l'ancienne Numidie* (1789).

Poiret, Pierre, *L'Œconomie de la providence universelle pour le salut de tous les hommes* (7 v. 1682).

Pommereul, F.-R.-J., *Mémoire sur les funérailles et les sépultures. Question . . . jugée par l'Institut* (An IX).

Porée, the abbé Ch.-G., *Lettres sur la sépulture dans les églises* (Caen, 1745).

Préfontaine, P.-A., *Discours sur la vénération due aux tombeaux* (An. IX; B.Nat. 8° YE pièce 5386–5465).

Prévost, the abbé Antoine-François, *Mémoires pour servir à l'histoire de Malte* (2 v. 1741).

——, *Œuvres choisies* (39 v. 1810). *Mémoires et aventures d'un homme de qualité* in Vol. I.

——, *Le Pour et contre* (5 v. 1734).

——, *The Dean of Coleraine* (E. T. 3 v. London, 1742; Bodl.).

——, *Le Philosophe anglais ou histoire de M. Cleveland* (8 v. 1744. First ed. 1731).

Quesnel, Pasquier, *Le Bonheur de la mort chrétienne* (Paris, 1688).

Rancé, the abbé de, *Relation de la vie et de la mort de quelques religieux de l'abbaye de la Trappe* (5 v. 1755). Has additions not figuring in the 1678 edition.

Bibliography

Rapin, Père, *La Vie des prédestinez dans la bienheureuse éternité* (1684).
Raunié, E., *Épitaphier du vieux Paris* (5 v. 1890–).
Restif de la Bretonne, N.-E., *Œuvres*, ed. M. Bachelin (9 v. 1930–2).
——, *Les Nuits de Paris*, ed. M. Bachelin (n.d. First ed. 1788–94).
Richeprey, J.-F.-H. de, *Journal des voyages en Haute-Guienne*, ed. H. Guilhamon, *Archives historiques du Rouergue*, 19 (1952).
Robert, *De l'influence de la Révolution française sur la population* (2 v. 1802, An XI; B.Nat. L³¹ 47).
Roissard, Père Nicolas, *La Consolation du chrétien* (2 v. 1775; B.Nat. D 1931–7).
Roland, (Marie-Jeanne Philipon Mme), *Lettres*, N. S. ed. Cl. Perroud (2 v. 1913–15).
——, *Mémoires*, ed. Perroud (2 v. 1905).
Rose, J.-B., *Traité élémentaire de morale* (1767; B.Nat. R. 18589–90).
Rousseau, J.-J., *Religious Writings*, ed. R. Grimsley (1970).
——, *Correspondance complète*, ed. R. A. Leigh (34 v. 1965–79, continuing).
——, *Œuvres*, ed. B. Gagnebin and M. Raymond (4 v. Pléiade, 1966–1969).
Rousseaud de la Combe, Guy de, *Traité des matières criminelles* (2 v. 1751).
[Routh, B.-R., S. J.], *Recherches sur la manière d'inhumer des anciens à l'occasion des tombeaux de Civaux* (Poitiers, 1738; B.Nat. J 1725).

Sabatier, A.-H. (called Sabatier de Cavaillon), *Poème sur la bataille de Lutzelberg* (1758; Bodl. 4°Σ 237).
Sabran, Mme la comtesse de, *Correspondance inédite de la comtesse de Sabran et du chevalier de Boufflers, 1778–88*, ed. E. de Magnieu and H. Prat (1875).
Sade, D.-A.-F., marquis de, *Dialogue entre un prêtre et un moribond* (1782, publ. 1795, ed. M. Heine, 1926).
Sainte-Marthe, Claude de, *Considérations chrétiennes sur la mort* (4th ed. 1713).
Sainte-Palaye, La Curne de, *Mémoires sur l'ancienne chevalerié* (2 v. 1759).
Saint-Fonds, *Correspondance littéraire et anecdotique entre M. de Saint Fonds et le président Dugas, 1711–39*, ed. W. Poidebad (2 v. Lyon, 1900).
Saint François de Sales, *Traité de l'amour de Dieu, Œuvres* (Pléiade, 1969).
Saint-Lambert, J.-F., marquis de, *Œuvres* (2 v. 1822).
Saint-Simon, Louis de Rouvroy, duc de, *Mémoires* (21 v. 1829).
Sarramon, A., ed., *Les Paroisses du diocèse de Comminges en 1786* (1968).

Sauri, the abbé Sauri, docteur en médecine, *Physique du corps humain, ou physiologie moderne* (2 v. Paris, 1778; B.Nat. Z 59759).

Ségur, L.-Ph., comte de, *Mémoires* (3 v. Stuttgart, 1829).

[Seigneaux de Correvou], *Essai sur l'abus . . . de la torture dans la procédure criminelle* (Lausanne, 1768).

Senancour, E. Pivert de, *Oberman*, ed. Monglond (1947).

Serpillon, F., *Code criminel, ou commentaire sur l'ordonnance de 1670* (4 v. Lyon, 1767).

Servan, M.-J.-A., *Discours sur l'administration de la justice criminelle* (1767).

——, *Discours sur le progrès des connoissances humaines . . . de la morale et de la législation en particulier* (1781).

Sévigné, Mme de, *Lettres* (3 v. Pléiade, 1963).

Sevoy, Père François-Hyacinthe, *Devoirs ecclésiastiques* (3 v. 1770).

Sinner, J.-R., *Essai sur les dogmes de la métempsychose et du purgatoire enseignés par les Bramines de l'Indostan* (2 v. Berne, 1771).

Sinsart, Dom B., *Défense du dogme catholique de l'éternité des peines* (1748).

——, *Recueil des pensées diverses sur l'immatérialité de l'âme* (1761).

Stendhal, *Mémoires d'un touriste*, ed. Y. Gandon (2 v. 1927).

Suard, J.-B.-A., *Correspondance littéraire de Suard*, ed. G. Bonno (Univ. California Publ. Mod. Philol. XVIII, 1934).

Sue, J.-J., *Recherches physiologiques et expériences sur la vitalité et le Galvanisme* (3rd ed. 1803; B.Nat. 8° Tb[11] 9).

Swinden, Tobias, translated by J.-F. Bion, *Recherches sur la nature du feu de l'Enfer . . . traduit de l'Anglais* (1728).

Tallement des Réaux, *Les Historiettes de T. des R.*, ed. MM. de Momergué and Paulin (5 v. 1862).

Tencin, Claude-Alexandrine Guérin, marquise de, *Mémoires du comte de Comminges* (1735).

Terrasson, the abbé Jean, *Séthos* (3 v. 1731).

Tesson de la Guérie, Jean, *Les Amours de Lucile et de Doligny* (2 v. 1769). Title-page 'par M. de Laguerrie').

Thiers, J.-B., curé, *Dissertation sur la clôture des chœurs des églises* (1688).

——, *Traité des superstitions qui regardent tous les sacremens* (3 v. 1704. First ed. 1696).

——, *Superstitions anciennes et nouvelles* (2 v. 1733).

——, *Critique de l'histoire des Flagellans (1703) et justification de l'usage des disciplines volontaires* (n.d.).

Thiéry, François (médecin), *La Vie de l'homme respectée et défendue dans ses derniers momens* (1787; Bodl.).

Thiroux d'Arconville, Marie-Geneviève-Charlotte Darlus, dame, *Mélanges de littérature, de morale et de physique* (7 v. 1775).

Thomas, Antoine-Léonard, *Œuvres de M. Thomas* (new ed. Amsterdam, 4 v. 1773).

——, *Œuvres* (5 v. 1822–3).

Thomassin, *Mémoire sur l'abus de l'ensevelissement des morts, par M. Durande, précédé de réflexions sur le danger des inhumations précipitées* (Strasbourg, 1789; B.Nat. Tc 54 12).

Tilly, Alexandre, comte de, *Mémoires*, ed. C. Melchior Bonnet (1965).

Tissot, S.-A.-A. D., *Traité de l'épilepsie*, tom. 3 of *Traité des nerfs et de leurs maladies* (1770. B.Nat. 8° Td⁸⁵ 78).

——, *L'Onanisme, ou dissertation physique sur les maladies produites par la masturbation* (1760).

Tourzel, Mme la duchesse de, *Mémoires, 1789–1795*, ed. the duc des Cars (2 v. 1883).

Toussaint, F.-V., *Les Mœurs* (1748).

——, *Éclaircissements sur les 'Mœurs'* (1762).

[Tribolet, Père Bernard], *Réflexions sur Jésus-Christ mourant pour se préparer . . . à une mort chrétienne* (1729).

Tronson, L., *Corresp.*, ed. L. Bertrand (3 v. 1904).

Troya d'Assigny, L., *La Fin du chrétien, ou traité . . . sur le petit nombre des élus* (3 v. 1751).

Turgot, *Correspondance inédite de Condorcet et de Turgot*, ed. Cl. Henry (1883).

——, *Lettres de Turgot à la duchesse d'Enville, 1764–74 et 1777–80*, ed. J. Ruwet *et al.* (Trav. Fac. Philos. Lettres Univ. Cath. Louvain, Histoire I, 1976).

Vasselin, G.-V., *Théorie des peines capitales ou abus et danger de la peine de mort et des tourmens* (1790).

[Vauge, Père G.], *Traité de l'espérance chrétienne* (1732 ed.; B.Nat. D 54087).

Vert, Dom Claude de, *Explication des cérémonies de l'Église* (2nd ed. 4 v. 1709).

[Verteuil, J. Deny, abbé de], *Derniers sentimens des plus illustres personnages condamnés à mort* (2 v. 1775; B.Nat. G 22629).

Vicq-d'Azyr, F., *Œuvres* (6 v. 1805).

Volney (= Chassebœuf, C.-F.), *Les Ruines, ou méditations sur les révolutions des empires* (1791).

Voltaire, *Œuvres complètes*, ed. Moland (52 v. 1877–85).

——, *Notebooks*, ed. Th. Besterman (2 v. 1952).

——, *Dictionnaire philosophique* (ed. R. Naves, 1967).

Bibliography

——, *Correspondence*, ed. Th. Besterman (101 v. Geneva, 1953–65). Except where otherwise stated, references are to this first edition.

——, *Correspondence*, new augmented ed. by Besterman (135 v. Paris, 1963–77).

Watelet, Claude-Henri, *L'Art de peindre, poème avec des réflexions* (1761).

——, *Essai sur les jardins* (1764).

——, *Dictionnaire des arts de peinture, sculpture et gravure* (5 v. 1792; B.Nat. 12 Θ 286).

Yart, curé Antoine, *La Poésie angloise* (2 v. 1749).

Yvan, V.-P.-A., *La Trompette du ciel qui réveille les pécheurs (recueilli par V. P. A. Yvan)* (Caen, 1711).

B. Secondary Works

(excluding articles and reference works)

Abensoir, L., *La Femme et le féminisme avant la Révolution* (1923).

Ackerknecht, E. H., *Medicine at the Paris Hospital, 1794–1848* (1967).

Agulhon, M., *La Sociabilité méridionale. Confréries et associations dans la vie collective en Provence orientale à la fin du XVIIIe siècle* (2 v. 1966).

Ariès, P., *L'Homme devant la mort* (1977).

——, *L'Enfant et la vie familiale sous l'ancien régime* (1960).

Armengaud, A., *La Famille et l'enfant en France et en Angleterre du 16e au 18e siècle: aspects démographiques* (1979).

Armigon, G., *Banquiers des pauvres* (n.d.).

Aubry, G., *La Jurisprudence criminelle du Châtelet de Paris sous le règne de Louis XVI* (1971).

Augustine, St., *The City of God*, trans. J. Healey, ed. R. V. G. Tasker (2 v. 1962).

Auzelle, R., *Dernières demeures: conception . . . du cimetière contemporain* (1965).

Aveline, C., *Les Mots de la fin* (1957).

Azais, *Bridaine et ses missions* (1882).

Babeau, A., *Les Artisans et domestiques d'autrefois* (1886).

——, *La Vie militaire sous l'ancien régime* (2 v. 1890).

Baehrel, R., *Une croissance: la Basse-Provence rurale* (1961).

Baloche, *L'Église Saint-Merry de Paris* (1911).

Baratier, R. (ed.), *Histoire de la Provence* (1969).

Bardet, J.-P., Chaunu, P. and Gouesse, J. M., *Histoire de la Normandie* (1970).

Bellet, R., Tetu, J.-F., *et al.*, *La Femme au XIXe siècle: littérature et idéologie* (Presses Universitaires de Lyon, 1979).

Bergues, H., Ariès, P., *et al.*, *La Prévention des naissances dans la famille: ses origines dans les temps modernes* (I. N. E. D.,) *Cahier* 35, 1960).

Bernard, A., *Le Sermon au XVIIIe siècle, 1715–89* (1901).

Bernier, P.-D., *Essai sur le tiers état rural ou les paysans de Basse-Normandie au XVIIIe siècle* (1891).

Bien, D., *The Calas Affair: Persecution, Toleration and Heresy in 18th-Century Toulouse* (1960).

Bila, *La Croyance à la magie au XVIIIe siècle en France dans les contes, romans et traités* (1925).

Billard, M., *Les Tombeaux des rois sous la Terreur* (1905).

Biraben, J.-N., *Les Hommes et la peste en France et dans les pays européens et méditerranéens* (2 v. 1975).

Birley, R., *Sunk without Trace* (1962).

Bloch, C., *L'Assistance et l'État en France à la veille de la Révolution* (1908).

Blond, L., *La Maison professe des Jésuites de la rue Saint-Antoine à Paris* (1965).

Bluche, F., *Les Magistrats du Parlement de Paris au 18e siècle* (1960).

Boguel, A., *La Faculté de Médecine de l'Université d'Angers, 1433–1792* (1951).

Bois, P. (ed.), *Histoire de Nantes* (1977).

Boisguilbert, Pierre de, various works published by the Institut Nat. d'Etudes Démographiques as *Pierre de Boisguilbert ou la naissance de l'économie politique* (2 v. 1960).

Bollême, Geneviève, *Les Almanachs populaires aux XVIIe et XVIIIe siècles* (1969).

Bongert, Y., Abbiateci, A., Billacois, F., *et al.*, *Crimes et criminalité en France au 17e–18e siècles* (*Cahiers des Annales*, XXXIII, 1971).

Boros, Ladislas, *The Moment of Truth: Mysterium Mortis* (1965).

Bouchard, Georges, *Prieur de la Côte d'Or* (1946).

——, *La Famille du conventionnel Basire* (1952).

Bouchard, Gérard, *Le Village immobile: Sennely-en-Sologne au XVIIIe siècle* (1972).

Bouchary, J., *Les Compagnies financières à Paris à la fin du XVIIIe siècle* (3 v. 1940).

Bourde de la Rogerie, M., *Le Parlement de Bretagne, l'évêque de Rennes et les ifs plantés dans les cimetières, 1636–7* (1931).

Bouteiller, M., *Médecine populaire d'hier et aujourd'hui* (1966).

Bouvet, M. and Bourdon, P.-M., *A Travers la Normandie, XVIIe et XVIIIe siècles* (*Cahiers des Annales de Normandie*, 1968).

Bowman, F., *Le Christ romantique* (1973).

Bibliography

Boyrea, J., *Le Village en France au 18ᵉ siècle* (1955).

Boysse, E., *Le Théâtre des Jésuites* (1880).

Bremond, H., *Histoire littéraire du sentiment religieux en France depuis la fin des guerres de religion jusqu'à nos jours* (11 v. 1916–32).

Brengues, J., *Duclos* (1971).

Brenner, C. D., *L'Histoire nationale dans la tragédie française au XVIIIᵉ siècle* (Univ. California Publ. Mod. Phil. 14(3), 1929).

Bromberg, W., *Man above Humanity:a History of Psycho-Therapy* (1954).

Brongniart, M., *La Paroisse Saint-Médard* (1951).

Brookner, Anita, *Greuze* (1972).

——, *Jacques-Louis David: a personal interpretation* (1974).

Brunel, L., *Les Philosophes et l'Académie française au 18ᵉ siècle* (1884).

Bullock, A. (ed.), *Faces of Europe* (1980).

Burgière, A., et al., *Mélanges en l'honneur de F. Braudel II (Méthodologie de l'histoire et des sciences humaines)* (1973).

Bury, J. B., *The Idea of Progress* (1955).

Busson, H., *La Pensée religieuse française de Charron à Pascal* (1933).

——, *La Religion des classiques, 1660–88* (1948).

Cabantous, A., and Messiaen, J., *Gens de mer à Dunkerque aux XVIIᵉ et XVIIIᵉ siècles* (1977).

Calvet, J., *L'Enfant dans la littérature française* (2 v. 1930).

Candel, J., *Les Prédicateurs français dans la première moitié du XVIIIᵉ siècle* (1904).

Carré, H., *La Noblesse de France et l'opinion publique au XVIIIᵉ siècle* (1920).

Carrière, Ch., Courdurié, M., and Rebuffat, F., *Marseille, ville mort: la peste de 1720* (1968).

Castan, Y., *Honnêteté et relations sociales en Languedoc, 1715–80* (1974).

Cauzons, Th. de, *La Magie et la sorcellerie en France* (3 v. 1861).

Champroux, S., *Le Vrai Moyen de vivre longtemps* (1885).

Chassaigne, M., *Le Procès du chevalier de la Barre* (1920).

Chaunu, P., *La Civilisation de l'Europe classique* (1970).

——, *Histoire, science sociale* (1974).

——, *La Mort à Paris; 16ᵉ, 17ᵉ et 18ᵉ siècles* (1978).

Chauvet, P., *La Lutte contre une épidémie au 18ᵉ siècle: la peste du Gévaudan, 1720–3* (Thèse méd. Paris, 1939).

Chérel, A., *Fénelon au XVIIIᵉ siècle, 1715–1820* (1917).

Chevallier, A., *L'Hôtel-Dieu de Paris et les sœurs augustines, 1650–1810* (1901).

Chevallier, P., *Loménie de Brienne et l'ordre monastique, 1766–89* (2 v. 1959–60).

——, *Les Ducs sous l'acacia, ou les premiers pas de la franc-maçonnerie française 1725–43* (1964).

Chomel, V. (ed.), *Histoire de Grenoble* (1974).

Clarkson, L., *Death, Disease, Famine in pre-industrial England* (1975).

Cobb, R., *Terreur et subsistances, 1793–95* (1964).

——, *Les Armées révolutionnaires: instrument de la Terreur dans les départements* (2 v. 1961–3).

——, *Death in Paris 1795–1801* (1978).

Cognet, L., *Le Crépuscle des mystiques* (1958).

Coirault, A. G. Y., *L'Optique de Saint-Simon* (1965).

Collas, G., *La Vieillesse douloureuse de Mme de Chateaubriand* (2 v. 1961).

Conlon, P.-M., *Jean-François Bion* (1966).

Corlieu, A., *La Mort des rois de France* (1873).

Corvisier, A., *L'Armée française de la fin du XVIIᵉ siècle au ministère de Choiseul: le soldat* (2 v. 1964).

Courdurié, M., *La Dette des collectivités publiques de Marseille au XVIIIᵉ siècle: du débat sur le prêt à intérêt au financement par l'emprunt* (1975).

Crocker, L. G., *Diderot's Chaotic Order* (1974).

——, *An Age of Crisis. Man and World in Eighteenth-Century French Thought* (1959).

Crubellier, M., *Histoire de la Champagne* (1975).

Cullmann, O., *Immortality of the Soul or Resurrection from the Dead?* (1958).

Cushing, M. G., *Pierre Le Tourneur* (1907).

Damilaville, E., *Voltaire à Paris* (1876).

Darnton, R., *Mesmerism and the End of the Enlightenment in France* (1968).

Dauvergne, R., *Les Résidences du maréchal de Croÿ, 1718–84* (1950).

Degert, A., *Histoire des évêques de Dax* (1903).

Delage, A., *Histoire de la thèse du doctorat en médecine d'après les thèses soutenues devant la Faculté de Médecine de Paris* (1913).

Delahante, A., *Une famille de finance au XVIIIᵉ siècle* (2 v. 1881).

Delaunay, P., *Le Monde médical parisien au 18ᵉ siècle* (2nd ed. 1906).

——, *La Vie médicale au XVIᵉ, XVIIᵉ et XVIIIᵉ siècles* (1935).

Delormeau, Ch., *Le Cimetière protestant de Montpellier* (1963).

Delumeau, J., *Le Catholicisme entre Luther et Voltaire* (1971).

——, *La Mort des pays de Cocagne: comportement collectif de la Renaissance à l'âge classique* (1976).

Desjardins, A., *Les Cahiers des États généraux en 1789 et la législation criminelle* (1883).

Desnoiresterres, G., *Voltaire et la société française au XVIIIᵉ siècle* (2nd ed. 8 v. 1867–76).

Desnos, E., *L'Histoire de l'Urologie*, in J. T. Murphy, *The History of Urology* (1972).

Dessens, A., *Les Revendications des droits de la femme . . . pendant la Révolution française* (*Thèse*, Toulouse, 1905).

Deyon, P., *Le Temps des prisons: essai sur l'histoire de la délinquence et les origines du système pénitentiaire* (1975).

Dollinger, Ph. (ed.), *Histoire de l'Alsace* (1970).

Dommanget, M., *Le Curé Meslier* (1965).

Donat, J., *Une communauté rurale à la fin de l'ancien régime* (1926).

Dornic, F., *Histoire du Mans* (1975).

Dowd, D. L., *Pageant-Master of the Republic. Jacques-Louis David and the French Revolution* (1948).

Doyle, W., *The Parlement of Bordeaux at the end of the Old Régime, 1771–90* (1976).

Dreano, M., *La Renommée de Montaigne en France au XVIIIᵉ siècle* (1952).

Dreyer-Roos, S., *La Population strasbourgeoise sous l'ancien régime* (1969).

Dufour, V., *Les Charniers des églises de Paris* (1884).

Dufresne, A.-S.-C.-M., *Notes sur la vie et des œuvres de Vicq d'Azyr, 1748–94* (*Thèse*, Bordeaux, 1906).

Dupâquier, J., *Statistiques démographiques du bassin parisien, 1630–1720* (1977).

——, (ed.), *Hommage à Marcel Reinhard: sur la population française au XVIIIᵉ et au XIXᵉ siècles* (Soc. de démog. hist., 1973), contributions by Armengaud etc.

Dupic, A., *Antoine Dubois, chirurgien et accoucheur* (*Thèse méd.* Paris, 1907).

Durand, A., *État religieux des trois diocèses de Nîmes, d'Uzès et d'Alais à la fin de l'ancien régime* (1909).

Durand, A., *Une paroisse mayennaise: Fougerolles sous la Révolution, 1789–1800* (1960).

Durand, Y., *Les Fermiers généraux au XVIIIᵉ siècle* (1971).

Égret, J., *Le Parlement de Dauphiné et les affaires publiques dans la deuxième moitié du XVIIIᵉ siècle* (2 v. 1941).

Ehrard, J., *L'Idée de Nature en France dans la première moitié du XVIIIᵉ siècle* (2 v. 1963).

Fairchilds, C. C., *Poverty and Charity in Aix-en-Provence, 1640–1789* (1976).

Farge, A., *Le Vol des aliments à Paris au XVIIIe siècle* (1973).

Favre, R., *La Mort dans la littérature et la pensée françaises au siècle des lumières* (1979). The thesis version (Ateliers reprographiques de l'Université de Lille III, 1978), is in 2 vols. and has fuller references. When a volume number is given I am quoting this earlier version.

Feipel, M. (ed.), Mandelbaum, D. G. *et al.*, *The Meaning of Death* (1959).

Fellows, O. E., and Milliken, S. F., *Buffon* (1972).

Ferté, J., *La Vie religieuse dans les campagnes parisiennes, 1622–1695* (1962).

Firth, Raymond, *Elements of Social Organization* (1951).

Flandrin, J.-L., *Famille, parenté, maison, sexualité dans l'ancienne société* (1976).

——, *Les Amours paysannes, XVIe-XIXe siècles* (1975).

Florkin, M., *Médecine et médecins au Pays de Liège* (1954).

——, *Un prince, deux préfets et le mouvement scientifique et médico-social au Pays de Liège, 1771–1830* (1957).

Forster, R., *The House of Saulx-Tavannes* (1971).

Fossy, P., *Les Catacombes de Paris* (1862).

Foster, W. D., *A History of Medical Bacteriology and Immunology* (1970).

Foucault, M., *Naissance de la clinique* (1972).

——, *Surveiller et punir: naissance de la prison* (1975).

——, *Folie et déraison: histoire de la folie à l'âge classique* (1961, new ed. 1972).

Francière, G., *Théophile de Bordeu (1722–1776)* (*Thèse méd.* Toulouse, 1907).

Franklin, A., *La Vie privée d'autrefois*:

——, *La Cuisine* (1888)

——, *L'Hygiène* (1890).

——, *Les Médicaments* (1891)

——, *Les Médecins* (1892).

Frêche, G., *Toulouse et la région Midi-Pyrénées au siècle des lumières* (1974).

Fulton, R. (ed.), Borkenau *et al.*, *Death and Identity* (1965).

Furcy-Raymond, Marc, *Inventaire des sculptures exécutées au XVIIIe siècle pour la direction des bâtiments du Roi* (1927).

Furet, F. (ed.), Brancolini, J., and Bouyssy, Marie-Thérèse, *et al.*, *Livre et société dans la France du XVIIIe siècle* (2 v. 1970).

Gabillot, *Hubert Robert et son temps* (1895).

Gaiffe, F., *Le Drame en France au XVIIIe siècle* (1910).

Gagnière, S., *Les Cimetières d'Avignon au XVIIIe et XIXe siècles* (1948).

Ganay, E. de, *Les Jardins de France et leur décor* (1949).

Gannal, *Les Cimetières depuis la fondation de la monarchie française jusqu'à nos jours* (1884).

Garden, M., *Lyon et les Lyonnais au XVIIIe siècle* (1970).

Gauchet, G., *Le Thème de la mort dans les romans de Bernanos* (1953).

Génévrier, J., *La Vie et les œuvres de Nicolas Chambon de Montaux, 1748–1826 (Thèse méd.* Paris, 1906).

van Gennep, A., *Manual of Folklore* (1943).

——, *Manuel de folklore français contemporain* (4 v. 1946).

Gille, B., *Les Sources statistiques de l'histoire de France: des enquêtes du XVIIIe siècle à 1870* (1964).

Gillet, J., *Le Paradis perdu dans la littérature française de Voltaire à Chateaubriand* (1975).

Girault de Coursac, P., *L'Éducation d'un Roi. Louis XVI* (1972).

Glas, D. V., and Eversley, D. E. C., *Population in History* (1968).

Glasser, R., trans. from German by C. G. Pearson, *Time in French Life and Thought* (1972).

Goncourt, E. and J. de, *La Femme au 18e siècle* (1862).

——, *La Du Barry* (1880).

Gorce, D., *Le Grand Siècle devant la mort* (1950).

Gordon, L. S., *et al.*, *Au siècle des lumières* (S. E. V. P. E. N., 1970).

Goré, J.-L., *La Notion d'indifférence chez Fénelon et ses sources* (1956).

——, *L'Itinéraire de Fénelon: humanisme et spiritualité* (1957).

Goubert, P., *Beauvais et le Beauvaisis de 1600 à 1730* (2 v. 1960).

——, Chaunu, P., Meyer, J., Desaive, J.-P., Le Roy Ladurie, E., *et al.*, *Médecins, climat et épidémies à la fin du XVIIIe siècle* (1972).

Goulard, R., *Une lignée d'exécuteurs des jugements criminels: les Sanson (1688–1847)* (1968).

Goulemot, J.-M., Launay, M., Eude, M., Andrews, R., Dautry, J., *et al.*, *Gilbert Romme et son temps* (Inst. d'Études du Massif Central, Fac. Lettres, Sci. hum., Univ. Clermont-Ferrand, 1966).

Gousset, Mgr, *Lettre de Mgr Gousset, archevêque de Reims, sur la communion des condamnés à mort* (Reims, 1841).

Granel, F., *Pages médico-historiques montpelliéraines* (1964).

Grange, H., *Les Idées de Necker* (1974).

Grannis, Valleria Belt, *Dramatic Parody in 18th-Century France* (1931).

Grar, E., *Histoire de la recherche et de l'exploitation de la houille dans le Hainault français, dans la Flandre française et dans l'Artois, 1716–1791* (3 v. 1847–50).

Greene, E. H., *Marivaux* (1965).

Grimsley, R., *D'Alembert* (1963).

——, *Rousseau and the Religious Quest* (1968).

Groethuysen, B., *Origines de l'esprit bourgeois en France: l'Église et la bourgeoisie* (1927). E. T. 1968 as *The Bourgeois: Catholicism versus Capitalism in Eighteenth-Century France.*

Grudet, V. R., *The Royal Provincial Intendants: a governing élite in 18th-Century France* (1968).

Gruman, C. J., 'A History of ideas about the Prolongation of Life: the Evolution of the Prolongevity Hypothesis to 1800', *Trans. American Philosophical Soc.* 56 (1966).

Gueranger, Dom, *Institutions liturgiques* (3 v. 1851).

Guerber, J., S. J., *Le Ralliement du clergé français à la morale Liguorienne: l'abbé Gousset et ses précurseurs, 1785–1832* (Analecta Gregoriana, 193, 1973).

Guerry, L., *Le Thème du 'Triomphe de la mort' dans la peinture italienne* (1950).

Guibert, L., *Les Confréries de Pénitents en France et notamment dans le diocèse de Limoges* (1879).

Guillois, A., *Pendant la Terreur, le poète Roucher, 1745–94* (1890).

Guitton, E., *Jacques Delille, 1731–1813, et la poésie de la nature* (1976).

Guomar, M., *Principes d'une esthétique de la mort* (1967).

Gutton, J.-P., *La Société et les pauvres: l'exemple de la généralité de Lyon, 1534–1789* (1971).

Hampson, N., *The Life and Opinions of Maximilien Robespierre* (1974).

Harrisse, E., *L'abbé Prévost, histoire de sa vie et de ses œuvres* (1896).

Hastings, Hester, *Man and Beast in French Thought of the 18th Century* (1936).

D'Haussonville, O.-B.-P.-G. de Cléron, comte, *Le Salon de Mme Necker* (2 v. 1882).

Hay, D. *et al.*, *Albion's Fatal Tree: Crime and Society in 18th-Century England* (1975).

Hepp, E., Bourguin, M.-H., *et al.*, *Aspects de la contrebande au XVIIIe siècle* (Fac. Droit Sc. écon. Paris, 1969).

Higounet, Ch. (ed.), *Histoire de l'Aquitaine* (1971).

——, (ed.), *Histoire de l'Aquitaine: Documents* (1973).

Hillairet, J., *Gibets, piloris et cachots du vieux Paris* (1956).

——, *Les 200 cimetières du vieux Paris* (1958).

Hoffmann, P., *La Femme dans la pensée des lumières* (1978).

Huard, P., and Grmek, M. D., *Science, médecine, pharmacie, de la Révolution à l'Empire, 1789–1815* (1970).

Hufton, Olwen H., *The Poor of Eighteenth-Century France, 1750–1789* (1974).

Hughes, J. P., ed., *Health Care for Remote Areas* (Kaiser Foundation, 1972).

Huillet d'Istria, Madeleine, *Le Père de Caussade et la querelle du pur amour* (1964).
Hunt, David, *Parents and Children in History* (1970).

Imbert, J., *Le Droit hospitalier de la Révolution et de l'Empire* (1954).
——, *La Peine de mort: histoire-actualité* (1967).
——, (ed.), Vidal-Hennequin, D., *et al.*, *Quelques procès criminels des XVIIe et XVIIIe siècles* (1964).
Ingersoll-Smousse, F., *La Sculpture funéraire en France au XVIIIe siècle* (1912).

Joppin, G., *Fénelon et la mystique du pur amour* (1938).
Jordanova, L. J., and Porter, R., *Images of the Earth* (1979).

Kaplan, S. L., *Bread, Politics and Political Economy in the Reign of Louis XV* (2 v. 1976).
Kaufmann, E., 'Three Revolutionary Architects: Boullée, Ledoux, Lequeu', *Trans. American Philos. Soc.* (1952).
——, *Architecture in the Age of Reason* (2nd ed. 1968).
Kerby, L. W. M., *The Life of Nicolas-Germain Léonard* (1925).
Krestovsky, L., *Le Problème spirituel de la beauté et de la laideur.* (1948).

Labande, E.-R. (ed.), *Histoire du Poitou, du Limousin et des pays Charentais* (1976).
Labrousse, C.-E., *Esquisse du mouvement des prix et des revenus en France au XVIIIe siècle* (1932).
Lachiver, M., *Histoire de Meulan et de sa région par les textes* (1967).
——, *La Population de Meulan de XVIIe au XXe siècle* (1969).
Laffay, E., *Le Poète Gilbert* (1898).
Lafu, P., *Le Prêtre ancien et les commencements du nouveau prêtre* (1967).
Lagrave, H., *Le Théâtre et le public à Paris de 1715 à 1750* (1972).
Lallemand, *Un chapitre de l'histoire des Enfants trouvés: la Maison de la Couche à Paris (17e et 18e siècles)* (1885).
Lancaster, H. Carrington, *Sunset, a History of Parisian Drama in the last years of Louis XIV* (1941).
Landry, A., Conan, J., *et al.*, *François Quesnay et la Physiocratie* (2 v. I. N. E. D. 1958).
Langlois, Ch., *Le Diocèse de Vannes au XIXe siècle, 1800–30* (1974).
Larroumet, *Marivaux* (1882).
Laurès, E., *La Municipalité de Béziers à la fin de l'ancien régime* (1926).
Lavaquery, E., *Le Cardinal de Boisgelin, 1732– 1804* (2 v. 1920).

Lavisse, E. (ed.), *Histoire de France* . . . *jusqu'à la Révolution* (9 v. 1902–10).

Le Bras, G., *Introduction à l'histoire de la pratique religieuse en France* (2 v. 1942).

Le Braz, A., *La Légende de la mort en Basse-Bretagne* (1883).

Le Breton, A., *La 'Comédie humaine' de Saint-Simon* (1914).

Lebrun, F., *Les Hommes et la mort en Anjou aux 17ᵉ et 18ᵉ siècles* (1971).

——, *La Vie conjugale sous l'ancien régime* (1975).

——, *Histoire d'Angers* (1975).

Lecercle, J.-L., Sgard, J., et al., *Approches des lumières: mélanges offerts à Jean Fabre* (1974).

Lecroq, Dom E., *Les Annonciades de Fécamp (1648–1792)* (1947).

Leflon, J., *Eugène de Mazenod, évêque de Marseille, 1757–1801* (3 v. 1957–65).

Le Gall, Béatrice, *L'Imagination chez Senancour* (1966).

Legrand, M.-A., *La Longévité à travers les âges* (1911).

Leith, J. A., *The Idea of Art as Propaganda in France, 1750–99* (1965).

Le Maître, M.-A., *Recherches sur les procédés chirurgicaux de l'école bordelaise* (1905).

Lenotre, G., *La Guillotine et les exécuteurs des arrêts criminels pendant la Révolution* (1927).

Léonard, E.-G., *Mon village sous Louis XV* (1941).

Lequay, E., *Étude historique de l'Ordre de la Charité de Saint-Jean de Dieu et de ses établissements en France* (1854).

Leroy Ladurie, E., *Les Paysans de Languedoc* (1966).

Lescure, M. de, *Les Maîtresses du Régent* (1861).

Levron, J., *Le Diable dans l'art* (1935).

Locquin, J., *La Peinture d'histoire en France de 1747 à 1785* (1912).

Longi, Olga, *La Terre et les morts dans l'œuvre de Chateaubriand* (Johns Hopkins Studies in Romance Literature and Languages, XXIII, 1934).

Lorédan, J., *La Grande Misère et les voleurs au XVIIIᵉ siècle: Marion du Faouët* (1933).

Lottin, A., *La Désunion du couple sous l'ancien régime: l'exemple du Nord* (1975).

Louw, G. van de, *Baculard d'Arnaud* (1972).

Loux, F., and Richard, P., *Sagesse du corps: la santé et la maladie dans les proverbes français* (1978).

Lovejoy, A. O., *The Great Chain of Being* (1936).

Lumière, M., *Le Théâtre français pendant le Révolution* (n.d.).

Luppé, Le comte de, *Les Jeunes Filles à la fin du XVIIIᵉ siècle* (1925).

Lüthy, H., *La Banque protestante en France* (2 v. 1959–61).

Macary, J., *Masque et lumières au XVIIIᵉ siècle: André-François Deslandes, citoyen et philosophe (1689–1757)* (1975).

McDermott, W., 'Infection and Malnutrition' in *Health Care for Remote Areas*, ed. J. P. Hughes (Kaiser Foundation, 1972).

McManners, J., 'France' in A. Goodwin (ed.), *The European Nobility in the 18th Century* (1967 ed.).

——, *French Ecclesiastical Society at the end of the ancien régime: a study of Angers in the Eighteenth Century* (1960).

——, *The French Revolution and the Church* (1969); Harper Torchbooks 1970).

——, *The Social Contract and Rousseau's Revolt against Society* (lecture, University of Leicester Press, 1968).

——, *Church and State in France, 1870–1914* (1972).

——, *Reflections at the Death Bed of Voltaire* (lecture, Clarendon Press, 1975).

Macquarrie, J., *Principles of Christian Theology* (2nd ed. 1977).

Maestro, M., *Voltaire and Beccaria as Reformers of Criminal Law* (1942).

——, *Cesare Beccaria and the Origins of Penal Reform* (1973).

Malley, C. P. O., 'Medical History of Louis XIV', in J. C. Rule (ed.), *Louis XIV and the Craft of Kingship* (1969).

Malraux, A., *La Voie royale* (1930).

Mandrou, R., *De la culture populaire au 17ᵉ et 18ᵉ siècles* (1964).

——, *Magistrats et sorciers au XVIIᵉ siècle* (1968).

Mann, A.-G. (ed.), *Histoire de l'Auvergne* (1974).

Manny, A.-G., *Histoire de Clermont-Ferrand* (1975).

Marion, H., *Dictionnaire des institutions de la France au XVIIᵉ et XVIIIᵉ siècles* (2 v. 1923).

Martial Levé, Mgr, *Louis-François-Gabriel d'Orléans de la Motte, évêque d'Amiens, 1683–1774* (1962).

Massé, P., *Varennes et ses maîtres, 1779–1842* (1956).

Mathorez, J., *Les Étrangers en France sous l'ancien régime* (2 v. 1919).

Maugras, G., *Lauzun and the Court of Marie-Antoinette* (E. T. 1896).

Mauzi, R., *L'Idée du bonheur dans la littérature et la pensée françaises au XVIIIᵉ siècle* (1960).

May, G., *De J.-J. Rousseau à Mme Roland* (1964).

Meerloo, A. M., *Suicide* (1962).

Meiss, M., *Painting in Florence and Vienna after the Black Death* (1951).

Mellor, A., *La Torture, son histoire, son abolition; sa réapparition au XXᵉ siècle* (1961).

Mercier, Raoul, *Le Monde médical de Touraine sous la Révolution* (1936).

Mercier, Robert, *La Réhabilitation de la nature humaine, 1700–1750* (1960).

——, *L'Enfant dans la société française* (1961).

Bibliography

Metzger, R. A., *Marie Huber: sa vie, ses œuvres, sa théologie* (Geneva, 1887).

Mevel, M., *Chirurgiens dijonnais au XVIIIe siècle* (1902).

Meyer, J., *La Noblesse bretonne au XVIIIe siècle* (2 v. 1966).

——, *Histoire de Rennes* (1972).

——, *et al.*, *Médecins, climat et épidémies à la fin du XVIIIe siècle* (1972).

Milner, M., *Le Diable dans la littérature française 1772–1861* (2 v. 1960).

Mollet, M. (ed.), *Histoire de l'Île de France et de Paris* (1971).

Mols, R., *Introduction sommaire à la démographie historique des villes de l'Europe du XIVe au XVIIIe siècle* (2 v. 1954).

Monglond, A., *Le Préromantisme français* (2 v. 1930; new ed., 2 v. 1965).

Morazé, C., *La France bourgeoise* (1940).

Morin, J., *L'Homme et la mort dans l'histoire* (1952).

Morineau, M., *Les Faux-semblants d'un démarrage économique; agriculture et démographie en France au 18e siècle* (*Cahiers des Annales*, XXX, 1971).

Mornet, D., *Le Sentiment de la Nature en France de J.-J. Rousseau à Bernardin de Saint-Pierre* (1907).

——, *Vies préromantiques* (1925).

——, *Les Origines intellectuelles de la Révolution française, 1715–87* (1954).

Murphy, J. T., *The History of Urology* (1972).

Naville, P., *D'Holbach et la philosophie scientifique au XVIIIe siècle* (2nd ed. 1967).

Neale, R. E., *The Art of Dying* (1941).

Nicholson, Majorie Hope, *Mountain Gloom and Mountain Glory, the development of the aesthetics of the Infinite* (1959).

Niderst, A., *Fontenelle à la recherche de lui-même, 1657–1702* (1972).

Nolhac, P. de, *Marie-Antoinette Dauphine* (1947).

Ostrogorski, M., *La Femme au point de vue du droit public* (1893).

Ozouf, Mona, *La Fête révolutionnaire, 1789–1799* (1976).

Palmer, R. R., *Catholics and Unbelievers in 18th-Century France* (1939).

Palou, J., *La Sorcellerie* (1957).

Panofsky, E., *et al.*, *Philosophy and History: Essays presented to E. Cassirer* (1963).

Parguez, J., *La Bulle Unigenitus et le Jansénisme politique* (1936).

Pariset, F. G. (ed.), *Bordeaux au XVIIIe siècle* (1968, being v. 5 of the *Hist. de Bordeaux*, directed by Ch. Higounet).

Parisse, M. (ed.), *Histoire de la Lorraine* (1978).

Paul-Albert, N., *Histoire du cimetière du Père la Chaise* (1937).

Payne, H. C., *The Philosophes and the People* (1976).

Pelletier, V., *Essai historique et critique sur les billets d'enterrement orléanais* (1861).

Pensa, H., *Sorcellerie et religion au XVIIᵉ et XVIIIᵉ siècles* (1933).

Perkins, Jean A., *The Concept of Self in the French Enlightenment* (1969).

Peronnet, M. C., *Les Évêques de l'ancienne France* (2 v. 1977).

Pérouas, L., *Le Diocèse de la Rochelle de 1648 à 1724: sociologie et pastorale* (1964).

Peter, J. P., 'Disease and the Sick at the end of the 18th Century', in Forster, R., and Ranum, O. (eds.), *Biology of Man in History* (1967).

Petit, C., *Les Cimetières de Saint-Dizier* (1937).

Pieper, J., *Death and Immortality*, trans. R. S. C. Winston (1965).

Pillorget, R., *La Tige et le rameau: familles anglaise et française, 16ᵉ–18ᵉ siècle* (1979).

Pingaud, L., *Les Saulx Tavannes* (1876).

Playoust-Chaussis, A., *La Vie religieuse dans le diocèse de Boulogne au XVIIIᵉ siècle (1725–1790)* (1976).

Plongeron, B., *Conscience religieuse en révolution: regards sur l'historiographie religieuse de la Révolution française* (1969).

——, *Théologie et politique au siècle des lumières, 1770–1820* (1973).

Poignant, Simone, *L'Abbaye de Fontevrault et les filles de Louis XV* (1966).

Poitrineau, A., *La Vie rurale en Basse-Auvergne au XVIIIᵉ siècle* (1969).

Pomeau, R., *La Religion de Voltaire* (1956).

Potez, *L'Élégie en France* (1898).

Purrat, P., *La Spiritualité chrétienne* (4 v. 1918–28).

Pra, J., *Les Jésuites à Grenoble, 1587–1763* (1901).

Prigent, R., Lannes, X., *et al.*, *Renouveau des idées sur la famille* (I. N. E. D., *Cahier* 18, 1934).

Proust, J., *Diderot et l'Encyclopédie* (1962).

——, (ed.), Fletcher, M., *et al.*, *Recherches nouvelles sur quelques écrivains des lumières* (1972).

Rabb, T. K., and Rotberg, R. T. (eds.), *The Family and History: an Interdisciplinary Enquiry* (1973).

Rather, L. J., *Mind and Body in 18th-Century Medicine: a study based on Jerome Gaub's 'De regimine mentis'* (1965).

Rawson, Elizabeth, *The Spartan Tradition in European Thought* (1969).

Rayez, A. (ed.), *Dict. de spiritualité, ascétique et mystique* (Vol. I, 1932, ed. M. Viller, continuing).

——, *Formes modernes de vie consacrée: Adélaïde de Cicé et P. de Clorivière* (1966).

Raymond, M., *Fénelon* (1967).

Razzell, P., *Edward Jenner's Cowpox Vaccine: the history of a Medical Myth* (1977).

Regnault, E., *Christophe de Beaumont, archevêque de Paris, 1763–81* (2 v. 1882).

Reinhard, M. and A. Armengaud, *Hist. générale de la population mondiale* (1961).

Rétat, P. (ed.), *L'Attentat de Damiens: discours sur l'événement au XVIIIe siècle* (1979).

——, (ed.), *Presse et histoire au XVIIIe siècle: l'année 1734* (1978).

Ribbe, Ch. de, *La Vie domestique: ses modèles et ses règles d'après les documents originaux* (2 v. 1877).

Ridgeway, R. S., *Voltaire and Sensibility* (1973).

Riguez, A., *Le Docteur Marat, 1743–83: son système physiologique* (*Thèse*, Paris, 1908).

Rivollet, C., *Adrienne Lecouvreur* (1925).

Robert, Ch., *Urbain de Hercé* (1900).

Roger, J., *Les Sciences de la vie dans la pensée française du XVIIIe siècle* (1971).

Rosen, G., *From Medical Police to Social Medicine* (1974).

Rosenau, H. (ed.), *Boullée's Treatise on Architecture* (1953).

Rosenberg, C. E. (ed.), *The Family in History* (1975).

Rosenberg, P., and Butor, N., 'La Mort de Germanicus' de Poussin, Catalogue (1973; B.Nat. V.8905(7)).

Rosenblum, R., *Transformations in late 18th-Century Art* (1967).

Rosenfeld, L. C., *From Beast-Machine to Man-Machine. Animal Soul in French Letters from Descartes to La Mettrie* (2nd ed. 1968).

Rosso, J. G. *Montesquieu et la féminité* (1977).

Rousseau, J.-J.-R., Comité National pour la Commémoration de J.-J.R., *Jean-Jacques Rousseau et son œuvre: problèmes et recherches* (1964).

Rowell, G., *The Liturgy Of Christian Burial* (Alcuin Club, 1977).

Royer, , *Voltaire malade: étude historique et médicale* (1883).

Sabatier, R., *Dictionnaire de la mort* (1967).

Sage, P., *Le Bon Prêtre dans la littérature française d'Amadis de Gaule au Génie du Christianisme* (1951).

Sareil, J., *Les Tencin: histoire d'une famille au dix-huitième siècle* (1969).

Savey-Casard, P., *La Peine de mort* (1968).

Schaer, A., *Le Clergé paroissial catholique en haute Alsace sous l'ancien régime, 1648–1789* (1960).

Schmitt, T. J., *L'Assistance dans l'archidiaconé d'Autun au XVIIe et XVIIIe siècles* (1952).

Bibliography

Schmitt, T. J., *L'Organisation ecclésiastique et la pratique religieuse dans l'archidiaconé d'Autun de 1650 à 1750* (1957).

Scott Smith, D., 'A homeostatic Demographic Régime', in Lee, R. Demos (ed.), *Population Patterns in the Past* (1977).

Seznec, J., *Essais sur Diderot et l'antiquité* (1957).

——, (ed.), Tisch, J. H., *et al.*, *Studies in 18th-Century Literature* (1974).

Shackleton, R., *Montesquieu* (1961).

Shryock, R. M., *A History of Nursing* (1959).

Sicard, A., *L'Ancien Clergé de France: les évêques avant la Révolution* (5th ed. 1912).

Singer, Ch., and Underwood, E. A., *A Short History of Medicine* (1962).

S'Jacob, Henriette, *Idealism and Realism: a Study of Sepulchral Symbolism* (1954).

Smith, D. W., *Helvétius: a Study in Persecution* (1965).

Snyders, G., *La Pédagogie en France aux XVIIe et XVIIIe siècles* (1965).

Souchal, F., *Les Slodtz, sculpteurs et décorateurs du Roi, 1685–1764* (1975).

Soulat, J.-F., and Laffa, J.-B., *Histoire de Tarbes* (1975).

Spacks, P. M., *The Insistence of Horror: Aspects of the Supernatural in 18th-Century Poetry* (1962).

Spengler, J. J., *Économie et Population: les doctrines françaises avant 1800* (1964).

Spink, J., *Essays in Honour of*, ed. E. Jacobs *et al*, *Women and Society in 18th-Century France* (1979).

Sprott, S. E., *The English Debate on Suicide from Donne to Hume* (1961).

Stannard, D. E., *The Puritan Way of Death: a Study in Religion, Culture and Social Change* (1979).

Starobinski, J., *L'Invention de la liberté, 1700–89* (1964).

Stavary, M. A., *Jacques Pierre Alexandre, comte de Tilly* (1965).

Stearns, P. N., *Old Age in European Society: the case of France* (1977).

Stewart, P., *Le Masque et la parole: le langage de l'amour au 18e siècle* (1973).

Stone, L., *The Family, Sex and Marriage in England, 1500–1800* (1977).

Suadeau, R., *L'Évêque inspecteur administratif sous la monarchie absolue* (2 v. 1940).

Sudnow, D., *Passing On: the Social Organization of Dying* (1967).

Sumeire, G.-J., *La Communauté de Trets à la veille de la Révolution* (1960).

Taton, R. (ed.), *L'Enseignement et la diffusion des sciences en France au XVIIIe siècle* (1964).

Tedeschi, P., *Saint-Aubin et son œuvre* (1968).

Temkin, O., *The Falling Sickness: a history of Epilepsy* (1945).

——, *Galenism: rise and decline of a Medical Philosophy* (1973).

Terisse, M., *La Population de Marseille, 1654–1830* (3 v. 1971).

Testud, P., *Rétif de la Bretonne et la création littéraire* (1977).

Thibaut-Payen, Jacqueline, *Les Morts, l'Église, et l'État dans le ressort du parlement de Paris au XVIIe et XVIIIe siècles* (1977).

Thomas, W., *Le Poète Edward Young* (1901).

Thompson, J. D. and Goldin, G., *The Hospital: a Social and Architectural History* (1975).

Tournier, Cl., *Le chanoine Maurice Garrigou, 1766–1852* (1945).

Toutain, J.-C., *Histoire quantitative de l'économie française*, I (ed. J. Marczewski, 3 v. I. S. E. A., 1961–3).

Trahard, P., *La Sensibilité révolutionnaire, 1789–1794* (1936).

Trousson, R., *Socrate devant Voltaire, Diderot et Rousseau* (1967).

Truchet, J., *La Prédication de Bossuet* (2 v. 1960).

——, *La Politique de Bossuet* (1960).

Tuot, J., *Le 'Plan Social' de Jean-Claude Chappuis: une utopie socialiste au XVIIIe siècle (Thèse, Paris, 1942).*

University of St. Thomas, Houston, *Visionary Architects: Boullée, Ledoux, Lequeu* (Catalogue, 1968).

Vallery-Radot, M., *Un administrateur ecclésiastique à la fin de l'ancien régime: le cardinal de Luynes, archevêque de Sens, 1753–88* (1966).

Valmary, P., *Familles paysannes au XVIIIe siècle en Bas-Quercy* (I. N. E. D. Cahier 45, 1965).

Vartanian, A., *La Mettrie's 'L'Homme Machine': a Study of the Origins of an Idea* (1960).

Veber, J., 'Malades et maladies à Lille, 1750–89' (typewritten thesis, Lille, 1971).

Veith, I., *Hysteria: the history of a Disease* (1965).

Vernière, P., *Spinoza et la pensée française avant la Révolution* (1954).

Versini, L., *Laclos et la tradition: essai sur les sources et la technique des 'Liaisons Dangereuses'* (1968).

Vial, F., *Une philosophie et une morale du sentiment: Luc de Clapiers, marquis de Vauvenargues* (1938).

Viallaneix, P. (ed.), *Le Préromantisme, hypothèque où hypothèse* (1975). Contains R. Mortier, 'Sensibilité neo-classique où préromantique?'

Viaud, J., *La Peine de mort en matière politique* (1902).

Villain, J., *Le Recouvrement des impôts directs sous l'ancien régime* (1932).

Vimont, M., *Histoire de l'église et de la paroisse Saint-Léo-Saint-Gilles à Paris* (1932).

Vivier, R. 'André Chénier, Rousseau et Foscolo', *Mélanges d'histoire et de littérature offerts à Henri Mauvette* (1934).

Vovelle, M., *Piété baroque et déchristianisation en Provence au XVIII* *siècle* (1973).

——, *Mourir autrefois: attitudes collectives devant la mort au XVII* *et XVIII* *siècles* (1974).

——, *Religion et Révolution: la déchristianisation de l'an II* (1976).

Wade, I. O., *The Intellectual Development of Voltaire* (1973).

Walker, P. D., *The Decline of Hell: 17th-Century Discussions of Eternal Torment* (1964).

Wallon, M., *Histoire du Tribunal révolutionnaire* (6 v. 1880–2).

Walzer, M., and Rothstein, M., *Regicide and Revolution: Speeches at the Trial of Louis XVI* (1974).

Wicker, C. V., *Edward Young and the Fear of Death: a Study of Romantic Melancholy* (1952).

Willard, N., *Le Génie et la folie au 18* *siècle* (1963).

Williams, C. G., *Literature and History in the Age of Ideas: Essays presented to George R. Havens* (1975).

Zink, A., *Azereix: la vie d'une communauté rurale à la fin du XVIII* *siècle* (1969).

Index of Places

Abbeville, 17
Africa, 50, 416, 419
Aix-en-Provence, 31, 44, 90, 99, 403, 405
Albi, 96
Alençon, 373
Alfort, 52
Algiers, 46
Alsace, 30, 91
Ambrum, 100
America, 41, 110, 118, 295, 296, 365, 391
Amiens, 223, 261, 282, 290
Angers, 26, 85, 90, 259, 271, 274, 290, 312, 313, 385, 410
Anjou, 8, 14, 20, 71, 89
Antilles, 351
Apt, 100
Arabia, 110
Arles, 17
Artois, 222
Auch, 91, 92, 255
Australia, 406
Auteuil, 300
Autun, 383
Auvergne, 18, 23, 91, 93, 99, 110, 222, 371, 461
Auxerre, 37, 93, 110, 261
Avignon, 45, 70, 232, 233, 315, 447
Azereix, 75

Barbary Coast, 297
Bâle, 50
Baltic, 46
Bas Quercy, 72
Basse-Auvergne, 73
Bavaria, 64
Bayeux, 228
Beaune-en-Gâtinais, 315
Betz, 346
Béziers, 31

Bois-de-Boulogne, 346
Bonfas, 45
Bordeaux, 11, 42, 69, 76, 92, 205, 300, 377, 441
Boulogne, 9, 142, 282, 332
Bourbonne-les-Bains, 33
Bourges, 111
Bourgogne, 371, 446
Breslau, 102
Brest, 7, 27
Brioude, 45
Brittany, 9, 12, 20, 26, 61, 89, 97, 222, 242, 273, 309, 446

Caen, 18, 41, 78, 85, 279, 306, 312, 371, 372, 387, 389, 407
Cahors, 386
Calais, 312, 381
California, 346
Camargue, 90
Cernon, 280
Cévennes, 102
Châlons-sur-Marne, 310
Charleville, 90
Chartres, 289
Châteaudun, 48
Château-Gontier, 409
China, 47, 116, 295, 296, 331, 345, 346
Civaux, 295
Cologne, 243
Condom (Diocese), 100
Congo, 419
Cotentin, 21
Corréjac, 45
Crulai (Normandy), 10, 71, 73

Dauphiné, 30, 112, 232, 371
Dijon, 7, 21, 93, 310, 371, 372, 387, 397
Dole, 92
Dunkirk, 315

605

Egypt, 298, 330, 333, 360
Embrum, 217
England, 22, 94, 95, 99, 177, 294, 300,
    319, 330, 331, 336, 345, 359, 399,
    429, 432, 434
Elne, 46
Ermenonville, 349, 350, 422
Ethiopia, 419

Ferrière (near Plantis), 232
Flanders, 12, 68, 222, 252, 405, 406
Fontainebleau, 277
Fontenoy, 390
Formosa, 419
Fougerolles, 282
Franche-Comté, 27, 222
France, central, 446
    south of, 272, 465

Gascony, 51
Geneva, 69, 102, 132
Germany, 94, 103
Gévaudan, 45
Great Britain, 98
Greece, 117, 297, 298, 307, 327, 328,
    352, 379, 426
Grenoble, 112, 371, 372
Guyenne, 30, 222

Hainault, 243
Halle, 50
Hanover, 113
Herculaneum, 328
Holland, 94, 177

Île de France, 93
India, 239, 296
Indies, 109

Japan, 459

La Flèche, 27
Langres, 93, 344
Languedoc, 13, 20, 30, 90, 93, 97, 223,
    232, 298, 371, 378, 405, 459
La Napoule, 100
Laon, 280
La Rochelle, 17, 97, 99, 410
La Trappe, 191, 236
Le Mans, 28, 90
Le Puy, 461
Levant, The, 68
Leyden, 50

Liège, 48
Lille, 16, 54, 103, 111, 223, 285, 300,
    313, 405
Limoges, 11, 232, 299, 383, 386
Limousin, 222
London, 117, 252, 428
Lorraine, 7, 91, 222
Low Countries, 103
Luçon, 314
Luxembourg (Palace), 249
Lyon, 10, 32, 41, 60, 71, 73, 92, 99,
    100, 112, 142, 205, 313, 383, 386,
    422, 430, 461
Lyonnais, 222, 371

Madrid, 352
Mâcon, 244
Malestroit, 33
Malta, 315
Marcillac, 33
Marly, 25
Marseille, 7, 23, 43, 44, 45, 67, 72, 90,
    96, 101, 217, 240, 301, 302, 310,
    313, 405
Maule, 232
Mende, 45
Méréville, 346
Metz, 11, 54, 395
Meulan, 10, 14, 22, 71, 72, 92
Midi, The, 106, 223, 446
Modena, 16
Monceau, 346
Montauban, 91
Montfaucon, 43
Montpellier, 6, 26, 38, 40, 51, 57, 80,
    103, 152, 304, 307, 310, 313, 384,
    386
Montrouge, 317, 366
Moscow, 441

Nancy, 92
Nantes, 26, 27, 50, 90, 310
Navarre, 294
Nice, 240
Nevers, 175
Noirmoutier, 312
Normandy, 28, 79, 89, 92, 107, 222,
    371, 378, 405, 446
Norway, 113

Orléans, 31, 97, 111, 281, 355, 359

Paray-le-Monial, 30

Index of Places

Paris
general, 169, 277, 282, 287, 303, 304,
306, 308, 310, 346, 355, 366
Police, 377
Punishments, 383, 384, 386, 387,
389, 391, 410, 423, 430, 431, 432,
441, 461
Palais Royal, 59
Châtelet, 373
Hôtel de Ville, 417
Cour des Aides, 371, 374
Medical, 9, 25, 27, 49, 51, 164; Body
snatching, 48; Faculty of Medicine,
315–16; Hospitals: Hôtel Dieu, 13,
30, 31, 33, 37, 55, 56, 273, 315; St.
Jean Baptiste de la Charité, 32, 42;
Public hygiene, 43, 48; Enfants
trouvés, 11, 68; Smaller hospitals,
54, 55, 56; Babies, 10, 11, 12
Parlement of, 21, 46, 76, 77, 99, 244,
278, 280, 284, 294, 309, 316, 322,
368, 370, 373, 374, 375, 389, 406,
407
Archbishop of, 284
Curés, 314
Churches: St. Sulpice, 102, 142,
259–301, 308; St. Roch, 271;
Notre Dame, 279, 285, 291, 301,
315, 316; St. Eustache, 329, 410
Monasteries, 244
Jews, 281
Population statistics, 90, 98, 99, 102,
272
Tax officials, 95
Press, 222, 223
Stage coach, 85
Diet, 18, 19, 22
Suicide, 259
Wills, 239, 240, 241, 242
Last rites, 249, 255, 260
Funerals, 283
Mourning, 60, 63
Pau, 91
Périgord, 18
Picardy, 222
Poitiers, 273
Poitou, 7, 28
Pompeii, 328
Potsdam, 266
Provence, 3, 7, 16, 25, 45, 90, 96, 146,
222, 223, 231, 232, 240, 241, 301,
371
Prussia, 162, 430

Pyrenees, 7, 273

Quimper, 9

Reims, 13, 90, 144, 209, 304, 371
Rennes, 13, 15, 27, 85, 90, 111, 197,
202, 232, 279, 387
Rhône Delta, 90
Riom, 91, 99
Rochefort, 55
Rodez, 33
Rome, 117, 170, 248, 297, 298, 308,
325, 327, 328, 330, 331, 379, 414,
415
Rouen, 17, 21, 42, 98, 99, 100, 181,
222, 307, 387
Roussillon, 46
Russia, 110, 400, 459, 461

Saintes, 177
St.-Amand-les-Eaux, 33
St. Brieuc, 28
St. Clément, 45
St. Dénis, 279, 285, 290, 353, 351
Saint-Jean-de Losne, 19
St. Malo, 18, 27, 366
St. Maurice-du-Désert, 21
Saulier, 310
Saumur, 371
Seine (river), 43
Seine (Dept. of), 362
Senlis, 281
Sennely, 74
Sens, 228, 284, 290, 322, 323, 326
Sérignan, 92
Sicily, 107
Sisteron, 45
Soissons, 247, 271
Sologne, 10, 20, 74
Spa, 48
Spain, 107, 108
Strasbourg, 22, 33, 54, 58, 77, 92, 93,
95, 156, 159
Sweden, 102
Switzerland, 348, 349

Tahiti, 451
Tarbes, 32
Toulouse, 19, 76, 91, 205, 311, 384,
397, 405, 424
Toulon, 43, 45, 54
Touraine, 92
Tours, 91, 97, 111

Index of Places

Uppsala, 50

Valais, 36
Valence, 261, 371, 384, 391
Valenciennes, 91, 96, 97, 405
Versailles, 5, 25, 26, 49, 60, 63, 64, 71,
    90, 112, 243, 249, 284, 299, 309,
    321, 411, 434

Vienna, 460
Vienne, 99
Villedieu-les-Poèles, 92
Vincennes, 416
Vitry, 149

Index of Persons
(not including modern writers)

Aaron (Old Test.), 294
Abelard (and Héloïse), 212, 361, 366
Aeneas, 323
Agricola, 171
Aguesseau, d', chancelier, 238, 300, 371
Aguesseau le Guerchoix,
    Marie-Madeleine de, 510, 511, 570
Aignan, E., 546, 556, 570
Aïssée, Mlle (=Charlotte-Elisabeth
    Aïcha), 521, 561, 570
Albon, comte de, 332
Alembert, Jean Le Rond d', 6, 12, 46,
    119, 159, 264, 267, 269, 320, 402,
    411–12, 527, 528, 570
Alexander VII (Pope), 325
Alexander the Great, 323, 328
Alix, 483, 487, 539, 544, 570
Amaury Duval, 363–4, 570
Ambrose, St., 214
Andry, Charles-Louis-François (medical
    writer), 561, 570
Andry de Boisregard, Nicolas (also a
    medical writer), 456
Antrechaus, chevalier d', 45, 478, 570
Aquinas, 116, 139, 142
Argens, Jean-Baptiste de Boyer, marquis
    d', 154, 163, 187, 500, 502, 508,
    525, 538, 560, 561, 570
Argenson, R.-L. de Voyer, marquis d',
    78, 486, 526, 552, 570
Aristotle, 148, 156, 163
Arnauld d'Andilly, R., 140, 201
Arnaud, F.-T.-M. de Baculard de,
    339–40, 570
Arria, 414
Artois, comte de, 317, 318, 332, 346
Astruc, J., 36, 476, 570
Aubert de la Chênaye Desbois, 533, 570
Augustine, St., 115, 135, 143, 149, 199,
    236, 254, 293, 305, 391, 425, 448;
    his mother, Monica, 293

Avril, Père d', S. J., 509, 570

Babeuf, 417–18
Bachaumont, 519, 521, 522, 525, 526,
    532, 533, 534, 537, 538, 539, 552,
    561, 571
Bacon, Francis, 116
Badou, 133, 134
Bailly, Jean-Sylvain de, 55, 481
Bailly, Louis (theologian), 521
Ballexsert, 470
Barbaroux, 417
Barbier, 237, 300, 384, 506, 517, 525,
    529, 532, 534, 551, 552, 571
Barbotin, 285, 531, 571
Barral, de, bishop of Castres, 46
Barry, Paul de, S. J., 569
Barthe, 263, 540
Barthélemy, J.-T., 325, 503, 571
Baudelaire, 325
Baudouin de Guemandeuc, 554, 571
Baudrand, 141, 500, 512, 571
Bayard, 328
Bayle, 36, 156, 163, 178, 258, 524,
    553
Beaumont, Christophe de (archbishop of
    Paris), 248, 260, 262, 484, 525
Beaumont, Élie de, 493, 571
Beaurepaire, 354
Beausobre, L. de, 571
Beccaria, 179, 376, 379, 392–4, 397,
    399, 402–4, 406, 553, 571
Bellarmine, 276
Bellefont, Mme de, 499, 571
Belloy, de, 327
Belmont, 153
Belshazzar (Old Test.), 199
Bentley, Thomas, 482, 571
Bergier, 124, 125, 128, 129, 131, 135,
    137, 138, 140, 141, 294, 324, 396,
    424, 425, 495, 496, 497, 498, 499,

Bergier – *cont.*
    500, 511, 533, 537, 538, 544, 554,
    560, 571
Bernard, St., 213
Bernardin de Picquigny, 512, 520, 522,
    571
Bernardin de Saint-Pierre, J.-H., 298,
    345, 351–2, 423, 436, 571
Bernini, 321, 325
Bernis, Cardinal de, 512, 571
Berry, duchess de, 247, 249
Berthier, G.-F., 193, 497, 509, 571
Bérulle, 212
Bichat, X., 58, 81, 487, 494, 571
Bienville, M. D. T., 479, 563, 571
Bion, 498, 505, 571
Bissy, comte de, 336
Blanchard, 520, 523, 572
Blessed Virgin Mary (including Our
    Lady etc.), 136, 138, 146, 199, 204,
    205, 232, 240, 456
Blondel, 333
Bodin, 94
Boerhaave, 150
Boesnier, 135
Boileau, the abbé J.-J., 512, 572
Boileau-Despreaux, N., 477, 572
Boindin, 261–3, 267
Boisguilbert, 17, 589
Boismont, 290, 509, 572
Boissier de Sauvages, 36, 40, 152,
    307–8, 476, 477, 501, 536, 572
Bonnet, 132, 159, 495, 496, 502, 572
Bordeu, 38, 49, 151, 273, 479, 501, 530,
    552
Bossuet, 115, 131, 214, 229, 288–9, 293,
    495, 532, 572
Boswell, 438, 562
Bouchardon, 326
Boucher, François (painter), 335, 457
Boucher d'Argis, 382, 394, 551, 554,
    572
Boudier de Villemert, M., 564, 572
Boudon, 572
Boufflers, chevalier de, 329, 585
Boufflers, duchesse de, 49
Bougeant, 156
Bouillon, maréchal de (also his son the
    Cardinal), 294, 322
Boula de Nanteuil, 99, 110
Boullée, Étienne-Louis, 333, 334, 366,
    540
Boullenois, 322

Boullier, 158
Bourbon, duchesse de, 285
Bourbotte, 417
Bourdaloue, 140, 500, 572
Bourdoise, 536
Boureau-Deslandes, 262, 266, 525, 572
Boursoul, 202, 205, 511
Brahmins, 183
Breteuil, baron de, 481
Breughel, the elder, 335
Brienne, Loménie de, archbishop of
    Toulouse, 311
Brion, 511, 514, 572
Brissot, 394, 403–4, 405, 406, 555, 556,
    572
Bruhier, 479
Brunet (actor), 356
Brutus, 426
Brydaine (or Bridaine), Père Jacques, 60,
    131, 133, 136, 497, 498, 499, 516, 572
Buffon, 10, 77, 86, 102–3, 111, 112, 114,
    149, 150, 154, 159, 169, 264, 436,
    451, 483, 486, 487, 488, 492, 493,
    494, 507, 534, 572
Bullet, 573
Burnet, Thomas, 177
Buzot, 417

Cabanis, 66, 78, 81, 82, 420, 481, 483, 486,
    487, 488, 495, 559, 573
Cadet de Vaux, 316
Caesar, 427
Cain (Old Test.), 396, 401
Calabre, 510
Calas, 267, 381, 393, 396, 424, 547, 589
Calderon, 182
Caligula, 184
Calmet, Dom, 132, 135, 157, 181, 496,
    497, 498, 499, 503, 534, 560, 573
Cambry, 361–2, 545, 573
Campan, Mme de, 506, 573
Camus, J.-P., 542
Canolle, 546, 573
Caraccioli, 60, 124, 130, 132, 159, 199,
    207, 238, 324, 334, 482, 487, 495,
    496, 497, 498, 499, 500, 504, 510,
    512, 532, 533, 538, 541, 573
Carignan, prince de, 247
Carmago (ballet dancer), 274
Cartouche (bandit), 386, 389, 402, 552
Caskellier, 557, 573
Castries, abbé de, 249
Cato, 414, 415, 416, 418, 424, 426, 430, 558

Index of Persons

Caussade, 206, 216, 218–20, 513, 514, 573
Caylus, comte de, 261
Cérutti, 347, 504, 544, 559, 573
Chambon de Montaux, 36, 476
Chamfort, 34, 54, 86, 447, 453, 489, 531, 565, 573
Chapeau, *curé*, 262
Chappuis, Jean-Claude, 494
Chardin, 457
Charenton, Pierre, 373
Charlemagne, 290, 305
Charles V, Emperor, 199
Charlevoix, 534, 559, 573
Charolais, Mlle de, 277
Charost, marquis de, 121
Charrière, Mme de (=Belle de Zuylen), 523, 573
Charron, 411
Chartres, duc de, 180, 346, 525
Chastellux, comte de, 329
Chateaubriand, 63, 87, 132, 303, 324, 350, 355, 359, 365–6, 483, 498, 530, 547, 560, 573–4
Chaulieu, 86, 263, 265, 350, 419, 574
Chaulnes, duchesse de, 287
Chaumeix, 154
Chénier, André, 358, 574
Chénier, Mme, 297, 352, 574
Chertablon, 204, 257, 509, 511, 517, 574
Chevalier, Claude, 494, 574
Chevassu, *curé* J., 138, 574
Chevert, François de, 329
Chevrier, F. A., 560, 574
Choderlos de Laclos, 83, 452, 458, 460, 468, 482, 496
Choiseul, 47
Chomel, 113, 487, 492, 496, 531, 533, 536, 560, 574
Christ (includes other titles), 124, 125, 127, 128, 132, 138, 139, 140, 176, 182, 199, 203, 204, 205, 207, 214, 218, 220, 225, 229, 230, 236, 240, 245, 249, 250, 263, 269, 293, 332, 356–7, 416, 425, 430, 456, 589
Cicé, Adélaïde de, 511, 516
Cicero, 115, 163
Clairon, Mlle, 339
Clavière, 417
Clément, 498
Cleopatra, 328, 414
Clichtove, 198
Clorivière, Pierre de, 510, 511, 516, 574
Clovis, 295

Coeuilhe, Jean Baptiste, 342
Collet, 130, 145, 194, 501, 509, 510, 520, 574
Colombier, Jean, 55, 208
Condé, prince de, 308
Condillac, 154, 155, 159
Condorcet, 55, 97, 118, 417, 449, 452, 491, 503, 528, 564, 574
Constantine, emperor, 305
Conti, prince de, 247, 284
Cook, captain, 346
Corday, Charlotte, 417
Cordemoy, 178
Coret, 510, 574
Cornaro, 112–13
Corneille, 168
Cosme, Frère (=Jean Baseillac), 32, 42, 58
Cournand, Antoine de, 335, 336, 541, 574
Court de Gebelin, 173, 332
Cottereau de Coudray, 531, 533, 540, 574
Coyer, 60, 317–18, 327
Crasset, 198, 203, 209, 244, 250, 482, 508, 509, 511, 512, 520, 522, 554, 574
Crébillon, Cl.-Prosper Jolyot de, 339, 421, 447
Creech, Thomas, 431, 561
Cressy, 551, 574
Croÿ, the maréchal duc de, 67, 242, 462, 520, 521, 574
Cubière de Palmezeaux (=Michel de Cubières), 542, 559, 574
Culant, Marquis de, 152, 173, 253, 502, 505, 523, 574
Cuppé, Pierre, 177–8
Curtius, 414, 426–7
Custine, general, 175
Custine, Mme de, 255

Dagobert, 354
Daignan, 66, 67, 68, 69, 75, 77, 81, 83, 483, 487, 492, 494, 575
Damiens, 368, 375, 381, 383–4, 388, 395
Dandré, Bardon, 323, 341, 538, 542, 543, 575
Dante, 338
Danton, 175
Daon, 515, 521, 551, 575
Daret, 478
Darius, 323, 328
Darthé, 417
Daubenton, 55
Dauphin, the (son of Louix XV, died 1765), 278, 284, 285, 290, 322–3, 326
David (Old Test.), 137, 192

David, Jacques-Louis (painter), 328, 356, 545
Davie, Jacques (surgeon), 478
Delafosse, 318, 333
Delamelle, 355, 358, 545, 575
Delandine, 575
Delille, 341, 345, 350, 353, 358, 543, 544, 545, 575
Delisle de Sales (=J.-B.-C. Isoard), 82, 113, 114, 183, 295, 337, 424, 430, 488, 494, 496, 501, 502, 507, 541, 559, 560, 561, 575
Démeunier, 495, 534, 554, 575
Denisart, 478, 531, 535, 537, 543, 557, 575
Deny de Verteuil, 523, 575
Deparcieux, 102-3, 492, 575
Desault, 58
Desbois de Rochefort, 58
Descartes (and Cartesianism), 41, 116, 135, 150, 151, 153, 155, 156, 158, 163, 165, 494, 563
Deshays (painter), 344
Deshoulières, Mme Antoinette du Ligier de la Garde, 169, 324, 575
Deslandes, *see* Boureau-Deslandes
Deslon (mesmerist), 411
Desmorets (executioner), 387
Desmoulins, Camille, 336
Desprez, Louis-Jean, 333, 515, 575
Destruissart, 547, 575
Desubas, pastor, 386
Détournelle, 363-5, 545, 575
Devil, *see* Satan
Diderot, 14, 58, 79, 81, 82, 85, 109, 119, 146, 157, 159, 160, 166, 167-70, 179, 181, 184, 245, 246, 256, 264, 326-7, 337, 339, 341, 344, 369, 379, 390, 400, 403, 414, 416, 424, 450, 451, 452, 457, 462, 482, 487, 488, 495, 501, 504, 520, 521, 523, 526, 527, 538, 541, 543, 547, 550, 554, 555, 575-6
Dido, 414
Dinouart, 479, 496, 576
Dionis, 523, 575
Dolivier, Pierre, 362-4
Donne, John, 429
Dorat, 329
Drelincourt, 208, 501, 512, 575
Drexelius, 192, 508
Dubois, Alexandre (curé), 576
Dubois, Antoine (surgeon), 478
Du Bos, the abbé J.-B., 203, 511, 575

Du Châtelet, Gabrielle Émilie le Tonnelier de Breteuil, Marquise, 82, 83, 460, 488, 576
Ducis, Jean-François, 221, 339, 544, 576
Duclos, Ch., 262, 264, 523, 576
Du Coudray, Mme, 54
Du Deffand, M. de Vichy-Chamrond, Marquise, 63, 174, 263, 266, 385, 431, 527, 551, 576
Dufort de Cheverny, Comte, 383-4
Dufour de Saint Pathias, J. M., 493, 576
Dugas, le président, 482, 508
Duguet, J.-J., 82, 197, 203, 205, 206, 225, 487, 496, 497, 498, 509, 511, 515, 576-7
Dulaure, J.-A., 540, 577
Dumas, Jean, 115, 426, 495, 560, 561, 577
Duns Scotus, 212
Dupaty, président, 396-7, 541, 556, 577
Dupont de Nemours, 157, 171
Durandus of Mende, 276
Duvary, 417
Duquesnoy, 417
Du Villard, 111, 492, 577

Élisée, père, 134
Emery, 142, 500, 577
Eon, chevalier de, 329
Epictetus, 140, 265
Erasmus, 163, 197, 234
Erlach, Rodolphe-Louis d', 113, 432, 494, 554, 558, 560, 561, 577
Estrées, duc de, 287
Eve (Old Test.), 446
Expilly, 98, 100, 491, 577

Faignet de Villeneuve, 109, 399, 493, 554, 577
Falconet, 169, 327, 504
Fauchard, Pierre (dentist), 478, 577
Fauchet, abbé, 291
Favart, Mme, 249
Félice, 493, 525, 577
Fénelon, 141, 214-16, 218, 330, 452-3, 513, 577
Ferri, 577
Ferrière, C.-J., 376, 547, 549, 577
Feutry, 336
Filassier, 221, 517, 520, 577
Flamen (of Lille), 285
Fleuriot de Langle, 352
Fleury, Cardinal de, 86, 290, 326, 330
Florian, 35, 476, 577

Index of Persons

Fontaine, P.-F.-L., 333
Fontane de Martel, Mme, 266–7, 519
Fontanes, L.-J.-P., marquis de, 344, 359, 520, 543, 577
Fontenelle, 86, 163, 164, 489, 504, 528
Fouché, 161, 545
Foucquet, Mme de, 29
Foucroy de Guillerville, 470
Fragonard, 452, 457
François de Neufchâteau, 577
François de Sales, St., 140, 211–13, 500
Franklin, Benjamin, 118, 268, 332
Frederick the Great, 258
Fréret, N. (=d'Holbach), 163, 504, 577
Fréron, 263
Fresnaye, Charles de la, 410
Freud, 3, 467
Fronsac, duchesse de, 237
Fuseli, 335

Gaiches, 498, 577
Galen, 26, 37, 38, 40, 51, 113
Galti (physician), 49
Gannier (executioner), 387
Garrison, Maurice, 511
Gastine (brothers), 315
Gaub, 150, 501
Gaudron, 145, 501, 577
Gaultier (Voltaire's confessor), 246, 267–9
Gauthier, Mme, 544
Gautier, J.-J., curé, 501, 577
Gayot de Pitaval, 397
Genlis, Mme de, 298, 515, 523, 534, 578
Geoffrin, Mme, 262
Geoffroy, the brothers, 51
Gérard, the abbé L.-P., 120, 238, 496, 578
Gérard, Sieur de Saint-Amant, Marc-Antoine de, 482, 578
Germanicus (death of), 328
Gertrude, St., 196
Gessner, 345, 352, 365
Gienet, 523, 578
Gilbert, M. E. (religious apologist), 578
Gilibert, J.-E., 527, 578
Girard, J., 362, 578
Girard de Villethierry, the abbé J., 293, 508, 512, 523, 533, 535, 560, 578
Girardin, R.-L., marquis de, 544, 578
Girodat, 480
Gobinet, 191, 508, 578
Goethe (Werther), 422
Goldsmith, Oliver, 557
Gonichon (printer), 271

Gossec (musician), 356
Goudar, Ange, 109
Gouges, Olympe de, 449
Goujou, 417
Goulart, 512
Graffigny, Mme de, 460
Grainville, Cousin de, 170
Grandjean, H., 49, 546
Graunt, John, 94, 100
Gray (Elegy), 336
Gregory of Tours, 248
Gresset, 339
Greuze, 256, 328, 457
Griffet, 138, 192, 196, 200, 496, 497, 499, 509, 510, 578
Grimm, 107, 246, 269, 287, 415, 416, 430, 435, 521, 525, 527, 530, 532, 533, 559, 560, 561, 578
Gros de Besplas, 123, 138, 258, 496, 499, 524, 578
Grou, 144, 194, 210–11, 220, 500, 509, 513, 578
Guesclin, marquis du, 287; 328; his ancestor the paladin, 292
Guilloré, 212
Guillotin (doctor), 407
Guyot, 524, 530, 536, 579

Haguenot, 307
Hallé, Jean-Noël, 57
Haller, Albrecht von, 151, 332
Hanard, Père Jean, 237, 238, 517, 579
Hardouin, 496, 579
Hardy, 521, 529, 532, 535, 551, 558, 561, 579
Harvey, William (d. 1657), 38
Hayer, 123, 154, 495, 496, 502, 579
Hecquet, 39, 182, 477, 507
Héloise (and Abelard), 212, 361, 366
Helvétius, 85, 161, 163, 171, 329, 402, 450, 503, 565, 579
Hénault, president, 327
Henri IV, 354
Henriette, Mme, 278
Hérault de Séchelles, 175, 526
Hercé, Urbain de, bishop of Dol, 60, 482
Hersan, 522, 579
Hervey, James, 336–7, 365
Hippocrates, 38, 487
Holbach, d' (see also Fréret), 154, 157, 161, 163, 168, 171, 179, 184, 251, 252, 327, 402, 433, 450, 453, 504, 506, 507, 552, 556, 579

Homer, 168
Houdry, 498, 532, 579
Huber, Marie, 179, 185, 187–8, 506, 507, 508, 579
Huet, bishop of Avranches, 139
Hume, David, 154
Humières, duchesse de, 277

Jacquin, 579
Jansenists (Jansenism, etc.), 140, 141, 145, 154, 156, 182, 197, 201, 203, 208, 253, 260–1, 280–1, 300, 388, 456
Jaquelot, 478
Jaubert, 108, 398, 493, 554, 579
Jeremiah (Old Test.), 294
Jesuits, 141, 156, 167, 208, 222, 232, 245, 247, 248, 253, 279, 386, 388, 589
Jews, 140, 253, 281, 389, 397
Joannet, 151, 155, 487, 495, 496, 501, 502, 503, 579
Job (Old Test.), 425
John, St., 204
John of the Cross, St., 212
Johnson, Dr, 438
Joly, Joseph-Romain (Capuchin), 394, 487, 495, 496, 503, 554, 579
Joseph, St., 234
Joseph of Arimathea, 294
Joseph II, Emperor, 48
Joubert, J., 435–6, 579
Jouenne (executioner), 387
Jousse, 380, 548, 549, 550, 579
Judas (New Test.), 137, 142, 143
Judde, Père Cl., 137, 138, 172, 197, 255, 497, 499, 500, 504, 509, 523, 579

Keranflech, 156, 502, 579
Kierkegaard, 1
Klopstock, 450

La Barre, Chevalier de, 389
La Barre, Poulain de, 450
La Baume-Desdossat, 133, 135, 139, 499, 579
Labille-Guiard, Mme, 460
Laborde, M. de (court barber), 346
Labrière, architect, 318–19, 332
La Bruyère, 392, 553, 579
La Condamine, 262, 264, 388
La Coste, 479
Lacretelle, 395, 399, 554, 555
Lacroix, 494
La Curne de Sainte-Palaye, 483, 585

Lafayette, 406
Lafitau, Père, S. J., 209, 520, 534, 580
Lafitau, P.-F., bishop of Sisteron, 509, 512, 580
La Fontaine, 83, 248, 366, 433, 488, 580
La Font de Saint-Yenne, 539
Laguerrie (=Tesson de la Guérie), 542, 580, 586
La Harpe, 269, 527
Lalemant, Père Pierre, 200
Laliman, Père (Dominican), 432, 561, 580
Lally-Tollendal, 239, 385, 386, 396, 397
La Marche, 141
Lamartine, 65
Lambert, Anne-Thérèse de Marguenat de Courcelles, marquise de, 488
La Mettrie, 46, 50, 162–3, 165, 166, 167, 252, 266, 405, 427, 449, 480, 501, 503, 560, 580
Lamourette, 508, 580
Landreau de Maine-au-Picq, 396, 398–9, 400, 405, 544, 555, 580
Languet de Gergy, bishop of Soissons, 201, 203, 209, 511, 580
Languet de Gergy, curé of Saint-Sulpice, 325
Lanthenas, 113
La Pérouse, 332
Lapeyronie, 26
Laplace, Pierre-Simon, Marquis de (astronomer), 55
La Place, P.-A. de, 539, 540, 580
La Reynie, 306
La Roche Aymon, Cardinal de, 242, 248
La Rochefoucauld, François duc de (1613–1680), 1, 214
La Rochefoucauld, François de (travels), 475
La Rochefoucauld, bishop of Beauvais, 299
La Rochefoucauld-Liancourt, duc de, 53
Lasne d'Aiguebelle, 238, 498, 510, 517, 580
Lasowsky, 357
La Tour d'Auvergne, cardinal de, archbishop of Vienne, 321
Laugier, 504
Lausausse, J. B., 497, 509
Lauzun, duc de, 224
La Vallière, duc de, 237
Lavoisier, 51, 56
Lazarus (New Test.), 293, 538
Lebas, 417

Index of Persons

Le Bret, A.-J., 488
Le Brun, 321
Le Camus, Antoine, 150, 501
Le Canu, 333
Lecat, Claude-Nicolas, 42, 494, 502, 580
Le Clerc, N.-G.-C., 41, 310, 477, 536, 580
Lecouvreur, Adrienne, 259, 329, 524
Ledoux, Claude-Nicolas, 366, 540
Lefebvre de Beauvry, 427, 478, 534, 560, 561, 580
Le Franc de Pompignan, J.-G., 353–4, 545, 580
Legouvé, 360
Lehoreau (of Angers), 551
Leibniz, 129, 162
Lelarge de Lignac, 155, 496, 580
Le Maître de Claville, 78, 79, 253, 485, 486, 487, 497, 523, 533, 580
Le Moine (painter), 434
Le Moyne des Essarts, N.-T., 397
Lenglet-Dufresnoy, 144, 460, 500, 580
Léonard, Nicolas Germain, 351, 422, 544
Leonardo da Vinci, 328
Le Peletier de Saint-Fargeau, 356, 401, 402
Le Pelletier, Claude, canon, 501, 512, 581
Le Pileur d'Apligny, 495, 530, 533, 534, 565, 581
Le Prévôt, canon of Chartres, 289–90, 532, 581
Leprince de Beaumont, Marie, 514, 581
Lequeue, Jean-Jacques, 333, 540
Lesbros de la Versane, 83, 339, 489, 542, 559, 565, 581
Lespinasse, Julie de, 423
Le Roy, Jean-Baptiste, 481
Le Sueur (sculptor), 347
Le Tourneur (translator of Young), 329, 336–8, 339, 540
Lévis, duc de, 50
Lezay-Marnésia, 340, 347, 544, 581
Lhéritier de Villaudon, Marie-Jeanne, 339
Ligne, Ch.-Joseph, prince de, 34, 329, 347, 350, 447, 476, 479, 544, 581
Limbourg, Philippe de, 48
Loaisel de Tréogate, 352, 353, 435, 541, 561, 581
Lobineau, Dom, 64
Locke, 150, 154, 155, 156, 168, 177, 178, 252, 345, 456, 581
Lombez, Père Ambroise, 140, 201, 210, 248, 500, 513, 521, 581
Longeville, Harcourt de, 112, 117, 494, 495, 581

Longueville, duc de, 237, duchesse de, 255
Lorrain, Claude (painter), 342
Lottin, 494, 581
Louis, St., 184, 293
Louis XIV, 24, 29, 30, 41, 50, 59, 83, 85, 91, 105, 108, 177, 247, 263, 279, 281, 288, 293, 299, 378
Louis XV, 26, 63, 76, 85, 126, 191, 194, 225, 241, 247, 248, 290, 309, 321, 330, 354, 368, 383, 388, 415, 431, 434 his Queen, 285
Louis XVI, 49, 54, 95, 331, 346, 350, 360, 374, 415
Louis, Dom, 189, 508, 581
Lucrece, 414, 426
Lucretius, 339, 390, 436
Lully, 263
Luxembourg, duc de, 277
Luynes, duc de, 66, 301, 384, 483, 521, 581
Luynes, Paul-Albert de, archbishop of Sens, 228, 248, 290, 516

Mabillon, Dom, 236, 243, 517, 520, 581
Mably, G. Bonnet de, 329, 401, 403, 555, 581
Macpherson, James (Ossian), 336
Macy, 156
Maillet, 166
Mailly, Mme de, 247, 300
Maine, duc de, 247
Maine de Biran, 63, 251, 522, 581
Malebranche, 182, 507, 581
Malherbe, 341, 543
Malraux, André, 4, 467
Mandrin (smuggler), 371, 391
Mangin, 248, 521, 581
Marais, 292, 530, 551, 581
Marat, J.-P., 152–3, 357, 394–5, 403, 404, 477, 494, 502, 546, 556, 581
Marcus Aurelius, 115, 328
Maret, H., 310, 536, 581
Maria Theresa, Empress, 460
Marie-Antoinette, 54, 350, 354, 506
Marin, F.-L.-Cl., 559, 582
Marivaux, 246, 390, 450–2, 454, 521, 582
Mark Antony, 414
Marmontel, 141, 186, 320, 329, 338, 458, 486, 542, 582
Marquis-Ducastel, curé, 537, 582
Marteille, Jean, 557, 582
Martin (farmer), 396

Massillon, 136
Masson, Dom, 510
Masson de Pezay, 341
Mauduyt, 57
Maugiron, Marquis de, 261
Maupertuis, 159, 165–6, 169, 411–12, 559, 582
Mazarin, duchesse de, 260
Mazenod, Eugène de, bishop of Marseille, 484, 597
Meister, J.-H., 86, 487, 488, 582
Menestrier, 293, 324, 533, 539, 582
Mercier, L. S., 43, 78, 80, 169, 339, 398, 410, 458, 461, 481, 483, 486, 494, 522, 529, 531, 541, 582
Merlet, 398, 582
Meslier, 127, 161
Messance, 7, 35, 99, 100, 103, 109, 110, 468, 492, 582
Métra, 519, 521, 525, 530, 537, 540, 544, 561, 582
Mezière, Nicolas Lecamus, 333
Miaczynski (veuve), 582
Michelangelo, 181
Milley, 216–18, 514, 582
Millot, J.-A., 582
Milton, 135, 168, 182, 338, 450, 542
Mirabaud, Jean-Baptiste de, 161, 582
Mirabeau, the elder, 332
Mirabeau, Victor, Riquetti, marquis de, 78, 168, 336, 354, 355, 403, 420, 504, 555, 582
'Moheau' (*see also* Montyon), 99, 100, 103, 480, 492, 582
Moléon (＝Le Brun des Marettes), 528, 582
Molière, 37, 366
Monaco, princesse de, 346
Montaigne, 156, 250, 255, 263, 392, 411, 446, 453, 454, 522
Montbailli (baker), 396, 397
Montesquieu, 6, 107, 109, 117, 156, 169, 248, 263, 267, 295, 330, 412–13, 415, 426, 429, 447, 450–1, 468, 526, 528, 582
Montesquiou, la maréchale de, 284, 553
Montfaucon, B. de, 479, 583
Montmorin, Mgr de, archbishop of Vienne, 321
Montpensier, duc de, 457
Montyon (*see also* 'Moheau'), 99, 110
Moreau, J.-N., 65, 236, 329, 492, 540, 557, 583

Morel, Dom Robert, 142, 210, 224, 500, 508, 509, 513, 583
Morelly, 186, 450, 508
Moses (Old Test.), 294, 396, 425
Moulin, Pierre du, 208, 512, 583
Mounier, Sophie, 336
Mulot, 363–41, 531, 538, 583
Muyart de Vouglans, 376, 379, 380, 403, 548, 549, 583

Napoleon I, 354, 363
Navier, 310, 536, 583
Necker, 55, 101
Necker, Suzanne Curchod, Mme, 174, 336, 350
Nepveu, Père F., S. J., 509, 521, 524, 583
Nepveu de la Manoulière, *curé*, 474, 583
Neuforge, 333
Newton, 164, 168, 330, 333, 460
Nicolas, Augustin, maître des requêtes, 392, 583
Nicole, Pierre (Jansenist), 131
Ninon de Lenclos, 225
Nivelle de la Chaussée, 454
Noailles, the maréchal de, 224
la maréchale, 237
Noé, Marc-Antoine, bishop of Lescar, 255, 331–2, 523, 583 .
Nonnotte, 139, 425, 433, 496, 499, 524, 527, 561, 583

Olivier, 536, 583
Olonne, duchesse de, 294, 519
Origen, 121, 135, 139, 176, 187
Orléans, duc de (d. 1723), see Regent
Orléans, duc de (d. 1786), 291
Orléans, duchesse de, 237
Orleans de la Motte, L.-F.-G. d', bishop of Amiens, 525
Orpheus, 182
Ossian, 336, 365
Ovid, 335

Panckoucke, 558 (for 'Pankouke', 577)
Parabère, Mme de, 60
Para du Phanjas, 120, 158, 496, 499, 500, 501, 502, 503, 583
Paré, Ambroise (d. 1590), 306
Parny, Evariste, vicomte de, 173, 505
Partz de Pressy (bishop of Boulogne), 138, 142, 158, 209–10, 499, 500, 513, 583
Pascal, 63, 234, 324
Pastoret, 359, 368, 403

Index of Persons

Paul, St., 125, 127, 131, 201, 207, 208, 250, 446, 448
Paul V (pope), *Rituel* of, 243, 274
Pélagie, Sainte, 341
Pergolese (*Stabat*), 338
Pernety, Dom, 81, 487, 583
Pernetti, J., 150, 501
Perreau, M., 399, 554, 583
Petty, William, 95
Philip of Macedon, 414
Philip IV (of Spain), 335
Philipeaux, 175
Piaron de Chamousset, 103–4
Piatolli, Scipione, 535
Picart, 497, 522, 528, 530, 534, 584
Pierre, Simon, 306
Pigalle, 170, 321–2, 538
Piganiol de la Force, 320, 329, 538, 584
Pilâtre de Rozier (balloonist), 332
Piles, Roger de, 541, 584
Pinto, M. J. de, 584
Piny, Dom Alexandre, 212–13, 513, 584
Piron, 64, 262, 329, 483, 506, 584
Plato (and Platonism), 148, 155, 176, 215, 458
Pliny, 419, 426
Pétion, 417
Pluche, 468, 584
Plutarch, 426
Poire, Père François, S. J., 316, 584
Poiret, abbé J.-L.-M., 297, 584
Poiret, Pierre, 186, 508, 534, 584
Polastron, Mme de, 101
Polignac, cardinal de, 29
Polignac, Mme de, 317
Pomelles, chevalier des, 97, 491
Pommereul, 362–3, 584
Pompadour, Mme de, 64, 248, 460
Porée, 306, 343, 536, 584
Porte, 247
Portia (wife of Brutus), 414
Poussin, 328, 340–2
Préfontaine, P.-A., 365, 584
Pressy, *see* Partz de Pressy
Prévost, 6, 46, 62, 84, 238, 339, 344, 429, 430, 515, 517, 542, 561, 584
Protestants, 201, 251, 315, 322, 329, 368, 386, 557, *see* Calas and Sirven
Puisieux, 452

Quakers, 396
Quesnay, François, 493
Quesnel, Pasquier, 201, 208, 238, 584

Racine, Jean (d. 1699), 264, 462, 526
Racine, J.-B., 430
Racine, Louis, 141, 251
Radicati, 522
Ramazzini, Bernadino, 14
Rameau, 263
Rancé, 236, 517, 584
Rapin, 132, 498, 585
Rast de Maupas, 313
Regent, the (duc d'Orléans), 60, 85, 247
Régius, *curé* of Gap, 516
Regulus, 427
Rembrandt, 338
Rémi, 171, 541
Renou (et Cie), 318
Resnel, abbé de, 329
Restif de la Bretonne, 63, 73, 79, 87, 238, 251, 271, 350, 382, 385, 418, 458, 479, 486, 487, 517, 529, 544, 551, 585
Riballier, 449, 452
Riccoboni, Mme, 451, 460
Richelieu, maréchal de, 86, 180, 246, 248, 521
Richeprey, 585
Richer de Sérezy, 360
Robbé de Beauvest, 388
Robek, 431, 561
Robert (author), 489, 493, 545, 585
Robert, Hubert (painter), 170, 341–3, 346
Robespierre, 175, 336, 362, 403, 417, 505
Robin (medical author), 476
Rochechouart, duchesse de, 300
Rochet (professor, Lausanne), 506
Roederer, 405
Rohan, cardinal, bishop of Strasbourg, 332
Roissard, 512, 517, 585
Roland, Mme, (Manon Philipon), 186, 336, 390, 423, 453, 484, 507, 585
Roland (husband of above), 417
Roman, the abbé, 47
Romme, 417–18, 559
Rose, abbé J. B., 121, 496, 585
Rosemberg (Trappist), 510
Roucher, 172, 341, 345, 505
Rouelle, Fr, 51
Rousseau, 26, 41, 47, 53, 54, 72, 81, 113, 154, 155, 173, 174, 176, 185, 189–90, 203, 251, 252, 253, 255–7, 302, 327, 328, 329, 344, 347, 354, 393, 416, 419–20, 421–2, 425, 435, 443, 450–2, 457, 458, 464, 476, 507, 523, 552, 566

617

Rousseaud de la Combe, 410, 557, 585
Routh, 585
Roux, Jaques, 417
Rubens, 204, 338, 507
Rühle, J.-P., 417, 559

Sabatier (=Sabatier de Cavaillon), 504,
    539, 585
Sabran, Mme de, 35, 251, 254, 277, 329,
    476, 479, 523, 585
Sachs, 58
Sade, 526, 585
Saint Albin, Charles de, archbishop of
    Cambrai, 247
Saint-Aubin, 502
Saint-Fonds, 482, 508, 585
Saint-Just, 168, 417
Saint-Lambert, J.-F., marquis de, 487
Saint-Marthe, C. de, 510, 585
Saint-Évremond, 160, 262
Saint-Pierre, the abbé de, 118, 264
Saint-Simon, duc de, 83, 254, 482, 521,
    522, 523, 530, 531, 585;
    Mme de S.-S., 59
Saint-Vincent, Mme de, 246, 521
Saladin, 199, 559
Samson (Old Test.), 425
Sanson (executioner), 387, 486, 552
Sarrau (Jesuit), 307
Saulx, cardinal de, 299
Sauri, 502, 586
Satan (and the devils), 180–2, 193, 203,
    213
Saxe, the maréchal de, 109, 320, 321, 330
Schoepflin, 320
Scipio, 417
Scudéry, Mlle de, 435
Sedaine, 398
Ségaud, 141
Ségur, the comte de, 517
    the comtesse de, 237
Seigneaux de Correvou, 550
Sénac, Jean (farmer-general), 264
Sénac de Meilhan, 56, 81, 487
Senancour, 78, 436, 486, 487
Seneca, 115, 335
Serpillon, 369, 547, 548, 550, 586
Servan, M.-J.-A. (jurist), 399, 401, 403,
    554, 586
Sévigné, Mme de, 8, 255, 462, 488, 523,
    586
Sevoy, 510, 586
Shakespeare, 327, 338, 339, 542

Sinner, J.-R., 503, 586
Sinsart, Dom, 137, 139, 142, 499, 500, 586
Sirmond, 141
Sirven (protestant), 396
Slodtz, Michel-Ange, 321, 325
Smith, Richard, 428
Sobre, Jean-Nicolas, 366
Socrates, 155, 266, 328, 416
Soubrany, 417
Soumille, 516
Spinoza, 162, 164, 503
Staël, Mme de, 422
Stahl, 151
Stendhal, 255, 523
Stephen, St., 125
Stoics, 411, 413, 415, 417, 426
Suard, J.-B.-A., 586
Sue, J.-J., 504, 557, 586
Swinden, 134, 506, 586

Tacitus, 171
Tallement des Réaux, 60, 482, 586
Talleyrand, 84, 446, 488
Tasso, 168
Tell, William, 332
Tencin, Mme de, 339, 410, 460, 542, 559,
    586
Tenon, Jacques, 55, 56, 481
Tertullian, 123
Terrasson, 264, 298, 330, 540, 586
Terray (Controller General), 96, 97, 110,
    322
Theocritus, 345
Thiers, J.-B., *curé*, 205, 482, 497, 506, 586
Thiéry, François (*médecin*), 539, 586
Thiroux d'Arconville, Mme, 337–8, 542,
    587
Thomas, Antoine-Léonard, 170, 291, 327,
    331, 483, 497, 504, 534, 538, 587
Thomas à Kempis, 197
Thomassin, 479, 587
Tillotson, archbishop of Canterbury, 177
Tilly, Comte de, 353, 545, 587
Tingy, M. de, 254
Tissot, 19, 36
Titon du Tillet, 330
Tournemine, 122, 153
Tourzel, duchesse de, 360
Toussaint, 83, 183, 185, 216, 507, 514,
    554, 587
Tremblay, 162
Tresmes, duc de, 271, 284
Tribolet, 508, 509, 517, 587

Tronchin, 266, 527
Tronson, L., 51, 206, 587
Troya d'Assigny, 139, 499, 587
Turenne, 332, 354
Turgot, 53, 97, 157, 289, 503, 587

Valazé, 417
Vanini, 262
Vasselin, 400, 554, 587
Vauban, 96
Vauge, 209, 216, 512, 514, 587
Vaugiron, duc de, 287
Vauvenargues, 264, 526
Velasquez, 335
Vert, Dom Claude, 482, 520, 587
Verteuil, 587
Vico, 1
Vicq-D'Azyr, 50, 52, 58, 479, 535, 536, 587
Vigée-Lebrun, Mme, 460
Virgil, 345, 426
Voisenon, 249, 262, 329, 525
Volland, Sophie, 166
Volney, 343, 543, 587

Voltaire, 41, 46, 86, 109, 110, 111, 115, 117, 123, 139, 140, 154, 156, 157, 167, 173, 178, 181–4, 237, 242, 246, 248, 252, 257–8, 262, 263, 265–9, 307, 329, 333, 337, 339, 354, 356, 369, 386, 390, 391, 393–4, 396, 399, 402, 403, 413–14, 416, 426, 427, 430, 433, 436, 443, 454, 458, 493, 503, 506, 517, 519, 524, 526, 527, 528, 552, 553, 561, 565
Vondel, 182

Watelet, Claude-Henri, 121, 181, 341–2, 345, 347, 496, 511, 534, 542, 543, 588
Watteau, Antoine, 263
Wille, Pierre-Alexandre, 257, 523
Winslow, 479

Yart, 343
Young, Edward, 4 (*Night Thoughts*), 335–8, 365, 524
Yvan, 487

Zeno, 426